The Golden Age of Buffalo Sports

1945-1950

DANIEL P. STARR

BUFFALO HERITAGE UNLIMITED

The Golden Age of Buffalo Sports.
First published in the United States of America in 2009 by Buffalo Heritage Unlimited.

Daniel P. Starr, Ph.D., is Professor Emeritus of History and former Director of Athletics at Canisius College, Buffalo, New York.

Book Design: Mary Lu Littlefield

Photo Editor: Thomas R. Stabler

Publishers: Joseph F. Bieron
Marti Gorman

Published by: Buffalo Heritage Unlimited
Buffalo, New York
www.buffaloheritage.com

Printed in the United States of America

ISBN 978-0-9788476-7-8

For Joanne, for a half century of support,
and for Kate, Lisa, Molly, and Jennifer –
all terrific pre -Title IX female athletes

Table of Contents

Introduction

Buffalo, New York in the 1940s was one of the major cities of the United States. It had been for a long time, for most of the 19th century and for the entire first part of the 20th century. Its rank in population in the 1940s placed it in the top fifteen in the nation. In that decade both during the Second World War and immediately after, the economy of the Queen City of the Great Lakes was booming. Unemployment was low. Industry was healthy and diverse. Tens of thousands of immigrants supplied the brawn necessary for manufacturing. They lived in thriving ethnic neighborhoods. Wealthy entrepreneurs lived in the mansions that lined Delaware Avenue, a sign of the city's status. The port of Buffalo continued to be one of the busiest inland ports in the nation. Railroads from all across the country converged on the city. Downtown Buffalo flourished. Department stores continued to expand and the entertainment district was vibrant. Cultural institutions were first class. The sports scene was exciting; venues were attractive, sport teams were successful and athletic events drew unprecedented numbers of spectators. Sports were viewed as a major asset of the city and Buffalo's sports were considered to be on a par with those of other major cities in the United States.

The period immediately following World War II was a Golden Age for Buffalo sports. Those years, 1945-1950, were more "golden" than at any other time in the city's history. The citizens had at their disposal major league professional football and major college basketball. The Buffalo Bills were charter members of the All American Football Conference (AAFC) organized at the end of the war. That conference was a worthy rival of the National Football League. The AAFC Bills fielded competitive teams that drew more spectators than most of the teams in both major football leagues. College basketball was played in Memorial Auditorium. The local quintets competed against the very best teams in the country and the crowds in the Aud were second only to those in Madison Square Garden. Buffalo also had the baseball Bisons and the hockey Bisons. Both were in leagues that were considered just a short step away from the major leagues. At that time only eleven cities were represented in the American and National Baseball Leagues. Four cities had two teams and New York City had three. Making up the rest of the major league 16 teams were Pittsburgh, Cincinnati, Detroit, Washington and Cleveland. Thus a city playing Triple A baseball, such as Buffalo, was in a much more elevated position than would be the case for a city playing in Triple A when the majors expanded to some 30 teams many years later. Buffalo was in a class with the likes of San Francisco, Los Angeles, and Baltimore. There was a much closer connection between the major leagues and the highest minors in the 1940s than there would be in later years. That was even more so in the case of professional hockey. At that time there were only four United States teams in the National Hockey League. Observers of the sports scene could be excused for thinking that the Buffalo Bisons or the Cleveland Barons were on a par with the Boston Bruins or the Detroit Red Wings. In addition Buffalo was the scene for major boxing and wrestling bouts, often staged in a capacity filled Memorial Auditorium. College football drew surprisingly large crowds to Civic Stadium as did midget auto racing and high school football. Buffalo also embraced the occasional sports event that drew thousands of spectators, such as a major bowling or golf tournament.

It was not just a time for large numbers of spectators but also a time when many of the teams and many individual athletes were successful on the field of play. Teams with winning records, teams contending for championships, and teams winning championships were not at all uncommon. Local heroes, some in individual sports and some on athletic teams, were in abundance. All of this added luster to the Golden Age in Buffalo Sports.

Unquestionably there were other times and other years in Buffalo's history when particular sports had their seasons in the sun, their own golden moments marked by superior achievement on the field of play. The Buffalo Bills of the mid 1960s and, without doubt, the four Super Bowl Bills teams of the early 1990s were such occasions. So were the Buffalo Sabres of the French Connection fame of the mid 1970s, and the Buffalo Baseball Bisons at the time of the opening of the splendid facility, Pilot Field, in the late 1980s. In college basketball the local teams had some truly outstanding accomplishments that included the three NCAA tournament teams of Canisius in the mid 1950s; the star studded St. Bona teams of the decade of the '60s and into the '70s, as well as the Niagara teams of the early 1950s and of the late 1960s. All those deserve all the accolades already bestowed upon them. That group also includes the University of Buffalo football team, the Lambert trophy team of 1958. One might also mention the Buffalo Braves of the NBA in the 1970s. A half century earlier, the 1920s, the Golden Age of Boxing, counted among its stars; Jimmy Slattery, Jimmy Goodrich, and Rocky Kansas.

Those were all wonderful teams and magnificent competitors that had Buffalo talking proud. But they do not fit into one convenient little niche, one small segment of the city's history as do the athletes and athletic teams of the late 1940s. No one era of the city's history can replicate the period immediately following World War II. No one era can equal the performances of the athletes and the teams or the enthusiastic fan support for all kinds of sporting events experienced by the citizenry in those years immediately following the Second World War. It was a unique period; it was a brief period. It began as soon as the Second World War ended, and drew to a close as the age of television, suburbs, and Sunbelt commenced. This book is about that Golden Age of Buffalo Sports.

I was privileged to have had two principal careers in my working life both of which I thoroughly enjoyed and both of which relate directly to the work at hand. One was teaching American History which I began doing in 1959, the second was serving as Director of Athletics, which commenced 15 years later. I retired from the latter in 2000. I continued teaching for a few more years, concentrating on the History of Sports.

In retirement, I decided that I would draw upon those two careers to research and write in the field of sports history. The City of Buffalo where I have spent most of my life was particularly inviting.

The 1940s appeared to be a good place to begin. The more I thought of the subject matter in those years the more convinced I became that there was a story to be told there. Moreover, in that immediate postwar period, I was an impressionable adolescent. Fond memories still linger from that era. The subject matter was very attractive to me.

I began my research almost five years ago. I started in the archives of the Buffalo Bills in Orchard Park, New York. As a teenager I thoroughly enjoyed going to the Bills games in Civic Stadium. The archives contained enough material to whet my appetite including team pictures, photographs of George Ratterman, season statistics and game reports. Next I began researching the microfilms of all the sports pages of Buffalo's leading newspapers, the *Buffalo Evening News* and the *Courier Express*. For the newspapers I used the collections at Buffalo State College and I also used the interlibrary loan services at Canisius College.

I greatly appreciate the assistance I received at the Canisius College Library and Archives from Ruth McGuire, Nancy Noel, Kathleen Delaney (the latter was also helpful in her previous position at Niagara University), and Donna Gesel of the Buffalo State Library. I am also thankful for assistance from Scott Stuart of the Alumni office at Niagara University, and at St. Bonaventure University from Joseph Flanagan of the Alumni office, Dennis Frank of the Archives and Don McLean; former "Voice" of the Bonnies. At the University of Buffalo Paul Vecchio, Charlie Donnor and Mike Jankowski were helpful as were Denny Lynch and Sandy Marzulla at the Buffalo Bills Archives. The assistance I received from Margaret Kraatz and Marsha Stokes of the Print shop and Alice Stelterman of the Chemistry Department at Canisius College has been invaluable as was that given by Pat Greenwald and John Maddock.

I researched in Toronto at the Hockey Hall of Fame and I thank Miragh Addis, the Archivist there for her help. At the Pro Football Hall of Fame in Canton, Ohio, I am appreciative of the assistance offered by Joe Horrigan, Vice President for Communications and Pete Fierle, AIC Manager. Pat Smyton of D'Youville College and Brian Cavanaugh and Warren Gelman of The Greater Buffalo Sports Hall of Fame provided important material; as did MaryJo Monnin, Jerry Sullivan, and Dave Valenzuela of the *Buffalo News*.

I would be remiss if I did not thank Bob MacKinnon, former Athletic Director and Basketball Coach at Canisius, for giving me my first paycheck in the field of athletics. When the Koessler Athletic Center opened in 1970, Bob hired me to help out with, among other things, the promotion of the Memorial Auditorium program.

During the course of my career in athletics, I befriended a considerable number of people who made their living in sports. Many of these individuals granted me interviews. In addition I communicated with many of the sports participants of the 1940s who lived locally as well as many who had moved away from Buffalo. I sent out initial inquiries to several hundred ex-athletes who had participated on Buffalo teams in the 1940s. Some of them proved to be very valuable sources of information. There were still others who though not involved actively in sports offered insight into the Buffalo scene at that time in history.

I also personally interviewed many Buffalonians whose memory I was able to jog and who then offered valuable perspectives on Buffalo in the 1940s. Some of these interviews took place some years ago, even before I began the actually writing of this book. A number of my interviewees have passed on to their eternal reward. I cherish their memory as well as their help.

Interviews were conducted in person or via telephone with the following: Tovie Asarese, Rick Azar, Don Barnett, Dennis Brinkworth, Joe Cardina, Bill Cotter, Wayne and Helen Reilly, Vince Christiano, Lou Corriere, Ed Gicewicz, Earle Hannel, Les Harrison, Don Hartnett, Susan Hunt, Ray Jacobi, Bob Jerussi, Jacki Jocko, Msgr Franklin Kelleher, Cy Kritzer, Connie McGillicuddy, Ray Manuszewski, Dick and Sally Munschauer, Ken Murray, Tony Rocco, Joe Scully, Oscar Smuckler, Dick Thompson, Ray Weil, and Cy Williams.

I was also provided with information, anecdotal material, photographs, and insights that enhanced my understanding of the period. Some people communicated with me by E-mail, others by cell phone, a few by old fashioned telephone or some other form of personal contact. Some even wrote letters — remember these were the 1940s. In alphabetical order I thank: Jim Burke, John Christiano, Chip Clover, Phil Colella's daughter, Christie Covelli, Frank Eberl, Pat Farrell, Larry Felser, Keith Herbst, Jim Hornung, Bill Hymes, Martha Lamparelli, Frank Offermann, Bob O'Neill, Bob Stoetzel, Jacek Wysocki, and J. B.Walsh.

I was privileged to be invited to the 55th reunion of Niagara University football players. Among those who shared experiences were: Dick Wojciechowski, Dick McCarthy, Dan O'Connor, Nick Stojakovich, Paul Miller, Frank Accardo, and Bob Rosa. I also attended a meeting of Ring 44, the Buffalo area boxing club, and there benefited from the recollections of Bob Caico, Angelo Prospero, Jack Green, Jim Brown, Jerry Collins, and Joe Cardina.

I am singularly indebted to those who read chapters and provided me with the benefit of their wisdom. These included: David Greenman, David Costello, Jerry Collins, Bob Miske, Don McMahon, Tim Warchocki, and Joe Wolf. I met with Joe Niland on a regular basis for several years right up until his death in 2007. His unbelievable memory served me well. I am grateful to all of them.

Finally, special thanks to those who put the final product together. Mary Lu Littlefield has provided her unparalleled talents indispensable for printing and publication. I am enormously indebted to Tom Stabler and Joe Bieron. Stabler's computer expertise saved me from disaster on numerous occasions. Bieron's encouragement kept me on an even keel. Both have been helpful in too many ways to recount here. My wife, Joanne, deserves many accolades for patience and support; my four daughters, Kate, Lisa, Molly, and Jennifer were helpful in ways they do not realize.

CHAPTER ONE

Buffalo
A Major U.S. City in the 1940s

Main Street looking North from Shelton Square. *Courtesy of Pat Farrell, www.travelingpictureshow.com*

Downtown Buffalo was a beehive of activity in the 1940s. Sports, entertainment, culture, and business were all part of that scene. The City of Buffalo was thriving. Buffalo, New York was one of the major cities in the United States. It had been for at least a century before World War II and it continued to be in the decade immediately following the war. As the city grew and prospered, so did its involvement with sporting activities, both professional and amateur. Eventually, just after World War II, Buffalonians entered a brief but intense golden age of sports.

During the last half of the 18th century, at the time of the American Revolution, the only cities were those that were along the Atlantic Coast. But in the early years of the 19th century, settlers began to move west, toward the Great Lakes. New settlements took root. One was a little community at the mouth of Buffalo Creek where it entered Lake Erie.That settlement was eventually called Buffalo.

Trade began to flow down the Great Lakes. To accommodate the needs of the growing commerce, the Erie Canal was constructed. The opening of Clinton's Ditch in 1825 helped to assure the supremacy of New York City as the major urban center of the country. It also led to Buffalo's growth. The population grew fairly rapidly. The settlement became a city in 1832. In the 1840s and 1850s the city experienced a large influx of immigrants; they came a mainly from Ireland and Germany, especially the region of Alsace Lorraine. They joined the thousands already here who had come, for the most part, from the New England area and from central and downstate New York in the early part of the century.

As traffic on the Canal boomed so did the City of Buffalo. Grain from the Midwest was shipped down the Great Lakes to Buffalo. To handle the ever increasing volume of corn and wheat and other grains, massive elevators were constructed in the Buffalo Harbor. Grain was stored and grain was milled and grain products were shipped down the Erie Canal to New York City.

The port of Buffalo became the busiest inland port in the country. Increasing numbers of the new immigrants found work there. Buffalo's reputation as a port city was mixed; business was thriving, but the canal district was a chaotic, bawdy, and sordid place. The heyday of the canal was rather short lived. Even before the Civil War the railroads had begun to have an impact on the canal routes and after the war the railroads became the premier commercial carrier of people and products.

Thousands of young men entered the army to fight for the Union during the Civil War. On the home front, commerce thrived and manufacturing, in its infancy, became increasingly important. In the closing decades of the 19th century the process of making steel was developed. Soon steel replaced iron as the most important product of the industrial era. Pittsburgh became the steel capital of the country and Buffalo was not far behind. Frank and Charles Goodyear were primarily responsible for the beginnings of the industry in Buffalo. They bought timber land and then built a railroad for access to the coal fields in Pennsylvania. They also acquired access to iron ore in the Mesabi Range. They put together parcels of land in South Buffalo and eventually produced steel.[1] Also at this time the use of the abundant waterpower of Niagara Falls was harnessed. The chemical industry in the cataract city was a big beneficiary. By the end of the century, Buffalo was the country's second leading rail center and was also second to Chicago as a livestock center as well as second to Minneapolis as a milling center. Buffalo had become known for its diversified economy.[2]

The city ranked eighth in population in 1900. Immigrants from southern and eastern Europe, the new immigration as historians labeled it, flocked to the shores of the United States, and thousands, especially from Poland

and Italy made their way to Buffalo where they were readily available as unskilled and semi-skilled workers in the labor market. Many were Jews and many more were Catholic; the composition of the city's population changed significantly. The old establishment, those primarily of Anglo Saxon heritage, was still in the driver's seat but the social fabric of the community changed drastically.

At the turn of the century the City of Buffalo was ready to flex its muscles; it was ready for a gala coming out party. Leading citizens of the Queen City of the Lakes recognized that it would be an ideal time to host the Pan American Exposition. The nation itself had just won accolades for its thrilling victory over Spain in the Spanish American War in 1898. As a result of that "Splendid Little War," the United States annexed the Philippine Islands and extended its hegemony over the whole Caribbean area. The United States was taking its place among the leading nations of the world, and indeed the nation was announcing that it was ready for, what historians would later call, the American Century. Buffalo too was ready to take its place among the leading cities of the booming country.

The city leaders who planned the Pan American Exposition in 1901 wanted to show off Buffalo's diverse industry with its countless and varied products. Especially exciting for the millions who attended was the Electric Tower. Thomas Edison only a short time earlier had invented the electric light bulb, and now, rising 389 feet over the fairgrounds, was this striking edifice ablaze with light bulbs. The phenomena of electricity along with the arrival of the President of the United States, William McKinley at the Pan Am, were what drew enormous crowds. On September 6, McKinley visited the Temple of Music and it was there, as Buffalo school children learned ever afterward, that the President of the United States was shot by the anarchist Leon Czolgosz. The President was immediately treated by available doctors and taken to the nearby home of John Milburn. He seemed to make some progress but then his condition worsened and he died a week following the shooting.

The Pan American Exposition ended up a bust; Historian Mark Goldman said it "ended in a nightmare." Things just seemed to unravel following the death of the President. By the time the fair closed in November, it had lost a substantial amount of money.[3]

But there was optimism afoot in Buffalo. A large company, Lackawanna Steel of Scranton, Pennsylvania, two decades later to be part of the Bethlehem Steel Corporation, was about to make its appearance. John Milburn and John Albright, acquired the Pennsylvania Company. Their efforts succeeded; the steel plant, located just south of the heart of the city of Buffalo, became fully operational in 1906.[4]

Buffalo's economy boomed in the first decades of the 20th century. It was not only steel, but a large number of other industries that accounted for Buffalo's successful and diversified economy. There were several small iron and steel companies in Buffalo. The port of Buffalo continued to be busy; indeed it remained the busiest inland grain port in the country. Shipping, storage and the making of cereal and other grain products continued to dominate the harbor scene. In various parts of the city independent breweries operated; the largest was owned by the Lang family, but also the labels of Simon's, Iroquois, Phoenix, Manru, Steins, and Magnus Beck were well known. They supplied the hundreds of ethnic taverns and other types of pleasurable emporiums in the city. Lumber was a major business, especially in North Tonawanda which was conveniently situated at the end of the Erie Canal, halfway between the cities of Buffalo and Niagara Falls. Much of the raw lumber was used as building materials, but some was used for furniture. The famous Kittinger Furniture Company opened for business at this time and quickly became world renowned for its quality product. Livestock remained big business, with the names Dold, Hughes, and Klinck among the most prominent. The famous Larkin soap company also was a part of the booming Buffalo economy.[5]

In the early part of the century, the making of automobiles focused attention on Buffalo. Best remembered was the Pierce Arrow company housed in a gigantic building on Elmwood Avenue conveniently located on one of the city rail lines. In Buffalo and especially in the city of Niagara Falls the chemical industry grew. In the years that followed, giant chemical companies: Union Carbide, Olin Mathieson, Hooker, Carborundum, DuPont, and others came into existence.

Along with the city's industrial growth and population increase, a significant downtown area developed. The electric streetcar played a major role in the making of the new downtown, the downtown of the 20th century. The streetcar brought people from every neighborhood in the city into the downtown area to work, to shop, to be entertained, to enjoy all the advantages of urban life. The streetcar went both ways. It allowed people to move away from their old neighborhoods and to settle in new areas of the city. New neighborhoods developed and new business districts blossomed.[6]

As the economy prospered in the first three decades of the century, so did the central business district in downtown Buffalo. It included office buildings, banks, department stores, and places of entertainment. In many respects, especially its physical features, it was the same vibrant downtown that Buffalonians knew after World War II, and well into the 1950s.[7]

In the fin d'siecle, two of Buffalo's best known and widely renowned buildings were erected. The Guaranty building, designed by the world famous architect, Louis Sullivan, was constructed on the edge of Shelton Square and nearby, on Main Street, the huge office edifice, the Ellicott Square Building was built.

Shelton Square along with Lafayette Square, just two city blocks to the North, were key focal points for identifying where one was in relation to downtown Buffalo. On or close to those squares were a number of significant Buffalo buildings, many that survived well into the post World War II period; some are still standing.

At Shelton Square were St. Paul's Cathedral, the Guaranty Building, the Ellicott Square Building, the Weed and Company building housing its famous hardware store and the Erie County Savings Bank. On the Main Street side of the square stood a solid block of businesses of various sorts including the Palace Burlesk, a vaudeville theater that later featured striptease entertainment that included the likes of Rose la Rose. A small building, popularly referred to as the shelter, stood in the middle of the square. It had restrooms and provided cover during inclement weather for those using public transportation. Shelton Square was a very busy place; it was the virtual transportation hub for the streetcars in Buffalo. The trolleys converged from all directions, and the square served as the major transfer station for users of the trolleys as well as the final destination for those who had business to conduct downtown.

A number of large department stores interspersed with some specialty shops and eating establishments marked the retail area, also known as the shopping district. Most were found along Main Street from Shelton Square north to a block beyond Lafayette Square. These included Adam, Meldrum,

Top: **Shelton Square.** ***Above:*** **Main Street; Palace Burlesk is at right.** *Photos: WNY Heritage*

and Anderson's (AM&A's), the J.N.Adam Company, known simply as JN's, William Hengerer's, Hens and Kelly's and a little further up the street, the Flint And Kent store, known for high end merchandise. Bank business was generally found toward the south end of downtown, epitomized by the Marine Bank, a towering structure built in 1913 at Main and Swan Streets. Toward the northern end of the shopping district stood the majestic Buffalo Savings Bank, capped off with a shimmering Gold Dome. Beneath the dome, was a huge and very attractive cavernous area, a very impressive interior. Parents loved to take their children there where they could ogle the massive sculptures on the walls and ceiling. The bank was located at Main and Huron where Genesee Street diagonally bisected both streets.

Lafayette Square was sometimes thought of as Buffalo's Times Square. It was bordered by Main and Washington Streets; the major arteries of Broadway and Clinton that extended far beyond the city line into remote villages to the east, terminated at the square. On the opposite side Court Street extended from the square a few blocks to Niagara Square with the McKinley monument as its

City Hall and Niagara Square - looking West from Lafayette Square and the Soldiers Monument. *Photo: WNY Heritage.*

centerpiece. Standing at Lafayette Square and looking down toward the monument one had a magnificent view. The land slopped gently downward; a person looking a few hundred yards beyond Niagara Square could see Lake Erie just as its waters flowed into the Niagara River. Later, when the massive art deco style city hall was built in 1932, one then looked directly at that towering seat of city government.

Lafayette Square itself was a large green space surrounding a concrete base; in the center stood the tall soldiers and sailors monument. The square was a pedestrians' delight; it was a place to rest, a place to meet friends, a place where crowds could gather to celebrate or protest or whatever their wish. Great buildings adjoined the square. On one side was the Brisbane Building, which housed offices on its top floors. On the first two floors was the Kleinhan's Men's Store, said to be the largest of its kind in the country. On the east side of the square was the Buffalo Public Library, and on the north and west sides were banks and other commercial establishments, notably Burns Brothers Clothiers where generations of Buffalonians had rented or purchased formal wear.

A thriving downtown would not be complete without first class hotels. At one corner of Lafayette Square was the Hotel Lafayette, considered to be one of the city's top hotels in the first half of the century. The original Hotel Statler, part of a chain of Statler hotels that were built in the major cities of the Northeast at this time, was constructed on the corner of Washington and Swan streets, a stone's throw from the Ellicott Square Building. It proudly advertised itself as the first hotel to offer a bath in every room. Later it was renamed the Hotel Buffalo, after the new Statler was built in the 1920s on Delaware Avenue at Niagara Square.

The entertainment district and cultural sites were also part of the downtown area. The 1920s saw the coming of Buffalo's "Great White Way" along Main Street. The anchor of the large downtown theaters was the impressive Shea's Buffalo. Close by were Shea's Great Lakes and Shea's Hippodrome. Across the street was the 20th Century Theater and around the corner, near Lafayette Square was Basil's Lafayette Theater. Next to the Hippodrome was the large Buffalo Billiards parlor. There were also a few stage theaters just off Main Street.

Athletic venues, in those days, were usually built a short distance from the downtown area. Offermann Stadium, the home of the beloved Buffalo Bison baseball team was built in 1925 at Michigan and Ferry Street.

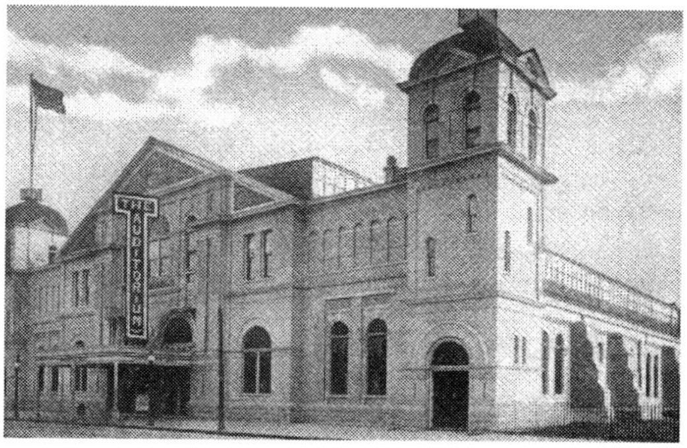

Broadway Auditorium - site of sports events in 1920s and '30s. *Photo : Commercial postcard.*

Earlier the Broadway Auditorium was built on Broadway just west of Michigan Avenue. It was the scene of many indoor spectacles and sporting events. Some of the most famous boxing bouts in the city's history were staged there. Canisius College played basketball games at the site and the famous six day bicycle races were an annual event in the old auditorium.

The economy continued diversified and prosperous through WWI and through the 1920s. The only ominous cloud on the horizon was the absentee ownership of some of Buffalo's largest businesses and manufacturing plants. The old standbys iron, steel, grain, and transportation remained prosperous. The more recent arrivals of the aircraft, automobile and chemical industries began to play a major role in the area's economy in the 1920s. Jacob Schoellkopf's development of cheap electrical power led directly to the establishment of the huge chemical plants strung along the Niagara River, at the point where the water began to form the rapids that rushed rapidly toward the Falls. World War I benefited the infant airplane industry in Buffalo. The Curtiss Wright Corporation became one of the country's leading airplane manufacturers.[8]

The roaring 20s, the decade of unprecedented prosperity in America, came to an abrupt halt with the stock market crash in 1929. Within a few years Buffalo as well as all major industrial cities, felt the full impact of the Great Depression. Industrial production ceased completely in some plants or slowed down significantly in others. Unemployment reached record levels. Thousands of citizens went on relief. Private sources of relief dried up as did those of the local and state governments. The Federal Government had to step in and it did. The New Deal, President Franklin D. Roosevelt's answer to the depression, brought tremendous benefits to Buffalo.

Various New Deal programs, especially the Works Progress Administration, the WPA, helped Buffalo to cope with the hard times in the 1930s. Millions of dollars were spent and tens of thousands of the local citizens were put to work. Among the impressive results were a large auditorium for civic and sporting events, the Memorial Auditorium, and a stadium to host outdoor athletic and other kinds of activities, eventually named Civic Stadium. The magnificent Kleinhans Music Hall was a beneficiary as was the Buffalo Museum of Science.

The local economy improved by the end of the '30s. Bethlehem Steel modernized and production increased. General Motors located a massive auto plant on River Road in the Town of Tonawanda that brought jobs and hope to thousands of the area's residents. The war in Europe broke out in September 1939. Buffalo's factories benefited tremendously. It would be two years and three months before the United States became directly involved in the global conflict. In the intervening period the United States became the arsenal of democracy, and Buffalo industry was a vital part of that arsenal.

Aircraft production was huge in Buffalo during World War II. Bell Aircraft began production at its Elmwood Avenue plant. One of its signature fighter planes, the airacobra, sat inspiringly on the lawn in front of the plant, a symbol of Buffalo's contribution to the war effort. Bell built another plant, a gigantic edifice, in the town of Wheatfield, near Niagara Falls. More than 30,000 were employed. Curtiss Wright built a plant on Kenmore Avenue and another on Genesee Street near the Buffalo airport. The company built the P-40s, known as the famous Flying Tigers, and also P-36s, and sections of the C-46s. The Curtiss plants employed over 40,000. Landing Craft Tanks (LCTs) were produced in record numbers by the Bison Shipyards in North Tonawanda. The Eberl Iron Works produced large quantities of parts for Army trucks. The steel plants, both Bethlehem and Republic, were in full production as was General Motors and Buffalo Arms and many smaller companies. Trucks, Jeeps, armament, weapons, ammunition, ships, and other sinews of war rolled off the assembly lines.[9]

World War II was total war. That was as evident in Buffalo as much as anywhere else in the country. The entire community became involved. Thousands of young men and many young women joined the military. Recruiting offices saw long lines of America's young people eager to serve their country.

Unemployment virtually disappeared in Buffalo. Those not in uniform played their part in the defense plants at home, including women, the Rosie the Riveters of Hollywood fame, who entered the work force in unprecedented numbers.

Many women stayed at home performing tasks that were part of the war effort; knitting clothing items, preparing packages to mail to boys overseas, and serving in the USO clubs and area canteens. Mothers made sure their children "knew there was a war on" as the popular saying of the day went. Kids collected and saved all sorts of things, lard, tinfoil, scrap material, soap, anything that might be used in the war effort.

Older Buffalonians helped out too. Some worked part time jobs to relieve others for the longer hours required in defense plants. Still others became air raid wardens. At nightfall they put on their pith-like helmets and walked the neighborhood streets making sure that the home lights were out and shades pulled down; they climbed up the gas light poles to dim the street lights. The story circulated that Buffalo, as a major industrial site, was high on the targets of Marshall Hermann Goering's Luffwaffe.

Civilians attended the smoke shows held in Civic Stadium in large numbers. Funds were raised to send cigarettes to the boys overseas. A pack of Camels or Lucky Strikes was one of the few pleasures that a homesick soldier could enjoy. At that time virtually everyone smoked; it seemed to be the natural thing to do once you reached the age of 15.

German POW's were kept at Fort Niagara. They had to be guarded. That was part of the war effort in Western New York. Military barracks were constructed at various places. Some were located adjacent to the airport; others were located in surprising places such at the Mang recreation fields in the village of Kenmore. Soldiers, sailors, and marines were seen throughout the area. Men in uniform were a constant presence in downtown Buffalo. Most visible were the hundred of sailors from the Sampson Naval Base on Seneca Lake in the Finger Lakes Region. It was one of the country's largest navy training sites. On weekend leave, sailors headed to Buffalo in droves.

Civilians had money now, wage earners made lots it; they were working fulltime and overtime. But there was little to purchase because of the scarcity of consumer items. So they saved money or bought savings bonds. Even small wage earners would buy special stamps and when they had the required number they turned them in for a war bond that cost $18.75 redeemable in ten years for $25. It was part of the spirited war effort on the part of a unified patriotic community.

The civilians at home followed the progress of the war news closely in the daily newspapers. Almost everyone had someone, a son, a good friend, a relative, in uniform. The news in the early months of the war was not always reassuring. But by end of 1942, the allies were on the offensive. Momentum was building. In Europe, following D Day at Normandy in June of 1944 the Nazis were pushed back out of France. By the spring of 1945 the allied forces had crossed the Rhine and were driving the enemy back deep into Germany. Meanwhile, in the southern part of the continent, American forces were forcing the Nazi troops northward out of Italy and into Austria and southern Germany, and from the East, the Russians drove the Germans back across Poland and into the outlying districts of Berlin. It was all over in Europe on V E Day, May 8, 1945.

But the war still raged in the Far East. The Japanese had overrun an incredibly large area of East Asia and the Pacific Ocean. In August of 1942, the American Marines were able to halt the Japanese advance in the South Pacific at Guadalcanal. Then the long way back, toward Japan's home islands, began. American forces battled the Japanese on the Burma Road and flew over the "Hump" into China to strike at the Japanese there. American soldiers under General MacArthur fought across New Guinea, and on to the Philippines, while the Marines and Navy under Admiral Nimitz began island hopping northward, to Tarawa in 1943 and the following year to the islands of Guam, Saipan, and Pelieu and then in February 1945, Iwo Jima.

At the very time that the Germans surrendered in Europe in May of 1945, the Americans were involved in the bloodiest campaign of the entire war on the island of Okinawa. The battle raged from April well into the month of June. The casualties, American, Okinawan, and Japanese, were enormous. By the time Okinawa was finally declared secure, it was obvious that Japan was not about to quit the war. The Japanese home islands would have to be invaded before the Pacific war could be ended.

Then in July the top secret atomic bomb was tested in the New Mexico desert. The test was successful. President Truman gave the go ahead and the A Bomb was dropped on Hiroshima on August 6 and three days later the second one leveled Nagasaki. On August 15 the Empire of Japan surrendered. The American boys in the Pacific as well as those in Europe with orders to travel to the Pacific, all of those hundreds of thousands of American service men, were grateful that the new weapon has ended hostilities. The A Bomb ended the war "pure and simple." President Truman made the announcement and the celebrations began. The celebrations across the country were incredible. Nothing like them had ever been seen, nor would their likes ever be seen again.

In downtown Buffalo, in the neighborhoods, in the villages and towns throughout Western New York people "went wild." It was pandemonium. Hirohito was hung in effigy in the Kensington-Bailey section of the city. The Broadway-Fillmore intersection resembled Times Square on New Year's Eve. People were delirious. Delaware Avenue, the main thoroughfare in the village of Kenmore, was typical. Automobiles seemed to be everywhere, coming for all directions and going nowhere in particular. Horns were beeping and blaring; people were leaning out of doors and windows and shouting and screaming, waving, and crying. It was bedlam. Pedestrians flooded the street too. People ran out of their homes banging pots and pans and anything else they could get their hands on, and made a beeline for Delaware Avenue, the heart of the action. Ecstatic men and women and children with happy faces were shedding tears of joy. Church bells were ringing, clanging endlessly; sirens on fire engines were whaling. The noise was overwhelming; it was deafening; it was louder than at any modern day rock concert.

People were yelling, praying, shouting. They mobbed the taverns, congregated on lawns, on street corners, in diners, wherever they could find breathing space. The churches were jammed with the faithful and the thankful, praising the Almighty that it was all over. People wanted to be with other people, they wanted to touch other people; they wanted to share their happiness and gratitude as best they could. The celebrating went on and on, into the night. It went on anywhere and everywhere. It was pure elation.

When the spontaneous celebrating finally stopped, there was still more celebrating to do. The following day the largest crowd in the city of Buffalo's history, well over 100,000, gathered in the meadow in Delaware Park for a victory celebration. Buffalo's most famous radio personality served as Master of Ceremonies. That was Clint Buehlman. Various dignitaries spoke. Mayor Kelly declared a civic holiday. Factories closed for the holiday. The making of instruments of war ceased abruptly. Workers took a much deserved holiday. Some took off an entire week. Many had saved tidy sums of money and were in no particular hurry to take new peacetime jobs. A vacation seemed in order. All rooms in the Niagara Falls area were booked for the upcoming Labor Day weekend. Many celebrated at Offermann Stadium watching the Bison baseball team.[10]

Finally the people of Buffalo and Western New York were ready to return to normal day to day activities. Things were good in Buffalo; the economy roared during the war. The expectations were high that the economy would continue to roar. The government and industry lost no time in converting from wartime to peacetime. In September civilian cars were rolling off the assembly lines in Buffalo area plants.[11]

The flour mills began operating at unprecedented heights. The American Machine and Foundry Corporation announced plans to purchase the Buffalo Arms plant in Cheektowaga and would spend millions to build new products.[12]

Entertainment returned to normal. The Erlanger Theater announced that sales were 30% ahead of the previous year; Shea's theaters were accommodating large crowds. Attendance at athletic events were already far above wartime levels. Buffalonians were again visiting nightclubs. One could splurge on a full course dinner at the new Town Casino for $1.50 while listening to the Mills Brothers or Lenny Paige.[13]

During the first peacetime Christmas shopping season, the downtown department stores did well. The *Buffalo Evening News* printed a photo worth the proverbial 1000 words. It showed a long line of people standing for several city blocks and ending up at the entrance of the J. N. Adam department store. They were waiting to purchase nylon stockings. Rarely had a woman seen a pair of new nylons during the entire war.

1946 opened with the announcement that $10 million was to be spent on the new Veterans Administration hospital in the Grover Cleveland golf course area. Buffalo's two largest department stores, Hengerer's and J.N. Adam's announced plans for expansion. Other stores that announced similar expansion projects included Bergers, Sattlers, Kobachers, and Sears and Roebucks. At the same time, a record home building boom began in Cheektowaga, Amherst, and in the Town of Tonawanda.[14]

A big concern was what would happen with the war time plants that had focused exclusively on military items. What would happen with all the surplus military goods? The answers came quickly. Bell Aircraft moved from its Elmwood Avenue site completely to its new plant on Niagara Falls Boulevard in Niagara County. Shortly thereafter President Lawrence Bell received the first ever contract to build helicopters. The Bell plant in North Buffalo was turned over to the War Assets Administration. It was used as the site for its warehouse. $150 million worth of machines, metals, chemicals, and consumers goods were to be sold or auctioned off there. Curtiss Wright made plans to move to Ohio. The Kenmore avenue plant was taken over by Western Electric, a division of A.T.& T. and the Cheektowaga facility was purchased by the Westinghouse Corporation. A giant auction was held; $3 million worth of wartime equipment was sold. A few months later, the DuPont Corporation announced a multimillion dollar expansion. More workers were hired. Smaller companies got into the act too. Fred Munschauer announced plans for the Niagara Machine and Tool works to convert from wartime machinery to making office equipment and washing machines.[15]

Not everything was rosy. A big steel strike took place in 1946 and thousands of workers were idled. The building materials' industry was hurt. The Housing shortage worsened. But things returned to normal fairly soon. Not all industries were destined to be successful. The Playboy Motor Corporation was determined to produce a

Bell Helicopter on display in front of Erie County Savings Bank. *Photo: WNY Heritage*

new automobile, an inexpensive convertible. It won a bid of $2 million for a Kenmore avenue plant purchased from the War Assets Administration. Only a few Playboy cars were built then the corporation went broke. There was also a sign of things to come. In mid 1947 AM&A's opened a branch in the University Plaza, one of the first shopping centers in suburbia. The *News* stated: "The Company has taken the lead among Buffalo Department stores in recognizing the necessity for suburban shopping centers."[16]

The year 1946 came to an end with Christmas buying showing a whopping 25% increase over 1945; the forecasts for 1947 were even better. And it was a better year. The Continental Can Company built a fiber drum plant on 40 acres of land at Colvin and Brighton in the Town of Tonawanda. Again there were more plant expansions and increased production. Even the railroads, among the biggest employers, spent more money on new equipment and facilities. Diesel locomotives rapidly replaced the old steam engines.[17]

Predictions for 1948 were even rosier. Westinghouse, DuPont, Yale and Towne, Western Electric, Donner Hanna, Ford, Pratt and Letchworth, Buffalo Pottery, National Gypsum, all announced plant expansion. High employment continued. Reflecting the high employment rates were the increases in population. It was not an official census year, but nevertheless the *Courier Express* noted that both the city and county had posted population growth gains of 12%, greater than the nation as a whole. This was due largely to the increased number of workers coming to the area for employment in the new industries.[18]

These were very good years both for industry and for home construction. By 1949 Bethlehem had emerged as the number one barometer for industry and business in the area. With its blast furnace smokestacks dominating the skyline at the western end of Lake Erie, the corporation set records in steel production in 1949; it also announced plans for the doubling of its steel capacity. Down the road on Route 5, the Ford Motor Company also made known its plans for a $35 million expansion. The Bethlehem and Ford projects were the greatest expansions in Buffalo's industrial history.[19]

Buffalo entered the new decade of the 1950s robustly optimistic about the future. Business had been good ever since the end of World War II. Productivity was up; employment was solid. Downtown was still the hub of Western New York. The Korean War broke out in June of 1950. It dragged on for three years. Big defense contracts were placed with many Buffalo firms. Continued economic prosperity was assured.

The City of Buffalo was still ranked in the top fifteen in the United State in terms of population. In 1900 it had ranked 8th, ahead of Pittsburgh and Detroit. It slipped a little in the next several decennial censuses but not a lot. In 1940 it was still ranked #14 with 575,901 and in 1950 it was #15 with 580,132. It was still in the upper echelon, still ahead of many of those Sunbelt cities that would overtake it by the end of the century.

Many of the buildings that marked downtown in the first part of the 20th century would remain a part of downtown in the period following World War II. A few were demolished; a few new ones were built. But the Buffalo that old timers, recall fondly today, the downtown of the 1940s and '50s, bore many similarities to the downtown that had been created earlier in the 20th century.

That was true of Buffalo's neighborhoods too. Ethnic neighborhoods solidified in the early years of the century. Actually neighborhoods in Buffalo as in other major cities were fluid, always changing but in the first half of the 20th century, they seemed to change less than usual. The Poles were the largest ethnic group. When one thought of Polish in Buffalo one automatically thought of the East side. The heart of Polonia was the Broadway-Fillmore area. Sattler's big three ring department store was at 998 Broadway. Across the street was the Broadway market, at that time largely on open air market featuring Polish food items and also produce, live poultry, and other farm products brought in almost daily from rural Erie County. A short distance away was the Polish Village restaurant, the center of Polish entertainment. Actually there was another Polish settlement in Buffalo, this one centered on Assumption Church, an impressive Roman Catholic House of Worship in Black Rock. Nearby on Grant Street stood St. Elizabeth's church, the focal point for the small Hungarian community.

The Old Italian neighborhood stood just a few blocks east of Main Street in the area marked by Michigan Avenue and Swan Street. A number of Black Americans moved to the city at the time of World War I and more at the time of World War II, and settled in that old Italian area. As their numbers increased, Blacks moved steadily to the North, toward Genesee Street and east toward Jefferson in the Willert Park area. Just north in the Humboldt Parkway area, many Jewish lived. Most Italians in the early part of the 20th century lived in the Lower Main Street /Canal district and in the area between Niagara Street and the Niagara River, known as the Lower West Side. By the time of the Second World War the heart of the Italian community had moved further up the West Side. Connecticut Street began to rival Niagara Street as the main focal point for Buffalo's Italians. The Germans, in the 2nd quarter of the century, by this time many second generation immigrants, were living in the fruit belt area and the streets around Humboldt Parkway. The Turn Verein on High Street announced that this was a German community. But by the time of World War II, many of those of German ancestry, had assimilated with others of northern and western European heritage and could be found living throughout North Buffalo, Riverside, in the Kensington-Bailey area and the University district. To the extent that there was an old German ethnic enclave it would be in the Genesee Street/Schiller park area. Al Hausback's restaurant was a popular meeting place for those of German heritage. Further east, actually in Cheektowaga was the Auf Wiedersehen restaurant, another

popular German gathering place. The Irish were still in the first ward and the "valley" but as the century lengthened the second and third generations could be found pretty much monopolizing most of South Buffalo.

The Buffalo of the late 1940's was in many ways a continuation of the previous decades. The Great Depression and the Second World War comprised an exceptional period for every city in the United States. Buffalo weathered the Depression and the War fairly well. Then it seemed that the city "took off" in the years that followed. Buffalo prospered; Buffalonians had a glorious time, and perhaps nowhere did things seem more glorious than in the field of sports. Those years immediately following World War II were a golden age for sports in Buffalo.

Buffalonians had been sports fans for generations. Baseball had been around for a century. Professional football had been played somewhat sporadically in earlier decades. Professional hockey had some ups and downs in the 1920s and '30s; on the eve of World War II it was coming of age. College football was a mainstay at all four area colleges since the early years of the century; likewise with college basketball. Boxing and wrestling had been a part of the Buffalo sports scene for quite some time. Individual athletes had occasionally made their mark on the local scene and sometimes their achievements had been celebrated well beyond Western New York. World War II had had an impact on all sports. Some had been suspended "for the duration."Others were curtailed in various ways. Now at the end of the war, a new era was about to begin. It was the dawn of the Golden Age of Buffalo Sports.

Top: Memorial Auditorium AKA the AUD. ***Above:*** **Civic Stadium, later known as the "Old Rockpile."**
Photos: WNY Heritage.

CHAPTER TWO

America's Past Time

— Buffalo's Past Time —

BUFFALO EVENING NEWS

18,000 Jam Bison Stadium For Opener Against Newark

Pre-war Enthusiam of Fans Returns with a Roar!

Buffalo Evening News, May 1, 1946

Home of the Bisons, 1925-60. Named after team owner, Frank Offermann.
Courtesy: Jim Hornung, Erie County Parks Commissioner

Baseball was big in Buffalo in the 1940s. Indeed Baseball was huge all over America in that decade. More than ever it was America's and Buffalo's pastime in the years immediately following World War II. It had been regarded as America's pastime for nearly a century. Recently records have been discovered that indicated that a type of ball game resembling baseball was played in Massachusetts in the late 1700s. Nevertheless the enduring myth, still embraced by many fans, is that Abner Doubleday conceived the game in Cooperstown, N.Y. in 1839. Actually it was Alexander Cartwright who formulated the rules of the game and with a group of young men called the New York Knickerbockers began to play what we know now as baseball. They first played in Hoboken, New Jersey. That was in 1845.

The game spread like wildfire. On the eve of the Civil War, in 1861, the game was being played by amateur baseball clubs throughout the Northeast. Joe Overfield, the official historian of the Buffalo Bison Baseball Club, states that the first baseball club, in Buffalo, called the Niagara, first played the game in the 1850s. By the mid 1870s professional teams were being formed. The first professional team in Buffalo, perhaps not surprisingly named the "Buffaloes," dates from 1877. Two years later, the team, now known as the Bisons, played in the National League. In 1886 the club secured some permanency by joining the International League where they remained until 1970. It is worthy of note that in 1887 there were several "Negroes" in the International League. Bison second baseman Frank Grant was the real standout of this group. "The Buffalo club, possibly because of Grant, strongly opposed" the move to bar all black ballplayers. But the effort was in vain and in the immediate years that followed, the black ballplayers were excluded.[1]

During the 1890s Buffalonians could watch Jimmy Collins, a product of St. Joseph's Collegiate Institute, play for their home team before he advanced to the Major Leagues. Collins was to become one of the great 3rd basemen of all time, and arguably the greatest player ever to come out of Buffalo.

Just after the turn of the century, in 1902, when the fortunes of the Bisons were quite low, George Stallings entered the picture; he secured the franchise with some help from Michael Shea, later to be known as the mogul behind the Shea's theaters throughout Buffalo. The baseball team under the knowledgeable Stallings did a magnificent job over the next few years, winning two pennants and coming close in other years. His final year was 1912.

In the World War I era, the Herd had two pennant winning years under the guidance of Patsy Donovan. But stiff competition entered the world of Buffalo baseball. A new Major League, a third one, the Federal League entered the picture with Buffalo as a member. The backers of the new league thought that it could exist along side the fairly new American League, born at the beginning of the 20th century and the venerable National circuit that had been organized in the latter part of the 19th century. The Buffalo club was aptly called the Buffalo Feds; the City of Buffalo now had a team at the top level of professional baseball. Unfortunately, after two rough years, the Federal League folded. But meanwhile the Buffalo Bisons too had suffered financial losses and there were some doubts about the club's future in the International League.

In 1920 several investors came to the rescue. A group led by Frank Offermann, a printing entrepreneur, and Marvin Jacobs, a concessionaire, purchased the Buffalo Baseball club.

The Twenties was a good decade for the Bisons. It was a terrific decade for all of baseball. It was marked by the towering achievements of Babe Ruth and the dominance of the New York Yankees. Fans flocked to the ballparks throughout the land. Baseball's reign in the sports world of the United States stood unchallenged. In 1927, the same year that was made famous by Babe's 60 home runs and the runaway of the Yankees with the American League pennant, was also witness to, what Joe Overfield states was "probably the greatest Bison team ever." The Bison manager was Billy Clymer, and his star player was first baseman Del Bissonette who hit a lofty .365 and led the league in several categories. Four years earlier, in 1923 the old ballpark, that had been used by the Bisons since 1889 was demolished. The Buffalo baseball team now had a wonderful new stadium built on the corner of Ferry and Michigan.

The Great Depression hit the nation in the 1930s. Initially the grim economic times took a toll on Buffalo baseball as attendance fell off sharply, but by the mid 1930s it was back up; well over 200,000 fans a year were again heading out to the ballpark. In part this was no doubt due to the performance of the team under the managerial skill of Ray Schalk whose charges won the pennant in 1936. One of the team's best performers was Ollie Carnegie. If there was one ballplayer that stood out and won the hearts of the Buffalo fans in the 1930s it was Carnegie. He didn't walk like a ballplayer and he didn't look like much of a ball player, but Ollie was a ballplayer, he was "old mister reliable."

In 1935 Frank Offermann who had done so much for Bison Baseball during the years he was part owner and President of the club, passed away. The stadium was renamed in his honor, a fitting tribute. Long after that grand edifice was gone, the words "Offermann Stadium" still resonated nostalgically with many, many Buffalonians and former Buffalonians. In that sense it was on a par with Crystal Beach in Buffalo folklore. Offermann's sons, Paul and Frank, continued the Offermann baseball legend, serving occasionally as assistant batboys, the envy of all Buffalo youth.

John Gehn, an old friend and colleague of Offermann's was named to succeed him as President of the ball club. In 1939, Isabella Offermann, widow of Frank, sold the family stock to the Jacobs Brothers, Marvin, Louis and Charles. Marvin Jacobs had the controlling interest in the baseball club as well as the real estate. World War II began in Europe in that same year; two years later, the United States was sucked into the conflict. Now it was total war, and this meant a scarcity of talent for baseball. This was true in

Top: **Aerial view of Offermann Stadium with the famous centerfield scoreboard, over 400 feet from home plate. The great Luke Easter belted one over it (in the 1950s).**
Bottom: **A typical Sunday doubleheader crowd.**
Photos courtesy of Frank Offermann Jr.

all sports, literally, as hundreds of America's best professional athletes became a vital part of the military forces needed to subdue the Axis powers.

The Bisons continued to field a team during World War II. President Franklin D. Roosevelt recognized the value of the sport; it was good for morale he said. In the words of baseball historian, Joe Overfield, "it wasn't good baseball, but it was baseball." Overfield is recognized as the authority on Bison baseball. In his summary of the war years, he notes that Bison manager, Bucky Harris used 40 players, "ranging from teenagers like Art Houtteman, Billy Pierce and Emery Hresko, to hoary veterans like Lloyd Brown (41) Ab Wright (39), and Henry Oana (37). He tried 4-Fs and Cubans as well. Even the venerable Ollie Carnegie came back for a final bow. Remarkably, at the age of 46, he batted .301 and hit four home runs." Major league fans may still recall that the St. Louis Browns even had a one arm outfielder by the name of Pete Gray, in their lineup.[2]

The war years were not spectacular. The colorful Eddie "Shovels" Kobesky replaced Ollie Carnegie as the clean up hitter, but Ollie's shoes were big ones to fill. The very likeable Greg Mulleavy served as manager. He led a rather motley team to a 7th place finish in 1943. Bucky Harris, future hall of famer, returned to Buffalo to manage the Herd to a 4th place finish in 1944. That squad was led by the hitting of Kobesky and centerfielder Mayo Smith. Harris' 1945 team did not do quite as well. Attendance during the war years was sluggish, but actually was not too bad, considering the fact that the country was engulfed in global war. Fans needed time out from their more serious concerns to catch a game now and then.

In August of 1945, at the same time that the Bison baseball season was drawing to a close, the Japanese were hit with the atomic bombs at Hiroshima and Nagasaki. The war ended a short time later, and the Bisons found themselves dwelling in the cellar of the league. Some of the erstwhile fans figured the future looked glum. However, knowledgeable baseball people had a more optimistic outlook. Cy Kritzer the *Buffalo Evening News*' beat writer for baseball expressed a glimmer of hope as he jotted down notes about catcher Eddie Modarski's perfect night at the plate in the Herd's triumph over Baltimore. A few days later, came the announcement by President Truman of the surrender of the Japanese. The President's message was read over the loudspeakers at Offermann Stadium. The crowd exploded in uproarious jubilation and the Herd responded with a victory won by 18-year-old pitching sensation, left hander Billy Pierce.[3]

Buffalo was still 29½ games behind the front runner, Montreal, but a few more Bison wins enabled the herd to pick up the pace and wind up in 6th place. Kritzer was correct; the Bisons were not "all that bad." In the final home game, Johnny McHale clouted a "Babe Ruth type Home Run." Then he, along with Pierce and Eddie Mierkowicz, who was named Player of the Year by radio station WGR, headed to the parent club, the Detroit Tigers, for the remainder of the major league season. This was quite an honor considering that Detroit won the World Series a few weeks later, besting the hard luck Chicago Cubs.

World War II affected all walks of life in the United States, baseball certainly was no exception. Many ball clubs found themselves in a dilemma; they had money to purchase players but the talent just could not be found. The war had taken its toll on the quality of baseball. The Bisons had some 43 players in the armed forces. Military service spared few players and no teams. Most of the superstars, including Joe DiMaggio, Ted Williams, Bob Feller, and many of the average players served in the military, a considerable number in actual combat, some paying the ultimate price. Now that the war had ended, ballplayers everywhere were anxious to get back to the good old days and to exchange their army fatigues for a baseball uniform.

The returning players were anxious to find a spot on the roster for the 1946 season. A baseball boom was in the making. In fact there would be so many ballplayers available that twenty new minor leagues were predicted for the first full year of peace. Ten minor leagues had actually been suspended during the war, they would return, and another ten were in the formative stage. Some 3,784 minor league players were serving in the armed forces and another 874 were working in war related jobs. That was a tremendous amount of manpower.

In the years immediately following World War II, the International League consisted of eight teams. The Toronto Maple Leafs and the Montreal Royals gave the league its international flavor. The Syracuse Chiefs and the Rochester Red Wings representing Buffalo's upstate sister cities were joined by the Baltimore Orioles, the Newark Bears, and the Jersey City Giants. To ready itself for the postwar era of baseball, the Buffalo Club hired the famous Gabby Hartnett to be the Field Manager. As Cy Kritzer put it, this former Cubs star catcher with 29 years of experience would hopefully "lead the Bisons out of the wilderness." The equally renowned Bucky Harris would stay on as the General Manager. The Bisons would now have two former major league manager/players, with decades of experience, in charge.[4]

Spring training for 1946 was held in Winter Haven, Florida. Joining the players and the front office personnel in the sunshine state would be some of Buffalo's media. Cy Kritzer of the *News*, his counterpart at the *Courier*, Billy Coughlin, and also sportscaster Jim Wells were there. As Kritzer reminisced decades later, the stay with the team in Florida, and the chance to observe the developments in the Grapefruit League, were great benefits or perks of his job.[5]

Winter Haven was close to the site used by the World Champion Detroit Tigers; this location would give the Bison management an opportunity to view some of the prospects that they assumed would find their way on to the Buffalo roster. The Bison brass was especially anxious to latch on to Anse Moore and Vic Wertz. Both did eventually join the Herd, first Wertz, and sometime later Moore, arrived on the local scene. Meanwhile Infielder Johnny Bero looked promising in camp, and John McHale who had come down from the Tigers looked good too. Actually fourteen Tigers were slated to make the trip to Buffalo, but first they all were guaranteed a 30 day trial with the Tigers, a provision guaranteed all returning war veterans. The Bison management took additional steps to beef up the roster; third baseman Johnny Antonelli and outfielder Coaker Triplett were purchased from the Philadelphia Phillies. Veteran pitcher Peter Appleton was also signed. He had been given his release by the Washington Senators. Following the rather routine spring training camp, the Bisons decamped and headed north to open the season at Newark. A good crowd of nearly 13,000 watched the Bisons pull off an 8 - 7 victory.

Several days later the Bisons opened at home. Opening Day of 1946 was truly a grand occasion in Buffalo, New York. It was the first one since the end of the global conflict. And what a day! Opening day was always a gala event in the Queen city, but this May it would be more gala than ever. It was a civic holiday for all practical purposes. To start things off, Wade Stevenson, perennial chair of the Welcome Home Bison Committee, hosted a pre-game luncheon at the Saturn club.

The dignitaries, the marching bands, and the drum and bugle corps, assembled on Woodlawn Avenue and marched into the stadium through a gate in the centerfield fence where they massed at the flagpole.

Throngs of fans poured through the turnstiles, or, as Tony Wurzer of the *News* reported, the crowd "just barged in bunches…like squashed grapes. They arrived in bunches, went through the gates in bunches, and sat in each other's laps in bunches. It looked like a nylon rush (a timely reference to the wartime shortage of that precious material for women's stockings) with no holds barred." Floral tributes abounded. Appropriately these were dispatched to various veterans' hospitals afterwards. The celebrities took their seats; Paul Fitzpatrick, State Democratic Chairman with his followers in one box, and Ed Jaeckle, Erie County Republican Chair in another. The Jacobs brothers and Lew Horschel and the rest of the city's elite were all decked out. The ceremonial battery had Mayor Bernard Dowd pitching, actually dribbling, the baseball to Wade Stevenson. The crowd kept coming; ropes had to be strung along the outfield to accommodate the overflow throng, necessitating a change in ground rules. What a crowd; it was unprecedented. Throughout the land, opening day baseball crowds in 1946 were smashing attendance records. Buffalo was no exception. The fans were back, at Yankee Stadium, at Fenway Park, at Ebbetts Field, and at Offermann Stadium. A record breaking crowd of 17,927 jammed into the ballpark. There was no doubt about it, as Cy Kritzer put it: "the prewar enthusiasm of the fans returned with a roar."[6]

Unfortunately, Team Buffalo did not do as well on the field against the Newark Bears. Trying to rebound from a hitless loss to Syracuse the previous day, the Bisons did little better, managing only one run. Pitcher Lou Kretlow, of whom great things were expected, did poorly as the Bears knocked out plenty of hits including two homers in their 5 - 1 victory. Some of the Bisons' worst teams have been victors on opening day and some of the best have let down the home opening day crowd. Most fans thought that that loss might be a good omen. The day ended with another tradition, the team was hosted by the Knights of Columbus at their annual Sports Night in the clubrooms on Delaware Avenue. Following the opening game, the Herd embarked on a roller coaster, they lost some and won some. By May 8 they were in 4th place. The season would continue that up and down trend.

Only a few weeks later, on May 19, Buffalo baseball had another grand occasion to celebrate, a kind of a second opening day in May. It was a watershed event for all baseball, indeed for all sports and for all America. Montreal, the farm club of the Brooklyn Dodgers, came to town with Jackie Robinson, a black ballplayer. Robinson had been a magnificent all around athlete at UCLA. He also was an army veteran, and a baseball star in the Negro Leagues. Branch Rickey, owner of the Dodgers, had previously signed Jackie Robinson; Rickey's plans called for bringing Jackie to the Majors once he had had a year of seasoning with the Brooklyn farm club in Montreal. Breaking the color barrier by Robinson was a milestone of monumental proportion.

Wherever Jackie Robinson played in the International League, the attention of the fans, indeed the attention of the entire host city was focused on him, focused on this Negro (as black Americans were then generally called) ballplayer, and on this rising star. This coming out party in the International League foreshadowed the 1947 debut of Jackie Robinson in the Major Leagues. Jackie's reception in Buffalo was very enthusiastic and certainly friendlier than in many other baseball cities. Indeed on the 50th anniversary of Jackie's breaking the color line, a major Canadian newspaper recalled that Buffalo's reception for Jackie Robinson was one of the most cordial in the United States. Certainly as Bob Stedler noted, it brought back memories for very old timers when "another Negro player, Frank Grant," was a big favorite locally as a member of the Bison team in the 1880s, just before the color barrier became a fact of life.[7]

A welcoming committee, which included many of Buffalo's prominent black citizens, welcomed Jackie, as did the spirited crowd of over 12,000. In between games of the doubleheader, Jackie was presented with a number of gifts. As far as his playing debut in Buffalo, Robinson fielded flawlessly, big league style, but did not have much of an opportunity to demonstrate his hitting skills. He singled once but was walked 4 times in his 8 trips to the plate. The Montreal team arrived at Offermann Stadium holding down first place, but the Bisons, on this grand occasion, took their measure twice, 7 - 3, and 5 - 4. Buffalo, like other Northern cities still practiced segregation; consequently Robinson had to rely on a group of local black athletes, including General Bass, to take him to Dan Montgomery's Little Harlem Hotel on Michigan Avenue. The rest of the team stayed, as was the custom for visiting teams at the Stratford Arms hotel on Utica Street, not far from the ballpark.[8]

The season proceeded through the summer with the Bisons' performance marked by several losing streaks and also several winning streaks. Fortunately for the Bisons, there were more ups than downs. The result was that the

Little Harlem Hotel. Jackie Robinson, playing for the Brooklyn farm club, the Montreal Royals, stayed here (segregation was still practiced then) on his first visit to Buffalo in 1946. *Photo: WNY Heritage Magazine.*

Herd hovered between 4th and 5th place for most of the season. It was obviously a better team than the 1945 version.

Pitching ace Art Houtteman was one of the big stars in the early part of the season winning his 9th by June 21. This feat caused some observers to comment that he was headed for rookie of the year honors. That was a bit premature since he did not notch his 12th win until July 20. On the other hand, Pitcher Lou Kretlow for whom there were also high hopes found himself packing his bags for Williamsport, Pennsylvania before mid season. In August the Bisons experienced a burst of success. Houtteman won his 15th and Pete Appleton performed yeoman relief work. Crowd turnouts reflected this success, some 11,166 turning out on August 11. The Bisons propelled themselves into 2nd place.

But then the bubble burst, and down the stretch the Herd lost a number of close ones. As the season wound to a close in September, the team found itself in 5th place, just missing the playoffs. The pennant race had been a tight one. The Herd's record was over .500 and they just missed 2nd place by three games. Moreover the team could boast of some individual accomplishments. First Baseman John McHale hit 24 home runs and had 94 RBIs. Right Fielder Vic Wertz, destined for stardom with the Detroit Tigers, batted .301, had 19 home runs and 91 RBIs. Art Houtteman compiled a 16-13 record on the mound. In addition, the attendance at the ballpark was the highest it had been in 43 years. Thanks in no small part to Jackie Robinson, the figure for the season hit 293,813. Baseball was emphatically back in Buffalo, New York. America's pastime was alive and well.[9]

The post season witnessed the expected changes. Bucky Harris resigned to take a post with the New York Yankees. Gabby Harnett retired from baseball; he headed back to Chicago and concentrated on his bowling enterprise. Bowling was a big activity in the Windy City. At the end of November Roger Peckinpaugh was named General Manager and a week later, the top brass in Buffalo and Detroit landed Paul Richards as the new Field Manager. Kritzer thought that the Richards' selection cemented the "once shaky alliance between the Herd and the Tigers."[10]

Richards' selection was a sound one and a popular one. He was an all around star catcher for the Tigers and one of the standouts for Detroit in their World Series victories the previous autumn. In fact he drove in four runs with a pair of doubles in the seventh game to lead the Tigers to a 9 - 3 victory over the Chicago Cubs and the World Series Championship. He was named to the Sporting News All Star team. Tiger Manager Steve O'Neill felt that Richards had much to do with pitching ace Hal Newhouser's success. Bob Stedler, the Sports Editor of the *News*, called the 38 year old Richards, "one of the best maskmen in the League." Stedler felt that Richards was a beneficiary of the good deal too since Buffalo was "one of the best managerial posts in baseball."[11]

Paul Richards, star catcher with world champion Detroit Tigers in 1945; Bison Manager, 1947-49; Won pennant in 1949. He later managed the Chicago White Sox.

Richards had other proven credentials. He had solid managerial experience; he had won two pennants as the boss of Atlanta of the Southern Association a few years earlier. During his career, this Waxahachie, Texas native had played every position in baseball except centerfield. Both Bucky Harris and George Trautman, who was manager of the Tiger farm system, were firmly in Richards' corner. At $13,000 he would be the highest paid manager in the International League; his bosses thought he was worth it. Cy Kritzer summed in up best: "In Richards, the Bisons hired an able handler of men, a proven success as manager, a catcher who should be a whiz with rookie pitchers, and a leader who has a distinguished record outside baseball as well" and "a tough disciplinarian of the John McGraw school" to boot. There were those who felt that Gabby Hartnett had been too easy on his players.[12]

Even the spring training site bore some blame for the rather ordinary 1946 season. Winter Haven was not suitable, the grounds were poorly maintained. Therefore Club Secretary Joe Brown worked out an arrangement for a site at Bartow, Florida for 1947.

The Bisons anticipated a good season in 1947. Their hitting had been more than adequate in '46. Coaker Triplett, Vic Wertz, Earl Rapp, and Ed Yount had battered over .300 and all were scheduled to return. The pitching had been weak but with Paul Richards at the helm the probability of vast pitching improvement was expected. And the fans were back in force. Attendance had doubled over 1945 when only 129,000 fans had trekked to Offermann Stadium.

Interest was up across the land. Baseball was widely acclaimed as being at the pinnacle

of the sports world. It achieved unrivalled popularity in the years immediately following World War II. Attendance and interest in other professional sports was not even a close second. It was not just the major leagues that did well. The minor leagues at all levels were drawing record numbers; from Triple A ball like the International League right down to Class D, like the Pony league. Hundreds of fans came from the rural areas of Western New York to watch games in Olean, Wellsville, Batavia and Jamestown. In Buffalo, throngs of boys were turning out to participate on MUNY and American Legion teams. Large neighborhood crowds turned out to cheer on their local favorites in Delaware, Schiller, Riverside, and Cazenovia Parks. There were even some glimmers of the future Little Leagues on the horizon as thousands of schoolboys played sandlot ball.

Buffalo Baseball fans couldn't get enough of the sport. When not attending the games in person, they got their box scores and highlights from the local newspapers. This meant the *Buffalo Evening News* and the *Buffalo Courier Express*. These were pre-television days; adults, and youngsters too, read the newspapers regularly, they counted on the newspapers for their news and sports. Radio played a role. Sport highlights would be given nightly over the radio and often parts of the Bison games would be broadcast. Mutual Radio also broadcast a game of the week, nationwide. Some of the radio broadcasts of out of town games passed through studios in Buffalo. Announcers would read off Western Union tickets and use some imaginative gimmicks to simulate crowd noise and the sound of the bat hitting a pitched ball. From the press box, listeners might think they heard the crack of the bat hitting the ball when actually it was an announcer slapping a piece of wood against a table. But it was the daily newspaper that served as the Bible for baseball fans. That was the source where the avid fan memorized the box scores, read the game stories, and agreed or disagreed with the opinion columns commenting on the play of the team.[13]

Buffalo fans had available plenty of material to read about their cherished Bisons. They were also furnished with considerable information about the Majors, especially the American League teams, and especially the Yankees, Red Sox, and Tigers. The Indians too were followed since Cleveland was less than 200 miles down the Lake Erie shore. It was the closest site for a Buffalo fan to catch a Major League game. In addition, the scribes from the local papers kept the fans interested in local boys who were either in the majors or who had the potential for professional ball. Sibby Sisti, Buddy Rosar, and Stan Rojek, were all watched closely.

Sisti was a regular for the Boston Braves and played in the 1948 World Series. He was recognized as a fine utility infielder. Rosar played several years in the Majors with four different teams. He started out as a catcher behind the great Bill Dickey of the New York Yankees; then Rosar became an All Star Catcher in his own right and in the post war period was a mainstay with the Philadelphia A's. Rojek was a regular with the Pittsburgh Pirates and batted at a .290 clip in 1948. Western New York fans also watched the newspapers closely for items relating to Jim Konstanty, a reliable relief pitcher from Arcade, New York who hurled for a number of different clubs in the Majors. He proved to be an excellent reliever in the 1950 season with the Philadelphia Phillies. Also Niagara Falls native, Sal Maglie, drew attention. Sal "the barber" had his best years in the 1950s, but his rather ill advised sojourn in the Mexican League in the late 1940s was often a hot topic of conversation. In addition to the aforementioned, a number of the Buffalo Bisons from the 1940s also spent time, of varying duration, in the Big Leagues. These included Art Houtteman, Billy Pierce, Ted Gray, Lou Kretlow, Saul Rogovin, Alex

Carrasquel, Lum Harris, Vic Wertz, Johnny Groth, Earl Rapp, Andy Seminick, Hal White, and Chet Laabs.[14]

When all was said and done, the one baseball player who stood out above all others in the minds and hearts of local baseball fans was Warren Spahn. He was universally regarded as Buffalo's greatest baseball native son. Warren Spahn, Spahnie, as he was sometimes called, had graduated from South Park High School, played some pro ball, served heroically in the armed forces overseas, and, in the late 1940s, he starred for the Boston Braves. Spahn's exploits with the Braves were followed diligently as he pitched season after season, on his way to becoming one of the great hurlers of all time, surely the greatest lefthander in the game. With his 363 victories he became a "shoo-in" for the Hall of Fame. Plenty of sports page coverage kept Buffalo baseball fans, many of them, like the Cy Williams' family, old friends of Warren Spahn, abreast of his many victories, his few losses, and his activities on and off the field. Indeed it was Cy Williams, a scout for the Detroit Tigers, and one of the truly outstanding Major League scouts, who helped to keep his hometown informed of the comings and goings of hundred of major and minor league players through the years.

Four Western New York Baseball Greats. ***Clockwise from top left:*** **Sal Maglie: Niagara Falls Native who pitched for New York Giants, known as "the Barber" for his close "shaves" against opposing batters. Warren Spahn: South Buffalo native – became greatest player ever to come out of Buffalo. Pitched for the Boston Braves and the Milwaukee Braves. Joe McCarthy: "Marse" Joe, arguably greatest Yankee manager ever. Often returned to his Amherst home on Ellicott Creek Road. Made many appearances at area sports nights. Cy Williams: Affable Irishman from South Buffalo. Served as chief scout for the Detroit Tigers for many years.**

What was true for Spahn, was equally true of Joe McCarthy. Marse Joe was an adopted Buffalonian. In the early part of the century, Joe McCarthy left the coal region of Pennsylvania and began to play the infield for the Bisons. He made his home in Buffalo in the upscale Gates Circle area. After a mediocre playing career, McCarthy, went on to become one of the greatest managers in baseball history. After the 1946 season, McCarthy retired from the Yankees, took a year off, and then returned to manage the Boston Red Sox from 1948 to 1950. By that time he had moved to Ellicott Creek Road in the rural Town of Amherst, a few miles north of the City of Buffalo. While still active in baseball, he would return home frequently. He and his wife loved their farm. Marse Joe was truly the gentleman farmer. His farm became a sort of shrine, a mecca for Baseball Dads for many years to come, who would drive by the farmhouse with their sons in tow and point and say: "That is where the great Joe McCarthy lives, one of the greatest baseball managers of all time." When McCarthy was inducted into the Baseball Hall of Fame in the late 1950s, the media flocked to his home making it a grand affair.

Joe McCarthy and Warren Spahn, and a host of others added zest and sparked additional interest in the sport of baseball in Buffalo. The local club benefited from this attention. As the Bisons headed to spring training they basked in the glow of the nation's pastime. Spring training, 1947, in Bartow, Florida, located in the central part of the state, initially appeared to serve the needs of the Bisons adequately. They won a few and lost a few in the Sunshine State but more importantly, new helmsman Paul Richards had a good opportunity to observe closely his prospects for the upcoming season. On April 17 the Bisons entrained north to open the 64th season of the oldest minor league in the country. They played Jersey City and lost, before undoubtedly the largest crowd ever to watch a Bison baseball game. Some 37, 000 people turned out, largely, it was claimed, through the strong arm efforts of the Boss Hague political machine of Jersey City.

After a few more road games, the Herd headed home for their own grand opening in Offermann Stadium. Joe Brown had the ballpark in excellent condition. The grass was firm and it seemed as though everything that should be painted, was. Kritzer even suggested that females had been taken into consideration in that Henry Perry, the handsomest Bison, was slated to pitch on opening day. Actually Billy Pierce did the honors. Mayor Dowd proclaimed a civic half-holiday. Students in the Buffalo schools were given a half day off. Had that not been the case, predictably a considerable number of grandmothers might have died that day so that young boys could have an excuse for not attending school.

The traditional parade from Woodlawn into the stadium was comprised of musical groups from the Fire and Police Departments, and the Shriners, as well as The St. Catharine's' Trumpet band, the Eagle' Drum Corps, the Colored Musicians Band, and the Buffalo Sports Boosters Band. The Illustrious Potentate of the Shriners, presided over the flag raising ceremony. Jim Wells WBEN Sportscaster was the Master of Ceremonies; Charley Bailey aired the game on WEBR.

Those in charge planned for a big crowd. Ticket sales in April were 35 % ahead of 1946 so it was not unreasonable for Joe Brown to predict an all time high turnout of perhaps 20,000 fans. Everyone and everything cooperated except the weather. It was a foggy, cool, rainy day. The result was a somewhat disappointing attendance of 15,012. The positive thinker would say that it was a surprise that so many fans did attend in view of the inclement weather.

To make matters worse, the Bisons blew a sizeable lead and lost 12 - 7. That seemed to set the tone for the next couple of weeks. The Bisons struggled. However once the ever popular Coaker Triplet got his bat going, the Bisons began to pick up steam. In the latter part of the month of May, with Triplett hitting a hefty .500, the Bisons climbed out of the cellar. By the end of the month they were tied for 5th and a week later they were in 4th place. To help out Triplett in the hitting area, outfielder Chet Laabs was bought from the Philadelphia A's. Laabs had been a star of the 1944 pennant winning St. Louis Browns. After a poor beginning in Buffalo, Laabs came on strong. At the same time Anse Moore began pounding the ball relentlessly. Eddie Modarski came alive too. Art Houtteman, was on his way back from Detroit to reinforce the pitching corps. Manager Richards got in the act too. Known for his fiery reputation, he lived up to that and then some, during the 1947 season. He was tossed out of a game in June for challenging a heckler; a short time later he received a five game suspension for his conduct berating an umpire. After returning he again was tossed out for arguing with a plate umpire. This time he was bounced just ½ inning after his reappearance. That was the 13th time he had been ejected from a game during the '47 season.

The Bisons held steady through the month

of August and made the playoffs, for the first time since 1944. In fact with the team comfortably in 4th position and yet no chance of being an actual contender for the pennant, Richards made a wise move. He rested the veterans during the last two weeks of the season. This worked magnificently; both the hitters and pitchers were ready for the playoffs. The Bisons had a tough task ahead of them. They had to open by playing the hottest team in the league, the Jersey City Giants.

Earl Rapp's homerun won the first game for the Herd, 3 - 2, the Bisons won the next despite Paul Richards' ejection; the Herd then returned to Buffalo. The fans were in a jubilant mood as they headed toward the ballpark. They embarked from the busses and trolleys and walked the last few hundred years down Ferry Street, past the offices of the Deco restaurants, across Main Street and on into the stadium. Hundreds of others came to Offermann from both directions on Michigan Avenue and from Main Street, while still more came over from Masten Avenue. Offermann Stadium was in an accessible location and it was located in a spic and span neighborhood. Years later, Cy Williams, venerable scout for the Detroit Tigers, noted that the old Germans in the area kept the streets and lawns neat and clean and virtually spotless. Williams' legions of friends from South Buffalo, would take the trolley down Seneca Street to Shelton Square, transfer to the Main Street bus or trolley, take that to Ferry Street and alight one block from the stadium.[15]

Those fans were on hand to watch the Bisons take games three and four from Jersey City. The crowds were enthusiastic; more than 10,000 and 14,000 respectively passed through the turnstiles. It was an impressive show of support and an impressive clean sweep for the hometown heroes over the Jersey City Giants.

Next the Bisons faced the Syracuse Chiefs for the Governors' Cup. A 14 — 1 blowout loss brought the Bisons back down to earth. But the resilient Herd rebounded nicely. They broke the Chiefs' twelve game winning streak by taking the second game. The Bisons then lost the third and won the fourth, lost the fifth, and won the 6th. It was a truly fine series for Buffalo; Coaker Triplett did his usual splendid job at the plate. Unfortunately for Buffalo, the Chiefs had Hank Sauer, future major league all star, leading them throughout the series. Syracuse took the 7th game.

Certainly there was disappointment with the final playoff loss but overall the 1947 season had been a good one. Buffalonians were pleased. Attendance was off slightly from the previous year but that was understandable in Buffalo as well as in much of the Northeast because miserable weather conditions prevailed in the spring of 1947. Still the fans had turned out and the final attendance was a respectable 267,012. The team had performed very capably. Paul Richards had showed that he indeed was a top notch field manager. In the fall, he was given a new title, that of general manager, replacing Peckinpaugh. Richards would also stay as field manager. Chet Laabs and Anse Moore had given the Bisons a powerful one-two punch. Each blasted 22 home runs and they totaled 149 RBIs between them. Coaker Triplett, who had hit .303 in 1946, upped his average to .315 in '47. Joe Overfield regarded Triplett as one of the best right hand hitters ever to wear a Bison uniform. Billy Pierce, the young left hander, finished the season at 14 - 8, in part due to Richards' expertise as a pitching instructor.[16]

Following the end of the season, Manager Paul Richards and others from the Bison front office were off for the long train ride to attend the annual baseball meetings in Miami. The lengthy trip was invariably enjoyable and rewarding. Old friends renewed friendships; new acquaintances established friendships. Baseball people got to know each other better; they could discuss leisurely their problems and could fraternize with other baseball people. The Yankee bosses, who were also on the train headed south, were a source of lively conversation. Train travel had its benefits.

Given the success of the team in 1947, the Buffalo fans looked forward to 1948 with lofty expectations. Spring training was moved to Waxahatchie, Texas, a pleasant little town of 15,000 some forty miles south of Dallas. It also was the home town of Paul Richards; indeed, he was regarded as its first citizen. The two previous spring training sites in Florida had had some drawbacks. Most glaring were the poorly kept grounds. It was almost impossible to conduct a well planned training program. Waxahatchie had to be an improvement.

The Bison rookies and veterans began gathering there late in March. The exhibition season rolled along without major problems. Optimism was in the air. Hometown boy, first baseman Frankie Heller who had played for Buffalo in the early war years, and in 1947 had hit very well while playing for the Williamsport team, was hoping to make a comeback with the Bisons. Masten High School all star Ken Fremming, was taking his highly regarded fastball to camp in Texas and was one of the young hopefuls. Centerfielder Johnny Groth who had a magnificent year in Williamsport seemed headed to Detroit but, it was hoped that he would have a year of seasoning in Buffalo before he made the big club. The regular season began on the road, as usual, and the Bisons lost again, as usual. They lost some more and by the time the Herd arrived home in Buffalo, their record was well below .500.

The home opener was planned with the usual amount of considerable fanfare. Ralph Hubbell, already a veteran radio voice, was the Master of Ceremonies, and the bugles and drums, and flags and flowers were all present. But then the clouds opened up and the rains lasted until game time, keeping attendance down to 13,554. But the Bisons did please their fans by winning the opener. Signs of what was in store for the 1948 season were the circuit blasts by Anse Moore, Johnny Groth and Coaker Triplett. That trio continued to pound the ball and in less than two weeks the Herd was in the first division. Chet Laabs, of whom much was expected, already had 7 home runs. Pitcher Saul Rogovin, an emerging star, had notched his third win, thus equaling his mark of the entire previous season.

Memorial Day, was customarily a big day for Bison baseball. The Herd took two from the Toronto Maple Leafs as 12,337 fans watched. That was a typical Memorial Day crowd and that figure did not include a hundred or so regulars who watched the action from the back porches on top of their garages on Masten Avenue and those who did so from their front porches across Woodlawn Avenue beyond the right field fence. They, of course, were part of the non-paid attendance figure. The club's top hitters went on a spree that culminated on June 20, in what Bison historian Joe Overfield called "an orgy at Offermann." On that warm sunny afternoon, the Bisons literally blasted the Syracuse Chiefs, 28 – 11, and 16 – 12. In the first game the Bisons hit a record 10 home runs, Moore got three, Groth and Saul Rogovin each had two. This outburst surpassed the old International League record of 7 home runs, also set by Buffalo, in the previous century. By the end of June, Chet Laabs had 27 round trippers and *Courier* Sports Editor Billy Kelly called him "one of the most dangerous sluggers ever to wear a Bison uniform." The Bisons were a great hitting ball club in 1948. Buffalo actually had a quartet of outfielders, Moore, Groth, Laabs, and Triplett, all of whom were batting over .315. With the team doing so well, the fans eagerly showed their appreciation. On July 4, 11,381 showed up, a week later, July 10, almost 10,000 fans were in the stands, and a week later, 16,444 were on hand.[17]

The summer of '48 also witnessed some discussion about the role of television in baseball in Buffalo. Television had made an initial appearance in the New York City area just before World War II, but the war itself put the development of the new phenomenon on the back burner. After VJ day, the technicians and businessmen began to accelerate rapidly the growth of the television industry. Television first came to Buffalo, and to WBEN, in mid 1948. Almost immediately this local station suggested a deal to tape delay televising some Bison games. The Bisons declined, fearing the adverse impact on attendance. Interestingly, it was only a decade earlier that top teams in New York City had debated over whether to even allow their games to be aired on the radio.

For the time being there would be no televised Bison games, but it seemed only a matter of time before that would change. Indeed, not long afterwards, the president of the International League, Frank Shaughnessy left no doubt where he stood. He stated that he would vote in favor of television for both the majors and the minors, saying "I believe that eventually TV will do nearly as much to boost baseball as did radio."[18]

By the time the dog days of August rolled around, the Bisons began to falter. They lost several games to league leading Montreal. Indeed the Royals even without Jackie Robinson were still the team to beat. In 1948, they had Don Newcombe and Sam Jethroe, future Major League all stars, on their roster. By the end of the month Montreal was in first place, 16 games out in front. The Bisons were four games out of the first division. Things got worse. The Bisons skidded downward on a nine game losing streak. Injuries hurt. Both Moore and Laabs were out for a spell. Their absence proved costly.

The Bisons did not make the playoffs. The Bisons had deficiencies that would have to be addressed before the next season. Billy Kelly had it right when he pointed out that the greatest needs were for pitchers and infielders especially at 2nd base and shortstop. Despite the disappointment, there were some bright spots. Coaker Triplett was the league batting champion with a hefty .353. Laabs and Moore hit 29 and 23 home runs respectively. Johnny Groth, one of the best players to ever wear a Bison uniform, hit .340 and had 37 doubles and 16 triples, and 30 home runs. As Joe Overfield so well put it, "Rarely had Buffalo fans seen a better looking young ballplayer than Johnny Groth. He was a graceful fielder with a powerful throwing arm; he could hit to all fields, and with power." Groth went on to a long major league career but unfortunately a number of injuries prevented him from reaching Hall of Fame status. He played in the Big Leagues, mostly with the Detroit Tigers from 1949 until 1960 and had a lifetime batting average of .279. Crowds at Offermann were once again solid, even better than 1947. Some 272,761 passed through the turnstiles. [19]

Meanwhile Buffalo baseball fans in the fall of 1948 could sit back relax, and follow the exploits of their hometown hero, Warren Spahn, who was pitching for the Boston Braves in the World Series against the Cleveland Indians. Spahn and teammate, Johnny Sain, did well for the Beantown boys but not well enough to win the series.

Spring training opened in March 1949, again in Waxahatchie. As usual there were more than a score of new faces hoping to make it in Triple A ball. The biggest story during the off season was the naming of Leo Miller to be Assistant to President John Gehn. Immediately there was speculation as well as some concern as to the meaning of this appointment, especially on the part of Paul Richards' supporters. What would Miller's role be? Richards and Miller had a lengthy conversation. As a result, it appeared that Richards was still the boss. Miller would be the money man, the one who decided how much players should be paid and deciding which, if any, contracts should be slashed. That left some observers confused.

Cy Kritzer knew the baseball mentality. He predicted that Richards' control would be drastically reduced, that things would come to a head at the end of the season, and predicted that Miller would be the big boss by the end of 1949. Cy was clairvoyant. But for the time being, the two, Richards and Miller, seemed to have a cordial relationship. To his credit Richards put any concerns he might have had behind him and concentrated on building a championship team.

Spring training proceeded without difficulty. Then the team moved north to open the season on the road as usual, and lost the opener, as usual. That was on April 20. Manager Richards welcomed the good news that Triplett was returning. He was very satisfied with his first rate outfield. Where he needed help was in the infield. In the person of Billy DeMars, who came down from the Philadelphia A's, he got an excellent shortstop. When Gene Markland inked a contract, Manager Richards had another first rate infielder.

The pitching staff had continued to improve under Manager Richards' watchful eye. League President Frank Shaughnessy noted that managers were always crying for more pitchers. If they were as good as Richards, they would not have much of a problem. He said that Richards was simply the best pitching coach in baseball. Richards was particularly pleased with the development of Aaron Silverman. For a young man who had never even pitched in high school, Silverman was progressing nicely. In addition Connie Mack, venerable boss of the Philadelphia Athletics, came through again and sent two hurlers to the Herd, Clem Hausman and Bobby Shantz. Hausman had actually had been with the Herd previously.

The 1949 Opening Day festivities in Offermann Stadium proceeded smoothly. The performance by the players had raised the hopes of the fans. Just a few days before the home opener, they pounded Newark 8 – 1 with a 15 hit attack, a healthy sign of things to come. They had emerged from the cellar before the home opener. Wade Stevenson gave his traditional pre game luncheon for the dignitaries, though this year it was at the Elks Club, a formidable stone edifice on Delaware Avenue. In addition to the usual flowers, bands, and flag raising, there were a host of prizes for various players donated by the likes of Victor Hugo's Restaurant, Schreiber's Brewery, the Touraine Hotel, The Ed Rose and Laux Sporting Goods Stores, and Jacobi Brothers Men's Wear. Ideal weather prevailed; it helped to bring out the 2nd largest opening day crowd "ever to see local lid lifter" in the words of the *Courier*'s Joe Alli. Some 16,897 fans showed up.[20]

The crowd let it be known that they came to see this promising team that Richards had assembled and to see it win. The infield included DeMars at shortstop, and Gene Markland at 2nd or 3rd base, reliable Marty Tabachek was behind the plate, and the outfield had top sluggers Anse Moore, Triplett, and Ray Coleman with the quirky Chet Laabs in reserve. The crowd would not be disappointed. The Herd pounded the Chiefs 14 – 4 and proceeded along the victory path during the opening home stand. Gene Markland was particularly impressive in the opener and would continue to be throughout the season. Former University of North Carolina football star Jack Hussey was a pleasant surprise. He drove in 5 runs. That night the players were feted as usual at the Knights of Columbus. That had become a tradition in the Queen city.

The team continued its winning ways defeating Syracuse again, then taking Jersey

City twice and splitting with Baltimore. Bison fans were especially happy to see their team get the best of perennial power Montreal. The win over the Royals on May 24 put Buffalo solidly in the first division. Memorial Day weekend was as big a baseball weekend as ever in Buffalo. 14,264 were on hand for a split with the Montreal Royals. The following day, the Herd swept the Toronto Maple Leafs before more than 10,000 fans.

In June the Herd continued its drive upward and after a sweep from the Chiefs on June 11, they gained the top position. The hitting barrage continued; heroes were abundant. On one day it might be Triplett in a starring role, another day it might be Laabs, and in other games in might be Moore or first baseman George Byam. The infield, escaping from its shabby past, was now a source of pride. Sports columnist Billy Kelly gave "much credit" to Manager Richards for engineering the deals to bring DeMars and Markland to Buffalo. By mid-June the Herd had won 16 of 22 home starts and was leading the league by 3 games. The July 4 weekend was another festive holiday affair. The Bisons beat the Leafs twice, before 9,476 fans. The pitching staff was doing nicely; both Hooper and Hausmann notched their 8th wins over the holiday weekend.[21]

However by the latter part of the month, the pitching staff began to grow a bit weary and the team faltered. Some of the pundits were predicting that the Bisons' success with those "old guys" in uniform would not last. By the end of July their six game lead was narrowed to just one game. The Bisons continued to appear shaky early in August. Thanks to the relentless hitting of Coaker Triplett, who was batting at .324, the club did not succumb completely. Saul Rogovin's pitching improved. Saul notched his 14th victory in August. Additional help arrived with the appearance of Alex Carrasquel, a 37-year-old Venezuelan pitcher. By August 9 the Herd had upped its lead to 5 ½ games. On that same day, Richards was suspended indefinitely for kicking dirt at an umpire. Fortunately the suspension was lifted 5 days later. Richards was welcomed back with a

Team Photo of the 1949 Bisons: International League Pennant winners in 1949 with 90-64 record. They set record attendance for Buffalo, 393,843 which was broken 10 years later.

rousing ovation from the fans. On August 16 attendance went over 300,000, an all time record for Buffalo.

The Bison hitting assault continued. By the end of August, the Herd was once again holding a 6 game lead. Hooper won his 17th game. A human interest story surfaced when Jim Wilson, a pitcher who had a brush with death and a long history of injuries, astounded the fans when he managed to pitch a no-hitter for Buffalo.

The Bisons were even in a bit of a cocky mood. They posed for a team photo even though they had not yet clinched the pennant. The old pros on the team had no hang ups about sitting for a "Championship" photo at this point of the season. They were confident that they would not blow the lead. The archrival Rochester Red Wings felt differently. They were not about to give up without a fight. On September 2, The Bisons and Wings engaged in a knock down, drag out slugfest which Buffalo won 10 – 8, and Hooper wound up with his 18th victory. This was a contest that Cy Kritzer called one of the "zaniest and most sensational ball games played by those belligerent rivals." Rochester was a "baseball mad city." The crowd that day sent the city over its all time attendance of nearly 400,000.

Four days later the Bisons beat Montreal thereby clinching the pennant. Manager Richards said simply that he was pleased with his "nine old men." Kritzer called winning the pennant a "modern miracle" in view of the fact that the Bisons were like "orphans operating on their lonesome without a major league alliance." At that time the Bisons had no solid ties with the Detroit Tigers or the Philadelphia A's.[22]

League President Shaughnessy praised Richards for his magnificent job. Kritzer said "it was the greatest personal triumph" of his career. He added that Richards had built and managed the team with skill and strategy. Sports Editor Bob Stedler added that the record attendance confirmed the fans' interest in good baseball. Team historian, Joe Overfield put it succinctly, saying that the 1949 Bisons "proved to be good '49ers' striking gold in the pennant race and at the gate." [23]

The team arrived back in Buffalo at the New York Central Terminal to a hero's welcome. The scene in the cavernous structure was reminiscent of the tumultuous crowds that greeted the throngs of returning servicemen following the end of World War II. As thousands cheered, acrobatic youth straddled the majestic Bison, the signature symbol of the Queen City, that dominated the vista in the terminal.

Thousands more cheered along the parade route that led from Paderewski Drive to Fillmore and Broadway then to Main Street and downtown Buffalo, when, indeed, there was a hustling, bustling downtown Buffalo. The city residents turned out in unbelievable numbers. The team, the Bison officials, the Mayor and other city dignitaries, boarded open automobiles outside the terminal and led the way. Bands aboard flatbed trailers followed as did floats of various types, a panoply of groups were involved including the Tonawanda Brownshidle Post Legion Band, the Lackawanna American Legion and, the Blackthorns of South Buffalo, the Knights of Columbus, the Lions Club, the Fire Department Drum Corps, the newly organized Buffalo Police Band, the Buffalo Sports Boosters, the Ismalia Temple band, and the prize winning Plewacki Post Band.

The playoffs were just ahead. For now the team and the city seemed to have everything in order for a great run. Buffalonians were cherishing a victorious team and celebrating a pennant winning season, in a manner befitting a big time American city basking in its glory in the immediate postwar era.

The playoffs opened with the Bisons trouncing the Jersey City Giants 10-4 before a crowd of more than 10,000 hearty fans. The chilly weather kept the crowd down Hitting at a .350 clip, the Bisons took the second came 12 – 10 before about 9000 well wishers. The 3rd game was a cliff hanger but the Bisons won again and then swept the series with a 10 – 1 rout in the fourth and final game.

Now, for the 2nd time in three years they faced the formidable Montreal Royals in the finals. The hometown heroes won the opener nicely, with a 9 - 3 win before more than 10,000. Then the tide turned. In game 2 the Herd lost a heart breaker 6 – 5. A Montreal home run with two out in the 9th won it for the Canadian club. That seemed to set the tone for the rest of the series. The Bisons lost the remaining games. Before the 1949 season had begun, the indomitable Branch Rickey, Brooklyn owner, had called his Montreal farm club the "greatest Triple A club ever assembled." He now had many believers in Buffalo. As Stedler saw it, the speed and youth of the opposition proved decisive. The Bisons seemed to have their number during the season, but now at playoff time, the Royals were virtually unbeatable. [24]

Nevertheless it had been a wonderful season, a wonderful way to close out the decade of the '40s. For a team that had been picked for 5th place in the spring, the Bisons of Manager Paul Richards had done very well, indeed. It was the first time the Bisons had finished the season in first place since 1936. The turnstile count of nearly 400,000, actually 393,483 was better than any previous season. The 1949 Bisons were a balanced team. Gene Markland cracked 25 home runs, Ray Coleman had 23, and Coaker Triplett and Chet Laabs each tallied 22 and first sacker George Byam had 19. Markland batted .305, walked 155 times, drove in 90 runs and was hit eight times. His "on base" average was a phenomenal .470. Three pitchers paced the Herd. Bob Hooper won 19 games and lost only three, Saul Rogovin was 16–6 and Clem Hausmann was 15 – 7.[25]

Accolades accumulated for the Bisons. Gene Markland, who was called up to the Philadelphia A's, was named Buffalo Athlete of the Year by the prestigious Buffalo Athletic Club at its annual sports night. Markland thus joined other luminaries of the post war 1940s that included Buffalo Bills owner, Jim Breuil, Bills' quarterback, George Ratterman, and Mike Broderick of the West Side Rowing Club.

The end of the season was a time for bestowing honors. It was a time for enjoying the thrill of victory, but also contemplating the future. The second guessing about Paul Richards' future with the Bisons, that briefly had surfaced earlier in the year, was now being discussed openly.

There was speculation that he might be named Chicago White Sox manager. He was seen in Toots Shor's in New York City, the nation's most famous watering hole for baseball celebrities, having dinner with White Sox management. A few days later it was confirmed that Richards was leaving to take a post with Seattle of the Pacific Coast League. Following that post, he would serve as manager of the Chicago White Sox from 1951 to 1954. Richards was too good not to make it to the Big Leagues; he continued to spend many years in the majors.

Cy Kritzer's prediction came true. Richards was leaving and Leo Miller was now running the show. Miller assumed complete control of the front office. He bought several rookies for the following season, and then he began to look for a new manager. He and President John Gehn arranged a meeting at the Lenox Hotel on North Street; there they signed Frank Skaff, to be manager of the 1950 version of the Buffalo Bisons. Skaff had had some success with Savannah in the Minors though his coming on board as manager raised some eyebrows. It was a departure from the practice of hiring a "name" baseball person for that position.

The raised eyebrows were right. The 1950 season was a complete disaster. As good as 1949 had been, 1950 was the reverse. The highlight of the season came on May 3, the date of the home opener. Some 16,000 fans watched the Commissioner of Baseball, Happy Chandler, help raise the pennant won the previous season. Jack Hussey's homer in the 9th, with two on base, gave the Herd a 7 – 5 victory.

From then on it was all downhill. The Bisons plummeted to the cellar; they stayed there. On May 8, before a meager Sunday gathering of only 6,000 the Bisons were forced to forfeit the game; the very first time this happened in their own stadium. Fans had been tossing tin cans and refuse at the umpire and they refused to stop. By Memorial Day, attendance was off 50% over the same period of the previous year. Two weeks later Bob Stedler noted that the Bisons had made "the most miserable showing of any Bison team within our memory."[26]

Something had to be done; the team had become an embarrassment. There had to be a scapegoat. So Frank Skaff was fired. Skaff had not assembled the players. Leo Miller had done that but Skaff was a much easier target. Top management turned, once again, to Ray Shalk, who had been manager of the Bisons more than a decade earlier. But that did not work. By the end of the season, the Bisons were 40 games out of first place; they were actually resting very comfortably in the cellar, eight games behind 7th place Toronto.

Late in December of 1950, the *Buffalo Evening News* in its annual year end summary of the sports highlights of the year, stated: "The year 1950 produced the biggest flop in Buffalo sports history." The Bisons had gone from first to last, attendance of nearly 420,000 in 1949 including the playoffs had, in 1950 fallen below 100,000. The outlook for the new decade looked bleak.

The post war '40s had been good years for the Baseball Bisons. The Bisons' teams in the Richards' era were winners. The 1949 pennant was the frosting on the cake in these golden years. Buffalo basked in the glory of the postwar boom in baseball; it was a boom shared by both the major and the minor leagues. In 1944, due to World War II exigencies, there were only 10 minor leagues that remained in operation in the country. In the boom years following the war, the minors spread into small towns and villages throughout America. At its peak in 1949 there were 59 leagues with 450 teams. The all time regular attendance record was set in 1949 with 39.7 million.[27]

In the 1950s many minor leagues simply ceased to exist. Many other minor league baseball cities experienced the same losses in attendance that Buffalo felt. By the end of the decade the minor leagues were a shell of their former self. Television took its toll. In its infancy following World War II, not many sports authorities feared the coming of television. Some welcomed it; most simply did not understand the impact it might have on the future of professional sports. The very first Buffalo television station arrived in mid 1948; very few homes in Buffalo had television sets in the late 1940s. But beginning in 1950, the purchase of television sets spread like wildfire. An example of what lay ahead could be seen in what had just recently happened in the Metropolitan New York City area. On May 18, 1948, a Jersey City Little Giants game, in the International League, drew less than 1700 fans. At that exact time, the New York Giants of the National League televised its game; it was received in 600 bars in New Jersey. Understandably minor leagues, especially in the East were becoming testy over the television policy of Major League Baseball. In January of 1950 the New York Yankees sold their Newark franchise, the Newark Bears of the International League, to the Chicago Cubs, to be thereafter located in

Springfield, Massachusetts. If minor league teams were going to survive they might have to do so in smaller cities, far removed from the overwhelming influence of the major leagues. Many baseball fans in the 1950s made a fateful decision. Rather than watch a minor league game in some urban ball park, they would watch a major league contest from a neighborhood saloon or from their living room couch at home. Rather than watch some fledgling pitcher toiling in the Pony League, they could turn on the TV set and watch Joe DiMaggio, or Mickey Mantle, or Willie Mays belting home runs out of Yankee Stadium or the Polo Grounds. Moreover they could hear it described vividly by Mel Allen, for the Yankees, as A White Owl Wallop or a Ballantine Blast. or, for the Giants, by Russ Hodges, as a round tripper by the "Say Hey" kid.[28]

Despite the horrendous 1950 season, better days lay ahead. Luke Easter, one of Buffalo's all time favorites and a truly great player had yet to don a Bisons' uniform. Another pennant would come with Kirby Farrell's formidable team in 1959. Then, too, there were some sad times. Offermann Stadium was torn down to make way for a public school. The Bisons then played, beginning in 1961, in Civic, renamed, War Memorial Stadium. The Bisons won the Little World Series that year. That venue proved to be a terrific setting for the great Baseball film, *The Natural*, but it was not very suitable for the continued success of a Triple A baseball franchise. The Bisons faltered for a few years then collapsed.

By the end of the 1970s, through the efforts of Mayor Jimmy Griffin and old baseball hand, Don Colpoys, baseball was resurrected in Buffalo. A franchise was acquired in the Eastern League and the Bisons survived there for several years before they had a complete rebirth in Triple A Ball in 1988. The construction of an awesome ballpark smack in downtown Buffalo symbolized the new era for Buffalo Bison baseball. Baseball was once again alive and well in Buffalo. In 1991, the Bisons, as a member of the American Association, set the all time Minor League attendance record for one season when 1,240,951 fans passed through the turnstiles of the new stadium.

By the dawn of the 21st century, Buffalo's major sports were the National Football League Buffalo Bills, and the National Hockey League Buffalo Sabres. Nevertheless minor league baseball was once again alive and well. It had survived some rough times. But it also had experienced some glorious eras, one of which was the period immediately following the Second World War, a truly Golden Age for sports in Buffalo, New York.

CHAPTER THREE

The First **Buffalo Bills**

BUFFALO EVENING NEWS

Browns Topple Bills From First-Place Berth Before Record 43,167

If Any City Belongs In Pro Football
It Is Buffalo, Says Rice.

Buffalo Evening News, December 29, 1949

SOUVENIR GRIDGRAM
BUFFALO BISONS
Member of the All-America Football Conference
All Home Games—Civic Stadium, Buffalo, N. Y.
Office
BUFFALO ALL-AMERICA CLUB
13 South Division Street
Ellicott Square Building
Buffalo 3, New York
Telephone CLeveland 5215

Professional football was born in the last decade of the 19th century. The City of Buffalo witnessed attempts by some of its citizens to field professional football teams at that time. Buffalo was among the very first cities in the United States to do so. Throughout the early decades of the twentieth century, professional football barely seemed professional; the sport simply struggled to stay alive. It was not until the immediate post World War II period that professional football achieved some recognition as a stable sport. It was also at that time that the pro game established some solid, viable beginnings in Buffalo. The result was the first, the original, Buffalo Bills professional football team.

With the end of World War II in sight, many professional football fans saw a bright future for the sport. Pro football had struggled through the Great Depression of the 1930s as well as the dislocations and disruptions caused by the war, and now Americans looked forward to a prosperous peacetime that would benefit athletes and spectators alike. One of the earliest questions was, would the existing National Football League, itself still on somewhat wobbly ground, expand to accommodate the growing interests in the sport, or would interested sportsmen and prospective owners have to go out on their own to form a new football league?

One thing was certain, there were going to be large numbers of potential professional football players returning from the war. Some had played college football and graduated, some had played and entered the service before concluding college; others had played pro football and now wanted an opportunity to resume where they had left off.

The military services themselves recognized the value of sports and encouraged athletic competition. Many athletes were assigned to combat regiments, but many others spent their tours of duty assigned to special services, simply representing their military unit in competition against other units in athletic events. The Great Lakes Naval Station's outstanding football team was perhaps the most famous example of a World War II service team. Many of the sport's future stars played for Great Lakes. Youngsters attending Saturday matinee movies in the local theaters could watch that team literally pummel all opposition including major college elevens. The Great Lakes team was virtually invincible.

There were also promoters who had been in the sports business since the halcyon days of the 1920s, who were looking forward to the postwar era. One of these was the highly regarded Arch Ward, sports editor of the *Chicago Tribune*. He had been an architect of the Golden Gloves boxing tournaments that began in the '20s and he was also a prime mover of the baseball and football All Star games that began in the '30s. In mid 1944 with World War II still in high gear, Arch Ward called a meeting of some wealthy businessmen to discuss the possibility of a new professional football league. Ward was one of those visionaries who saw the potential of a large crop of football players becoming available after the war was over. Ward's invitees, soon to be organized as the All America Football Conference, or AAFC, met on June 4, just two days before D-Day. Those present included representatives of Los Angeles, San Francisco (significantly two West Coast teams) and also Chicago, Cleveland, New York, Buffalo, and Baltimore. Their plans made headway. A few months later, Joe Crowley, a member of the Four Horsemen of Notre Dame, arguably the most famous college football backfield of all time, was named the commissioner of the new conference. Perhaps it was just a coincidence that at that same time, another of the Four Horsemen, Elmer Layden, was the Commissioner of the National Football League. A short time later, Eleanor Gehrig, widow of the famous Yankee first baseman, became the Vice President of the AAFC. She was the only woman executive of a major sports enterprise at that time.

The Buffalonians at the Chicago meeting were Jim Breuil and Sam Cordovano. Breuil, a wealthy oilman, was a native of Philadelphia. He arrived in Buffalo in 1929 and formed the Frontier Oil Company. He built terminals on River Road in Tonawanda. Breuil's company struggled through the Depression but continued to increase refining capacity and by the time of WWII the company had some 300 employees and was doing quite well. Sam Cordovano, former local football star and college coach, was involved in the construction business in the 1940s. Some months before the meeting with Ward, Breuil and Cordovano had taken their own initiative to try to obtain an NFL franchise. They deposited a check for the requisite amount, said to be $25,000, to the NFL along with a formal application for a franchise. According to Cordovano the check was turned down, the NFL representatives saying "Buffalo is a minor league town." How many of the existing NFL owners shared that view is not known, but the slap at the city would remain, like a festering sore, with the franchise during its entire existence in the 1940s. Cordovano and Breuil were very pleased to join with Arch Ward's group. They became "leading instigators" of the new football league. The Buffalo entry was to be called the Buffalo Bisons.[1]

Buffalo's representatives had good reason to take offense at the treatment received from the NFL. There were some cities in the NFL at that time whose small crowds hardly made them big league. Several of the cities did not have a football tradition the equal of Buffalo's. Buffalo could point to a history of interest in and involvement with professional football that predated the very beginning of the National Football League.

Professional football originated in Western Pennsylvania at the end of the 19th century. A number of teams were organized there as well as in Eastern Ohio and Western New York. The Buffalo Niagaras and the Rochester Jeffersons were two such squads. These teams were informal; they had no front office; a team captain handled scheduling and finances. In reality they were neighborhood teams, the Niagaras hailed from Buffalo's West Side. The players made little if anything at all in terms of financial compensation; perhaps an occasional free meal is what made them "professional." The players were content just to play football in their time off from their regular jobs. In the early years of the 20th century, some of the teams became a bit better organized; usually their home base was in an athletic club or some local industry. For example, there was a team based in the Oakdale Club, an athletic association in South Buffalo. At the same time the Buffalo Prospects, led by Tommy Hughitt, had a team that played in the Western New York area. [2]

Clubs from the Ohio towns of Massillon, Akron, and Canton were the leading teams in the World War I era and indeed their Ohio League was considered by some to resemble a professional football league. The development of those teams along with others in Pennsylvania and Western New York led to the beginnings of the National Football League that we know today. The NFL dates from a meeting of businessmen, including George Halas and Joe Carr, at an auto agency in Canton, Ohio in August of 1920. Representatives of teams in Canton, Akron, Cleveland and Dayton formed the American Professional Football Conference; teams from Buffalo and Rochester that had applied to join by letter were also admitted.[3]

The team from Buffalo, the Buffalo All-Americans, fared very well in the first season of the NFL. There were ten teams in that inaugural season, and the Buffalo contingent ended up with a 9 – 1 – 1 record, just behind the champion, Akron Pros. In the second season the Buffalo squad again was a contender but the Chicago Stanleys were recognized as the champs. The All Americans changed their name to the Buffalo Bisons in 1924 and again changed the name to the Buffalo Rangers in 1926. There apparently were two teams in 1926 in Buffalo, one playing under the name Buffalo Bisons and the other the Buffalo Rangers. The Rangers quickly folded and the Bisons later succumbed to the hard times of the Great Depression.[4]

Obviously the NFL was very unstable in the 1920s, with some clubs exiting the league and new ones entering on a yearly basis. Teams would play a schedule that included some opponents in the NFL but also some that were not. It was very difficult to assess which teams were really the strongest.[5]

A semblance of order was brought to the NFL in 1934 when the League was organized into two divisions of five teams each. This relative stability lasted into the years of World War II, but it was only relative. Teams continued to enter and leave the NFL though not as frequently as in the 1920s. Also rival leagues surfaced from time to time. One, called the American Football League, included the Buffalo Indians in 1940 who compiled a 1 - 3 record and one forfeit, and in 1941 the Buffalo entry was called the Buffalo Tigers and their record was 2 - 2.

Meanwhile, Buffalo's efforts to be involved in professional football on a more permanent basis were helped out during the Depression when the New Deal of President Franklin D. Roosevelt's administration gave the green light to the Works Progress Administration to build a stadium in Buffalo. It was to be an all purpose facility, modeled somewhat after the Berlin Olympic Stadium of 1936. The WPA edifice was constructed in 1937 and was named Roesch Stadium, after Buffalo's mayor. Soon thereafter it was changed to Grover Cleveland Stadium, and a short time later to Civic Stadium which it would remain for the 1940s and 1950s. In its final years, it was renamed War Memorial Stadium. As it aged, not very well, it became known affectionately, and for some a bit sarcastically, as the "Old Rockpile."

Civic Stadium had its drawbacks for hosting a football game but they seemed minimal in its early years. Buffalonians were satisfied to have a major facility; and the NFL attested to the usefulness of the new stadium. In those years NFL teams were considered "2nd class citizens." They often had to use their home city's baseball facility. This meant that frequently football teams, in order to secure favorable dates, would play some of their games in cities that happened to have an adequate football arena. Buffalo was one such city. Less than a year after the stadium officially opened, the first professional game was played there. On September 14, 1938, the Philadelphia Eagles beat the Pittsburgh Pirates, later renamed the Steelers, 27 - 7. Professional football games, both exhibition and regular season, continued to be played in Civic Stadium in the years that followed. Attendance was fairly good, often games played in Buffalo drew more spectators then games played in official NFL cities.

With a satisfactory stadium, with a tradition of football in the city that was at least the equal of any NFL city, with a prosperous economy and an expanding population, and with many young men being mustered out of the military, some of whom were eager to be involved in football, Buffalo had the ingredients to become a successful football franchise.

The ground work for the AAFC was done in 1944 and early 1945. With VJ Day coming suddenly in August of 1945 the planning by the football brass swung into high gear. "A major break" for the AAFC came in December when Dan Topping, who just happened to be the owner of the New York

Buffalo "Brass" Coach Dawson, Owner Breuil, and Francis Dunn, as featured in the inaugural program of the AAFC. Known in 1946 as the Bisons, the club changed its name to the Bills in 1947.

Yankees Baseball Club, took his football team out of the NFL and joined the AAFC. This meant that now the new league had a big name venue, indeed Yankee Stadium was the premier venue in all sports.[6]

Grantland Rice, the Dean of American sportswriters in this era, stated that a war with the NFL was inevitable, and he noted that only four of the NFL teams had made money recently, so a costly recruiting war was looming. The AAFC showed that it meant business. A signing war took place and the AAFC was surprisingly successful. Some 100 former NFL players joined the AAFC. The new franchises were especially successful in signing some of the former NFL players who were in the process of mustering out of the military service. Moreover, of the 60 players who were on the roster of the All Star squad in Chicago, 44 signed with the AAFC. Back then the College All Star-Pro football game was a major event. Buffalo did its part by signing Notre Dame's big star from the 1941-42 season, Steve Juzwik. He had been on the Washington Redskin's roster in 1942; later he starred for a military service team.

Jim Crowley, newly appointed AAFC Commissioner, gave a speech in New York in which he indicated that he was convinced of the great potential for the growth of pro football, regardless of what the old Guard in the NFL might think. In September of 1945, Commissioner Crowley indicated he too was ready for a fight, and recognized that raids on rosters were fair game, since the old league would not cooperate with the new league. A fortnight later, the great Jim Thorpe, who had been the very first Commissioner of the NFL, predicted the success of the AAFC in a speech he made at St Joseph's Collegiate Institute in Buffalo.[7]

The year 1946 opened with the Buffalo officials pressing forward. General Manager Sam Cordovano and Owner Jim Breuil went South and West to scout the players at the Bowl Games. They continued building the Buffalo franchise, doing considerable recruiting, and spending large sums of money. According to Cy Kritzer, Breuil and Cordovano would spend some $300,000 by the time the first game was played.[8] In May Sam Cordovano suddenly resigned. His own explanation was that as President of Globe Construction Company he had become "tied up with outside business interests" and it was imperative that he tend to them. Within 24 hours Owner Jim Brueil was in Chicago signing Lowell "Red" Dawson as head coach. Dawson had coached at Tulane and the University of Minnesota. A few days later, Coach Dawson was off to Ithaca in the Boss's private plane where he waited for Al Dekdebrun, star quarterback for Cornell, to finish his final examinations. He then signed the Western New York native.

Dawson next hired his assistant coaches, the most noteworthy being Clem Crowe, an early exponent of the T-formation. The Bison coaching staff and their recently signed prospects reported for their first preseason training camp in mid-August. The training camp was located in Oconomowoc, Wisconsin, on the grounds of a Cistercian Monastery.

Preseason camp was spirited but uneventful. The fact that so many of these young men were returning war vets, eager to see what they could still do with a football, heightened the enthusiasm. Nine players who had been on the 1945 Fleet City Bluejackets, a national service championship team, attended. This group, led by quarterback Harry Hopp and guard Rocco Pirro, was already seasoned enough to provide a core of unity for the new professional team.

Coach Red Dawson was especially pleased with the all around performance of Vic Kulbitski, his ace recruit. Kulbitski had been a member of two national college champions, the 1941 University of Minnesota Golden Golphers, and the 1943 University of Notre Dame Fighting Irish. He had attended Notre Dame as a marine cadet. Kulbitski was destined to be one of the top rushing backs for Buffalo. Interestingly enough, a small item appeared in the local newspaper on the last day of August mentioning that Cleveland Brown Coach Paul Brown, had traded Chet Mutyrn to Buffalo. Cleveland did not have room on the roster to keep Mutyrn. Neither Brown, nor anyone else could have realized how important Chet Mutyrn would be for the future of the Buffalo football team.

Meanwhile other future Buffalo players were practicing as members of the 1946 College All Star team. Western New Yorker Al Dekdebrun, had a standout performance in that contest. The majority of players on the all star roster were bound for AAFC teams rather than NFL teams; so many observers saw the game as an important indication of the prestige of the new football conference; even more so since the All Stars were victorious over the NFL champion, Los Angeles Rams.

The official AAFC season opened just after Labor Day in 1946. In one of the very first AAFC games played, the Cleveland Browns swamped the Miami Seahawks, 44 - 0. That game was played before 60,135 fans, the largest crowd to ever watch a pro football game up to that time. The AAFC was making itself heard; the owners had reason to feel optimistic.

In Buffalo, the community showed it really had warmed to professional football. The Buffalo Sports Boosters staged a mammoth parade with more than 40 bands and drum and bugle corps. The parade was led by one of the most colorful heroes of World War II, Admiral "Bull" Halsey. The parade took the familiar route up Main Street from Exchange to North Street. A number of other celebrities were on hand, including the political hierarchy of the city. Reports said that some 100,000 viewed the event. The Bison football team and their opponents in the season opener, the Brooklyn Dodgers, were the big hits of the parade. Van Patrick, the city's premier radio sports announcer, broadcast the parade activities from Lafayette Square.

On September 8 all things seemed to be in order to inaugurate a successful beginning for the AAFC in Buffalo, except perhaps the team itself. Many of the players were simply untested. No one quite knew what to expect as the Bisons prepared to kickoff to the visiting Brooklyn Dodgers. Harry Hopp at quarterback and Steve Juzwik as the main ball carrier did quite well. They brought the Bisons back to tie the game at 14 - 14 in the last quarter. Unfortunately that score did not hold up. The game hero, Dodger Glenn Dobbs, threw some spectacular passes as he engineered his club to two touchdowns in a three minute span. The result was a 27 - 14 victory for the visitors.

Despite the defeat, Buffalo fans were not downcast. A pretty good crowd of 25,489 had witnessed the Bills outplay their opponents offensively. *Courier Express* reporter Ray Ryan called it a "thrilling" game, and his sports editor, Billy Kelly said it was an "auspicious" beginning for pro football in Buffalo. His counterpart at the *Buffalo Evening News*, Bob Stedler, labeled it a fine performance and said Buffalo had a "truly worthy team of major caliber." [9]

There were a couple of "What ifs." If the field would have been in top shape, the Buffalo rushing game might have been much better. A rodeo had been held there a few days earlier, and before the field could be repaired the rains came and the result was that a portion of the playing surface was in poor shape. And what if there had been instant replay. Of course no such technology existed. Television was in its infancy and there was simply no television in Buffalo yet. But there were game films and when the films were shown two days later they showed a bizarre sequence. The Buffalo quarterback had actually crossed the goal line, the film did not lie. However the referee had ruled no touchdown, and so the Bisons tried a field goal and missed. Then the Dodgers, on the missed field goal, ran the ball back 102 yards for a touchdown. The actual rule said that once the ball was in end zone, it had to be ruled down. It was not ruled that way. Again the film showed clearly what actually had happened.

The Bisons, next traveled to New York City where they lost to the New York Yankees, 21 - 10. The Yankees were led by Spec Sanders who demonstrated clearly why he would emerge as one of the premier all around backs in the AAFC. The Bisons returned home and were whitewashed, 28 - 0, by the Cleveland Browns. The Browns showed why they were on their way to becoming the dominant team in the entire AAFC. As a matter of record, the Browns would become the best team in all of professional football. The Browns showed too that they had the league's best passing and running game in Otto Graham and Marion Motley. The Browns' pass defense was, obviously, no slouch either. The Bisons gained a measly 49 yards in the air. In the next contest, against the Chicago Rockets, the Bisons cranked up their offense. They scored 35 points, unfortunately Chicago scored 38. Honchy Hoernschemeyer, the ex-Navy star, led the attack for the winners; he was ably assisted by Elroy "Crazy Legs" Hirsch. Chet Mutyrn ran well for Buffalo as did Vic Kulbitski and Steve Juzwik.

A tie with the Los Angeles Dons gave a bit of a reprieve to the Bisons. Buffalo's passing was ineffective again, but the running game put them in the lead early in the game. The Dons stormed back to gain the 21 - 21 tie. Another loss to the Sanders' led Yankees showed that the Buffalo defense had some huge holes in it. As the Bisons continued to lose, more and more fans continued to stay away. This situation worsened when the inept Miami Seahawks knocked off the even more inept Bisons. A field goal in the final minute sealed the Bisons' fate, 17 - 14, before a meager 5,040 fans in Civic Stadium. Some observers began to wonder if Buffalo really was ready for professional football.

Finally an upset occurred. The Bisons pulled off a solid victory against the San Francisco 49ers. Pinpoint passing by hometown hero, Al Dekdebrun and the all around playing of a consistent Chet Mutyrn led the way. Dekdebrun engineered a score in the final minute to give Buffalo the 17 - 14 victory, before the lonely 6,101 fans. The poor fan turnout was accompanied by rather skimpy press coverage.

Billy Kelly insisted that Buffalo had gotten some bad breaks; he felt that the team was better than its record indicated. Bob Stedler at the *Buffalo Evening News* echoed Kelly's pleas to get fans out to the game. Stedler emphasized civic pride noting it would be a big blow to the entire community if the team were to vacate Buffalo.

The team and its fans responded in the final home game of the season. 15,758 paying spectators turned out on October 27. The breaks went Buffalo's way as the Bisons thumped the hapless Chicago Rockets 49 - 17. Even the Buffalo defense played well.

There were still five regular season games to play; all of them on the road. Such a road trip would be unthinkable today. The team flew to the West Coast to play San Francisco, then back to the East Coast to Brooklyn, then to the Southeastern tip of the country to play Miami, then back North to play Cleveland, and then all the way to the Southwest to play Los Angeles. The incredible mileage that the team accumulated on planes, trains, and busses, to those road games, was magnified by mid week trips back to Buffalo for practice. This surely helped to explain why the Bisons were only 1 and 4 on that trip, their sole victory being, a 17 - 14 win over Brooklyn. The losses to San Francisco, 27 - 14 and to Miami, 21 - 14 were at least tolerable. The game with the Browns was a hopeless 42 – 17 thrashing. All the Browns' stars shone brightly that day. The season finale was even worse. The L.A. Dons ran up a record breaking score, 62 - 14, in crushing the Bisons in Memorial Coliseum. The Dons "squeaked out" 625 yards on offense. Surprisingly, the Bison's passing game was better than usual, but the ground game was totally inept. In later years, this season ending performance by the Buffalo football team would have been referred to as a "Run for the Bus" game.

The end of the first season of competition for the Buffalo Bisons and for the entire All American Football Conference called for a review. The Cleveland franchise was a spectacular success. The New York Yankees and the San Francisco 49ers did fairly well. The other teams, including Buffalo, needed to do significantly better in the future. For Miami there would be no future. Baltimore would replace that city in the AAFC in 1947. With 117,000 fans passing going through the turnstiles, the Bisons finished 6th in attendance, just ahead of Brooklyn. Miami, with a total home attendance of only 50,000, was securely in last place. The NFL was not doing much better. Grantland Rice noted that in the NFL, Detroit, Los Angeles, and Boston appeared particularly shaky.

At the end of the year, Tony Wurzer who had covered the Bills for the *Buffalo Evening News* for most of the season speculated that only a handful of the '46 football players would be returning for the 1947 season. Vic Kulbitski who was 3rd in the AAFC in rushing with a 6.24 average and Steve Juzwik who was 7th with a 6.14 average were secure as was Falto Prewitt, a stalwart at Center. Surprisingly no mention was made of "little" Chet Mutyrn.

If 1946 ended dismally for Buffalo's professional football team, then 1947 would start and end in wonderful fashion and the same held true, generally, for the All American Football Conference. The Buffalo organization was not going to fold its tent, nor was the conference to which it belonged. The AAFC was in the battle with the NFL for the long haul. The AAFC mounted a positive front as 1947 moved along. Just a few days into the new year, Billy Kelly, the Sports Editor of the *Courier Express*, asserted boldly that the AAFC rested on solid beginnings. He noted that the NFL's first twenty five years were very wobbly and that the AAFC was able to learn from all the mistakes of the older league. The infant conference was surely entitled to a few mistakes of its own; the planting of an ill-begotten franchise in Miami being the most glaring. That was rectified when Baltimore took over the Miami franchise. The appointment of a new commissioner, Admiral Jonas Ingram, was viewed as a positive step for the conference, for it allowed Jim Crowley to leave the commissioner's post to help shore up the faltering Chicago Rockets by becoming coach and part owner.

Occasional stories continued to circulate about the possibility of the Buffalo team folding, but these were quickly dismissed as unsubstantiated rumors. Francis Dunn, a spokesman for the Buffalo Bisons, talked of the team's future and in so doing articulated what would become a recurrent theme. He said that while the Buffalo football team would stay in Buffalo, how long the team would stay was up to the fans.

The Buffalo front office and the coaching staff had considerable work to do. They would prove equal to the task. Bills' personnel made preparations to attend all the bowl games. Their pockets were full with plenty of money to sign a host of new players. Everyone recognized that game attendance had to increase. The schedule makers did their part; six of the seven home games for 1947 were slated for Sunday afternoons. The Friday night games in the previous season had been disastrous from an attendance point of view. There would be no more five game marathon road trips.

The Buffalo organization was ready to shed just about everything, even its nickname. A contest was held to give the Buffalo team a new nickname; part of the reason was to distinguish the footballers from the Baseball Bisons and the Hockey Bisons. As a matter of fact, the professional basketball team, recently deceased, was also called the Bisons, as was the Roller Derby squad. The winning nickname was the Bills. It was selected to depict the team members as a posse of Buffalo Bills, after the great Western Frontier legend, Buffalo Bill Cody. Cody symbolized the old frontier of the Wild West days. The Buffalo team, the Bills, would symbolize a new frontier, in Western New York sports, the Niagara Frontier. Appropriately the team was sponsored and owned by the owner of Frontier Oil.

It had become obvious to the Bill's staff that a top notch quarterback was the key to a good team and a successful season. Frankie Albert of the 49ers and Otto Graham of the Browns were clear evidence of that. Buffalo had a gaping hole to fill here. A number of prospects, some with good pedigree, had been given a shot at the position but none indicated promise of being a consistent performer. The quarterback position was one that had been clearly up for grabs. Any new prospect, with even a glimmer of potential, would have a golden opportunity to take over the post.

Enter George Ratterman. The biggest news for the Buffalo Bills in 1947 was the signing of George Ratterman, an excellent quarterback prospect from Notre Dame. Ratterman was signed in June to a two year deal at $11,000 per year, a mighty tidy sum in the 1940s. It was hoped that he would take the Bills to the Promised Land; he almost did. With

George Ratterman: First Buffalo Bills "Superstar" – Quarterbacked Bills from 1947-49. *Photo: WNY Heritage*

Ratterman the Bills got a gem, a player on whom you could build a franchise. In 1946, Ratterman had played at Notre Dame as a back-up to the legendary Johnny Lujack. He had actually directed the Fighting Irish to 14 of its last 16 touchdowns. Hugh Devore who had coached Notre Dame in 1945 indicated that he actually preferred Ratterman to Lujack.

Ratterman was handsome, intelligent, and an all-around athlete. Besides football, he played tennis, baseball, and basketball. In fact, "he was the last of only four students in Notre Dame History to earn letters in four different sports." Legendary football coach Frank Leahy called him "the greatest all-around athlete in the history of Notre Dame." He was named to the Madison Square Garden All-Star basketball teams in 1945 and in 1946. He had played in Buffalo's Memorial Auditorium against Canisius College. He also participated in the finals of the National Intercollegiate Tennis Tournament in 1946. Dick Leous, a former Bennett High School Star in Buffalo, and friend of Ratterman's at Notre Dame, recalls that he was also a top notch golfer and billiards player.[10]

Before the ink was dry on Ratterman's signature, the NFL cried foul. It claimed that Ratterman could not become eligible until 1948. The AAFC ruled that he was eligible as soon as his class at Notre Dame had graduated and since his class completed its work in three years under the accelerated war time program, Ratterman's class graduated June 9, 1947. Buffalo signed him the following day; too bad for the NFL! Ratterman's own explanation for signing on in 1947 before he finished at Notre Dame was that "I wanted to marry my hometown sweetheart only I didn't have any money. For another the Bills offered what seemed a dizzying salary. At the age of nineteen, I became no longer single, and no longer an amateur."[11]

Owner Jim Breuil put his money where his mouth was. His mouth was saying that he had given the green light to his coaches to buy the best talent possible. At a Buffalo Club luncheon he boldly asserted "This will be either THE year or the last year for Buffalo in the AAFC." The coaches were given a free financial hand to find the best talent possible, and they were doing just that. Now it was up to the fans. Buffalo fans knew where the owner stood. Breuil had lost $285,000 in his first year as Bills' owner. He said the Bills needed to average 28,000 home game admissions to cover expenses. Stedler put it succinctly, in thoroughly modern sports language: "Pro football is Big Business." The message was clear, if you want to be a big time sports town, you had better get behind Breuil's team. A committee of leading civic and business leaders formed a Quarterback Club. The aim was to get the community leaders involved and to enlist the community in support of the team.[12]

While community support was growing, Coach Red Dawson and his staff continued to sign prospects and when preseason camp opened on July 21, fifty four hopefuls appeared.Training camp proceeded as well as could be expected in view of the fact that key recruits, including George Ratterman, were missing for three weeks in August while they were practicing for the College All Star game. That game was a terrific advertisement for the AAFC and for the new Buffalo Bills. The All-Stars shut out the NFL champion Chicago Bears, 16 - 0. Ratterman gave a convincing demonstration that he was worth every nickel that Breuil was paying him; he played a major role in the victory; completed 8 of 12 passes for 150 yards.

Bills' preseason camp was held in Hamilton, Ontario in 1947. Dawson was pleased with the camp; he was especially gratified with the work of his prize recruit, George Ratterman. He was also impressed with Julie Rykovich, the star of the most recent Rose Bowl game and with Buckets Hirsch, a Buffalo boy, who has been a standout on Northwestern University's team. Hirsch too had performed splendidly in the Chicago All Star game; Dawson recognized that he had the potential to be an All Star Buffalo Bill.

As the official 1947 season was about to get underway, the confidence exhibited in Buffalo was shared by the other teams around the league. Shortly before the season opened, Commissioner Ingram again proposed a championship game, a charity benefit contest, with the NFL. Bert Bell turned it down flat. Lawton Carver the sports editor for *International News* was very critical of Bell for taking it upon himself to turn down the AAFC proposal. Carver took the occasion to point to the NFL as a "worn out circuit made up of older and in many ways, worthless players." Carver said that the collegians led by the young AAFC recruits "all but ran the Chicago Bears out of the park last week." He said that the Browns, 49ers, and Yankees were all better than any club in the NFL. Time would prove him to be a prophet. Carver fired a parting shot at Bell, who he said was beholden to the owners. He asserted that the NFL was under the domination of Tim Mara, George Halas and G.P Marshall. All three had worn out ball clubs.[13]

Meanwhile the Bills fans were demonstrating that they were anxious for the season to begin. An intrasquad game at North Tonawanda High School drew more than 4,000 fans.The Bills returned to their Hamilton, Ontario training camp and two weeks later played another intrasquad game; this time in Hamilton before 5,800. Next the Bills played two exhibition games, the first was a 9 - 7 loss against the New York Yankees in Newark, the second a 29 - 20 victory over the Baltimore Colts in Hershey, Pennsylvania.

A few days before the season opener, Arch Ward, *Chicago Tribune*'s sports editor, addressed the Quarterback Club in the Hotel Lafayette. He lavished praise on the Bills, and recalled how "Ratterman lifted the all stars right out of their boots and made them great." Ward said that Ratterman was as good as any quarterback he had seen in the last three decades of football. Echoing Bills' management Ward told the Quarterback Club members that Buffalo had to support the team this year. This could be the "last chance to prove it's a major league city."[14]

The season opened on August 31. A record crowd of more than 30,000 was predicted. To accommodate this, the local transit company, the IRC, provided a large number of extra busses to run from all major points in the city. The Bills' home opener was truly a promoter's dream. The New York Yankees, well financed by the Baseball Yankee Czar, Dan Topping, were coming to Civic Stadium. The Yankees would feature their star rookie, Buddy Young, billed as the fastest man in football. They would be facing the Bills led by their rookie sensation, George Ratterman, the magician passer from Notre Dame. Both these acclaimed rookies were making their professional football debut in the Queen City of the Great Lakes. The game was also billed as a contest between the single wing Yankees and the T-formation Bills. The Bills' coaching staff regarded Ratterman as the leading exponent of T-quarterbacking.

The game, all aspects of it, lived up to its advance billing. It was called a "spectacular grid duel." 32,385 watched the lead change hands as the two teams ran and passed up and down the field. The Yankee all star backfield of Spec Sanders, and Frank Sinkwich, in addition to BuddyYoung excited the fans but not nearly as much as Quarterback Ratterman and his accompanying cast of runners, Lou Tomasetti, Julie Rykovich, and Chet Mutyrn. The fans were on their feet screaming in the last quarter. Harvey Johnson nailed a field goal to put the Yankees ahead and then Ratterman led his troops to the "come from behind" victory with his dazzling play calling in the final minutes that culminated in a short pass to Chet Mutyrn in the corner of the end zone. That was the game winner; final score: Bills 28 - Yankees 24. It ranked with the best in the annals of Buffalo Bills football.

Billy Kelly spared no superlatives in his post game commentary. "Never have we seen such sensational nerve-tingling, jumpy see-sawing of the lead, each advantage on either side being accomplished without flaw or 'the breaks' but by honest, rough and tough play." Kelly praised Coach Dawson for using Buckets Hirsch at fullback on defense. Buckets earned a niche for himself in Bills' folklore by leveling Buddy Young with a devastating tackle in the final quarter. Young was forced to leave the game.[15]

The Bills second game of the season was a very different story, especially in the first half. Cleveland rode roughshod over the Bills and held a 27 point lead at halftime. The Bills behind Mutyrn stormed back with 14 points of their own in the 3rd quarter, enough to scare the 61,442 fans in Municipal Stadium, but not enough for a Bills' victory. The final score was 30 - 14. Ratterman had an off day; the lack of adequate pass protection did not help matters. Chet Mutryn now the league leading rusher with an 8.6 average was coming into his own; he would continue to be a dominant force for the rest of his AAFC career. Mutryn surprised Coach Paul Brown as much as anyone. The Cleveland coach admitted he made a mistake in trading Chet or "Little Chet "as the press now liked to call him.

In the third game of the season, the Bills beat the Chicago Rockets 28 - 20, and again set a home attendance record, 33,648. Again Chet Mutyrn played exceptionally well, and receiver Alton Baldwin gave indications that he too was moving into a starring role. Ratterman ran the team well. Unfortunately for Chicago, their star quarterback, Angelo Bertelli of Notre Dame fame, suffered a knee injury and would be out indefinitely. The Bills then followed the Rockets back to Chicago for the 4th game of the season, and this time Buffalo won convincingly, 31 – 14. Ratterman surpassed Otto Graham's one game record by passing for 294 yards, while striking for four touchdowns. Obviously Ratterman impressed the pundits. Tony Wurzer who covered the Bills regularly for the *Buffalo Evening News* referred to him as "the most amazing rookie that ever stepped into the pro gridiron ranks." Wurzer looked for him to set an all time world record before the season was over. In a related story, Wurzer congratulated Assistant Coach Clem Crowe for bringing together one of the best 1-2 punches in football. Crowe was credited with enticing Mutyrn to come to Buffalo and for influencing Ratterman to sign a two year contract. [16]

The Bills returned home to face the highly regarded San Francisco 49ers; another record breaking crowd was anticipated. Extra busses were provided and increased auto parking was arranged at the Sears' lot at Main and Jefferson with free shuttle service to the stadium. Automobiles were just beginning to make their presence felt in the postwar era, the issue of where to park large numbers of cars was a new problem. Those who could not get to the stadium at all would have to listen on the radio. Sig Smith was handling the play by play for Bills' games. A good crowd of 36,099 attended and was immediately put in a jubilant mood as the Bills rushed to a 24-7 lead. The fans became less jubilant as the 49ers gradually got back into the game and then the fans became rancorous as they watched the opponents storm ahead with 20 points in the last quarter. The final score was San Francisco 41- Buffalo 24. The Bills had played three quarters and then quit, the 49ers played all four. Mutyrn ran well again, but there was little else to cheer about.

The Bills rebounded the following week in Los Angeles where they upset the Dons, 27-25. Ratterman, "The Kid," as he was increasingly referred to in the local press, especially by Mike Kanaley of the *Courier Express*, combined excellent field generalship with "brilliant passing." The Dons actually outplayed the Bills in the 2nd half, but cool headed Ratterman took two safeties to take the wind out of the sails of the fired up Dons. Rykovich had been injured in practice just before the game, but Steve Juzwik came up with a solid rushing game At this point of the '47 season, the Bills, in four home games had drawn more fans than they had in the entire '46 season. The AAFC was doing very well versus the NFL in what was sometimes called the "Battle of Gate Receipts." The upstart league was averaging 40,726 to 31,475 for the NFL.[17]

On October 12 the Bills hosted the Baltimore Colts and the Bills eked out a close victory, 20 - 15. Bud Schwenk, the Colts quarterback had a terrific game. Ratterman had a pretty fair game himself, and the Bills running attack led by Mutyrn, Jozwik, and Rykovich was superb. Bills' defensive star, Niagara Falls native, Vince Mazza had another great game. The real game story though was the "riotous finish." Just before the final gun sounded, the Colts led by former Bills' quarterback Bud Schwenk marched into Bills territory. Schwenk on the final play of the game fired a pass to Racehorse Davis on the 30 yard line and the Colts thought he raced into the end zone. However the official on the spot ruled that Davis stepped out of bounds on the 1 yard line just as the game ended.

Pandemonium ensued. Spectators, officials, and players were all involved. The irate owner of the Colts loudly announced that he was filing a protest with the Commissioner. While that protest was making its way to the League office, the game films became available. The controversial finish of the game created so much interest that the quarterback club luncheon at the Chez Ami had an overflow crowd. Fans lined up on Delaware Avenue trying to get into the famous revolving bar restaurant to catch a glimpse of the film clips. As expected, at least by Bills' fans, the game films showed clearly that the official's call was the correct one. Commissioner Ingram's statement stated the obvious. The *News* and the *Courier* reinforced the point and printed photos that clearly showed Davis being out of bounds.[18]

Next, the Bills traveled to Ebbetts Field for the first of a home and home contest with the Brooklyn Dodgers. The Bills thought they had the first one in the bag. But in the 4th quarter, Hunchy Hoernschemeyer, the former Navy star, ran 84 yards to pay dirt to earn a 14 - 14 tie for the Dodgers. A week later, in Civic Stadium, the Bills hammered the Dodgers 35 - 7. The Bills were dominant in all phases of the contest. The game was also a kind of coming out party for Lou Tomasetti, a fan favorite, who rushed for 72 yards.

The Bills were doing quite well, so well that Buffalo fans were looking positively and confidently toward the meeting with the Cleveland Browns on November 1. The local press hyped a huge buildup for the game. Civic Stadium officially seated 37,500. Some 8,000 seats were added on the track that circled the playing field. The Browns were 10 point favorites but Buffalo fans paid no attention to that. The greatest advance sale in local sports history took place. Billy Kelly called the Cleveland game the climax of two years of building to our claim to Big Time Sports, to show the world that "Buffalo ranks well up there when they talk of good sports towns." 43,167 fans, the largest crowd ever to attend a sports event in Buffalo, turned out for the game. The game itself perhaps was anti-climactic. The Browns won 28 - 7. They were simply a better team. Billy Kelly called Cleveland's victory "a display of perfection, performance, and finesse." The Bills played well, but the strong Cleveland line was superior and so were the Browns' receivers. Cleveland's infamous 99 yard play, etched in the minds of Buffalo sports fans ever after, sealed the Bills' defeat. Graham, with the ball on his own one yard line faded back and hit Mac Speedie in the flat. With four blockers in front of him, the swift Speedie sped down the sidelines untouched.[19]

The final home game of the season, against the L.A. Dons, was held on November 9. The area's first snowstorm of the season arrived at the same time. Civic Stadium was a mess. The playing field was covered with snow and slush. Fans had to clear several inches of snow from their seats. The stadium management sought help from the city but municipal workers were tied up throughout the area with snow removal. Harsh criticism was directed at both the stadium and city hall. The press cried that it was a big disgrace. Yet, despite the horrible conditions, a surprisingly good crowd of 21,293 showed up at game time. In retrospect, the poor field conditions helped the Bills forward wall offset the 20 pound weight advantage held by the Dons. The Bills mustered their best pass defensive effort of the season which was largely responsible for the 25 - 0 victory over the Los Angeles team.

The Bills spent the final three games of the season on the road. As they exited Buffalo, they were still in the running for the Eastern Division title. The Bills pounded Baltimore 33 - 14. Poor field conditions once again may have aided the Bills' running game in administering this thrashing to the Colts. Chet Mutyrn scored twice and Buckets Hirsch scored on an interception. Next the Bills had to tackle the high flying downstate rivals, the New York Yankees, led by Spec Sanders, the top offensive player in the AAFC. Spec was not only leading the conference in scoring, rushing, and total offense, but was also one of the top passers and a leading return man. Sanders did not disappoint his fans; he scored three touchdowns while his teammate, future Bills' coach, Harvey Johnson kicked 5 points after touchdowns, for a season total of 47, a league record. In addition, the Yankees' defense did a job on the Bills' vaunted running game. Final score was 35 – 13; the loss spelled elimination for the Bills from the AAFC title race. The final game of a season featured a passing duel between two of the conferences' premier quarterbacks, Ratterman and Frankie Albert of the 49ers. In a thrilling fourth quarter both the Bills and the San Francisco team each scored 14 points and the result was a 21 - 21 tie.

Despite the fact that the Bills did not make the playoffs the team was a success in a number of ways. Mike Kanaly remarked that the Bills' season was "an outstanding success artistically and financially" and the Bills' accomplishments marked "one of the most rapid strides in the history of professional football." Commissioner Ingram seconded that view. In its end of the year round up, the *Buffalo Evening News* asserted that the Bills' football success proved that Buffalo "is a Major League Sports City." The Buffalo Athletic Club at its annual sports night, the premier event of this type in Western New York, honored the Bills as the team of the year, and honored George Ratterman as the Buffalo Athlete of the year. The Bills were at high tide.[20]

It was clear that the Buffalo fans were developing a very close relationship with their Bills. Attendance was up almost 100% over the 1946 season. In 1947 the Bills drew 217,656 fans while the previous year they had only drawn 117,954, and even that figure had been padded with many giveaways.

The 1947 Buffalo Bills were making an impact. Appropriately Grantland Rice wrote a story in which he discussed the financial difficulties faced by many of the pro teams in both leagues. Rice mentioned to Chicago Bears' owner, George Halas, the possibility of a 14 team league that would include Buffalo, Brooklyn and Baltimore. Halas took issue with those three. But Rice countered: "I believe

Buffalo and Baltimore can be strong centers, given high grade teams." Rice went on to say that only four teams in the NFL really made money out of the more than 20 teams that had appeared in the National Football League in the previous two decades.[21] The facts clearly indicated that the new league was doing very well in terms of fan support and in some ways it was doing much better than the old one. On November 10 the New York Yankees hosted the San Francisco 49ers before 37,342 and on that same day, also in New York City, the Giants hosted the Philadelphia Eagles before 29, 016.

Tim Mara, owner of the Giants, was one of the biggest critics of the AAFC, and so the Buffalo press took delight in poking fun at Mara. At one point, Mara said he would welcome only San Francisco and Cleveland into the NFL and was steadfast against the suggestion of two leagues. Billy Kelly called him "one of the NFL's most bitter foes" of the AAFC. Bob Stedler of the *News* said it was another "bitter pill for Mara" when the Yankees- Browns game drew a record New York crowd of 70,060 while the haughty Giants and arrogant Bears, on the same day, were drawing only 27,939 in Gotham. A week later, November 30, 1947, a New York Yankees-Buffalo Bills game drew 30,012 while a New York Giants-Chicago Cardinals clash drew 28,744.[22]

The time seemed favorable for another proposal for a title game between the two league champions. This time the invitation came from the city of Los Angeles. The AAFC accepted, while NFL Commissioner Bert Bell flatly rejected the offer. The NFL felt that it had too much to lose. The war of the professional football leagues would continue into 1948. The AAFC teams were outdrawing their NFL counterparts; financially the teams in the new league were in better shape that those in the NFL.This meant that for the foreseeable future, at least for the 1948 season, and probably for 1949 too, the AAFC was going to continue to function. The NFL would have to live with escalating costs in the gridiron war until it was ready to work out an accommodation with the new, despised kid on the block. The AAFC had arrived.

The Buffalo Bills were determined to continue their success. Early in 1948, Jim Breuil named Jim Wells to be his executive assistant and treasurer. These were new titles. Wells had been a sportscaster with WBEN for nearly a decade; he was well known to Buffalo sports fans. Not long after the Wells' appointment, Bus Owens the Bills' General Manager who had done so much to improve the Bills in the 1947 season, left to take a similar position with the Chicago Rockets. A primary consideration for this move was that Illinois was the home turf of Owens. Wells assumed Owens' duties. Another effort to enhance the profile of the team came with the organization of an All-Star Band with Lou Pepe as music director. The *Courier Express* and its radio station, WEBR, were the principal promoters of the band, and saw to it that some of the best talent in the local area was put to good use. The band was featured in a big parade in downtown Buffalo that kicked off the 1948 preseason for the football team.

The Bills' staff also demonstrated its awareness of the drawing power of signing local talent. Jerry Whelan who had played at Canisius College was considered an excellent prospect for center and linebacker. Lou Corriere, "Lockport Lou," perhaps the greatest University of Buffalo player of his era was also signed. Corriere had a decent preseason but was cut before the regular season began. The Bills were loaded at his position. Whelan played throughout the '48 season and did a pretty good job. The Bills also inked a future all-pro, John Kissell, top lineman in the East out of Boston College. Kissell would be an all star in the years ahead.

The Seymour Knox estate in East Aurora

was the site of the preseason camp. The setting was distinctly advantageous over the previous preseason sites. It had well groomed practice fields that previously were used for polo games, and it had privacy, yet it was easily accessible to Buffalo. The East Aurora High School provided locker rooms and equipment storage. The players stayed at the historic Roycroft Inn. Following the opening day's practice, some 350 members of the East Aurora Athletic Association honored the Bills at a dinner at the Roycroft.

Preseason 1948 moved along rather methodically. In the first preseason contest against the New York Yankees, the Bills displayed offensive striking power and ended up with a 28-28 tie. The Bills hosted the Brooklyn Dodgers in the next exhibition game. A surprisingly good crowd of 27,630 turned out to watch the Bills clip the Brooklyn club, 21 - 19. In their final pre-season tussle against the Cleveland Browns in the Akron Rubber Bowl the Bills were losers to their Lake Erie rivals, 35 – 21.

The 1948 and the 1949 regular seasons were quite similar in some ways. In '48 the Bills record was 8 wins and 8 losses; that included a win and a loss in post season play. In 1949 they compiled a 5-5-2 record which included one post season loss. Attendance in both years, while below the 1947 mark, compared favorably with the rest of the AAFC and with most of the NFL.

In 1948 the Bills lost twice to each of the Conference powers, the Browns and the 49ers. They beat the teams they were supposed to beat each time that they played, the Chicago Rockets, and the Brooklyn Dodgers. They split with the other three conference foes, the Baltimore Colts, the Los Angeles Dons, and the New York Yankees. In post season play they won their first ever playoff game over the Colts. That victory entitled them to be clobbered by the powerful Browns.

The Bills opened the 1948 season at San Francisco by getting walloped by the 49ers, 35 – 14, then returned home to pulverize the star-studded Chicago Rockets, 42 – 7. That was the first of five consecutive home games. In the next contest, the Browns dominated the Bills, 42- 13, a game in which George Ratterman was just plain awful, completing only 3 of 9 passes for 20 yards. As usual Otto Graham and burley Marion Motley were standouts. Buffalo's own Tommy Colella, who had starred at Canisius in his college days, was also one of Cleveland's stars, scoring one of their touchdowns. The following week, the 49ers came to town and flew away with a 38 – 28 victory. A week later the Bills knocked off the Brooklyn Dodgers, 31 – 21. Only 17, 694 showed up for that game. The following week the Bills hosted the Yankees and only 18, 825 attended. To make matters worse the Bills blew a 13 point halftime lead, and lost 14 - 13. Ratterman had a sub par performance, marked by his errant passing.

It was at this point in the '48 season, that a team-disruptive controversy, involving Ratterman, hit the local headlines. George Ratterman loved football, but it was not his only interest. Ratterman was a well rounded person, a virtual renaissance man. Sometimes his other interests got in the way. He loved music. He was an accomplished pianist. He made his debut as a concert pianist in Buffalo's renowned Kleinhan's Music Hall under the direction of Maestro Robert Schulz. His performance was widely acclaimed. Unfortunately this debut took place shortly after his poor quarterbacking in the New York defeat. To add to the confusion, at that very time, it also became known that Ratterman was beginning to serve as a television commentator for college football games. Television had just recently arrived in Buffalo, in mid-1948, at WBEN-TV.

Unrelated but coincidental, *Look Magazine*, one of the nation's leading general readership publications, published a very flattering article about the Bills' quarterback. In it, Tim Cohane, Sports Editor of the magazine, stated that "Ratterman did more than win football games. He gave a new league a shot in the arm." He called George "the greatest rookie ever to enter pro football."[23]

Some critics were quick to blame Ratterman's outside activities for his poor quarterbacking and for the Bills loss to the Yanks. A *Buffalo Evening News* story, headlined "Ratterman Benched, Told to Quit outside Activities," stated that team officials were said to be critical of Ratterman's attitude. One official warned that George had better change or he would be traded. Others, also unnamed, saw Ratterman as a scapegoat for Coach Dawson. The "law school" issue also surfaced. George Ratterman was still studying law at Notre Dame and while there in the spring, he had been assisting Coach Frank Leahy with spring practices as well as helping with football clinics in other parts of the country. Presumably this detracted from his commitment to professional football. George was determined to earn a law degree, which he eventually did, and he was determined to pursue a career in the legal field, which he eventually did.[24]

Fortunately the episode did not get out of hand. Jim Wells played down the controversy and said that officials were simply restoring the authority of the coaches. Head Coach Dawson was silent. Jim Wells held a five hour conference with the coaching staff. The upshot was that Ratterman was absolved of all charges of insubordination. The music and sports program issues were ignored, though his career as a concert pianist and television sports commentator came to an end for the time being. Backup quarterback Jim Still was named to start in place of Ratterman in the next football game. George would be 2nd string temporarily. He said he was satisfied with the outcome.

In that next game, on October 17, the Bills lost to Cleveland, 31 - 14. However, Ratterman came off the bench in the 2nd half and played well. The Cleveland press praised his performance. Dawson obviously was pleased. George was back as the number one quarterback. He would remain there for the rest of the season, and the rest of the season went quite well for the Bills. They won three in a row, over the Dons, 35 – 21, over Baltimore, 35 – 17, and over the Dodgers, 26 – 21. A loss to the L.A. Dons, 27 – 20, was followed by a Thanksgiving Day victory over the Chicago Rockets, 39 – 35. Just three days later the Bills went to New York and thumped the Yankees 35 – 14, more than avenging the one point loss to the Yankees earlier in the season. In the regular season finale, the Bills looked forward confidently to defeating the Baltimore Colts, a victory would have assured them the Eastern Division title. They had defeated the Colts easily earlier in the season; however, this time the shoe was on the other foot; the Bills got zonked, 35 - 15.

The Bills and Colts ended the season tied with a 7 -7 record necessitating a playoff game. Again it was played in Baltimore; this time the Bills won. It was a gratifying first-ever post season victory and the thousands of fans who welcomed the Bills home at the Buffalo airport saw to it that their team was duly acclaimed for its feat.

On December 19, the Bills had the unenviable task of playing the Browns in the AAFC championship game in Cleveland. Trainloads of Buffalo fans followed their heroes to Cleveland; it didn't help. The Bills lost 49 – 7. The Browns finished a perfect season, fifteen victories and no losses. The trouncing at the hands of the Browns notwithstanding, the Bills had a pretty fair season themselves.

The 1949 season packed even more drama than 1948, some of it again involving the star quarterback. There seemed to be little question but that George Ratterman was the most important player on the team. He was as close to being indispensable as one player could be. That became evident when his spectacular rookie season, 1947, was compared with the dismal record of the Bills in the previous season. When the 1948 season ended Ratterman did not have a contract for the 1949 season. Surprisingly, no one seemed particularly alarmed. As the 1949 preseason approached, there was still no acute anxiety about Ratterman. Indeed some observers viewed Jim Still as an adequate replacement for Ratterman. Still, a star at Georgia Tech, had joined Buffalo in a trade with Los Angeles. In August, in the Bills preseason camp, Still was said to be constantly improving. Meanwhile George Ratterman was back in South Bend, Indiana, studying law. Ratterman was interviewed and he indicated that he was taking a required law course that was only offered at that particular time. He did allow that "if they would make it worthwhile for me to postpone my law studies, I would."[25]

The preseason did not go very well for the Bills. A loss to Baltimore was attributed to a poor passing attack, and the next game, a loss to San Francisco, saw no semblance of a passing game whatsoever. The 49ers' coach gleefully remarked that "the best thing Breuil did for us was not to pay Ratterman the $25,000 he wanted."

The 1949 regular season kicked off with the Bills traveling to Chicago to face the underdog Hornets. Chicago upset Buffalo as the Bills were out-passed 198 to 66 yards. Jim Still was still at quarterback for the Bills. George Ratterman had driven in from nearby South Bend to watch the game as a spectator; presumably he had some time to study his law briefs at halftime. Apparently Jim Breuil recognized that he had to act. On August 29 he personally flew to Indiana to sign Ratterman. Owner and quarterback quickly came to terms. Ratterman hopped into his automobile, drove nine hours and arrived in Buffalo at 3:00 AM. He reported for morning drills.

George Ratterman was ready for the Bill's first home contest of the 1949 season. In fact the entire Buffalo Bills team was ready. So was the multitude of Buffalo fans. The entire community was ready for the Labor Day meeting with the Champion Cleveland Browns. Ticket sales had skyrocketed since the announcement of Ratterman's return. An overflow crowd at the Quarterback Club's luncheon was overjoyed with the appearance of the sleek, popular quarterback. The entire Buffalo team was in good shape. Lou Tomasetti, who had been nursing an injury, was scheduled to be back in the starting role at fullback. Three former Brown players were now dressed in Bill's uniforms and ready

Tom Colella, greatest player ever from Canisius College. Starred for the Cleveland Browns – played final season with the Buffalo Bills in 1949.

to go. One was punter and defensive back, Tommy Colella, one of the best football players ever to come out of Western New York. Paul Brown knew that the ex-Canisius star would be retiring after the 1949 season. He released him so he could play his final year before his hometown fans.[26]

The Bills were going to need to be in top shape. They were going to have to play a near perfect game. They were going to need all the help they could muster. They were facing one of the greatest football teams of all time. Since the league began in 1946, the Browns had compiled a record of 38 victories, 3 losses and one tie. They had an unblemished record of 15 victories in 1948. They had pummeled the Bills unmercifully in three of those games. The Browns were paced by one of the great quarterbacks in professional football history, Otto Graham. Marion Motley was at fullback and he too was recognized as one of the best ever at that position. At the halfback slots were the Jones boys, Special Delivery and Dub. The ends were Mac Speedie and Dante Lavelli. The outstanding linemen included Lou "the toe" Groza, Lou Saban, Bill Willis, Lou Rymkus, and Chubby Grigg. At 280 pounds, Grigg was the heaviest player in the AAFC. Like Ratterman, Grigg spent time with both the Bills and the Browns. Ratterman recalls that Coach Red Dawson used to say at the end of practice: "Run that last play again and then everyone take two laps around Grigg."

Of course, the coach was the incomparable Paul Brown. He had put together an awesome team. It seemed that everything Brown and his Browns did was first class. One observer, who served the needs of both the Cleveland Browns and the Buffalo Bills, recalled that the Browns' playbook appeared to be the size of the local telephone directory. It was further observed that their trainers were first rate and their equipment was top shelf; even their water buckets were far superior to those used by the rest of the teams in the league. The Browns were favored by 14-16 points; many thought the figure should have been twice that.[27]

But the Bills were ready. They were not about to be cowed. The game itself was one for the ages. To the delight of the Buffalo fans and to the horror of the Browns' fans the Bills rolled to what seemed to be an invincible lead, 28 – 7 going into the final quarter. The Browns actually scored first shortly after the opening kickoff, then the Bills tied the game, and the score stood at 7 – 7 at the half. The third quarter was all Buffalo. Ratterman and company simply startled the Browns; the Bills' defense throttled Cleveland's vaunted offense as few teams had ever done before. Ratterman scored twice on quarterback sneaks and a rout seemed to be on. To add insult to injury, end Vince Mazza stole the ball out of Graham's hand. That gave the Bills a first down on the four yard; two plays later the Bills had a 28 – 7 lead.

The game was not over. The Bills fans had begun to celebrate prematurely. Cleveland showed why it was at the top of the football world and Graham showed why he was without peer. Graham began to pass and then pass some more. He completed 18 of 21 passes for three touchdowns. The game ended in a tie.

Tony Wurzer in the *Buffalo Evening News* put it this way: "Buffalo had come within six heartbreaking inches of staging the sports upset of the decade." It was a fantastic game. Both sports editors, Billy Kelly of the *Courier* and Bob Stedler of the *News*, viewed the game as a moral victory. The fans could hold their heads high. After the 49 – 7 slaughter by Cleveland in their previous outing at the end of the 1948 season, the 28 – 28 tie with those same Browns, however it was played out, was encouraging.[28]

George Ratterman was back and Buffalo was happy. Two weeks following the Cleveland game, the Bills knocked off the high flying 49ers, 28-17. The largest crowd of the season, 32,097, turned out. The Bills offense shone brightly. Ratterman went 15 of 20, for 224 yards and two touchdowns, and Mutyrn, Bumgartner, and Cline all ran well. Unfortunately the Bills surrounded these achievements with some horrible losses, to the Dodgers, the Colts, and the hapless Chicago Hornets. Owner Breuil's patience was being tested. On October 9, the Bills played in Los Angeles and suffered a humiliating 42 - 28 pounding at the hands of the Dons. That brought Breuil into the locker room following the game. He asked for and received Coach Red Dawson's resignation. Assistant Coach Clem Crowe took over.

The LA game resulted in more than another addition in the loss column, and it resulted in more than the loss of a pretty good coach, it also resulted in the team, in Billy Kelly's words, being "soundly trounced and badly hurt physically." Dawson supporters might alibi that the injuries really were responsible for the defeat but it seems clear that Dawson had been having difficulties before the trip to Southern California. Earlier losses to three weak teams and general player discontent were two obvious signs of trouble. The Bills' all star running back, Chet Mutryn recalled that "Red Dawson was a bit of a curmudgeon, and didn't know how to communicate with the players."[29]

The new coach, Clem Crowe was given a free ride for his first game, against the formidable 49ers. The Bills were without their three starting running backs. The predictions that they would be smothered by the Niners, proved painfully accurate. The final score: Bills lost 51 - 7. San Francisco, led by one of the all-time NFL great running backs Joe Perry, chalked up 310 rushing yards. Buffalo's makeshift rushing game ground out a measly 11 yards. As one newspaper put it, San Francisco's "brutally strong 49ers ran roughshod over Buffalo's battered Bills."[30]

Nevertheless Clem Crowe was deemed a worthy successor to Dawson. Crowe was not saddled with the horrendous loss to the 49ers. Crowe had quality football credentials; he was respected by the players, he had a better rapport with the players than Dawson and the fans liked him. He had played with the famed Four Horsemen at Notre Dame; Knute Rockne had had high praise for the future Bills' coach. In Lafayette Square, in busy downtown Buffalo, Clem Crowe was given a

Buffalo Bills team picture of 1949. ***Left to right, front row:*** **Larry Joe, Joe Sutton, Ed (Buckets) Hirsch, Abe Gibron, Vito Kissell, Alex Wizbicki, Chet Mutryn;** ***second row:*** **Joel Hunt, Paul Gibson, Ollie Cline, Lou Tomasetti, Wilbur Volz, Chuck Schuette, Rocco Pirro, Hal Herring, Rex Bumgardner, Clem Crowe (coach);** ***third row:*** **Bobby Brown, Art Statuto, Al Baldwin, Chet Adams, Jim Still, Jim Lukens, John Kissell, Jack Kerns, Al Stanton, Bob Oristaglio, Tony DiRosa;** ***fourth row:*** **Red Dawson, Bill Schroll, Odel Stautzenberger, George Ratterman, Tommy Colella, John Maskas, Jack Carpenter, Vince Mazza, Vic Vasicek, Hank Reese. The Bills reached the height of their success in 1949 – tying champion Browns twice.** *Photo: Buffalo Bills Archives*

rousing welcome by fans shortly before his first home game as coach. The Bills responded by beating the L.A. Dons, 17 - 14. Led by a "fantastic" Ratterman, they far outplayed the visitors. Lou Tomasetti rushed for 188 yards.

The Bills went on a roll, winning four and tying one. Following the L.A. win, came a victory in New York City over the Brooklyn Dodgers (the Brooklyn club had been combined with the New York Yankees at the beginning of season). After that triumph, the Bills traveled to Cleveland where their outstanding play earned them a 7 – 7 tie with the perennial champions. The following week Buffalo shut out the Chicago Hornets, 10 - 0, and a week later they finished the regular season at Baltimore, rolling over the Colts, 38 - 14. Ratterman was 22 of 30 for 218 yards and 3 touchdowns, out dueling future Hall of Famer, Y.A. Tittle, who was 12 of 26 for 235 yards and 2 touchdowns.

The strong showing in the second half of the season earned the Bills another shot at the Cleveland Browns in the post season on December 4. Thousands of fans took the 190 mile trip along the southern shore of Lake Erie to Cleveland's mammoth Municipal Stadium. Many went by auto, but many more boarded the special trains that left from the towering New York Central Terminal on Buffalo's East Side. It was truly a tremendous show of Buffalo fan support in this golden age of Buffalo sports.

Again the Bills played very well, as did the Browns. The game featured two of the best quarterbacks in the business. Ratterman put on a fine performance; but, unfortunately for Buffalo, Graham played even better, leading the Browns over the Bills, 31 - 21. Together, Otto Graham and George Ratterman, put on a record passing spectacular. 85 passes were thrown, a sign of things to come in the game of professional football. Graham passed for 326 yards and two touchdowns, and Ratterman had 293 yards and three TD's.

In the final analysis pass defense proved crucial. Cleveland simply was better. It was a "not to be ashamed of" game for Buffalo. The Bills fans left satisfied, knowing they had witnessed a memorable performance against arguably the very best team in all of professional football.

The Buffalo Bills had definitely arrived as a solid professional football team. Two ties with the well nigh invincible Cleveland Browns, and a "respectable" loss to that same team in postseason play, were clear evidence of the caliber of the Bills' team. Buffalo's success must have sent shivers and anxieties into the NFL hierarchy who it appears were planning to take only Cleveland and San Francisco into the NFL when the time for the end of the grid war arrived. The Bills had proven that they could compete with the best. Unfortunately the splendid on-field performances of the Bills in 1949 were being overshadowed by more far reaching questions. Would Buffalo actually have a team in 1950? Would there be an AAFC in 1950? The long festering Grid War was heading to a disastrous conclusion for Buffalo. It had been a behind the scenes, off again/on again, scenario ever since the birth of the All American Football Conference. At the end of the 1949 football season the war was ready to explode.

Back at the end of World War II when the AAFC was being organized, the National Football League paid scant attention to the new kid on the block. During its inaugural season, 1946, the fledgling conference continued to be ignored by the senior conference. The AAFC was happy just to survive its shaky first year. Occasionally it floated a trial balloon for some sort of accommodation between the two football leagues, but the NFL took no notice, other than to utter an occasional condescending remark. The NFL itself was still somewhat wobbly, not all of its own member franchises were financially successful by any stretch of the imagination.

Things changed the following year. The AAFC had a very successful season in 1947. The new conference looked as though it was here to stay. Indeed the AAFC was recruiting top stars from the college ranks, drawing more fans, and winning the all important war of gate receipts. The Grid War was heating up and the senior conference did not like it. To be in a good bargaining position for the day when peace talks should arrive, the Bills' organization, along with those of other AAFC clubs, was going to have to build upon the 1947 successes.

The concern for Buffalo's professional football future was relatively muted as the 1948 season began. Then, in a rather bizarre episode, owner Jim Breuil blasted America's most renowned sports writer, Grantland Rice, for his alleged criticism of Buffalo's status as a "big league city." Breuil sent an "open letter" to the sports editors of Buffalo's two daily newspapers. The letter was addressed to the general public and in it the Bills' owner was hypercritical of Rice's September 8th syndicated column that had appeared in the *Buffalo Evening News* as well as in many other newspapers around the country. He accused Rice of negativity toward the Bills as well as toward the AAFC and alleged that Rice had referred to Buffalo as minor league. Both newspapers published the full text of the letter. The *Courier* had little comment, but Bob Stedler in the *News* took issue with Breuil's broadside. He said Rice's column did not spread "malicious propaganda" about the AAFC or Buffalo and, indeed, Stedler pointed out that Rice was a firm believer that there should be two recognized leagues in football and that there should be a championship game for all professional football honors. Stedler did give the Bills' owner the benefit of the doubt saying that Breuil had misinterpreted Rice. It appears that Breuil was not only inaccurate but he was also unusually sensitive. He was still losing money and he wanted larger crowds, and he also wanted wider acceptance and recognition that Buffalo was "Big League." The Buffalo newspapers certainly sympathized with Breuil's goals. Stedler promised Breuil that he would keep Rice as informed as he possibly could about Buffalo's status to prevent future misunderstandings.[31]

Just a week later, in another syndicated story, Grantland Rice stated "we have always felt that...Baltimore and Buffalo were capable of holding their own." He added: "there is certainly room and a direct need for two leagues where Baltimore and Buffalo belong. Both have been Big League Cities for many years." In support of the AAFC he noted that Cleveland and San Francisco "can outmatch" Chicago and New York in the NFL. Rice left little doubt in the minds of his readers that he was a firm supporter of the AAFC, of a peace agreement, and of a merger that would include the Buffalo franchise.[32]

Attendance at Buffalo's first five home games in the '48 season was off some 13,000 compared with the previous year. Rumors circulated questioning the future status of the Bills. But Jim Breuil promised that the Bills would be in the AAFC in 1949 and he further noted "we have lost little financially this season" compared with 1946. Breuil continued optimistic that peace could be worked out with the NFL. He hoped for larger crowds for the remaining two home games to bolster the Bills' position. Unfortunately the Baltimore game drew 23,694 and the final home contest against the LA Dons drew 23,725. These turnouts were better than many cities experienced on the corresponding days, but still, for a city looking to secure its place in pro football, the crowds should have been larger.

Mike Kanaley, *Courier Express* reporter, in a related story, said that the NFL was hurting as much as the AAFC and pointed out that on the most recent Sunday the NFL in 5 games drew less than the AAFC drew in just 4 contests. On November 5, Carl Lindquist, *United Press* sportswriter, noted that most pro football clubs had suffered a decline in attendance from 1947 to 1948, and confirmed that the losses of the senior circuit were larger. The Chicago Bears alone in the NFL showed an increase, whereas Baltimore, Brooklyn, and San Francisco in the AAFC all showed gains; Lindquist felt this itself was an impetus for peace. In his end of the season column captioned "Pro Football Closes Financially Disastrous Schedule," Grantland Rice took the occasion to reemphasize his conviction that two leagues with a total of 16 teams, including Buffalo was the answer. He again took issue with the NFL bosses who did not want two leagues.[33]

Some observers sensed that an armistice was near. It was fairly common knowledge that both leagues were discussing plans for some sort of accommodation as 1948 drew to a close. A number of plans and proposals were hatched at this time. A week before Christmas, the AAFC bosses at their annual meeting in Cleveland suggested that the Chicago Cardinals and the Boston Yanks be put in the AAFC and recommended that the Brooklyn Dodgers and Chicago Rockets be dissolved. Each league would then have 8 teams. A common draft was part of the plan. About this same time, an Associated Press story out of Cleveland said it had a "top secret report" showing that the NFL was worse off than the AAFC and this was prompting the AAFC owners to continue operating in 1949. Meanwhile a report out of the NFL annual meeting in Philadelphia noted that the senior league was still willing to take only Cleveland and San Francisco in a 12 team set up. Other than that, there was no consensus in the senior league. The grid war ground on as 1949 unfolded. Owners complained about diminishing revenues and increasing costs; players did not complain about their higher salaries.

Meanwhile Jim Breuil had left for a vacation in Florida. From there he sent back some reassurances, saying: "I can say professional football will stay in Buffalo." A short time later, he added, "Buffalo has demonstrated that it is a better big league city than most of the NFL....We are in Pro Football and will stay in."[34]

By February of 1949 it appeared that the grid war was an accepted fact for at least another season, and so the posturing about peace moves and possible plans for new league arrangements were put on hold. Occasionally a statement would be made or a new source quoted about some peace overture but nothing essentially changed. In April Arch Ward of the *Chicago Tribune* said that the AAFC was stronger than at any time in the past and a two league system was guaranteed. Ward continued to boost Buffalo, as did Art Rooney, the convivial owner of the Pittsburgh Steelers. Rooney came to Buffalo to participate in a meeting of an Irish fraternal organization, the Knights of Equity. Certainly Rooney was not an unbiased bystander, but he took the occasion to remark to Billy Kelly that Buffalo is a major league city and ranks well with major league cities elsewhere.[35]

It had become clear that Buffalo would field a team in '49 but it also was clear that Buffalo had to make a big push at the box office to demonstrate that it would continue to be a big league city. Buffalonians had to show that they were behind Breuil and his football Bills, and that they were also going to help with his other bills, his financial bills. It appeared that Breuil had fought hard for the Bills' survival in the 48-49 league talks, now it was time for the fans to ante up, to purchase tickets, to fill as many of the stadium seats as possible for each of the six home games in the upcoming season.

In May 1949, plans for a season ticket

campaign were announced. A committee was set up. Its very simple goal was to sell a record number of season tickets. The Buffalo newspapers jumped into the effort wholeheartedly. Stedler used a full column trying to stir up interest. Stedler sounded the alarm, he made reference to the fact that Dallas and Cincinnati were interested in obtaining pro football franchises, and warned that "it behooves all to do everything possible to avoid making Buffalo the laughing stock of the entire sports world." Billy Kelly in the *Courier* spelled out the details of the Committee's operation; some 200 business and civic leaders would break down into twenty smaller groups; and then they would canvas virtually everyone who was any sort of a prospect whatsoever.[36]

Both editors saluted Breuil's past efforts, took note of his financial losses, and urged fans to show support. The *Courier*, foreshadowing arguments that would be heard often decades later, noted how vital professional sports were for a city like Buffalo. Sports were important if Buffalo were to be considered one of the great cities of the country; it was important for the team and the city's name to be mentioned on every radio and in every newspaper throughout the land. Sports had come to exercise a "tremendous hold" on great numbers of Americans in their daily conversation. Surely the Buffalo newspapers were on the cutting edge of modern hype. Both papers noted that the cold war in football was heading for a hot solution by the end of the year. Stedler, a short time later, put it bluntly. He noted that last year Buffalo had had 5300 season tickets holders, "far less than many other cities." The city had reached a turning point: "the test of whether Buffalo wants its professional football team."[37]

The big ticket push appeared to get off on the right foot. Mayor Bernard Dowd bought the first ticket and then issued a proclamation proclaiming "Buffalo Bills Citizens' Committee Week." A well-publicized downtown kickoff luncheon was held. The Jaycees, 1000 members strong, joined the campaign. Businessmen from the largest banks, the M & T and the Marine, as well as leaders from Oil, Steel, and Auto industries played committee leadership roles. Tommy Colella, a celebrity now back in his hometown, was brought on board to make a sales pitch for tickets. The "Albion Antelope" as he was famously called, had been a local hero since his days at Albion High School and at Canisius College in the years before World War II. The ticket drive was being launched in a grand manner.[38]

Then a strange think happened; as a matter of fact not much happened. Very little was heard about the campaign again as those late spring days gave way to summer. A few hundred season tickets were sold, the drive was extended into July but then it just fizzled.

Buffalo fans turned their attention to the Bills' preseason. Over 31,000 turned out for the Bills first exhibition game against the Jersey City Giants. The Bills pummeled the hapless minor league team, 79 – 0. Both the score and the size of the crowd were good omens. However at the next preseason game, another victory, this time over the Bethlehem Bulldogs, only 12,697 turned out. That was not a good omen.

The Bills, minus George Ratterman, lost the official 1949 season opener played in Chicago. But the following week, Ratterman played in the home opener and the powerful Cleveland Browns and the Bills played to a 28 - 28 tie. It was a superb football game. 31,839 fans purchased tickets for the game. Unfortunately that was 12,000 short of the 1947 Cleveland game, and 4,000 fewer than the 1948 game. The following game was against the New York Yankees, and the Bills lost 17 - 14 before 30,410. After two home games the Bills actually led the conference in attendance. Next the Bills defeated the San Francisco 49ers before 32,097 in Civic Stadium. Buffalo had done fairly well attendance wise in the first part of the season. If Buffalo could continue to average over 30,000 then the Bills' franchise would be in good shape.

Then the Bills traveled west, they were blown out by the L.A. Dons, and Dawson was fired. In the following game against San Francisco they were again blown out under new head coach Clem Crowe. Back in Buffalo the Bills turned their season around on the playing field, but, unfortunately, not at the box office. Attendance took a nosedive. Only 21,310 showed up to watch the Bills defeat Los Angeles and in the final home contest the Bills defeated Chicago before a mere 18,494 die hard fans. Weather was partly responsible, but that did not show up on the statistical chart. In fact the weather was so miserable for the Chicago game that the size of the crowd, small though it was, was viewed as a tremendous show of support and appreciation for Breuil and his team. In the Bills' final game of 1949, the Bills lost to the Browns in a postseason contest. More than 3000 rabid Buffalo fans traveled to Cleveland in adverse weather conditions to cheer on the Bills. Certainly this was another indication of Buffalo's willingness to support professional football. Attendance at pro football games was off generally. Buffalo's was not off as much as in most cities. The problem was that for Buffalo to secure a more permanent place in a professional football league it would have to demonstrate a better drawing power than most other cities. That's just the way it was.

Grid peace and the merger of the football conferences had been mentioned, on and off, for many months. Things appeared comparatively quiet during the final days of the 1949 season. Then, on December 9, without warning, without any sort of rumors circulating for days or even hours before, the figurative bombshell was dropped on Buffalo. In Philadelphia the merger of the NFL and AAFC was announced. Cleveland, San Francisco, and Baltimore would join all ten teams in the National Football League. The new set up was called the National American Football League, the NAFL.[39]

The merger was no such thing; it was quite unlike what would be the 1970 merger of the AFL and the NFL. At that time the interests of both leagues were accommodated. In 1949 the NFL simply allowed in as new members of its organization, three teams from the AAFC. It was an obvious victory for the older league. Of the 17 cities represented by teams in the two leagues, Buffalo was the only city not represented in the so-called merger. Each of the other cities had at least one franchise representing it. This was a cruel blow to the city's ego. It helped to explain the bitter reaction of the Buffalo fans.[40]

Apparently Horace Stoneham, the owner of the Baseball Giants, and of the Polo Grounds was the catalyst behind the final decision. Two of the NFL teams played their home games there and both lost money. Stoneham summoned Bert Bell and J. Arthur Friedlund, AAFC Commissioner Kessing's representative, to talks in New York on December 6. The following day they traveled to Philadelphia and met "round the clock" until they arrived at the December 9 merger decision. Bell announced that the new league would come into existence on December 19, on the day following the NFL championship game.

Jim Breuil apparently had at least a little advance notice. On the same day that the merger was announced, he dispatched an "Open Letter" to the *News* and the *Courier*. Both papers published the complete text on December 10. After thanking the thousands of loyal fans, the Bills' owner said he wanted to explain what happened "by relating the simple truth." He enthusiastically had brought football to Buffalo in 1946, but he had not anticipated the "drain on my physical and mental resources" that affected him over the subsequent months. He reached his limit by the end of 1948 and "quickly conveyed" his predicament "to a sizeable group of civic-spirited men who immediately set forth to form a corporation which would assume the responsibility of operating the Bills. The initial enthusiasm...was so great that I was convinced it would meet with success and personally pledged Buffalo to the All America Conference for 1949." Breuil stated that for reasons unknown the movement collapsed, but he had made a pledge and against the advice of business associates and his doctor he fielded the1949 team. That team under Coach Clem Crowe was the best yet of the Buffalo teams, but "the same old problems were present behind the scenes – additional demands on my time, money and energy far beyond what any man could endure." [41]

Anticipating that many questions would be raised and fingers pointed, Breuil continued with the following puzzling statement: "Someone asked, 'Why wasn't the public informed of this? The needed funds could have been raised by subscription to carry the load.' In answer, I can only state that the amount of guarantee demanded by the Conference is $250,000, a lot of money. And assuming the funds could have been obtained; there wasn't time to arrange a responsible corporate set-up prior to the mid-December meetings in Houston." Then Breuil noted, somewhat strangely, there was a silver lining in that Buffalo would have the exclusive rights to Cleveland's three preseason games. Cleveland would be the host team for the games in Buffalo. And Breuil, disingenuously, said that the people of Buffalo would be "virtually on a par" with the Cleveland fans who would be limited to five home games. Perhaps this is what Breuil meant, when he said some months earlier, that Buffalo would continue to have football.

Billy Kelly in his first column following Buffalo's beheading, praised Breuil for his great efforts in bringing pro football to Buffalo and keeping it here for four years. He agreed with Breuil that providing pro football was too great a burden for just one man to bear. Bob Stedler took a different tack. He thought that the interest of local fans in the Bills was clear evidence that the area would support a major league team, certainly more so than in many other cities. "Had any intimation been give the local public," Stedler continued "that additional capital was desired, or that the Buffalo franchise was on the market, there would have been a ready response here to produce the required amount." He had received inquires in the past weeks about the future of football in Buffalo, but was unable to give any encouragement for lack of information as to the intention of the owners of the Bills. Stedler had no doubt that Buffalonians would have come to the rescue of the franchise but they were not given the chance ahead of time to do so. The merger announcement came as a complete surprise and a shock. Buffalo had lost prestige in the sports world. Stedler predicted that "It will doubtless be a long time before another major league football franchise is obtained for the city." He further added, "One cannot blame the owners for protecting their interests." Perhaps with a touch of sarcasm he noted: "Evidently they believe they gave the city a fair trial."

There was a slight ray of hope. The new league, the NAFL, would hold its first meeting on January 19, 1950. Jim Breuil mentioned that a franchise might be available in the new league if sufficient capital, that is, $250,000, were raised before the new league held its initial meeting. When the *Courier*'s Mike Kanaley asked Bert Bell "point blank" if Buffalo might be accepted if it raised $250,000, Bell responded that "the biggest obstacle is the schedule."

The Buffalo fans reacted quickly and vigorously to this little glimmer of hope, however farfetched it might actually be.

January 19 was the day of reckoning, the day on which the NAFL would make its final decision as to whether to go beyond 13 members. It was only five weeks away. Could Buffalo make a strong case for being granted a franchise, for becoming the 14th member of the new league? Buffalonians were determined that they could.

On Monday, December 12, the citizenry was galvanized into action. Early that day the Quarterback Club, and the Buffalo Sports Boosters, joined forces with interested citizens including civic and business leaders and formed the Buffalo Bills Football Club, Inc. Dr. James Ailinger and Dave West were named co-chairmen of the Citizens Committee of the club and Arthur Rich was named secretary treasurer.

The new committee met at the Buffalo Athletic Club, under the banner "Keep the Bills in Buffalo" and announced that capital stock, 100,000 shares of it, would go on sale at a mammoth rally to be held that very evening in Memorial Auditorium. The rally would start at 5:00 pm; shares would be priced at $5.00 each. This would give the public a chance to own its own ball club. Mayor-elect Joseph Mruk and out-going Mayor Bernie Dowd, and Council President Democrat Peter Crotty, and Republican council member, George Raikin all came aboard pledging "fullest cooperation."

The rally was a jubilant affair. A huge outpouring, well over 10,000 fans, jammed enthusiastically into Memorial Auditorium. One report said the figure was actually 20,000. Buffalonians from all walks of life, young and old, male and female, laborers and professional people handed over their money to 42 volunteer bank clerks. $74,700 was raised outright, and $125.000 was pledged. This $199,700 was well on the way to the goal of $250,000.

The initial response certainly was overwhelming. Billy Kelly called it "spontaneous, astonishing, and monumental." The media was so energized with the response that even the man in the street eager to part with a five dollar bill was enthusiastically recognized. Five dollars here, and ten dollars there, were given as much recognition as the occasional $100 bill. George Ratterman's mother sent a check for $10. A local steelworker bought a $5 stock for his son. A postal employee took his pretty young daughter by the hand to purchase a stock certificate. It went like that. But not many big timers made their presence felt, rarely was a purchase of more than $100 made. That may have not been a good sign.

The huge Aud turnout and the quick results of nearly $200,000 impressed Bert Bell enough for him to state that Buffalo was at least entitled to a hearing. Again he cautioned that a unanimous vote of all thirteen members was needed. He said that he would meet with a Buffalo delegation in Philadelphia, before the January 19 deadline. The commissioner suggested that Buffalo's case would be helped if money were also raised for season tickets, and not just money for operating expenses. Sales of stock continued in the days that followed. The three largest banks, M & T, Marine, and Liberty, all major department stores, the *Courier* and *News*, and the major labor unions would all act as outlets for selling tickets as well as stock certificates. All across the United States sports fans cheered on the impressive efforts to save the Bills. Red Smith, celebrated sports writer for the *Herald Tribune*, devoted two columns to the plight of the Bills and the fervid response of the city to save the team.

But then the drive slowed a little. It was observed that the "little guy in the street" was carrying the burden toward the first $250,000. Art Rich said "big business must step up to help," in fact, he added "Big Business must make sizeable donations." $250,000 was the original goal, but more was needed to convince the NAFL brass. Bob

Stedler kept urging everyone on, the drive "must not fail." Once again the newspapers were solidly behind the effort. They spelled out the stakes as clearly as possible.

Thirty three men, representing a cross section of business, banking, industry and labor were set up as a Board of Incorporators, making the Buffalo Bills Football Club a reality. This group would select a delegation to meet with Bert Bell. Subsequently a group of five; J. Eugene McMahon, lawyer, Albert T. O"Neill, President of Buffalo Niagara Electric Corp, David West, local businessman, Dr. James J. Ailinger, dentist and Buffalo sports figure, and Jim Wells, assistant to Breuil, met with the commissioner in New York City. They met in the offices of the State Democratic Chairman, Paul Fitzpatrick, in the Hotel Biltmore on December 20. The committee exited the meeting with the feeling that Buffalo had an "excellent chance" for a new franchise. They could not find an owner who was against the Bills. Tim Mara, New York Giants' owner, and a good friend of Paul Fitzpatrick declared his support on the spot.

Meanwhile Grantland Rice, in his syndicated column for the *North American Newspaper Alliance*, continued to plug for a two league concept with eight teams in each, mirroring major league baseball. Rice was clearly in Buffalo's corner, saying "If any city belongs in football it is Buffalo." He referred to Buffalo as "a bustling community with close to a million souls and a civic spirit many other cities lack."

Unfortunately Commissioner Bert Bell was not as optimistic as the Buffalo community. The New Year began on a pessimistic note. Bell was still trying to work out a 14 game schedule. He told the Courier that he was burning the midnight oil "in an effort to fit Buffalo into the 1950 professional football picture." But the schedule remained the sticking point, it apparently was more difficult to work out a fourteen than a thirteen team schedule because of the game traditions and loyalties and preferences. The commissioner of all football declared "I am not encouraged." He mentioned that "it was a simple thing to work out a schedule but it is another thing to please the teams." On January 3 Bell said he had actually worked out a schedule but the rub was that it would lead to financial chaos; no one in his right mind would agree to it.

The Buffalo community would not be deterred. The stock subscription drive had reached $255,535 but in the New Year, the concentration would be on the season ticket drive. The goal was to sell at least 12,000, and hopefully as many as 15,000 season tickets, a formidable undertaking considering that the previous high was 5300 tickets in 1948. Bell had stressed the importance of advance ticket sales because this would assure enough revenue at each game to pay the bills for visiting teams.

With great exuberance a season ticket drive was outlined. Dr. Ailinger was named head of the Season Ticket committee. Ailinger was an excellent choice; he had a long time involvement with Buffalo sports, especially with professional football. He went right to work on what was now being dubbed the "supreme test" for tickets. The drive got off to a slow start causing Stedler to remark that he was disappointed and even amazed that there has been so little response from those in industry. But then things picked up, ticket sales surged ahead and optimism once again became the order of the day.

On January 6, it was announced that approximately 4,000 season tickets had been sold, on the following day the total was more than 7,500, and on the day after that, 9,219 was the number. The following day, the total hit 12,414. By January 10 the total neared 15,000, causing Tony Wurzer to remark that the drive "is one of the most amazing 5-day responses in the history of sports." Big industry had begun to respond to the ticket drive, especially with payroll deduction plans.

Bell again stated that he was impressed with the Bills' civic pride and indicated he would make an effort to produce an acceptable 14 team schedule.

A week later Ailinger, McMahon, O'Neill and Murray headed to Philadelphia to make the Buffalo presentation. Bus Owens accompanied them. Should a franchise be granted, he would represent Buffalo in the player draft. On the eve of the meeting O'Neill indicated that he had canvassed a number of owners and said he had found no one opposed to Buffalo, though some did take a wait and see attitude. Furthermore the Buffalo contingent met in Philadelphia with good friend Art Rooney who told them he had a bloc of seven owners who would help get all the others on Buffalo's side.

In the City of Brotherly Love, on Wednesday the day before the official meeting of the NAFL, O'Neill delivered the facts for Buffalo's case. The figures presented were 15,008 season ticket pledges; he had $177,600 on hand in stock subscriptions, and $86,000 in pledges. Mike Kanaley noted that if the NAFL owners rejected Buffalo's bid, it would have to be for reasons other than attendance and finances.

On the eve of D-Day, things seemed to be tilting in Buffalo's favor. The season ticket total had surpassed 15,000. To put that in perspective, Washington topped the NFL with 20,000 season tickets and Chicago had approximately 15,000. All the others were far below that mark. Some of the owners with real clout, notably Marshall of the Redskins, Rooney of the Steelers, and Mara of the Giants, had indicated that they were in the Bills' camp. The cities of Dallas and Houston had previously submitted applications; both had dropped out of the running. The Bills' representatives felt reasonably confident. They would have been much less so if they had known that each of the NAFL owners came to Philadelphia armed with his own preferred schedule.

The end came quickly and it was bitter. At the plenary meeting on January 20, the 13 NAFL owners and Commissioner Bell discussed a two division set up and the scheduling concerns. The motion to increase the league from 13 to 14 teams was defeated. No written tabulation was made because a unanimous vote was needed and as soon as there was one vote against, then the motion failed. In his official announcement, Commissioner Bell said that in the morning session the tide swung against Buffalo over the schedule issue. A satisfactory schedule could not be worked out. Traditional rivalries stood in the way of approving a workable schedule. The owners wanted to know ahead of time which division they would be in and who they would play. That was it. As best as could be determined the final vote was 7 for and 5 against and one not voting.

Dan Reeves of Los Angeles was the lone owner who voted against, who was willing to offer a reason; he placed the blame on Bert Bell because the commissioner failed to produce a 14 team schedule as he had promised. "I was not against Buffalo…I voted no because there was no schedule."

On January 20 the headline in the *Buffalo Evening News* read: "Football Owners Reject Bills' Bid." A ground swell of resentment swept through the city. As one would expect, the Buffalo fans that were canvassed far and wide, let it be known that they were shocked, disgusted, indignant and even hostile. Mike Kanaley, in the *Courier Express*, summed up the demise of the Bills as well as anyone: "Pro football in Buffalo died today after a lingering illness...Stricken December 8 after being stripped of all protection through a merger... the late franchise experienced a period of alternate rallies and relapses...at a moment when the battle appeared won the last breath was knocked from a prone body."

The *Courier Express*, after reviewing the scheduling dilemma, editorially stated "our own idea [is that], after all the promises and assurances that Buffalo would get a favorable vote...the owners have not forgotten the four lean and hungry years they suffered" because of the AAFC war with the NFL. So "they had a chance for partial revenge. It was a shabby, vengeful, and selfish treatment of our town."

The *Buffalo Evening News*, in its lead editorial on the editorial page, reviewed the admirable civic campaign, then concluded "it was a shocking disappointment when the decision ...was announced...somewhere there was duplicity." Stedler said that though it was a losing fight, "it still remains as the greatest effort ever made for a sports proposition in the entire history of Buffalo."

Two main questions continued to agitate. Why did the Bills not get a franchise on January 20? Why was their solid proposal to obtain a franchise and to become the 14th member of the NAFL not accepted by the owners in that league? Secondly, why were the Bills even in that situation in the first place? In other words, why were the Bills not included along with Cleveland, San Francisco, and Baltimore in the original so-called merger on December 9?

The simple answer to the first is that the NAFL owners did not want to make any concessions that they felt would deprive them of having their own preferred schedule, playing their traditional rivals on preferred weekends. It apparently was difficult enough to fit Baltimore as the 13th member into the schedule; they were not about to stress out over a 14th member.

Jesse Linthicum the sports editor of the *Baltimore Sun* thought Buffalo never had a chance. Thirteen was the number of teams agreed upon well in advance, he asserted. Louis Effrat of the *New York Times* could only say, "thirteen Moguls...after 3 days of wrangling were unable to agree on major issues." There does not seem to have been any particular animosity or dislike for Buffalo itself. The owners were businessmen, perhaps greedy in some cases, but primarily concerned with not wanting to continue to lose money on their football franchises. Most of them had lost money, and it was time to show a profit. The grid war was estimated to have cost ten million dollars making it the costliest "box office battle in the history of sports."

Bert Bell shares some responsibility. Several statements he made during the time of the Bills' limbo, from December 9 to January 18, were confusing, and sometimes misleading, even if not intentionally. Bert Bell seems to have been guilty of some double talk, perhaps unwittingly. At the very least he raised some false hopes for Buffalo. Perhaps Bell really did feel that the Bills had a chance. He seems to have been genuinely impressed with the success of the civic drive to support Buffalo's bid for a new franchise. He encouraged Buffalo's hopes. Bell had said he would do his best to develop a 14 team schedule; however he never did present such a schedule to the owners on January 20. He did note that the unanimous consent of all 13 owners was needed to admit a new member. And then he said that "in my opinion, that unanimous consent will not be granted." Bert Bell seems to have been unsure of the situation. As commissioner he was faced with an unprecedented situation; he was trying to accommodate a city's bid for a new franchise, a city that had had a solid team in the old AAFC, a team that was more successful than most of the teams in the NFL.

Buffalo's application for a franchise in the new league was rejected on January 20. But why was Buffalo even in this situation in the first place? Who or what was responsible for the Bills being in the predicament they found themselves in after December 9, 1949, of not being accepted in the so called merger with Cleveland, San Francisco, and Baltimore on December 9.

No one would argue that Cleveland and San Francisco did not deserve a place in the

NFL. Cleveland outdrew, and most observers figured the Browns could outplay, any team in professional football. San Francisco's attendance was above average and the 49ers had played well also. Probably more important was the fact that a team from the Bay Area was seen as a beacon for the NFL on the booming West Coast. Baltimore was a different story. Baltimore had not done very well, but in the final analysis it appears that George Marshall, one of the heavyweights in the NFL, considered Baltimore as being a natural rival for his Redskins. Why was Buffalo not included? Many football people recognized Buffalo as, "a success on the field and at the gate." Stan Grosshandler claims that "the one club really shortchanged" in the NFL-AAFC merger was Buffalo. Robert Peterson, in his authoritative study on the early years of pro football noted that Cleveland and San Francisco were solid franchises and the Buffalo Bills, "were coming on strong." The Bills had developed a solid fan base, they outdrew almost all of the NFL clubs, and "improved so much that they tied the Browns twice, and extended them to the limit in the playoffs before losing, 31 - 21." Buffalo certainly had good credentials for inclusion in the December 9th merger. So why were they left out. Billy Kelly referring to talks involving NFL officials said "It was quite apparent that Jim Breuil had little to say about the details." By the time the merger was arranged, Breuil was not a major player anymore.[42]

Breuil certainly deserved such praise for bringing the AAFC franchise to Buffalo and maintaining it for 4 years. Breuil received accolades from Buffalo leaders even after the whole affair was over. But was he as forthcoming as he could and should have been? Breuil was not always candid and may have been guilty of doubletalk. If not that, then at least he was confused and out of the NFL owners' loop.

Tony Wurzer, who had covered the Bills for most of their existence, pointed to Breuil's decision to go with Cleveland rather than to try to secure a franchise for Buffalo as an important factor behind the rejection. Wurzer was convinced that Buffalo had actually been written off back in November of 1949, because at that time at a secret AAFC meeting, Breuil said he would not go on with Buffalo in 1950 and just wanted to get out of football. Wurzer quoted Breuil as saying that he had earlier offered to "turn the franchise over to a Buffalo group...but nothing was done." Breuil added that he was losing money and time and so he told the AAFC that he was finished and then he received an offer from McBride of the Browns for a minor share, which he accepted. Furthermore Breuil admitted that he had even tried earlier, in 1948, to get out, but there were no takers. Ray Weil, close friend of the Breuil family and prominent Buffalo sportsman himself, recalled that Breuil was concerned that he was beginning to lose more money because tax write-offs were being lost in 1949 and the government was coming down on him and he could not afford the Bills anymore.[43]

Jack Ledden in a special to the *News* from Cleveland claimed that Breuil had decided several weeks earlier to abandon the Buffalo franchise. He told Cleveland friends "that he tried unsuccessfully to interest civic groups to help carry the financial load." It appears that Breuil had had enough and just wanted out.[44]

Breuil was only partly responsible for the situation in which Buffalo found itself in late 1949. Another problem that Buffalo had was the lack of leadership from the business community. No one stepped forward when Breuil was ready to give up the ship. No one was willing to take control of the franchise when Breuil was ready to simply give it away. Earlier when Breuil gave stern warnings of the need for more season tickets and more revenue, he approached directly the leaders of the business community. Unfortunately that group failed miserably.

In a broader sense, Buffalo's cause also seems to have been handicapped by the lack of one wealthy individual representing the team in the discussions and with Bell and at the NFL meeting. Buffalo did not have that one entrepreneur, like a Mara or a Marshall, who could relate directly to the old boys who ran the NFL. Buffalo was fortunate to have had Jim Breuil five years earlier, but he was out of the picture now. Big Money may not have been very important in pre-World War II days in professional football but it was becoming very important in the post-war years.

The Buffalo fans did step forward after the guillotine had been lowered in December. It was a magnificent show of support, but it was too late. And even then it was the little guy who was purchasing stock and pledging money for season tickets; business leaders were conspicuously scarce.

AFTERMATH

The Golden Age of Sports in Buffalo, as far as professional football was concerned, came to an abrupt end in January of 1950. Buffalo's AAFC team was not part of the so-called merger. Its bid for a new franchise in the newly formed NAFL, which, incidentally, would revert to its old title, the NFL, a short time later, was rejected.

In the aftermath of Buffalo's decapitation, Commissioner Bert Bell held out still another carrot of sorts, saying that if the 13 team set up fails, then "Buffalo would deserve first consideration" for a new spot. There was, of course, some talk about the NAFL expanding in the future. A number of officials agreed with Bell that Buffalo would be at the head of the line. Actually Bell felt that the 13-team league would stand "without change in future years." It stood for one year; Baltimore dropped out of the league. Buffalo was not offered a franchise. The league returned to 12 teams. No mention was made of Buffalo. In 1951 the New York Yankees were transferred to Dallas. That move lasted one year then the Dallas franchise moved back to Baltimore under a new owner.

Others tried to put a better light on the disastrous end of professional football, saying that now local colleges could have an easier time scheduling games in Civic Stadium. Canisius had played all its games there in the post war years, and Niagara and Bona played some too. Local college football was quite successful in that golden age of Buffalo sports just after World War II. But fate was cruel. Less than 3 weeks following the Bills' demise, Canisius College dropped football. A year later Niagara University did also, and St. Bona followed suit a year after that. The University of Buffalo did play some games at the corner of Jefferson and Best, but appeared to be content to play most of their games on campus near Main and Bailey.

Those old Bills' teams of the 1940s are long gone but some fond memories remain. Some talented players passed through the locker rooms at the old Rockpile as members of the original Buffalo Bills. A number of local college products had tryouts for the Bills and a few actually made the squad. Jerry Whelan, from Canisius College, played with the Bills in '48, and Bob Stefik of Niagara, played with the Bills during that same season. Tommy Colella, an All American when he starred at Canisius, played his final year, 1949, as a pro for the Bills. Previously he had starred for the Cleveland Browns. Paul Brown, arguably one of the greatest coaches in the history of pro football, coached the Browns from 1946 to 1962. He stated that Tommy Colella was "one of the 15 players I rate as the best ever to play on my pro teams."[45]

Chet Mutyrn was a three year all conference halfback, George Ratterman was the #3 all time passer in the conference behind Otto Graham and Frankie Albert and Al Baldwin was the #5 receiver after being in the conference for just three years. In 1949, the final season, Ratterman ended up second only to the great Graham in the passing department, Chet Mutyrn, the "butcher boy from Cleveland" ended up just behind the future Hall of Famer Joe Perry in rushing, and Baldwin wound up second to the Hall of Famer, Mac Speedie, in receiving. The Bills averaged 26,000 fans per game that year which was significantly above the NFL average of 23,000. Cy Krtizer in a story in the *Buffalo Evening News* in 1963 interviewed the Bills' coaches of the 1940s, Red Dawson and Clem Crowe. Each asserted that the Bills by 1949 were close to being a great football team.[46]

Buffalo fans would have to wait a decade before they would once again have their own professional football team. In the meantime they could become, perhaps a little bit grudgingly, fans of the Cleveland Browns. More than a few Buffalo natives took great delight and a sense of sweet revenge when, just nine months after the purging of the Bills, the Cleveland Browns clobbered the reigning NFL champion Philadelphia Eagles, 35 – 10. That essentially was the same Cleveland team, with the addition of a few Buffalo Bills, that the old Buffalo team had tied twice during the previous season, and then lost by only ten points in the AAFC playoff game. No other team had ever done that. As a matter of record, 19 of the Bills on the final squad of 37 players, continued on to play in the National Football League and three did so in the Canadian Football League.[47]

Nine years later, when another American Football Conference was being organized, an out of town businessman came to Buffalo's rescue. Detroit native, Ralph Wilson, had hoped to buy into his hometown franchise, but that was not available. He next was interested in securing a franchise in Miami in the proposed new conference, but others, well versed in professional football, advised him that Buffalo was a first class sports town and would be a much better investment. Almost a half century later, Wilson was still in charge of the Buffalo Bills professional football team. The new conference began operation in 1960 and television assured its survival. Indeed television assured that the peace settlement with the NFL, later in the 1960s, would amount to a true merger, not some sort of window dressing.

Back in 1948 when television made its debut in Buffalo, Alfred Kirchofer, editor of the *News*, asked for permission to televise the Bills'games. The *News* wanted to promote its recent acquisition, WBEN-TV. Breuil responded "Why doesn't he just ask us to committee suicide?"[48] Not many had any clue as to how revolutionary television would be for the future of organized sports. A decade later, 75 % of American homes had a television set, and by the 1960s television networks had millions of dollars available for football telecasts. The AFC survived; the AAFC did not. Back in the late 1940s, television was simply an infant looking for a home, for a niche in American society.

CHAPTER FOUR

Local College Football

— Never Better —

Courier-Express

Record Throng of 35,089
Sees St. Bona Beat Canisius

Buffalo Courier Express, November 4, 1946

The November 4, 1946 Canisius - St. Bonaventure game in Civic Stadium. *Photo: Canisius College Archives.*

College football in Western New York in the immediate post World War II years provided thrills and excitement for surprisingly large numbers of fans. The University of Buffalo, Niagara University, St. Bonaventure University and Canisius College, each operated athletic programs that were classified in the University Division of the NCAA. Each fielded competitive football teams in those years. Each played at least some of their games before sizeable crowds in Buffalo's Civic Stadium. When not playing there, they played at campus sites where fans demonstrated loyal support. St. Bonaventure, the University of Buffalo, and Canisius College consistently had winning seasons. Niagara did not fare quite as well in the won-loss column but the Purple Eagles had some shining moments and were rarely embarrassed on the gridiron. The University of Buffalo at the time was a private non-denominational institution; the other three were private Catholic institutions and were regarded as members of the Little Three, even though that designation had no legal standing. Rather it was simply an informal grouping.

Football was the nation's number one college sport and had been for a number of decades. It had come a long way since that first intercollegiate "football" contest between Rutgers and Princeton in 1869. In retrospect, that 6 – 4 contest that Rutgers won was more reminiscent of a soccer game. In the following decade Harvard University and McGill University of Montreal experimented with rugby type changes, and in the 1880s and '90s, Walter Camp, the coach at Yale University, and the father of American Football, modernized the game and made it distinctively American.

The college game began to attract large followings by the last decade of the 19th century, especially among supporters of those colleges that would eventually form the Ivy League.[1] Indeed the Big Three, Harvard, Yale, and Princeton, dominated the sports pages in the East at that time. In the early decades of the 20th century, Notre Dame with Knute Rockne at the helm as well as the teams representing the service academies at Army and Navy began to make their mark on the national scene. They were joined by many of the state institutions from the Midwest, the Far West, and the South. Many of those built large stadiums to accommodate their legions of fans.

The Roarin' Twenties ballyhooed many aspects of America's social and cultural life; sports were no exception. The decade of the 1920s marked the emergence of college football as a huge spectator sport. The tens of thousands, who cheered on the Four Horsemen and Red Grange, were right at home with the throngs who cheered on Jack Dempsey, Bill Tilden, and Bobby Jones as well as the millions who idolized Babe Ruth. College football was beginning to be referred to as "King Football." It was, without doubt, the most popular college sport.

The four Buffalo area colleges participated in the growth of intercollegiate football in the '20s. Students at Bona, Niagara and Canisius had been playing organized football since the time of the First World War. U.B. had actually played the game as early as 1894. It dropped the sport for a few years and then renewed it in 1915. By the 1920s, each of the local institutions was playing a very respectable brand of football. Their supporters continued to grow in numbers. Even during the Depression Decade of the 1930s the game continued to increase in popularity. On the eve of the Second World War college football seemed destined to have a rosy future.

World War II put many civilian activities on hold. Football vanished from many college campuses, or as the favorite expression of the day put it, football "was suspended for the duration." Physically fit young men of college age either enlisted or were drafted into the military service. Many of the football players from the area schools went off to serve in the armed forces. For instance, all 42 members of the 1942 Canisius College team went into the military. Other area institutions were not far behind. It was that kind of an era.

Once peace returned in 1945, it was only natural that the local colleges would make plans for the reestablishment of their football programs. They shared the national view that college football was the number one sport. Meanwhile, college basketball had continued to gather support in the Buffalo area. The old view of a basketball team being just a bunch of guys running around in short pants, perhaps a cut above tennis, was waning. Still basketball played second fiddle to football.

Most college athletic teams had few problems reestablishing themselves immediately after the war. But football was different. Football virtually had to start from scratch. Most of the teams had gotten rid of their uniforms and equipment. Finding new sporting goods to purchase for the teams was very difficult. In fact sporting goods, like many consumer items, were so scarce that it was virtually impossible to outfit a team in the months immediately following the end of the war. An even bigger problem was the scarcity of players.

The fall semester of 1945 began so quickly following the conclusion of the war that college enrollments remained unprecedented small. There was much uncertainty as to which former players would be returning and when they would do so. A similar situation prevailed in the coaching ranks. In some instances, new coaches would have to be hired. What with the shortage of supplies, equipment, and personnel, the colleges were forced to postpone whatever plans they might have had of restoring football programs in 1945. It was unrealistic to think otherwise.

Nevertheless, the football fans in Buffalo were geared up to watch their favorite sport. Fans were anxious for the "good old days to return." Buffalonians wanted football. Even during the war, fans turned out in impressive numbers to watch the Buffalo High Schools compete in their championship games in All High Stadium. On Thanksgiving Day in 1945, 11,792 hearty fans trekked to All High stadium for the Harvard Cup championship, the first High School championship held after V. J. Day. Despite the awful weather conditions, this was the best crowd ever for High School football in Western New York. It was merely a harbinger of things to come.

Momentum for college football quickened in1946. The University of Buffalo was the first of the local institutions to take steps to start up the sport once again. That was understandable since U.B. had Jim Peele as both coach and athletic director. He had been in those positions at U.B. since 1936 and he continued to wear those two hats after the war. For many involved with the University of Buffalo, it seemed that athletics and Jim Peele were synonymous. Peele announced that his institution would hold spring practice in 1946.

The Little Three colleges meanwhile were in the process of recruiting new head coaches. Niagara University hired Jim Moran, while he was still serving in the Navy. Moran was an ex-Notre Dame footballer and had played for the Washington Redskins, before entering the military service.

Canisius College announced that Earl Brown would be hired to coach both football and basketball, a dual position quite common in the decade of the 1940s. Brown had outstanding football credentials. Like Moran, he was a product of Notre Dame where he had been an All American end. He served on several coaching staffs, then again like Moran, he served in the Navy.

Above: Earl Brown coached Canisius in both football and basketball immediately after WWII. He left Canisius to be head football coach at Auburn.

St. Bona landed the big fish, Huge Devore of Notre Dame. Devore had been head coach of the Irish in 1945 while Frank Leahy was serving in the Navy. He signed with St. Bona for the then incredible salary of $8,000 though *Courier Express* Sports editor Billy Kelly quickly noted that St. Bona got more than $8000 worth of publicity just for the hiring. The university held a banquet welcoming Devore to the Olean campus. On this festive occasion, the Bishop of Buffalo, Most Rev. John O'Hara, former President of Notre Dame, was on hand as was legendary coach, Frank Leahy and several other Notre Dame notables. The banquet was a testament to the high esteem in which football was held on the Bonaventure campus. Fittingly, Fred Forness, former Mayor of Olean and a big time local businessman, announced he would give $100,000 to Bona for a new stadium.

In April a gala Little Three football dinner was held in the Golden Ballroom of the Hotel Statler in downtown Buffalo. Before the sellout crowd, it was formally announced that gridiron competition was being renewed. The public reacted enthusiastically to the announcement by indicating their intentions to purchase tickets.

Meanwhile, large numbers of young men were being mustered out of military service, and a considerable number of these war veterans indicated their eagerness to report for preseason practice. By mid summer the coaches were getting a pretty good picture as to the prospective players that they would have available in the fall of 1946. Some were returning from action in Europe, others from in the Pacific, others from the various bases stateside. Some fought the enemy; others played football for service teams. Some did both. There also was the occasional maverick who added color to the scene. Such was Darrell Braatz, popularly known as "Smiley." The peripatetic Braatz may have seemed unusual but there were other veterans who had somewhat similar experiences. Braatz arrived at Canisius after a dizzying several years. Smiley had played at Wisconsin with Elroy "Crazy Legs' Hirsch, he then played for Earl Brown at Dartmouth. In fact three days after he initially reported at Dartmouth, he played in the Yale game and was promptly voted the best back in the game. A little later, he was with the Marines on Okinawa, earning a Purple Heart. Now, a year later he showed up with his old mentor, Earl Brown, at Canisius. In addition to the wartime vets, there was the usual crop of 17-18 year old high school graduates eager to demonstrate that their prowess on the scholastic gridiron could carry over to the college game. It would be a huge challenge for them.[2]

Hugh DeVore , Head Football Coach at Notre Dame in 1945 and at St.Bonaventure, 1946-49.

In the second week of September, Cy Kritzer, *Buffalo Evening News* Sports Reporter, began what would become an annual ritual, his preseason reports from the various college training camps.His first stop was at Niagara University where fifty hopefuls reported to Coach Jim Moran. The majority were ex-servicemen. Kritzer referred to the Purple Eagles as a small but fast squad. Coach Moran put his hopes on Dick Doherty. Many familiar with Doherty thought that his previous experience as a player at Boston College might make him the best quarterback in the Little Three. He was referred to as "the spinning back and the ball handler" in Moran's T formation. Doherty had just returned from the Navy having survived on a ship twice torpedoed in the Atlantic. Niagara fans hoped that Doherty's luck was a good omen for their football team. Unfortunately, Doherty suffered a knee injury in preseason camp and would remain inactive for part of the season.

At Canisius College, Coach Earl Brown was pleased with the 76 candidates who reported for practice on August 7. He and his two assistants split the squad into three groups, Brown took the ends, Assistant Coach John Williamson took the backs, and Walter Marshall handled the lineman. The Griffs practiced on the Villa field, directly behind Old Main. Even before the war, Canisius had begun to play its home games in Civic Stadium, which was only a little over a mile from campus, directly south on Jefferson Avenue. The old Villa grandstands were on their way to Olean to be used in Bona's new stadium. Actually not exactly 100 percent of the stands left the Canisius site, players continued to pick up nails on the practice field for the next few years.

Cy Kritzer thought the Griffs had good reason to be optimistic. He surveyed the 6 squads of prospects and concluded that the Griffs had "the biggest, strongest, and fastest squad every assembled at the Villa." War veterans would play a big role in Canisius football, just as they would in most of the nation's college teams. Veterans of the 1942 Canisius team Dick Mazuca, Jim Naples, and Frank Acquino looked like they were ready to step into starting jobs. So was Felix Centofanti who was voted team captain in 1946. The average age was 23, and with so many good players returning from the pre war squads, it was understandable that a number of high school hopefuls did not make the team. One who did and was destined to become a college all-star was Ray Jacobi. He had earned a scholarship as a result of his stellar play on the great St. Joe's Collegiate team of 1946. Years later, Ray recalled being amazed at the size and maturity of the veterans.[3]

The turnout at the University of Buffalo was even larger. More than 100 prospects reported to camp. Jim Peele had good reason to be just as optimistic as Earl Brown. He had his big star from pre war days, Lou Corriere, back in uniform. Lou would play two more seasons. By the time he finished his outstanding career, he was hailed as the best all around athlete ever to wear the blue and white of the University of Buffalo. Peele was especially high on the Bulls' aerial game, led by Corriere and quarterback Vic Manz. Corriere's star power was such that Cy Kritzer figured it was one reason that U.B. shifted five of its games to Civic Stadium. Kritzer was impressed with U.B.'s entire squad; in words very similar to those he had used to describe Canisius, Kritzer called the Bulls, "the biggest, fastest, and most experienced squad" in U.B. history.

At St. Bonaventure fifty hopefuls showed up for tryouts. Coach Devore was optimistic. He said that he could count on a "very spirited" group. The fans in the Allegheny foothills were just as spirited, "football fever is burning in the beautiful Cattaraugus hills," Kritzer commented. People from the countryside, some 400 of them on average, attended each Bona practice, and the new college President, Rev.Tom Plassmann, made an appearance at every practice. The Booster Club, popularly known as The Gridiron Club, some 1500 strong, had already gobbled up thousands of dollars worth of tickets. Part of the attraction was Hugh Devore. Kritzer, a Bona alumnus and a Devore devotee, knew that Devore's name had a touch of magic to it. He claimed that Devore was "regarded as the nation's best coach…because of his marvelous work with below-par material at Notre Dame."[4]

The only cautious words came from the Bona coaching staff. They warned that the players were still trying to get in top shape. But Devore had a classy group of veterans returning, some were military veterans, others were veterans of previous playing experience; some fell into both categories. Bona was loaded, asserted Kritzer, perhaps it was the "greatest team" ever seen in these parts. Devore had Eddie Hlasmack , formerly of Miami University, ready to operate as a T formation quarterback. He was schooled during the summer by Frank Dancewicz, who was Devore's quarterback at Notre Dame. Devore also had Nunzio Marino who played in the backfield at Notre Dame. At fullback he had Hugh Marcolini who played with the Cherry Point Marines.

With many good players returning, and with the high caliber of experienced coaches at the area colleges, there was ample justification for the air of optimism that pervaded the football atmosphere, when the sport returned to the college campuses in the fall of 1946.

The Golden Griffins were the first of the local teams to take the field in the 1946 season. Many fans shared Cy Kritzer's lofty evaluation of the Griffin players. Many thought that the Griffs were the team to beat in Western New York. With solid depth at every position, there was good reason to rate the Griffs highly. The Griffs were loaded both with players and plays. Big George Doyle at right end and Al Chorny at the other end position could be counted on to make their mark early in this renewal of football. Coach Brown tabbed two other veterans with solid gridiron experience for starting roles John Martinelli, and Al Petrella. The coach also announced that he would be using two versions of the single wing and two versions of the T formation. He figured his choice to start at quarterback, Smiley Braatz, could handle this. Ray Ryan noted that newcomer Braatz, was actually already a known quantity to the coaches. "Still got that old floating power" remarked Assistant Coach Williamson, in a show of familiarity as he was observing Braatz in practice.[5]

A large crowd, in fact the largest in school history, was expected for the Canisius home opener, against the University of Western Ontario, on September 20. The Mustangs had the reputation as being a pretty fair Canadian football team so there was the prospect that it might be a close game. It wasn't. Canisius won 34 – 3. Despite the score, the Canadian players tried to make a game of it and they were battling at the end of the game just as hard if not harder than when the game began. More than 10,000 fans attended. That crowd included large groups of students as well as many fans from all walks of life in the Buffalo area.

The Griffs did what they would become known for in these post war years, piling up big offensive statistics, especially in the rushing category. The Griffs rolled up over 500 yards. Coach Brown used 43 players and a number of stars emerged. Braatz's running, passing and kicking, earned him the label of triple threat. He excelled on defense as well as offense. Howie Willis, a seventeen year old from New Jersey, had 89 yards in nine rushing attempts. Surely this was a sign of things to come for this rising star. Bud Agnew of East Aurora, substituting for Braatz, gave a good accounting of his ability at quarterback. Frank Acquino "a powerful spinning back," performed well. Canisius also uncovered an unheralded back in Tony Rocco, "lately of Notre Dame" who did a good job.[6] At one point the Griffs used an ambidextrous passer, Sam MacNeil of Williamsville. He passed for consecutive first downs, once in southpaw fashion and the other with the right hand. Such was the passing game in the 1940s.

It was an impressive opening game victory for Canisius. Nevertheless not everyone was in agreement that Canisius was the team

The 1946 Canisius College Football Team. ***Left to right, front row*****: George Doyle, Felix Centofanti, Dick Mazuca, Bob Sanders, Al Perella, John Marinelli, Al Chorny.** ***Back row:*** **Howie Willis, Bill McGreevy, Frank Acquino, Si Palumbo and Darrell Braatz.**

to beat. The Brown Indians gave promise of being the cream of the crop in Western New York. Bona had a new campus site for its home games, Forness Stadium. The Brown Indians also had a new coach with impressive credentials, not the least of which was his recent coaching experience at Notre Dame. Bona also had some proven football players on the roster, and a formidable schedule starting with a tough, well known opponent. Everything seemed to be in order for a grand coming out party. A capacity crowd of 8,800 jammed Forness Stadium. Bona kicked off on September 28 against Youngstown, a traditional powerhouse. The home team showed right off the bat that the prognosticators were on target. They scored two quick touchdowns. Unfortunately for the Brown Indians, the early success was costly. On the first touchdown drive, Bona's s ace passer, quarterback Ed Lhalsnack, went down and out with a twisted knee. Nuncio Marino, former "Notre Dame flash" scored the next one. A short time later, he was carried off with a knee injury. Those injuries opened the door for the opponents. Youngstown dominated the second half, and won 20 – 14.

That same weekend, the University of Buffalo kicked off its season with an awesome demonstration of offensive power. The Bulls showed a balanced attack, scoring three times through the air, and three times on the ground. They wiped out Moravian College, by a score of 40 – 7. Another impressive crowd of 7000 sweltering fans in Civic Stadium looked on. Not unexpectedly Lou Corriere led the way. The Lockport sensation had not missed a beat from his pre-war days on the gridiron. One particular touchdown of his had the fans on their feet cheering wildly. Quarterback Vic Manz, faded back to pass and just as he was about to be tackled, he flipped to ball to Corriere "lurking nearby." "Lockport Lou," as he was popularly called, circled the field then headed for the goal line 49 yards away, was hit four times but retained his balance, tight roped down the sideline and scored. Frank Nappo and Vic Cleri were also major contributors to the Bulls' victory. Coach Peele continued to substitute but the scoring also continued. All told the Bulls chalked up over 400 yards in the combined air and ground attack, and another 167 in return yardage.

Twenty miles to the North, Coach Jim Moran's Niagara University squad easily topped visiting Valpariso, 31 – 0. Moran had made a last minute move and it paid off. He announced two days before the opener that Jim Lindsay, who had played for Moran at the University of South Carolina, would start at quarterback. Lindsay along with Guido Filicetti and Les Dugan in the backfield demonstrated that the Purple Eagles also had some genuine offensive power. Filicetti galloped 69 yards on the first play from scrimmage and the Eagles never looked back

In September of 1946, just one year after VJ Day, Buffalo area fans had been treated to a glorious rebirth of college football. The four Western New York elevens all fared well on the gridiron in their season openers. College football was up and running and looking good. Fans eagerly looked forward to many rewarding autumn afternoons on the gridiron in the weeks that lie ahead.

The Griffs played their second game against Brown University, on the latter's home turf in Providence, Rhode Island. They came close to defeating this respectable Ivy League team. The Griffs took an early lead with George Doyle's touchdown reception courtesy of Howie Willis. The Griffs received an additional boost from Smiley Braatz who played almost the entire sixty minutes with a broken hand; he played a stellar game on defense. But it turned out to be an unlucky day for the Griffs. A costly Griffin fumble led to the go ahead touchdown for Brown; the final score was 14 – 7. However the Griffs quickly rebounded. They devastated their next two opponents, shellacking St. Mary's of Minnesota, 31 – 0, before nearly 9,000 fans at Civic Stadium, and then shutting out Alliance College of Ohio, 42 – 0. Bud Agnew's passing earned good marks and the running game of Howie Willis, Tom Kretz, Nipper Castine and Smiley Braatz proved virtually unstoppable.

Meanwhile the Purple Eagles of Niagara also showed that they could provide plenty of offense. They played Ithaca College, a perennial small college powerhouse, before 5000 spectators on the Niagara University home field. The game turned out to be a breather for Niagara. Led by Dick Dobmeier and Dick Doherty, Niagara lowered the boom on the visitors from "high above Cayuga's waters," 41 – 0.

The big game in the first half of the 1946 season took place on Columbus Day weekend. It was a Little Three contest featuring Niagara and St. Bona. The Brown Indians took the well worn 65 mile trip north on Route 16, better known as the Olean Road, to meet the Purple Eagles in Civic Stadium. More than 16,000 saw this first postwar resumption of Little Three football. Unfortunately, those looking for a typical Little Three contest were disappointed; Bona had just too many horses. Phil Colella, ex-Notre Dame player, set the tone when he raced for a 47 yard touchdown in the early minutes of the game. All the Bona stars operated in high gear. Dave Curtin, referred to by Ray Ryan of the *Courier Express*, as a "Daniel Boone marksman" did a great job at quarterback. Hugo Marcolini, a burly fullback, drove for valuable yardage, and Mitch Smiarowski, who was on his way to becoming one of the best centers in Little Three annals, also proved his worth as a kicker. He blasted two kickoffs into Niagara's end zone. Coach Devore had his subs play more than half the game. Still Bona was able to coast to a 29 – 7 victory.

The following week, Buffalo football fans were again treated to a Little Three contest, this one pitted Canisius against Niagara. Coach Brown converted Bud Agnew, a two- year navy veteran, to a T formation quarterback. Agnew made his start against Niagara. Brown also planned to feature Howie Willis, the 162 pound, 17-year-old ace from the Philadelphia area. The Griffs were heavily favored, but the Purple Eagles were up for the game. They played much better than they had against Bona. The game turned out to be a thriller for the 12,979 onlookers. Niagara led 2- 0 until the last quarter. Ray Ryan likened the Niagara defense to the Russians who held at Stalingrad as the Purple Eagle defense repeatedly stymied the high powered Griffin offense. In the first half the Griffs were held to 39 yards rushing and zero passing. Meanwhile the Niagara offense rolled up yardage, behind Jim McKinnon's passing and the running of Bruno Pacini and Guido Filicetti. Things looked bleak for Canisius. All but the most loyal Griffin supporters had pretty much given up. Canisius loyalists wondered what happened to the changes that Coach Brown had talked about. Then, in the final quarter, the Griffs came alive. A Howie Willis to Bud Agnew pass and a 56 yard scamper by ex-Kensington High star, Nipper Castine accounted for two Griffin touchdowns and allowed the Griffs to pull off a 14- 2 victory. The Griffs knew that they were fortunate to escape with a win. The newspapers praised Moran's coaching, and noted that Canisius was outplayed in every department except the score. Possibly this close call would serve as a wake up call for the Griffs as they contemplated their showdown for the Little Three title against St. Bona, a few weeks hence.

Before the much anticipated November Little Three clash, several other contests were played by the Western New York elevens, some against very high quality teams. Jim Peele's U.B. Bulls made a courageous effort to withstand the assault of a powerful Bucknell squad. A colorful parade down Main Street, and a homecoming crowd of 8000 in Civic Stadium, inspired the U.B. players, but not enough to enable them to spring an upset. Bucknell won 20 – 0. The Bulls also lost, a much closer contest, to Wayne State, 25 – 20 before 4500 fans. But this time the Bulls could find a bit of an excuse in that their great all around sensation, Lou Corriere, was not able to play because of an injury. However the Bulls then proceeded to chalk up some impressive victories. They knocked off Rensselear Polytechnic Institute of Troy, New York, 28 – 13 and defeated Hobart 20 – 7. Then, on November 2, with Lockport Lou back in action they clobbered Bethany 32 – 6. Lou scored twice on dazzling runs. A short time later, Lou again was the star as the Bulls upended previously undefeated Alfred, before 3000 in Civic Stadium. The Bulls continued on the winning path by shutting out both Carnegie Tech and Johns Hopkins. With "lopin" Lou Corriere "in the saddle" U.B. traveled to Pittsburgh where they ran herd over a hapless Carnegie team, 28 – 0. The Bulls then finished the season in similar fashion. Again Corriere starred, he initiated the scoring with an 80 yard run before 4,000 chilled fans at Civic Stadium; he and his teammates dominated Johns Hopkins University, 36 – 0. One could easily understand why Ray Ryan called Lou Corriere, "Lockport's gift to U.B. athletics."[7]

Niagara, after losing to its Little Three opponents, played an excellent game against a very strong John Carroll University team, and came out on the winning end, 14 - 6. The Purple Eagles also defeated a good Waynesburg team in convincing fashion, 19 – 0, and finished the season with two shutouts, over Hobart 25 – 0 and over Scranton 12 -0.

Meanwhile, down in Olean, Bona continued to rack up the points and draw in the fans. 8500 watched Bona shutout St. Vincent's 26 – 0 behind the stellar play of Phil Colella and Hugo Marcolini. The Brown Indians now stood at 3- 1, and appeared to be ready for their next trip to the big city on the Eastern end of Lake Erie. However before the Bona-Canisius showdown, the Griffs had to square off against a major foe from the Midwest. They played a strong Bowling Green eleven at Civic Stadium on October 24. It was the first time that the Ohio team had ventured east to play. They were billed as a high profile team, led by a fierce defense. The Griffs too could boast of a tough defense. In fact, the Golden Griffins had not allowed a touchdown since the Brown game. Western New York fans looked forward to a spectacular game. Unfortunately a miserable, rainy night kept the crowd down to 2,000. Those stalwarts who did endure the poor conditions were rewarded.

The Griffs looked like a well oiled machine in the first half. Their offensive line blocked crisply and enabled the backs to run and pass efficiently. The Griffs scored first, toward the end of the first quarter. Bud Agnew's passes to Jim Naples brought them downfield, then, Norm "Nipper" Castine dove in from the three yard line. Unfortunately the tide changed following the intermission. In the 3rd quarter, Bowling Green intercepted a pass and went 76 yards for a touchdown. In the 4th quarter, the visitors again scored, this one on a freak play that sealed their victory. The Bowling Green quarterback threw a pass into the end zone. It looked as though Bud Agnew had batted it down harmlessly. But the ball struck Smiley Braatz who was lying flat on the ground in the end zone, the football bounced up in the air and landed in the hands of Norm Welker, the Bowling Green receiver, who was also lying flat on the ground next to Braatz. The referee realized that the ball had not hit the ground at any point, and signaled touchdown. For the Griffins, it was a heartbreaking loss, courtesy of the strange bounce of the pigskin. Canisius had more than twice as many first downs, and outplayed Bowling Green for most of the game. Unfortunately, the final score stood at 13 – 7 in favor of the Ohio team.

The Indian Summer Days passed and as October turned to November, chilly weather and the threat of snow became part of the weather forecast. Western New York football fans now turned their attention to the upcoming battle between Canisius and St. Bona. The setting was Civic Stadium, Sunday, November 3. The Griffs had been playing quite well but St. Bona had been playing even better. In fact since the opening loss to Youngstown, the Bona team had been smothering the opposition. One big reason was "Mr. Smear" himself. That was the moniker given to Mitch Smiarowski, the Bona center, who seemed to eat up opponents. Mike Reilly, highly regarded former Bona coach, called him the best center ever to play for Bona. The odds makers had Bona favored by 21 points. Cy Kritzer dissented; he felt that the Griffs matched up quite evenly with the Brown Indians. The Olean team had a better backfield, but Canisius had depth and its defense had been outstanding, a good match for its Bona counterpart. Billy Kelly, *Courier Express* Sports Editor, agreed with Kritzer. The great tradition between the two institutions would make nonsense of that 21 point prediction, he asserted. Kelly tagged it the game of the year. Area fans anticipated a bruising, closely contested game; they were not disappointed.[8] All predictions indicated that this game would have all the trappings of a major football contest. Thousands, in fact as many as 10,000 fans were expected to arrive from the Allegheny foothills to cheer on the Bona team. To galvanize the Canisius faithful, at least those who may have needed some galvanizing, a rally was held at the Villa and a gala homecoming dance took place in one of the Queen City's major downtown hotels. Enthusiastic Canisius students headed downtown to do more celebrating. They milled about Lafayette Square and came in contact with like minded Bona students who spilled out from their lodgings in the Lafayette Hotel. The usual taunts from both sides followed; fortunately things did not get out of hand.[9]

Indeed November 3, 1946 turned out to be a great day for college football in Western New York, arguably one of the best in Western

New York football history. Even the weather cooperated. A balmy, 70 degree temperature greeted the 35,089 fans who entered Civic Stadium. It was a record throng, in fact the largest ever to see any kind of athletic contest in Buffalo to that time. It continued to be a record turnout for any kind of college athletic contest into the 21st century.

The first half of the historic game was scoreless. The Griffs stymied the vaunted Bona attack. Coach Brown had set up a fluid defense that checked the Brown Indians each time they crossed the 50 yard line. Canisius fans had visions of an upset as they watched the teams sweep back and forth during the first half. The Canisius hopes rose to a crescendo as Howie Willis took the second half kickoff three yards in the end zone and raced 51 yards; then Braatz and Oldenburg and Agnew moved the ball to the Bonnies' 32 yard line but there the drive was halted. Bona then took command and, aided by Griffin fumbles, the whole complexion of the game changed.

Nunzio Marino and Phil Colella, both former Notre Dame backs, went to work and chalked up some important yardage. Hugo Marcolini helped out too. Ray Ryan noted that Bona's tremendous line, did a superb job opening up gaping holes for the running backs and also providing solid protection for Dave Curtin, the quarterback. Curtin was not known for the number of passes thrown, in fact he seldom tossed the ball downfield. But in this game he made his few passes count. Curtin also was a competent play caller. Phil Colella, the great running back, collided with stalwart Al Petrella of Canisius. Both were laid out and had to be removed from the game. Then an unsung hero emerged for Bona. Coach Devore looked over his bench, and picked George Chatlos to replace the seemingly irreplaceable Colella. Chatlos had been a Tech Sergeant with General George Patton's Third Army and had fought in the Battle of the Bulge. Battle-toughened Chatlos emerged as an unexpected hero in the Bona-Canisius game. Chatlos picked up yardage on several plays, and his efforts culminated in a plunge from the one yard line. That was Bona's first touchdown and it was enough for the win. Bona added an insurance touchdown later. Canisius threatened late in the 4th quarter but could not cross the goal line.

It was essentially hard running and solid defense that enabled the Brown Indians to come up with their victory. The final stood at 13 – 0. Among the many heroes, beside Chatlos, who would have received the mythical game balls were defensive stars Steve Cipot and Frank LoVuolo of the Brown Indians and Feliz Centofanti and Al Chorney, the outstanding linemen for the Griffs. Bob Stedler, *Buffalo Evening News* Sports Editor, in his postscript for November 3, called this "The most important day, athletically, in the history of the Little Three institutions."[10]

Despite the loss to Bona, the Griffs had had quite a good season. In fact, it was a very favorable return to college football for the Main Street institution. Scranton was all that remained on the Griffs' schedule. That contest ended in a 13 – 13 tie. St. Bonaventure had an even better season. Following its victory over Canisius, the Olean school defeated a rugged Bowling Green club, the same team that had previously defeated Canisius by a touchdown. The Bona 13 – 9 victory was highlighted by Phil Colella's 67-yard sensational gallop for a touchdown. Coming off the line of scrimmage, Colella was hit by three Bowling Green players; he then tiptoed along the sideline and with the aid of LoVuolo's block, went in for the score. A week later Bona capped its regular season schedule by pulverizing the United States Merchant Marines 26 – 0.

All four Western New York football teams had acquitted themselves very well in 1946, this first season of renewal following World War II. Each had a winning record, U.B. stood at 7 – 2, St. Bonaventure and Niagara each had a 6 – 2 record, and Canisius College ended with a 4 – 3 – 1 record.

Good teams with good records and outstanding players, often playing before sizeable crowds were the order of the day for Buffalo area college football. At the top of the galaxy of stars was Phil Colella who was named to the first team of the Little All American squad. Hugh Devore had recruited Colella when he had been a high school student in Pennsylvania. Following his military service, he played under Devore in 1945 at Notre Dame and then played baseball in South Bend in the spring of 1946. By that time Frank Leahy was the head football coach and Devore was on his way to St. Bonaventure. Colella said he found it difficult to juggle baseball and spring football practice. Colella said that Leahy "didn't need me." So Phil and five other Notre Dame players decided to join Devore at St.Bonaventure.[11]

In an interview with Colella, Cy Kritzer confirmed some of the information that Canisius quarterback Tony Rocco had provided earlier. Phil indicated that he had some problems with Notre Dame Coach Frank Leahy in spring practice. According to Rocco, Leahy ordered Colella to attend spring practice or else. Colella found out what the "or else" meant when he reported late to the Notre Dame team in September. Coach Leahy said he did not need him. Collela turned in his equipment, talked to Devore and then headed to Olean, New York.

The Kritzer story also noted that an American torpedo plane had fished Phil out of the waters off Guam after his army transport ship was sunk by the Japanese in March of 1945. He was mustered out of the service a few months later, and reported to Devore who was then the Notre Dame Coach. Kritzer stated that Phil went on "to become the most publicized back in 1945," after Doc Blanchard and Glenn Davis, the fabulous Mr. Inside and Mr. Outside of the powerful

Phil Colella and Frank LoVuolo – Co-captains and future Hall of Famers at St. Bona. *Photo: 1948 game program*

Army teams. In that 1945 season, on his very first carry, Colella galloped 45 yards for a touchdown against the University of Illinois. He continued to do well for the Fighting Irish and in the 6-6 tie with Navy he almost became legendary. He carried the ball for what some thought as the winning touchdown only to have the effort nullified after one of the officials claimed he had not actually crossed the goal line.[12]

Phil Colella was not the only standout for Bona in the 1946 season. Bona's 210 pound guard, John Quinn, was named the MVP of

Little Three Football, by the sports media people at a Buffalo Athletic Club luncheon. Quinn was responsible for wreaking havoc on the Niagara offense and, in the Canisius game, he was a star both on offense and defense. It was Quinn with help from Mitch Smiarowski and Herb Dintiman, who cleared out the center of the line and made Bona's longest gains of the season possible. Bona dominated the All Western New York team. Colella, Quinn, and Smiarowski were accompanied by teammates, Cipot, Marcolini, and George Hayes. They were joined by U. B.'s Lou Corriere, by Dick Mazuca and Al Chorney of Canisius, and Peter Hulub of Niagara and the quarterback was Jimmy Kehoe of Alfred.

The regular football season was over, numerous accolades had been given, and many trophies handed out. Equipment had been turned in and football collegians returned to their studies to concentrate on the first semester final examinations.That was true for all but the St. Bonaventure football team. The strong showing of the Brown Indians earned them a bowl bid.

In New York State, the Bonnies were ranked second in intercollegiate football. Only the great Army team, an undisputed national power, was ahead of them. Not only was Bona considered a very good football team but it also had drawing power. In its two appearances in Civic Stadium some 52,000 fans watched them. On their home field, Forness Stadium, every game packed in some 8,000 plus fans. The Brown Indians reward for the successful season was a trip to the second annual Tobacco Bowl in Lexington, Kentucky. The Bona opponent was slated to be either Muhlenberg College of Pennsylvania or the University of Kentucky. Muhlenberg owned an 8 – 1 record while Kentucky was 7 – 3, but with a much tougher schedule. Bona's opponent turned out to be the Muhlenberg Mules. The two clubs seemed to be fairly well matched.

The southern tier was overwhelmingly

St. Bonaventure Team members. ***Left to right, starting at top:*** **George Chatlos, M. Curtin, Hugo Marcolini; Leo Hagerty, Chris Scaturo; Joe Pavilkowski, George Hays; and Mitch Smiarowski.**

supportive of the Bona Bowl bid. The Bona students and the Olean locals were ecstatic. More than 2000 fans signed up for the trip to Kentucky. The gridiron club of Salamanca held a banquet honoring the Bona team at the historic Hotel Dudley in Salamanca; a similar festivity took place at the Olean House, the number one hotel in Olean. Other smaller local communities climbed aboard. The enthusiasm for Bona football was electrifying. The game was set for Saturday, December 14. On Thursday evening the Bona team left on the Erie Railroad in three sleeping cars. Other trains followed, Bona fans filling them to capacity. The Erie Railroad was still thriving in the late 1940s. Busses and automobiles joined in the massive exodus out of Olean.

If fans enjoyed offensive football, it seemed that they would get a pipe full of it in the Tobacco Bowl. The game lived up to expectations. The *Buffalo Evening News* called it a "newsreel thriller" with both teams racking up spectacular gains. The statistics were quite even, Bona rolled up 414 yards, 301 of them rushing, while the Mules had 374 yards, 240 of them rushing. The ball went back and forth throughout the game and so did the score. Unfortunately the breaks went against Bona. They had two touchdowns called back. Then, ironically, Muhlenberg went ahead in the final period by a touchdown which it scored courtesy of its own fumble. A Mule back fumbled when hit on the Bona 22 yard line, he kicked the ball forward, and another Mule player picked it up on the 3 yard line and walked into the end zone for what proved to be the winning touchdown. With less than five minutes to go the Brown Indians almost found redemption. Bona marched down the field and scored but the place kick for the point after that would have tied the score was wide right. Down one point, with less than two minutes to go, the Brown Indians again marched down the field but a Bona pass was intercepted on the 5 yard line and run back to the 10 yard line. The Mules were able to kill the clock and the final score read 26 – 25. It was a tough loss for St. Bonaventure. But it had been a magnificent season for the Brown Indians as well as for all college football in Western New York.

The summer of 1947 was uneventful from the standpoint of college football on the Niagara Frontier. Since the 1946 season was such a success, there was no doubt that the players and fans looked forward to the '47 season with great anticipation. There just was not much for the media to write about during the off season. Specific sports were not considered virtually "year long" affairs as they would become by the end of the century. College football players returned home once classes ended in June, obtained summer jobs, and sometimes even participated in baseball or some other activity.

Athletic Departments were seldom very busy during the summer months. However one problem, faced by administrators, involved football scheduling; the scheduling of appropriate football opponents. Indeed it would be a recurrent problem for area institutions in the years that lay ahead. The local teams had proven that they could defeat highly regarded teams, so to some extent they were victims of their own success. They frequently found that name teams that they wished to play simply had no interest in taking a trip to Western New York where they ran the risk of suffering a defeat. It would look bad for their programs. To minimize scheduling difficulties there was talk of the possibility of the Western New York institutions forming a football conference along with schools from the central part of the state, such as Hobart, Ithaca, and Alfred. But the conference idea never got beyond the talking stage. Different institutions had different objectives for their football programs, in addition to winning games; consequently the conference never materialized.

As the 1947 football season approached, it was time for speculation as to how the local teams would fare. The overall preseason assessment of the *Buffalo Evening News* was that each of the four college elevens would be even better than they had been in '46, perhaps 25% better.[13]

The team that would show the least improvement would be St. Bonaventure, but only because it had done so well the previous season. The *News* felt that Bona would be the most powerful of the upstate teams. Most of their stars would be returning so there was not an awful lot to be improved. Coach Devore's problem was not with players but with arranging a suitable schedule that would bring the recognition to the team that it deserved.

Among the returning Brown Indians was the sensational open field runner, Phil Colella. Also returning and having some Notre Dame experience were Nunz Marino, and Frank Ferris. Bona fans were also glad to see that Hugo Marcolino and Dave Curtin were back. Marcolino was a former army sergeant who had played on the all service team with Otto Graham and Charlie Trippi, and Dave Curtin had served on a destroyer in both the Atlantic and Pacific theaters. Also returning was first string end, Steve Charsky, who had been a member of the Navy's Underwater Demolition team. He was one of several players from the Triple Cities' area of downstate New York: Binghamton, Johnson City and Endicott. Bona recruited many of its players from that area and from the small towns throughout New York State as well as from those in Pennsylvania, and New Jersey.

Canisius began preseason practice on September 1. The Griffs were in a situation similar to St. Bona. With so many fine veterans returning, they were bound to have another fine season. Jimmy Hutch the legendary trainer found that the team reported for practice in the "best shape ever." This was no mean compliment from a wise experienced trainer. The quarterback spot was a question mark. There would be a battle for that position. Frank Acquino had graduated and Bud Agnew was not returning. Both would be missed because they had adjusted fairly well to the T formation. On the other hand the single wing was still widely used, so a great passing T formation quarterback was not nearly as essential as it would become later. Initially Zeke Palumbo and Bob Martineck were the leading candidates but Tony Bolognese, a 22 year old sophomore, promised to give them stiff competition. Jim Oldenburg, weighing 220 pounds, was impressive at the fullback post. Jerry Whalen, a whale of a ballplayer at most any position was converted to center where he was needed. Dick Mazuca would be back. He was not only a fine lineman but was a great cheerleader and his peers credited him with infusing spirit into the Griffs. Back too was one of Coach Brown's first recruits, Bob Jerussi of the Bronx. Jerussi had played at Cardinal Hayes High School then transferred and played at Power Memorial High. Four players who had had brilliant rookie years were returning: two linemen, Ray Jacobi and George Eberle and two halfbacks, Chet Kwasek and Howie Willis.

Jim Peele, U.B.'s veteran coach, was just as optimistic about the upcoming season as his peers were. He had both size and quality and he also had recruited well. One of the local high school stars, Les Molnar, a Harvard Cup standout, and a hefty 235 pound lineman, was an outstanding prospect. Peele could not help but be pleased with his returning veteran backfield that included Bill Rudick,Vic Manz, and the magnificent Lou Corriere. Peele also looked for great things from Frank Constantino, a sophomore who played on defense with his nose three inches from the ground. Teammates said he resembled a submarine as he drove through the opposition like a torpedo.

Niagara, too, would have a holdover cast,

Members of the Canisius Squad. ***Left to right from top*****: Don Mackinnon, George Eberle, Ray Jacobi, Dick Mazuca; Darrell Braatz, Bud Agnew; Al Chorny, Bob Jerussi; and Chet Kwasek.**

and like U.B. coming off a 6 -2 campaign, was at least as optimistic as the Bulls were. The Purple Eagles had been beaten only by their two Little Three rivals. World War II veterans would continue to play a major role for Niagara. These would include Guido Felicetti, Army sergeant, Les Dugan, Marine orporal and Bronze star winner, Big John Walsh, 225 pound tackle from Aquinas Academy in Rochester, a navy vet with 9 battle stars, as well as Murph Pitaressi, from Niagara Falls, an army staff sergeant, and Robert Reddon who had served in the Navy. All anticipated that their senior year, 1947, would be a rewarding one. It was also thought that running back Les Dugan, and fullback Jim Russ, both of whom missed much of the previous season because of injuries would

Niagara University Purple Eagles; ***right to left from top:*** **Les Dugan, Jim Russ; Richard Dobmeier, Guido Filicetti; Jack Ross, James McKinnon; Robert Rosa, and Nick Stojakovich.**

be major contributors. Three others who had shown well in their freshmen season also raised the Niagara hopes: these were Bruno Pacini, a "fancy stepping" halfback, Bob Rosen, a sturdy anchor in the line and Jim McKinnon, a promising quarterback.

The 1947 college football season opened with Niagara and the University of Buffalo facing each other in Civic Stadium on Friday night, September 19. Favored Niagara would be playing U.B. for the first time since 1934. The two had played in eight previous games, with Niagara on the winning side five times. Area fans, encouraged by the hype of local sportswriters, looked forward to this much anticipated renewal of local football. Many hoped it would lead to Canisius and Bona scheduling the University of Buffalo. The crowd of 14,919 at Civic Stadium was an indication of how welcomed this game was for area fans. Dick Johnston of the *News* stated that the crowd was "believed to be the largest ever to see a U.B. game."

Niagara scored first. Fleet footed Guido Filicetti led the way for the Eagles as they marched steadily toward the goal line. However, U.B. roared back and kept right on roaring on its way to a "stunning upset." Sal Amico, one of many local high school graduates playing that evening, ran well for the Bulls as did Felix Spiezega, a transfer from Bucknell. Lou Corriere reeled off several spectacular runs, some from scrimmage and some on punt returns, on his way to scoring two touchdowns. The Bulls won 27 – 14. In fact the headline in the *News* boldly asserted that the win established "U.B. as a WNY Grid Power."[14]

The real story of the game was Lockport Lou. A week following the game, it was revealed that Coach Jim Peele had pulled off a "Win for the Gipper" at halftime of the U.B. – Niagara game. Lou Corriere and Peele had a solid friendship established when Lou was at U.B. for two years before entering the military in World War II. Peele had helped Corriere with tutors in his studies, and boarded him free when he ran out of cash. When in the service, Lou and his coach corresponded. In one of the letters Lou told how appreciative

he was of the help that the coach and his wife had given him and hoped he would some day have a chance to repay the coach. "I miss the university and the boys, but some day, coach, I'll play a great football game, that's a promise." In Civic Stadium at halftime of the U.B. – Niagara game, Peele produced the letter and said "I want that great game you promised me Lou, tonight." Lou did, indeed, produce.[15]

U.B. proceeded to have a magnificent season, ending up the campaign with eight wins and just one loss, that being to Wayne State, 32 – 12. The Bulls had fairly close contests with Moravian, 7-0, and with RPI, 14-7, but their offense rolled into high gear against Hobart, 54 – 0, Alfred, 40 – 7, Bethany 40 – 6, and St. Lawrence, 50 – 7. They climaxed their season with a thrilling upset win, on the road, against an always strong Bucknell eleven, 14 – 6. It was the best season the Bulls had ever had.

Lou Corriere had continued his heroics for U.B. Lockport Lou picked up big yardage regularly and scored often. An injury caused him to miss several games. Fortunately the Bulls had other first rate backs to help fill the gap. Bill Rudick, Sal Amico and Eddie Mittelstadt proved to be excellent ground gainers. Local fans appreciated their quality of play. Even the game against little known Bethany, drew some 4500 fans to Civic Stadium. Indeed football was popular enough that local radio station, WWOL, with Al Haley at the mike, began to broadcast the Bulls' games that season.

The records for Canisius and St. Bona were almost as dazzling as U.B.'s. Canisius ended up 7 – 2, and Bona was 6 – 3. The Griffs kicked off their season in almost identical fashion to the way Bona had in 1946. Like Bona they played Youngstown on the road. And like Bona they took the early lead, this coming on a spectacular 54-yard gallop by Chet Kwasek. Youngstown countered with their own 6 points a short time later, and then the two teams slugged it out until the Ohio school scored the go ahead touchdown in the final quarter and "eked out" a 12 – 6

***Above, left to right starting at top* are Niagara players Jankowski, Rosa, Pacini, McMahon; and McCoy.**
***Facing page:* Canisius College Football Squad – *Left to right, first row:* Centofanti, Hurley, O'Brien, Castine, Willis, Kwasek, Ferraro, Luciani, Calendrelli; *second row:* Co-manager Cloutier, Marino, Dobmeier, Tautkus, Jacobi, Sexton, Jerussi, Bolognese, Austin, Nasser, Co-manager Wagner; *Third row:* Hutton, Schaus, Sweeney, Wactowski, Measer, D'Arcy, Greaves, Minihan, Eberle, Brinkworth, Trainer Hutch; *Fourth row:* May, Bajak, MacKinnon, Casey, O'Neill, Moffat, Swistak, Yavicoli, McShane.**

victory. The Griffs then proceeded to enter the record book, breaking their all time scoring record, with a 79 – 0 thrashing of a hapless Rider team. Ten different Griffins scored touchdowns; three different Griffins kicked extra points. Every player in uniform played in that game. The locals were delighted to see the Griffin rushing machine racked up 467 yards to a paltry 10 for the New Jersey school.

The Griffs next won two close contests, the first over St. Vincent's, 10-7. In this one Smiley Braatz, who had been used chiefly on defense in recent games, got called into action on offense and his power running proved to be decisive. The student newspaper was elated that Braatz had developed into the kind of performer that had been hoped for. The Griffs then took to the road, and defeated a perennially tough Marshall University team, 25 -20. Tony Bolognese, injured in preseason, had a chance to show his stuff. He did so by passing the Griffs to victory over this previously undefeated powerhouse from West Virginia. The Griffs proved to be just as tough as their opponents. During the contest, Griffin defensive stars, Jerussi and Naples, collided. Naples had to go to the sidelines since he was bleeding profusely. Team physician, Dr. Edward Lyons sewed up Naples' lower lip with needle and thread but used no pain killer, and sent Big Jim back into the game. Face masks were not yet in style in the 1940s. The athletes were tough, but as one veteran noted, it you really wanted to know about "toughness" you should have been in the Battle of the Bulge.

Meanwhile St. Bonaventure had started the season on the right foot, blanking St Vincent's 21 – 0, with Quarterback Dave Curtin showing the way with three touchdown passes. The men from Olean then lost to a highly regarded team from the University of Cincinnati, 20 – 14. The Brown Indians soon returned to their winning ways by thumping Kings Point, 25 – 0.

These favorable beginnings for both the Golden Griffins and the Brown Indians set the stage for their Little Three showdown. As expected, the game was hyped in the local press. It was called the "collegiate game of the year" and Chet Kwasek and Dave Curtin were singled out as the key men for their respective teams. They received plenty of ink. Kwasek, a local favorite since his record breaking days at McKinley High School, had been playing

extremely well as of late for the Griffs. Curtin, a sophomore star transfer from Syracuse, was the backbone of Devore's T-formation attack.

As if to underscore the seriousness of the game, Coach Earl Brown took his team to a foreign country for secret drills. Alabama under fabled coach Bear Bryant did not even do that. Actually the Griffs, courtesy of J. Walter Koessler, a Canisius alumnus and an avid supporter, stayed overnight at the Buffalo Canoe Club in Crystal Beach, Ontario where they could relax and watch game films.[16]

As game day approached, it was reported that some 7500 fans set out from Olean to make the trek to downtown Buffalo where hotel space was at a premium. As was their custom, the Bona team stayed in the always popular Lafayette Hotel, at Lafayette Square, in the center of downtown Buffalo. Many of the fans stayed there too so as to be not far from the Jazz emporiums on Washington Street and the bright lights of Buffalo's own Great White Way along Main Street.

Griffin fans too were out in full force as the game time drew near. Students formed a 45 car motorcade and drove from the Main Street campus to City Hall for several laps around Niagara Square. Later many Griffin fans frolicked downtown at the Statler Hotel; others did so on the outskirts of downtown at the ever popular Troop I Post. Close friends of the football players would congregate near the campus, at the celebrated "hangout," known as Benny Powers' saloon at the corner of Main Street and Lafayette.

The game was played on October 19 before nearly 20,000. The game lived up to expectations. For almost the entire first half the contest was marked by a vicious battle of the lines. Then the great Phil Colella, always dangerous in the open field, received a punt on his own 37 yard line; he broke several tackles, sped down the middle of the field then over to the sidelines and 66 yards later Bona was ahead by a touchdown. But not for long; the lead changed once again. Coach Brown put Tom Kretz, with fresh legs, on the field for the ensuing kickoff. Kretz took the ball on his 7 yard line, and sped up the middle, convoyed by a bevy of blockers, and according to Ray Ryan received a key block from Nipper Castine, who "Indianized the last Bona who had a shot at him." Kretz scored. It took 13 seconds; then he went to the bench from whence he had come, playing a total of 13 seconds in the game. Bona then received the kickoff and fumbled, when the runner was belted solidly by Ray Jacobi. For good reason, Jacobi was recognized as the outstanding lineman of the game. A few plays later, Howie Willis kicked a field goal.[17] Bona then regained the lead in the third period. This time it was a Curtin to Frank LoVuolo 28 yard pass play that did the trick. With Bona ahead, 14 – 10, the Griffs were not to be denied. Jacques Austin passed to Smiley Braatz for 21 yards, then Coach Brown sent in Jim Oldenberg and on a fourth down gamble he tossed a pass to Chet Kwasek who snared the ball on the 16 and took it into the end zone. A little bit of luck helped out; just as Kwasek caught the pass the Bona defender slipped and Chet was home free for the score. The Bona fans still held out hope. With a minute and a half left, a Dave Curtin to Steve Charsky pass play covered 41 yards. The Bona fans went wild as the ball came to rest on the Canisius 14 yard line. However on the next play, Tony Bolognese intercepted a Curtin pass and the Griffs were able to control the ball for the remainder of the contest, thus assuring their victory. The final score was 17 – 14.

Coach Earl Brown had to be very satisfied with his victory over fellow ex-Notre Damer, Hugh Devore. Brown was given considerable praise in the local press. One move was singled out: his decision to send Tom Kretz into the game for just one play, and it turned out to be the 93-yard kickoff return for a touchdown. Henceforth the hero of the moment would be called Tom "One Play"

Kretz. Brown's overall strategy was called "superb'. Cy Kritzer noted that by "brilliant handling of his well-manned squad, he had a fresh, inspired and hard hitting eleven on the field at all times."[18] In the final analysis the game was won in the trenches with Ray Jacobi and Captain Dick Mazuca spearheading the Griffin assault. The teams fought bitterly right to the finish. It was a heated contest. Some punches were thrown and some unsportsmanlike penalties levied. That was all part of the frenzied atmosphere of this Little Three contest. The *Courier*'s Ray Ryan called it "the most thrilling football game of a series that is notable for thrilling football." The thousands who attended were happy that the game lived up to its expectations.[19] Both teams still had to face Niagara later in the season before a Little Three champion could be crowned. Niagara was not going to be a pushover. They had given some indication that they were on a par with their rivals. In one of the great football games in Niagara annals, the Purple Eagles lost a heartbreaker to Syracuse 14 – 7. The two foes battled to a 7 – 7 tie in the first half. In the second, Niagara marched down the field to the 21 yard line of the Orangemen, then luck ran out for the Purple Eagles. Syracuse recovered a Niagara fumble and that miscue set up the winning score.

The Niagara team did not allow the painful loss to the Orangemen to linger for long. Led by Captain Les Dugan, Niagara stormed back with a convincing victory over Ithaca, 26 – 6. Though they lost to Scranton, 39 – 6, they recovered nicely with a 27 – 7 win over Waynesburg with the hard driving Dugan again spearheading the attack. Then the week before the Bona contest, Niagara and St. Vincent's College played to a scoreless tie.

Meanwhile, the Brown Indians hosted the University of St. Louis football team. Fans in Olean anticipated a titanic struggle between the Missouri Valley Conference co-leaders and their local heroes. 9,200 fans crammed into Forness Stadium. The game lived up to expectations in the first half; it was a close game with both sides playing aggressive football; but then Bona turned the game into a rout in the 2nd half. Phil Colella scampered for two touchdowns. The Bona ground attack simply bowled over opposing linemen. The final score read 47 - 13.

That set the stage for another trip to Buffalo for the Bona athletes, this time to take on Niagara's Purple Eagles. The game turned out to be a bit of a surprise. The men from Monteagle Ridge put up strong opposition. Field general Jim McKinnon paced the Eagles, while the Niagara defense constantly harassed Bona quarterback Dave Curtin. In fact quarterback Jim McKinnon, handled the Niagara team so well that it outplayed the Bona team, for a considerable part of the game. Niagara was ahead 6 – 0 before Bona woke up. The Brown Indians came to life by their usual route, pounding away on the ground with Leo Haggerty and Phil Colella doing much of the running. Ultimately, before the more than 7,000 in Civic Stadium, St. Bona emerged with a 13 – 6 victory. It was another close one, another valiant effort by the Eagles, but another disappointing loss. Mike Quinlan, sports editor for the *Niagara Falls Gazette* noted: "The Eagles played very, very well . . . showed surprising spirit."[20]

Bona continued on the victory path, defeating a strong Bowling Green team, 21 – 14, as Dave Curtin threw three touchdown passes, two to LoVuolo and one to Colella. The following week, the Brown Indians again won by a single touchdown, this time over the University of Scranton, a team that had previously defeated the other two Little Three teams. Despite poor weather, the Bona team showed it could still draw a crowd in Olean. 8,800 watched Colella, Curtin, and company rally to defeat the Pennsylvania team in the last quarter 13 – 7. In their final game of the 1947 season, Bona lost a cliffhanger to the University of Dayton by a 7 – 6 score.

The Canisius football team had a letdown in the games that followed their defeat of archrival St. Bonaventure. In the game with the University of Scranton, the Griffs protected a 7 – 6 lead until a minute and a half left in the game. Then Scranton quickly marched down the field and scored the winning touchdown. The Griffs could not mount a comeback; Scranton held on for the win. In their next outing, Canisius traveled to Ohio to face a weak Steubenville team. The Griffs must have been over confident, perhaps a bit cocky. They were fortunate to emerge with a 7 – 0 victory over a team that fought courageously right to the bitter end.

Meanwhile the Purple Eagles hosted John Carroll University in Niagara Falls the week following the loss to Bona. Niagara was defeated 41 – 26. Despite the recent losses, Coach Moran's players held their heads high. Indeed their spirits rose and their confidence returned as they prepared for the Little Three finale.

As the 1947 football season headed toward its conclusion, the attention of area fans turned to the Niagara-Canisius game. The local press again demonstrated its ability to drum up support for a game. For several days prior to the Sunday, November 16th kickoff, the newspapers discussed the chances that each team had to win. Canisius was the clear favorite but Niagara had played well against Bona and could not be counted out. The Niagara coach, Jim Moran, spoke of how well his players were holding up despite their several losses. The mere fact that it was a Little Three game gave Niagara supporters reason to hope. Ray Ryan, a veteran of covering Little Three contests for more than 2 decades, lent encouragement to the Niagara fans by noting that they had the important psychological factors on their side.

Both squads featured players of star quality. The Griffins dressed some of the best rushers in the State of New York, including Kwasek. Braatz,Willis, Oldenberg, and Jacque Austin. Niagara had two dependable running backs in Les Dugan and Guido Filicetti. The Purple Eagles also had a fine passing quarterback in Jim McKinnon. In fact "Stop McKinnon" was the buzz phrase that circulated around the Villa practice field. Canisius also was celebrated for its powerful line. Walt Marshall, assistant coach of the Griffs and another ex Notre Damer, was proud of his superior upfront crew and pointed to it as the key to victory. He cited George Eberle and Ray Jacobi as the two best tackles in the area and praised the great defensive play of center Jerry Whelan and guard George Kuhrt. These linemen did not make mistakes; on defense they plugged up holes and caused fumbles, on offense, they were the reasons that the backs made sizeable gains and that Canisius was such a dominant rushing team.

The game was scheduled for the second weekend in November, the weekend when Buffalo, traditionally, got its first taste of winter weather. Weather, at that time of the year, was often a crowd determinant. It was hoped that well over 20, 000 would attend. The Louise de Marillac Guild of Sisters Hospital was the game's sponsor; guild members were turning over every stone they could in order to sell tickets. Local sportsman, Jimmy Dunnigan, was doing his part to assist. He lined up hundreds of orphans who would be his guests. They came from some of Buffalo's well known orphan asylums, as they were then called. These included Father Baker's, the German Roman Catholic Orphan Asylum, The Protestant Home, St.Mary's School for the Deaf, and The Working Boys Home.

Unfortunately the huge crowd that had been anticipated did not materialize. Weather indeed was the big factor. The day was dismal; 13,235 chilled spectators watched under gloomy skies. The stadium lights were turned on after half time to aid the players and also so that fans could actually see who the players were. In fact even though it was a Little Three contest, a number of fans left early, some headed for popular watering holes where they could relax with a Roast Beef on Kimmelweck and a pitcher of Iroquois. That seemed more appealing than sitting in miserable conditions in Civic Stadium.

Despite all the pre-game posturing, the game was a blowout. The Griffs were not overconfident, they were simply better; they just went out and played hard. Moreover Coach Brown had too many reserves for the undermanned Eagles, he was able to keep fresh backs coming into the game at regular intervals.

The Eagles threatened to score only once, and that was in the second quarter. Guido Filicetti advanced the ball to the 22 yard line; that was as close as Niagara would get. The rest of the game went the Griffins' way; they emerged the victors with a 27 – 0 score. There was no one standout for the winners, many shared the spotlight. The line, led by Jacobi and Eberle, was awesome. Several opponents were knocked out of the contest, at least temporarily. Les Dugan, Jim Russ, Jim McKinnon, and Jim Lindsay were all sidelined. As expected the Canisius rushing backs did well, Braatz, Willis, Kwasek, Castine, Austin, each contributed. Even the Griff passing game, dormant for most of the season, came alive for two scores, with Willis and Jim Oldenberg being the key operatives. Again Coach Earl Brown was lauded for his play calling. Brown now had another Little Three title to add to the basketball one he had earned the previous winter.

Canisius and Niagara each had one more game to play. Niagara took to the road for a trip to Indiana where they faced Valpariso. The Purple Eagles lost, 27 – 7, thus bringing to a close a rather disappointing season at 3 - 6 – 1.

In its season finale, Canisius had to face a powerful Toledo team. The Ohio team arrived in town as the favorite having won eight previous contests and lost only once, that to John Carroll. Among Toledo's victims were some highly reputable teams: Great Lakes, Akron, Youngstown, and Dayton. Scouts warned that the passing attack of the Rockets was highly regarded. Their quarterback, Lee Pete, was hailed as one of the best in the Midwest, and certainly the top passing quarterback that the Griffs had yet to face.

Early on, Lee Pete seemed to live up to his reputation. He completed a couple of long bombs that awed the crowd, but those simply woke up the Canisius defense. It promptly went to work and Pete ended up with his poorest performance of the campaign. He completed just three passes. He also had two interceptions, both by Nipper Castine. A gloomy, cold afternoon kept the crowd down to just over 4,000 but those hearty fans, after watching their favorites play up to peak performance, left the stadium in a good mood. Kwasek and Willis, the elusive Griffin backs, put on a storybook performance with their open field running. They were the heroes along with Castine and all the Griffins who carried out to perfection a great pass defense plan devised by Coach Brown. The final score read Canisius 21 and Toledo 13.

The press attributed the surprising Canisius victory primarily to the coaching of Earl Brown. Cy Kritzer asserted that no coach ever made better use of the unlimited substitution rule than Brown did all season long. Kritzer noted that the victory over Toledo improved Canisius' rating in the state just behind Army and Columbia which made it the highest rating ever earned by a Canisius football team, "it was smart, vicious, superbly coached." [21]

Western New York football fans once again had been treated to some first rate college football during the 1947 season. With the exception of the Niagara team, the season had been a successful one for the Western

New York elevens. And even Niagara, despite the losing record, could hold its collective head high in view of some terrific games they did play, especially against Syracuse, Ithaca, Waynesburg and St. Bona. The Brown Indians were good with a 6 –3 record, Canisius better at 7 – 2 and U. B. was best, at 8 – 1. The Purple Eagles ended up with a 3 – 6 - 1 record. Fan support was satisfactory, but it could have been better. Unfortunately the weather for some of the most attractive games was so dismal that attendance was down from the 1946 season. Nevertheless, almost all observers would agree that the 1947 season was quite successful.

Buffalo Evening News sports editor, Bob Stedler, reviewed the season. He noted that the area was fortunate to have four outstanding coaches. A by-product of their success was the fact that the rumor mill had already begun. There was talk of Brown returning to his alma mater, Notre Dame, should Frank Leahy retire. Another story had Hugh Devore headed for Holy Cross. Earl Brown eventually did leave to take the head coaching job at Auburn University. Stedler also called attention to some of the highlights of the Little Three contests but he was particularly effusive in his praise for the University of Buffalo. Not many expected U.B. to beat Bucknell in the season finale, but the U.B. players came through with flying colors and put their school in the limelight nationally. Stedler remarked that that historic win might mark the beginning of more widespread recognition in football circles for the boys who attended school on the Main/Bailey campus. Certainly the students who frequented hangouts like Leonardo's Grotto Restaurant, across from the campus, hoped so.[22]

As expected many of the players from the area colleges merited special citations for their superb performances. The All Western New York selections included Quarterback Dave Curtin of Bona who had accumulated some of the top statistics for a passer in the East, and Phil Colella, whom Jim Naples, the giant end for Canisius, called the cleverest runner he ever faced. Joining the two Bona backs were two from U.B., Bill Rudick an effective blocking back and steady runner, and Eddie Mittelsteadt, a pile driving fullback, who was the leading scorer in upstate football. This meant that equally deserving backs including Howie Willis, Chet Kwasek, and Jacque Austin, of Canisius and Hugo Marcolini of Bona as well as Lou Corriere of U.B. just missed making the first team. Corriere had been sidelined with injuries for much of the season. Frank LoVuolo of Bona

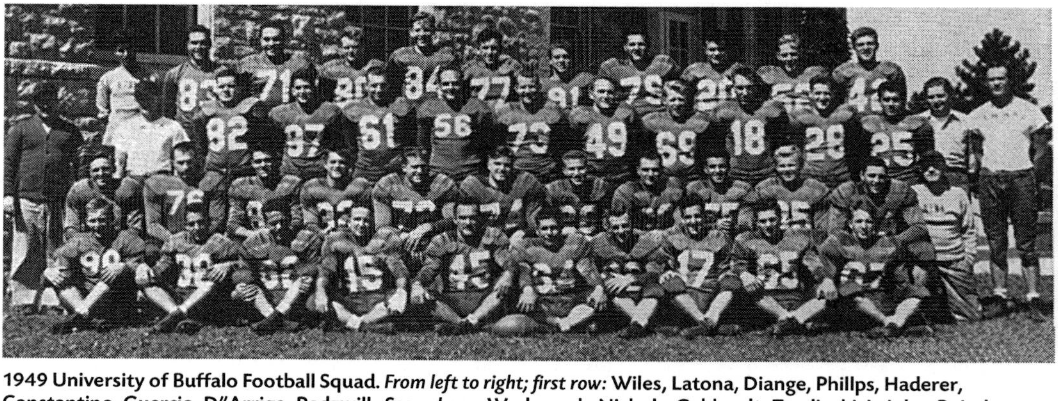

1949 University of Buffalo Football Squad. ***From left to right; first row:*** **Wiles, Latona, Diange, Phillps, Haderer, Constantino, Guercio, D"Arrigo, Radzwill.** ***Second row:*** **Wodarczak, Nichols, Gebhardt, Zwolinski, Leipler, Beitelman, Nicosia, Morano, Ferrintino, Olson, Gugino, "Mac."** ***Third Row:*** **Trainer Hanlon, Assistant Coach Gibson, Rhodes, Szyklowski, Landel, Chotoff, Meyer, Walsh, Dingboom, Weser, Panzica, Rich, Manager Lipp, Coach Clair.** ***Top row:*** **Assistant Manager Caruso, Markey, Saltzman, Cameron, Gicewicz, Grottanlli, Derme, Molna, Holland, Mueller, Licata.**

and Naples of Canisius were named to the end posts. Lo Vuolo was a standout receiver; he also picked up considerable yardage on end around sweeps and could justly be considered a fifth back. The tackles, Eberle and Jacobi of Canisius were shoo-ins, as was their teammate, guard George Kuhrt. The other guard was Al Massey, who was the key to the Bulls' very successful ground gaining attack. Mitch Smiarowski of Bona repeated at the center position. The competition was so close that four first team selections of 1946, Marcolini and Corriere, as well as end Al Chorney of Canisius, and the dynamite guard of Niagara, Bob Rosa, wound up on the second team. Bruno Pacini was named the MVP by the Purple Eagle players and was honored at Ye Olde Tavern as well as at the Block N banquet held at Luigi's.[23] Almost all of those great football players from the 1947 squads would be around for the 1948 campaign. It certainly appeared to most observers that Western New Yorkers would again be treated to some exciting and well played football games.

Football news in the waning weeks of 1947 focused, naturally, on the bowl games. Michigan, Texas, Georgia Tech and SMU were all favored in the New Years' Day classics. Penn State tied Southern Methodist in the Cotton Bowl, Georgia Tech knocked off Kansas, 20 – 14; the other two favorites won handily, Texas over Alabama, 27 – 0, and the Wolverines bombed USC, 49 – 0 in the Rose Bowl. Notre Dame was not a bowl participant but Johnny Lujack had a terrific day leading the East to a 40 – 9 victory over the West in the annual Shrine Bowl Charity game in San Francisco. Items of special local interest during the football off-season included Charlie Trippi's visit to Buffalo to see his family. That was a page one news item since Trippi was one of the biggest football stars of the decade. He was a consensus All American at the University of Georgia and was under contract to play pro ball with the Chicago Cardinals.

Other off-season news included a trial balloon by Buffalo State administrators indicating they might start a football program. They had seen the enthusiasm with which the sport was received at other local institutions and thought it a worthwhile idea to explore. However, when submitted to the Buffalo State students for a vote, the proposal lost. It was fairly close but not enough to reconsider.

By Christmastime the banquets were over, and the seniors who had played their final game were hitting the books hard so that graduation would become a reality in the spring. The football players who planned to return for the 1948 season could count on an abbreviated spring practice. Varsity athletes who wanted to keep in good physical shape would do so on their own schedule, establishing their own regimen of exercise and weight lifting, perhaps at a local YMCA, but without having the prying eyes of an assistant coach spying on them. Such were the good ol' days of amateur sports.

Coaches, even head coaches who held full time jobs at their respective colleges, usually had other chores. Many of them might also be athletic directors or assigned to some other administrative duties, while a number of them coached one or two other sports. The age of specialization had not yet arrived. However signs of a new age were beginning to appear.

Earl Brown coached both football and basketball at Canisius College. He was successful at both. He had just been named Coach of the Year for college football in Western New York. In January of 1948 he was midway through the basketball season and his team was having a fairly good year. Suddenly, like a bolt out of the blue, an announcement from Auburn University in Alabama, on January 20, stated that Earl Brown would be the new Auburn football coach.

Earl Brown loved basketball but he was first

and foremost a football man. He had done well at Canisius in both sports; in football he had had one satisfactory and one excellent season, but he knew that Canisius was not headed for the big time. Even the Ivy League, for a long time recognized as big time in football, had recently announced that it was scaling down. The Canisius administration was aware of Brown's leverage. They knew that he would probably not remain at Canisius for very long. Word had it that he had talked to people at the January football meetings. Brown was friendly with many football coaches especially a number of those in the Southeast Conference.

Brown had kept his negotiations secret. When the news finally became public, the ire of the Canisius administration was aroused as was that of Ray Ryan, regular college beat reporter for the *Courier Express*. Ryan was harsh; he referred to Brown as "the peregrinating Earl Brown" and said his quitting in midseason was almost without precedent in college sports. On the other hand, Ryan's counterpart at the *News*, Cy Kritzer, allowed that Brown had to make an important decision. He recognized that the way sports had been developing the same individual could not really do a satisfactory job coaching both football and basketball at the top level. Brown favored football in part because it paid better than basketball. Kritzer noted that at that time not many college basketball coaches were paid very well. Kritzer indicated that Brown recognized that the Canisius' football program was in the red. Despite the success of the team on the field, it was difficult for a school the size of Canisius to continue major financial support for college football.[24]

The problem for many people was the timing of Brown's decision. It came midway through the basketball season. Had the decision come at the end of the season it would not have caused as much rancor. On the other hand many players, basketball and football, accepted the decision in stride. Once Brown had solidified terms with Auburn, he informed his basketball team. The basketball and the football players liked and respected Brown. He was generally regarded as a "class act."

Joe Niland took over the basketball reins immediately upon Brown's exit, but Canisius took its time in finding a new football coach. There were some quality coaches available and the Canisius job was perceived to be a good one. Down through the years the story has persisted that Vince Lombardi wanted the coaching job at Canisius but was turned down. Larry Felser, long time football writer for the *Buffalo News*, and a nationally recognized football authority addressed that issue.

Back in 1961, before either party had become famous, Felser encountered Lombardi at a site in California in the Palo Alto area. Both the Buffalo Bills and the Green Bay Packers just happened to be practicing nearby for their respective upcoming games against the Raiders and the Rams. Felser and Lombardi engaged in a couple of hours of conversation. When Felser told Lombardi that he had gone to Canisius College, Lombardi "almost winced." As Felser remembers it, Lombardi said that "Canisius gave me the greatest disappointment of my career…I was a plebe coach at Army then, and when I came to Canisius for my interview carrying a recommendation from my boss, Colonel Red Blaik, and a degree from another Jesuit school, Fordham, I felt pretty good about my chances on the way home. Then they hired some lawyer who had coached the team before the war. I had never been more disappointed."[25]

The person Lombardi referred to was Jimmy Wilson. By the end of March Canisius had decided to rehire Jimmy Wilson. It was viewed both as a good move and a popular one. Wilson was a native Buffalonian and had starred in football at Cornell University.

He had coached the Canisius freshman team from 1934 to 1938 and was head varsity coach from 1939 until 1942 when the program was suspended due to World War II. After Canisius dropped football in 1942, Wilson was employed by Bell Aircraft as the Director of Recreation. He organized several sports at the giant corporation. Earlier he had coached at Lafayette High School, followed by a stint at the University of Buffalo. At Canisius he had coached Tommy Colella, arguably the greatest football player to ever wear a Canisius uniform. He had also coached Dick Poillon and Bill Piccolo. All three played in the professional ranks. In retrospect, it was probably "a given" that Wilson would be appointed the new Head Coach.

Canisius' Coach Jimmy Wilson

Wilson took over in time to hold spring drills. He proceeded to hire Piccolo and Al Dekdebrun as his assistants. Wilson was familiar with Dekdebrun as he had coached him in a few service games during the war. Dekdebrun was a local favorite; he starred at Cornell University and played with the Buffalo Bison professional football team in 1946. Wilson chose Bill Piccolo as his line coach. Piccolo had been captain of the '42 Griffin team, and after graduation he had played with the New York Giants for three years. Another assistant, hired later by Wilson, was Jim Hogan, class of '39. Hogan had been a star running back under Coach Hiker Joy. Hogan was also a renowned oarsman for the West Side Rowing Club.

Later in the spring, the University of Buffalo also announced a coaching change. Jim Peele was leaving his post as head football coach in order to devote his time and energy, as the Director of Athletics, to the expanding athletic program at his institution. In fact Peele already had other responsibilities as the Head of the Department of Physical Education at U.B. The University of Buffalo hired as its new head coach, Frank Clair. Like his predecessor, Clair was a Big Ten product. He had played at Ohio State and then in the pro ranks with the Washington Redskins. He played and coached while in the military service in World War II, then he served on the staff at the University of Miami of Ohio and in 1947 he coached the ends at Purdue. Clair was a proponent of the T formation by the time he landed the head position at U.B.

The coaching situation in 1948 found one new face, Frank Clair, one familiar coach returning to the school where he had coached a few years earlier; Jimmy Wilson, and two veterans returning to the same positions they had held in 1947. All four coaches had many veteran players returning. They also might find some prospects from among the increasing number of students registered to attend their college. All the area colleges were reporting record enrollments. In fact, each of the four local football playing institutions counted an enrollment in the 2000 range, which meant at least double what it had been before World War II. Niagara University, like its sister institutions, continued to set postwar enrollment records. In 1946 Niagara set a school record with 1701 students and the following year, 1947, the count was 1654; that number included 959 male vets and 8 female vets. With a growing pool of students to choose from, many of whom were mature war veterans, football teams representing relatively small institutions found themselves experiencing vintage years.[26]

The University of Buffalo continued to draw most of its players from the Buffalo Public School system. A few came from the Niagara Frontier League, which, with North Tonawanda and Kenmore High Schools leading the way, was then the toughest suburban football conference in the area. Only occasionally would there appear a player from elsewhere in Erie County such as Amherst or Cheektowaga, and rarely one from out of state. Canisius, similar to the University of Buffalo, drew many of its players from City of Buffalo public high schools though, unlike U.B., a number also hailed from Canisius High School and St Joe's Collegiate Institute. A few came from the satellite cities and a sprinkling from out of state. Niagara and St. Bona had dormitories. Niagara drew a number of its students from the City of Niagara Falls. But other than that neither institution drew many students from the communities nearby. The vast number of students at those two schools, both football playing students and non-footballers, came from downstate, principally the New York City area and from elsewhere in the state itself.

By mid August of 1948 the squads were ready for pre-season drills. Cy Kritzer made his annual rounds of the preseason camps and reported that none of the squads suffered heavy losses. Since this was the third postwar year, all four of the area football teams would continue to be stocked with wartime veterans most of whom would now be in their junior year of college. Those who were in their senior year or those who had graduated were young men who had played before the war and then returned to complete their eligibility.

The Canisius team would have all of its starters back again and that augured well for another successful season with the possibility of another Little Three championship. Kritzer said that no one could find a weakness in the line, but that if the Griffs did have a soft spot it was in the air. There was no outstanding passer or kicker. The Griffs had speed and striking power overland especially with Kwasek and Willis. They would be operating from the single wing Michigan system rated by many as the best in football for a sustained running game. It accented the magic of ball handling and split second timing. It fit the Griffin personnel very well.

St. Bonaventure too looked to a host of outstanding junior lettermen returning. The list included Phil Colella, Frank LoVuolo and a number of quality linemen. The one noteworthy absence would be Dave Curtin, who had performed superbly as one of the top passers in the East. His loss worried Coach Devore as he looked over his prospects. He was hopeful that Chris Scaturo would be able to fill Curtin's shoes; that would be a very large task. Kritzer remarked that enthusiasm was once again high in the Cattaraugus hills that surrounded the picturesque St. Bonaventure campus.

The situation with U.B.'s personnel was remarkably similar to that of Canisius and St. Bonaventure. Many war veterans were still on the squad. Excellent linemen, both on offense and defense, were returning. The one major loss was Lou Corriere, but other fine running backs, notably Bill Rudick and Sal Amico were ready to step in and fill the giant cleats left by Lockport Lou. The Bulls' passing game was questionable. Kritzer noted that the Bulls were loaded with confidence and they had an energetic young coach. The biggest problem for the Bulls was time. Would the players have enough time to learn rookie coach Frank Clair's system before they met Colgate in the season opener? That issue was compounded by the fact that the Red Raiders were coming off their most disastrous season in history; they were smelling blood.

The situation for the Niagara Purple Eagles was different. Their dismal 1947 season was in large part due to a lack of depth and a swarm of injuries. But in preseason 1948 the Eagles were on the upbeat. Coach Jim Moran had some solid linemen returning, including Bob Rosa, and Big John Walsh, a 235-

pounder. Moran also had a promising crop of sophomores. He was particularly impressed with the development of Dick McCarthy of New York City at the center slot. Kritzer suggested that Niagara's hopes for a successful season might well rest with their passing game. Jim McKinnon, who had a splendid year as one the East's best passers, would be returning; he would be pressured by John Theobold, new to the Niagara campus, who had been an excellent quarterback when he was starring for Kenmore High School.

Kritzer summed up his observations on the eve of the season stating that "to all indications, 1948 will be a season dominated by the breakaway backs and fast, big lines. The aerial department will be secondary."[27]

The big news for the upcoming football season was the introduction of television. The new medium would eventually revolutionize the game of football; in fact it would have a huge impact on the entire sports world. Television had only recently made its debut in Buffalo, actually in mid 1948. It was only a few weeks later that the local colleges, Canisius and UB, agreed to have all their games that they played in Civic Stadium televised on WBEN-TV. The first college game ever to be televised locally would be the Canisius season opener.

Very few Buffalonians owned television sets in 1948. The big surge in sales would not come until the following decade. With only one local station, and a very limited program schedule, and the technology very primitive, the average citizen did not see himself in a position to use his hard earned wages, to purchase a Philco, or an Admiral, or any of the other television brands then coming on the market. Automobiles and kitchen appliances took precedence. Avid followers of the game of football, as well as just curious observers of the new medium, would line up on Delaware Avenue or Hertel Avenue, or on Seneca Street or Bailey Avenue or any of the other commercial strips in Buffalo and stand in front of the showroom window of a furniture dealer or appliance dealer and watch whatever appeared on the tiny screen of the display television set that was being advertised. Other fans might find their way into a local saloon or bar, and watch a sports program while imbibing a favorite product from one of the several local breweries. Regardless of where you watched a game on television, you ran of risk of not seeing much of the game itself. The screen was often quite snowy, in fact one might think the football game was being played in a snowstorm, at times it was impossible to identify the ball itself. Boxing and wrestling, given the confines of the ring, fared somewhat better.

Bob Stedler gave a plug to the colleges' decision to have their games seen on television. He noted that, unlike some of the professional sports people, the college administrators were not fearful of attendance being hurt by televised games. It was welcomed as a way of creating wider public interest. Further, in keeping with the spirit of the times, it was thought that televising games was a service to many people, especially disabled war veterans who were unable to attend; it was a morale booster. In addition, high schools agreed to have some football and basketball games televised and the colleges did the same for their basketball games in Memorial Auditorium. Television was in its infancy but athletic administrators were beginning to see its possibilities. But in the 1940s, the number of viewers was miniscule.

The Canisius College Golden Griffins opened the 1948 season on September 19 against St. Francis of Pennsylvania. It was a historic event if for no other reason than it was the first local college game ever to be televised. Unfortunately, in a scrimmage just a few days before the opener, Ray Jacobi, 1947's MVP in the Little Three, suffered a hand injury and would be out for at least the opener Other than that, the Griffs were in top shape. Coach Jimmy Wilson had always been a strong proponent, indeed an extremely zealous proponent, of physical conditioning. Jimmy Hutch, a 42-year veteran of athletic training, said he had never seen a team in such good condition. Hutch himself was a long time, colorful figure on the Buffalo sports scene. Several of his former players claimed that he had a secret salve that he used on injured muscles, a formula of his own concoction. Bob Jerussi, star Griffin football player and later a renowned chemist, tells the story that Hutch had a letter from Doc Cramer of the Boston Red Sox who asked Hutch for some of his salve and promised not to give it to anyone else. Hutch refused; his salve was his own secret.[28]

The St. Francis team came to town with a line that heavily outweighed the Griffs. Other than that there was not much that the Canisius staff knew about their opponent. As things turned out, that was not a problem. The Griffs mauled the St. Francis team, it was strictly speaking, no contest, as the final score read 61 – 0. Unlike Coach Earl Brown, Coach Jimmy Wilson allowed his quarterbacks to call the plays. The Griffs surprised the opposition by unveiling a passing attack. Six different Griffins completed passes. Combined they completed 50% of their 16 passes, St Francis hit on just one of 10. This was a nice turn of events considering that a passing attack was virtually non existent throughout most of the previous season. The starting eleven played little more than a quarter. The game was marked by free wheeling substitution and scoring. Another surprise was Johnny Wactawski, previously unknown. He carried the ball only twice, but each time he scored, once on a 63 yard run and the other on an 80 gallop. It was learned later that the equipment manager had given Wactawski shoes two sizes too large. It obviously did not hamper him. All the Griffin backs ran well, piling up a total of 443 yards by the rushing route.

Naturally Jimmy Wilson was pleased with this first victory in his second stint as coach of the Griffs. So were the more than 9,000 fans who attended. The Griffs had an abundance of talent. Some observers thought that the coach would have had a problem trying to decide which players to use and when to use them. It was the kind of problem that Coach Wilson did not mind.

The other three colleges played more difficult teams in their season openers. St. Bonaventure hosted the Dayton Flyers, always a tough opponent. The game was played before a record crowd of nearly 10,000 in Forness Stadium. The *Courier Express* called it the largest crowd ever to watch a sports event in Western New York outside of Buffalo or Rochester. Frank LoVuolo, at end, and rookie Chris Scaturo who took over the quarterbacking chores for the departed Dave Curtin, starred for the Brown Indians. The Olean team was able to squeak out a 7 – 6 victory. It was the identical score of the previous year, but this time Bona was on the winning end.

U. B. opened on the road against a formidable Colgate team, and was promptly whitewashed by the Red Raiders 25 – 0. It was a cruel baptism for rookie coach, Frank Clair, but he would rebound nicely in the months that followed. Actually the loss was not as one sided as it appeared. U.B. played a decent game but a couple of miscues early on led to Colgate scores and the Bulls then were doomed.

On that same day, Niagara also traveled to Central New York to take on the Syracuse Orangemen, before 25,000 in Archbold Stadium. Syracuse was favored; it was no surprise that they quickly took the lead. Bernie Custis, "Syracuse's Negro triple-threat," led a 79-yard march to paydirt. The Purple Eagles then changed the whole tone of the game. Their group of talented sophomores took over. One of those sophomore stars, John McCoy, slashed his way across the goal line; that put Niagara ahead. The Eagles continued to outplay the Orangemen. Quarterback Jim McKinnon, a native of Massachusetts, was masterful. As Ray Ryan colorfully put it, McKinnon "flimflammed them all over the premises with a Houdini exhibition of faking, passing, and running." With his precision and dangerous bootleg running, many fans thought that McKinnon reminded them of the popular professional player, Frankie Albert. Late in the game Syracuse scored again. With time running out the Orangemen held a slim 13 – 9 lead. Niagara simply would not give up; they moved the ball downfield, just one yard from the goal line. On the next play it looked as though Bruno Pacini scored. The Niagara fans were sure of that. But it was a disputed call, the referee ruled fumble. There was no instant replay camera and no official's challenge. Syracuse had the ball and time ran out. It was a heartbreaking loss for the persevering Purple Eagles. As Ray Ryan put it "This upset would have lived long in song and story above the gorge." If there was ever such a thing as a moral victory this was it. Syracuse had been favored by as many as 21 points. The Niagara Student newspaper called it "the biggest heartbreaker in Niagara University history."[29]

The Niagara squad returned to Varsity Stadium where they had played their home contests since 1932. They faced Ithaca and vented their pent-up anger, routing them, 41- 0. The Eagles' scoring leader of the previous year, Bruno Pacini, led the Eagle attack. He scored three touchdowns. Unfortunately the rest of the season would not be as glorious for Niagara. Both Little Three opponents shut out the Purple Eagles. There were few bright lights in the remainder of the season, other than a 13 – 13 tie against the U.B. Bulls.

On the other hand, the University of Buffalo stormed back from its walloping at the hands of Colgate to administer a like walloping to Hobart, 39 - 0, before 3500 in Civic Stadium, and then proceeded to knock off RPI, 39 – 21. With all this scoring going on, it was no wonder than new backfield stars were emerging. These rookie Bulls included Jules Licata, used mainly at quarterback, and Frank Nappo and Vic Cleri, who the U.B. Bee, the university newspaper, referred to as "Volcanic Vic." In addition, veteran Ed Mittelsteadt continued to do some fine running. Spurred on by these Bulls, U.B. then defeated an always strong opponent, Alfred University, by a score of 8 - 0. That victory was followed by a stunning upset, when U.B. trounced Washington and Jefferson, 41 – 14. According to Bob Stedler, U.B. had entered that game as a 20 point underdog.[30]

Next the Bulls traveled to Kentucky, and in an even bigger surprise they easily trounced Louisville, 48 - 13. That still stands as one of the great wins in U.B. history. Ed Gicewicz, the star end for the Bulls and a vital figure in U.B. athletics for many decades, recalls the 19 hour train ride to Louisville. An "awful lot of poker was played" and that relaxed the players and put them in the right frame of mind to handle their formidable opposition. The way that the Bulls were playing boded well for the showdown with Niagara.[31] Still, it was a local rivalry. With the Bulls on the upswing, and Niagara heading in the other direction, it was difficult to predict what would happen when the two teams clashed on November 6. They played in Civic Stadium on the day following the Canisius - Bona tilt; the field was a sea of mud. Despite the atrocious conditions, the teams put on a good offensive show. Statistics were fairly close. The Eagles scored first, on a Dick Dobmeier plunge from the 2 yard line. Fritz Price tied the score on a 35 yard run and then the Bulls went ahead on Jules Licata's quarterback sneak. The game bogged down for a while. Then, late in the game, the Eagles composed themselves and marched down the field. But in a hotly disputed call, the U.B. defenders were called for interference with Niagara star receiver, Dick Wojciechowski. Niagara got the ball on the one yard line and after the Bulls stalwarts held twice, MacKinnon fired a pass to Pacini for the tying scoring. The scoreboard read 13 - 13, and the game ended a few minutes later. The anger of Bulls supporters over the officiating continued well after the final gun. The UB band struck up "Three Blind Mice," which reflected the sentiments of many of those exiting Civic Stadium. The protests continued loud and vigorous long after the final whistle.

St. Bonaventure, like the University of Buffalo, was having a good season. Following the squeaker over Dayton, the Bona team journeyed east to face a heavily favored Boston College eleven. The game was well played; it ended up as a 7 – 7 tie. Boston College scored on the opening second half kickoff. St. Bona quickly retaliated with Chis Scaturo again leading the way to pay dirt. Cleo LaChappelle continued to do a great job for Bona calling the defensive signals.

St. Bonaventure then had an easy time in its 13 – 0 victory over Wayne University. It was considered a necessary breather, coming between the tough Boston College contest and the upcoming clash against heavily favored William and Mary, the Southern Conference champion.

The game between St. Bona and William and Mary was played in Forness stadium. It was a bitterly fought contest, highlighted by Mitch Smiarowski's 57 minutes of extraordinary football. "Mr. Smear" was "a raving demon on defense" according to the *Courier Express*. With just 6 seconds to go in the first half, and Bona trailing 6 – 0, Chris Scaturo threw a 53 yard pass to Phil Colella who made a dazzling catch on the 7 yard line and strode into the end zone. Ever reliable Frank Ferris kicked the extra point and that was the margin of victory. Bona remained unbeaten by pulling off this dramatic 7 – 6 win. The Brown Indians then traveled to St. Louis where they expected another cliffhanger. Instead, they had a fairly easy time. They shut out the St. Louis University football team, 21 – 0.

Then they turned their attention to archrival, Canisius College. The November battle promised to be one of the great games in Little Three history. Bona had been prepping very well for the game; so too had the Golden Griffins.

The week following the season opening slaughter of St. Francis, the Griffs tangled with the ever dangerous Youngstown University team. Youngstown gave the Griffs a taste of their own medicine, rushing for two first quarter touchdowns. Led by Castine, Braatz, and Willis the Griffs fought back valiantly. The Griffs had a wide margin in first downs, and certainly played as well as their opponents. Unfortunately penalties were costly, stopping drives by the Griffs, and, in turn, leading to touchdowns for Youngstown. The breaks went against Canisius, the result was a 33 – 21 loss. But the Griffs learned from this close defeat.

The Griffs went on a roll. They shut out St. Vincent's, 19 – 0, then they knocked off a powerful Fordham club, 31 – 21, they whipped Niagara, 19 – 0, and also demolished Scranton, 32 – 7. They stood at 5 – 1 as they prepared to face the 4 – 0 – 1, St. Bonaventure team.

The Canisius victories showed just how formidable the Griffins' football team could be. The score against St, Vincent's could have been much greater. The Griffs held them to just one completed pass and racked up 21 first downs to just three for their hosts from Latrobe, Pennsylvania. The usual rushers starred for Canisius, Willis, Kwasek, and Castine. Also Johnny "Shoes" (his new nickname) Wactawski played well.

Bob Jerussi was called the "best lineman on the field." In the Fordham game, the Griffs rushed to a 30 – 7 lead and then held on for the win. Jack Sweeney, a Kenmore lad, emerged as a top receiver in this game. Even tackle George Eberle got into the scoring act when Kwasek flipped him a lateral and he rumbled into the end zone.[32]

The Bona game was still two weeks away, but Canisius knew that it could not afford to look past the upcoming Niagara contest. Coach Moran had some fine veterans and also had more depth than he had had previously. He counted on the large number of maturing sophomores to back up his upper-classmen. Canisius wasrated a slight favorite. Most fans felt they could count on watching a typical Little Three thriller. Unfortunately for them, the game was a mismatch. The headlines following the game blared: "Even Griffin Rooters are astounded by the ease of the Griffs' 19 – 0 victory." Howie Willis, the 155-pound dynamo from Philadelphia, proved very maneuverable on the muddy turf. He emerged as the game's big star. Willis ran for two touchdowns and passed for another. Kwasek and Sweeney helped considerably, and Don MacKinnon, no relation to the Niagara quarterback, shone brightly at the center slot.[33]

The Willis heroics continued as the season moved along. The game against the University of Scranton the following week could have been dubbed "the Howie Willis show." A crowd of nearly 8,000 (actually 7, 828) saw Willis execute three dazzling plays in the first half. He scored on a 53 yard punt return, a little later he returned a 95 yard kick off for a touchdown and then he tossed a pass to Jake Austin, a play that a covered 54 yards. Moreover the Griffs put up a great pass defense against a team known for its strong passing attack. Scranton managed to complete only 8 of 24 passes. Austin put the game out of reach when he intercepted Mike Denola's pass and raced 97 yards for a score.

Howie Willlis, Canisius triple threat. The little guy, 5′ 7," was a huge star. *Photo:The Griffin, Canisius College Archives.*

The Griffs were in top form as they prepared for their showdown with archrival St. Bonaventure.

As expected, the Western New York community looked forward to the Canisius-Bona game with great anticipation. Both teams had been having excellent seasons. Bona was undefeated and the Griffs only loss had come at the hands of highly-rated

Youngstown. The November 7 showdown was literally the talk of the town. Underscoring this was the success that promoters had in obtaining advertising for the game program. Everyone wanted to get in on the act. Cole's Restaurant, Chet Brunner's Tavern, the Blacksmith Shop, the Braemar Room of the Hotel Markeen, the new Crystal Room in the Hotel Touraine, the Hi-Gate, and Duff's Bar Fiesta and Patio, and MacDoels' Drum Bar Lounge, all helped to hype the big college game. All hoped to share in the spin-off business they anticipated would come with the game. Dick Fisher's three sporting good stores, one downtown, one in Tonawanda and one on Falls Street in Niagara Falls, joined in the hoopla. Dick Fischers'competitors, including Ed Rose's Sporting Goods Store, the Strauss-Dilscher Sporting Goods Store, and Edwards Sport Center in the Edwards Department Store, all wanted a share in the spotlight. So too did Culliton Ice, Weckerle Dairy, Lang's Creamery, and Stegmeier's Bakery (four locations duly noted). Finally Kleinhans Men's Store was not going to miss a chance to promote its college shop. Its ads featured corduroy sport coats for $19.95, available in the most popular colors: brown, tan, green, and, of course, maroon. Just about every college student felt obligated to have, at least, one of those "fashionable" garments.

On that first weekend in November Bona supporters, students as well as fans from Olean and throughout Cattaragus County, caused a virtual traffic jam as they traveled up Route 16 en masse, ready to make their presence felt in downtown Buffalo. The Hotel Lafayette, unofficial headquarters for Bona people, was overflowing. Students from the Franciscan institution could be seen driving around Shelton Square and Niagara Square in their old LaSalles and Studebakers; some were in revved up Fords and Chevrolets. The better heeled alumni sported their post war Buicks and Lincolns. A flock of the Brown Franciscans made the trip to assure that the Brown Indians had plenty of spiritual and moral support. The campus they left behind was cluttered with leaflets urging the Bona followers to "Stay in the hills, Brown Indians," because Canisius was destined to win. The Blue and Gold Club had chartered a small airplane to drop the leaflets. Days earlier some Bona fans had white washed the buildings on the Canisius campus. The colorful college atmosphere of these halcyon days of football was up and running.[34]

The coaching staffs of each institution were cautious. Coaches almost always are. Both coaching staffs were lamenting the superior forces they had to face and they were full of compliments for their opposite numbers. Both Canisius Coach Jimmy Wilson and Athletic Director, Doc Crowdle, acknowledged to Cy Kritzer that Canisius had some terrific linemen and backs and excellent ends in Bob Schaus and Jack Sweeney but cautioned that Bona's personnel matched up quite well. A few days before the big game, Kritzer drove to Olean and interviewed Coach Devore. The story he wrote was headlined: "Unbeaten Bona Weaker, Griffs Stronger Then Last Year, Devore Says." The Bona coach claimed that Canisius was 25% stronger than a year ago. He pointed out that the Griffs had the most varied offense that Bona would encounter in the 1948 season. Devore did admit that he had more strength at tackle than he had had in 1947 and that would help against the standout Canisius line. His troops would be up for the game but physically they would show some signs of the exhausting 25 hour train ride from St. Louis following their recent game there the previous Saturday. The players were given Monday off just to try to get back to normal. The Griffs had had no game that weekend so that would be to their advantage. Devore would not predict a winner but he did predict that this would be the "greatest game ever played in the series."[35]

The fans also gave their opinions. The *Buffalo Evening News* headline blared: "Fans

Rate Bona line tops, Give Edge to Griffin Backs." The story then cited the skills and performances of some of the leading players on each team as seen by their supporters. The following day, the main sports page of the *Buffalo Evening News* bore this headline: "Bona faces stern task to check air offensive of 9 Canisius passers." With the T formation still a novelty and the I formation not even heard of, Canisius used the single wing, and sometimes the double wing. Those formations provided the offensive backfield with a variety of passers. Jack Collins, one of the Griffs' all time gridiron greats who had played early in the century, commented on Jimmy Wilson's superb coaching job, and noted that before the season began it did not look as though Canisius would have a capable passer or a reliable punter. Now, Collins told the News, under Wilson's tutelage, nine capable passers and four decent punters were available.[36]

On the other hand, the Bona offense had not had much of a chance to open up earlier in the 1948 season because they had had so many close contests. But some observers thought that the Canisius game would be different. They looked for Chris Scaturo to do more passing and they looked for more offense simply because of the presence in the lineup of Phil Colella. The fabulous Bona back had been recovering from injuries for some time but he would be ready to go full steam ahead against Canisius. Bona received some bad news a few days before its big game with Canisius. It had to suspend its star punter, Jack Collins, one of the best in the East, for playing organized professional baseball. The complaint came, not locally, but from someone in the Albany area who had seen Collins play in the Boston College game and remembered that Collins had played with Schenectady in the Class C Canadian-American League.

With the football season at its height and with the excitement building for many days before actual game day, a big turnout was expected. There was a very large advance ticket sale. These were the best of years for Little Three football. Bob Stedler noted that the Little Three fan base had increased over the years; it now extended well beyond the 100 mile limit and involved many more supporters than just students and alumni. It was the 29th meeting of the archrivals and they entered the game with their best cumulative records in history. A very large crowd was on hand; 32,541 fans attended the classic. Indeed the turnout would have been larger had it not been for very high winds and threatening clouds. Indeed the all time attendance record of 35,000 in1946 might have been exceeded. Still the attendance was impressive. Its sheer size added luster to Little Three mythology.

At kickoff time, the Brown Indians were rated as slight favorites. But the Griffs refused to be awed. With the fans on their feet and electricity flowing throughout Civic Stadium, the Griffins struck first. Howie Willis tossed a 26 yard pass to Jack Sweeney for touchdown number one. Bona scored next when Tony Bolognese's punt was blocked and Joe Romansky, one of Bona's top linemen, fell on the ball in the end zone. The Griffs then struck for the second score, this one coming on a one yard plunge by Jake Austin. The game bogged down; Canisius maintained its lead. When the final whistle blew, the scoreboard at the Jefferson Avenue end of the stadium read: Canisius 14 – Bona 6.

The scribes were in agreement that the game was won up front, in the trenches. As usual Kuhrt, Eberle and Jacobi, as well as Bob Jerussi and Joe Bajak, were exceptional and they were flanked superbly by Chorny, Sweeney, Schaus, and Eddie Casey. The Canisius wall held the Brown Indians to just 3 first downs, and a total of 76 yards on the ground. The longest run was a 13-yard sprint by Stan Zajdel. The Canisius student newspaper, the *Griffin*, noted that Bob "lightening" Jerussi was under the punts and covering them before a Bona back could get a handle on them. His vicious tackles "jarred even the fans." The paper added that Bob Schaus' downfield tackling was so spectacular that it "brought huzzahs from the Canisius stands."[37]

A *Buffalo Evening News* headline seemed to be particularly jarring to the Bona authorities. It pointed out that the defeat cost Bona a "$50,000 Bowl Game," a sizeable figure back then. The bowl under consideration was the Cigar Bowl in Tampa. Had that materialized it would have made for an interesting story: first the Brown Indians participated in the Tobacco Bowl, and two years later the Cigar Bowl. What a different era![38]

A few observers thought the outcome of the game was an upset. Possibly it was, though it was hardly of the magnitude of the Truman victory over Governor Dewey in the presidential election of 1948 that had occurred just days before. Most fans were not surprised that the Griffins pulled off the victory. Coach Jim Moran, whose Niagara team was dismantled earlier by the Griffs, predicted the outcome. Jim Peele, the U.B. Athletic Director, had boldly asserted that Army "is the only team in the East that can take Canisius"[39]

Bona fans, disappointment written all over their faces, dragged themselves back down to the Southern tier. As Kritzer put it, "the road back to Olean is enveloped in broken dreams,"as thousands from the Cattaraugus hills had just witnessed the fatal blow to their hopes for an undefeated season. Some stayed around to enjoy the bright lights of downtown Buffalo and drown their sorrows at such celebrated hot spots as the Town Casino, or the Long Bar at the Lafayette Hotel, some went to hear the sounds of Mickey Dee and Skinner at Snowballs on Buffalo's West Side, some met friends from Canisius at the Everglades on Hertel Avenue where they listened to Jackie Jocko, the up and coming songster and pianist. They all knew that sooner or later they had to accept defeat and rally 'round and plan for another day. The St. Bonaventure Brown Indians were never down for long.

Bob Stedler put the game in much broader terms. He said that some of those in the vast crowd who had attended the game wondered if this might not have been the best Canisius team ever. The Griffs had suffered only one loss and that a close one to Youngstown, recognized as the best team in the state of Ohio, outside of the Buckeyes of Ohio State. Stedler's column reminded his readers that football experts had foreseen that the real test for Canisius would come against St. Bona. Only three touchdowns had been scored against the Brown Indians all season long. They had one of the outstanding football coaches in the country and a very rugged schedule. Stedler concluded that both clubs fought tenaciously for the full 60 minutes of play. It was cleanly contested; Bona and Canisius demonstrated the high caliber of football played in the Western New York area.[40]

Not to be outdone, Billy Kelly, *Courier Express* Sports Editor, used his column to congratulate both teams for a well played game and to praise the victors, calling Canisius the "most compact, well conditioned, and effective football team ever turned out" by the Jesuit school as it "rolled to victory over its most fabled and formidable rival." Many in the press box at Civic Stadium even stated that Canisius "would suffer nothing by comparison with the best teams in the East – or anywhere."[41]

The University of Buffalo football team also had cause to celebrate. It closed its season before 3,000 at Civic Stadium by whipping Bucknell University, 47 – 13. It was one of the worst clobberings ever administered to the team from Lewisburg, Pennsylvania. Standouts for the Bulls were Vic Cleri and

Fritz Price. Each scored twice. Cleri, another Lockport gift to the Bulls, picked up 140 yards rushing. The Bulls amassed over 400 yards of offense. The victory over Bucknell climaxed another successful season for U.B. Despite the fact that 6 of 8 games were played in the mud, the Bulls posted the best scoring mark in recent years, totaling 236 points. Coach Frank Clair had good reason to be very proud of his rookie 6 – 1 – 1 season. The players themselves, many of them products of Lafayette, Technical and other Buffalo public schools, found convenient outlets for their exuberance at Cole's on Elmwood and the Royal Pheasant on Forest Avenue.[42]

A week later, St. Bona hosted Niagara; and the Brown Indians were not very cordial hosts. They met on November 14, the weather was nasty, and the hearty crowd of 8500 shivered throughout the contest. Niagara played a pretty good game, better than the score would indicate. They held the Bona ground attack in check for the better part of the game; Bona was ahead only 7 – 0 at halftime. But a couple of Niagara miscues led to Bona scores and put the Eagles in the hole for good. The Brown Indians won, 21 – 0. In their final home game of the season, the Purple Eagles waged an all out battle before losing to a tough Scranton team, 27 – 14 in the "Anthracite metropolis." The 2 – 6 – 1 season was obviously a disappointing one for Niagara fans.

The St. Bona team then proceeded to defeat St. Vincent's 28 – 12 and in the season finale they defeated the University of San Francisco, 20 – 14. Led by Leo Haggerty and Frank LoVoulo, the Brown Indians scored two touchdowns early and forced San Francisco to play catch up ball. The victory over the highly regarded West Coast team was an impressive way to end a successful season. The friendly hometown crowd, another full house of some 9,000 fans, was pleased. Bona ended up with a formidable 7 – 1 – 1 record.

Meanwhile, Canisius too continued its winning ways. In what had to rank as a major accomplishment, the Griffs defeated powerful Toledo, for the second consecutive year. Chet Kwasek performed brilliantly; he scored three touchdowns in the 26 – 21 victory. In the following game, the Golden Griffins experienced a let down against Marshall University, the perennial West Virginia powerhouse. Perhaps the Canisius players were affected by the 18-hour train ride in sleeping cars from Buffalo to Huntington, West Virginia. The Marshall eleven took the opening kickoff and raced 80 yards for a score. The Griffs put together some decent offense but the big defensive line of the Thundering Herd repeatedly frustrated the Griffs each time they approached the end zone. Fortunately the Griffs had Nipper Castine patrolling the defensive backfield. He took a punt and raced 79 yards to even the score. Canisius had to settle for the 7 – 7 tie.

Canisius' players Austin, Willis, Bajak, MacKinnon, Castine and Kwasek on the eve of the Great Lakes Bowl.
Photo: The Griffin, 1948.

The Golden Griffins ended their regular season with a 7 – 1- 1 record. The Griffin victories over strong opponents were enough to earn them a bid to the Great Lakes Bowl, the first bowl invitation ever received by a Canisius football team. The game was to be played in Cleveland on December 4 against John Carroll University. The inaugural Great Lakes Bowl, the previous year, had seen Kentucky defeat Villanova. 14,900 spectators showed up. It was felt that having John Carroll, located in Cleveland, as the host team, a larger crowd could be attracted. That was a big order since cavernous Municipal Stadium, situated on the shores of Lake Erie, had a capacity of 85,000. The game was sponsored by the Knights of Columbus, and perhaps, a sign of the times, the proceeds were to go to fight Juvenile Delinquency, a big political issue and community concern in that era.

In the days leading up to the game, the momentum and excitement continued to build. A sizeable part of the Canisius student body made plans for the trip down the lakeshore to Cleveland, as did large numbers of alumni and various community groups. Officers of the alumni association were the main sponsors of the excursion; George Martin, one of the chief promoters, estimated that 3000 would make the trip, by automobile or train, making it the largest sports excursion ever to leave Buffalo. Two special trains, holding some 1400 fans, were provided by the New York Central Railroad. One of the trains was exclusively for students. Some of the recent alumni classes sponsored their own railroad cars on the other train. Also on the trip to Cleveland were groups from the Humboldt Club, Tuttle Motors, Bernie Flynn's The Place, Sisters Hospital, the local Knights of Columbus, the Blackthorns, and Joe Dudzick's tavern. $12.00 covered the round trip train fare as well as a box seat at the game. Meals were on your own; students were busy buying up dozens of Freddies' donuts, especially peanut sticks, by the carloads. Some also purchased Paul's Pies, others bought hamburgers from the White Tower, "Buy 'em by the bag full" was the slogan, and some even tried a brand new gastronomical delight, called Pizza, pioneered locally at the Bocce Club. The college atmosphere around the Main Street campus was festive. Typically, in those days of the 1940s, college related activities often took place in downtown Buffalo. The Junior Class held a dance honoring the football team at the ever popular Elks Ballroom on Delaware Avenue. Mel's Men's Store, on Main Street downtown, even got in the act. Canisius fans could purchase a suit for just $10.00 and along with it get a turkey for Thanksgiving.

The sports calendar was especially active in Buffalo in the late autumn of 1948. In fact Buffalo may just have been concluding one of its best sports years in its history. Not only was the Griffin football team basking in glory but it shared the limelight with other sports teams, especially the Buffalo Bills. The Bills had just defeated handily the New York Yankees, and were in the running for a playoff berth in the AAFC. Area colleges were going full speed ahead with their basketball season; large crowds, often more than 10,000, were showing up for the doubleheaders at the Aud. It was also Golden Gloves time in Memorial Auditorium. The national amateur boxing event was more popular than ever; it drew spectators in numbers commensurate with those that attended the Little Three basketball games. The Buffalo Bisons of the American Hockey League drew similar crowds in the same facility. A trip to an athletic event in downtown Buffalo was a hot ticket item in those days. Shelton Square was a veritable beehive of activity as automobiles, streetcars, and busses jockeyed for position, and pedestrians on the way to some sporting event feared for their lives what with all the motor traffic downtown. Since the Christmas shopping season was in full swing, the department stores were jammed. Thousands of shoppers walked along Main Street, many of them stopping to rest their eyes on the Christmas displays in the store windows, something that had become a cherished Buffalo tradition. Snow rarely had a chance to settle on the sidewalks.

The Griffin players practiced at the Villa; when conditions warranted they used the Delavan Avenue Armory. The team, at full strength and in a jubilant mood, departed on

Saturday, December 3. Coach Jimmy Wilson said the team was in good shape, there were no major injuries. The coach acknowledged that there had been somewhat of a letdown after the peak performance against St. Bona. That was evident in the Toledo and Marshall games. However Wilson was confident that the team had put that behind them and was now ready to roar. The John Carroll team also was reported to be in top shape. The Blue Streaks were pleased to have Don Shula, one of their best runners, back on the roster. He had missed the two previous games because of a rib injury. Later, Shula, as coach of the professional Miami Dolphins, would become the winningest coach in professional football history.

The Great Lakes Bowl game of 1948 was a closely fought contest; in fact, it could be labeled a spine tingling clash for the full 60 minutes. A crowd of nearly 18,000 watched intently. The Blue Streaks scored first on a Bob Kilfoyle pass to Jim Moran. The Griffs threatened twice in the first half but had to wait until after intermission for their first touchdown. Midway through the third period Don MacKinnon intercepted a Kilfoyle pass and raced 28 yards for a score. Just four minutes later, the Griffs scored again when Captain Zeke Palumbo sprinted 22 yards into the end zone.

The Griffs held a 13 - 7 as they entered the final period. The Streaks then found a vulnerable spot. George Kuhrt, the superb Griffin guard, had been hurt earlier in the game. He suffered a broken nose. He returned but was not quite the same. John Carroll took advantage of this and rushed Carl Taseff on slants through the Griffin line. Taseff, who later played in the National Football League, racked up important yardage; eventually he scored. The point after was good and proved to be the difference in the John Carroll 14 – 13 victory. The Griffs suffered some miscues, in fact two passes, which seemed to be sure touchdowns, were dropped in the end zone. But the opposition had miscues of its own. The mistakes balanced off and the overall game statistics were fairly even.

Canisius had played hard and their thousands of faithful fans who made the 190 mile trek down the Lake Erie shore were rewarded with a valiant effort in a nip and tuck game. The only thing better would have been a victory. The Golden Griffins could hold their heads high. They licked their wounds on the train ride back to Buffalo then were met by hundreds of supporters who cheered them as they walked through the massive New York Central Terminal on Buffalo's East side. Locally the college football season was officially over. It had been a very good one for Western New Yorkers.

All that remained was the awarding of post season honors.

Two Canisius players and two Bona players received Honorable Mention, on All American teams, no small achievement for small schools. George Kuhrt and Howie Willis represented the Griffs, and Frank LoVuolo and Joe Romanowsky were the selections from the Brown Indians. They were in good company. The really big names nationally on the 1948 All American team were Charley "Choo Choo" Justice of North Carolina,

***Above:* Program cover for the Great Lakes Bowl, 1948.**
Courtesy: Canisius College Archives

and Doak Walker of SMU. Dick Rifenburg, Michigan's big end, later to be a celebrity sports announcer for many years in Buffalo, was also in that elite company.

LoVuolo, the sensational pass catching end, reached an even higher peak when he was chosen as a first team selection for the Little All America team. All who had seen him play, recognized that this was a well deserved honor for the former field artillery sergeant. LoVuolo had served in five major battles in Europe and then he returned home to become one of the all time great athletes in Brown Indian History. On Christmas night, LoVuolo started for the North squad in the North-South Charity All Star game in the Orange Bowl. He certainly did not embarrass himself even though he was in the august company of Chuck Bednarik of Pennsylvania and Terry Brennan of Notre Dame.

The *Buffalo Evening News* also named a Western New York All Star team and, as expected, Canisius, and St. Bona, closely followed by U.B., dominated the team.

In Olean, 1200 St. Bonaventure supporters attended the Gridiron Club dinner at which Mitch Smiarowski was name the standout Bona player of the year. On the day before Christmas, Howie Willis was named unanimously the outstanding football player in the Little Three by a board of sports writers and sportscasters: Kritzer, Ryan, and also Charley Bailey of WEBR, Tom Benton, of the AP, Jack Horrigan, of the UP, Ralph Hubbell of WBEN, Gene Korzelius of WBNY, Sig Smith of WGR, and Bill Mazur of WKBW. Kritzer said that if the "will-o'-wisp" Willis was wearing the uniform of a major football team, he would be recognized as one of the best backs in the country. Ray Ryan who had been covering Canisius football since 1928, said Willis could do more things better than any back Canisius ever had. Dick Stedler, sports editor of the Union and Echo, called Willis the best all around back since Tommy Colella.[43]

As the year 1948 drew to a close, not all was roses. In an end of the year summary one of the local newspapers concluded that the two City of Buffalo teams, Canisius and U. B., had had perhaps their best seasons ever. But then the column, noted, somewhat ominously, that attendance could have been better, especially at the Civic Stadium games. Weather was not always ideal, indeed it was a big factor in the disappointing attendance overall. Moreover it was becoming widely known that all the local teams were operating at a financial loss. It had been a very bright season, but there were some gray clouds gathering on the horizon.

As usual Buffalonians joined the rest of the nation in following the major bowl games on New Year's Day, 1949. In the Cotton Bowl, SMU defeated Oregon, in the Sugar Bowl, Oklahoma beat North Carolina, and in Miami at the Orange Bowl, Tom Landry led Texas to a victory over Georgia. In the granddaddy of the bowl games in Pasadena, the Big Nine representative, Northwestern, surprised California. Not long afterwards, the Big Nine announced that it admitted Michigan State, thereby becoming once again the Big Ten Conference, at least for the 50 - 51 season.

Once the New Year's Day Bowl games were over football issues appeared to go into hibernation. One exception involved the professional war between the AAFC and the NFL. Some thought that the new league might fold, even though it appeared to be doing as well financially as the equally unstable NFL. Others thought that a truce would be called and that a merger of some sort would result. Rumors spread and some discussions did take place but nothing of consequence materialized. On the college front, there was continued concern of the escalating expenses of football, especially the costs of scholarships and of travel. There were even reports that mentioned that some small colleges were thinking of dropping the sport.

There was one local football development that had not been unexpected. Niagara Coach Jim Moran resigned following the '48 season to take a job as an assistant at Holy Cross College. Soon after, Niagara hired Jim Miller to be Moran's successor. Miller had played at Purdue. He served in the Navy during the War, and then briefly he was a coach at Wabash College of Indiana. Earlier he had played at Massillon High School for Paul Brown, the future coach of the Cleveland Browns. Miller was a devout disciple of Paul Brown. He worshipped him and patterned his coaching after the great master. When Niagara was looking for a new coach, a Niagara emissary went to Paul Brown to seek his input and Brown recommended Miller. Brown would come to be recognized as one of the most influential figures in football in the 20th century, certainly on a par with George Halas of the Chicago Bears.

The end of August, 1949 saw the various college prospects report for preseason training. As was traditional, the squads were previewed in the local press. The St. Bonaventure camp was the first visited. Huge Devore spoke about his team as they were being sent through drills at the McGraw-Jennings practice field on the Olean campus. Devore, as usual, was cautious. He needed to find replacements for such stalwarts as Frank LoVuolo, Steve Charsky, and Phil Colella and dependable place kicker, Frank Ferris. The first three signed professional contracts, while Ferris joined the Franciscan Order. But a number of fine veterans were returning. Chris Scaturo would be back as the T formation quarterback, the other backs included Lou Salley, Leo Haggerty, and George Chatlos. Mitch Smiarowksi and George Hays were named co-captains for the Bona squad, top linemen joining them were Ernie Virok, Joe Romansky, and Al Lesko. No one doubted that Bona would have another very good team. [44]

U.B.'s situation was similar to Bona's. Coach Frank Clair said he was pleased that he would have a "strong, experienced line." Les Molnar, Charley Dingboom, Don Beitelman and Bob Leipler were all returning to their forward wall positions. But some big shoes in the backfield would have to be filled. Sal Amico a dependable and at times explosive running back was returning and Jules Licata, back from the injured list, would be able to handle the quarterback chores from the T formation, but Bill Rudick, Fritz

U.B. Football Players. ***From left to right:*** **Rhodes, Szydlowski, Cameron, Dingboom, Gicewicz, and Nichols.**

Niagara players, *clockwise from top left:* Nick Wojciechowski, Dick McCarthy, John D'Arcy, and Johnny Theobald.

Price, Eddie Mittelsteadt and Vic Cleri were all gone. Clair was optimistic about his fine crop of sophomores who were eager to play regularly. These included: Don Holland, Matty Sydlowski, Big Ed Gicewicz, and Russ Gugino

The enthusiasm for college football was as heated as ever at Canisius as the 1949 season approached. 500 supporters had shown up for the Canisius Bloc C dinner at the Statler Hotel, the traditional dinner at which athletes received their awards. Billy Kelly noted that it was the largest turnout since Knute Rockne spoke to the Bloc C back in 1930. The Griffin athletic teams were enjoying considerable success. Large attendance at the annual banquet attested to that.

Canisius players were in good physical shape as preseason drills began at the Villa. Most of their star players of the great 1948 team would be returning. Don MacKinnon who had played well at center in the past was practicing hard and ready to be the permanent first string center. Ray Jacobi, star tackle for the past three years, now fully recovered from an injury that forced him to miss part of 1948, was back and deservedly wore a new hat; he was now the captain of the Golden Griffins. Coach Jimmy Wilson had thought of jumping on the college bandwagon and installing the 2 platoon system, but decided against it and said he would rather keep his "best players in there as long as possible." While many of the country's football teams were adjusting to the T formation, Wilson stuck with the single and the double wing formations. In a preseason scrimmage, the Griffs fared well against Ivy League Champion, Cornell. Chet Kwasek looked good for the Griffs, while Hillary Chollet paced the Big Red. Unfortunately George Eberle and Johnny Wactowski suffered injuries.

Missing from the Niagara team would be Charlie Pacini, Les Dugan, Nick Stojakovich, and Bud Stefik, but there were some fine veterans returning. These included up front: Dick Wojciechowski, Bob Rosa and Dick McCarthy, and backs, Jim Russ, Dick Dobmeier, Bruno Pacini, and John McCoy. At quarterback, Coach Jim Miller would have to fill the slot vacated by Jim McKinnon. Johnny Theobold seemed to be the most likely candidate.

A proverbial baptism of fire awaited the Niagara head coach in his debut. The Purple Eagles opened their 1949 season against the Big Red of Cornell. The game was played in Ithaca before 15,000. Veteran halfback Hillary Chollet, brother of the famous Leroy of Canisius basketball fame, raced 70 yards for the opening touchdown for the Big Red. Cornell ended up blanking Niagara, 27 – 0. But the score was misleading. Niagara had more first downs than Cornell. Niagara drove to within the six yard line on three different occasions, but then simply could not score. Misfortune seemed to be an old story for Niagara.[45]

The St. Bonaventure Brown Indians were more fortunate. They got off to a rousing start for the '49 season. They faced the University of Scranton before 9000 fans on the Olean turf. Bona's solid defense kept Scranton from mounting any sort of meaningful drive. On offense, Chris Scaturo's passes paced the host team to a 26 – 0 rout over the boys from the coal region of Pennsylvania. The Brown Indians overwhelmed the visitors in the statistics' column too.

With so many solid veterans returning, the Griffs had reason to feel confident as they prepared for the 1949 season. Canisius went on the road for their opener. They played the always formidable Youngstown College team. It was a see-saw game, but the Griffs rose to the occasion and emerged with the victory, 28 – 26. Jake Austin was the big star for the Griffs. He scored all four touchdowns. Kwasek ran well, as usual. Willis suffered a broken finger during the course of the game but Nipper Castine filled in admirably for Willis, as he had often done in previous seasons.

The following week, Coach Wilson put Castine into the starting lineup for the home opener against St. Norbert's. The former All High Kensington player and army veteran would team up with Chet Kwasek, and Jake Austin. These three would furnish the running game and Tony Bolognese would direct the attack. Bob Jerussi, a senior from the Bronx, and an excellent downfield blocker, would help spearhead the assault along with center Marty Breen. Wilson also unveiled a pleasant surprise, a sophomore tailback from Niagara Falls, Dick Luciani. He was all over the field making plays. He appeared to be the latest triple threat for the Griffins until he was carried off the field with a game ending injury. It was another story of short-lived fame. They Griffs quickly jumped into the lead and tallied four touchdowns before the opposition from Wisconsin tallied a six pointer of their own. The final score was 26 – 6. Unfortunately only 3650 fans witnessed the win in Civic Stadium.

U.B. started its season with a big, though not unexpected loss, to Colgate, 32 to 0. The U.B. team was in good shape for the game. The Bulls practiced at Archbold Stadium in Syracuse, stayed overnight at the nearby Hotel Onondaga, then bussed to Colgate. U.B. had a horrible outing. Fumbles were the main culprit for the Bulls; the slippery ball caused four of them. Moreover U.B. completed just one pass and that went for a loss of nine yards. Things would have to be better for the Bulls the following week, and they were.

The month of October opened with local rivals, Niagara and the University of Buffalo, playing each other in Civic Stadium. Frank Clair and Jim Miller, the respective coaches, were old friends; that fact added a little extra zest to game preparations. Moreover the Niagara alumni were anxious to see their team regain supremacy over U.B. The two teams had played 16 times from 1918 to 1934. In that span, NU had scored 168 points and held U.B. scoreless. The series was renewed after World War II, and to some a bit surprisingly, U.B. was in the driver's seat. In 1947 the Bulls won and the following year Niagara was fortunate to earn a tie with them.

Coach Clair had reason to count on his line to get the job done against the running game. One of the stars in the U.B. loss to Colgate was Les Molnar, a 235 pound tackle from powerful McKinley High School. Joining Molnar in the interior line were two real heavyweights, U.B.'s heavyweight wrestling champion, Don Beitelman, and also former heavyweight boxer, Matty Ferrentino. Clair also knew he had to beef up his pass defense. He focused on containing Niagara's ace passer, John Theobold. Clair succeeded. Niagara's lone score came on a 2 yard sneak by quarterback Theobald. Meanwhile the U. B. offense did its job. Carl Markey caught two passes for touchdowns, and Frank Nappo came up with the game's most exciting play when he took Ray Siembida's punt and raced 75 yards for a score. The real game story was the coach himself, Frank Clair. Sports reporter Ray Ryan wrote that Coach Clair did a masterful job when three times he drew five-yard penalties deep in enemy territory, in order to get a play into the game, and he came up with a touchdown each time. The final score stood at 26 – 7; nearly 9,000 fans were on hand in U.B.'s favor.

On October 8, U.B. played RPI and handily defeated the men from Troy, 26 – 2. A week later they pulled off a convincing win over archrival Alfred University, 32 – 6. More new stars were coming into the picture for Coach Clair. These included two excellent ends, Ed Gicewicz and Matty Sydlowski and also a fine running back, Ray Weser. Against Alfred, Weser had a day to remember; he scored three touchdowns. The Bulls appeared to have fully recovered from the Colgate bashing, and were now shifting into high gear.

Meanwhile the Niagara team was headed in the opposite direction. The week following the loss to U.B., the Purple Eagles were demolished by Scranton, 32 – 0. An impressive home crowd of 4500 enjoyed the warm afternoon but that is all they enjoyed. The Purple Eagles could do nothing right, it was a game of frustrations for fans and players alike. In the next game the Eagles did not fare much better; they lost toYoungstown, 27 – 7.

The first Little Three contest of the 1949 season, this one featuring Canisius and St. Bona, took place on October 16 in Olean. This was the first of two meetings of the arch foes in the 1949 season. The reason they scheduled each other twice owed to difficulties of scheduling enough suitable opponents. Officially only the second contest counted as a part of the Little Three Conference standings.

In the pre game rituals both coaches cried the Blues. Coach Jimmy Wilson claimed that his charges were victims of mounting injuries; he was particularly distressed by the loss of his key guard, George Kuhrt. Moreover he refused to accept the fact that the Griffs were a slight favorite over Bona. That was no doubt due to their early season victory, over formidable Youngstown University. Coach Hugh Devore also sought sympathy. Even though Bona has just defeated Wayne University, the Bona coach pointed out that he had lost his two previous outings, to the University of San Francisco, 34 - 21 and to Dayton, 28 -13. Regardless of what the experts might predict, most fans anticipated a close game, virtually a toss up. Canisius alumni and students gobbled up hundreds of tickets. Many bought them as part of a package deal that included a trip to Olean on the Erie Railroad. Others planned to take busses or automobiles. Olean would be a very busy little city that weekend, a veritable metropolis on the Southern tier.

The Golden Griffins headed south into Cattaraugus County. They must have sensed an ambush coming. As they drove on the Bona campus, they saw a huge Indian, a piece of mechanical art, who was sawing away at the body of the mythical Griffin. At Forness field a few hours later, that is pretty much what happened. The Griffins were pulverized.

But it did not happen right from the opening whistle. Bona led by senior, Leo Haggerty, their leading ground gainer with a 6.7 average per carry, scored first. The Griffs retaliated and actually went ahead for the only time in the game. Bona then regained the lead and led at halftime, 13 – 7. Following the second half kickoff the roof fell in on the visitors from the metropolis to the North. Leo Haggerty and Lou Salley established a solid running game. Chris Scaturo fired three touchdown passes. Joe Pavikowski, the big end, intercepted a pass and ran it back 100 yards for a touchdown. Coach Devore used plenty of substitutes in the second half but they, too, continued to pick up considerable yardage. The score climbed and when the final whistle blew it was a 46 – 13 win for the home forces. The overflow crowd of more than 12,000, which included hundreds of alumni on hand for homecoming, could not have been more delighted. After losing in the final quarter in his two previous games, to Dayton and San Francisco, Devore said "we had this one coming to us."The Franciscan community praised the Lord; the alumni who jammed the Castle Restaurant and other nearby watering holes were ecstatic.

Canisius was absolutely humbled; 46 points were scored against its vaunted defense. It was one of the worst defeats in Canisius history. Fortunately, in a perverse sense, the Buffalo Bills lost the same day, 51-7 to San Francisco. So there was some commiseration among Buffalo fans, except those who cheered for Bona. The Canisius Coach graciously said "We met a great ball club today." As Jimmy Wilson left the southern tier he could only hope that with Willis, Austin, and Eberle back in the lineup for the return bout in two weeks, the outcome would be different.

Following the slaughter in Olean, the Brown Indians journeyed north to Niagara Falls and perpetrated another massacre, this time against the Purple Eagles. They shut out Niagara, 41 – 0, before 3500 shocked homecoming day fans. The Niagara forces simply could not mount a serious scoring drive as they lost their fifth straight. Bona's defense was relentless; it forced two mistakes by Niagara that led to two quick touchdowns in the first few minutes of the game, one on a fumble and the other on a blocked punt which skidded into the Eagles' end zone. On Bona's part, there was no one standout. As Canisius scout, Al Dekebrun put it, when you play them, "You have to concentrate on all eleven men." Bona's victory over Niagara was a thoroughgoing team effort.

On that same October weekend, Canisius rode roughshod over the University of Scranton, dealing them one of their worst losses in years, 32 – 0. It seemed as if the Griffs were taking out their frustrations from the Bona loss on the unsuspecting Pennsylvanians. Bona scouts could not help but notice that Howie Willis was back in shape again, though the day really belonged to Chet Kwasek. Most of the 7500 in the stands in Scranton would have agreed that Kwasek was the best all around player on the field. His play was spectacular. Art Calandrelli had an extraordinary day punting for the Griffs.

The University of Buffalo, meanwhile, was feeling pretty confident with its 3 – 1 record as they headed into their game with St. Lawrence University. Most observers figured that the Bulls would have little trouble with the squad from Northern New York State. They were wrong. U.B. lost 13 – 7. Perhaps U.B. was looking ahead to its next encounter against Bucknell. The Bulls had the awesome assignment of trying to defeat Bucknell for the second year in a row. The visitors were rated as a legitimate Eastern power in 1949, their only loss being a one pointer to Temple. If Bucknell needed any motivation at all it was that they had been swamped by U. B. in 1948 by a 47 – 13 score. It was one of their worst defeats ever. The display of pictures from that humiliating loss served as additional inspiration.

The Bulls faced the Bisons before 5,200 in Civic Stadium. Bucknell struck first, but with Sal Amico and Ray Weser, doing some steady ball carrying. U.B. tied up the game and then the brilliant U. B, defense went to work; it held Bucknell in check for the major part of the game. However, in the last quarter Bucknell pushed across two touchdowns and won 21 -7. The Bulls had put up a valiant effort. In his Monday column, Sports Editor Bob Stedler praised the Bulls' aggregation, especially the linemen, who constantly frustrated a very strong Bucknell team. Stedler remarked that when one considered the many injured players on the Buffalo roster, the Bulls "did remarkably well."[46]

The day following the Bulls' valiant effort, Civic Stadium was again host to a big game. It was the second Bona-Canisius meeting of the season. Because of the annihilation of the Canisius team by the Brown Indians just two weeks earlier, there were some big questions to be answered. Had the Griffs recovered? Could the Griffs stay with the fierce Bona team? Could they conceivably win the game? The excitement, as usual, had been building for several days. Downtown hotels started to register the out of town alumni, several of the hotel ballrooms held pre-game parties. The spirit of the student bodies of both institutions clicked into high gear. The *Griffin*, the Canisius student newspaper, cited the efforts of Max McCarthy, John Brady, Donny Hawkins, and the Gold Key club for providing spirited leadership. Bona students, with their throngs of followers coming from southwest of Buffalo were not to be outdone. They arrived in record numbers, coming from Bradford, Wellsville, and Angelica and from Salamanca and Jamestown, and even from Killbuck and Limestone, as well as a huge outpouring from Olean itself. Bona was a 13 ½ point favorite and these denizens of the hills south of Buffalo smelled blood.

Bona began the game looking as though it would have no trouble covering the spread. In the opening minutes Bona picked off a Canisius pass and took the ball to within striking distance of the goal line. But then things changed. After seven thrusts that produced just one first down, the Griffin Blue Wall still held. Indeed it held "with a show of tackling fury that Canisius men will talk about in awed tones for years to come." Don McKinnon, Bob Jerussi, Bob Schaus, Joe Bajak, they were all demons on defense. They turned the tide. From then on, the Griffs were dominant. The mighty defensive line got a big boost from Art Calendrelli. Once again his booming punts were a significant factor. One actually traveled 71 yards from the line of scrimmage. The Griffs played at their peak. MacKinnon played such a superb game at center that his teammates voted him the game ball. Junior Bill Minihan turned in an excellent performance at tackle for the ailing George Eberle. That same Bona team that had run up 46 points against the Griffs just two weeks earlier was now blanked. It seemed only right that the two outstanding Canisius senior running backs, Willis and Kwasek, each scored one of the touchdowns. Arguably they were the best running duet in Canisius history. The final score stood at 14 – 0. Cy Kritzer called the game "one of the most fantastic form reversals of modern times." He further noted that the 20,125 in attendance saw a Devore's Bona team shut out for the first time in his four years as head coach.[47]

Coming off this high, the Griffs next had to face their other Little Three opponent, the Niagara Purple Eagles. Despite the poor season Niagara had been having, the team was not about to toss in the towel. The week before they were to play Canisius, Niagara defeated Wayne University. In that game, Johnny Theobold's precision passing was a big factor, as was the running of John McCoy whose two touchdowns led the Eagles to the 14 – 6 victory. The men from Monteagle Ridge were feeling pretty good about their chances as they prepared for the showdown in Civic Stadium with Canisius.

The Canisius - Niagara game was the subject of considerable publicity. As expected, the Griffins were the heavy favorites. Griffin footballers wanted to be part of history by winning the Little Three championship three years in a row. Nine of the Griffin starters were taking their final bows. On the other hand, the pundits warned that anything could happen in a Little Three contest. One could hear or read of such dire warnings to Canisius as: "Don't be overconfident" and "beware of the upset," and "an upset would make the season" for the otherwise downtrodden and dispirited Purple Eagles. In practices before the game, Coach Jimmy Wilson warned against being overconfident. He called attention to the fine play of Theobold and McCoy in the Niagara victory over Wayne University. Most keen observers refused to predict a Canisius rout. The more perceptive analysts indicated that despite the lopsided losses that Niagara suffered earlier in the season, the team was getting better with each game. There were some very good athletes on the team, and, to paraphrase the old cliché, on any given day, they could perform miracles. That is almost what happened on November 6, 1949.[48]

From the opening whistle, the Griffs knew they were in for a battle. Niagara's great running back, Johnny McCoy, took the kickoff and raced 62 yards to the Griff 27. Then Niagara's ace passer, Johnny Theobold, hit McCoy on the 9. Luckily for the Griffs, defensive signal caller, Joe Bajak, got his team off the hook by recovering a Theobold fumble. However after that the Griffs' luck pretty much dissipated. Time after time the Niagara defense stymied the Canisius attack. All told the magnificent Niagara defense turned back Griffin drives seven times inside the 20 yard line. All the scoring took place in the 3rd quarter. Castine, Bob Schaus, and Tom Ferraro, all played important roles. On a crucial and surprising play that started at midfield, Schaus lateraled to Bob Jerussi, who took the ball to the 2 yard line. Ferraro bulled his way into the end zone. Howie Willis kicked the extra point. Niagara retaliated immediately. Theobold led a 61 yard scoring drive. McCoy and Bruno Pacini played key roles, the latter diving in from the one yard line. Unfortunately for the Purple Eagles, the PAT was missed.

There were many stars for the Purple Eagles that afternoon but John Theobold shone the brightest. On defense, he personally was responsible for choking off three touchdowns. In one instance, the Griffs marched 88 yards, only to be thwarted by a Theobold interception in the end zone. He also recovered two fumbles to halt Griffin drives. On the other side of the line of scrimmage Theobold passed beautifully, slippery ball notwithstanding, to set up Niagara's touchdown.

The Griffins won, 7 – 6. The Griffins had an overwhelming edge in statistics. But it was simply the point after touchdown that spelled the difference. Cy Kritzer said that if there ever was a moral victory, this was it for Niagara. It was a shame that one of the best local college games ever, was played on a cold, rainy, dreary day. The miserable weather reduced the size of the crowd; only 3,551 showed up. But those brave souls were treated to a Little Three classic. It turned out to be a well played game despite the awful field conditions.[49] That was the last big game between local rivals in the 1949 season. But there were more games to be played by Western New York's quartet of teams, some against very difficult opponents.

Many Canisius seniors were saying good bye to their college football days; most of them had participated for four rewarding seasons. Unfortunately the season finale for the Griffs was not especially memorable. Canisius hosted John Carroll University, their conqueror by a single point in the Great Lakes Bowl just eleven months earlier. The John Carroll team came to Buffalo looking for its fourth consecutive win. Once again they were led by Carl Taseff who had been so instrumental in their victory over the Griffs in the 1948 bowl game. Taseff was a legitimate candidate for Little All America honors; he was in the top echelon of rushers for small colleges in the entire nation. Taseff lived up to his reputation in this game. He ripped, slashed and tore apart the Griffins' gallant line, putting the Blue Streaks ahead comfortably early in the game. The Griffs mounted two successful scoring drives in the second half giving hope to the faithful that their team might make a heroic comeback.

The Howie Willis to Jack Sweeney passes were big factors. Following the second touchdown, on the ensuing kickoff, rookie Denny Brinkworth spilled Taseff and a fumble resulted. The Griffs had the ball. What looked to be a third successful drive for a touchdown got underway. The Griffs' threat was snuffed out when "hard running Don Shula" intercepted a Willis pass. That ended the Griffs' hopes. When the game ended, Taseff had gained 236 yards in 39 attempts as he sparked the John Carroll team to a 26 – 12 victory. It was a tough loss for the seniors who had given fans such a wonderful display of exciting football over the past 4 years. Unfortunately only 3517 fans witnessed the finale. [50]

As Bob Stedler put it, the football fans of the 1940s would long remember the more than two dozen veterans who "gave their all as members of the team for the brilliant and hard fought contests they produced here and on other fields. They rate as one of the best football teams in the history of the college. They served well, effectively, and brought honor to the school, the city, and themselves." Fittingly the Alumni honored the Football Griffs at a banquet at the Buffalo Trap and Field Club on Cayuga Road near the Buffalo Airport. That was the first of several tributes held in honor of, arguably, the greatest collection of athletes in Canisius football history. The *News* on November 9, prophetically, noted that the game against John Carroll at Civic Stadium "rings down the curtain on the most successful era in Canisius football." Three months later Canisius dropped the sport of football.[51]

Meanwhile Niagara had two more games to play. In their contest with Waynesburg, the Purple Eagles managed their second victory of the campaign, a nice way to close out the home season. The final score was 24 – 6. Niagara's usual stars John Theobold, Johnny McCoy, and Bruno Pacini performed well Niagara's final game was against the Quantico Marines, played at the famous Marine base in Virginia. Perhaps the game was a commentary, and a sad one at that, on Niagara's disappointing season. The Purple Eagles were just plain unlucky. They lost 27 – 19 but they could just as easily have won if some breaks had gone their way. Niagara drove 99 yards the hard way for a score, and the Marines raced 90 yards with a kickoff return for their first score. That was how the game progressed until the last period when the host team scored the final two touchdowns.

The University of Buffalo had a very successful campaign. Following its loss to Bucknell, the Bulls finished out the season in a blaze of glory, with three victories, the last two on the road. In their final home game, the Bulls shut out Washington and Jefferson, 26 – 0 before a slim turnout of 2600 of the faithful on a chilly November evening. One of the highlights was the honoring of the 20 seniors who were taking their final bows before their hometown fans. The U.B. band, fifty strong and dressed as Joe College types, with blue dungarees and white shirts, received kudos from the local press for creating a festive atmosphere. UB was bidding good bye to a host of excellent seniors but the Washington and Jefferson game showed that some future stars were already on board. Tracy LaTona pitched three touchdown passes to Ed Gicewicz and this underclassmen combination spearheaded the 26 – 0 triumph. It was a strictly local duet, LaTona from Seneca High School and Gicewicz from Technical High School. The latter would come to be widely acknowledged as one of U.B.'s all time great football players.[52]

The following weekend found the Bulls on the road playing at Rhode Island College. Coach Clair made good use of his emerging stars. Quarterback LaTona, ends Gicewicz and Carl Markey, and running backs, Sal Amico and Ray Weser, all performed very well. The Bulls clobbered the Rhode Island team, 39 – 7. U.B.'s latest victim thus ended

U.B. All-Star End Ed Gicewicz. *Photo: Game Program*

an ignominious season; they failed to win a single game. The Bulls, on the other hand, continued their winning ways. However their next opponent reckoned to be much more difficult.

The U.B. Bulls traveled to the Buckeye state to play Ohio University in the 1949 season finale. The home team was the favorite, as well they should have been. Its victims included West Virginia, Western Michigan, Kent State, and Butler; all solid teams. Still Frank Clair was optimistic. His Bulls were looking forward to pulling off their first major upset of the season. It would be a grand finale for UB's 20 seniors. The Bulls were as confidant as their coach. They took a very relaxed bus trip from Buffalo to Athens, Ohio. In the locker room before the game, Jim Peele, Director of Athletics and former Coach, approached each senior individually, shook hands and thanked each of them for how well they had played for him and for Coach Clair and then urged the players to "give us this one to remember" you. They did just that. In the first half, the teams played an even game. Ohio U. struck first but just before intermission, the Bulls tied the game. The second half was a different story. The UB defense held firm, stifling drives and recovering fumbles. Bob Leipler, Matty Ferrentino, and Les Molnar all performed like blocks of granite. It was a total team effort. Some unheralded players, made a name for themselves. Al Zwolinski, filing in for the ailing Sal Amico, and Mike Rhodes, who played with all sorts of aches and pains and was referred to as "the magnificent wreck" by Cy Kritzer, provided additional inspiration for the Bulls. The 20 – 7 victory gave the U.B.'s senior corps a memorable end to their college playing days. It was a game to "reminisce about" for decades to come. Cy Kritzer called it one of the richest upsets in the history of U.B. football.[53]

The St. Bonaventure team took a path similar to that of the University of Buffalo, finishing its season in a blaze of glory. Bona beat Houston 20 – 14, then traveled to Fenway Park to play a strong Boston University eleven and the Brown Indians shut them down completely, 19 – 0. The victory over Boston University was particularly satisfying. The home team was a heavy favorite. The Brown Indians played the role of spoilers once again. The Terriers' only previous loss was, by one point, to a strong University of Maryland team. The headline in the local press hit the nail on the head when it blared this alliteration: "Bonnies Blast BU Bowl Bid." The Brown Indians were led by the brilliant quarterbacking of Chris Scaturo. He teamed up with another senior playing his final game, Leo Crampsey, on two touchdowns strikes and Scaturo ran in the third himself. On the other side of the line of scrimmage, the Olean team was able to put up a stiff pass defense against one of the country's All American passers, the much-heralded Harry Agganis.

The University of Buffalo and St. Bonaventure University ended their campaigns with identical 6 – 3 records. Canisius posted a 5 – 2 season, and Niagara, unfortunately, ended up with only 2 wins while losing 7 games.[54]

As the college football season came to an end, and the college basketball season began, the attention of the football world focused on the future of the All American Football Conference and the National Football League. For Buffalonians it focused directly on the future of their own Buffalo Bills. Anxious times prevailed in December, 1949 and January, 1950. Fans hopes were high. It seemed as though supporters from all walks of life got behind the cause. Unfortunately their hopes were dashed. Despite the best efforts on the part of the local citizenry, the Buffalo franchise was lost. Buffalo would no longer have a professional football team; at least not for the next ten years.

Not many figured that the same future might await some of the local college teams, but that is exactly what did happen. Just a few weeks after the Bills' heartbreaking exodus, the morning newspaper headlines blared the shocking news that Canisius College was dropping football.

The official announcement was made on February 8, 1950 by the President of Canisius College, the Reverend Raymond Shouten. The President indicated that he had recently consulted the Jesuit faculty and also met with his Board of Trustees before arriving at the decision. The President's announcement rang with Newmanesque overtones as it called attention to the highest purpose of higher education while noting that football was not an essential part of that purpose. The Shouten statement said that "it was unfair to the academic development of the college and to the student body as a whole to utilize the funds of the college to carry on a sport that cost so much and interested so few." The President said that the college did not exist for football, and added that "too few saw the team perform and the expense was beyond all proportion to the accidental good." The President also asked: "Was the contribution made by football sufficient to warrant the financial sacrifices imposed on all the students and on the college and thereby causing educational deprivation?" Obviously the President of the college thought it did not. The emphasis in the announcement clearly was on the mounting costs of the football program. The equally emphatic conclusion was that those expenses far outweighed revenue. Indeed the President was careful to note that the alumni had been informed two years earlier that the sport was running in the red.

The response on the local sports pages and from sports fans was one of great disappointment but tempered with understanding of the reasons for the decision. The *Courier Express* called attention to the fact that Canisius had just won the Little Three Crown for the third consecutive year, something no institution had ever accomplished. Perhaps it was a bit poignant that the sport was dropped just as it had reached the pinnacle of success. But the morning newspaper did point out that the Canisius decision was similar to that taken by other institutions that shared similar characteristics. All were small, most were private and Catholic and some were Jesuit. Among those that dropped the sport about the same time as Canisius were Loyola University of Chicago, St. Joseph's of Philadelphia, Creighton, DePaul, St. Louis, Manhattan, Gonzaga, Providence, Steubenville, and Portland. They all dropped football for basically the same reason; they simply felt that they could not afford it anymore.

Billy Kelly, the *Courier*'s sports editor, also

had a column on February 8, in which he indicated that he regretted but understood the Canisius decision. He reiterated the factors that others did, and he also called attention to the horrible weather that had occurred at the time of the most recent Canisius - Bona game in Civic Stadium. Had that contest been played on a pleasant day, Kelly thought that the Stadium might have been sold out.

The *Buffalo Evening News* story that reported the Canisius decision added scheduling difficulties as a factor in the decision. In fact the *News* noted that U.B. and Canisius were on the verge of scheduling each other and hinted that that might have saved the program. Certainly a U.B. - Canisius football game would have drawn well. But it is a stretch to say that it would have saved the Canisius program and put it in the black. Cy Kritzer, the insightful scribe for the *News*, who had covered local college sports for two decades, offered the opinion that the success of Canisius in basketball, and the enthusiasm that the student body demonstrated for the round ball sport, may well have entered into the college's decision.

Most football fans had not yet recovered from the loss of the Buffalo Bills; still many of them were disappointed with the Canisius decision to drop football. Canisius students were stunned, and of course the football players were too. Indeed anger may have been the key word to describe most football players, and that anger stayed with them for years afterwards. Many alumni were upset with the decision and voiced their dissatisfaction. The *Buffalo Evening News* too reported that alumni officers were stunned by the suddenness of the administration's decision. On the other hand some alumni did indicate that they understood the reasons for the decision and a few alumni leaders voiced their support of the administration. Dropping a major college sport always invites some backlash. The college student newspaper, *The Griffin*, sought out answers with respect to the decision. It stated that "the alumni were not consulted" on the football issue. To this allegation, President Schouten responded that he had sought the advice of his, all Jesuit, Board of Consultors as well as the Jesuit Faculty.[55]

A number of factors entered into the decision of the college to drop football. No one would take issue with cost being the major factor. As soon as Canisius had reinstituted football following World War II, Coach Earl Brown called attention to the huge expenses required in order to outfit a squad of 75 young men. Travel expenses also were a factor, increasingly so. As scheduling became more difficult, travel expenses increased. Nor was the Canisius decision an isolated one made in some sort of vacuum. The Canisius type institution that had resumed football after the war found that it now, at the beginning of a new decade, was facing obstacles that had not been apparent or anticipated when the war ended. In effect, a chain reaction among similar types of private institutions was set off.

Costs, obviously, might be offset by revenue. The source of revenue for a college sports program came primarily from gate receipts. If thousands of tickets were sold for all home games, then revenue was significant. The balance sheet for Canisius football immediately after the war seemed fairly rosy. Fan turnout for most games and especially for Little Three contests was solid. Indeed that was true of attendance at small college football games generally. However, as the decade came to a close, attendance dipped. The total attendance at the Canisius home games in the final season was only 32,000. Well over half that figure, in fact, 22,000, of those were at the Bona game. Most games were broadcast over radio but the income from that source was slim. Even though games were shown on television and that included many of those played in Civic Stadium, TV revenue in those fledgling days of television was negligible.[56]

The declining number of war veterans in college as well as the rising costs of recruiting football players were also important considerations. They were directly linked in those years. The number of World War II veterans who comprised the majority of football players on many college teams just after the war had peaked by the end of the decade. On Canisius, as well as on the other local football teams, well over half of the participants on the squads were war veterans. In effect, those vets were on full scholarships. The fabulously successful G.I; Bill covered their college expenses. Most of them continued to play for three or four years. At the end of the decade, the great majority of those football playing students had graduated. The footballers mirrored the general student body. For example, the 1950 graduating class at Canisius had the largest number of graduates up to that time; a significant number of them were wartime veterans, some played football, some did not. 1950 was the peak year. All local institutions saw their student enrollment drop precipitously in the 1950s. With significantly smaller enrollments, the coaching staffs would have to expand their recruiting efforts to fill out the rosters on their football teams. Recruiting costs were already beginning to escalate.[57]

The other local institutions were affected by the Canisius bombshell. Niagara and Bona were especially so, since their annual Little Three showdown with the Golden Griffins was a sizeable part of their meal ticket. Each institution issued the expected statements regretting the Canisius decision and the loss of their old Little Three rival from their schedule.

When queried about Niagara's future, the President, Reverend Francis Meade, noted that Niagara University was in a different position than Canisius. Niagara had its own stadium and was supported by an on-campus student body. There was little doubt that those factors aided Niagara football in its efforts to cut costs and increase attendance. Was that enough to assure the continuation of football at Niagara? Meanwhile at St. Bonaventure, President, the Reverend Juvenal Lalor, indicated that his institution had no intention of dropping the sport. Bona had a large solid base of fans for home games in Olean. Bona would try to schedule some big name teams for Civic Stadium to cover the large guarantees that the gate receipts at Forness Stadium would not be able to cover. Scheduling was an especially important concern for St. Bona, but, in 1950, the school administrators felt it could be dealt with satisfactory.

At the University of Buffalo, Director of Athletics Jim Peele took a different slant. He indicated that student fees covered most of the costs of sports at the university. He said that he planned to look into the possibility of playing more games in Civic Stadium. If it appeared that U.B. could increase its attendance by scheduling big name opponents, he would pursue that. The *Buffalo Evening News* noted two weeks later that there were positive discussions between U.B. and Bona officials about scheduling a game in Buffalo. Both football programs were hopeful at the time, but eventually nothing materialized from these discussions.

Actually it appeared that St. Bonaventure University was doing some soul searching of its own. On February l, 1950 The President of St. Bonaventure University announced that he had accepted the resignation of Hugh Devore as the Head Football Coach, "with regret." Devore was devoted to St Bona and vice versa. He had done a great job at Bona; he raised the profile of the institution. So the announcement came as a surprise as well as a severe disappointment. There were stories that Devore was having some problems with interference from the athletic department. These were not substantiated. The truth appears to be that Devore had family concerns. He still had a home in New Jersey and he wanted employment closer to home. Nevertheless, it appears that for a brief period following Devore's departure, the coach's loss was hard to swallow for the ardent Bona fans. There were even some rumors that the school was seriously considering abandoning the sport.

The Bona faithful were reassured when Joe Bach was hired in March. Bach was hired on the advice of the Athletic Director Father Silas Rooney. Rooney was a member of the famous Rooney football family; he was a brother of Art Rooney the Pittsburgh Steeler owner. Joe Bach had been head coach of Pittsburgh in the 1930s. Bach also served with the professional New York Bulldogs as line coach. Bach was an All American tackle at Notre Dame and he coached at Niagara University before World War II. In 1950, he had his work cut out for him; he would have to literally rebuild Bona as some 25 members of the 1949 squad including the entire starting team, would be gone.

The University of Buffalo was also experiencing some difficulties in its athletic program. Athletic Director Jim Peele and Head Coach Frank Clair had strained relations. It appeared that Clair wanted more money for various things, and Peele was getting fed up. He accused Clair of using U.B. as a stepping stone. A published report said that Clair's record was not good enough. In his two years at the helm, he was "only" 12 – 4 – 1. The report also said that Clair was blamed for "friction" in the athletic department. Both Clair and Peele leveled charges against each other. The faculty committee on athletics in a split vote recommended that Clair be rehired, but the split vote necessitated that the recommendation be sent to the administration where it was turned down. Clair then left to take a position with the Canadian Football League, and by March, stories were circulating that Jimmy Wilson might be hired. His name had been mentioned in connection with the Bona job also. Former U.B. players who had played for Wilson when he coached at U.B. in the 1930s were behind a campaign to bring him back; Bob Rich, the captain of the 1933 team led the drive. Wilson met with the U.B. Faculty Committee on Athletics and was given a contract as the new Head Coach of the Bulls.[58]

The Canisius decision to drop football sent shivers through the Western New York football community. But Niagara University, the University of Buffalo, and St. Bonaventure University appeared determined to continue with their football programs. They vowed not only to continue but to take up the slack that had been left in Buffalo's football world. Nevertheless the halcyon days of football that followed the end of World War II appeared to be over by 1950. The Buffalo Bills were gone, so were the Canisius College Golden Griffins. The remaining local teams were, already in 1950, experiencing some major difficulties.

Even as they recruited new players and filled out game schedules for the fall season of 1950, costs continued to increase. Recruiting was becoming expensive. The pool of World War II veterans who attended college on the G.I.Bill was fast diminishing. Meanwhile another war had broken out. Manpower for sports teams again became a concern. The Korean War broke out in June of 1950 and by the end of the year, young men of college age were being drafted into the armed forces. Institutions of similar size to those in Western New York continued to eliminate their football programs. Scheduling was, thus, being made increasingly difficult. To make matters worse, the big time college football games were flooding television every weekend. Rabid football fans preferred to watch a Southern California - Notre Dame game, on a Saturday afternoon, rather than venture to Civic Stadium to watch a local contest. As the 1950s wore on, crowds at small college football contests were no longer really crowds.

Nevertheless with the 1950 college football season about to open, the Western New York teams went about their business as usual. They had complete schedules and reasonably full rosters. Bona's new coach, Joe Bach, was optimistic for the fall season despite having a very competitive nine game schedule and despite losing all but two of his regulars. Kritzer had great praise for the high powered offense, but noted that the defense might not be as good as in past. Bona would be led by Jerry Hanifin, a gifted open field runner, and by Ted Marchibroda, a 19-year-old sophomore sensation from Franklin, Pa. Marchibroda was destined to become one of the great passing quarterbacks in Eastern College football. In 1950 he led the East in forward passing yardage and in total offense.[59]

Coach Jimmy Wilson, at the University of Buffalo also was cautiously optimistic. He had lost plenty of stars but he was hopeful that his solid crop of returnees could fill the void. He had dependable quarterbacks in Tracy LaTona, and backup Don Holland, and some excellent linemen in Ed Gicewicz, Carl Markey, and Matty Ferrentino. He also had hoped that Les Molnar would be back, but the hefty tackle had entered the Marines by the time the fall season rolled around. Niagara had endured some rough times in the 1940s but the 1950 season looked more promising. Coach Miller was particularly pleased with the maturing of quarterback John Theobold. Miller also figured that he could count on the running ability of John McCoy, and he had some solid linemen in center Dick McCarthy, and tackle Paul Miller

One of the big games locally in 1950 would feature Niagara against U.B. in Civic Stadium. The game took place Saturday night, October 7. It was a perfect time and setting for a major event. The game was sponsored by the *Courier Express* and WEBR and promoted by the *Courier*'s Goodfellows' fund. The citizenry seemed to be going all-out to prove that Buffalo was still a major football city. Just about all of the area's business executives were involved. Wade Stevenson, chair of the Goodfellows, predicted a complete sellout. Well known sportsman, Eddie Atwell, in his capacity as ticket chairman, regularly furnished optimistic reports on ticket sales. Individuals and businessmen were asked to buy packets of 200 tickets. Additional ticket outlets were opened, including two in Niagara Falls. Business leaders looked for a record turnout in what was being billed as the "Best Street Bowl." A special dinner at the Buffalo Club preceded the game. A "Who's Who in Buffalo" attended. Buffalo's most popular men's store, Kleinhans, conducted a popularity contest in connection with the game. Mayor Joseph Mruk weighed in, saying that the game is a "test for Buffalo."He noted that big time football people would be paying attention to Buffalo's premier game of the season. Both institutions also arranged for a number of special promotions.

The game itself was well played. Niagara won, 27 to 13, primarily on the passing arm of Johnny Theobold. The game drew 24,217. That was a respectable crowd but still some 10,000 short of expectations. Weather was not a factor.

A month later the other big game of the season was held, again, in Civic Stadium. This time, it was the Little Three, now the Little Two, St. Bona played Niagara. The awesome offense of the Brown Indians, led by Ted Marchibroda's passing, and Jerry Hanifin's running, accounted for the 41 – 20 beheading of the Purple Eagles. The game had been hyped extensively in the local press. Various promotions were staged. The Buffalo Chamber of Commerce stepped into the picture to promote the contest. The Chamber was an old hand at this, having sponsored earlier games, including the very first one played in Civic Stadium between Tulane and Colgate in 1937. Admonitions were issued to the public to get out and support local football. Sports Editor Billy Kelly in his column in the *Courier* stressed that not only did the "fate of…area wide collegiate football in this city, but a vast potential of intersectional contests" depended on a very large turnout. He added that "convincing numbers" must attend if good local college football was to continue. Unfortunately only 13,195 showed up.[60]

Overall the three Western New York institutions that had continued football fared well in the 1950 season. Though not quite as impressive as the previous few years, the University of Buffalo posted a winning season at 5 – 3. Bona did better, winning 7 and losing only to Xavier and Duquesne. Niagara actually had a rebirth of sorts, winning 6 games and suffering 3 losses. Local fans also relished the heroics of the outstanding football player on the local scene, Ted Marchibroda, Bona's sophomore sensational quarterback. He entered the record books as the all time passer for the Eastern Collegiate Football Association. Incidentally many sports observers thought that the Eastern Association carried more prestige than the NCAA at that time.

However, despite promotional efforts, attendance was not as good has had been hoped. The *Buffalo Evening News* in its annual end of the year summary of the local news highlights of the year called attention to the disappointing support for football. In fact, other than college basketball and professional wrestling, most all other sports suffered a drop off in attendance.[61]

Two months later, Niagara University announced that it was dropping varsity football.

On March 6, 1951 The *Buffalo Evening News* published the official announcement issued by the President of the University, Reverend Francis Meade. It was not a complete shock. Some observers had surmised that something might be in the works, since two weeks earlier Head Football Coach, Jim Miller, had resigned and offered no reason.

In issuing the statement Father Meade indicated that Niagara "hoped to resume once the present emergency is over." The emergency referred to by Niagara's president was, of course, the Korean War. Conscription was the law of the land again, and several promising underclassmen were lost to the draft.

The Korean War had started in June 1950 and within a few months it was apparent that a quick end was not in sight. Once the Chinese entered the conflict near the end of 1950, the United States had to increase its manpower commitments tremendously. Hundreds of thousands of young men of college age were once again called up to serve Uncle Sam. The colleges felt this manpower pinch. Enrollment at colleges dropped off. Fewer young men were available for football teams.

Less than a year later, and in fact, exactly two years after the Canisius announcement that it had eliminated football, Bona followed suit."St. Bonaventure chose the hour of its zenith in the college basketball firmament to announce the decision to "suspend" varsity football because of financial losses and the national emergency."[62]

The President, Fr. Juvenal Lalor, estimated the college had lost $300,000 since WW II. In today's terms, that would be in the millions. It was also obvious that with Niagara and Canisius no longer playing football, Bona's revenue and its scheduling ability were adversely affected. The Bona president pointed to the 20,000 attendance figure in the 1951 season which was the low point for attendance in the post war era for the four games on the home field at Forness Stadium, and a disappointing 9000 in Buffalo for the Quantico Marines game. These were major reasons for the suspension. When queried about the rising interest in basketball, the President replied that the college would be able to concentrate on basketball as its major sport. Bona's 1951 football season was successful, but the 5 – 4 record was not nearly as impressive as its record in the previous seasons in the postwar era. Bona had to struggle to complete its schedule. Though it played 9 games, two of those, tellingly, were against the service teams from the Quantico Marine Base and Camp LeJeune.[63]

As the decade of the 1950s proceeded, major changes took place in college football. Smaller institutions simply could no longer compete on a par with the big boys and therefore had to accept the elimination of the sport or adjust to play at a "lesser" level with a scaled down schedule. The major institutions did experience some financial problems at the very beginning of the decade when television, still in is infancy, was not controlled and college football games were shown almost continuously each weekend. But once the NCAA, under the guidance of its first full time executive director Walter Byers, realized it could operate as a cartel, similar to baseball, then television was controlled and the cash began to roll in. Tens of thousands of fans filed into the huge college stadiums each Saturday afternoon, and the athletic departments waited eagerly for the thousands of dollars that would come their way courtesy of television contracts. Western New York college football did not share in the gold rush. During the 1950s, major college football flourished along with Major League baseball. Those two sports dominated the American sports scene. Major College football continued to outdraw professional football. In fact it was simply no contest.

The University of Buffalo stayed the course in the 50s, though at a lesser level. The Bulls had scheduling difficulties just as their local counterparts had had. They played what was called a college as contrasted with a university schedule; there was no divisional structure at that time. Large sums of money were not poured into the Bulls' program. U.B. suffered through some rough seasons in the mid fifties, then in 1958 had a terrific season and earned the Lambert Trophy symbolic of small college superiority in the East. The U.B. program had some ups and downs in the 1960s; the sport was dropped in 1970. Meanwhile Canisius, Niagara, and St. Bona had begun club football teams, and when the NCAA formalized the division structure in the 1970s, Canisius and U.B. entered football teams in Division III. Buffalo State also established a Division III team. Each of those Division III institutions experienced some successful football seasons in their comparatively brief histories. By the end of the century the U.B. authorities saw fit to elevate the U.B. football program to the highest level, Division I A, in the NCAA.

But there was never again a period like the one immediately following World War II. The 1946–50 era witnessed successful college football teams playing an important part of the Western New York sports scene. Nothing like it had occurred since that time. Those were truly golden years.

CHAPTER FIVE

College Basketball in the Aud

— Second only to Madison Square Garden —

Courier-Express

Record 12,053 Crowd Sees Canisius Tip Niagara, 49-47

MacKinnon Produces Key Baskets; Griffs Overcome 9-Point Deficit

Buffalo Courier Express, January 19, 1950

MacKinnon scores, surrounded by Niagara's Johnston (26), Moran (21), Birch (11), and Smyth (27). That one Last point! *Photo: Mott, Game Program.*

Leroy Chollet, Zeke Sinicola, Hank O'Keefe, Taps Gallagher, The Nilands, Ken Murray, Jack Chalmers, Len Serfustini, Eddie Milkovitch, aka Melvin, Hube Coyer. Those are some of the legendary figures, names that still evoke the glory of the golden years, of sold out basketball doubleheaders, of local teams defeating some of the very best college basketball teams from every corner of the nation.

College basketball became big time in post World War II America and especially so in Buffalo. Indeed it became unbelievably successful. In point of fact Buffalo was second only to New York City as a mecca for spectators eager to watch top ranked collegiate teams. More than anything else what enabled Buffalo to achieve such lofty heights in basketball was pure and simple, the Aud. The downtown arena, officially Memorial Auditorium and popularly known as the Aud, was a wonderful showplace, one of the best in the nation in the 1940s. It was considered state of the art. It had been built at the end of the previous decade, a gift of the Works Progress Administration, the WPA, of the New Deal. The massive doors of the Lower Main Street arena opened just as the first shots of World War II were fired.

Cy Kritzer of the *Buffalo Evening News*, who covered college basketball for many decades, affectionately referred to the Aud in its early years as the "Pretty Lady of Lower Main Street." It acquired a number of nicknames, attesting to its special place in the community. Sometimes it was referred to as "The Glamour Girl of Lower Main," and years later "The Old Gray Lady of Main Street." The Aud was a godsend to college basketball, especially to Canisius College. Without the Aud, Canisius College would have been simply another one of a number of small colleges playing an increasingly popular sport with a modicum of success. To a lesser degree that was also true of Niagara University, St. Bonaventure University, and the University of Buffalo. Canisius was the key to the Aud because it was the host team; it was the institution responsible for arranging the Aud's most prominent feature, the doubleheader basketball program. It was also centrally located, smack in the middle of Buffalo. Niagara University, after Canisius, was the most frequent participant in the Aud program.

All the Western New York colleges had been playing the sport of basketball since the early years of the 20th century. It was only a short time before, in 1891, that the sport was invented by Canadian James Naismith. He had been teaching at Springfield College in New England and he was challenged to provide an indoor game for the youth in that area of the country during the long months of inclement weather. With a round ball in his possession, and a conveniently available peach basket that he promptly affixed to a pole, he invented the game of basketball. The sport very quickly became popular. Western New York, with its fair share of inclement winter weather, enthusiastically embraced the game. Canisius established its first team in 1903, Niagara did so two years later, and U.B. did so in 1915. St. Bona followed with its first basketball quintet four years after U.B. did. Buffalo State Teachers College, for many years popularly called State Teachers, established a team a few years after that.

By the 1920s, a period of great expansion for spectator sports in the United States, the various college quintets in Western New York were upgrading the caliber of their competition, and playing as many as 15 games each season. The Great Depression of the 1930s caused major economic problems throughout the country, but still the local colleges continued to field competitive teams. Canisius, Niagara, and Bona began to play each other on a fairly regular basis, entitling themselves to be members of a mythical conference, that soon came to be known as the Little Three.

Most games were played in the on-campus gymnasiums of the respective institutions. However Canisius in the 1930s, had begun to play a number of games each season, against opponents of national stature, in the Broadway Auditorium, a large barn-like structure on the fringe of downtown Buffalo. In fact on February 4, 1936 Dr. James Crowdle, the Graduate Manager of Athletics at Canisius College, staged the first college doubleheader program in the Broadway Auditorium. It featured a St. Bona victory over Niagara (37 - 23) and a Canisius victory over Georgetown (43 - 36). Unfortunately, poor weather, including gale force winds clocked at 70 miles per hour, prevented much of a turnout for the event. Attendance in the Broadway arena averaged about 4,000 fans for most contests; it was much larger when Notre Dame, Stanford, and Nebraska came to play. The auditorium, located on Broadway near Michigan Avenue, hosted a number of athletic events in the 1930s, especially in the years immediately before the Memorial Auditorium was constructed. Most famously were the six day bike races, a fad of the decade. They regularly drew several thousand spectators to the Broadway edifice.

Dr. James Crowdle came to Canisius College in 1919 as a chemistry professor. Shortly thereafter, and completely by accident he became involved in intercollegiate athletics. The college needed someone to do the scheduling of intercollegiate athletic competition and the job fell to Crowdle, ever after known as Doc. In the 1920s he scheduled basketball and football games and in 1930 he arranged the first Canisius-Niagara basketball game. He became known as the father of the Little Three, the informal arrangement that involved St. Bonaventure as well as Canisius and Niagara in athletic competition. In the 1930s, he scheduled football games at the Villa field, located directly behind the Old Main building of Canisius College on Main Street. He scheduled basketball games at St. John Kanty Auditorium and at the Elmwood Music Hall, as well as at the Villa and eventually in the Broadway Auditorium. The construction of Memorial Auditorium signaled a new direction for Doc Crowdle and college basketball in Western New York.

Doc Crowdle , Director of Aud doubleheader basketball program.
Photo: Game program - Canisius College Archives

Meanwhile in New York City, Ned Irish, a local sportswriter, originated a doubleheader basketball program in Madison Square Garden, at the promptings of the usually debonair, sometimes crooked, but always colorful, Mayor of New York, Jimmy Walker. The proceeds were to help the economically depressed kids of the big city. The crowds were phenomenal. Ned Irish emerged as the chief mogul of the Garden during the 1930s. When Memorial Auditorium opened in 1940, Irish saw a golden opportunity to expand his basketball empire.

At that time in American history, as any Buffalo schoolboy might recall from grade school social studies class, Buffalo was a major railroad center in the United States, second only to Chicago. The day of air transportation was just beginning, athletic teams did not yet travel by air, or, if they did it was only in exceptional circumstances. Trains were the travel mode of choice and numerous trains of several major railroads passed through Buffalo each day. First and foremost was The New York Central, but there were also the Lehigh Valley, the D.L. and

W., the Erie, and the Nickel Plate. Hundreds of trains came into Buffalo each week from Chicago and other points in the West and then continued on to New York City, less that a day's journey, and to other large cites along the Eastern seaboard. Irish saw the potential of Buffalo with its first class railroad connections and its brand new 12,000 seat arena.

Ned Irish traveled to Buffalo to work out arrangements with Doc Crowdle, and thus the Aud Doubleheader Program was born. Crowdle bore the title of Graduate Manager of Athletics; he ran the Aud program; he took personal charge of scheduling. The Reverend Timothy Dineen, Director of Athletics, handled other athletic matters. Crowdle and Irish worked in tandem for more than a decade. They began the scheduling of major teams from the West and Southwest to play in Buffalo, and then a second game in New York City, and sometimes a third game, on their Eastern Swing, in Philadelphia. This made economic sense, and it also gave great exposure to the big time state institutions coming from the Midwest and beyond. A team from California or Wyoming could plan a road trip to the East and the expense could be justified in the athletic department budget. A potential All American could now get exposure before the famous New York City Press, and his team could fill out its schedule by adding games in Buffalo and Philadelphia.

Adding to the luster of Eastern exposure was the opportunity to play before members of the National Invitation Tournament committee. The NIT had just been founded in 1938. In its early years and at least until the early 1950s, it was the premier post season basketball tournament in the country. The NCAA held it first championship basketball tournament in 1939 but it would be a number of years before it began to attract large followings.

In 1940, the very first doubleheader was held in Memorial Auditorium. It featured Buffalo State against Wake Forest, and Canisius against the City College of New York, CCNY. The State players were up for the history making debut of the Aud; they fought valiantly in a losing effort. The newspaper headlines put it best: Wake "nips plucky State," 42 - 39. In the second game the Griffs were ahead throughout most of the contest but lost a cliffhanger to CCNY, 43 - 42. 4,228 fans had a delicious taste of things to come, of the exciting doubleheader evenings that lay ahead.

More doubleheaders were scheduled but the promising beginnings of big time basketball fizzled and the program had to be put on the backburner because of the outbreak of the Second World War. Because that war meant total war, the Aud's development as a top notch sports arena, had to mark time while that global conflict was being resolved. The great days for the Aud's fabulous doubleheader program would have to wait until World War II was over.

During the war, colleges shrank in size. College students, including many athletes, lined up at recruiting stations in unbelievable numbers. Some athletic teams, especially football, were suspended for the "duration of the conflict." There was no choice; there were not enough athletes. Other teams, that had lesser manpower requirements, such as basketball, were continued at some institutions, but played an abbreviated schedule. In fact several of the opponents of the local college athletic teams in these war years would be teams from military installations such as Fort Niagara, or the Sampson Naval Base.

Coaches too had their careers directly affected by the war. John "Taps" Gallagher, already on his way to becoming a legend at Niagara University, was called to serve in 1943. Gallagher had been coaching at N.U. since 1931. Niagara suspended its program in 1943 then Ed "Bus" Flynn took over the coaching chores for the following two seasons, playing a 13 game schedule with a 7 – 6 record in 1944-45 and a 19 game slate the following year with an 11 - 8 record. Bona's legendary Mike Reilly who had started coaching at Bona in 1928 left in 1943. Bona suspended its program in 1943-44; it started up again the following season with Fr. Anselm Krieger at the helm. Bona played just ten games in 1944-45, going 3 - 7, and then improved to 12 - 3 in 1945-46. The University of Buffalo had been coached by Art Powell ever since the basketball program's inception in 1915. Powell coached until 1943 and then Buffalo suspended its program for the '43-'44 and '44-'45 seasons. Buffalo State dropped its program in 1942 and did not start up again until 1945-46.

Canisius continued its basketball program as best it could during the war years. Several of its key players were in the military. Coach Allie Seelbach who had come to the Golden Dome in 1933 continued with a schedule that included several service teams. His 1943-44 squad was good enough to earn a berth in the NIT. Unfortunately this outstanding coach met an early death from cancer a short time later. Canisius then hired Art Powell, ex-U.B. mentor, who proceeded to coach the Griffs in 1944-45 and 1945-46.[1]

World War II came to a close in August of 1945. The troops started to return from overseas in large numbers but still many servicemen had to remain in the military for several more months, and some for more than a year. Athletics Directors planning for the 1945-46 basketball season had to confront some vexing questions. When would the former coach be mustered out? Which former players would return to college, and when would they be available to participate in basketball? Would it be possible to field a competitive team in 1945-46 or should plans be made for the following year? Which opponents would be ready to compete and when? Could a reasonably full schedule be arranged?

Plans went ahead and local teams in Western New York began to organize. Several coaches were still serving on an interim basis. Bus Flynn continued at Niagara, Art Powell stayed on for another year at Canisius, Fr. Anselm did the same at Bona, and U.B. was coached for one year by Robert Harrington, who had been captain of the Bulls back in 1930. Several of the athletes who had played before entering the military service, returned shortly after the war and were ready to take up where they had left off. Others would not be mustered out of the service until many months later, the exact time uncertain. Schedules were developed and were somewhat similar to prewar years though there were some gaps.

Despite the uncertainties, the1945-46 college basketball season in Western New York began rather smoothly. It proved to be a sign of good things to come. Ray Ryan, who would continue to cover college basketball for many decades for the *Courier Express*, wrote in November that the most ambitious schedule ever, awaited Western New York basketball fans. Canisius was anxious to take advantage of its role as primary participant in the Aud doubleheader program. Canisius was slated to host a number of big time teams and the Buffalo community eagerly awaited the return of a full schedule of games in the downtown arena. The Junior Chamber of Commerce announced that it would help to promote the Christmas holiday doubleheaders in the Aud. It was becoming clear that a new era was dawning for college basketball in Buffalo.[2]

Canisius got untracked more quickly than the other WNY institutions. The college received a boost with the return of Tommy Niland. Niland had played in 1942 then left to join the Army Airborne troops. He parachuted over Normandy, and his battalion fought its way across France and then at the Battle of the Bulge, he was wounded. Niland received several military commendations including the Purple Heart. Just one year after he had led troops against the German juggernaut at Bastogne, he was ready, even with his paralyzed arm that was the result of a battlefield wound, to lead the Griffs into action in the Aud. Niland was named team captain. He was far from being the only war veteran or the only hero. In fact the *Buffalo Evening News* published a photograph of five players that presumably might start for the season, and headlined it: "ALL VETERAN, ALL VETERAN TEAM AT CANISIUS." Bill Melvin, Jim Mauro, Joe Trimboli, and Joe Nasal, were pictured with Niland. The quintet had been awarded several pounds worth of military medals, including battle citations and purple hearts. Not only were they war veterans but they were veterans by virtue of having played for Canisius prior to their military service. Other Western New York institutions also had a heavy enrollment of war veterans.[3]

Tom Niland and Bill Melvin: Top Canisius stars immediately after the war. *Photo: Game Program – Canisius College Archives.*

The Memorial Auditorium program for college basketball in the first year after the end of the war usually featured Canisius College. Canisius played eleven of its home games in the Aud, and Niagara played four. The other local teams did not play any in downtown Buffalo in this initial season of renewal.

The 1945-46 Aud doubleheader program opened with the Griffs losing to Cornell, the class of the Ivy League. The game was played before a record opening night crowd of 8,563, a harbinger of things to come. Many of the local fans expected a win; they were pumped up after the Griffs' surprisingly easy victory over Oswego, 71 - 22 the previous week. Tommy Niland, who would be the mainstay of the Griffs for the next two years, did not disappoint. Ray Ryan was very impressed with Niland's hard work. Ryan also had some praise for Bill Rudick's good set shot, wryly commenting that Rudick was only recently discharged after serving 2 1/2 years in the submarine service "where he had little opportunity to practice basketball in a submarine." However Coach Art Powell looked to Jim Mauro, Bill Melvin, and Joe Trimboli for scoring punch but all three had a horrible shooting night. Combined they made just one in twenty nine attempts. With 6'10" Buffalo native, Ed Peterson at the center position doing a great job for Cornell, and with the Griffs' inability to find the basket, it was a relatively easy win for the Big Red. Cornell coasted to a 77 – 51 victory. In the other game Oklahoma A & M defeated Westminster.

A week later, only 2,518 hardy fans braved the severe winter weather to watch the Utes from the University of Utah defeat the Griffs,

50 - 39. Joe Nasal hit double figures on the strength of his "push shot." Niland's great all around play continued, and Don Hartnett, a frosh just out of St Joe's Collegiate, was impressive off the bench as he bagged 5 quick points. However Utah was simply bigger and better. A short time later, at the end of December, 6,526 fans got their money's worth as they watched Canisius lose a cliffhanger, 35 - 34 to Colorado, a game marked by a wild finish. The Griffs' Jake Cwick, made a shot at the buzzer that would have taken them to overtime. But the official disallowed it asserting that he had called a foul before the ball left Cwick's hand. The foul shot was made and the Griffs lost by a point. Obviously the Colorado players could not complain that the game was a "home job" for the Griffs.

Calendar year 1946 opened with Canisius fans witnessing the continued development of two Canisius stars, Bill "Bumps" Melvin, the first Black basketball player to play for the Griffs, and Frosh Don Hartnett. Tom Niland played his usual consistent game. Despite their excellent showing, the Griffs could not stop the much taller Brigham Young team. The inability of the home team to handle the height of the visitors would be an oft told tale in years to come. Melvin tossed in 21 points, and Harnett played with tremendous hustle, but the Griffs went down 62 – 52. A week later the Griffs got on the winning side of the ledger by whipping Scranton before 3,263 with Niland again leading the way with help from Rudick. The two Griffin backcourt men were mainly responsible for limiting the Scranton team to 31 points while the Griffs collected 51.

The New Year also witnessed the return of Niagara University to the Aud after a three year war-time absence. The Purple Eagles produced a team not dissimilar to the Griffs, in terms of war vets and basketball vets. Fred Schwab, a star on the 1942-43 squad, returned from military service to lead the Purple Eagles. Schwab was a former POW; he felt very fortunate to be alive. His outfit of 40 soldiers was ambushed by the Germans in Italy, 30 were killed, Schwab was wounded and taken prisoner. Now the 6'5" star was back home in a civilian uniform.

Eddie Keim also was back in a purple uniform; he would prove to be a remarkable guard with great passing and ball handling ability. He had, like Niland, been in a paratrooper unit and been involved in several battles, but suffered no major injuries. Then, ironically, on his way home to be discharged, he suffered a severe arm injury playing basketball. There was the possibility he might even lose the arm. Fortunately he pulled through the operation satisfactorily. He would proceed to become a Hall of Fame basketball player at Niagara.

The Purple Eagles met their traditional rival, St. John's University from New York City on January 19. The Redmen were coached by a genuine legend, Joe Lapchick, the star center of the Original Celtics in the 1920s and early '30s. Lapchick had been at St. John's as coach since 1936. The game was a rude awakening for the Eagles. They suffered an embarrassing loss by an 80 – 37 score. Seldom would they ever again lose a game by such a large margin. In the second game, the Griffs lost but fared a bit better, losing by just six points, 51 - 45 to the New York University squad coached by another well known mentor, Howard Cann, in his 23rd season at NYU. The Violets, at 10 – 1 in the current season and rated in the top ten nationally, were heavily favored over the Griffs. They were led by their "big guy," 6'5" Dolph Schayes. The eight sports reporters from the New York City press, who took the train to Buffalo, were a testament to the importance attached to college basketball in the nation's metropolis back then.

Meanwhile, Hube Coyer, recently discharged as a Major in the U.S. Army, returned to

coach Buffalo State again. State had not had a team since 1942 but now made a solid re-appearance with Coyer at the helm. The big news in the early season was State's lopsided victory over cross town rival, U.B., 47 - 31. A sell out crowd packed the Elmwood campus court; so many were crammed into State's gym that U.B.'s Athletic Director Jim Peele, who came late, could not squeeze in. At the end of the season, U.B. hosted the return game. Before the largest crowd, 1,500, ever to see a basketball game in Clark Gym, the Bulls defeated Buffalo State 54 – 44. Jake Schaefer led State with 21 points but Lou Vastola, State's star, was held to just nine.

The highlight of this first postwar season in the Aud, was the Notre Dame – Canisius game. It was always a red letter day when the Fighting Irish came to town; February 7, 1946 was no exception. Throughout the first half the Griffs played even with the Irish and were behind by only one point at the intermission. Led by All American Vince Boryla, the Irish stormed back and easily dispatched the Griffins, 69-47. But the big story was the record turnout. 10,038 attended. A bonus was that the Notre Dame staff showered praise on the Aud, on the facility and on its operation, an indication that the Fighting Irish would be willing to return. George Ratterman managed to score 7 points, that same George Ratterman who shortly would emerge as a huge star for the Buffalo Bills of professional football.

The Golden Griffins finally won a big one. It was called "a major upset," when they nosed out Syracuse 43 – 41. Tom Niland, and teammate, Jim Quinlan, an ex-Marine who had served on Iwo Jima, and like Niland a Purple Heart recipient, did a superb job of holding the #3 team in the nation to just 41 points. At the beginning of the second half, the Orangemen went scoreless for nearly ten minutes. Unfortunately only 4,035 fans were on hand to witness this great feat. The Syracuse team did not take kindly to this humiliation; in the final game of the season played in the Salt City, revenge easily could be gleaned in the 62 - 32 defeat the Griffs suffered.

After a close loss to Long Island University in Madison Square Garden, the Griffs, back on their home court, quickly rebounded under the marksmanship of Joe Trimboli. Joe was "hotter than a $2.00 pistol" as his 18-point first half spearheaded the Griffs to victory over CCNY, one of the nation's top teams, 53 - 40. Only 3,780 fans showed up, an indication that in this early going just after the war, those much talked about "every Saturday night sellouts" that alumni reminisced about years later, simply did not occur, at least not every Saturday night. In the final doubleheader of the first postwar season, 5,06l fans saw Niagara beat Toronto, 67 – 58 and Baylor knock off the Griffs, 59 - 47. Baylor with its 25 - 2 record showed why it was a top ten team. Canisius could be proud however that it did not back down when the Southern school threatened to raise an issue about the Griffs using Bill Melvin, who happened to be a black athlete.

Cy Kritzer of the *Buffalo Evening News* wrote a season ending summary. Kritzer reminded his readers that Canisius had kept alive the doubleheader program during the war; he noted that even though the Griffs had lost several games to major powers during the just completed season, they were paving the way for bigger and better competition in the future. At face value, the record of 8 – 11 did not appear very impressive. However, the Dunkel rating noted that Canisius had the toughest schedule in the East. Two opponents, Syracuse and West Virginia were in the NIT and three others, Colorado, Baylor and New York University, were in the NCAA. The Griffs lost to Cornell, Utah, Brigham Young, West Virginia, Notre Dame and Baylor usually by 10 points or less. They lost close ones to Colorado, to NYU, and to LIU and split with Syracuse and among their other victims was the highly regarded CCNY team. The record was not spectacular, but the effort could not be questioned.

The war, having been only recently concluded, had an effect on the schedule makers. Both Bona and U.B. played weak schedules in '45-'46; Niagara's was somewhat stronger. The Purple Eagles played most of their games in St. Vincent's gym, their on-campus facility, but they did play four games in the Aud. Canisius played most of their games in the Aud and thus was able to schedule major competition. Bona compiled a 12 - 3 record, losing only to Alfred, Gannon and Niagara. Its wins were over smaller institutions from Central and Western New York. The University of Buffalo's 5 - 10 record was compiled against similar opponents. Niagara's 11 - 8 record included losses to Cornell, Syracuse, and St. John's. It split with Bona and its victories were over various New York State institutions. Canisius, perhaps surprisingly, did not play any of the other local institutions that season.

The Memorial Auditorium college basketball doubleheader program was off to a pretty good start. It was successful enough so as to prevent the professional basketball circuit from establishing a team on a permanent basis in Buffalo. A professional team, the Buffalo Bisons, made an attempt to establish itself in Buffalo in late 1945 but before the calendar year was over it had packed its bags and left for the Tri City area in the Midwest. Its presence had caused a bit of a stir. Ned Irish, the impresario of Madison Square Garden who, with Doc Crowdle, was responsible for the college program's viability in Buffalo, was opposed to the pros playing in the Aud during the college season. He felt, apparently with good reason, that the city could not support both college and professional basketball. Since the pros relocated before the end of 1945, the issue was resolved for the time being, only later to recur during the Buffalo Braves presence in the NBA in the early 1970s.

One more issue remained to be resolved. It was understood that it was only a matter of time before Canisius would hire a new coach to replace the elderly Art Powell. After the war, as things began to get back to normal, Doc Crowdle, began to send out some feelers to find out who might be available; hopefully he could land a big timer, someone who could handle both the head football and basketball chores. It was not uncommon back in that era for the same person to handle more than one coaching position. The age of specialization was coming but had not yet arrived in full force.

In 1945, Doc Crowdle learned about the availability of Earl Brown from his friend in New York, Ned Irish. Brown then was a Commander in the Navy and he also served as Head Coach at the Merchant Marine Academy. Brown had impressive credentials. He had been a splendid athlete at Notre Dame in the 1930s where he had been an All American end on the football team. He also was the captain of one of Notre Dame's best basketball teams, and played against Canisius twice in the Broadway Auditorium. Subsequently he had coached at Harvard; then as head coach at Dartmouth he guided the New Hampshire institution to championships in football and basketball. Just before being called into the military service, he was head coach at Brown University. During the 1945-46 season, Ray Ryan of the *Courier Express*, broke the story that Brown would be coming to Buffalo. Like Kritzer at the *News*, Ryan covered college sports for the *Courier*, especially college basketball, for nearly half a century. Ryan was also a close friend of Doc Crowdle's. Ryan reported that Earl Brown came to Buffalo to meet with Crowdle; he liked what he saw, especially Civic Stadium and Memorial Auditorium "two of the nation's finest athletic plants." On February 28, 1946 Brown signed on to coach both football and basketball at Canisius College.[4]

The 1945-46 basketball season ended in March; the basketballs were put in storage to remain there losing a little air and collecting a lot of dust during the following months. There were some summer basketball programs in the 1940s, but hardly like the deluge in future years. Most basketball players engaged in other sports during the summer. Not much would be heard from the college athletic offices until the fall semester rolled around. The equipment room was locked up tight. Some avid Buffalo sports fans turned to watch the hockey season wind down; others were reading reports coming out of the South about the Bison Baseball team at its spring training camp.

Meanwhile the World War II veterans were returning to civilian life and enrolling in colleges in record numbers. The local teams already had shown that the war veterans would play a major role in college basketball. The G.I. Bill, one of the most far-reaching pieces of legislation ever enacted into law in the United States, was proving to be fantastically successful. Student enrollment climbed to new records in area colleges. In 1945, there were 856 students enrolled at Canisius College, in 1946 there were 2,184. At Niagara University in 1945 there were 673 and in 1946 there were 1,336, of which 1,071 were veterans. With so many new students, bigger crowds were predicted at games in the forthcoming season.[5]

When the 1946 fall semester began, interest in college sports picked up. The annual pre-season reports that appeared in the local newspapers forecast excellent basketball teams for both Canisius and Niagara. The other area colleges were also predicted to have better than average squads. More talent, but also better coaches and a higher grade of schedules were the order of the day.

Coach Earl Brown, in his rookie season at Canisius, had a splendid supporting cast. Hank O'Keefe and Leroy Chollet, both whom had made the *Sporting News* All Americans teams when, during the war, they were service cadets at RPI and Loyola respectably, would provide the offensive punch for the Griffs. O'Keefe had already had experience with the Griffs as a member of the 1942 team. Tom Niland and Mort O'Sullivan could be expected to excel on defense. They would be joined by Bob MacKinnon, widely acknowledged to be the best basketball player to come out of a Buffalo High School in a decade. With such highly regarded personnel, some said that Canisius would be the best college team in the entire state of New York.

Taps Gallagher, Head Basketball Coach at Niagara University. *Photo: Pat Smyton.*

Niagara's success would depend to a great extent on Fred Schwab's condition. He had suffered frozen feet while a German POW and was having some difficulty getting back in shape. Harry Foley would be back in the lineup too, and would be joined by Paul Yesawich, Eddie Keim, Bill Holroyd, and Lloyd Paterson, all future Hall of Famers at the Monteagle Ridge institution. Keim, Yesawich and Holroydhad all played at Niagara before they entered the military. The biggest boost for the Eagles was the return of the highly regarded John "Taps" Gallagher. Former Navy Commander Gallagher was once again Coach Gallagher. The student newspaper, The *Niagara Index*, noted that he was "one of the greatest contributors to the success of Little Three basketball" and that "his stirring duels" with Mike Reilly of St. Bonaventure and Allie Seelbach of Canisius "laid the foundations for the great appeal of the Little Three." A bonus was that Taps, a St. John's University graduate with New York City connections; would be of great help in bringing downstate teams to the Aud.[6]

The University of Buffalo hired Mal Eiken, a former star at the University of Minnesota, to be its new coach. Eiken would introduce a rough, contact style of play that he had experienced in the Midwest. He looked forward to a large turnout that would include many war vets and a number of U.B. football players. Lou Corriere, the star running back for the Bulls' football team, was also an excellent basketball player. "Lockport Lou" would be joined by Frank Nappo, Bob Eldridge, and Benny Constantino as well as Len Serfustini, aka "Surf," who would one day become a legendary coach at his alma mater. At 6'1", "Surf" was the tallest regular reporting for tryouts in the fall of '46. The Bulls upgraded their schedule which now included four Aud dates.

St. Bonaventure University named Harry Singleton as its new coach. He replaced Fr. Anselm who returned to other duties including recruiting. Fr. Anselm had vowed to improve the basketball team and he did so. He had some familiarity with the New Jersey area. Football coach, Huge Devore was from West Orange, New Jersey. Fr. Anselm's prize find in that area was Ken Murray. Another fine recruit, Frank Ready was also from the Garden State. Murray said that he had no idea where St. Bonaventure was located. He recalls that when he took his initial trip from New Jersey to Olean, he arrived on board the Erie Railroad at 3:00 AM. He found himself alone in the middle of the main street in Olean and later reminisced that it reminded him of a scene in the film, High Noon. The rest is history. Murray stayed on for four years and became one of the truly great basketball players in Bona history. Murray, and Frank Ready, along with Sam Urzetta, Eddie Donovan, and Tony Iacovino would be the mainstays of the Bona teams beginning in 1946. When Eddie Milkovitch arrived as coach the following year, Murray states that the coach made 'overachievers" out of them. They were a vital part of the foundation of the rich basketball tradition that developed at St. Bonaventure.[7]

Ken Murray, Bona's first superstar and first Hall of Fame member. *Photo: Game Program, Canisius College Archives.*

Buffalo State Teachers was going to build its squad around two fine athletes, Lou Vastola and Jake Schaeffer. Dutch Stellrecht and Clair Westcott promised to be of some help to Coach Hube Coyer. Buffalo State, or State Teachers as it was generally referred to at that time, did not compete at the same level as the other four areas institutions. Nevertheless, under Hube Coyer in the years immediately following World War II, Buffalo State was very successful on the basketball court.

The Western New York season opened with a rather bizarre game, a 20 – 13 Niagara victory over Oswego. One of the glass backboards had shattered just before tip-off.

Only a wood backboard could be found as a replacement; so now there was one wood and one glass backboard. To add to the zaniness of the evening, Niagara played a possession game. The Purple Eagles held the ball for a full 25 minutes because Oswego refused to come out of its zone.

The first Aud doubleheader of the 1946-47 season was held on Saturday, December 7 and featured Canisius facing the previous season's national champion, Oklahoma A & M, coached by legendary Hank Iba. The entire starting five on the Oklahoma squad were over 6'4;" height would prove the difference in the outcome of the game. Canisius was ahead at halftime but the taller Aggies wore down the Griffs. Another setback was suffered when an ailing Tom Niland had to be taken out of the game by Coach Brown. The Griffs saw their four point lead vanish; they lost 40 – 32. In the other half of the twin bill, Niagara led by its veterans from the great 1942 - 43 season, Paul Yesawich, Fred Schwab, and Eddie Keim, defeated Georgia, 59 - 51. A new Aud attendance figure, words that would be repeated often in the ensuing years, numbered 10,196.

The next doubleheader saw a fired up Niagara team easily dominate Montana State, 64 – 39, while the Griffs lost to Texas, 52 -46. Once again, Canisius was ahead at the half, by three points this time, but Texas started hitting their shots and the partisan crowd of 7,796 left the Aud disheartened. In the next action at the Aud, one of the occasional Thursday night doubleheaders, Canisius crushed Bona 53 - 35 before a surprisingly sparse gathering of some 3,517 fans. A stellar defense held the Bonnies to just one field goal in the first half. O'Keefe and Chollet led the way on offense and Mort O'Sullivan came off the bench to give the Griffs a good shot in the arm. *Courier* reporter, Ray Ryan, remarked that Canisius "unearthed an apparently valuable operative" in O'Sullivan. As he frequently did, Coach Brown "opened the gates of mercy" and allowed everyone on the squad to play. In the first game of the doubleheader, Lou Vastola, on his way to becoming one of Buffalo State's all time great basketball players, tallied 21 points. That performance allowed Buffalo State to dominate McGill University of Montreal, 54 - 40.[8]

A marquee doubleheader took place on December 21. 5,669 fans watched with delight as the Griffs upset previously unbeaten Louisiana State University, 59 – 50. Chollet put on a 21 point display for his friends from Cajun country. Mort O'Sullivan, in his first start, excelled on defense and made a significant contribution with his seven points. In the first game, Niagara lost to the Oregon Ducks in overtime in what Ray Ryan claims was one of the best Aud games ever. NU went ahead with two minutes to go on a hook shot by Paul Yesawich but the Oregonians stormed back to tie. The taller Ducks prevailed in the extra period for a 67 - 60 victory.

The day after Christmas, a unique doubleheader was held in the Aud, unique in that the first game involved no local teams; rather two teams from West of the Mississippi, UCLA and Wyoming, were pitted against each other. The very fact that two big name schools from the West came to Buffalo to play one of their regular season games was a testament to the attraction of Memorial Auditorium. UCLA, led by All American candidate Don Barksdale, beat the Wyoming Cowboys 54 – 41. In these pre politically correct days, Barksdale was referred to as the "6'6" Negro center," one of the "slickest operators" to appear that season. He had 19 points. 6,538 fans were on hand, a clear indication that attendance continued to be better than the previous season. In the evening's second contest, the Canisius Golden Griffins fell to a highly touted Utah quintet, 37 - 31. Utah's All American Arnold Ferrin was held to nine points, but the taller Utes, paced by another All American Vern Gardner, prevailed. Utah would continue to dominate their competition throughout the season; they capped a storybook year with a win over Kentucky in the NIT championship.[9]

Two days later, Oregon State in overtime tipped the Griffs, 48 – 40, before 4,656 fans. Bill Melvin, a Lackawanna native, who was referred to in the media as the "Negro Ace" furnished the drive and the spark in the second half that enabled the Griffs to tie the Beavers at 25 and again at 31. Then Captain Tommy Niland took command. He knotted the game at 37 and sent it into overtime. In the first game, Buffalo State Teachers defeated Allegheny College 43 – 42. Captain Jack Schaefer led the way with 16 points. On January 1, Southern California led by Fred Bertram beat Canisius, 60 – 51 before 7,653. O'Keefe and Chollet each bagged 13 in the hard fought, losing effort. U.B. hosted Southern Methodist University in the other half of the doubleheader and lost.

A few days later a couple of upsets took place that had to please the nearly 10,000 fans. The Griffs defeated a solid Cornell quintet, 50 - 40. O'Keefe starred on offense, and Mort O'Sullivan had one of his best defensive efforts in holding Hillary Chollet, Leroy's brother, to just one field goal. Coach Brown cleared the bench, seventeen Griffs saw action. In the first part of the twin bill, Lou Corriere's 26 points led the University of Buffalo Bulls over Carnegie Tech, 45 - 31.[10]

Doc Crowdle announced that at this stage of the season, attendance was up 55% over the previous year. The Saturday night doubleheaders were attracting large crowds and developing a virtual mystique. Saturday night was the night to go out in Buffalo. The place to go was the Aud and the purpose was to see the college basketball doubleheaders. The fans would get their money's worth. Chances were that at least one of the games would be a thriller; perhaps both would be. If not, the disheartened fan could always drown his sorrows at the bar in the first floor lounge at the Aud or simply leave the site and visit a dingy saloon on Lower Main Street. Thursday night games did not draw nearly as well. Only 3,482 showed up for the Colgate-Canisius game; despite the fact that Colgate was led by a consensus All American, Ernie Vandeweigh, who excelled in the Red Raiders' 52 - 44 victory.

The local quintets had their ups and downs as the New Year progressed. On January 11, the Griffs suffered their worst defeat of the season. Nothing went right in the 63 - 43 drubbing at the hands of West Virginia. All American Fred Schaus poured in 17 points for the Mountaineers. Schaus was one of the most outstanding of the several All Americans who appeared in the Aud in the 1940s. The 7,823 fans would readily attest to that.

A week later the Griffs played a much better game against a powerful Western Kentucky team before an almost identical crowd, actually 7,857. The team from the Bluegrass state was coached by Ed Diddle. Not only was Diddle a colorful personality but he was easily one of the best coaches of his era. A late rally did the Griffs in. They lost a heartbreaker, 52 - 50. That same evening DePaul defeated its sister Vincentian institution, Niagara University,

Above: **Jake Schaefer, Buffalo State Co-Captain; World War II combat veteran and star at Buff State.**
Photo: Game Program, Canisius College Archives.

by a score of 58 – 51. The Blue Demons were led by Everybody's All American George Mikan, the veritable giant of his day at 6'10", who tallied 14 points. Next a spirited, nail biter took place between Little Three rivals, Canisius and Niagara. Before 9,079 spectators, Hank O'Keefe's 14 points led the way to a Griffin victory. The 51 - 50 score indicated it was another Little Three classic. Niagara's Bill Smyth had 17 points and he helped keep Niagara in the lead for a good part of the game.

The basketball season had hummed along smoothly. The calm was shattered on January 26, 1947. Buffalonians woke up to their Sunday morning *Courier Express* and were startled to read, on the front page no less, that a near riot had taken place in the Aud the previous evening. The Headlines in the *Courier* stated boldly: "Aud Fights Quelled by Police Squad."[11]

Long Island University, rated #2 in the East, came to town with legendary coach Clair Bee at the helm. Bee watched in disbelief as his team suffered its worst defeat in his long coaching reign, 72-48. Most of the 9,471 spectators also watched with a certain amount of disbelief but tempered with satisfaction. Toward the end of contest, an LIU player committed a flagrant foul against Hank O'Keefe. The great Canisius forward was having one of his very best games; at that point he had 34 points and was shooting for a new Aud record. LIU sent in a substitute, "a spear carrier," who sent Hank flying against the uprights. Some observers said this was retribution, alleging that Tom Muller had struck LIU's star center, Dick Holub from behind, earlier in the game. Hank's younger brother, Tim, a fiery Irishman in his own right, came off the bench, and swung at the LIU player. Both benches erupted. Police dashed to the scene restoring a semblance of order but then some fans stormed on to the floor and took over the LIU bench. Even Coach Bee was roughed up a bit. Again the police quickly got things under control. O'Keefe made his two free throws then Brown removed him with only a minute to go.

Cy Kritzer noted that Bee was singled out in official reports as "the instigator of the tension" that resulted in the free for all. Throughout the game, it appears that Coach Bee and some LIU people were protesting, sometimes actually railing, against every call that an official made. Bee had no comment. The controversy simmered in the pages of the Buffalo and the New York City newspapers in the days that followed. Doc Crowdle acknowledged that Tom Muller had struck LIU's star center, Dick Holub, from behind earlier in the contest. He quickly added that both the crowd in the Aud and the officials shared some responsibility for the incident getting out of hand.[12]

Relations between LIU and Canisius remained tense in the weeks that followed the near riot in Buffalo. The Griffs may have been concentrating on their upcoming contests with their downstate rivals, NYU, CCNY, and LIU once again. All three were on the Griffs' schedule during the next two weeks. Evidently they overlooked their mid-state rival, the Syracuse Orangemen. On February 8, before 8,239, Syracuse beat Canisius, 45 - 40. The Orangemen were flying high with a record of 14 - 2. Less than a week later, the Griffs hosted New York University. Tom Muller found himself again in the role of villain. He decked Dolph Schayes, the star of the NYU squad. Some claim that Schayes did the shoving, and others said that Muller did. But Muller took the swing; he was the culprit. The Griffs won the game 61 - 54 but the New York City Press had a field day.

Dan Parker, noted scribe for the *New York Mirror* said "New York college teams now scuffle off to Buffalo" asserting that "another near riot was incited by an uncontrollable Griff student body that fired Tom Muller into a fight" with Schayes. The Brooklyn Eagle scolded Canisius and referred to the "peculiar behavior" of the fans and Canisius students. The *New York Journal*'s headline ran: "NYU 2nd Cage KO Victim of Canisius." Dick Young in the *Daily News* said "The puzzling, unconscionable anti-New York bitterness which simmers in this town boiled into another fist-flailing near riot" in the NYU game. What was Canisius to do? Coach Earl Brown had taken the microphone and pleaded with the crowd to behave responsibly. But his words fell on deaf ears. Muller was obviously a problem, Father Dineen, the Director of Athletics and Doc Crowdle, the Aud Doubleheader program impresario, agreed that Muller had to be removed from the team. Crowdle sent letters to NYU and LIU, indicating that Muller was dismissed from the squad. Muller also indicated that he was leaving school. Meanwhile New York University dropped Canisius from future scheduling.[13]

Two days later the third of Gotham's triumvirate of basketball powers, CCNY, came to the Aud to play the Griffs. Tension filled the air. The contest was close, but cool heads prevailed. Fortunately the contest was trouble-free. Another near record crowd of 10,394 watched happily as the Griffs came from behind to defeat powerful CCNY 52 - 49. The Griffs were playing very well. The sports editor of the school newspaper, the *Griffin*, waxed alliteratively when he remarked that Hammerin' Hank (O'Keefe) and Leapin' Leroy (Chollet) the "Twin Tornadoes" led the team.[14] Chollet, especially, earned accolades for his great game. Joe Lapchick of St. John's, and Nat Holman of CCNY, had high praise for Leroy Chollet. Lapchick said that Chollet "could become one of basketball's all time great players." Cy Kritzer, in the *News*, noted that the "Bayou Beauty" won the praise of the visiting New York press. "The olive-skinned curly head" from New Orleans was viewed as the cleverest operative they had seen this season. The O'Keefe-Chollet duo combined for 135 points against the three New York teams and executed expertly. Gotham's coaches noted that Canisius was the first team to defeat all three subway powers, CCNY, NYU, and LIU, during the same season. Indicative of the attention now being given to college basketball was the fact that Western Union Morse code operators sent more than 20,000 words to the New York City newspapers. That was some sort of a record in this pre-laptop computer age.[15]

Leroy Chollet , Canisius standout, Louisiana native, aka "the Bayou Beauty," twice Aud MVP.
Photo: Canisius College Archives

While Canisius was battling the sports writers, Niagara was having mixed results on the basketball court. On the same evening that LIU and Canisius engaged in fisticuffs, Niagara and Georgetown engaged in a terrific battle. NU trailed 62 - 54 with three minutes to go. Smyth and Yesawich led a great comeback to bring Niagara within two points in the final minute. NU declined a foul shot (a peculiar rule back in the '40s) and opted to take the ball out of bounds. Eddie Keim let go a near half court shot – swish game tied and headed for overtime. The Canisius crowd joined the Niagara supporters in a huge standing ovation. Unfortunately, the Eagles lost in OT, 66 - 62. Fans might have considered that a "good" loss. A week earlier Niagara suffered a "bad" loss when, St. John's defeated them, 46 - 36. The Eagles experienced what Ray Ryan termed "an execrable off night," not being able to hit a basket from almost any range. Large Harry Foley, Harry "the Horse," he was called, playing in his initial college game, came off the bench to lead a rally but it fell short.[16]

As the basketball season entered the homestretch, the Griffs showed new life. Just a short time earlier, the Griffs were thought to be out of the race for a tournament bid, but this late surge over the New York powerhouses put them right back in the race. A clean sweep of four victories over the New York teams might be the clincher. Next up was the return "bout" with LIU. Relations between LIU and Canisius were still not cordial. The Big City press did not help matters much. The New York newspapers keyed in on Canisius. A quarter page cartoon in the *New York World Telegram* depicted an angry Griffin with talons wrapped around the New York City teams, and its body hovering over bags of money representing the Invitation Tourney in Madison Square Garden. The cartoon stated that the Griffin "was a creature, the guardian of the Scythian gold, and the Canisius Griffin is handling his appointed task (as far as our MET teams are concerned) in a manner to do his old biographer, Herodotus, proud."[17] LIU got the revenge it sought, legitimately, on the court. They blasted the Griffs, 68 - 52, before more than 18,000 in the Garden. Dick Holub, Muller's fisticuff victim in the earlier game in Buffalo, was the hero with 32 points, a record for the Garden that season. Hank O'Keeffe also had a hot hand. He became the first player in Canisius history to reach the 300 point mark in one season. Kritzer called attention to the pro scouts who "were excited" by O'Keefe's play. The fact that Hank's mother and several friends from his hometown of Malvern, Long Island, were in attendance must have been an inspiration.[18] *New York Times* correspondent, Louis Effrat, noted that "in an obscure corner of the Eighth Avenue Arena sat…a disconsolate figure …Tom Muller, 22-year-old freshman who had punched…Holub and…Schayes...and had been dropped from the squad." Effrat did add that Muller had apologized to Schayes before the game and was going to do likewise with Holub.[19]

Red Smith, of *The Herald Tribune*, and one of the most highly regarded sportswriters of his generation, added his voice to the controversy. He had anticipated another slugfest. His column on February 20 was marked by wonderfully poignant humor: "reports from Buffalo…suggested that the rugged delegates from that sector have developed a revolutionary playing technique based on the scientific principle that the best defense is a swift poke in the chops. In matches in Buffalo, Canisius had scored knockout victories over L.I.U. and N.Y.U. and defeated City College on points. The record indicated that this was the most promising amateur team since Joe Louis turned pro." But Smith did acknowledge that this second LIU-Canisius meeting turned out be a very gentle contest, though it was marked, unfortunately, by too many whistles from the officials. Smith even criticized the spectators in the Garden for their loud and impartial booing of Canisius rooters and players. Smith added his praise for some of the Canisius players, for Tom Niland and especially for Hank O'Keefe. He said that O'Keefe played the sort of game that made the hecklers look foolish. Smith called him a slim, tireless, deft athlete and a standout on the court. He also congratulated Tom Muller for recognizing that he was wrong and standing up to the consequences.[20]

The Griffs returned home to prepare for combat with a stellar Notre Dame team. The Fighting Irish came to town with the newspapers gleefully noting that this was the first sellout ever. 11,029 tickets were sold, and more than 1,000 disappointed fans milled about the Terrace Entrance Lobby trying to find a ticket to purchase. George Ratterman's name must have helped. By this time his was a name readily recognized in the Buffalo community. The promising quarterback was pictured in his Irish uniform in the local press, however he was not a factor in the game. The Irish won, 45 - 39 with their center, John Brennan, the dominant player. He scored 16 points. The Griffs had to travel to Syracuse to get back into the victory column; they beat the Orangemen 67 - 58, with O'Keefe and Chollet, once again leading the way. They received a helping hand from little heard of Mauro Panaggio, who scored 15.

The Griffs then beat Hawaii 45 - 43 before only 3,690 fans. This was supposed to be a breather for the hosts, but the touring Hawaii team, gave the Griffs a rude awakening. Hawaii played to win, and the fans were on their feet screaming as the game came down to the wire. Coach Brown got caught flatfooted; he used his reserves for much of the game, then Hawaii got hot, hit 14 straight points, and the Griff regulars had to be rushed back in to regain the lead. They just barely did so. It was a frantic game right up until Bob MacKinnon pivoted and hit the winning basket with 16 seconds to go.

The grand finale in 1946-47 was played before another record crowd. 11,891 fans turned out to watch Canisius led by Chollet's 16 points defeat Niagara, led by Schwab's 13. The final score was 52 - 44. The hero of the game was Captain Tommy Niland, playing in his final home game. He did it all; dribbled to the basket for left handed push shots, hit from the outside, and ran the team on the floor. Among the most memorable moments in Aud history was the huge standing ovation for Tommy Niland when he was taken out with less than two minutes to go. In the first half of this "Big Four" doubleheader, U.B. defeated Buffalo State, 51 -37. Each team ended the season with a respectable record, this was U.B's 12th victory in 17 starts, and it was just the fifth loss for the Bengals in 16 outings. The Bulls were led by Bill Rudick, who though playing slightly injured, did a commendable job of holding the great State star, Lou Vastola, to just 8 points. Rudick had 11 and Lou Corriere had 14 points for the winners.

In fact all the local quintets ended up with winning records in 1946-47 except for St. Bonaventure. The Brown Indians had to settle for a mediocre 10 – 11 season; their home games were in the "infamous" Olean Armory, and on the road, for the most part they played small schools in New York and Pennsylvania. None of their games were in the Aud. Niagara finished with a 13 – 8 record. The Griffs, who had played 5 of the top 10 teams in the United States, wound up with an 18 – 13 record.

As was customary, the end of the season saw several honors bestowed on the Western New York basketball players. "Louisiana Leroy," a new moniker for Chollet, was voted the Most Valuable Player to appear in Memorial Auditorium in the 1946-47 season. At Transit Valley Country Club, the University of Buffalo Boosters, named Lou Corriere the most outstanding U.B. athlete. Buffalo State College held its athletic banquet at the Hotel Lafayette and named Lou Vastola, most valuable athlete. Dick Fisher, one of Buffalo's premiere sports promoters acted as Master of Ceremonies and Doc Crowdle was the main speaker. Eddie Keim was

Lou Corriere, Outstanding UB basketball and football player, before and after the war.
Photo: Game Program, Canisius College Archives.

voted the MVP for Niagara. Keim averaged but seven points per game but his greatest assets were his defensive ability and his leadership.

It was truly a splendid season for Western New York college basketball. The teams played well, the players earned richly deserved recognition, and the fans turned out in increasingly large numbers. *The Courier Express* reported that 142,371 had witnessed nineteen doubleheaders in the Aud, for approximately a 7,400 average. It was better than 1945-46; even better years lay ahead.

Six months later, the Aud schedule for 1947-48 was announced. Canisius would play in the downtown arena seventeen times and its other home games would be played at the Villa or at Canisius on Delaware (as Canisius High School was then called). Niagara would play ten times in the Aud with the remainder of its home games at St. Vincent's gym on campus. St. Bonaventure, the University of Buffalo, and Buffalo State each would appear several times on the Aud doubleheader program; other games would be on their respective campuses.

Many of the Aud games would be on radio station WKBW with play by play by Sig Smith. Kleinhan's, Buffalo's premier Men's Store, would be the sponsor. In a humorous moment in one particular game, Sig had Kleinhan's scoring a go-ahead basket. Edwards Department Store, one of Buffalo's main downtown department stores, across the street from the Statler Hotel, announced that it would be awarding, a "New Little Three Trophy." That trophy was on display in the Sporting Goods Department. At that time, Edwards was one of the principal sporting goods outlets in Buffalo and was also a major outlet for the sale of tickets to all downtown sporting events, second only to the famous Mathias Cigar Store. There were those who felt that the Mathias Ticket outlet had an unfair advantage because of its key location on Main Street at Shelton Square adjacent to the Palace Burlesk. A visit to the Palace was regarded as a rite of passage for young men of the Buffalo area. There were those who speculated that some male fans might be more interested in applauding Rose La Rose or Bubbles Darlene than Leroy Chollet.[21]

The Western New York quintets were looking forward to the upcoming season with considerable optimism. Bona upgraded its schedule. That was good news for the Aud as well as for downtown Buffalo. Bona also had a top notch team leader returning in Ken Murray and a veteran supporting cast: Frank Walsh, Frank Ready, Ed Kraus, and Eddie Donovan. The even bigger news in the off season for St. Bonaventure was the hiring of a new coach, Eddie Milkovitch, later to be known as Eddie Melvin. This was a positive indication that the Olean school wanted to upgrade its program. As time would show, the Bona administrators made the right decision in hiring the rookie coach.

Ray Ryan reported in his preseason column that Buffalo State fans were also very hopeful. The *Courier* reporter referred to "the most talented squad in the history of Buffalo State Teachers' basketball." Big George Doyle had transferred to the Elmwood Avenue College from Canisius. He would be joining Captain Jake Schaefer, the only senior, and Dutch Stellrecht, Sam MacNeil, and Frank Riccio. This made for a solid team. Unfortunately it was not ready for the early season clash with Bona. The Brown Indians manhandled the State team, 50 - 30. Cy Kritzer of the *News* considered Milkovitch's debut as a "big surprise" and hailed him as an enthusiastic bench cheerleader as well as a capable coach.[22]

Canisius fans too were optimistic for 1947-48. What else could they be with the dynamic duo of Hank O'Keefe and Leroy Chollet returning to lead the team? Reliable Joe Trimboli and the indomitable Tom Niland had graduated but Mort O'Sullivan was returning at one guard spot and Bob MacKinnon was ready to take over the reins as floor general of the Griffs. Tom Muller, a sophomore, held out some promise as a big man in the middle. Muller had been allowed to return to school, presumably he had been rehabilitated in the off season and would not be the center of controversies as he had been the previous year. Dan Parker, popular New York sports writer, noted that Knishes are hot mashed potatoes and, like knishes, Canisius dropped both NYU and LIU from its schedule but also reinstated Muller who was the storm center of two rhubarbs involving those teams. Parker added: "Now he is back and the two teams are dropped. If those are the wishes of Canisius, then everything is delicious, but henceforth Muller shouldn't be so vicious."[23]

Niagara University had good reason to be the most optimistic of all the local quintets. The same players who had done so well the previous year would be returning. Fred Schwab, Paul Yesawich, Eddie Keim, all stars in their own right, were joined by reliable Bill Holroyd, and Lloyd Paterson. Coach Taps Gallagher knew that his team had a very good chance of being rated the best team in Western New York.

At the University of Buffalo, Lou Corriere would be joined by veterans Bob Eldridge, Frank Nappo, Benny Constantino and Len Serfustini. Newcomers Paul Brady and Bill Rudick might determine if the Bulls could pull off another winning season.

As usual the Western New York colleges tipped off the season by playing "warm up" type games against smaller state schools or teams from nearby Canada. The initial program in the Aud took place on December 6. It was a marquee doubleheader featuring two powers from west of the Mississippi. Niagara played Brigham Young University and found itself in the hole, down by 21 points in the second half, only to battle back and then loose by a single point 54 – 53. In the second contest, the Griffs, in the lead for much of the game, lost by two points, 50 - 48 to Pacific Coast Champion, Oregon State. All American Candidate, Cliff Crandall led the Oregon attack with 14 points. 10,281 fans attended and they agonized over the two heartbreaking losses

1948 Canisius College Varsity Basketball Team. ***Left to right; Front row:*** **Co-Captain O'Sullivan, Coach Niland, Co-Captain H. O'Keefe.** ***Middle row:*** **Masino, T. O'Keefe, Konrad, MacKinnon, Mauro, Chollet, Knab, Calak.** ***Back row:*** **Manager Murphy, Asst. Manager J.B.Walsh, Schaus, Muller, Kamp, Beebe, Powell, Hartnett, Killeen.**
Photo: Canisius College Archives.

The coaches, Earl Brown and Taps Gallagher, were not discouraged. Gallagher's seasoned veterans knew how to regroup following the one point loss to one of the country's best teams. Coach Brown had been experimenting with various player combinations in his attempt to find the best lineup. He felt he found his answer in the next outing, against the University of Scranton. Scranton played a very respectable schedule in the 1940s, and was considered a very competitive team. In this early season contest they fought the Griffs tooth and nail for the better part of the game. Then the Griffs found an answer. Don Hartnett had recently been discharged from the army. He was warming the bench waiting for his opportunity. He got it; he propelled his team to a 14 point lead. Canisius proceeded to win handily. Hartnett would eventually end his basketball days as one of the all time Canisius greats.

In mid-December, Canisius faced a major power from the south, Louisiana State University. 8,346 fans turned out to watch the Griffs put on a stellar performance upending the mighty team from Baton Rouge, 59 – 44. In the first half, Hank O'Keefe's "masterful one hand shooting" led the Griffs. In the second half, it was Cajun Leroy Chollet's turn. He poured in 17 of his game high 20 points after the intermission. The Griffs' great victory over LSU was offset by a horrendous loss to Washington State the following week. The score was 48 - 37 but could have been much worse as some 7,391 dejected fans watched the Griffs shoot just 14%.

The University of Utah, the Utes, the previous season's National Invitation Tournament champions, were next on the Aud program. Once again, they were led by their two All Americans, Arnold Ferrin and Vern Gardner. They lived up to their advanced

Don Hartnett goes all the way up against Scranton. Chollet and Muller stand by to assist. *Photo: Canisius College Archives.*

Chollet surrounded by LSU players scores two. *Photo:Canisius College Archives.*

billing. They dominated the boards, and helped Utah eke out a 41 - 37 triumph over Canisius. In the first game, Niagara nipped the University of Southern California, 46 - 43. Captain Eddie Keim's last minute shot sealed the win, giving the Purple Eagle fans among the 10,619 in attendance, a one day late Christmas gift. The belated gift was gratefully accepted by the Niagara fans but they were not surprised. The colorful, clutch shooting Keim had performed similar feats in the past.

The teams from the conferences in the Western states liked to come east in the early part of their season. Their games in Buffalo and New York City prepared them for their conference schedules in the second half of their season. Accordingly, Kansas State and the University of Missouri, the top teams from the Big Seven Conference, also known as the Missouri Valley Conference at that time, came to town just after Christmas. Unfortunately the host institutions were a bit too kind to the visitors. Canisius lost to Kansas State by a bucket, 47 - 45 and the University of Buffalo lost by just one point, 51 – 50, to the University of Missouri. The local fans, some 5,483, were disappointed but not completely disheartened because they witnessed superb efforts on the part of both local teams.

New Year's Day, 1948, saw the Griffs get back on the winning track. Some 5,934 fans braved a severe winter storm and were rewarded with a 59 – 50 victory over highly rated Arizona. Morris Udall, future national political figure from that state, led with 17; Hank O'Keefe out dueled him by bagging 26 points. Local fans were given an additional treat by watching a thrilling first game featuring UCLA and Cornell. The Big Red lost by just three, 50 - 47. Cornell did not return to their Finger Lakes home empty handed. Two days later they rebounded by defeating Canisius in the Aud before 9,151 fans, 41 – 37. The Griffs were limited to just one field goal in the second half.

Mort O'Sullivan, Outstanding Canisius defensive player.
Photo: Game Program, Canisius College Archives.

The best doubleheader of the year took place two days later. A large crowd of nearly 10,000, actually 9,895, were rewarded with a thoroughly exciting evening of basketball featuring Canisius against Georgetown and Niagara against West Virginia. In the Canisius game Mort O'Sullivan nailed a long set shot that put the seal on a 40 -39 victory over the Hoyas. Mort had been in and out of games, often handicapped by a recurring injury. Now he had a moment of stardom that inspired a young columnist for the *Buffalo Evening News*, Dick Johnston, to devote some richly deserved accolades to O'Sullivan. Mort was described as a steady player, one who was "a nifty ball handler and a tricky dribbler." These were skills he had learned at Power Memorial High in New York City. He heard about Canisius College while he was in the army in World War II. He had teamed up with Joe Niland while playing basketball at Camp Cooke in California. Joe persuaded

Mort to come to Canisius. Mort proved to be a fine addition to the Canisius program; a good basketball player and an eminently likeable Irishman.[24] Ray Ryan called the other half of the doubleheader, the best game of the season. The Eagles' starting five of Schwab, Yesawich, Foley, Smyth and Keim put on a dazzling display of team basketball. Unfortunately it fell just a point short as West Virginia nipped Niagara, 59 – 58.

Playing just two days later in Niagara Falls, Ontario, the Purple Eagles rebounded nicely with a 54 - 52 win over Bona. Fred Schwab's two pointer in the waning seconds of the game sealed the win. The Golden Griffins were not as fortunate. They followed up their thrilling victory over the Georgetown Hoyas with a horrible drubbing at the hands of perennial nemesis Western Kentucky. The 74 - 52 win was certainly no fluke for Coach Ed Diddle's team. By the end of the season the Hilltoppers had amassed an enviable 28 – 2 record and wound up third in the NIT. Three days later, the Griffs flew to Ithaca, a first ever flight for the team, and lost a close one to Cornell, 56 – 51 despite Bob MacKinnon's 18 points.

On January 20 came the startling news that Coach Earl Brown would be leaving Canisius. He had decided to take the position as Head Football Coach at Auburn University in Alabama. Brown's negotiations with Auburn had been secret but it was widely recognized that Brown was primarily a football coach and that if a major college job were offered, he would probably take it. Ray Ryan commented that a coach's leaving in mid-season "is almost without precedent." Brown's departure was a surprise only in its suddenness. Some observers wondered if the Canisius administration would allow Brown to stay on to coach in the upcoming tilt with Niagara. But this proved to be a non-issue. The players liked Earl Brown; they gave him a silver serving set in a special presentation before the Niagara game. Then they went one better and presented the departing coach with a convincing 59 - 39 victory over archrival Niagara. The entire team played well in tribute to the coach. Brown left the next day to begin planning for spring football practice at Auburn, taking with him an unblemished record over Niagara, three basketball and two football victories.[25]

On January 25, 1948, Canisius College announced the return of Joe Niland as Head Basketball Coach. Joe was widely acknowledged as one of the all time great basketball players at Canisius College. He had completed his playing days at the beginning of World War II. He entered the army serving as a tank commander, a member of General George Patton's famed Third Armored Division. After the war he returned to be an assistant coach at his alma mater. At the beginning of the 1947-48 season Joe was hired as head basketball coach at Gannon College in Erie, Pennsylvania. Joe compiled an 8 - 5 record, and was well liked by the Gannon administration. They acknowledged his attachment to Canisius; a clause in his contract stated that should a job open at his alma mater, he would be released from Gannon. That is what happened.[26]

For his maiden road trip, Canisius Coach Joe Niland, journeyed to Olean and lost to the St. Bonaventure team. It was a close one, 45 to 42. Joe felt that his new charges were not working hard enough. He achieved some initial notoriety by making his practices more strenuous. His next game was a win and perhaps fittingly, it was over his former employer, Gannon College, 58 – 45. It was played in the Villa on the Main Street campus. The Griffs had a rough time for most of the rest of the season, the losses outnumbered the wins. In mid-February it was time for the annual contests against New York City teams. Unfortunately the success of the previous season was not repeated. On February 14, over 9,000 (actually 9,059) fans watched a closely contested Aud doubleheader. In the first game CCNY defeated Niagara, 56 - 52 and in the nightcap, the St. John's Redmen defeated the Griffs 41 - 38. Less than one week later, the same Western New York quintets visited Madison Square Garden and before more than 17,000 both lost again. This time Canisius faced CCNY. The Griffs played well, were down by only four points with four minutes, then collapsed and lost 51 – 39. St. John's led by the highly regarded Dick McGuire knocked off Niagara 57 – 48.

After a rough fortnight, the Griffs caught a reprieve. They faced Syracuse in the Aud and came away with a 55 - 48 overtime victory. Chollet, O'Keefe, and Muller combined for 46 points. The Griffs made it two in a row when they defeated St. Bona by four points, 39 - 35 before 8,398. Ken Murray tallied 13 points but it was not enough to match Chollet's 11, and O'Keefe's 10. In the first game of the Big Four doubleheader, Niagara defeated U.B, 69 to 49. Niagara's four top guns, Keim, Schwab, Yesawich, and Smyth tallied 52 points.

Notre Dame visited Buffalo for what had become an annual trip; and left with what seemed to be an annual result, a 64 - 53 victory over Canisius. 11,519 watched the rough, hard fought, foul filled contest. The much celebrated Irish lad, consensus All American Kevin O'Shea, was held to 7 points but his teammate, John Brennan, canned 22. The Griffs followed this with a well deserved victory over the Orangemen at Syracuse, 59 - 58 with Tom Muller tossing in the clutch baskets. On March 4, a Thursday night doubleheader featured Manhattan against Bona with the former winning 35 - 31, and U.B. beating Alfred, 50 - 39. The highlight of the evening was the bowing out, after a magnificent career, of U.B.'s Lou Corriere. Lockport Lou's grand finale was marked by a characteristic display of speed and shooting ability. Fittingly he was high scorer that night with 17 points. Unfortunately only 1,579 were on hand to witness this.

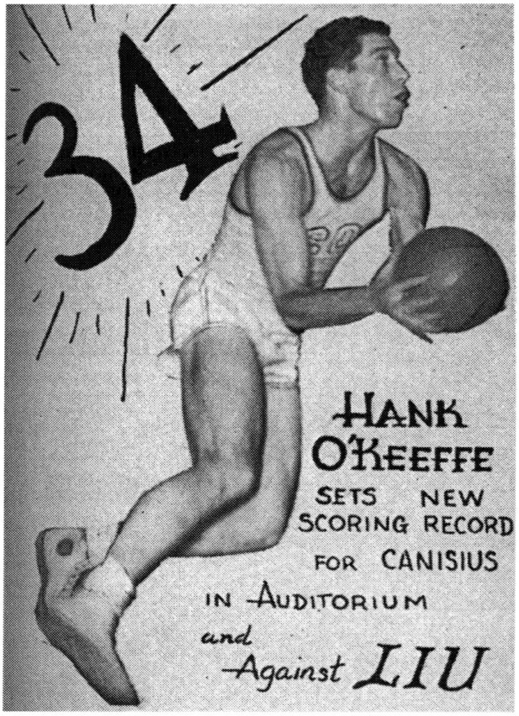

Hank O'Keefe, Canisius star, 1942-43; 1946-48.
Photo: Scrapbook - Canisius College Archives.

The final game of the year saw Canisius play Niagara before 11,634 fans, the second largest crowd in Memorial Auditorium annals. It was a typical Little Three contest, fought hard to the bitter end. With so many fans crammed into the Aud, it seemed as though the building was rocking. Niagara, led by Fred Schwab, playing his final game, overcame a 14 point deficit to come out on top, 49 – 42. It was also the swan song for Lenny Kamp and Bill "Bumps" Melvin of Canisius and for Paul Yesawich and Eddie Keim of Niagara. All received warm send-offs. It was also Hank O'Keefe's final game, the Long Island native who had provided so many thrills to Buffalo fans. While Griffin fans enthusiastically said their good-byes to Hank, many of the Niagara rooters, felt obliged to give him a solid booing. According to Cy Kritzer, NU partisans had picked Hank as their favorite target all season.

Post season, 1947-48, saw Leroy Chollet, once again, named Aud MVP. Up in Niagara Falls, two Purple Eagles were earning Most Valuable Player honors, Eddie Keim was named MVP by the Knickerbocker Club of New York at the "Ye Olde" Tavern" a favorite watering hole for Niagara loyalists, while Fred Schwab was named MVP in a student/faculty poll.

The area teams had performed well. Bona's record of 12 - 10 included several wins over average teams, a closely contested loss to a very good Utah State team early in the season, a split with Canisius and two losses to Niagara. Eddie Milkovitch, in his first season at the helm of the Olean school, could take some satisfaction in that the team record was better than the previous year. He would be heard from in the future. Mal Eiken in his second season at U.B. again had a respectable record of 13 - 8. Taps Gallagher's squad recorded the best won-loss record of the local teams that played at the major college level, at 15 – 9. The Purple Eagles victims included Southern California, Scranton, and Siena, in addition to the two conquests of St. Bona and a split with Canisius. The Griffs under two different head coaches ended the season at 10 - 15. Though posting a losing record, the wins were something of which to be proud and included conquests of Louisiana State, Arizona, and Georgetown and two victories over Syracuse. Their overall record was not as good as that of their local counterparts, but many pundits felt that their strong play against some of the nation's powerhouses earned them high marks.

Buffalo State came through with the best record of the Western New York quintets, with 14 wins and only five setbacks. Most of its games were played on the Elmwood Avenue campus, but the Bengals did venture into the Aud for two contests. Both were victories, one over Carnegie Tech and the other over Grove City. State concluded its very successful season with its 9th straight win when "Dutch" Stellricht's memorable shot earned his team a 55 – 54 victory over Western Ontario.

Overall college basketball was strong in Western New York. Memorial Auditorium in downtown Buffalo continued to pack in thousands of spectators, on a fairly regular basis. The size of the basketball crowds attending games in Memorial Auditorium continued to increase in the years following World War II. Each season recorded larger numbers than the preceding one. Elsewhere in the nation the immediate postwar boom in sports appeared to be leveling off. That was not true for Western New York. The increasing number of fans coming into downtown Buffalo for the basketball doubleheaders showed no signs of weakening. Buffalo had arrived as a place of national recognition for hosting major basketball games. It was no surprise that the area continued to be acclaimed as one of the real hotbeds of college basketball.

Sports teams, sports writers, and sports fans all liked to visit Buffalo. The city was more than just a place to watch an athletic event. Downtown Buffalo was the focal point of entertainment in the 1940s. Sporting events, the big movie palaces, and a variety of nightclubs including some "hot" jazz spots, all drew people to the area. "Going downtown" was a big deal in those years for some people, for others it was a regular event. Many Buffalonians attended parties either before or after a sporting event in one of the downtown hotels. Most often these would be held in the Statler, the Lafayette, and the Buffalo. The Hotel Lafayette was a favorite for celebrity seekers. A number of visiting teams, including those from St. Bonaventure and the University of Notre Dame stayed there. The "Olde English Grille" at the Buffalo was a favorite after the game; the fans who traveled from Olean preferred the Hotel Buffalo for

Hotel Markeen Braemar Room
"Where Good Fellows Get Together"
Main at Utica
ANVIL BAR
The Blacksmith Shop
628 Delaware Near North
Jimmy Smith's Cafe
"The Best of Everything"
260 Pearl Street
CHET BRUNNER'S TAVERN
3889 Main Street
Eggertsville, N. Y.
"THE WINNER"
PARKRIDGE RESTAURANT AND GRILL
300 Parkridge Avenue
Famous "Peter Stuyvesant Room"
Excellent Food and Entertainment
245 Elmwood Avenue
MEYER'S TAVERN
Famous Roast Beef
1391 Delaware Avenue
. . . Where to Go After the Game . . .
The Coral Room
Appetizing Snacks and Delicious Drinks
Hotel Westbrook — Delaware and North
HOTEL BUFFALO
For Your After the Game Snack
Washington at Swan
Checkerboard
BAR — RESTAURANT
1403 Main Street
DUFF'S BAR FIESTA and
DUFF'S SHERIDAN PATIO
Millersport Highway, Eggertsville, N. Y.
Pat and Ruth Slater's "DUBOIS"
22 West Eagle Street
"Roast Beef on Kuemmelweck"
Hotel Touraine Coffee Shop
"Superb Food Always"
Delaware Ave. at Johnson Park
Meet Your Friends at
JOE DUDZICK'S TAVERN
770 Seneca Street

Where to go after the game . . . *Photo: Game Program, Canisius College Archives.*

overnight since it advertised "Free Radio in Every Room." Sometimes the Hotel Worth, because of its proximity to the Aud, would be booked by a booster club. Other fans, often college students on dates, or young married couples, would have dinner before the game at the Grotto, or Leonardo's, or perhaps Laube's Old Spain. Post game parties were also common. They were billed as victory parties; they were held regardless of the game's outcome. Students, away from the observing eye of the college administrators, could be found liberally imbibing quantities of the products of the local breweries. Genesee, Iroquois, and Kochs seemed to be most popular. The college crowd left the Manru, Steins, and Simon Pure for the older generation. Buffalo was also an ethnic city, so neighborhood saloons abounded in those years. The Polish dominated the East side, the Irish in South Buffalo, the Italians on the West side, and a mixture of Germans, Jewish, Irish, and others in North Buffalo. Sports fans discussing heated sports events were commonplace in the neighborhood watering holes.

The big name basketball teams from the West were unquestionably a popular attraction. But the Little Three games were something else again. More and more Western New Yorkers were becoming fervent fans of the Little Three. It mattered little if or where they went to college, they just wanted to be part of exciting basketball. The Little Three provided it on a regular basis. The Little Three had been around, unofficially, for decades. But, in point of fact, it always was and always would be a mythical conference. There was no constitution or by-laws. Nothing bound the three institutions together other than the competitive spirit in the athletic arena and the accompanying tradition that was being ever enhanced. That spirit and that tradition were alive and well in the 1940s. Unfortunately there would be periods in later decades when other interests of the institutions undermined that spirit and tradition.

In the 1948-49 season, for the very first time, all Little Three contests would be played in the Aud. It was what the local fans wanted; it was only fitting that the schedulers complied. All three teams were loaded with talent. For the Griffs the "Bayou Beauty" as some liked to call Leroy Chollet, was back for his final year. Bob MacKinnon who was often referred to as "the greatest schoolboy basketball scorer ever produced in the Buffalo schools" was also back and he was joined by Mort O'Sullivan and Al Masino, reliable defensive specialists. A new speedster from Erie, Pennsylvania, Johnny DeLuca would also become an integral part of the team. Tom Muller was back in school so the center problem might be solved if he were to have a solid year. True, Canisius lost one of its most famous players to graduation, that was, of course, Hank O'Keefe. But the wealth of experience from others would offset that. Niland was committed to improving upon the previous 10 – 15 season. A three year contract for Joe Niland, underscored the administration's confidence in the young coach He was able to celebrate by indulging in a "Big Thick Steak" at McVan's Supper Club on Niagara Street and for just $1.50. The players would be content to celebrate down the street at Sauerweins, especially popular with the Black Rock and the Riverside crowd, or perhaps at Benny Powers Saloon, a famous hangout for the college crowd. Benny Powers place was literally a stone's throw from the Canisius campus; actually many students thought it was part of the campus.[27]

Some pundits may have thought that the outlook for Niagara was not very rosy. Niagara lost four of its stars. However Coach Taps Gallagher said no one should shed any tears because he had some smart, scrappy ballplayers ready to take over. These included a spectacular trio of sophomores from New York City: Jim Moran, Tom Birch, and the charismatic Emilio "Zeke" Sinicola. Ned Irish, New York City's basketball guru, regarded this as the best trio to come out of basketball's mecca in a long time, perhaps ever. Coach Gallagher also had two top notch veterans returning, the rugged 6'4" center, Harry "the Horse" Foley, and the ever reliable Bill Smyth. The Purple Eagles looked like a sure bet to better their 15 – 9 of 1947-48.

St. Bonaventure under the guidance of Eddie Milkovitch was gaining respect. Its schedule continued to improve and some excellent players were returning. Coach Milkovitch himself had become quite a drawing card. Cy Kritzer called him one of the best shows in town, and said there was "plenty of ham in his antics." Obviously many fans liked the ham that Coach Eddie served, since there was a heavy demand for tickets near the Bona bench. Milkovitch felt confident that he would better last year's, 12 - 10 record.[28]

U.B. too looked forward to another good season. Coach Mal Eiken, like his WNY peers, felt he would improve on the 13 - 8 season of 1947-48. U.B. would have Paul Brady and Bob Eldridge back, two solid players, as well as veterans Frank Nappo, Benny Constantino and Len Serfustini. They would be joined by a newcomer with tremendous potential, Jack Chalmers.

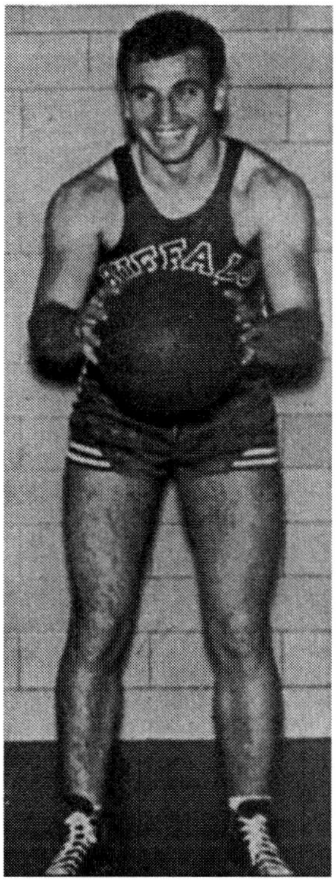

Len Serfustini, U. B. star and future coach. *Photo: Game Program, Canisius College Archives.*

The outlook for the Western New York basketball teams was bright. It did not take long to see that this optimism was not unfounded. In the very first double-header of the season, some 9,213 fans saw that it was for real. Niagara, on a last second shot by Jim Moran, knocked off Denver, the Skyline Conference favorite, 58 - 56. Canisius beat Baylor, the South-west Conference Champion, 55 - 45. Chollet and DeLuca each bagged fourteen points. It was a great way to start the season, two wins by the locals over two big name schools from the west.

The Canisius – Baylor game was the first televised basketball game ever in Western New York. Television had only recently arrived in the Buffalo area. It made its debut in mid-1948 and in the months that followed, various experiments in programming, including some with sporting events, took place. The basketball telecast was welcomed and the authorities did not seem worried that the new medium would have a deleterious impact at the box office. The fact of the matter was that almost no one had a sense as to what the impact of television would be. It would not be until the 1950s that the American public began to buy television sets in large numbers for use in their private homes. The revolutionary impact of television would then begin to be appreciated.

The following week an even larger throng, 9.689, attended the Southern Methodist-Niagara; Canisius-Arkansas twin bill. The Eagles were defeated 67 - 57 but the Griffs earned praise for beating a highly regarded Arkansas team, 60 - 51. Bill "Moose" Hymes had a superb game, scoring 16 points and nicely handling the boards, while Chollet and DeLuca each chipped in with 14 points.

Canisius continued its winning ways in the next doubleheader, clipping Bona, 58 - 54. Future Bona Coach Eddie Donovan came up with a game high ten points. But their ace, Ken Murray was held to just three. Tom Muller and Bill Hymes were the Canisius keys to victory. It was a typical Bona-Canisius clash, one marked by plenty of fouls. In the first game, Niagara rebounded nicely from the loss to SMU by edging a very tough Dayton team. A disappointing crowd of 5,991 watched a legend being created as Zeke Sinicola sparked the Purple Eagles with 20 points in the 62 – 59 victory. Zeke raced up and down the court, his black hair flowing freely as he ran, then either stopping abruptly and throwing up a 30 foot set shot or darting to the basket for a lay up.

Another solid doubleheader, before 7,349 fans, saw the University of Buffalo put forth an excellent effort, though in a losing cause, as they went down to defeat at the hands of the University of Georgia, 56 – 51. Again the Griffs knocked off a major opponent, this time it was Iowa State, 58 - 45. Another creditable performance by Moose Hymes was a big factor in the Canisius victory.

Once again the stage was set for the Golden Griffins to break into the magical Top Ten. In the latest Associated Press poll they were ranked # 11. They had already defeated some national powers and Canisius stood at 6 – 0, ready to face Western Kentucky. The Hilltoppers were ranked in the top three in the country. It came as no surprise when an Aud sellout was announced.[29]

Unfortunately for Buffalo fans, the game did not live up to expectations. Canisius struggled from the opening gun. Both Tom Muller and Bill Hymes got into foul trouble early trying to contain the taller Bob Lavoy, the 6' 7" All American candidate. The Hilltoppers lived up to their nickname; their height was just too much for the Griffs to handle. Coach Niland protested that big men were being protected by the officials but, of course, those protests fell on deaf ears. DeLuca had 16 and Chollet had 15 in the disappointing 65-55 loss. There was better news, in fact very good news, for the University of Buffalo in the first game. The Bulls had a "hot hand," they blasted Lafayette College, 65 – 39 behind stellar performances by Jack Chalmers, and Bob Eldridge; the latter had a game high 19 points.[30]

As the calendar year 1948 drew to a close, Canisius, led by Johnny DeLuca's nineteen points, beat Miami of Ohio 68 – 56 before 5,470 fans. In what was referred to as an "outsider's" game, Utah swung by the Aud on an Eastern trip and beat Cornell 52 - 44. In the 1940s, Cornell usually had a very good basketball team, and if they wished to host a power from outside the Eastern region, they traveled to Buffalo's highly regarded Memorial Auditorium to do so.

A sensational doubleheader featuring Canisius against Syracuse and a Little Three contest, Niagara versus Bona, was on tap for January 6. More than 10,000 were expected to pass through the turnstiles. Unfortunately, a vicious blizzard earlier in the day kept the crowd down to just 5,711. Those who plodded through the lake effect snow along lower Main Street could be excused for thinking they might have taken the wrong turn and were somewhere in the frozen tundra. Fortunately those hardy souls were rewarded with two top notch games. Canisius continued to dominate the Orangemen, defeating them 59 – 52, thus making the lifetime record against Syracuse, 7 - 2. Syracuse had pinned its hopes on Royce Newell, the 6'8" giant from Jamestown, New York. They reckoned without Tom Muller. The Canisius center did a good job on Newell, committing just one foul against him and matching Newell's 12 points with a dozen of his own. In the other game, in what was coming to be called a typical Little Three game, the score was tied nine times. Bona, on a last second shot by Eddie Donovan, clipped Niagara, 61 – 59.

The following day the St. Louis Billikens, the number one team in the land, arrived in Buffalo for a Saturday night game against the Golden Griffins. St. Louis University was another one of those Jesuit institutions of higher learning that discovered that it could outfit a basketball team that in that era could compete on a regular basis with the largest institutions in the country. In that respect, St. Louis was similar to the Little Three schools. The Canisius-St. Louis game was the earliest sellout in the brief history of the Aud. In fact fans were hanging around the Terrace Street lobby offering $15.00 (five times face value) for a ticket. 11,538 fans passed through the turnstiles. That huge assemblage made itself heard. It was on the verge of hysteria as the Griffs came from 13 points down to tie the Billikens at halftime. However in the second half St. Louis went ahead for good. Tom Muller, who had been doing a decent job on Ed McCauley, fouled out. The 6'8" McCauley, with the moniker "Easy Ed," showed why he was everybody's All American. He tallied 16 points and he used his height to nail down the victory. The Billikens outscored the Griffs, 64 – 55 and increased their unblemished record to 9 – 0. In the first game, West Virginia beat Niagara, 71 – 66. Zeke Sinicola rallied the Eagles. As usual there was excitement when Zeke played. But his 23 points did not quite match the 28 point output of consensus All American, Fred Schaus, of the Mountaineers.[31]

A week later Niagara rebounded sharply over a high flying DePaul team. The Blue Demons showed signs of overconfidence. They had just defeated Notre Dame by 21 points. Against Niagara they proceeded to bolt into the lead and hold it for three quarters. Perhaps one could not fault them for being a little cocky. They had Zeke Sinicola under control but they reckoned without Bill Smyth and Tom Birch. Those two took over, and Smyth with 21 points and Birch with 15 led the Purple Eagles to a 57 - 53 stunning upset.

Another Little Three donnybrook was set for January 20. Both Niagara and Canisius had been doing quite well against major competition. Team leaders, Zeke Sinicola and Leroy Chollet were ranked one and two in scoring in Western New York, just one point separating them. Another sellout was expected. 11,686 passed through the turnstiles. As usual, electricity filled the air. The lead changed hands several times. At the final buzzer, Jim Moran tipped in the winning bucket and Niagara nipped the Griffs, 49 – 48. Chollet was held to eight points, and Zeke had just six, so their scoring race did not match the game's excitement.

There were many thrilling games in those years and almost all games were satisfying. Occasionally local fans had to sit through a disastrous game but rarely a disastrous doubleheader. However such was the case when Canisius faced LaSalle and St. Bona faced Loyola of Chicago. Canisius was thoroughly thrashed by the LaSalle Explorers, the #7 team in the nation. The Griffs appeared to be beat physically after the Niagara game. The players looked as though they had played just hours earlier. The Explorers, their roster composed of "all Philadelphia schoolboy stars" won easily, by a score of 59 – 43. Ray Ryan said that LaSalle "simply had too much height, speed, and shooting ability" for Canisius. In the first game, Loyola of Chicago thumped Bona, 48 points for the Windy City quintet, and a measly 34 for the losers. Some 6,739 fans showed up for the evening of humiliation.[32]

The Big Four doubleheader on February 3 provided much better entertainment. This time many of the 11,523 fans watched in astonishment as the U.B. Bulls pulled off, what Ray Ryan called the "upset of the season." Led by Kenmore's Bob Eldridge who scored 15 points, and sophomore center star, Jack Chalmers' 13 points, and aided by a superb defense, the Bulls defeated Niagara, 59 – 53. Mal Eiken demonstrated that he was no slouch as a coach. Eiken called on his fastest guard, Jumping Jack Gushue, to handle Zeke Sinicola, and he rose to the occasion.[33] The other half of that twin bill pitted the Golden Griffins against the Brown Indians and, as usual, the air in the Aud was filled with tension even before the whistle blew. Canisius held a pretty good lead most of the game. However with less than two minutes remaining, trouble broke out. Tempers flared and players scuffled in front of the Bona bench and police rushed out on the court. Fortunately, the rebellious crowd was disbursed before it turned violent. Canisius won, 53 - 44. The game was highlighted by Bob MacKinnon outscoring Bona's ace, Ken Murray, for the 2nd time that season.

A victory over a Little Three opponent was always a cause for jubilation. Perhaps the Griffs did a little too much post game celebrating, because just two days later the Griffs lost to Toledo in the Aud by the score of 59 – 49. But redemption came quickly. The Griffs left almost immediately for a road game in Madison Square Garden where they handily defeated the St. John's Redmen, 59 – 48. Chollet led the way with 23, DeLuca chipped in 13 and Al Masino added 11. For the young Canisius players, it was regarded as a big thrill just to play in Madison Square Garden; to defeat St. John's on their home court was no small feat; it was like frosting on the cake.

The Griffs returned to the Aud to face Nat Holman's formidable CCNY team. Holman told the press that his team was hitting its peak. Surely Canisius would not have argued with that assessment after the Griffs were zapped 70 - 54. *The Herald Tribune* said that this was "City Basketball at its best." CCNY shot 52% and used the fast break and "weaving magic" to bedazzle the Griffs while the defense was holding Chollet to just one field goal. Another packed house of 11,374 looked on. The fans took some comfort in Niagara's narrow victory over St. John's, 56 – 55. The Redmen committed a number of fouls allowing Niagara to capitalize at the charity stripe. The New York press took a different view, asserting that the "redmen beat themselves;" they blew a number of easy shots.[34] A week later the Griffs rebounded with a convincing victory over the Manhattan Jaspers. 6,247 fans were on hand to watch Leroy Chollet etch his mark in the Canisius record book, by becoming the first player ever to reach the 1,000 point plateau. A rousing ovation was a fitting tribute to the star player who had done so much to bring Canisius basketball into the national limelight. In the other contest, U.B. outscored Bucknell, 58 – 50 making it another sweep for the home teams.

Canisius and Niagara then went on the road, Canisius to Syracuse where they lost, 70 – 58, and Niagara to New York City, where they found success. The Purple Eagles played a whale of a game against CCNY. Before 16,000 in the Garden, they found themselves down by 9 with less than 2 minutes to go.

The indomitable Zeke Sinicola went to work. Niagara tied the score just before the end of regulation time. In overtime, Zeke's 35 foot set shot won the game. The final score was 66 – 64. Zeke had a total of 25 points. But it was that last shot, that 35 footer that won the game, that added to the growing sense of immortality. It was an ending for the ages. Not only on the campus in Lewiston, but on Main Street and on Falls Street in downtown Niagara Falls, the legend of Zeke was growing larger and spreading throughout Western New York.

The next week the Griffs got back on the winning track by defeating St. Francis of Brooklyn, 51 – 46. The bigger news was that Niagara University chalked up its 20th win of the season with a convincing triumph over the Bona Brown Indians, 54 – 46. Indeed the Purple Eagles had reached a milestone. It was the very first time that a Niagara team had ever won 20 games in a single season.

Just two days later, on February 26, Notre Dame Coach Ed "Moose" Kraus brought his Fighting Irish to Buffalo for the annual tussle with Canisius. As usual, there was a considerable amount of fanfare leading up to the game. The local Notre Dame Club assembled to help bring down the "thunder." As usual also, the Fighting Irish walked away with the victory. Another record crowd, 11,921, was on hand. The Griffs shot only 25 % and they learned that that kind of shooting was not going to win many games,

Canisius Coach Joe Niland and Notre Dame Coach Moose Kraus at their annual basketball game in the Aud – always a sellout. (Middle party not identified.) *Photo courtesy of Martha Lamparelli, Joe Niland's daughter.*

especially against the likes of Notre Dame. The final score was 59 – 51. Jim O'Halloran with 18 points and John Foley with 17 led the way for the Irish. The locals took consolation in Bob MacKinnon's spectacular game; he had 21 points while holding the great Kevin O'Shea to just seven.

On March 5, the Griffs entertained Boston College before 7,054 fans. It was a topsy - turvey game in the first half with the Griffs trailing by one point at the intermission but then Bob MacKinnon went to work and his game high 24 points broke the game open. It was the first time that season that the Griffs came back to earn a victory after being behind at halftime. They won easily, 63 - 49. In the other game Villanova, sporting a 21 – 3 record, and ranked in the Top 10 nationally, knocked off St. Bona, 43 – 36. All American Paul Arizin led the Wildcats.

The grand finale of the year would once again be the Canisius-Niagara game. With both teams doing well, there was more than the usual pre-game fanfare. The alumni of each institution held a joint luncheon at the Hotel Lafayette, just a few days before the game. Ned Irish, the father of the doubleheader program in the United States was the guest speaker. He passed out praise liberally. He saluted Joe Niland as "America's most up and coming young coach" while reminding his audience that Coach Niland, even with his team at a distinct height disadvantage, had produced several significant upsets. Irish also heaped praise on Buffalo, calling it "America's most enthusiastic basketball city." There would have been wide agreement with Ned's remarks, both locally and nationally.[35]

The game was a sellout, naturally. Leroy Chollet started his 83rd consecutive and final game of his college career. He had 19 points and was able to reach the 400 mark for the season, the first Canisius player ever to do so. The Griffs played well. Al Masino, always a defensive standout, shut down Zeke, outscoring him 6 – 4. But Birch, Smyth, and Foley took up the slack. Each had 13 points and Niagara won, 57 - 52. Niagara had better reserves and they just wore down the Griffs. With less than a minute to go, the entire Aud erupted, giving Chollet a roaring, standing ovation as he exited the game. Niagara partisans joined enthusiastically in the stirring tribute. The *News* remarked that "on that harmonious and sporting note, the greatest doubleheader season in Buffalo's history ended."[36] In addition to being a sellout the game was seen, reportedly by 50,000 fans, on television on WBEN-TV. If that figure was even close to being accurate, it meant that many viewers must have watched the game either at local bars or in large groups in homes fortunate enough to have a television set. There were simply not many television sets in private homes in Western New York in 1949.

The captain of the Golden Griffins, Leroy Chollet, was able to nose out Zeke Sinicola as the college basketball scoring champion of Western New York. Chollet finished the regular season with a 14.99 points per game average. Sinicola was a fraction behind with 14.29. Zeke scored 443 points, an all time high for an upstate player, but he had played in four more games than Chollet. It seemed only appropriate that two of the greatest, most colorful, most popular players ever to set down their sneakers on the Aud court should be involved in such a heated, season-long scoring race.

The season ended on a high note for Western New York fans. Niagara's 24 – 7 record was its best ever and promised to remain at the top of the record books for a long time. They lost only one out of their final 13 contests, a remarkable streak. Joe Niland, in his first full season, also did an excellent job. He coached his squad to a 16 – 12 record and as usual knocked off some of the leading cage powers in the country.

Second year coach Eddie Milkovitch achieved 18 wins and lost only 8 games, a record of which he could be justly proud. The University of Buffalo, with Mal Eiken calling the shots from the bench, won 11 and lost 9. To say that basketball was alive and well in Western New York was an understatement. The *Buffalo Evening News* called 1948-49 one of the best seasons ever.

Canisius' Leroy Chollet was listed on the Honorable Mention Associated Press All American team. The great Chollet gathered in numerous awards: MVP in the Aud, All-Western New York, All-Little Three, and as the school newspaper the Griffin noted: "Honorable Mention on All-American squads too numerous to mention." Certainly Bob MacKinnon reinforced his star status in the 1948-49 season. A fitting end to the season for MacKinnon came in the Jesuit Mission benefit game. Even though Holy Cross was victorious over Canisius in that fund raiser, Bob MacKinnon was named MVP over Bob Cousy. The Griffs had something to boast about since the "Coos" was recognized, universally, as the premier guard of his generation.

Attendance throughout most of the nation had declined slightly during 1948-49, but not so in Buffalo. The *Griffin* newspaper of March 4, 1949 reported that Buffalo continued to set records for doubleheaders. For the 2nd consecutive year, the record mark in attendance was broken. Buffalo's average attendance jumped from 7,000 to over 8,000. Nearly 180,000 had shown up for the Aud doubleheaders. New York City went from, 17,000 down to 15,000 and Philadelphia went from 9,000 to 7,000 on average. Television possibly may have aided in the attendance. Record crowds were established on the nights that games were telecast, and the smallest crowds were on Thursday nights when video was denied the public. *The Sporting News*, arguably the leading sports vehicle in the country in the 1940s, interviewed Doc Crowdle on the subject of Buffalo's preeminence as a college basketball center. Crowdle reviewed the Aud program and cited factors responsible for its success. He singled out the facility itself, the fervent Buffalo fans, and the cordial working relationship with Ned Irish. This national recognition added to the luster of the Aud and to the city of Buffalo.[37]

Impresario Ned Irish was right, nationally renowned coach Clair Bee was right, college basketball experts were correct when they labeled Buffalo, a hotbed of college basketball. The Aud was second in the nation in attendance. Only the Garden, Madison Square Garden in New York City, the mother venue of all college basketball, surpassed Buffalo's downtown arena in the late 1940s as a mecca for college basketball fans. 179,699 had passed through the turnstiles in the Aud. The Queen City of the Lakes had reason to be proud. Year after year, the local institutions, especially Niagara and Canisius, were fielding competitive teams, and managing to be victorious regularly against some of the very best teams in the nation. Bona had become competitive and had upgraded its schedule and the University of Buffalo showed that it could play with top rated teams too.

Looking ahead to the 1949-50 season, there was good reason for Western New York sports fans to be cheerful. Nineteen doubleheaders were scheduled. There would be one every Saturday night during the season except for Christmas Eve. Some Thursdays would also be included. Thirty one of the nation's top teams would participate, including the NIT Champion, the University of San Francisco Dons; NIT finalist Loyola of Chicago; Oregon State, Pacific Coast Champion and Final Four participant; Washington State, runner-up to Oregon State in the Pacific Coast Conference; the University of Denver, Mountain State Conference Champion; Kansas State, Big

7 champion; and Western Kentucky, the Ohio Valley Champion. As usual, Syracuse, the 1948-49 winner of the Seelbach Trophy, indicative of upstate basketball supremacy, would be on the Aud schedule. The heyday of the Aud doubleheader program was continuing.

Niagara had all their stars returning from their outstanding 24-7 team. Their stretch run of 12 wins in the last 13 games should have assured them a post season tournament. Why they were not invited boggles the mind. The Purple Eagles would be first rate once again. The trio of sensational sophomores: the electrifying Zeke Sinicola known for his set shots and his daring drives to the basket, Tom Birch, with his accurate one hand shot from 20 feet away, and Jim Moran, a strong rebounder, would be back for their junior year. Back with them for their senior year would be Harry "the Horse" Foley, noted for his aggressiveness under the boards, and playmaker and Captain Bill Smyth.

At Canisius, Joe Niland, in his second full season, would have more height than usual, a rare luxury for the Main Street school. Randy Sharp, at 6'9" and 6'5" Herm Hedderick, were the tallest. Joining them, all over 6', were John Krochmal, Mike McGuire, and Bob Stoetzel. Another strength for the Griffs was the veteran backcourt led by Captain Bobby MacKinnon, and ably assisted by Mort O'Sullivan and Al Masino.

Back for their senior year at St. Bona would be Ken Murray, and a quartet of steady veterans, Frank Ready, Ed Krause, Fred Diute, and Sam Urzetta. Murray continued to be the leading scorer and the team's sparkplug, Ready was a defensive ace, Urzetta, a set shot artist, and Diute and Krause were, respectably, 2nd and 3rd in scoring. Coach Milkovitch was quite happy with his returnees.

At the University of Buffalo, Coach Mal Eiken would be without his top scorer, Bob Eldridge, but he had 6'4" Jack Chalmers back. Chalmers had become a prolific scorer, himself. Jack Reid, Bill Needham, and Hal Kuhn all could be counted on to provide valuable assistance.

The 1949-59 season in the Aud was tipped off as was customary with a warm up doubleheader over the Thanksgiving Day weekend. 5,243 fans were on hand to watch Canisius easily defeat Western Ontario. With Al Masino hitting a high of 16 points the Griffs demolished the Canadian squad, 60 – 24. Washington and Jefferson defeated the University of Buffalo, almost as easily. The U. B. squad, riddled by injuries made a "good game" out of it for a half. The score was tied at halftime but the Presidents went on to whack the Bulls, 64 – 40. U.B. just did not have the depth to keep up with the opposing team. Ed Gicewicz who had just finished playing football the previous Saturday, scored 6 points and proved to be "a willing and aggressive" player, a welcome addition to the squad.[38]

The "real" season got underway on December 3 with a couple of blockbuster games. The locals performed up to expectations. In the first game, Texas A & M pulled ahead of Niagara early and led comfortably for much of the contest. Then Niagara woke up. The Purple Eagles blanked the Texans in an eight minute stretch. The Aud became just plain bedlam as Joe Smyth and his fellow Purple Eagles stormed back wiping out a 13 point deficit in the final five minutes and ended up winning 53 – 50. In the nightcap the Griffs knocked off Oregon State, 58 - 45 behind the stellar all around performance of Bob MacKinnon and an 18 point output by Herm Hedderick. The crowd of 10,331 was a healthy omen for the 1949-50 season.

One week later, 11,127 watched another thrilling pair of games. Niagara led by Moran, Foley, and Birch beat Southern Methodist University, 55 - 47. The Griffs followed up, a few hours later, with a 54-51 win over Kansas

State. Johnny DeLuca's "peerless exhibition of set shooting" aided by Don Hartnett and Al Masino accounted for 38 of the Griff's points. Ray Ryan called the game, a "heart stopper." Those who followed the local teams on their home radios were able to share some of the rousing excitement because now Bill Mazur had arrived in Buffalo. Sponsored by the Atlantic Refining Company he broadcasted the games over WKBW on a regular basis. Mazur's spirited enthusiasm became a hallmark of his broadcasts. His success in Buffalo catapulted him to the top of the sports radio business in New York City years later. Some fans claimed that he may have been seen him as a forerunner of Dick Vitale.[39]

Next, the University of Southern California arrived in town. The Trojans were led by Bill Sharman, said to be the West Coast's best player since Hank Luisetti, Stanford's jump shot artist, who had revolutionized the game in the 1930s. Sharman lived up to this billing. His 27 points led his team over Canisius 69 - 55. Sharman had perfected an all but unstoppable reverse pivot shot. At the conclusion of the season, Sharman was named a first team All American. As part of that doubleheader, 6,415 fans saw Niagara eke out a 55 – 54 victory over Denver. It was another thriller for Niagara and once again Sinicola's 14 points led the way. Zeke's long set shot, with just 29 seconds to go, proved to be the winning bucket. Denver's big center, 6'6" Dale Toft had been having a fine game; he had 24 points and was looking for more in the final seconds. Denver had the ball and set up Toft for the final shot. Toft got the shot off but, as Ray Ryan noted he "was knocked off the court and off his feet by Sinicola on the play, but no foul was called." Kritzer tersely added: "Sinicola racked him up."[40]

Two days later, Canisius faced the University of California Golden Bears before 6,983 paying customers. DeLuca set the pace for the Griffs in a spectacular 55 - 53 win. Randy Sharp had two clutch baskets including the game winner. Griff fans were delighted; they now had some "hope in a big guy" in their future. California had an All American Candidate, Captain Bill Hagler, whose one handed shooting netted 25 points. In the first game, Washington State beat U. B., 56 - 44. U.B. led at the half. Chalmers with 9, Gushee with 10, and Needham with 11 played their hearts out. But those three had to play almost the entire game and they became exhausted. The Cougars simply had too much bench strength. Nevertheless it appeared that the Bulls partly regained some confidence they might have lost in the rout to Washington and Jefferson in the season opener.

At this juncture in the campaign, Canisius at 6 - 1 was rated # 11 in the country directly behind Western Kentucky. The Hilltoppers just happened to be the next opponent for the Griffs slated for the day after Christmas. The Kentuckians were led by 6'7" All American Bob Lavoy. He had a super night; he went to work immediately and accumulated a total of 34 points while leading his team to a 74 - 61 victory. The devastating loss was a blow to the Top Ten hopes of the Griffs. It was a double disappointment in that it was a repeat of what happened the previous season when the Griff's hopes to crack the Top Ten were thwarted by the same institution. In the first game the Temple Owls, one of the best of the Big Five teams from Philadelphia, easily defeated the U.B. Bulls despite Chalmers 23 points. Bill Mikvy had 26 for the Owls.

The Western Kentucky team, in a forecast of the future, flew to Buffalo on a chartered airline. In the 1940s most teams visiting Buffalo from any great distance still came by railroad. In fact that was one of the chief reasons that Doc Crowdle was able to construct an outstanding schedule. Teams from the west and southwest had splendid connections through Chicago and to Buffalo and then on to New York City and Philadelphia. In the following decade that would change drastically as rail travel dwindled and air travel grew by leaps and bounds. The Western Kentucky team stayed at the Hotel Buffalo which was one of the closest hotels to the Aud, so a natural choice. That too would change in the years ahead, as various hotels in downtown Buffalo would close for lack of business and would then give way to chains of motels and hotels located on the outskirts of the city, some near the airport.

The Brown Indians of St. Bona came into the Aud on December 29. They posted an impressive victory for Coach Eddie Milkovitch as they nipped Brown University 54 - 51 behind Murray's 18 point performance. In the nightcap of that Aud twin bill, the Griffs got back on the winning track; for the first time ever they defeated Utah. They did so handily, 49 - 39. A solid Thursday night crowd of 6,645 watched Bob MacKinnon and Don Hartnett lead the way in handing the Utes their worst defeat of the season.

Canisius College and the University of Utah had a cordial relationship that dated back to the NIT tournament in 1944 in Madison Square Garden. Both teams were knocked out of the NIT, Canisius by Oklahoma A. & M. and Utah by Kentucky. But the Utah squad, subsequently, received a bid to the NCAA tournament. Utah faced a crisis. It did not have enough basketball shoes. In the midst of World War II there was a severe shortage of rubber. The Canisius Coach at the time was Allie Seelbach. He came to the rescue; he said "take ours" and they did, and the Utes ended up wearing Canisius College sneakers and won the NCAA tournament defeating Dartmouth. Did this mean that a part of Canisius actually won the NCAA tournament? Moreover, in a special Red Cross World War II benefit game, Utah, the NCAA champion defeated St. John's the NIT champion. Utah again was partly outfitted by Canisius.

On New Year's Eve, 1949, more than 10,000 fans saw the locals drop two close encounters. The Griffs lost to Ivy League power, Cornell, 47 - 43. The first half was just plain ugly, it was appropriately called "a chamber of horrors basketball game." It was said that neither team "could have thrown the ball into the Buffalo Harbor...not far from the scene of carnage." Canisius, in the first half shot 4 of 29 while Cornell was 6 for 24. The second half was only slightly better. MacKinnon and Hartnett each managed to tally 13 points. In the other game, Niagara lost to a powerful University of San Francisco team but the fans got their money's worth. San Francisco rushed to a big lead and continued to lead much of the way. Then Niagara staged one of its classic comebacks; urged on by the traditional din coming from their cheering sections, the Eagles struck with stunning suddenness. Niagara hit 6 points in just 24 seconds. But it was just not quite enough. San Francisco held on for a 52 – 48 victory. Moran had 15 and Birch and Zeke had 11 each.[41]

Canisius and Niagara quickly redeemed themselves. The Griffs knocked off the highly touted Billikens of St. Louis before 10,993. The Griffs scored one of their epic victories. They came from behind with just over a minute to play and pulled off a 55 – 50 win. Hedderick, DeLuca, and MacKinnon led the Main Street forces. Earlier that evening, once beaten Niagara had defeated West Virginia, 70 – 63 behind the scoring of Zeke and Harry Foley. Each had 21 points. Taps' troops also made up a second half deficit in earning the win. With a capacity crowd on hand, and with the locals winning closely contested games, it was the kind of doubleheader that Buffalo fans would reminisce about for decades. In fact while listening to fans wax nostalgic many years later, one might have concluded that at least 500,000 fans attended such a doubleheader.

Notre Dame, always a big attraction came to town on January 14 and played Canisius before 11,031. Notre Dame had been making an annual appearance for several years and though Canisius always gave the Irish a good battle, the Irish invariably departed with a victory. This year the outcome was different. The game was hotly contested for the full forty minutes. Lanky Randy Sharp was having a difficult time against the tough Irish defense. Coach Niland substituted Tom Muller near the end of the game and Muller played probably the best few minutes of his entire career, pouring in six crucial points and acting like a tiger around the backboards. Canisius won, 53 - 50.

With both Niagara and Canisius playing top flight basketball, the first clash of the season between the two arch rivals reckoned to be a thriller. It was just that. Over 12,000 packed the Aud, 12,053 to be exact, and the rooters from the Cataract City cheered lustily as their team surged ahead by nine points at the beginning of the second half. The Griffs stormed back; it became a closely fought contest right to the final buzzer. Bob MacKinnon's key baskets secured the win for the Griffs, 49 - 47.

Another doubleheader saw undefeated Bona defeat its sister Franciscan institution, Siena College, by the score of 52 - 47. Canisius thrashed Georgetown, 58 - 41 in the other game, a contest that saw Frank Pleto come into his own as a star for the Griffs. Pleto led all scorers with 16 points but it was more than just putting the ball in the hoop that earned him the fans' admiration. Pleto played at an explosive pace, literally just about knocking himself out, running up and down the court faster than anyone else. The spectators loved it as Frank ran and ran and then ran some more. 7,485 witnessed this performance.

At this halfway point of the season, Cy Kritzer was convinced that the Little Three was one of the strongest conferences in the nation. His column noted that the three schools had an amazing winning mark of 84%. Bona was still undefeated at 9 – 0, Canisius stood at 11 – 3 and Niagara at 12 – 3. The Little Three schools had chalked up 32 wins in 38 games. The Aud was selling out, not always but often.

Canisius began the second half of the season on a winning note, notching its fifth straight, this one over a stubborn Scranton team. Pleto, DeLuca and Hartnett led the attack. The University of Connecticut in the first game, a game filled with foul shots, bested the University of Buffalo, 56 – 40. U.B's center, Jack Chalmers, who had been racking up double digits regularly, was held in check with just 3 points. Obviously that hurt the Bulls' cause. The smallest crowd of the season, a mere 4,876, was on hand.

On February 2 all the major local teams played in what, decades later, would be known as a Big 4 doubleheader. A new record crowd of 12,065 turned out. Bona put its eleven game winning streak on the line against Canisius. The Griffs demonstrated why they were one of the top defensive teams in the East. The Brown Indians lost four men on personal fouls, and Canisius lost none. Despite Ken Murray's 18 points, the Brown Indians fell to Canisius, 49 - 42. The first game of the twin bill was even more exciting. It was a true heartbreaker for the U.B. Bulls. They led Niagara for 39 minutes and then fell, 51- 49. U.B. had lost three of their regulars on fouls and the substitutes could not stand up to the Niagara press, and that allowed the Eagles to fend off the upstarts seeking the upset.

Two days later, the Bona team showed its resilience as it downed Loyola of Chicago, 55 – 51, to go to 11 – 1 for the season. This time Ken Murray and his 27 points would not be denied. In the other half of the program the crowd of 8,181, watched Syracuse beat Canisius, 59 – 49. The Griffs' six game winning streak came to an end; Syracuse won the game at the foul line making 21 of 24, an unusually high percentage for the Orangemen. The Griffs had only half as many opportunities from the charity stripe. The

Orangemen were having a very good year. A few days later they convinced any remaining doubters, when they defeated Niagara at Niagara 60 - 55 to end the Eagles' home winning streak at fifty-one games.

The first part of February saw both Canisius and Niagara trying to cope with the great Bob Zawoluk, St. John's outstanding center. Zawoluk poured in 22 points as he broke the St John's single season scoring record at 382. The game was played in Madison Square Garden. The Redmen won 62 - 50. It was a rough, tough contest, with plenty of close body contact between Herm Heddrick and Zawoluk but once the game was over, both teams, on friendly terms, boarded the same midnight sleeper to Buffalo for games at the Aud the following night. The New York press saw it somewhat differently. *The Daily News* stated that "What might have been one of Buffalo's best Golden Gloves squads was merely the Golden Griffins of Canisius who manhandled St. John's something awful." *The Daily Mirror* claimed that "a great football game was turned into a mediocre basketball game" by the officials. "Zeke Zawoluk had more black and blue marks on him than points...Canisius was belting the Redman line with its single wing attack." *The Herald Tribune* stated "anyone watching the first half of the scrap between the Bushwack tribesmen and their Buffalo rivals would have been excused for doubting that Canisius had abandoned football." It undoubtedly was a tough game but even the Redmen ballplayers admitted that Canisius was not the roughhouse outfit that the hostile New York City press alleged.[42]

A short time later in Buffalo, St. John's faced Niagara. On the same twin bill, Canisius hosted the highflying CCNY squad. Again another Aud record was established, as 12,105 saw Zalowuk lead the highly rated Redmen to a 72 - 63 victory over Niagara. The big guy's 38 points skewered the Eagles. In the nightcap, the Griffs downed the CCNY Beavers. Frank Pleto had an excellent game but it was Randy Sharp who was the man of the hour. The lanky Canisius center sank three field goals near the end of the game to secure the win. The pundits noted that Joe Niland coached brilliantly as he forced Nat Holman's club to play his style of ball.

In the final weeks of the 1949-50 season, Niagara seemed to be faltering. An NIT bid was still a possibility for them and something they wanted badly. The NIT was the premier tournament, especially in the eyes of the Eastern teams. In fact, the colleges in the New York City area seemed to have preferential treatment for a berth. With only 12 spots available it was rather difficult to make the cut in those years. But the Purple Eagles were hopeful. With that in mind Niagara felt it was facing a must win situation when it traveled to New York City to play CCNY. 18,000 were in the Garden and watched Niagara upset the home team despite a 23 point performance by Ed Roman, the dominant center for the locals. It was not enough to offset the performances of Sinicola and Birch who had 15 each. The Purple Eagles were now in a good position to receive the bid.

It was still winter in Buffalo. The weather was cold and blustery especially in the vicinity of the Aud. Nevertheless 6,751 fans hardy souls turned out to watch U.B. beat Hawaii 69 - 50, and Canisius top Manhattan, 52 – 50. Jack Chalmers emerged as the top scorer in U.B.'s history, passing the legendary Lou Corriere. In the Canisius game, the Griffs, behind the steady work of guard Al Masino won in overtime. Meanwhile in Niagara Falls, the Purple Eagles reached the 18 - 6 mark, with a 58 – 45 bashing of Bona.

Canisius too had felt that it was in the running for an NIT bid. Unfortunately for the Griffs their prospects dimmed and then crashed in the games that followed. In a double overtime contest Bona nipped the Griffs 52 - 51 before 10,942. Don Hartnett had one of his finest nights ever in a Canisius uniform, pumping in 28 points. Hartnett's heroics were in vain as Ken Murray, old Mr. Reliable for the Brown Indians, put in the winner in the second overtime. Incredibly, Bob MacKinnon was blanked, the first time ever since he had become a starter. A week later the Griffs took the four hour bus ride to Cornell, lost in a rout 65 – 43 and returned to prepare for the grand finale with Niagara.

An inspired and perhaps rowdy crowd could be expected to be on hand for the final Aud game of the year, the traditional end of the home season for Niagara and Canisius. The fans tramped through the snow down Main Street from Shelton Square in record numbers. The bitter winter weather was no obstacle. Ray Ryan called it "the greatest crowd in the history of Buffalo basketball." 12,111 watched the Griffs' tournament aspirations receive another crushing blow; in fact it was the final nail in the coffin.[43] Zeke had a great game; the crowd loved it. It was called a classic "Zeke the Zipper" performance, one marked by his long sets swishing the nets and further enhancing the Zeke legend. Niagara won 51 – 42. The fans came too, to pay their respects to some of the graduating seniors of both teams. Unfortunately the timing was poor for one of the greatest Canisius stars of all time. Bob MacKinnon was not able to get the recognition he so richly deserved. He was taken out with just a minute to go, but at that very instant someone called timeout and so the entire Canisius team was around Bob as he sat down quietly. A short time later, with the game nearly over, the whistle blew. Mort O'Sullivan had possession of the ball. In a warm gesture of sportsmanship, Mort presented the ball to Captain Bill Smyth of Niagara. It was a fitting climax, as Smyth hugged Mort, two more great players in their last Aud appearance.

Niagara's spectacular six game stretch drive capped with the decisive victory over

Zeke Sinicola, Niagara set shot artist. *Photo: Pat Smyton*

Canisius earned them a bid to the National Invitation Tournament. Canisius was definitely out of the running after the loss to Niagara. Any hopes that Bona had for a tournament were also dashed when the Brown Indians lost to Seton Hall, 42 - 41.

The Griffs showed they had at least a little gas left as the beat Syracuse 65 - 64 for their 17th win. They also showed they could actually make a high percentage of free throws. They made 21 of 28, their usual performance was below 50%. Summing up the Griffs' 1949-50 season, Jack Laing the new sports editor for the *Courier Express*, put it succinctly, "They played a terrific schedule all the way, facing many of the country's top quintets...but we believe that they are just beat out."[44] It was the final home game for Lew Andreas, Syracuse's well liked and respected coach. Andreas had coached for over a quarter century at Syracuse. The Orangemen went on to the NIT defeating LIU and then succumbing to Bradley in the quarterfinals.

Meanwhile Niagara relished its well deserved bid to the NIT. The student body on the picturesque campus overlooking the Niagara River gorge was elated. The joy spread throughout the Cataract City from Flynn's famous downtown shoe store to the stately Hotel Niagara to Luigi's famous watering hole. Niagara fans provided considerable support. The squad would need it. The Purple Eagles had their work cut out for them. They would be playing the # 2 seed, Western Kentucky, in a field that had many of the top 20 teams in the country. But Niagara would feel right at home, as a majority of their players were natives of the New York City area. The game itself was a thriller. Niagara fought valiantly against the tall Kentuckians. The game was marked by several ties, but Big Bob Lavoy was just too much to handle. His 32 points sparked their 79 - 72 victory. Western Kentucky continued to be a menace to Western New York teams.

CCNY won the NIT and CCNY also won the NCAA tournament that year, in fact in the same month; the first and last team to ever do that. Unfortunately that magnificent accomplishment by Nat Holman's team would be forever marred. A year later the infamous basketball scandals broke. Some CCNY players were central figures in what proved to be a devastating gambling, point spread, disaster. The CCNY team's future was ignominiously clouded.

1949-59 was another banner year for Western New York basketball in the Aud. The 19 doubleheaders had drawn an average

Niagara Team, 1949-50. ***Left to right: First row:*** **Tom Birch, Joe Smyth, Jim Moran, Capt. Bill Smyth, Harry Foley, Ed Murphy, Zeke Sinicola.** ***Second row:*** **Jim Jennings, Wally Rooney, Frank Powers, John Spanbauer, Art Hutson, Jim Brennan, Trainer Bill Dascoulias.** ***Third row:*** **Taps, Merv Mink, Jim Delaney, Walter Johnson, John Donohue, Jim Sotis, Manager Don Statt.** *Photo: Pat Symton.*

of 9,281 spectators. That was the best Aud attendance in history. Individual players accumulated laurels too. Bob MacKinnon was named on the All American second team published by the *Sporting News*. Ken Murray of St. Bona was named to the 4th team. The native of West Orange, New Jersey, was the first Bona player ever to reach the 1000 point mark; his number, #13, was retired. Niagara's Sinicola also received richly deserved post season honors.

There was no reason to anticipate that the 50-51 season would not be just as successful as the recent campaigns. Television, still in its infancy in Buffalo, had not shown any signs of hurting college basketball attendance. Suburbia was just beginning to boom throughout Western New York. It was not yet viewed as a threat to the commercial and entertainment dominance of downtown Buffalo. The Korean War broke out in June 1950 and by the time the basketball season was underway American troops were committed in large numbers. United Nations forces, led by U.S. troops, had rescued the South Koreans at the Pusan perimeter and by the end of 1950 had pushed the North Koreans back across the 38th parallel and up to the Yalu River. Then the Chinese Communists entered the conflict in massive numbers and in 1951 the war bogged down. Despite the fact that many college age men were either drafted or recruited in this first major "hot" conflict of the Cold War, the impact of the loss of manpower on college sports was nowhere near what it was in World War II. Indeed the Korean War was a spurt to the local economy. Buffalo continued to be a major site for the manufacture of war material. Overall Buffalo continued to appear to be a vibrant city. The 1950 census would show that Buffalo had the largest population in the city's history.

The Aud basketball schedule was announced in September. The 21 date card was highlighted by the first time appearance of Bradley University. Bradley was the runner up in both the NIT and the NCAA the previous season and was expected to vie for the number one position in the country in 1950-51. Duke would make its first appearance; several other big name institutions from the South and West would again be represented. Canisius would play in 20 of the 21 doubleheaders, Niagara would play in 10 and Bona and U.B. would play in 6 each.

The downtown arena promised some excellent basketball in the upcoming season. The coaches and players were well prepared and the fans as usual were eager for the excitement of big time college basketball. Crowds of ten to twelve thousand were now the norm. College basketball was strong. It was growing even stronger. All local teams had acquitted themselves well in 1949-50. A few great names passed from the playing scene and into the record books. Bob MacKinnon and Ken Murray were achieving legendary status as alumni of their institutions. Other standout players remained on the active rosters, and potential stars had been recruited and were in the wings getting ready to contribute during the upcoming campaign. All of the Big Four coaches were returning. Eddie Milkovitch at Bona had posted an excellent 17 - 5 record, and Taps Gallagher at Niagara had done even better, reaching the magical 20 win mark, with a 20 – 7 record. Both Joe Niland at Canisius at 17 - 8 and Mal Eiken at U.B. at 15 - 10 could be proud of their accomplishments. Buffalo State, though rarely on the Aud program, ended up with a fine 12 – 6 record, with Hube Coyer continuing as head coach. It was surely as good a group of coaches as had ever been assembled for basketball in Western New York.

Canisius was slated to boast their tallest team ever, and the key would be 6'9" Randy Sharp. He had shown improvement but he needed to be more consistent. In the backcourt, Don Foreman had shown signs of being able to step in to be a major contributor. Ed Milkovich's Bonaventure teams had improved steadily during his three seasons of coaching at the Olean school; the prediction was that they would be even better in 1950-51. Captain Fred Diute, second in scoring to Ken Murray, figured to be a star upfront. Some terrific sophomores would be available; Bob Sassone, Mike Bednar, and Bill Kenville. Bona could be the biggest surprise of the campaign. It was also predicted that the University of Buffalo team would be better than last year. Mal Eiken's team would have more height, stronger reserves and more team speed. Jack Chalmers, the first Bull ever to reach the 1,000 point mark would be back for his senior year. He would be joined by Hal Kuhn, sophomore of the year in WNY in 1949-50. Like Chalmers, Kuhn would eventually be a member of the 1,000 point club. Both would one day be inducted into the U.B. Hall of Fame. Coincidentally both averaged 15.2 points over their college career. As far as Niagara University was concerned, Taps Gallagher would be short on depth but his starting quintet would be top notch. The trio of Sinicola, Birch and Moran would lead the way, just as they did into last year's NIT, and would be ably assisted by Joe Smyth at center and John Spanbauer at forward. Cy Kritzer stated that "it's a slick team that should run most of its opponents into the boards." Hube Coyer at State would miss Captain Clair Westcott, but five returning veterans would be the cornerstone of his team.

Sometimes too much success brings problems. Father Dineen, Canisius director of athletics, had to deal with student complaints about the seating selection in the Aud. Students were allotted a portion of the premier side brown, floor level, seats. Seniors had preference. Late comers and underclassmen had to settle for corner blue and side gray, at the nose bleed level. Students voiced their concerns saying that they felt they deserved more of the good seats. In an open letter to the students, Dineen noted that college basketball was now a business so it was necessary to save a number of the best seats for those willing to pay full price. If there was not sufficient revenue to cover the costs of operating in a big public arena, such as the Aud. "This could be the last season of college basketball…" Dineen made a veiled threat, he told the students that if they insisted on a new seating arrangement that would mean decreased revenues and fewer receipts and then less desirable teams coming to play. "We will end up playing in our gym with a minor league classification." Those strong words quieted the students temporarily. But the issue never did go away; it would be reiterated by students at NCAA institutions ad infinitum.

The Aud season opened on Thanksgiving weekend. The Canisius game against Western Ontario was played the way it was supposed to be. It was a warm up for the Griffs. Presumably the authorities were not too disappointed that the crowd was only about 4,000, given the level of competition. As expected, Canisius trounced the Canadian team, 78 - 45. Randy Sharp sharpened his skills for the season by scoring 13 points and reliable Don Hartnett chipped in with 11, all available Griffs saw some action. The Canadian universities did not pay much attention to the sport of basketball in that era, but they were always "good sports." Years later the Canadian schools would develop some outstanding blue chip players. The other half of the doubleheader proved much more entertaining. The University of Buffalo Bulls rallied from a half time deficit 36 – 24 and made a real game out of it, before losing to Washington and Jefferson by just two points, 64 – 62.

The first big doubleheader of the season took place the following week and matched two western powers against the Golden Griffins and the Purple Eagles. In the first game Brigham Young University, the Skyline Champions, defeated Niagara, 84 – 69. Mel Hutchins, a legitimate All American Candidate, paced the visitors with 28 points. Niagara fell behind early. The famous fast break led by Zeke and Smyth, together they accounted for 37 points, rallied the Eagles but not enough to close the gap. Niagara did not get much help from its bench and that was a factor in the 84 – 69 loss. BYU had its third win of the season and its 21st in a row. Brigham Young's success continued throughout the 50-51 season culminating in its winning the NIT championship in March.

Local fans, and there were more than 10,000 of them, received some satisfaction in the second game as they watched the Griffs, rather easily knock off Oregon State, 59 – 47. Herm Hedderick had 14 and Don Hartnett 13, but it was the excellent defense put up by Coach Joe Niland's forces that spelled victory. Less than a week later, Hedderick and Hartnett again led the Griffs attack, this time against the Texas A & M squad. The score changed hands several times, then, unfortunately the Griffs made some huge mistakes at crucial junctures that led directly to defeat. They had the ball stolen from them and, as Ray Ryan noted in the *Courier*, the Aggies struck "with cobra speed and precision for two baskets in the last 30 seconds."[45] Jewell McDowell, a slight 5'9" guard, picked off a pass and laid it in with seconds to go to allow the Aggies to escape with a 45 – 44 victory. Perhaps it was surprising that the score was so close since the Griffs shot a lowly 25%. In contrast to the mistake prone Griffs, the Brown Indians played very well against Valpariso. The boys from Olean were "smooth, flawless and effortless" as they "whaled" Valpariso, 79 – 61, behind the "phenomenal set shooting and driving ability" of newcomer Bob Sassone. The bespectacled 19-year-old, Long Island native clicked for 25 points. As Ryan put it, Bona "unveiled a young man who will be heard from in the future." Indeed Bob Sassone would be a vital part of the Brown Indians' basketball program for years to come.

Two nights later, nearly 10,000 turned out for a Canisius-SMU and Niagara-Denver twin bill. They were not disappointed. Niagara clipped Denver, 50 – 44 in a game that was a "tribute to Taps superb defensive strategy." Joe Smyth turned in a big job at center by outscoring Denver's All American Candidate, Dale Toft, 14 – 6. Zeke Sinicola contributed 18 points. Canisius supporters were still moaning over the previous loss, some called it a 'give-away," to the Texas Aggies. Gradually their mood improved as they watched their heroes rally behind Milan Miller and Don Hartnett in the SMU game. An additional spark was furnished by Randy Sharp; the Griffins defeated the Mustangs, 64 – 55.

Another Thursday night doubleheader, sparsely attended, saw the locals win both ends of the program. The Griffs were in top shape in their 59 to 45 victory over the University of Texas. They cast aside their slipshod manners and they "looked like a smooth, integrated machine." The exciting offense threw five fast breaks at the Longhorns. Milan Miller and Don Foreman were right on the money with their precision passes. Coach Niland was especially pleased with Sharp's performance; he wanted to see if the lanky center had the stamina to play virtually the entire game. Sharp did and he contributed 20 points. In the first game, the University of Buffalo was victorious over the University of Delaware by a score of 54 to 38. It was an easy victory for the Bulls. Their star, Jack Chalmers, accounted for half the Bulls' points. An interesting sidelight; a Western New York native, Jim Konstanty, the Philadelphia Phillies' ace relief pitcher, officiated the first game. The consensus was that he did a good job. Not bad for one who was honored nationally as athlete of the year for his superb season in baseball.[46]

Just two days later, on December 16, the same two teams again served as the hosts in the doubleheader program. This time U.B. had to take on a strong Washington State team. They were trounced, 70 – 49. The Cougars used their height to good advantage, kept a steady lead and allowed 11 of their players to break into the scoring column. The old reliable duet of Chalmers and Kuhn paced the Bulls. In the nightcap the Griffs gained their 6th win of the season against perennial nemesis, Utah. The Griffs surged in front early, had a one point advantage at halftime, received some timely help from Jerry Stockman and John Krochmal, and pulled away for a 49 – 43 win.

Basketball then took a short Christmas recess. Fans could join the multitude of other shoppers who crowded downtown Buffalo for some last minute Christmas shopping. Kids by the thousands flooded the downtown department stores, dragging their parents along in their effort to determine which of the big stores had the best, or the real Santa, and which store had the best model railroad display. Usually Lionel won out over the American Flyer brand, and Hengerer's, and J.N. Adams fought a close race for having the number one Santa. As the decade of the 1950s got underway, Buffalo remained one of the nation's major cities with major spectator sports and a bustling downtown.

The day after Christmas, Canisius took on the undefeated Wildcats from the University of Arizona. The Griffs were ready; they won victory number eight while ousting the Wildcats from the ranks of the unbeaten. Milan Miller was the hero; "the dynamo from Gowanda" Cy Kritzer labeled him. Ray Ryan added that, "The cinderella guard whipped three scoring passes in such mystifying fashion that his opponents were "befuddled" in this night of his "greatest performance." In the other game, the UB Bulls suffered their fourth defeat, 61 –51, this one at the hands of the University of Connecticut. The Huskies, while upping their record to 9 and 1, put up a good zone defense which nullified the Bulls' inside game. Chalmers had 13 and Kuhn 12 in the losing cause.[47]

On the night before New Year's Eve the Griffs, going strong at 8 – 1, faced an unbeaten Cornell team. Ardent Griff fans saw their team, once again, at the threshold of breaking into the Top Ten. The Big Red, last year's Seelbach trophy winner, had a very good team throughout most of the post World War II era, and this year was no exception. In fact Cornell may have been one of the best in the entire East. But Niland thought he had the players to get the job done. Indeed Niland never backed down from any opponent. He was confident in the work of the improving Randy Sharp and Milan Miller, and he could always count on the dependable Herm Hedderick, Bob Stoetzel, and Don Hartnett. Miller complied with 15 and Hedderick did so with 20 points but Sharp was shut out completely and Hartnett was limited to 2 free throws for the evening. The Big Red defense had done its job. Cornell traveled back to Ithaca with a 58 - 49 victory and with the jubilant feeling that came with playing before the largest crowd of the season, 11,697. In fact many hopefuls mulled about in the Terrace Street lobby hoping a ticket would turn up. Some 2,500 fans were turned away. In the first game, Bona did much better than its Little Three cohorts. Playing another nemesis of the Western New York teams, the Western Kentucky Hilltoppers, the Brown Indians were sharp. Team leader Fred Diute had 18 points, and Bob Sassone chimed in with 12. Bona won 62- 57. It was a rare defeat for the Hilltoppers on their annual Northern swing.

On New Year's night, 1951, a crowd of 6,557 turned out for a premiere doubleheader, and watched the Griffs return to the victory path by downing the Duke Blue Devils, 69 – 57. Sharp was sharp; he used his height to great advantage for tap-ins and wheeling hooks. His teammate, Herm Hedderick was the master of the outside one-hand shot; he riddled the Dukes' defense with 8 of them for his 16 points. Ray Ryan said Griffs' fans were elated as they watched the Griffs "flashing a gaudy second half rally." Dick Groat, the Dukes' sure bet for All American honors was limited to 11 points. He had been averaging 21 points per game and would, two months later, be named the college player of the year. Captain Johnny DeLuca and Don Foreman did a great job containing Groat. They forced him out on fouls with 12 minutes to go. The Griffs shot a nifty 43 % from the field. Unfortunately the Purple Eagles were not so fortunate; they fell to the University of San Francisco Dons, 53 - 45. The Niagara fast break was just not the same without the injured Sinicola. Without Zeke, it was tough for the Purple Eagles to keep up with the Top Ten team. Niagara made a game of it but Cappy Lavin put on a dribbling exhibition to the delight of much of the crowd. The Dons' waived nine fouls to retain ball possession, and Cappy saved the victory with his ball handling.[48]

On January 6, 1951, another blockbuster doubleheader was held. 11,113 fans were on hand to watch Canisius face the St. Louis University Billikens, and Niagara take on the University of West Virginia Mountaineers. St. Louis came to town boasting a 10 – 2 record including a win over powerful Kentucky. The Billikens stayed at the Hotel Lenox, spent a day sightseeing at Niagara Falls then got down to business. They had scouted the Griffs well. They produced a shifting front line defense that prevented the Canisians from getting the ball inside. The Griffs could not hit from outside. Overall they shot just 20% from the field against the foes' 39%. That was the difference. St Louis won easily, 52 – 40. The first game was a fast tempo affair. Zeke was back in the lineup; he played all 40 minutes and led the Eagles with 20 points. Smyth and Spanbauer had 17 each. They tried to run the Mountaineers into the ground but the visitors had brought an oxygen tank with them which they used during the time outs. It helped but not enough to earn them a win. They also had a terrific player in 6'9" Mark Workman, who, despite having four fouls called on him in the first half, ended up with 32 points for the night. That too was not enough to defeat the Eagles. Niagara won 83 – 76. Meanwhile the Brown Indians continued undefeated. They managed to lure Seton Hall into the Olean Armory where they "scalped" the Pirates 74 – 61 for their eighth straight.

The doubleheader program was going so well that its promotion and its operation attracted widespread interest. Personnel from Chicago, New York and Philadelphia recently visited Buffalo to obtain information about its success. Doc Crowdle, the program's architect, gave them the tour. He took them behind the scenes and provided them with details about the operation[49] The out of town visitors were extremely impressed with the efficiency of the small staff. There was really only one full time worker, and that was Dion Rahill, the office supervisor of the athletic association at Canisius. Rahill was in charge of tickets, the box office, and seat planning in the Aud. Ned Irish called him the "best box office man in America." Connie McGillicuddy, a Canisius High School coach, and Math and Latin teacher, was in charge of tickets at Canisius College. Connie "Mack" who had "a memory that astonished everyone," was able to indicate where so and so sat and how long that fan had had those tickets. He could do that for the entire Memorial Auditorium.[50] The numerous other workers at the Aud including the statisticians and the press box attendants were part timers. They liked their job, they did not do it for financial gain; rather they just liked being part of the action. When visitors looked over Rahill's financial statements they were amazed that such a major operation could be conducted with such little overhead. They were surprised too that even when there were sellouts Canisius still made sure that there were several hundred tickets available at 60 cents per ticket for various high schools in the area.

In addition, Western New York basketball was well served by radio and newspapers, still the major communication vehicles, though, by 1950, television was coming on fast. The sports staffs of the two local newspapers were headed by long time veterans of the sports scene. Billy Kelly was the sports editor at the *Courier Express*; his counterpart at the *Buffalo Evening News* was Bob Stedler. Ray Ryan was the chief college basketball beat writer at the *Courier* and his friendly rival at the *News* was Cy Kritzer. Each had been around for many years. Radio men included Ralph Hubbell, Van Patrick (briefly), Roger Baker, Charlie Bailey and Sig Smith. Near the end of the postwar era, Bill Mazur arrived in town. College sports were well served by the local media.

A Big 4 doubleheader was scheduled for January 11, 1951. It was preceded by an alumni luncheon at the Hotel Buffalo which featured remarks by all four area head coaches. Big Four and especially Little Three get-togethers were quite common in those post war years; those gatherings were an important reason behind the success of the Aud program. The University of Buffalo though not officially a member of the unofficial Little Three had excellent relationships with Canisius, Bona, and Niagara. The local media warmed to events such as the downtown basketball luncheons. They were good preparation for game night.

Another 10,000 plus crowd swarmed into the downtown arena for the Big 4 twinbill. Favored Niagara, operating like a well-oiled, smooth functioning machine, swept U.B. 59 – 41. All Niagara starters were major contributors. Niagara was sharp in its shooting and in its play execution; its defense was able to contain U.B.'s top stars Jack Chalmers and Hal Kuhn. The Canisius - St Bona game was a nail bitter. It would go down as another of the many great Little Three games played in the Aud. It was close throughout the first half, then in the early part of the second half, the Bonnies looked like they could name their score, they went up by 14 points. However the Griffs, led by Frank Pleto, anointed "the swift one," came roaring back to get within two points. There was pandemonium in the Aud. The Griffs pulled even at eight minutes into the second half, and then it was touch and go the rest of the game. The Griffs were ahead 66 – 64 when Coach Milkovitch made a surprise move. He sent in a sophomore, Roger Davies, for his one and only play of the night. With 12 seconds to go, Davies took an 18 footer, "swish." The game was sent into overtime by "One Play Davies." In the extra period, the Brown Indians were able to take the lead and hold it for a 77 – 72 victory. Canisius was led by Pleto who had 17 and Harnett who tallied 20. Captain Fred Diute led the Bonnies with 18 counters. Veteran observers said it was the most exciting Little Three game ever played.[51] Second guessers were now second guessing Joe Niland. Especially irritating was the fact that Tony Gregory had come off the bench and given a great lift to the Griffs. Then Niland had pulled him. In answer to his critics the coach said Gregory had asked to be pulled because of an asthmatic condition that he had.

The Griffs and the Eagles did not have much of a chance for a rest because another major doubleheader was scheduled two days later. Canisius hosted the Boston College Eagles, and Niagara took on the number one team in the nation, the Bradley University Braves from Peoria, Illinois. Bradley had just recently won the Sugar Bowl tournament defeating St. Louis, and had surged to the number one spot in the nation. They came into Buffalo with a 15 – 1 record. The Bradley appearance had been making headlines for several weeks. The standout player for the Braves was Gene Melchiorre, who was sometimes called the Midget Mikan, because, at only 5' 7" he often played the pivot position. He led his team to 32 wins the previous season when Bradley ended up number two in the rankings and was the runner up in the NIT and the NCAA.

As expected, another record crowd was on hand, 12,147. Niagara played very well; the lead changed often. With less than three minutes to go, Bradley broke a 72 – 72 tie with two quick baskets and then went into a freeze and held on for a 78 – 74 win. Zeke played brilliantly, "perhaps the greatest exhibition of an illustrious career," and scored 26 points. The fans were pleased; they saw a supreme effort against the nation's top team, in a free wheeling game with the accent on the fast break. Tom Birch did a great defensive job on Melchiorre; he was all over him. In the second game, Canisius outlasted the Boston College Eagles, 56 – 54. The game was marked by a host of fouls in the final minutes as BC tried to get back into the game. They kept fouling and Canisius kept waiving off the fouls to retain possession. The strategy worked. The Griffs held on for a two point victory.[52]

The arena in downtown Buffalo had hosted three doubleheaders in the span of eight days. 33,378 spectators had turn out for these affairs. That made history. Extra police had to be called to clear lobbies so that ticket holders could get through the turnstiles. The Associated Press commented on it this way: "if you want your money's worth, go to a basketball doubleheader in Buffalo. That goes for the man who paid $50 for two $2.50 seats." Fifty dollars was an astronomical amount back then. Buffalo was a big time city in college basketball.[53]

The Little Three games were usually the biggest draws but not every Little Three contest was played in the Aud in those years. In January of 1951 Niagara and St. Bonaventure met in a momentous clash played high above the Niagara gorge in the student center gym. The Brown Indians had not lost a game in the current season; they were confident; they smelled victory. But they reckoned without Zeke Sinicola. Zeke seemed to score from everywhere on the court on his way to scoring 28 points that led to the upset victory. Zeke was carried off the floor as the capacity crowd of 3,000 howled with joy because the Eagles had dealt the Bonnies their first defeat of the season. Tom Birch contributed 21 points and played his usual fine floor game. The final score was 72 – 57 though the game was actually much closer than the score indicated.

The Niagara team got a taste of their own medicine when they faced an aroused Griffin team in the Aud a few days later before 12,166. The Griffs came from behind and won 71 – 61. Niland was cautious about the unpredictable Randy Sharp but thought if his tall center could come up with the kind of game he did against Duke the Griffs would win. Niland gambled with Sharp and it paid off. But there were some anxious moments. With less than four minutes left in the game, Randy had made only 4 of 20 shots. But then he went to work. Sharp ended up scoring 17 points, 14 in the second half, and several at crucial times inside the four minute mark. Niagara could simply not stop Sharp's hook shots. The fans were elated; they carried him off the court. Actually Canisius had other heroes too; Don Foreman did a fine defensive job on Zeke and Herm Hedderick was top scorer with 21 points. Niland's coaching was at its best as he matched wits with Taps Gallagher. Niland used his superior bench depth to play a significant role on his way to earning his 11th win in 15 engagements.

On January 27 Canisius lost to Georgetown, 87 to 71, and Toledo beat Bona 70 – 56. The 6,042 fans were disappointed, Georgetown had been an up and down team.

They had just lost to Gannon. But they regrouped against the Griffs. They raced off to an 18 point lead early in the game, kept it by playing almost flawless basketball and by hitting on 47% of their shots. Georgetown tallied more points against the Griffs than anyone had in recent years. Good playing by Tony Gregory, who had 15 points, all in the 2nd half, helped the Griffs make a comeback, but it was not enough. Earlier in the evening, Bona had been blitzed by a superior, tenacious and highly ranked Toledo team. That shutout the Olean squad down the middle. The Brown Indians could not counter from outside.

Things turned around for Canisius on the first weekend in February. The Griffs eked out a 51 – 50 win over Manhattan; in doing so they earned their 12th victory. Tony Gregory again came through in the second half, scoring 10 points. He and Herm Hedderick with 16 counters, paced the Griffs. In the first game, Bona lost to Loyola of Chicago in overtime, 58 – 50. Loyola led most of the way, as Bona tasted its 4th defeat in 17 starts. A week later, on February 10, 1951, before 10,516, the Griffs went down to defeat at the hands of the Redmen of St. John's 57 - 49. Bob Zawoluk, who held the Aud scoring record, had 27 points in leading St. John's to its 12th straight victory, and its 18th in 20 starts. The Griff fans readily agreed with the polls ranking St. John's in the Top Ten. The Redmen were simply a very good versatile basketball team and played as though they knew that they were tournament bound. The Griffs played well but it seemed every time that the Griffs mounted a rally, and they mounted a few of them, the Redmen would come right back to put a damper on them. In the first game Niagara made its record 14 – 7 by throttling John Carroll, 79 – 49. Niagara's Big Three, Zeke, Birch and Smyth ran up big numbers, 20, 19, and 17 respectively.

In the middle of the month, the Eagles and Griffs boarded the train for the annual doubleheader appearance in Madison Square Garden. Niagara played St. John's and another of the metro area's top powers, CCNY, hosted Canisius. The invaders from upstate stunned the crowd by sweeping the doubleheader. Presumably the "upstaters" were aided by the large number of fans who followed them to the Big City. Billy Kelly, just recently retired as Sports Editor of the *Courier Express*, called it the largest Buffalo delegation "since the days of Jimmy Slattery's fights." Hundreds boarded trains for the excursion. They were ready for a grand celebration in the Big Apple and they got their reason to celebrate. It was the first time that a pair of invading teams had ever carried off two overtime triumphs in New York. The Griffs spurted to a deadlock in the final minute and then in overtime, unsung hero, Bob Stoetzel who was having a bang up game with his scrappy play, was a key factor in the win. Stoetzel had 17 points for the evening. The final was 67 – 64.[54] The

Bob Stoetzel, front line stalwart with Herm Hedderick and Larry O'Connor, continued Griffs' success into the 1950s. *Photo: Game Program. Canisius College Archives.*

second game with Niagara topping St John's in double overtime was even more exciting. Zeke played one of his greatest games. He scored 29 points, two of them off a driving lay up with less than a minute to go that sent the game into the first overtime. Sinicola's performance was such that veteran reporters in the Garden, unanimously acclaimed it to be "the most amazing little man performance ever seen here." But Zeke was not the only hero. Niagara went all the way with just six men, and at the jubilant finish, with Niagara students swarming on the floor, the Purple Eagle vets raised sophomore Johnny McMahon to their shoulders and carried him into the dressing room. McMahon, the 6th man, bagged 9 points in a tremendous effort. The Purple Eagles won 77 – 75.[55]

With the season winding down, basketball talk focused on the National Invitational Tournament. The Little Three teams were doing well, each had legitimate hopes for the post season. The winner of the mythical conference would be in the driver's seat to receive a bid. The Griffs faced nemesis, St. Bona, on Saturday, February 17. A crowd of 9,932 saw the Brown Indians conquer the Griffs for the 2nd time that season, 64 – 57. Sassone and Kenville led the way, each in double digits; high man for the game was Don Hartnett, who had 19 points for the losers. In the opener the U. B. Bulls came from behind to defeat traditional opponent, Lafayette College, 69 – 55. Jack Chalmers, who held season and career scoring records for U.B. tossed in 25 points. It was a well earned upset win for U.B. and the margin of victory enabled Coach Mal Eiken to clear the bench. It was U.B.'s 11th victory in 17 starts.

Next it was Niagara's turn to face the Brown Indians. The game would determine the winner of the Little Three. On February 21, Niagara took the long bus ride to the Southern tier to confront St. Bona in the Olean Armory. The Purple Eagles had reason to feel confident since they had upset the Brown Indians by 15 points earlier in the season. But that was on the small court on the Niagara campus. Now the situation was reversed, and with a vengeance. The Purple Eagles had to face the Brown Indians in the famous, for opponents it was the infamous, Olean Armory, scene of countless Bona victories and very few defeats. Moreover Bona would be at peak strength. In the earlier contest, one of their stars, Fred Diute, had been in the hospital with pneumonia. He was now back in uniform and eager to play. As expected there was considerable hoopla over the game. Throngs of Niagara fans made the trip to Olean only to be wedged like sardines in the armory seats, with barely enough breath left to cheer on their heroes. It was a typical Little Three barnburner. Bona edged Niagara, 54 – 51.

Meanwhile the chances for a post season bid for Canisius were becoming dimmer with each game. A veritable cage debacle took place in the Aud before 4,425 fans on Thursday, February 22. The Syracuse Orangemen hammered the Griffs, 71 – 55. It was a nail in the coffin game for the Griffs. The Syracuse candidate for All American honors, Jack Kiley, helped his cause with a terrific exhibition of set shooting; he hit on 6 of 8 from far out range. The Griffs never got very close in this one. However, on the plus side, young Larry O'Connor came off the bench and put on his best performance of the season, scoring 7 points and showing that he would have to be reckoned with in the future. It the early game, the Deacons of Wake Forest ripped the University of Buffalo, 77 - 55. They led U.B. all the way, though the Bulls did make a good run at it and came within four points in the later stages of the game. Wake Forest had too much speed and its shooting was red hot. For U.B. Chalmers was held to 7 points, abnormally low for him. Hal Kuhn had 14.

Next up for the Golden Griffins was the

annual game with the University of Notre Dame. The Irish had won the first four games played since the end of the war, but the Griffs had won in 1949-50, and were determined to show that last year's victory was no fluke. Only 7,024 fans were on hand, a surprisingly small turnout for an Irish-Griffin game. But those present saw some great coaching by Joe Niland. His scouting paid off. He recognized that the Irish had lost their ace backcourt man earlier in the season. They were no longer an outside threat. This meant that their big forwards were now their top scorers. So Coach Niland had his players clog up the middle. The Irish forwards were limited to a total of 15 points. Niland also used the same tactics he had used in his upset over CCNY, a switching, driving attack, that forced the opponent to commit personal fouls. The Griffs won 60 – 53. Pleto and Hartnett, singled out for praise by the Irish players, led the Griffs in scoring. In fact 11 of the 12 Griffs who saw action broke into the scoring column. Center Larry O'Connor come through nicely for the second week in a row. Niland could now look to him with confidence in future games.

As had become traditional, the last Aud game of the season would pit Canisius against their arch rivals from 20 miles down the Niagara River, the Purple Eagles. The game sold out in advance. Box office boss Dion Rahill said the demand for tickets was the greatest since the days of the Rocky Kansas-Jimmy Goodrich boxing rivalry. The sell-out crowd caused Cy Kritzer to remark that there was renewed confidence in the local game of basketball despite the national news about the bribery and gambling scandal that hurt attendance elsewhere. "If there were any doubt as to Buffalo's future as a major basketball center, that sellout crowd convinced college authorities here and elsewhere of the deep faith of the public." More than 12,000 turned out for the annual March donnybrook. The actual figure was 12,166. Many held Standing Room Only tickets.[56]

As usual there was a full week of hype leading up to the March 3 classic clash. Not surprisingly Sinicola's name was the one most frequently found in the headlines. The colorful Zeke was the first Niagara player to ever reach the 1000 point mark in his career. It was possible he would set a new single season scoring record in the Canisius game. He set the existing mark at 443 points in a single season two years ago and at this point of the current season he had 432. Zeke was one of several graduating seniors. Captain Jim Moran, the excellent rebounder, and Tom Birch, a national leader in assists joined their Niagara classmate. From the Canisius team Captain John DeLuca, who starred at both forward and guard, and Frank Pleto, the flashy exponent of the fast break, would be playing their final game along with one of the all time Griffin greats, Don Hartnett. Cy Kritzer liked to call Hartnett "the Enforcer," a tribute to this solid, rugged, all around player. The veteran *News* scribe thought of Harnett as a block of granite under the boards. He knew how to score too; he held the single Little Three game scoring record, having put in 28 points against St. Bona in 1949-50.

The game itself was a good one, a typical hotly contested Little Three contest. Tom Birch played one of his greatest floor games and directed the Niagara attack. The Purple Eagles rushed to an early lead and maintained it. Don Foreman held the great Zeke to 11 points, but the Canisius offense could not penetrate Taps' well conceived defenses. Smyth had 14 for Niagara and Bob Stoetzel put in 16 for the Griffs. Niagara won 51- 46.

The 1950-51 Aud season was over, but the locals still had the remainder of their schedules to complete. The Griffs went on the road to face Cornell and for the second time that season the Big Red beat the Griffs. The score was 72 – 60. It was not much consolation for Canisius to know that

Cornell's victory was its 19th of the season, against just 5 losses, the best record of any basketball team in the history of that scenic institution located high above Lake Cayuga's waters.

The Griffs then traveled north along the Finger Lakes route to Syracuse for their final game of the season. The Griffs surprised a sparse "crowd" of 1,131 in the Syracuse Coliseum with a 69 – 66 triumph. It was the 15th victory against 10 defeats. Sophomore Larry O'Connor continued to show great promise; he collected 16 points and Senior Frank Pleto had 15. Canisius had the depth and the hustle. Syracuse did not.

Meanwhile Niagara ended its season on a down note in Albany succumbing to Siena by a 58 – 44 score. The largest crowd ever to witness a basketball game in the Albany Armory, 5,800, watched a nip and tuck game for the first 30 minutes then the Indians shot ahead and put a hammer lock on the game by freezing the ball for several minutes. The win made Siena's record, 19 – 6 and gave them a shot at a post season tournament berth. Niagara ended its season with an 18 – 10 record; Zeke did manage to break his own Western New York single season scoring record, though he was held to just nine points.

The U. B. Bulls closed their season with a sound thrashing of Hobart, 83 - 51 in Clark Gymnasium. In that game, Jack Chalmers, the Williamsville, New York native, closed his brilliant career with 37 points giving him the new single game scoring record for his school. He also set the season record at 396 points; he reached a career mark of 1,003, thus becoming the first Bull ever to top the 1,000 mark. His teammate, Hal Kuhn, also played in his last game. Though a junior, Kuhn had decided to join the Air Force Cadets.

For its last game of the regular season, St. Bona traveled to Philadelphia to play in one of college basketball's best known facilities, the Palestra. There they took on the Wildcats from Villanova and pulled off a major upset 74 – 69. That victory was enough to earn them an NIT invitation which they immediately accepted. NIT committee members were in Philadelphia for the game and they concluded that the Bona performance more than made up for the loss to Siena the previous week.

Western New Yorkers rallied behind the NIT bound St. Bonaventure Brown Indians. The fans were not disappointed. The Olean school represented Western New York very well. The Little Three Champs pulled off a stunning double overtime win over the University of Cincinnati. Nearly a thousands partisans cheered on from the Garden stands. It was a great team effort with Bob Sassone's 18 points leading the way and special cheers went up near the end of the game when Mike Bednar of Binghamton put away two crucial buckets and Leo Corkery of Jamestown, locked up the win with three points in the final minute of regulation time.

Two days later St. Bona met top seeded St. John's. Bona led by 10 at halftime and seemed to be running the Redmen right out of the arena and on to Eighth Avenue. But in the final stages of the game, St. John's coach Frank McGuire used a full court press and that got his team back in the game. All American Bob Zawoluk's shot in the final seconds gave the Redmen a 60 – 58 victory. It was a heart breaker for all Western New York fans.

All in all 1950-51 was another banner year for all of Western New York Basketball. The Bona team was the best. The others were not far behind; all having acquitted themselves quite well. Coach Eddie Milkovitch's forces had chalked up major victories over Western Kentucky, Seton Hall, and Villanova. They had twice conquered Canisius and earned a split with Niagara. In post season play, they pulled off a magnificent double overtime win over Cincinnati in the NIT. Then they suffered a wrenching loss, perhaps it was also a moral victory, over highly ranked St. John's to conclude the season. Niagara ended up at 18 – 10 and that included victories over Denver, West Virginia, St. John's, and Colgate and splits with Canisius and Bona and Syracuse, and a close loss to top ranked Bradley. Sinicola, Birch, and Moran, arguably the most famous trio ever to play for Niagara University, closed out their illustrious three year career with a 62 – 24 record. Fittingly their jersey numbers were retired and hung in the Niagara field house for later generations to admire.

The University of Buffalo had a 13 - 8 season with quality wins over Delaware and Lafayette, and losses to some big time schools, notably Washington State, Wake Forest, and the University of Connecticut. The Canisius record at 15 – 10 did not appear overly impressive. However when one considers that the Griffs winning season included several victories over nationally ranked teams, then the record appears surprisingly good. The Griffs defeated SMU, Duke, Oregon State, Utah, Texas, Arizona, Notre Dame, Boston College, CCNY and Syracuse. Probably no other team in the history of Western New York basketball had ever achieved such an accomplishment, such a list of wins over big name national competition. Unfortunately, from the point of view of tournament committees, the stellar victories were offset by just a few too many losses especially those occurring late in the season. That is what hurt Canisius' chances for an NIT bid. Joe Niland was, in the minds of many basketball experts, the best coach in college basketball in that time period who never received a bid to a post season tournament. Don Hartnett was voted most valuable player to appear on any team in Memorial Auditorium. In New York City, Zeke Sinicola was accorded a very high honor by being voted the best visiting player of the year in Madison Square Garden by the Metropolitan Basketball Writers Association.

College attendance overall was down for the 1950-51 season. The Associated Press stated: "blame it on television, the international situation, or repercussions from the fixed games' scandals, but attendance at college basketball games showed a decline for 1950-51 compared with a year ago." The AP compiled figures for the 8 big city arenas that hosted doubleheader programs. Buffalo showed the least drop off in attendance, approximately a 4% drop. The Boston Garden doubleheaders fell off 36%, the Cleveland Arena was down 41.1% and Madison Square Garden was off 24.8%. Buffalo's attendance dipped from 176.370 to 166,611, but still Buffalo had an average of 7,933 and maintained its place as second leading basketball center in the nation. Elsewhere in the country there were actually some basketball arenas that showed gains in attendance. Ominously for places such as Buffalo's Memorial Auditorium, those were the large new field houses on big state campuses, such as Kentucky and Kansas State. That was the wave of the future.[57]

Meanwhile the great gambling, game fixing scandal had been unfolding. On January 18, 1951 an item appeared in the press about a Manhattan College player, Junius Kellogg, who had reported a bribe attempt to the District Attorney. The public waited for more information as the season rolled along. Questions were asked. How many schools were involved? Was the scandal limited to New York City? One of the primary concerns was that the scandals would damage big city arenas. Of course, there was concern in Buffalo. But Doc Crowdle was confident that the Aud was not involved. Crowdle attended the National Basketball Coaches meeting in Minneapolis, late in March of 1951, and returned stating that the doubleheader program would go on substantially as it had in the past. With an eye on Madison Square Garden's problems, Doc noted that the Aud in Buffalo had always met NCAA requirements for off-campus sports; the Aud games had always been under college control. The President of the College, the Reverend Raymond Shouten backed up Crowdle's comments. The Aud doubleheader program was not tarnished. Coach Joe Niland continued to receive scheduling requests from his friends in the coaching ranks for a spot on the doubleheader program.

The point shaving scandals struck widely, far beyond New York City. Gambling had been a part of big time sports, professional and college, since sports had become big time. Following World War II, with more people having more money and more disposable income, gambling flourished. Boxing and college basketball seemed to be especially favorable targets. In Buffalo the gamblers were so brazen that they could be seen openly at ringside of boxing bouts in the Aud. The Police Chief in Buffalo sounded the alarm in 1948 and made a concerted effort to get rid of the gamblers in the Aud. The situation was cleaned up.

But in New York City gambling was more widespread than anywhere else. It was carried on openly. Around Madison Square Garden, inside and outside the arena, black suited gamblers decked out with white ties and dark fedoras, flocked like ants. It was a scene right out of the popular Broadway play, Guys and Dolls. The newly recognized point spread system of wagering on games was infusing new life into gambling. It was fairly common knowledge that college basketball games were frequently the targets of gamblers.

When the Manhattan College story broke in January of 1951 it could not have been much a surprise to many New York City observers. Junius Kellogg, the Jaspers' star, who declined tainted money, went to his coach, Kenny Norton. The police were informed; the District of Attorney was brought in and the news was out in the open. Initially it appeared that only the metro New York teams were involved. CCNY, LIU, NYU, and Manhattan, were the institutions that housed the culprits; the players who were taking money to shave points. But within months the scandal spread far beyond New York City. Players from Bradley and Toledo, Midwest powerhouses, were guilty. Adolph Rupp, the great Baron of Basketball, had indicated that his boys would never be tainted by the type of sordid activity that had been uncovered in those urban dens of iniquity in New York. It did not take long for Baron Rupp's face to turn red; within a year, Kentucky's star players admitted to being deeply involved.

The results of the scandals were catastrophic. Some of the New York City institutions hastened to deemphasize basketball. The glory days of the Big Three, NYU, CCNY, and LIU, now entered the history books. Presidents of the large educational institutions from the West and Midwest indicated they would no longer play in the Garden. Some said they would fly to the East coast only as the situation warranted. Athletic departments soon found out that they could make more money by playing more games on their home courts.

After the 50- 51 season changes did begin to take place in the world of major college basketball. They took place gradually rather than abruptly. During the '50s the local teams began to play more of their games at away sites. Canisius had played as few as four road games in the late '40s, now they began to play six or seven and by the end of the 1950s decade they would be playing about half of their games on the road. The same held true for Niagara University, St. Bonaventure University, and the University of Buffalo. All three had played home games on campus and some home games in the Aud, but as the fifties wore on they played more games on the road. Buffalo's famous Aud, a symbol of Big City status, the "Glamour Girl of Lower Main

Street" as Cy Kritzer appropriately dubbed the building, was beginning to lose a little of its appeal. At the same time, and perhaps more importantly, many colleges built arenas on campus that could seat more than the typical 3,000 that the old fashioned college gyms had held. Buffalo's extremely successful doubleheader program of the 1940s changed slowly, almost imperceptibly, in the decades that followed.

To some extent the changes were brought about by changes in the New York City programs, changes that came about in reaction to the point shaving scandals that began in Madison Square Garden. But the changes in Buffalo's Memorial Auditorium program also reflected broader social and economic changes.

The American people were adapting to air travel. So were athletic teams. No longer did a team from West of the Mississippi need to spend 10 days or more, traveling to the East coast, by railroad, stopping in Buffalo, then on to Philadelphia and New York City. By the mid-1950s, a West Coast team could fly directly to an East Coast city, play a game, then return home, all in a matter of three days.

As far as the Aud program in Buffalo was concerned, the doubleheader program began to include fewer and fewer of the big name institutions from the West and South. The schedule now included the likes of Dayton, Seton Hall, and LaSalle, instead of Texas, Utah, and Denver. Doc Crowdle continued, for a few more years, to be the main man directing the Aud program. But he did so without Ned Irish. In the wake of the college scandals, Ned Irish turned his basketball interests to the New York Knicks and the fledgling National Basketball Association. The direct New York City – Buffalo connection became a thing of the past. Crowdle stayed on until a new Canisius administration figured out a convenient way to remove him from his Aud duties, alleging that Doc had to spend more time in the Chemistry Department of which he was the chairman. It was also said that some members of the administration wanted to gain control over the revenue that had previously been handled by Doc Crowdle. Familiar faces, such as those of Irish and Crowdle were leaving the scene at the same time that the days of a Southern California, an Oregon State, or a Wyoming team coming to Buffalo and continuing on to New York City were passing. This was occurring at the same time that Buffalo's leadership position in the field of railroad travel was giving way to air travel in the 1950s.

The Aud itself, as a central attraction in downtown Buffalo continued to be the scene of major basketball doubleheaders for many years to come. Now, however, the opponents came chiefly from the East coast or from locations in the nearby Midwest. Occasionally a distant foe would participate, but not like "the good ol' days," not like in the 1940s. The changes did not mean that the caliber of basketball played by the local teams had slipped. All of the local institutions continued to have some banner years in the decades that followed. In the '50s and '60s, both Niagara and St. Bona were fairly regular participants in the NIT. The Brown Indians reached the Final Four of the NCAA in 1970. Canisius was the pride of the city in the mid-'50s, earning bids to three consecutive NCAA tournaments

But the Aud program in downtown Buffalo was not quite the same. The Little Three teams, as well as the University of Buffalo, had some truly fine teams in the decades that followed. But they were not all first rate at the same time. The opponents, too, were different. Other changes occurred. Niagara and Canisius had a falling out over Aud revenue distribution. At times Niagara had the better team and drew very well but did not receive a satisfactory percentage of the revenue. This squabble led to the Eagles absenting themselves from any participation in the Aud program for nine seasons, from 1957 to 1966. By the time Niagara returned to the Aud program, St. Bona had built its Reilly Center. This on-campus facility could hold 6,000 for the Brown Indians' home games. St. Bonaventure no longer felt the need to play more than a handful of games in Buffalo. Niagara was of the same mind when the Convention Center opened in downtown Niagara Falls. There the Purple Eagle would play many of their home games beginning in the 1970s.

Certainly some individual local teams in some years could be considered superior to their predecessors of the 1940s. The same was true for individual players. The Bona teams of the Stith brothers or the Bob Lanier led teams of a few years later, were first rate, as were the Niagara teams of Larry Costello in the '50s and the teams that Calvin Murphy led, close to two decades later. Similarly the great Canisius teams led by Johnny McCarthy, and Hank Nowak had their day in the sun and could, indeed, be compared favorably with the Griffin teams of the '40s. Jim Horne of U.B. as well as Greg Saunders of Bona, and Charlie Hoxie and Ed Fleming of Niagara, all were terrific ball players and Randy Smith of Buffalo State was in a class by himself. But the teams at all four local institutions in the late 1940s, collectively, were unique. They all did very well, all in the same years, the Golden Age of Buffalo Sports.

It was also true that Western New York continued to be blest with first rate coaches. Eddie Donovan and Larry Wiese put their indelible mark on Bona in the '50s and '60s; as did Taps Gallagher at Niagara in that same time period and Frank Layden a little later. At Canisius, Joe Curran had a sensational run in the '50s followed by Bob MacKinnon's splendid seasons a decade later. Len Serfustini made his mark at U. B. in the '60s; some years later, Dick Bihr did so at Buffalo State.

But the years immediately following World War II were exceptional. College basketball in the post war era of 1945-51 experienced a golden age in Buffalo. Quality teams from each of the local institutions coached by nationally acclaimed coaches, and each squad having legendary players in the lineups, played teams from nationally recognized institutions on a regular basis from every corner of the United States. This comprised a situation that was unique to the Aud doubleheader program in those years. It is no wonder that the City of Buffalo with its Memorial Auditorium was widely acclaimed as the second leading basketball center in the nation. The Aud itself was second only to the mother of all sports arenas, the legendary Madison Square Garden.

CHAPTER SIX

The Ice Bisons

— Prelude to the Sabres —

BUFFALO EVENING NEWS

Ice Herd's 36th Victory Sets All-Time AHL Record

Buffalo Evening News, March 11, 1946

The Buffalo Bison Hockey team of the American Hockey League was another of the Buffalo sports that made the Queen City a major sports center in the Post World War II era. The success of the Hockey Bisons both on the ice and at the box office had much to do with giving credibility to Buffalo's claim as one of the nation's premier sports cities.

During the 1940s and 50s, hockey's major professional organization, the National Hockey League, stood frozen in time with just 6 teams, four American and two Canadian. The league, the NHL, obviously cherished stability after having endured many years of instability. It had been organized in 1917, and like other professional sport leagues, notably the National Football League, the NHL, in its first two decades experienced a number of teams joining and then leaving the league. By the time of World War II, six teams had survived. The Original Six, as they liked to refer to themselves, represented Canada's two largest cities, Toronto and Montreal, as well as four of America's largest metropolises: New York, Chicago, Detroit, and Boston. The Original Six continued as the NHL's only members for the next quarter of a century. Expansion then came rapidly in the mid to late 1960s.

With the National Hockey League not prepared to foster expansion in the 1940s, the American Hockey League served as hockey's principal minor league. Many of the star players who participated in the AHL had either come down from the Big League or were building their resumes on their way to participate with the Big Boys. In fact the line between the two hockey leagues was not always clear. It was sometimes said that the strongest teams in the AHL, usually Buffalo and Cleveland, were on a par with teams in the NHL. Cleveland and Buffalo drew crowds that were as large as those for some of the NHL teams. Many knowledgeable observers thought those two cities deserved consideration for membership in the NHL. But the original six had closed minds.

In the 1940s, several of the AHL cities ranked among the top dozen cities in the entire United States in terms of size and importance. Philadelphia (briefly a member of the AHL) was in the top five, and Cleveland, Pittsburgh, St Louis, and Buffalo were not far behind. In future decades, those rustbelt cities from the Great Lakes region, would find themselves rapidly overtaken by the emerging sunbelt cities. But in the 1940s the situation was quite different. In the years following World War II, Buffalo was virtually big time in hockey, just as it was in other sports.

Nor was Buffalo a johnny-come-lately on the hockey scene. Buffalo, figuratively and almost literally a stone's throw from Canada, had experienced the sport of ice hockey for many years. Hockey of course began in Canada where it was played in an amateur way on the rivers and ponds of Ontario and Quebec in the 19th century. Sports historians would refer to hockey in its early years as a folk game. In the early 20th century there were some "professional" leagues organized in Canada. The leagues were hastily established; many of the teams were transient. Understandably, some Buffalonians, just across the Niagara River from Canada, became attracted to the sport. The Nichols School took the lead and organized a team as early as 1910. After playing on frozen Delaware Park Lake and an assortment of "iffy" ponds for a few years, Nichols built an ice rink. Just a few years later, in the 1920s, across the river in Fort Erie, Canada, an artificial indoor ice rink was constructed. The ferryboat operating in the Upper Niagara River was the mode of transportation for Buffalo hockey players wanting to play in Fort Erie. In 1927 the Peace Bridge opened; that meant that the Fort Erie arena was within minutes of downtown Buffalo. The very next year the Buffalo Hockey Club entered a team in the Canadian Professional Hockey League and finished 5th out of 8 teams in the

1928-29 season.

The following year the Canadian Professional Hockey League became the International Hockey league and the Buffalo Bisons, as the team was appropriately nicknamed, was included as a member. Initially the Bisons performed fairly well, but as the Great Depression ground on, the club found itself financially strapped. Then, nature made itself felt. The infamous St. Patrick's Day snowstorm of 1936, one of the most memorable ones of the 20th century, caused the collapse of the Peace Bridge arena in Ft. Erie. That disaster forced the Bisons to play their games at the Niagara Falls arena. They did so until December of 1937 when low attendance and financial difficulties forced the Buffalo club to withdraw from the league.

The hockey club would have to await the largess of the New Deal before it could begin play again. The New Deal is perhaps best remembered for many of the public works projects that were constructed with federal money by various alphabetical agencies of the federal government. The projects put to work thousands of the unemployed, and the resultant public edifices were clearly of great benefit to local communities as well as to the nation. The Works Progress Administration, the WPA as it was popularly called, was one of the most memorable of the numerous New Deal agencies. One of its enduring successes was the Memorial Auditorium in downtown Buffalo, actually on Lower Main Street, not far from the busy harbor.

The Memorial Auditorium, or the Aud, as it soon came to be popularly called, opened for business in the Fall of 1940. At about the same time the old International Hockey League transformed itself into the American Hockey League, the AHL. The resurrected Buffalo Hockey club was now owned by Louis Jacobs, whose rise to entrepreneurship started as a peanut vendor in Offermann Stadium, home of the Bison Baseball team. Jacobs continued to own the Hockey team until 1955. Jacobs also served on the Board of Governors of the AHL. He continued as the CEO of his growing sports concession empire, known as SportService Inc. Jacobs ran his business, including the Buffalo Bisons Hockey club, out of an office at Main and Tupper Streets in downtown Buffalo. Visitors to the office were amazed at the simplicity of the Lou Jacob's office, replete with cartons and boxes stacked in the corners, simple wooden chairs and a plain desk. These hardly would seem to be the trappings of one who would become a giant in his field of business.[1]

By 1940 everything seemed in order for the beginning of a grand new era for the sport of ice hockey in Buffalo. Everything seemed in order, that is, except the World Order. World War II had just begun in Europe, and first Canada, as a member of the British Commonwealth of Nations, and then the United States became embroiled up to their proverbial necks in the conflict. The new hockey league, with Buffalo as a member, did manage to get off the ground. Buffalo played its first game in the Aud, November 3, 1940, a little over a year after Hitler had instigated the Second World War by invading Poland. Hockey continued to be played but at a "lesser" level during the war years. Many Canadian and American boys, who otherwise would be zipping up and down the ice, were trudging up and down the mountains of Italy, scaling the cliffs of France, and wading ashore on the islands in the Pacific. Those hockey players who were not in the armed forces continued to participate in the sport. The Ottawa government thought that hockey's continuation was good for the country's morale. Washington. D.C. concurred.

During World War II, membership in the American League varied, reaching a low of just six teams in the 1943-44 season which coincided with the peak period of the global conflict. When peace returned in

September of 1945, the league had grown to eight teams, divided into an Eastern and a Western division. The mainstays continued to be Buffalo, Cleveland, and Pittsburgh. The former two were regularly the best teams in the league and drew the largest crowds. Indianapolis became a stable franchise; Indy drew good crowds and usually had a competitive team. Providence was similar to Indy in several ways, the size of the city itself, the size of crowds that attended games, and the team performance. Hershey, Pennsylvania was somewhat of a fluke in the hockey world. It was a rather small city, perhaps better described as a large town best known for the delicious chocolate candy bars that flowed from the site. Hershey drew well considering its size and it rarely embarrassed itself on the ice. Many saw the Hershey Bears as the football Green Bay Packers of the hockey world. New Haven and Springfield, average sized cities, also had teams during some of the immediate postwar years. Finally, Washington, Philadelphia, and Cincinnati were members of the AHL briefly in the 1940s.

Buffalo's first two years in the new American Hockey League were mediocre. However, the team soon became a regular contender for the championship trophy, the Calder Cup. The Bisons actually won that Cup in 1942-43, and again in 1943-44, then lost in 1944-45 in the playoff finals to arch rival Cleveland. The Buffalo Bisons seemed poised once again to make a run at the championship in 1945-46 just as World War II came to an end and peace returned.

In the fall of 1945 the Bisons opened their preseason camp in St.Catharines, Ontario. The key figures in the front office were S. Edgar Danahy, President and Art Chapman, General Manager. The Head Coach was Frank Beisler. Danahy had been involved with hockey in Buffalo for many years. He would remain as President well into the 1950s. Art Chapman had played for the Bisons and then coached them under General Manager Eddie Shore during the war years. When Shore left, Chapman became GM and hired Beisler, a former Bison player, to be his coach.

The Hockey club had a few solid holdovers from the 1944-45 season returning, notably Paul Mundrick and Doug Lewis. The front office knew they needed reinforcements, so they busied themselves in the off season searching for new blood. Jack Laing, the *Courier Express* beat reporter, who covered the Bisons in the postwar years, paid particular attention to the purchase of Freddie "Fritz" Hunt, a native of Brantford, Ontario. Hunt had performed well for the New York Rangers the previous season but the Rangers had ample talent returning from the military service. Hunt was put on waivers and claimed by Montreal. However the Canadians also had such a wealth of right wing talent that they listened to and accepted a deal from the Buffalo Bisons. Hunt was purchased for a "sizeable sum." That was fine with Fritz. He had played for Buffalo in the 1943-44 season and rolled up 80 points, an all time record for a Bison up to that time. Jack Laing called him "the whirling dervish on skates" and said he was like a little wraith who packed a "wicked scoring punch." Hunt had terrific speed and was regarded as one of the best defensive forwards playing the game. Hunt had other Buffalo connections too; he had married "Sis" Frank of the Queen City. The Hunts were happy to be home in Buffalo.[2]

Fred Hunt, Played in the 1940s and served in administrative capacities with the Bisons and Sabres. *Photo: Tim Warchocki*

Hunt was joined in camp by two other

key additions to the 1945-46 roster: Murdo MacKay and Tommy Cooper. Chapman and Beisler had to be very pleased. MacKay had been on the Bisons' squad in the early 1940s. The native of Fort William, Ontario, then served in the Canadian military for the duration of the war. Now he was back and ready to show off his talents as a playmaker and scorer. Tommy Cooper made his name as a youngster playing in St. Catharines. Laing quickly noticed his great speed and skillful stick handling and predicted that he would have a great career. Cooper was rated one of Canada's best amateurs. A week before the opener the Bisons added more scoring punch with the acquisition from the Detroit Red Wings of veteran Larry Thibeault.

There was guarded optimism about the team's prospects. *Buffalo Evening News* Sports Editor Bob Stedler in his annual preseason outlook column called attention to the large numbers of players who were returning from military service. They meant an immediate increase in the quality of players at all levels. Buffalo certainly would benefit. GM Chapman spoke confidently of winning another Eastern title. Tony Wurzer, Laing's counterpart as beat hockey writer for the *News*, predicted that the Herd would chalk up plenty of goals. He cited Chapman as indicating that the Bisons would have greater scoring punch than at any time in the previous three years. That might have been going out on a limb since in those years the Herd had won two league titles and one Eastern Division title. As if to confirm these predictions, the Bisons in their first preseason game in St. Catharines bombed Eddie Shore's New Haven Eagles by a score of 9 – 2.[3]

Eddie Shore was a well known name in the hockey world, as much so in Buffalo as anywhere else. He had played for many years in the National Hockey league. He was highly regarded as a tough, first rate hockey player. Proof of his toughness was the fact that in his career he had 978 stitches, his nose broken 14 times, his jaw shattered five times, and lost every tooth in his month. Shore was responsible for developing Buffalo players during the war years; he coached Buffalo to two Calder Cups. However Shore secured ownership of the Springfield hockey club that was destined to begin operations in the 1946-47 season, once the United States Army had vacated the hockey arena. It was understood that Shore would then leave the Buffalo area for New England. He thus had first gone to New Haven as head man then the following year, as scheduled, he would take over the reins of the Springfield club.[4]

The 1945-46 American League hockey season opened on October 17. Opening night was an overwhelming success. It was also a sign of things to come. The season home openers, at Buffalo, Hershey, Providence, and Pittsburgh, saw 27,499 ticket holders jammed into the four arenas of those cities. Buffalo's attendance was the largest, at 8,946. The American Hockey League offered convincing evidence that it was the top minor ice circuit in North America. Post World War II hockey was off to a glowing start

Buffalo hosted Indianapolis in its face-off game. It was a well played contest, one that was up for grabs until the final 18 seconds. Actually, a bit earlier in the game, with the Caps up 2 – 1, the Bisons seemed on the verge of rallying to tie the contest. Murdo MacKay fired a shot that most observers thought went in the net. That would have knotted the score. The Goal Judge flashed the red light. But the Referee ruled that MacKay's shot had hit the goal post and therefore did not count. That ruling shifted the momentum. A bit later, the Bisons, losing 2 – 1, gambled, they pulled the goalie to increase their scoring punch. The gamble backfired. The Caps scored, and the Bisons lost 3 – 1. But there was a silver lining. Tommy Cooper lived up to advance billing; the crowd saw a new Bison star emerge. Wurzer concluded "For an amateur, the bristle black haired youngster was easily the best pro on the ice and that included the Caps Jud McAfee, who had been on the Detroit Red Wings first line last year." Cooper scored the first goal, midway through the first period giving the Bisons a 1 – 0 lead. The veritable "whirlaway on skates, quickly caught the fancy of the crowd as he skated in and around the Caps. Cooper's name was on the tongues of fans throughout the evening.[5]

The Bisons struggled in the early part of the season. They lost on consecutive nights to the Pittsburgh Hornets. In one of those losses, the Bisons had 59 shots on goal and still could not come up with the win. Pitt goalie, Roger Bessette was sensational. He could be flat on his face and still stop shots. It was a puzzling first few weeks. The Bisons had difficulty finding the right combination. Chapman continued to try to work deals with NHL clubs in order to bring some first rate players to Buffalo. He contacted Chicago and Detroit, and finally he had some luck with Montreal and was able to swing a deal that brought the Bisons two husky Canadian defensemen, Frankie Eddolls and Wilf Field. Their arrival seemed to signal a turnaround for the Bisons. They promptly went out and thrashed the New Haven Eagles, 9 – 1, for the first victory of the season. There seemed to be more cohesion on the club; they had worked out the kinks. Though they were unaware of it at the time the Bisons were off and skating on their way to a sensational, record breaking season.

At the next game, 9,478 fans, the largest crowd yet of the new campaign, turned out to watch the Bisons hand the powerful Hershey Bears their first defeat of the season. Goalie Frankie Ceryance was the local hero shutting out the Bears in the 4 – 0 win. He earned a standing ovation from the crowd. Tommy Cooper had a hand in 3 of the 4 goals and played perfect position hockey all evening. His work earned praise from the *Courier*'s Jack Laing who stated succinctly "the kid was TERRIFIC." The new defensive duo of Field and Eddolls also made a big hit with fans. Eddolls who would endear himself to Buffalo supporters for many years was a fine defensive player, one of the best in the league. He had played with Hershey two years earlier. That was followed by service with the Canadian Air Force and then he joined the Montreal Canadians. Eddolls added a "little extra" to the team, he was something of a rarity, namely a chatterbox and bench jockey. Chapman said he resembled a baseball player, in his "riding" the opposite players, and the way he encouraged his own teammates.[6]

In November the Bisons got hot. On November 4 they played their best hockey of the season to date, thumping their arch nemesis, the Cleveland Barons, 7 – 3. The game was played before the largest crowd of the season, 10,055. Unfortunately it cost them the services of ace defenseman Wilf Field. He was checked hard and severely injured his right arm. He would be out for several weeks. A few days later, the Bisons trounced Providence, 6 – 1, for their third straight victory on home ice. It was a penalty filled contest, in fact in the third period alone, there were 10 penalties called. The fans showed their disapproval by showering the ice with countless programs and whatever else they could find to toss at the poor officials. The following night, the Bisons traveled to Providence and again beat the Reds on their home ice by a score of 5 – 2. On November 11, the Bisons continued their onslaught, setting 5 scoring records in a 10 – 3 triumph over St. Louis. The usual suspects, Hunt, McKay, and Cooper, played well but the evening, scoring wise, belonged to Kenny Mosdell and Johnny Horeck. Each had a hat trick. Another record crowd of 10,184 was on hand, perhaps because it was Armistice Day, a national holiday also celebrated as Remembrance Day in Canada. Jack Laing's column was full of WWII analogies perhaps because of the recent memories so many had of the war. He likened the Bison victory to the atomic bomb, descending with a roar of fury and then crashing on the hapless Flyers. The thousands of spectators were "stunned by the trail of wreckage and devastation left in its wake." Words such as pilot, tail gunners, and navigator permeated the column. Even the 500 people, who were turned away from the Aud because all the standing room was sold out, were likened to "500 persons running from the scene of carnage even before the bomb fell."[7]

The blistering pace continued. A record midweek crowd of 8,526 turned out to watch Buffalo top the Indianapolis Caps, 5 – 3, behind the so-called "Money line." If there was a money line in the AHL, Buffalo had it. Center Kenny Mosdell, Rookie Tommy Cooper, and Johnny Horeck were the trio that earned that label. That trio was the "swiftest thing on the ice" in a long time. They accounted for 4 goals in the surprising triumph over the front running Caps. They scored in every contest since they were put together as a front line eleven games earlier, as they paced the red hot Bisons. A disgruntled goalie, Tommy Wilson said "You just couldn't see those guys fast enough. I hope I never see 'em again." Buffalo's chief scout called it the "only National League line playing in the American Hockey League." They were that good.[8]

Following a 3 – 1 road victory over the New Haven Eagles, the Bisons returned home and chalked up their seventh straight; this one against Cleveland. Betwixt and between a large number of penalties and fistfights, the Bisons and the Barons managed to score 13 goals, the Bisons earning the 8 – 5 win over their opponents. The turnout was another record, a capacity crowd of 10, 251, including a number of standing room only attendees. More than 800 fans were turned away. The poor showing of the early part of the season was a thing of the past. This latest victory climaxed an uphill fight. Now the Bisons were tied for the league lead. Mosdell bagged a hat trick, two of the goals coming within 47 seconds, and McKay, tallied twice, the goals coming within a 17 second span.

After a successful stretch in early November, the Bisons found out, once again, that they were human. They traveled to St. Louis and in a wild, chaotic contest, marked by 18 penalties and the ejection of Bison Coach Frank Beisler, the Flyers tied the Bisons 4 – 4. Pittsburgh ended the Bison seven game winning streak with a 4 – 1 victory. The league leading Indy Caps pummeled the Bisons, 9 – 4, and the new month of December did not start off any more promising for the Bisons. The Hershey Bears battered the Herd, 7 – 1.

Some changes were needed. The really big news came just before Christmas when the Bisons received two wonderful holiday gifts. Connie Dion and Mike McMahon were on their way to join the Herd. McMahon would make an immediate impact; Dion would begin to do so in a month. Both would become immensely popular with the Buffalo fans, and would, in time, become veritable legends in Buffalo Bison hockey lore.

Dion arrived on the scene with considerable experience. He came by way of the St. Louis Flyers. Previously he had been with the Indianapolis Caps and also had played with Montreal and with Detroit. Mike McMahon was often referred to simply as "Wide Mike," and occasionally was tabbed "Mr. 5 x 5." He made his debut in the Aud on December 8 before 9,028 fans. He contributed 4 points in the victory over New Haven and was immediately hailed as the answer to the Herd's defensive woes. Mike was no Dick Button on skates, but he was very difficult to knock down. One burly New Haven defenseman who tried to flatten Mike failed to do so but did receive a penalty. On the way to the penalty box, the player said "interfering with that guy is like picking on a runaway boxcar. They should give me a medal not a penalty." Wurzer noted that city carpenters made repairs to the hockey boards because McMahon "has an uncommon thing for driving opposing players against the planks." Wurzer quoted the New Haven coach saying "you can't score when you are busy pulling yourself out of the boards. That guy McMahon is strictly a one-man team wrecker."[9]

By the end of 1945 it had become clear that hockey had become a very popular sport. The AHL was thriving. Shortly after the first month of play, attendance figures were released that indicated that the league was headed for a new attendance mark. At that juncture it stood at 400,000. Buffalo led the way with 72,000. That was 15% ahead of the previous year. Little Hershey, Pennsylvania was only 2,000 behind in attendance and both Indianapolis and Cleveland, were near the 60,000 mark. Once again there were rumors about Cleveland and Buffalo being invited into the NHL. A player who had just come down from the Detroit Red Wings said he failed to see any difference between the speed of the Buffalo forwards and the forwards in the NHL. However the Original Six were content with the status quo. Moreover the issue of territorial rights in the case of Toronto was a known factor. That would continue to be the case.[10]

It was becoming very difficult for the sports writers to single out individual Bisons for praise. There were plenty of heroes. Tommy Cooper continued to excel. His hat trick led the Bison over the Cleveland Barons in a 6 – 3 win before 10,233 in a late December game. By the end of the year, the Bisons were again on a winning streak and were solidly in first place. Roger Leger was as steady a hockey player as one could find. Many of his peers regarded him as one of the top defensemen in the entire league. Besides he was a prolific scorer. He already held a number of scoring records for a defenseman. Indeed he only trailed Murdo MacKay in team scoring. Freddie Hunt always performed well; he had recently scored the 100th goal of his career.

The Herd began the new year of 1946, on the right foot, or right skate, by blasting Hershey, 7 – 2, for its fifth straight victory. The high flying Bisons were leading the league, not only in games won but also in goals scored. A few days later another overflow crowd again saw the Bisons blast the Bears, 6 – 1. Then the largest week night crowd in Bison history, 10,178, many of them standing behind the back rows of the red seats, saw the Bisons increase their league lead when they knocked off the Western Division leaders, the Indy Caps, 4 – 2. Big Roger Leger led the winning attack, sniping two of the goals. Dion and Eddolls were key contributors. Dion made 32 saves, some of the miraculous type, and Eddolls could be observed checking the opposition players everywhere on the ice.

Unfortunately success is often accompanied with problems. In mid January Murdo MacKay, the leading goal getter on the Bisons, and number two in the entire League, was traded to the Montreal Canadians. He tested well there. The Canadians decided that Murdo was rugged enough to remain in the big league, so they said they would work a deal that would send Wide Mike McMahon back down to Buffalo in time to play against Pittsburgh. He had been on loan to Boston. Unfortunately Wide Mike left his skates in Boston so he could not play in the January 20 contest against the Hornets. A sellout crowd of 10,229 watched as Pittsburgh defeated Buffalo for the fifth straight time in the 1945-46 season. Wide Mike McMahon quickly redeemed himself. In an 8 – 1 pummeling of Providence, he had a mighty big hand. As Tony Wurzer commented, McMahon was "something of a leisurely moving human steamroller on skates." While Mike was knocking down opponents, his teammates were scoring goals in clusters.[11]

The end of the season was coming into focus. The Bisons were getting ready for the final drive, anxious to secure their first place position and ready themselves for the playoffs. Murdo MacKay and Vic Lynn both were returned to the Bisons. Also General Manager Chapman announced that Bob Blake, a hard hitting defenseman, star of the championship Herd three years earlier, was coming back. He had recently been released from the U.S. Army. Blake was scheduled to arrive by train in St. Catharines and then get himself in shape for the playoff run.

The Bisons continued to chalk up victories in February. They suffered an occasional setback; usually it seemed to be at the hands of their old nemesis, the Pittsburgh Hornets. On February 6, the Bisons drew a record weekday crowd of 10,242 for a game with Indianapolis. The throng included 1,000 *Courier Express* paperboys, and another 1,500 youngsters from the Ft. Erie area. The Canadian neighbors from just across the Niagara River were reliable supporters of hockey in Buffalo. The thousands on hand saw one heck of a battle between the division leaders. In a wild bitter contest, the Bisons downed the Caps, 4 – 2. The game included four major penalties and a match misconduct which was handed to the Caps' Tony Bukovich after his vicious battle with Fritz Hunt. Bukovich slashed Hunt and then they both started slashing each other. Both got cuts that necessitated stitches. Each received a five minute penalty and Bukovich's was upped to a match misconduct for unsportsmanlike conduct which put him out of the game. The hero of the game was Kenny Mosdell who was playing his final game before heading for Montreal. He scored the go ahead goal following some terrific skating and stick handling. Near the end of the contest, the Caps pulled their goalie, and Mosdell promptly fired another counter into an empty net.

The streaking Bisons ran into their jinx, the Pittsburgh Hornets, on Sunday, February 10, before a season record crowd of 10,278. The Bisons lost, 4 – 2. It was the third time Pittsburgh defeated Buffalo on the latter's home ice. The fans, with little to cheer in the actual game, made the most of other opportunities to vent their feelings. For example, when a Pittsburgh goalpost came loose, the officials attempted to get it back in position to no avail, so equipment manager Shorty LaLonde "stalked majestically over the tricky ice floes, the customary seegar clenched in his teeth." He fixed it pronto, and the fans gave him a great hand. A little later, a board was knocked loose and again "Shawty" came to the rescue and again the fans cheered.

The Bisons returned to the victory trail and closed in on the Eastern Division Crown. The high scoring club added to its reputation for also being a very hard hitting club. Wide Mike McMahon was already known as a physical presence to be reckoned with. His fellow defenseman, Art Lessard, joined him as one of the tough guys in the Bison arsenal. Lessard was the one time French-Canadian amateur heavyweight boxing champion. During a game against Cleveland, the Barons got Lessard's dander up. Lessard claimed that twice in the game he heard Cleveland players say: "We get by this Lessard easy. He is easy mark. Hah, I show who is easy mark, by gar." While Lessard dealt out his physical punishment, the defense as a whole did a good job in leading the Bisons to a 3 – 2 victory.[12]

Connie Dion was also proving to be an outstanding goalie. Wurzer called him "the best little goalie in the AHL." Connie really was a little guy; he stood five feet five inches and weighed 140 pounds. Since he joined the Herd, in mid December, the Bisons won 17, lost 5 and tied 3. Dion had a goal per game average of slightly more than 2. Wurzer was impressed with Dion's own view of a goalie's role. Dion wrote an article on goalies for his hometown newspaper, in Asbestos, Quebec, circulation of about 200. Connie was referred to as the sports editor. In his commentary, Dion stated "A good goalie must have the sensitive feeling...like...like a musician.... he must be able to foresee in advance what another man is about to do...he must be alert and his hands, quick and sure, like an alligator hunter."[13]

The Bisons were riding high at this point. A 5 – 0 win over St. Louis before 8,904 in the Aud saw Leger break the record for defensemen in the AHL with his 20th goal. Next the Bisons traveled to Indianapolis and womped the Caps, 8 – 1. Then the Bisons encountered major problems with their defensemen. Kenny Mosdell and Frankie Eddolls were called up to Montreal. They would be missed not only because of their playing ability but also because they were likeable guys who added "a little something extra" to the team. They were guests of honor at a farewell party at the Stage Door, one of Buffalo's many popular downtown restaurants in the 1940s. Players, sports writers, sportscasters, and fans were on hand to wish the players well with Montreal and presented them will wallets stuffed with green bills. At the same time Art Lessard suffered an injury and Mike McMahon was called home because of a death in the family. That left just Leger and Field, as the only regular defensemen. So Bob Blake who had been getting into condition in St. Catharines, joined the team and did well despite the fact that he did not have much time to get his legs in condition.[14]

The Bisons managed to survive the dearth of defensemen nicely. March started out well for the Bisons. On the first day of the month, Murdo MacKay fired two goals into the net to cap a 5 – 4 victory over the St. Louis team. The Bisons were now firmly in control of their own destiny. A few days later, in the Aud before a new record crowd of 10,371 they faced their nemesis, the Pittsburgh Hornets. In the locker room, Coach Frank Beisler gave a pep talk emphasizing that "there's $1000 at stake there tonight for each of you." The players got the message. In one of the fastest and most exciting games of the season, they finally defeated the Hornets. The Bisons were led by 5"5" Doug Lewis, the smallest guy on the squad, even shorter that Dion. Lewis scored the first and the last goals in the 4 – 2 victory. The Bisons now had a six point lead overall and moved within four points of an all time record for best winning percentage in league history. They had at least an additional $1,000 each for earning the playoff spot; that was big money back then.[15]

The Bisons next met New Haven. Hopelessly out of the playoffs, the New Haven club fought as if the title were at stake. Never before had any Eddie Shore team, any team he played with, coached, or managed, failed to win a single game on an opponent's ice for a full season. That dubious honor came to Shore when Buffalo once again defeated his squad, 2 – 1. Poor Eddie was in the record books again, though this time not by choice. The win clinched Buffalo's very first AHL championship. Even if all the other contenders won all their remaining games they could not equal the Bisons 77 points. Moreover, the Bisons had tied the mark for most wins in a season at 35, and there were still four more games to go.

Two days later, the Bisons played at Hershey and before the second largest crowd of the season in the Chocolate City, the hometown Bears tied the Bisons. On March 10 the Herd continued its assault on the record book by defeating Providence. The victory was number 36, a new all time AHL record. The victory also set a new league mark of 80 points. Capacity or near capacity crowds continued to come out to the games. And the usual stars continued to satisfy those loyal fans. Popular Roger Leger registered 57 points, a new record for a defenseman.

The Bisons won their 37th on March 14, this one over New Haven again, by a 5 – 1 score. Home town favorite "Little Freddie" Hunt bagged two goals. The final game of the regular season was held on St. Patrick's Day. As usual, or so it seemed, it was a victory for the Bisons. They beat Hershey 10 - 6 thus recording their 38th victory of the season and racking up a total of 84 points.

This first peacetime hockey season was truly a glorious one for the Buffalo Bisons. They had played well consistently and had delighted their numerous fans.The community loved the Bisons. But there was more work to be done. Next on the agenda were the American Hockey League Calder Cup playoffs. The Buffalo Bisons were the odds on favorites.

In the first round, Buffalo was matched against the Western Division Champions, the Indianapolis Caps. The Caps themselves had reason to expect that they could pull off at least some upsets. One reason for this optimism was that they were led by Les Douglas, the league's individual scoring champion, and unanimous selection for the all star team.

The first game started out to be a hard fought contest. Wurzer said "the game had everything but a beheading." It was as a frenzied affair at least until near the end of the second period. Then the Caps became disorganized and the Bisons began to find the net. They ended up decapitating the Caps with ease, 5 – 1. The cast of heroes was led by Connie Dion. Unfortunately Dion lost his shutout with only 18 seconds remaining.[16]

Connie Dion, Bison star goaltender of the '40s. *Photo: Tim Warchocki*

The next game was a grueling affair. The Bisons managed to win, 1 – 0, but it was costly. Doug Lewis was lost for the remainder of the playoffs when he was carried off the ice with two broken ribs. Coach Beisler made a good adjustment, he moved Bob Blake up to defenseman. The gamble paid off; Blake hit the lone tally.

The Bisons then ran into a buzz saw and got clobbered 7 – 1. It was a decisive defeat but on the bright side it served to give the Bisons incentive for the following contest. Buffalo rebounded nicely, and in the 4th game, they defeated the Caps 4 -1 before 7,822 Hoosier fans. In the fifth, the Bisons earned a berth in the final round with a 4 – 2 victory over the Caps. Connie Dion again was singled out for his stellar work in goal. The victories over the Indianapolis team were particularly gratifying for Dion. He had been somewhat of a castoff from Indy and now he had been able to make them eat crow. As Dion put it, "They say I am too small to play goalee. I show them, eh?" The Bisons had several injuries but still managed to survive nicely. In fact, Fred Hunt, as usual, came to the rescue, playing very well against the Caps. Wurzer called Hunt,"the squad's chief money player." The fans were definitely pleased; more than 10,000 came out for each game.[17]

Winning four out of five games in the first round was pretty much what most pundits would have predicted. As Buffalonians prepared to assess their team's prospects in the final round "for all the marbles" some grew a bit apprehensive. The Cleveland Barons were the opposition. They had not had a particular good regular season, certainly not on a par with their performance in recent years. However the Barons had succeeded in knocking Pittsburgh out of the playoff picture and the Barons always gave Buffalo a tough time.

The championship series was set. The Buffalo hockey squad boarded the train for the 200 mile ride along the Lake Erie shore to Ohio's largest city. The Bisons were well rested. Roger Leger and Art Lessard were both able to recuperate nicely from their injuries, and they joined the travel group that included the well known sports director of WEBR, Van Patrick, who would broadcast the games back to the fans in Buffalo. The team was focused on winning the Calder Cup; the team also coveted the $14,400 cash prize. The Bisons were in the playoffs for the fourth straight year. It they needed an additional incentive, they had one. Last year the Barons knocked them out of the series in the first round.

Alas, things did not go as planned for the Bisons. They went through a tough practice in Cleveland that turned out to be disastrous. Defensemen Bob Blake and Wilf Field came up with leg injuries, Vic Lynn suffered a broken nose. Roger Leger suffered a twisted knee. Doug Lewis was still at home with his cracked ribs. Against the injury ridden Bisons, the robust Barons had reason to be confident. They were referred to affectionately in the local press as the nine old men; the fact is that nine of the Baron players had more than 10 years of experience. They were money players, cold and calculating veterans who did not get overly excited even when the stakes were high.

An all time record crowd of 12,359 was on hand for the opening game in Cleveland. The locals did not disappoint their hometown fans. They defeated the "Redshirts," as the Bisons were sometimes called, by a score of 3 – 2. The Bisons skated as though they were going to put the game away early, unfortunately their shots were off target, some even missing the open net. Buffalo did go ahead 1 – 0 but the Barons then presented a screen play. The players gathered around the Buffalo goalie, so much so that Dion could not even see the puck. Then a Baron would sneak up on the outside and shoot. The Cleveland strategy paid off.

The Bisons squared the series back on their home ice, routing the venerable Barons, 8 – 2. The aging Barons simply could not keep up with the opposition. The Bisons were very gentlemanly about it, skating carefully around and past the Barons, but refusing to hit them or rough them up. Wide Mike McMahon said: "it would be like body-checking your father. It's not done in polite circles."

The aggressiveness that the Bisons, especially Tommy Cooper and Murdo MacKay, demonstrated in the second game was lacking in the third contest. After bolting out in front the Herd's defense collapsed and allowed the Barons back in the game. Cleveland tied the contest at 4 goals a piece, and came away the winner in overtime. Ex Bison Fred Thurier led the way with a hat trick.

Two nights later, back in Cleveland, the Herd again stormed into what seemed to be a safe lead, only to see it vanish. The Bisons took a 3 – 1 lead in the first 14 minutes of play. They seemed to have had hit their stride. They circled the veteran Barons with "astonishing ease...then came a strange interlude." Wide Mike McMahon was sent to the penalty box for what certainly any loyal Bison fan would claim was no more than a threatening gesture. The referee saw it differently. The Barons promptly, in fact within 20 seconds, tied up the game with two rapid goals. Each team added to its score, but the Bisons seemed to be playing without heart. They ended up losing by a 7 – 5 score.

The Barons were now in the driver's seat with a 3 – 1 lead in the series. Just one more victory and the Barons had the coveted cup. Comments began to be made about dissension among the Bison players.That was denied. Still, even the coaches were baffled. What happened to this powerhouse hockey team that had set records and had ridden into the playoffs as such a dominant force? No one had the answer. General Manager Chapman said: "The players themselves don't know why the team is falling to pieces." Wurzer concluded that it was not so much the Bisons, as the fact that the Barons would just not quit. He called them "A bunch of wily veterans who were about as hard to discourage as the old-time magazine salesman."[18]

Whatever the problem, the Bisons quickly solved it. In the next game the Bisons rebounded strongly and steamrolled the Barons, 6 – 1. One answer might have been that Connie Smyth and Dirk Irvin, of the Toronto Maple Leafs and Montreal Canadians were in the stands watching and they were known to strongly dislike players playing out of position. The fact is that those NHL big shots were closely observing several Bisons including Murdo Mackay, Tommy Cooper, Vic Lynn and Roger Leger. The result was that all the Bisons stayed in their positions, even after Buffalo had the lead, unlike in the two previous games. Bob Stedler's column following the fifth game reinforced the view that the Bisons were playing together. Rumors of dissension were just that. The Bisons were money players. In the 6th game the Bisons traveled to Cleveland and outplayed the Barons again, earning a closely-checked, 4 – 3 victory at Cleveland. Paul Mundrick put in the goal that clinched the Bisons' victory; thus setting the stage for the grand finale back at the Aud.[19]

If there was ever any doubt that Buffalo was a big time hockey town, those views should have vanished on Sunday, April 15, 1946, the date for the final AHL game of the season, the final of the championship series. Billy Kelly reported in his column, that mobs of people lined up to buy tickets for the final game. The ticket windows opened at 10 AM. Fans began gathering at 6 AM, outside of the Bisons' office at Niagara and Pearl Streets. Noting that he had seen long lines of patrons for all kinds of sports events in Buffalo, Kelly said that nothing ever equaled "the patient hopefuls who formed at Pearl and Niagara Streets, opposite the hockey club's offices and then extended along Niagara Street to Shelton Square, thence west on Church street to Pearl, thence north to midway between Church and Niagara Sts, then crossing to the west side of Pearl St. and heading toward Church St. and thence all around the block of Church to Franklin, to West Eagle to Niagara St. to Pearl and the ticket windows. Surely such loyalty and enthusiasm are without precedent in the Buffalo sports field." All the tickets were gone in two hours. Unfortunately, the authorities had to enforce the fire prevention laws, so standing room tickets could not be sold. The attendance at the game was 9,445. [20]

The Bisons won the game, 5 – 2. They scored first and were never headed. But that did not mean that the game was an easy one. Throughout the three periods, the determined and hard hitting Barons kept the fans on the edge of their seats. Bison star forward Vic Lynn scored two goals helping him earn a ticket to the NHL the following season. Dion, as often, was one of the stars along with Bob Blake and also Freddie Hunt with his amazing back-checking. That trio played major roles in the last two Bison victories of the playoffs. Overall it was the story of a Bison team that skated much faster that the veteran Barons. The Bisons rained 55 shots on net, a new high for the year. Both teams hit hard, but the checks were clean, and Referees Rabbit McVeigh and Eddie Burke did not hand out a single penalty

The final buzzer sounded at 10:38 on Sunday night. Pandemonium followed. A thunderous cheer went up, rocketing from wall to wall, a veritable avalanche of sound occurred, that included horns, whistles, sirens, anything else that could make some noise. Programs from all sections of the Aud were tossed down on the ice. Jubilant fans mobbed poor little Connie Dion. The *Courier Express*'s Jack Laing would customarily put the final story together immediately following a game. This night he simply took time out to observe the celebrations. He watched as the players left the ice to rousing applause, noting "the players rewarded their admirers by tossing their sticks into the crowd as souvenirs. It was a grand windup to a truly great season." The Bisons had won their third title in four years. This time they did it the hard way, coming back to win the last three games. They broke their own record of 48 playoff goals by scoring 50.[21]

It was a magnificent season for the Buffalo Bisons. There had been some skepticism about the team before the season opened. Art Chapman was new in the managerial role, and had succeeded the popular Eddie Shore. The team needed an infusion of new blood. Many thought Buffalo's prospects were questionable. But that quickly changed and eventually the highest honors in the American League were brought home to Buffalo culminating in the first championship for GM Chapman and Coach Beisler. The attendance and loyalty of the fans was excellent. Many capacity crowds were the result. Only Cleveland outdrew Buffalo, and that was because its arena had more seating capacity. The Bisons drew 321,162 fans for an average of 6,451 per home game.[22]

The evening following the championship game, a farewell banquet was held in the Hotel Lafayette where the players gathered for a farewell party. The festivity was a grand affair. Dr. James J. Ailinger, Vice President of the Buffalo Hockey club, was the toastmaster. He announced that already season ticket sales for the following year were three times greater than this past season. By winning, each player would receive about $850 in playoff money, as well as a sapphire ring and a $100 victory bond. Player salaries averaged about $3,000 per year; they could usually count on another $1000 or $1500 from summer jobs. So this playoff bonanza was heartily welcomed.

The following morning the players went their separate ways. A few stayed in Buffalo. Freddie Hunt had married a local girl and would go on a short honeymoon and then return to Buffalo. Len Halderson who married a Buffalo girl would do the same. Others dispersed for points throughout the Eastern United States and Canada. Coach Beisler would leave to help out his father in the funeral business in Connecticut. Equipment Manager, Shorty LaLonde, headed for Syracuse to help out his father in his liquor store. Mike McMahon went to Saskatoon to work as an iron welder, and Art Lessard worked in a fruit store in Montreal, Vic Lynn would work as a carpenter in Toronto and Paul Mundrick was employed in a chocolate factory. Murdo MacKay would work as an employee of a grain company in Ft. William Ontario, and Wilf Field would serve as a golf pro at a country club in Pt. Arthur, Ontario. Doug Lewis was hired by the Canadian-Pacific Railroad.

It would be five months before the hockey players would report to training camp. Many of the star players from the championship season would return for the 1946-47 season;

in fact many remained with the Herd throughout much if not all of the postwar period, that is until 1950-51. These included Fred Hunt, George Pargeter, Murdo MacKay, Len Halderson, Doug Lewis, Bob Blake, Tommy Cooper, Wilf Field, Art Lessard, and Connie Dion. In addition, Roger Leger, Paul Mundrick, Mike McMahon, Frankie Eddolls, and Floyd Curry, played at least a few seasons in a Bison uniform. Toward the end of the postwar period, Grant Warwick, and the Great Abe DeMarco joined the herd and played major roles. That was also true of Paul Meger, Sid McNabney, Gordon Pennell, and Les Hickey. A few had very brief stints with the Bisons simply because they were so good; they advanced to play the major part of their career in the NHL. Such were Doug Harvey an outstanding defenseman with the Montreal Canadiens in the 50s and Tom Johnson, another defenseman who also made the grade with Montreal. Both were future Hall of Famers. The stability served the Bison organization well during the 1940s. Fans and the entire community got to know the players very well unlike later years when players on all major sports teams would come and go whenever the money beckoned.

Generally the Bisons also maintained a fairly high degree of stability and consistency during the post war period in the front office. Ownership remained in the hands of Louis Jacobs. Edgar Danahy continued to serve as President. Dr. James Ailinger served as Vice President until mid 1947, when the demands of his dental practice required him to resign his Bison post. John Sweeney then filled that post. Sweeney was a local banker and a former amateur sports star.

The stability did not extend to the coaching staff. Frank Beisler, and Leroy Goldsworthy were the most familiar names in the period. But there were others who took a turn at the head coaching position. On the other hand, the decade of the '50s was marked by even more volatility in the coaching ranks.

The Calder Cup Champions were not able to duplicate the success of the 1945-46 season again in the immediate post war era. However, with the exception of the dismal 1948-49 season, they did manage to make the playoffs each year. They did have some very good seasons.

The Bisons and their fans looked forward to the 1946 – 47 season with great optimism. Hockey had arrived big time in Buffalo. Fans were eager for it. The Western New York community was ready for more ice hockey at all levels of play and competition. The two major newspapers followed the sport closely and devoted ample space to the Bisons. Bob Stedler, *Buffalo Evening News* Sports Editor, recognized the hockey boom and its popularity in the Buffalo area. The caliber of play was improving as expected, what with the return of so many veterans. The minor leagues benefited from the surplus that the major league teams now had. During the war, it was pretty much a matter of letting play whoever was available. Looking to the future, Stedler noted that there would have to be more minor leagues organized. Stedler also recognized the need for more rinks for the youngsters in the community. The youth of the area reflected the enthusiasm for Bison ice hockey by playing plenty of pick-up games wherever they could find a sheet of ice. Stedler urged that rinks be constructed and that high schools and colleges develop teams. Citing one of the public's main concerns, that of juvenile delinquency, Stedler thought that the availability of more hockey rinks could be an antidote to that problem.[23]

Bison Vice President, Dr. James Ailinger, quoted in Billy Kelly's column in the *Courier Express* added his two cents. He urged that high school hockey teams be formed. Ailinger even suggested that an ice plant could be put in Civic Stadium and that two artificial rinks be constructed there. Further, Ailinger even offered to have the

Bisons supply coaches for the teams, and furnish equipment and then added a familiar tune, saying that "they talk about juvenile delinquency around here. Well, for Pete's sake, that's the best way to combat it."[24]

Ailinger and the Bisons kept their word. A few months later, the Buffalo Hockey club announced that Maxie Bennett had been signed to a fulltime contract. His main job would be to work with the Municipal Hockey League. Hockey had always been Maxie's career and his first love. Maxie was an Auditorium original, he had been on the very first Bison team in the Aud and played until an injury in 1944, ended his playing days. He was one of the AHL's most colorful and most popular players. The Hockey Club felt that hockey owed Maxie Bennett something. This new position would be ideal for him. Moreover it was viewed as a wonderful move for the local area youngsters, something very positive for the community. Maxie would work directly with the junior chamber of commerce, the official sponsor of the Muny league.

In July Ailinger traveled to New York to attend the annual hockey meetings. He announced the expected, that Frank Beisler would be back as coach for the 46-47 season. His rookie year had been a superb one. Besides he was popular with the fans, that relationship dated from the time he had been the captain of the Bisons' first championship team during the war years. Ailinger also announced that Buffalo would shift its United States Hockey League affiliation from Dallas to Houston. He also confirmed that the AHL was expanding; its new members, Philadelphia and Springfield, would make it a 10 team circuit.

Upon his return, Ailinger met with the press and expressed his opinion that the Bisons were going to have their greatest season ever on the ice and in the stands. The sports reporters shared the optimism but were a little more cautious. Ailinger also pointed out that it was still summer and the club had already sold 500 reserve season seats in the grays, something not done previously. A short time later, Dr. Ailinger, accompanied by GM Chapman went to Montreal; there they worked out a favorable working agreement with the Canadians.

As opening day approached, there continued to be reports that the Bisons were signing recruits. Chapman stated that there would be some 100 prospects in camp, including at least 60 rookies. Many hockey players continued to be mustered out of military service in 1946. The Bisons had other good news too. Though they would hold preseason camp in Ottawa, the Peace Bridge arena was scheduled to be re-opened in November. This meant that they would be able to practice in-season at that site. Unlike in the past, they would have ice available every day.[25]

The regular season got underway on October 16. The season opener against the Indianapolis Caps ended in a hard fought 1 – 1 tie. The following night the Bisons won, 3 – 1, this time at Indy. The Bisons had a much easier time and it appeared they were ready to roll, just as many had predicted. However things did not go as expected. The Bisons lost, then lost again and then battled the Providence Reds to a 4 – 4 tie, in a game that typically reflected Bison frustrations in the first weeks of the season. Freddie Hunt was playing well, got his second goal of the evening and the Bisons seemed to be coasting to a 4 – 3 win but Providence evened the score shortly before the final buzzer. The Bisons had to wait until the end of the month before they registered their first home victory. That was a 2 – 1 win at the expense of St. Louis. 8,000 fans turned out in the Aud. That was an average figure for the first part of the season. Attendance was healthy though not quite as high as the previous season. But the victories were not as numerous either. The

Herd's biggest rival offered no consolation. The Bisons faced the Cleveland Barons three times within a week, and lost two, 2 – 0, and 5 – 2, and tied one, 3 – 3. The Barons took 5 of 6 points in the series; and dealt a hefty blow to the self esteem of the Bisons.

By the second week of November, it appeared that the Herd had turned things around. On November 9, they blasted the hapless Philadelphia Rockets, one of the new entries in the AHL, 9 – 3. The next day, they scored only once, but it was enough since Connie Dione served up a shut out against the high flying Hershey Bears before the largest crowd of the season, over 10,000.

A few days later the Herd earned a point by tying the Indianapolis Caps but it was a costly point because Frankie Eddolls who had just come down from Montreal to help the struggling Bisons suffered an eye injury. He had to be carried from the ice. The game then degenerated into one of the wildest and roughest affairs in which the Bisons were ever involved in the Aud. Twelve penalties were called in the first two periods. Tony Wurzer said "it was hockey stripped of any semblance of a game." By the third period the two teams were so exhausted that one wondered if they were actually playing hockey. Things got worse. The Herd lost to Cleveland on November 17, 6 – 3, and the following day they lost to Pittsburgh, 4 – 2. They found themselves in last place. Obviously they were not playing like champions; in fact they did not even resemble champions. The Bisons skated out of the cellar by pounding the Philadelphia Wings 7 – 1. That was not a great achievement as the Philadelphia club boosted a 2 -17 record, and had an average of 8 goals per game against them. Wurzer remarked that the Wings "displayed as much vigor as a damp firecracker." He added that "the defensemen were distinguishable from innocent bystanders solely because they wore numbers and frequently fell on the ice." Freddie Hunt was one of the exceptions. He got the hat trick, and that accomplishment entitled him to a new hat at one of Buffalo's downtown haberdasheries, as well as a dinner at a local ale house. Hunt continued to be a bright light.[26]

By defeating some of the weaker teams the Bisons were, at least, able to stay out of the cellar. Coach Beisler was able to continue his unblemished record against New Haven. In his two years of coaching the Bisons he had never lost to New Haven. On December 1, Buffalo once again defeated the Connecticut club. But things did not really get much better. Frankie Eddolls returned but briefly. He suffered another injury, this one to his knee. This would put him out of commission for several more weeks. The team lost to Hershey, to Springfield, and to Providence. Then the Bisons did turn things around. They defeated Providence, 4 – 2, and followed that with a victory over the Hornets, 5 – 3. Then they squeezed a 1 – 0 win over Springfield, giving Connie Dion his second shutout of the season. More wins and ties followed. As the month of December drew to a close, the Bisons once again were drawing 10,000 fans to their games in the Aud. On New Year's Eve the Bisons faced the Indianapolis Caps. Entering the final period Indy was ahead 6 – 2, but the Bisons came alive and blistered the net for three goals. The tying goal seemed not far behind; unfortunately time ran out. It was a tough loss but all things considered 1946 ended fairly well for the Buffalo Bisons. Now at the midway point of the season, the Herd was in the middle of the AHL standings. Cleveland and Hershey were sitting atop their respective divisions with 48 points each.

On the first Sunday of the New Year, the Bisons faced the seemingly indestructible Cleveland Barons. A near capacity crowd, as usual, filled the Aud. For two periods the Barons did seem to be invincible. The Bisons, trailing 3 – 1, appeared to be a beaten team. However the third period turned out to be one for the ages, or at least one for the record books. It was not recorded what might have been said in the locker room to the players, but they came out as if a "Win one for the Gipper" speech might have been made. They immediately seemed to be a much inspired group. The fans quickly discerned that and most of them were on their feet cheering lustily and veritably rocking the building for the entire final period. The Bisons had been strengthened by the addition of Center Jimmy McFadden and Winger Les Hickey. Both made their presence felt in the third period, especially McFadden, the sensational rookie from Ottawa. The Bisons clocked a record 8 goals in that period and held the Barons scoreless. Wurzer thought that the unfortunate Cleveland goalie, Roger Bessette was "whirling like a dervish." The crowd loved the high scoring spree, even more so since the victim was Buffalo's greatest rival and the league leader. Buffalo picked up four points over the weekend, having defeated another nemesis, Pittsburgh, the previous night. Now the Herd was solidly in third place.

In fact second place was clearly in sight. On January 6, the Herd beat St. Louis 5 – 4 for its 9th victory in 11games. The newcomers to the team began to make their weight felt. The Bisons next victory came over Springfield, and McFadden had a hat trick as the red hot Bisons reeled off a 4 – 1 victory, before the usual 10,000 in the Aud. They extended their unbeaten streak in the calendar year, 1947, to 4 – 0 – 1. Then they faced the Indy Caps in a terrific game, a dazzling back and forth, up and down the ice affair, with the lead changing several times. The Bisons led by Tommy Cooper and Jerry Brown, who each scored a brace of goals, skated away with a 5 – 3 verdict and a tie for second place.

The Bisons continued to jostle with Pittsburgh and especially with Indianapolis for sole position of the second spot. The Eastern Division was as tight as ever. The Bisons tried to remedy this; Buffalo defeated Cleveland, on January 19, 5 – 2 with Hub Macey leading the way. It was another sellout crowd for a home game with the Barons. Next they pummeled the Providence Reds, 8 – 2 with MacKay getting the hat trick and then they trounced the Rockets, 8 – 3. Still the Bisons remained tied for 2nd place with the Caps and just one point ahead of the Pittsburgh Hornets. By mid February the playoff picture still had not clarified. A dozen games remained. The Herd next played the Hornets to a scoreless tie, and the game was most noteworthy because the sellout crowd in the Aud became irate after a Bison goal had been disallowed. Newspapers, programs, coins, and whatever else the fans could get their hands on, were tossed on to the ice and the game had to be delayed. But the tie held up.

A short time later the Bisons had to face the two division leaders, the Cleveland Barons and the Hershey Bears. Several hundred Buffalo fans took the train to Cleveland and several hundred other fans motored down the lakeshore to the Barons' arena. More than 12,000, the largest crowd of the season was on hand to watch a very exciting contest. Buffalo's Jerry Brown was able to score in the final minutes to give Buffalo a 2 – 2 tie. Back in Buffalo, a few days later, the Herd defeated the Hershey Bears before the usual 10,000. The Bisons played an all around splendid game and the victory enabled them to secure a spot in the playoffs.

The Herd plastered St. Louis, 7 – 0 and this victory combined with a Pittsburgh loss to Cleveland enabled the Bisons to take over second place. The second spot was now between Buffalo and Indianapolis. The season was coming down to the wire. A win over Indy would put the Bisons just two points behind the league leading Barons. But a lost to Indy would drop the Herd into a tie for third place with Pittsburgh.

The Bisons entrained for Indy and were ready for the Caps. The easily outscored the host team 7 – 0, and Dion had his 6th shutout, most in the AHL, for the season. But the game and the scoring were purely coincidental. The game was full of all sorts of fisticuffs; the police had to step in to stop what had the makings of a general melee. The *Buffalo Evening News* story was headlined: "full period devoted to fighting during Herd's 7 - 0 triumph." Amidst the near riotous situation there was even a little humor. At one point Doug Lane was slashed by Frankie Eddolls. Lane retaliated, but he mistook McFadden for Eddolls, and knocked McFadden down. McFadden yelled: "What was that for?" Lane skated into the penalty box and said "That's for looking like Eddolls."[27]

In the final week of the season, the Bisons defeated Cleveland and Springfield and earned a 2 – 2 tie with Providence. They lost to New Haven, perhaps because the Ramblers were so desperate for a win. They needed another victory more than Buffalo did in order to secure a playoff spot. Then on March 16, in the season finale, the Bisons again defeated Pittsburgh, thereby clinching 2nd place. The usual stars shone that night. Mundrick and McMahon each got a brace of goals, and MacKay added the other. McMahon was in particularly good form, perhaps because it was the eve of St. Paddy's day. Wide Michael after all was from County Clair by way of Brockville, Ontario. He literally wore his green on his sleeve as did many of the other 10,000 spectators. In addition to scoring two goals, Mike landed some hard elbows on the opponents. One wonders if he might not have had some of the Irish spirits before the game.

The season thus ended on a high note for the Bisons. By finishing in 2nd place, each player would get the grand sum of $100. Murdo MacKay would get a little more. It was announced at the last game that MacKay was the winner of the MVP award, based on fan voting. His prize would be a golf bag and clubs donated by Rose Sporting Goods. The regular season was over. It had started out poorly but finished up quite well. The Herd secured 2nd place, just two points out of first. They seemed ready for the first round of the Calder Cup. There was certainly no reason for anyone to be jittery since this was their fifth consecutive AHL playoff appearance. They headed for Massachusetts in a good mood to face their old friend, Eddie Shore and his Springfield Indians.

Wide Mike's Paddy Day's spirit continued in Springfield. Before the capacity crowd of 6,500, McMahon, with just 36 seconds remaining, fired a long hard shot from just over the Blue Line. It landed in the net and gave the Herd a 3 – 2 victory. Back in the Aud, two days later, the Bisons had an easier time of it. They coasted to an 8 – 4 victory, thus sweeping the first round in the playoffs. Paul Mundrick, one of the heroes of last season's playoffs, was the big gun, getting the hat trick. Old reliable Tommy Cooper caged a pair of goals. But it was a costly victory. Freddie Hunt was injured; he suffered a fractured right cheekbone and would miss the rest of the season. Hunt was a good big game player; he was one of the league's best back checkers. He was known for his reckless speed that back checked many an opponent out of a goal.

In the Calder Cup semifinals Buffalo faced Pittsburgh. Since Buffalo had ended the season on a high note, and Pittsburgh did not, the Bisons were labeled the favorite. They promptly got smeared in the opener, 5 – 0. The Bisons were stopped cold by the Hornets' all star goalie, Bas Bestien. He bagged his 8th shutout of the season. Back in Buffalo for the next game, the Bisons felt confident. Why not? They had won 21 straight home games; in so doing they had tied the AHL record. That accomplishment did not phase the Hornets. They finished off the Bisons with a 2 – 1 win. The Herd did not go meekly; they played their hearts out; they were all over the Pittsburgh end of the ice, but simply could

The 1946-7 Buffalo Bisons. ***Left to right, front row*****: Gauthier, Cooper, Lewis, Eddolls, McFadden, Mahaffey, Hunt, Agar and Dion;** ***Back row:*** **Trainer Dipperty, Hickey, Fields, Brown, Shill, Blake, Portland, MacKay, Mundrick, McMahon, and Coach Biesler.** *Photo: Tim Warchocki*

not get a break.

Pittsburgh advanced to face the Hershey Bears in the finals. The Chocolate City team proved to be worthy Calder Cup champs for the 1946-47 season. The Buffalo players settled for a farewell banquet in the Hotel Touraine in downtown Buffalo. The affair was marked by a mixture of condolences and congratulations. The Bison players lost out on $700 by missing the final round but they received $500 for winning the first round. Three of the Bisons headed for the Big Time, joining the Stanley Cup playoffs, then in progress. Jimmy McFadden headed to the Detroit Red Wings, while Murdo MacKay and Frankie Eddolls reported to the Montreal Canadians.

It was disappointing for the Herd to be eliminated in two straight games in the play-offs. But overall, it was a fairly satisfactory year. Yet, they did not win the Calder Cup. Therefore the Hockey club officers kept busy during the off season; busy arranging for new blood for the team, and busy promoting the club. Dr. James Ailinger, vice president of the Bisons was always on the go. He practiced dentistry but on off days and in the evenings, one could find Dr. Ailinger, speaking at sports banquets, honoring various youth hockey teams, representing the Bisons at various sports nights in the area, or making appearances before troops of Boy Scouts, war veterans organizations or any of a number of other groups.

In July, Dr. Ailinger's exhausting schedule caught up with him. He submitted his resignation so that he could devote the necessary time to his profession of dentistry. Ailinger was also a national collegiate football official and he wanted to continue his work as a head linesman at leading college football games each fall. Ailinger was a genial, diplomatic, capable sportsman; he was "well liked by the public and the newspapermen with whom he came into frequent contact." For many decades he continued to be a valuable ambassador for the city of Buffalo.[28]

Following Ailinger's departure, various reorganization measures were taken. Art Chapman, the hockey club's General Manager announced that John J. Sweeney, a local banker at the Manufacturers and Traders Trust Company was appointed treasurer of the club. The office of Vice President was eliminated. Sweeney took over most of Ailinger's duties. In addition Robert Harrington, a local attorney was named the secretary of the club. Chapman also noted that a new coach would be appointed in the near future. Frank Beisler had resigned and taken the coaching position with Washington, a new entry in the American Hockey League. There Beisler would have more control over hockey matters than he had had in Buffalo. In mid August the appointment of Leroy "Goldie" Goldsworthy, as Head Hockey Coach was announced. Goldsworthy was a full blown hockey veteran. He had broken into the profession ranks in 1929 with the New York Rangers. Subsequently he played for a number of other teams in the years that followed. His playing career included a year with the Buffalo Bisons in 1941-42. During the war years, he coached minor league teams in Baltimore and Dallas. Rudy Pilous was appointed chief scout.

Meanwhile, from May to August, the hockey players spent their waking hours playing golf, working at a variety of jobs, and trying to keep in good physical shape for the hockey season that lay ahead. The Bison hockey offices in downtown Buffalo remained open; General Manager Art Chapman and the newly appointed Hockey club officers kept fairly busy. They completed their farm system with the purchase of the San Diego team of the Pacific Coast hockey league. At the time that league was equivalent to the senior circuit in Ontario. They continued to retain their affiliation with Houston of the United States Hockey League.

By the end of the summer, the Hockey staff had made the necessary preparations for the return of the players to preseason camp at Barrie, Ontario. A total of 82 prospects would be available for selection. In camp, the press noted that some of the defensemen were making their weight felt, and one, Harold Jackson, who liked to demonstrate how to physically beat up on other players, would actually make the squad and become the Bisons' tough guy for the season. By early October the front lines were coming together nicely. The Bisons were very pleased that they were getting a solid front line, in tact, from Montreal. The line included the popular Murdo MacKay, and also Leo Gravelle and Joe Bell, brother of the more widely known, Gordie Bell. The *Courier Express* announced that Charlie Bailey would be back to do hockey announcing on game nights from 10:30 until 11:15 over WEBR. The *Buffalo Evening News* also announced that Jim Wells would do play by play of Bison hockey on WBEN-FM. He would be broadcasting from a precarious roost on the catwalk, high up in the rafters of the Aud. The Bisons played an ambitious preseason schedule that included two games with the Montreal Canadiens and one with the Toronto Maple Leafs. The Bisons showed that their skills were pretty good, but the preseason contests also revealed that many of the players were woefully out of shape. This was especially true of defensemen like Mike McMahon and Bob Blake.[29]

The 1947-48 season opened for the Bisons in Cleveland on October 14. The Bisons won, 4 – 3. Reliable Murdo MacKay led the way with two goals. Then the Herd returned to Buffalo for its own home opener the following night, again against Cleveland. The game marked the return of Leroy Goldsworthy to the Aud and his debut as a head coach in the AHL. Four of the five defensemen, among the toughest in the AHL, were wearing Bison uniforms for the first time. This quartet consisted of Leo Lamoureaux, Hal Laycoe, Hal Jackson, and Bob Currie, all seasoned veterans and strictly major leaguers. Only Bob Blake was back from last year's squad. Another newcomer, goalie Paul Bibeault, had an excellent preseason camp. In fact it was good enough to give him the nod over Connie Dion. The *Courier's* Jack Laing said that some felt that the Bisons had "their most powerful club...in many years."[30]

In the eyes of the 8,000 plus fans who attended the home opener, the Bisons lived up to expectations. The Herd dominated the Barons, 8 – 1. Bobby Thorpe and Joe Bell each had a brace of goals. Paul Bibeaut had 61 saves. The owner of the Barons attended the game in Buffalo and declared it was the "strongest Bison team" he had ever seen. On the other hand, the Cleveland squad was composed of a number of old veterans, some very good players but not quick enough to keep up with the Bisons. In his account of the game, Tony Wurzer noted that as the game wore on, Buffalo's youth and quickness began to tell. Bobby Thorpe, the speedy rookie, scored and then Defenseman Hal Laycoe "played the puck for a full minute around the Baron net like a coon hound circling a scent: When he finally let fly, Bessette (Roger the goalie) was in the wrong corner." Then Bell followed a minute later with his second score of the game, and "the Barons might as well have been in Peoria after that."[31]

Following their very successful opening weekend against the Barons, the Bisons experienced an up and down type of season. It was a season in which they were, once again, in a constant battle with the Pittsburgh Hornets for second place in the Western Division. Occasionally there seemed a slight chance that they might even catch the league leading Cleveland Barons. Tim Warchocki, Bison hockey authority, noted that it was a season marked by frequent line-up changes and turnover in personnel with considerable traffic to and from Montreal and Houston. When the season was only a week old, two popular members of the team volunteered to help out the Houston farm club, a team beset by injuries. Connie Dion and Bob Blake wanted to play themselves into condition. Bibeault had been playing most of the time so Connie needed to get some playing time in, and Blake who was recovering from an injury needed to get in shape too.[32]

On the second weekend of the season, the Herd played St. Louis in a home and home series, first losing to the Flyers in St. Louis, 5 – 3, but then back in Buffalo they returned the favor 4 – 2. In that game, the Bisons were all over the Flyers, often the latter were on their backs on the ice. It was a rough game that produced five sets of double penalties. Wurzer said: "The boys came off the ice in pairs, like policemen on the old waterfront beat." The Bisons also showed that they had a welcome addition to their offense in the person of Leo Gravelle, "the sensational new young blond star" down from Montreal. Gravelle was the hero in the St. Louis victory; he tallied twice. Wurzer referred to him as "the blond antelope on skates." In the early part of the season, Gravelle was close behind Murdo MacKay, the league leader in scoring. Jack Laing devoted much of one of his "Passing the Puck" columns to MacKay. He noted that if Murdo continued to play well, as he did last spring with Montreal in the Stanley Cup finals against Toronto, he no doubt would be back with the Canadiens soon. That prediction came true a month later.[33]

The offense was doing its job. But Coach Goldsworthy felt he needed some improvement on defense. He sought out Art Lessard, who had retired from professional hockey and was working with amateurs in the Quebec area. Goldy liked the idea of having a "hardworking bloke" like Lessard "just to scare the opposition." This is exactly what the big French Canadian did well. Goldy succeeded in talking Lessard into returning to the Bisons.

At the end of the month of October, the Bisons did not appear to be playing up to their potential. They dropped a 5 – 2 decision to Caps. The story in the *Buffalo Evening News* noted that Bibeault had a rough night in goal, and implied that Dion who was having a successful time in Houston might be recalled to Buffalo. The following night in St. Louis, the Bisons tied the Flyers. MacKay's goal rescued the Bisons but otherwise the Herd did not play well. Tony Wurzer remarked that the Herd was listless, just going through the motions. The fog was the big story because it was hot both inside and outside the arena, very unusual for late October. The fog gave the customers something to discuss. The fans' chief interest seemed to be "will the fog settle low enough to hide the players... Unfortunately, it didn't."[34]

With the Herd not playing well, hockey talk turned to peripheral matters. It might be weather conditions, or it might be injuries to goalies without face masks. This was the case after a game in which the Bisons topped the Flyers, 4 – 3. Paul Bibeault was in goal for Buffalo and his opposite number was lanky Hec Highton. Both goalies played well and each suffered facial injuries. Highton was hit on the left side of the face by a puck. He dropped to his knee and after receiving first aid from the trainer ambled over to the bench and took a healthy belt from the water bottle. He received a fine ovation as he returned to his cage. Bibeault was injured when he was inadvertently clipped by a Flyers' stick as he leaned forward in his cage. He withdrew to the dressing room and play was suspended for two minutes while two stitches were taken in his lower lip. Then he returned. Goalies were hardy athletes back then.[35]

On October 29, the roof fell in. The Bisons suffered their worst ever defeat on home ice as they were crushed by the Caps 9 – 1. Laing said that Goalie Paul Bibeault had a red face and a red neck, the result of "red light sunburn" from all the goals scored. His counterpart at the *News*, Tony Wurzer, called it a "new home ice record in futility." General Manager Chapman was upset. He had just returned from a week with the Houston farm club. From what he saw at the game gave him clear evidence that some changes were needed. Indications were that Defenseman Bob Blake and Goalie Connie Dion would be brought back from Texas. But no sooner had the Herd suffered this embarrassing defeat than their fortunes changed once again.[36] For whatever reasons, November seemed to usher in a different Bison team. The Bisons began with a five goal first period assault on the hapless Washington Lions and then cruised to a 7 – 3 victory. A couple of days later the Bisons executed another seven goal game. This time the victim was the Providence team. Joe Bell and Les Douglas each got the hat trick. It was a hard fought but clean game with plenty of bruises and stitches on both teams.

Joe Bell appeared to be on his way to stardom. He was the top Bison scorer with 29 points. At that pace he would set an AHL record. Bell was from Portage la Prairie; Tony Wurzer called it a little antelope stop in Manitoba. The New York Rangers had found Bell playing in the amateur ranks in Portage la Prairie. Following a year in the NHL with the Rangers he served in the Canadian army for two years, next he played with Montreal. The Canadiens shipped him to Buffalo where he now was the left winger on Buffalo's most dangerous line; Les Douglas was at center and Tommy Cooper at right wing.[37]

By mid November the Herd had rolled up five straight victories and was tied with Pittsburgh for first place; the Cleveland Barons lurked closely behind in the third spot. The two co-leaders of the pack got ready for a show down on November 15. Meanwhile the Bisons experienced some major personnel changes. Both MacKay and Gravelle, were on their way to play for the parent Montreal club. Chapman took that in stride saying they had earned another chance at the National League "big time." To compensate, the Canadiens sent down a pair of highly prized rookies, wingers Ted Campeau and Floyd Curry. They were two of the highest scoring amateurs ever to come out of the hard hitting Quebec senior hockey association. They had sparked the Montreal Royals of that circuit to a championship the previous year. The Canadien brass felt that the rookies needed more seasoning. Meanwhile, as fate would have it, the Bisons were not yet ready for the showdown with Pittsburgh. The Hornets shattered the Bison win streak coasting to a 6 - 2 victory. But the resilient Bisons, on the following day, knocked off the Eastern Division leaders, the Hershey Bears, by a 6 – 3 count. Les Douglas paced the Herd with his hat trick, his second consecutive one on home ice. Connie Dion was back in goal; he won his first game since returning to Buffalo.

The Bison ride on the seesaw continued. They trimmed the Caps 5 – 2 before a sellout throng, largest of the season. More than 1,000 fans were turned away. Many fans viewed this as a grudge match, since Indy had literally clobbered the Bisons a month earlier. Tommy Cooper led the Herd with his two goals. The Bisons bowed to Cleveland in what was essentially a two separate hockey game evening. During the initial phase that lasted into the beginning of the second period, the Bisons dominated play. The Herd was ahead 3 – 0. But the Barons stormed back with six unanswered goals. That 6 – 3 loss was followed by a squeaker, a 4 – 3 win over New Haven. Then the Herd received a shellacking from Philadelphia, 5 – 0, but promptly retaliated with a 7 – 4 win over the same team.

The seesaw tipped in Buffalo's favor in December. The Bisons opened the month with a 3 – 2 victory over the Indy Caps. The Caps were bigger than the Bisons; they were rough and tough and they liked to demonstrate their physical superiority. But the Bisons kept their tempers in line and played good hockey. Jack Laing called it the greatest game of the season. The crowd was kept in a constant state of excitement as the Caps went all out in the closing minutes to try for the tie. With a minute to go, they pulled the goalie and had six forwards on the ice but the Herd's stalwart defense held. Two nights later, the Bisons traveled to the Chocolate City and survived with a 4 – 3 victory over Hershey. They won by the same score over the Springfield Indians in their next outing. They then beat the New Haven Ramblers, 5 – 3, lost at Indy 5 – 3, lost to Philadelphia, 7 – 3, and defeated Springfield, 4 – 3.

The Bisons were now busy getting ready for their mid December showdown with the Pittsburgh Hornets. The Buffalo brass thought the Herd needed more scoring punch. Murdo MacKay could provide that. He had seen little action in Montreal, and so was ready to come back down to Buffalo. Wurzer recognized his value; he called MacKay "the seige gun" and said he had "the most feared shot in the American League."[38]

Buffalo also arranged for a new defenseman to join the lineup. This was young, 190-pound Doug Harvey. He had played with the Montreal Royals last season and had been valuable in helping them win the coveted Allan Cup. In fact Harvey was voted the most outstanding athlete of Canada. Buffalo was now simply the next step in his hockey career that would lead ultimately to enshrinement in the Hockey Hall of Fame. He would be recognized as the greatest hockey defenseman in the history of the game until Bobby Orr came along. For its needs, Montreal called up three very good players, Hal Laycoe, Floyd Curry, and Bobby Fillion. Some fans felt consternation over these changes with Montreal. Cy Kritzer, of the *Buffalo Evening News* staff defended the moves. Kritzer said that Chapman felt Buffalo got the better of the deal; Chapman added that "In Doug Harvey we acquired the best defenseman in the league...the Maple Leafs would give $25,000 for him."[39]

The showdown with Pittsburgh came on Wednesday, December 17. Jack Laing said it was another great game, one of the best he had ever seen. The game featured the return of Murdo MacKay and the debut of Doug Harvey. Both played key roles. The number one star went to MacKay who scored the go ahead goal and overall put on a terrific show to key the 4 – 2 victory. The Bisons were now three points behind Pittsburgh. It appeared as though the season was going to be all about the struggle for first place between Buffalo and Pittsburgh. Indianapolis was in third place and the Cleveland Barons seemed to be somewhat forgotten in fourth as the 1948 calendar year began. In their next outing, the Herd defeated Philadelphia, 4 – 3. A Detroit Red Wing official observing the contest was so impressed with Doug Harvey that he predicted that he was on his way to being one of the best in the business.

It was the Holiday season, and as usual, or so it seemed, the Bisons were hot. The Bisons played another sensational game beating the Barons, 6 – 3 just before Christmas, before a SRO crowd of 11,656, biggest of the year in Cleveland. Dion was brilliant. He turned away 35 shots, many from close range. A few days later, the Herd rode roughshod over the Hershey Bears 5 – 1, leaving them only one point behind league leading Pittsburgh. Dion again shone brightly. In fact, Laing said that the way he stopped the Bears in the first period was a veritable "bare faced robbery." The crowd, that numbered 9,846, was the largest of the year in the Aud.[40]

The Herd spent New Year's Eve in Indianapolis and lost 4 – 2 but then started out the New Year of 1948 on a good note by knocking off Cleveland, 4 – 3. The Herd was within two points of Pittsburgh. Another donnybrook with the Hornets was next on the schedule; a victory would put the Bisons in a tie with the Hornets for first place. On Wednesday, January 7, one of the biggest mid week crowds ever, almost 10,000, watched the Herd defeat the Hornets, 4 – 2. The "Smoky City Boys" outplayed the home town team in the first half of game; Buffalo roared back with three goals by the end of 2nd period and added another in the 3rd period. Hard working Len Halderson was the big gun, sniping two counters.

The Bisons next were victorious over Philadelphia, 4 – 0. Connie Dion earned his first shutout of the season. It was a game in which the fans smelled blood. They knew that Art Lessard and the Rockets' Ed Bush, the league leading "bad man," did not like each other. Last time they met they staged a slugfest. The bloodthirsty crowd did what it could to egg them on. Finally near the very end of the game, Hal Jackson of the Bisons, not Lessard, and Ed Bush got into it. After the usual huffing and puffing, and groping and punching, both went to the penalty box. Some fans rushed the penalty box and police had to be called. Then, something happened for the first time in the history of Memorial Auditorum; Bush and Jackson were spirited out of the penalty boxes and into the dressing rooms to avoid any more fan outbursts. Three fans were ejected from the Aud. Meanwhile Art Lessard seemed to be content with scoring; his two goals paced the Herd. That same night, Pittsburgh lost to New Haven. Now the Bisons were in first place by two points but getting there was costly because George Pargeter was hurt in the victory over Philadelphia. Pargeter was relied upon as a penalty killer, and even more so since Freddie Hunt, their number one penalty killer, was off on a scouting mission.

On January 18, another capacity crowd saw the Hornets tie the Bisons. The crowd was on its feet ready to cheer Connie Dion for his second consecutive shut out on home ice, but with less than two minutes to go, Pittsburgh scored. The tie cracked the 10 game home winning streak of the Herd.

The contest for the top spot in the Western Division continued unabated. Buffalo lost to Cleveland a few days later and now was in second place with both Cleveland and Indy close behind. In fact the Barons were on a roll and would soon be in first place and would not relinquish that spot for the rest of the season. The Cleveland team, despite its rough beginning, proceeded to have one of the very best seasons ever for any team in the AHL.

Meanwhile the Bisons went into a minor slump. Wurzer at his sarcastic best noted that something nice about hockey was that there was something new everyday. "The latest creation, tried out Wednesday before 7,340 customers in Memorial Auditorium was one period hockey." He thought that the Bisons were saving themselves for the next big game, so in this one against Providence they did not exert themselves. All the scoring took place in a 5-minute framework in the second period. Other than that the Bisons and Reds just kind of lulled around. They all looked like tired business men after their annual outing. The Bisons were content to fore-check, and the Reds seemed content just to skate around without the puck. The Bisons managed to defeat the Rhode Islanders, 2 – 1.[41]

Things brightened up for the Herd in February. The Bisons scored their first win of the season on Indianapolis ice, 4 -2; it was a quick, exciting game played before almost 10,000. Once again the dynamic duo paced the Herd; MacKay got the hat trick and Dion was superb in goal. Buffalo next faced Pittsburgh in the Aud. They lost to the Hornets, 3 – 1. This was a particularly tough one to swallow as it ended one of the finest unbeaten home streaks ever compiled by the Bisons. The Herd had reeled off 13 victories and a tie dating back to mid November. Obviously they had not performed well as a road team. That trend threatened to continue. In mid February the Bisons went on the road and lost two in a row. It looked like their encounter with the St. Louis Flyers might be number three. The Bisons seemed to be standing still for the first two periods. Wurzer called it the laziest first two periods in the history of hockey. In fact between the 2nd and 3rd periods, GM Chapman literally barged into the locker room and suspended Joe Bell one of those who was barely exerting himself. Joe Bell then watched from the stands. The team came out for the third period fired up; Cooper scored within 5 seconds and the Herd proceeded to win 7 – 4.

The next game was just as bizarre. Most of the scoring took place in the first two periods; the final was reserved for a wild player - spectator brawl, the likes of which had not been seen since the days of Eddie Shore. Ironically no players on the ice were involved. The outbreak occurred when Jerry Brown completed the hat trick for the Bisons. He was skating by the New Haven bench when the Rambler Coach, Lynn Patrick, reached out and tugged at his jersey. Fireworks followed. The Ramblers' bench erupted. Rambler players and their coach got in a tussle with the fans. The local police finally quieted things down. The New Haven coach was ejected. Buffalo defeated New Haven, 7 – 3.

The Bisons did very well for the remainder of the season. Unfortunately, the Pittsburgh Hornets also did very well and the Cleveland Barons did even better. The Barons were all alone in first place in March and ended the season with a record number of wins. Buffalo and Pittsburgh continued to slug it out for second place; Indianapolis had fallen back comfortably into the fourth slot. Meanwhile the Providence Reds ran away with the Eastern Division title. Interestingly, Providence had the same number of points in first place as Buffalo did in third place. 86 was the number.

The final stretch to the playoffs was marked by some noteworthy accomplishments. In the March 2nd Bison 8 – 5 victory over Providence, a very odd sequence occurred. Midway through the final period, before more than 9,000 thrilled spectators, Murdo MacKay had a breakaway when his team was short handed. But he was hauled down from behind by one of the big Reds' defenseman. Murdo was sailing along fast and his momentum as he went down carried him into the Providence goal. In the crash that resulted, Goalie Harvey Bennett's right ankle was pierced deeply by the point of Murdo's skate. He bled profusely, so he had to retire from the game and went into the locker room for stitches. Bennett actually helped McKay. To Bennett it looked as though MacKay would break a leg if he crashed into the iron post so he moved away from it to give MacKay more room and in so doing was injured himself. That meant that one of the Providence's forwards had to play goalie for the remainder of the game. Murdo was give the penalty shot, the very first one of the year in the Aud. MacKay made it and with it the hat trick. The Bisons were now just a single point out of second place.

Good news in early March for the Bisons came with Freddie Hunt's return to action. He immediately teamed up with MacKay and Jerry Brown and became part of one of the hottest lines in hockey. Earlier in the season Hunt had not been performing up to par so the Bison administration decided to use him in a scouting capacity. He traveled to Northern Ontario to check out future prospects.Then the front office did an about face, deciding that Hunt was not "washed up" after all. Hunt got back in shape and proved he was still one of the fastest wingers in the game. In fact Jack Laing noted that the "most amazing spurt by local snipers" was being staged by Freddie Hunt. In less than a month Hunt had scored 8 goals and 13 assists, proving that he was a real "money player." Laing said he was just what the doctor ordered for Calder Cup play and added that Hunt was a "hard and popular performer ...and is about the ablest penalty killer in the league." He had a 100 mph shot, and said he owed that to his golf activity. Hunt was only 5'8", and 155 pounds, but he had such powerful wrists that they "well might belong to a blacksmith." Hunt referred to golf as the great summer month conditioner for hockey players. He was a native of Brantford, Ontario and played much of his golf on the courses spread out over the Niagara peninsula. He was regarded as one of Canada's top amateur linksmen.[42]

The Bisons kept up their red hot pace. Before nearly 10,000 fans, the Bisons closed out the season with a 6 – 3 win over Springfield on March 21. In so doing, the Herd set two records, 28 wins on home ice, and a total of 86 points. Unfortunately Pittsburgh also won and ended up in second place for the season, two points in front of Buffalo. The Cleveland Barons had done even better, having secured first place earlier and ending the season with an amazing 98 points. The final standings in the Eastern Division showed that the leader was Providence with 86 points, the same as Buffalo, followed by New Haven with 69 and Hershey with 63.

At the end of the regular 1947-48 season, Tommy Cooper was voted the most popular player and won the traditional golf bag and a set of clubs. Murdo MacKay earned first string honors on the Players' All Star team, voted by the League players. MacKay and Les Douglas tied for Bison scoring honors with 76 points each, Mackay led with most goals, Douglas had most assists.

In the first round of the playoffs, Buffalo faced Hershey. In the opener; the Bisons seemed to have little trouble, winning 5 – 3. The second game proved more difficult. Hershey was at full strength while the Bisons had some injured players including Len Halderson, Paul Mundrick, and Wilf Field. Nevertheless the Bisons prevailed, 3 – 2, before more than 9,000. Doug Lewis, "Little Dougie" as the press like to call him scored two goals including the game winner. Hershey was eliminated and the Bisons advanced to the next round.

Meanwhile New Haven had knocked Pittsburgh out of the race and thereby qualified to visit Buffalo to open the second round of the playoffs. The opening game was a fiercely fought contest. Finally at 4:35 of the second overtime period, Les Hickey proved to be the fair haired boy as he pleased 9,950 fans with his game winning goal to give his team a 2 – 1 sudden death victory. In the second and final game of the series, the injury riddled Bisons spotted the New Haven Ramblers one goal, then stormed back and defeated the Ramblers 6 – 2. Freddie Hunt had two goals.

The Herd now had the unenviable task of taking on the formidable Cleveland Barons in the Calder Cup finals. The Barons set several records in the 1947-48 season, chalking up 43 victories and going through 30 straight games without a defeat. To make matters worse, the Bisons were not in good shape. Art Lessard and Len Halderson were out with injuries. There were other issues, too. Laing referred to the Herd as the harassed Redshirts, commenting on the fact that several Bisons were involved in a post game brawl in a New Haven restaurant, following the final game with the Ramblers. Five Bison players were charged in the disruption but the charges were dropped on all but Wilf Field. He had to return to Connecticut to post bail.

Buffalo and Cleveland would be battling it out for the championship for the third time in five years. Buffalo won in 1946 and in 1944. This time, despite their good in-season record, they were not up for the Barons in post season play. The Barons riding the crest of one of the most amazing seasons in hockey history sunk the Bisons in the first game, 6 – 1. Then in the second game, again before a packed house of nearly 12,000 fans in Cleveland, the Bisons lost. 5 – 3. The Bisons played better but had to compete with just three defensemen for part of the contest. Hal Jackson drew a 10 minute misconduct penalty for fighting with a ringside spectator who tried to snatch his stick. Jackson let him have it, not the stick but a good hard punch. In the final period, the Bisons gambled with a five forward attack in the last two minutes of the game but to no avail.

Back home for the third game, the Bisons performed well before a full house but again not well enough. It was a rather sad game for the Bisons. They outskated and outplayed the Barons in the first part of the contest but then when Mike McMahon was sent to the penalty box disaster struck. The tide turned abruptly and it did not turn back. The Barons, paced by the sensational rookie, Bobby Solinger, scored two goals within 36 seconds and later, he skated the entire length of the ice and scored again, demonstrating why he was named the Rookie of the Year. Cleveland won 3 – 1.

The Bisons were down three games to none but would not toss in the towel. In the fourth game the Bisons and Barons fought tooth and nail for two periods. Halfway through the final period with the score knotted at 2 – 2 the tie was broken by the Barons and the flood gates were opened for four more goals. Perhaps Tony Wurzer of the *Buffalo Evening News* summed it up best when he said the Barons won "because they had too much class, finesse, scoring punch, savvy and know how" not to. Another capacity crowd of nearly 10,000 witnessed the 6 – 2 finale.[43]

Cleveland had won its second Calder Cup in the past four seasons. The Barons genuinely deserved this one, having dropped only one game in the last 36 starts. The two teams lined up to exchange hand shakes in the best tradition of the game while the organ played Auld Lange Syne. Some of hockey's best known figures, including NHL president Clarence Campbell, King Clancy a prominent NHL referee, and Eddie Shore, Mr. Hockey himself, smiled approvingly. Jack Laing in the *Courier-Express* added the final footnote saying "Hockey faded out of the local sports picture for the season as Cleveland's wonder team completed its sweep of the Calder Cup Playoff finals."[44]

Each Bison pocketed about $950 from the playoff pool and departed on their separate ways. Coach Goldsworthy left for his job as golf pro at the splendid Jasper Park Lodge in the Canadian Rockies in Alberta. Wilf Field and Les Hickey headed home to Winnipeg. Art Lessard resumed his duties as a member of the Montreal Provincial Police. Mike McMahon would stay in the Buffalo area as a salesman for a local brewery, and Jerry Brown toiled at the same occupation in Cornwall, Ontario. Goalie Paul Bibeault remained local as a wholesale meat salesman whereas Connie Dion left for his lumbering business in Quebec. Freddie Hunt would go into partnership with Foster Brooks, who one day would be a nationally known comedian, in the operation of a refreshment stand at Delaware and Sheridan Drive in Kenmore. And so it went, some remained in the Western New York area, others left for homes and jobs throughout Canada. Little would be heard of hockey or written about it for the next several months. That is the way it was back then; things have changed drastically.

Sports fans and the local sports writers turned their considerable attention to America's pastime. By the time September rolled around, the playoffs for the International league were underway and a short time later the 1948 World Series began. The Cleveland Indians faced the Boston Braves. Local fans followed closely Bob Feller and Lou Boudreau of the Indians and, of course, there was a huge following for the pride of South Buffalo, the Braves' great southpaw, Warren Spahn. Meanwhile the football season had begun. About that same time, hockey fans in Buffalo began to read about the Bison hockey club opening its preseason camp. After a few exhibition contests, the Herd was ready for the official beginning of the 1948-49 AHL season. It would last until mid March, to be followed again by a few weeks of playoffs to determine the Calder Cup Champion. Then the cycle would repeat itself. To think that hockey games or basketball games would still be played in June was, well, it was unthinkable.

During the off season, General Manager Art Chapman emphasized the need for a more youthful look for the Bisons. He minced no words in saying that few of last year's team would make the squad. That surprised some observers since the 1947-48 team reached the finals of the playoffs.[45] The big change, of course, was in the Buffalo head coaching position. GM Chapman signed Leroy Goldsworthy to be General Manager of the Houston Huskies. Chapman named Toe Blake, the Bisons' new coach. Toe Blake was one of the greatest left wingers of all time, part of Montreal's famed Rocket line that included Rocket Richard and Elmer Lach. Blake was nicknamed the "Old Lamplighter" because of his scoring talents. In his 12 seasons with Montreal, he won the Hart trophy and the Lady Byng trophy and was named to numerous NHL All Star teams. Early in the 1947-48 season he broke his leg playing in the NHL so he went to Houston as their coach. He led that team to its first United States Hockey League championship.

Coach Toe Blake recruited some defensemen and was happy to have them joined by such old hands as Dion, MacKay, Halderson, Pargeter, Douglas, and Cooper. The Bisons also acquired the services of Ab DeMarco, a veteran prolific scorer. The Bisons played exhibitions in Barrie, Ontario. They lost three times to the parent club, Montreal, and then lost a fourth contest to Springfield. They finally got on the winning side of the ledger by whipping the squad from Shawinigan Falls, Quebec 5 – 1.

The regular 1948-49 season began on October 12. The players assembled at the towering New York Central Terminal in East Buffalo for the long train ride to St. Louis where they would open a three game road trip. The revamped Bisons would be facing the Flyers, another revamped team. The St. Louis squad had high hopes for their season. They had finished in last place in the West for the previous four years, and were determined to get off on the right foot. They did, they beat the Bisons 4 – 0, registering their first shutout in two years. The Bisons traveled to Indianapolis and lost again. They moved on to Pittsburgh; the losses continued. Coach Blake wondered what happened to his scoring punch. "We have plenty of scoring power on paper but the trouble is they won't let you play the game on paper" he told the *Buffalo Evening News*.[46]

Following the disastrous road trip, the Bisons were grateful to be back in Buffalo for a home stand. They faced the Hershey Bears, a team that was having troubles of its own. The Herd appeared to be a rough and ready beast; their determination reinforced by GM Chapman who was sitting up in the grey seats, with axe in hand, making sure his players knew he meant business. Chapman and Coach Blake had revamped the front lines. On one of the lines, MacKay was back at a center post with Hunt and Pargeter on wings. That line worked very well. George Pargeter score a pair of goals to lead the Bisons, and MacKay tallied one, in the 3 – 1 victory over the Bears before 8,328 of the faithful.

The next foe was much more formidable. The Providence Reds were a high scoring machine; in fact they were leading the league, averaging six goals a game. They were led by Carl Liscombe, who had set an all time professional scoring record of 118 points the previous season. The Bisons were up to the task. They whitewashed the Reds, 5 – 0. Dion earned the shutout, turning in one of his finest games ever as a Bison. George Pargeter also was brilliant; he was responsible for four goals, three in less than a seven minute span.[47]

Success did not last long, however. The Bisons played at Washington and managed to hand the lowly Lions their first win of the year, a 3 – 1 decision. It had to be sweet revenge for former Bison coach, Frank Beisler, who now was at the helm in Washington. The Herd treated the Hershey Bears the same way. The Bears won their first game of the season at Buffalo's expense, a 4 – 2 verdict despite a stellar performance by Murdo MacKay. The Buffalo ace had two goals before suffering a minor injury that forced him to leave the game. The Herd returned again to the comfort of home ice but it was not much of a comfort this time around. It was the fourth outing in five nights. The Bisons played rather listlessly and managed only a 2 – 2 tie with the St. Louis Flyers. After a much needed week of rest they hosted Washington. The Bisons got revenge for the humiliating loss they suffered less than two weeks earlier. They pounded the Lions 10 – 0, tying their record for goals scored in one game. MacKay got the hat trick and Hunt and Agar each got a brace.

The Bisons seemed to have turned the corner. The Bisons beat the Reds, 3 – 2 at Providence and piled on two more road wins, over New Haven and over Springfield, then returned home and defeated New Haven again. They were now out of the cellar in the Western Division. As if to underscore their return to respectability during the first half of November, the Bisons went on a record breaking spree against the Philadelphia Rockets. On November 12, the Bisons literally overwhelmed the men from the City of Brotherly Love, 16 – 4. Nine goals were scored in the second period, tying an AHL record. The 16 goals in one game was also a record. MacKay had the hat trick and Hunt and Pargeter each had two goals. The only thing that seemed to break the "monotony" of scoring was the physical tussle between the teams' two "bad guys," Art Lessard, and Eddie Bush. The Herd was now tied with Indianapolis for third place.

The changes were paying off. The MacKay, Pargeter, Hunt line was doing what was expected of it. The local sportswriters were singing its praises. Wurzer devoted considerable space in one of his columns to Freddie Hunt, "the old veteran." Recalling that he had started his career 12 years ago, and that he had been "an amazing utility player" for the past two seasons, Wurzer said that it was great to see him back with MacKay and Pargeter. The line proceeded to score 22 goals in a dozen games, and lifted the Herd out of the doldrums. MacKay was playing like the MacKay of old, he was scoring regularly; in fact he tied Carl Liscombe for the league lead with 25 points. Hunt and Pargeter were right behind. Laing seconded the praises for Murdo, noting that he was on course to set new AHL scoring records.The Bison upsurge continued. They next faced the Indianapolis Caps who featured their sensational goalie, Terry Sawchuk. Sawchuk had been voted the most outstanding rookie in the United States League the previous year. The Redshirts were not intimidated. They routed the Caps 9 – 3. The victory was their 8th in 9 games and gave the "Hot as a Pistol" Bisons a tie for 2nd place.[48]

Despite the recent successes, Buffalo faced a serious problem. Injuries had reduced their number of able bodied defensemen to just three. Coach Toe Blake came to the rescue. He would play himself. He was known to have been a model for his teammates when he was a star player for the Montreal Canadiens; now he would serve as a model again. Toe took to the ice in the Aud before 9,504 well wishers in a mid November game against Springfield. The Bisons won, 4 – 1, or as the press phrased it in those not so politically correct times: "Herd Scalps the Indians." Blake proved his worth. He seemed to have a knack to be where the puck was, he played "spotless defense." Toe was heartened by the way the players had rallied around him. The money line of MacKay, Hunt, and Pargeter scored three goals and Lessard, displaying raw courage, as he played with an injured back, was spirited on by his Coach and he scored the fourth.[49]

The Bisons continued to do fairly well as the month of November drew to a close. They split their weekend series with Pittsburgh, losing in the Steel City then winning at home before 9,826. In so doing they regained third place. It was the ninth game at home without a defeat. Next they took on the New Haven Ramblers. For the 8 years since the Aud first opened, the Ramblers were viewed as a soft touch. But that was the past. Now they proved to be a tough opponent. The Herd felt fortunate to earn a 1 -1 tie. The Bisons then beat Hershey, 3 – 1 in a game in which Connie Dion got "dazzling support" from his defense. The next night, on home ice, the Herd made it two in a row over the Bears, winning 5 – 2. The two squads struggled in a 2 – 2 tie for almost the entire game then with just seven minutes to go the Bisons showed flashes of their old offensive brilliance by netting three goals

The Western Division standings were nip and tuck in December and would continue to be so for the remainder of the season. St. Louis was in sole position of first place but Buffalo and the other three teams were separated by a mere four points. Things improved briefly for the Bisons near the end of the year. On December 28 Indianapolis came to town and battled the Herd to a 2 – 2 tie. The Herd had a number of opportunities but rookie star Terry Sawchuk kept coming up with fantastic saves. As Tony Wurzer put it "On a good night he looks like Detroit's Harry Lumley, and Wednesday night he had one of those good nights." The year ended on a winning note for the Bisons. This time they had better luck against Indianapolis and shutout the Caps, 3 – 0. They also opened the New Year with a victory over Philadelphia. MacKay was playing up to par; he picked up 4 points in the scoring race in the previous two games and was now only 4 behind league leading Carl Liscombe. At the same time league statistics showed that Dion was still one of the best goalies ranking second just behind Baz Bastien of Pittsburgh and slightly ahead of Terry Sawchuk. On January 4 the Bisons and Caps duplicated their game of a week earlier, another 2- 2 tie. The game was marked by spectacular goaltending by both Dion and Sawchuk.[50]

In January, 1949 the Bisons received the welcome news that the Peace Bridge Arena in Fort Erie, Canada was finally reopening. It had collapsed during the famous or in-famous St. Patrick's Day snowstorm of 1936. There had been delays in the rebuilding caused by mechanical difficulties and wartime priorities. It was officially opened on January 15, 1949 at a cost of $105,000. It had a seating capacity of 2,300 and the rink itself was 80 feet by 180. In the new arena, the Bisons had their own equipment room. Some families of players already had begun to move to Fort Erie to be near the facility. The arena was only about one mile from the entrance into Canada and about five miles from Memorial Auditorium. This was a distinct advantage over having to drive to either St. Catharines or Welland to practice. Both those Ontario cities were some 25 miles from Buffalo. The new Fort Erie arena would also provide more ice time for amateur teams and for public skating.

A few days later, a bombshell hit the front pages of the local papers. The Buffalo Hockey Club announced the resignation of Head Coach Toe Blake. General Manager Art Chapman said it was "like a bolt out of the Blue." At the formal press conference the official statement said: "The contract…has been terminated by mutual consent of both parties concerned. Blake did not 'quit' his job, nor was he dismissed....The agreement to terminate the contract was reached after Blake told GM Chapman that he did not think that he could be of any further value to the organization. It was agreed then to terminate the contract."[51]

Commenting on the coach's decision, Bob Stedler said that Blake "walked out of Buffalo last night with all the sureness, grace and dignity that made him Montreal's favorite son." He removed a well chewed cigar from his mouth and said: "I didn't quit. I just said I couldn't get 100% out of some of the Buffalo players. I suppose that left Art Chapman no other choice then to relieve me. After all, he's got a job to do; he's boss." Chapman did try to talk Blake out of leaving but to no avail. Blake shook hands with all the reporters, and as he left said: "you know fellows, this kind of thing just happens in sports." Many truly great players essayed the role of coach or manager and failed." Toe Blake had had a spectacularly successful career as a hockey player. He would go on to have a fantastically successful career as coach of the Montreal Canadiens. Under his tutelage the Canadiens would be at the pinnacle of the hockey world winning eight Stanley Cups from 1956 - 1968. His interlude with the Buffalo Bisons was a difficult one to understand. It seemed that Toe felt frustrated. The Bisons were in a scoring slump. They were not playing poorly but they were not playing well either. As Blake indicated, some players were simply not playing at full throttle. They were not going all out which is the way he had always played. He found that difficult to accept.[52]

Toe Blake had no immediate plans. He went to Toronto to watch his old team mates, the Montreal Canadiens, defeat the Leafs. A couple of days later, a small item in the *Courier Express* said that Toe indicated he was glad to be through as coach of the Bisons but that he wanted to stay in coaching and would "listen to the highest bidder." A few weeks later it was announced that Toe Blake signed to coach Valleyfield of the Quebec Senior League. That was the beginning of the road back that would culminate in his Stanley

Cup successes.

Leroy Goldsworthy returned from Houston to take over the head coaching position once again. In his first game Goldy's forces faced New Haven. The Bisons dominated for 56 minutes and 31 seconds but the Ramblers fought back with two goals near the very end of the game, to earn a 3 – 3 tie. It was a tough return for Goldy. Many fans were in a belligerent mood. Catcalls were abundant. The Herd traveled to Pittsburgh and before a standing room only crowd the Hornets zipped five goals into the net in the very first period. The Bisons came back with three of their own but then Pittsburgh cruised to a 7 - 4 win. Fortunately the Washington Lions were next on the schedule, the "lowly" Lions. They were not so lowly for two periods as they held the Bisons in check, but in the third, the Herd rode to a 4 – 1 victory and the 7,476 fans could leave the Aud reasonably content.

The Herd seemed to have emerged from its offensive doldrums. On February 2 the Bisons stampeded the Barons, 11 – 3. It was their first victory over the Barons in over a year. Excellent team spirit prevailed, something that had been conspicuously lacking. Young Tommy Johnson and Floyd Curry set the pace each getting a hat trick. MacKay added two goals; Joe Lund made an impressive debut by scoring a brace. Lund, born in Finland, came to Ontario and played amateur hockey with Barrie, then he moved up to Indy and then on to Buffalo. He was a big rough guy and a welcome addition to the Buffalo club. The Barons got some revenge the following night before more than 11,000 in Cleveland by beating the Bisons 3 – 1. It was a bruising battle marked by many penalties including three on Lloyd Finkbeiner, and two on bad Eddie Bush. Meanwhile it was announced that Wilf Field was returning from Houston, to help with the Buffalo defense.

At this juncture the hockey career of one of Buffalo's most popular players, Fred Hunt, headed down another fork in the road; this one led to Hershey, Pennsylvania. In the words of the historian of the Buffalo Bisons, Tim Warchocki: "On February 12, Art Chapman made one of the hardest decisions of his managerial career. Fred Hunt who was the team's all time leading scorer was sold to the Hershey Bears." In an immediate sense, the move was a good thing for Hunt. He would get a cut of the playoff money since the Bears were assured of a spot in the playoffs. Hunt's departure was a big loss for Buffalo. He had become widely admired within hockey circles and throughout the community. Fortunately Fred Hunt would return to Buffalo a few years later and become an even more vital part of Buffalo hockey, first in a managerial capacity with the Bisons and then with the Buffalo Sabres. By the time of his sudden death in the mid 1970s, Fred Hunt had become a Buffalo Legend.[53]

Throughout February of 1949 the Bisons continued to struggle to gain a playoff spot. When the month of March began, the Bisons still had an outside chance for postseason play. The fact of the matter was that the team standings in the Western Division were extremely close throughout the season. Buffalo, the dweller in the cellar, was usually just a point or two behind fourth place Cleveland which was just a point or two behind third place Indianapolis, which in turn was just a point or two behind second place Pittsburgh. St. Louis the, front runner all season long, was secure in the top spot.

In the Eastern Division the Providence team was far out in front. The Rhode Islanders came to town on March 3. The Reds beat the Redshirts, 7 – 4 and the AHL's leading scorer, Carl Liscombe got the hat trick. In so doing he also set a new AHL record with his 53rd goal of the season. Two days later, in Pittsburgh, the Hornets took a 5 - 0 lead in the first period and coasted to a 6 - 1 victory over the Bisons. But the following night the

Herd pulled off a surprise by clipping the Barons 4 – 2. It was one of those games where the Bisons seemed to emerge from hibernation in order to humble their old rival. Joe Lund, who had been playing better than most of his teammates in recent games, got another hat trick. The Bisons still mathematically had an outside chance to make the playoffs.

The disappointing 1948-49 season sputtered to its conclusion. The Bisons beat Washington, lost to Hershey and St. Louis, beat Cleveland again, lost to Indianapolis and went out on a mini-winning streak by defeating Springfield and Philadelphia. In his postscript to the 1948-49 season Jack Laing wrote: "The curtain dropped on the most dismal season in Buffalo hockey history as a die-hard crowd of 7,000 saw the Bisons ride roughshod over a hapless Philadelphia Rockets, 9 – 4 at the Aud." It was a run for the bus game and a wait until next season for the Bisons, although it was not even that for the dismal Rockets. It was announced after the game that the Philadelphia franchise would be suspended and the Rockets disbanded. Some Bisons did shine in the final game. George Pargeter scored 4 goals. Murdo MacKay scored two, for a total of 84 points for the season. That was the highest ever for a Bison, breaking Hunt's record of 80 points set back in 1943-44. MacKay suffered a mid-season slump, otherwise he probably would have been right up there with the top scorers in the AHL.[54]

Murdo MacKay was named to several All Star teams. He was also one of four Bisons called up to Montreal for the Stanley Cup playoffs. The others were Connie Dion, Floyd Curry and Tommy Johnson. MacKay would appear in his third Stanley cup series. He did quite well. In fact in the Canadiens' 3 – 2 win over Detroit, MacKay put in the winning goal. Connie Dion was named the most popular player by the fans. He received the E. J. Rose trophy along with a golf bag and clubs. Leger won it in '45-'46, MacKay in '46-'47, and Cooper in '47-'48.

Murdo MacKay - top Bison goal scorer.
Photo: Tim Warchocki

In his "Passing the Puck" column, Jack Laing concluded that it was sort of a sad season all around. Sometimes the defense would be playing at a peak and the offense would be in a slump, at other times the situation would be reversed. Some nights only Connie held them up, otherwise there would have been more losses. When things went bad the "Booers" made their appearance, something not witnessed in past seasons. The resignation of Coach Toe Blake in mid season was another unfortunate development. The inability to win more home games was costly. There were eight ties on home ice. A tie may be as good as a win for a visiting team but not for the home squad. General Manager Art Chapman made a succinct "off the cuff" assessment of his team's play. After one of the lackluster performances by the Bisons near the end of the season, Chapman was making his way out of the Aud and was heard to mumble: "No drive, no fire that was the problem all season long...but we're building. And next season we will be good. Believe me."[55]

Some thought that the way the Bisons performed in the final games offered a ray of hope. Beating Cleveland twice near the end of season and almost knocking them out of the playoffs was heartening to Buffalo hockey fans. Many were also impressed when 7,000 fans showed up for the final game between two teams that were far out of contention. In that final game, the Bisons and Rockets put on a great effort and never let up until the final buzzer. It was a good way to end a disappointing season. Some ardent supporters also pointed out that had the Bisons been in the Eastern Division they would have wound up in second place, just behind league leading Providence.

During the off season, the front office kept busy while the players went their separate ways. The Bison coaching staff sometimes seemed to go almost overboard to land a recruit. In May Rudy Pilous, chief scout, went to Port Colborne and boarded the Steamship Brampton, a large wheat carrier, and signed Bully Buschlen to a Buffalo contract. Buschlen was a deckhand on the Brampton in its runs between Port Colborne and Montreal. He had played amateur hockey in St.Catharines in the past season. In addition to being a recruiter, Pilous also maintained contact with the roster players during the off season and provided information on their whereabouts. MacKay was building houses in Port Arthur, Ontario. Curry was selling men's clothes in a Montreal department store. Tommy Johnson was working in his father's gas station in Winnipeg. Locally, Len Halderson was working in the Lackawanna steel plant, and Tommy Cooper was with a local coal firm.[56]

In the summer of 1949 the New York Yankees and the Boston Red Sox were engaged in one of their classic pennant races in the American League. The Joe DiMaggio led Yanks defeated the Ted Williams led Sox and then proceeded to defeat, in the World Series, who else? The Brooklyn Dodgers! Meanwhile the Buffalo Bison Hockey Club finalized plans for the preseason. Forty rookies reported to the new Fort Erie Arena just after Labor Day. Daily workouts began there, under the scrutinizing eyes of General Manager Art Chapman and Head Coach Leroy Goldsworthy. Various veterans arrived at various times over the next several days, the last being Murdo MacKay, George Pargeter, and Ab DeMarco, who together comprised most of last year's scoring punch.

The Bisons' record in the preseason contests was a good one. They ended up with four wins and four ties and just one loss. The defeat was at the hands of the World Champion Toronto Maple Leafs, 2 – 1. The first preseason home game in Fort Erie was against Pittsburgh. It ended in a 2 – 2 draw. But the 2,000 fans who crammed into the arena were rewarded with exciting play by some of the newcomers. The top prospects on display were forwards Paul Meger, Sid McNabney, and Gordie Pennell. The youngsters skated wild and fast, determined to make the team. The *Buffalo Evening News* called them "a collection of wild skating, eager beaver rookies." Eight veterans joined them; they were all in top physical shape. The team was placed in the Eastern Division for the 1949-50 season. Previously Buffalo had been in the much stronger Western Division. Washington and Philadelphia formerly in the Eastern Division were now defunct. Cincinnati was brought into the AHL as a new franchise and was placed in the West. Since Buffalo was the easternmost city in the West Division, it was logical from the geographic point of view, and also in order to have an equal number of teams in each division, that Buffalo now move to the East.[57]

The Bisons opened the 1949-50 home hockey season with more fanfare than usual. Indeed it was the most colorful inaugural since Memorial Auditorium was officially opened in 1940. A parade sponsored by the Buffalo Sports Boosters preceded activities inside the arena. Then, at center ice, President Edgar Danahy thanked the fans for their continued support and predicted a first place finish for the team. The Deans of Harmony sang their favorite barbershop quartet selections. In view of the popularity of Barbershop quartets in the decade after World War II, (In fact the Buffalo Bills Barbership Quartet was rated number one in the nation) that too seemed appropriate. Then the players were introduced. The home opener featured the Indianapolis Caps. The home team outplayed the visitors and held a 2 – 1 lead well into the final period. Then, one of the Bison stars from last season, Joe Lund, now with the Caps, plunked in the tying goal. No doubt his previous experience with the Bisons enabled him to fake out Connie Dion. The Buffalo fans did not like the tie, but were satisfied with the play of newcomers, McNabney, Pennell, and Meger. Chapman was pleased with their play too.

During the first two months of the season the Bisons hovered between first and last place.They closed out the month of November by losing to New Haven, 2 – 1. That loss dropped them into third place. They played "one of the worst games they ever played locally." Only 4,933 disgruntled fans showed up to watch this effort in futility. It was the lowest attendance since the war and perhaps that was a good thing because the front office showed some concern for the decreased attendance.[58]

Hockey attendance in the Aud had been down in the first month of the new season. Instead of drawing crowds of 9,000 – 10,000 on a regular basis as they had for the past three years, the turnstiles regularly counted 5,000 - 6,000 customers. The top brass were naturally concerned. General Manager Art Chapman, and team treasurer John Sweeney met with Bill Veeck, the president of the Baseball Cleveland Indians. Veeck was widely known for his promotional activities that ranged from the clever to the bizarre. Some sports officials regarded him as a genius, others thought he was a screwball. When someone asked Veeck if he thought that money being tight might be a factor in low attendance, the Cleveland prexy laughed saying "I am convinced there is no saturation point for the money fans will spend for sports." Veeck offered the Bison brass some suggestions such as don't sell all your tickets as season tickets, save some of the good ones for new customers. That is one way to make new fans. Don't let the concessionaires talk you out of between- period promotions because of their claim that they stood to lose money at the concession stands. They won't lose; in fact ask them how many hot dogs they would sell if the stands were empty. Don't advertise your special attractions in advance, let the fans buy a ticket and then come to the game wondering what type of crazy event will occur.

The Buffalo club did try more promotions. Things improved in December. The Bisons defeated Indy 3 - 2. Then they tied the New Haven Ramblers. A good crowd was on hand which included more than 2,000 boy scouts. Those youth were in the stands cheering on the local heroes. Tommy Johnson was back, having been sidelined with a leg injury for a month. He was a favorite of the youngsters. On December 10 the Bisons beat Springfield 4 – 2 before 5,767 in the Aud. The Herd stormed back in the third period with three goals to win it. The victory still left them tied for 2nd. Such was the nature of the tight, up and down, race in the Eastern Division.

Next they faced the division leaders, the Providence Reds. Coach Goldsworthy decided to use a little of his own psychology. Prior to the Providence game, he put up a clipping in the locker room from a newspaper and then paraphrased from it saying: "Some say I'm harboring dead wood. What are we going to do about it?" He added more choice words. The team responded by walloping Providence, 4 – 1. They were now tied for the lead in the East with the Reds.

On December18, Connie Dion shutout the Bears 4 – 0. A line composed of MacKay-McNabney-Lewis paced the Herd. Dion had his third shutout. By Christmas the Bisons were in the number one spot in the East; on Christmas night they hosted the first place team from the West, the Cleveland Barons. There was no Santa Claus for the 6,987 fans as their team got clobbered, 7 – 3. The size of the crowd and MacKay's two goals were the only things for the locals to be happy about. Some good news was announced a few days later. Grant "Knobby" Warwick, a seasoned right winger, who had played seven seasons with the New York Rangers, was acquired from Montreal.[59]

New Year's Day, 1950, was a gala one for Buffalo Hockey. The largest crowd of the season, 8,261, turned out. They were treated to a trouncing of the Pittsburgh Hornets, 6 - 3. Of particular interest to the locals, was the appearance in the Hornet lineup of Tim Horton. The Pittsburgh defenseman closed out the night's scoring with about the "sweetest solo rush" seen in a long time. Hockey fans would remember Tim Horton for many, many years to come, as a great hockey player, a future Buffalo Sabre, and as a name associated throughout Western New York and all across Canada with long lines of automobiles waiting for fine coffee and donuts.

January was a good month for the Bisons. On January 5 a late game goal from Paul Meger gave the Herd a 2 – 2 tie with the Ramblers. Two days later the Bisons were in a scoreless deadlock with Springfield until the final period. Then a three goal onslaught by MacKay, Warwick, and Meger took place. The Bisons won and Gordie Bell earned his first shutout since taking over for Connie Dion and the team was just one point back of Providence. They skated into first place a few days later with a 5- 0 win over New Haven. Knobby Warwick picked up a brace of goals and Bell got his second consecutive shutout at home.

On January 19 the Herd picked up another win; this one a 4 - 2 victory at Indianapolis. It was a red letter day for Murdo MacKay. He got his 200th goal of his career. The Bisons continued to win more than they lost. They pulled off another big victory over Eastern Division arch rival, Providence 3 – 1 then lost 5 – 3 at New Haven. Emil, the Cat, Francis, in goal as usual for the Ramblers, was the culprit. He stopped 33 shots fired by the Bisons. The Herd rebounded with a 2 – 1 victory over Springfield. The month ended with Buffalo in first place by three points.

If January was a good month for the Bisons, February was better. The Herd maintained a solid hold on first place throughout the month. Attendance at the home games increased significantly. On February 1 Buffalo faced arch rival Cleveland. The Barons, as was frequently the case in these years, were dominating the Western division. Cleveland had beaten the Bisons regularly; in fact they chalked up victories against the Bisons almost at will. Not this time. The Herd broke the Cleveland jinx, and did so in a convincing manner, 5 – 2, before 6,613 fans delirious Auditorium fans. Right from the opening face off there was no doubt who was going to win. The Bisons smacked in three goals before the first period was half over. The DeMarco, Warwick, Meger money line led the way.

The 1948-49 AHL champions, The Providence Reds, came to town on February 15. Coach Goldy confronted them with a newly fashioned line consisting of Gordie Pennell, Sid McNabney, and Les Hickey. They were capable, they were fast, and they were young. In fact, Pennell and McNabney, were not even old enough to drink alcoholic beverages in Canada yet but they did know how to score. This newly formed line spearheaded the 7 – 1 victory. One could say that they put on the heat which was absolutely needed as the Aud was frigid. There was no heat due to the coal shortage. The game was quick and clean, only one penalty was called. Buffalo was now basking in first place with a 10 point lead.

In a home and home series with the Cleveland Barons, the Bisons traded victories. The game on the Barons home ice was filed with penalties, 16 were called. The Bisons lost 6 – 2. Back in Buffalo the tables were turned and the Herd won, 5 - 2. A five goal spurt by the home team in the first period was more than enough to assure a victory as well as to help warm up the still freezing auditorium. Despite the wintry conditions, the largest crowd of the season turned out. 8,856 hearty supporters such as these enhanced the mythology of Buffalo's rugged blue collar fans. Perhaps the crowd was augmented too by some curious non-hockey fans who showed up to watch Ezzard Charles, World Heavyweight champion, drop the puck for the start of the game. He was in town to box Freddie Beshore a few days later in the Aud.

The final month of the hockey season began with the superb Murdo MacKay scoring his 30th goal for the fifth straight season. That had never been done in the AHL. Buffalo continued to hold down first place in the East. It was good they had a solid lead because now the fortunes of the Buffalo hockey team turned ugly. The Bisons were upset on home ice by the St. Louis Flyers before 8,200. Then the Ice Follies took over the Aud for its traditional two week run. The Bisons hit the road for 10 days. They lost to Cincinnati and to Indianapolis. They still needed one more win to nail down the Eastern title. They succeeded in Pittsburgh when they clinched it with a 2 – 1 victory. It marked the first win in the Steel City in over 2 years. Gordie Bell was a standout. A few more losses followed and then the March 15th season finale was played against Providence. The Bisons figured to use the game as a warm up for the playoffs against Cleveland. Unfortunately they lost. The groans from the 6269 fans were a clear indication that this was not a good way to tune up for the Cleveland Barons. As the playoffs approached, the *Courier's* Jack Laing gave his estimate of Buffalo's chances. The "Bisons' wobbly finish portends rough going," he said. The Herd lost too many games in the final weeks of the season. They eased up to prevent injuries, but they eased up too much. Laing predicted a difficult time against the Barons, especially in the first games.[60]

Injuries to the Bison players were probably no more widespread than they were for other teams in the AHL. Fortunately the Bisons had the services of Frankie Christie, the highly regarded Bison trainer, who had been doing yeoman work all season. Christie had a remarkable career in Buffalo. He was born in New York City to Greek immigrants; he arrived in Buffalo in 1947 after having spent four years in military service in World War II. He remained with Buffalo hockey well into the Sabres era. Armed with bandages, adhesive tape and a bottle of liniment Christie worked minor miracles. At one point in the season, three players had injuries that could have kept them out of action. But the players wanted to play and Christie effectively ministered to their ailments. Pargeter had a shoulder injury, Warwick had six vertebrae in his neck out of place, and Meger had a skate cut back of his knee. Paulie Meger re-injured himself and certainly his absence helped to account for the dismal performance of the Bisons in March. Christie got him ready for the playoffs. The fact that he was ready to rejoin the DeMarco-Warwick line kept alive Bison hopes for success in the playoffs.
The *Buffalo Evening News* expressed the hope that the Money Line could perform in a big

way, otherwise the Bisons stood no chance at all. The Cleveland fans were cocky. So were the players. They were confident that they could take the Bisons without much trouble; even those who showed at least a little respect for the Bisons thought that the series would last only five games.

The playoff opener seemed to confirm the Cleveland thinking. The Barons battered the Bisons 7 – 1. The Barons simply continued doing what they had been doing all year, scoring lots of goals. The Bisons regrouped and played much better for most of the second game. They took a 4 - 1 lead into the closing moments of the third period, then with just three minutes to go, the Barons scored three goals to force an overtime session. The Barons scored again and had a 5 – 4 victory. To compound the disappointment, Knobby Warwick, who scored two for the Bisons, was injured in the overtime period and knocked out of action. Back home in the Aud, the Bisons decided to win one for little Knobby, and they did. They came from behind and defeated the Barons 3 – 2 before 9,246 satisfied customers. But the hopes for a follow-up victory quickly evaporated as the Barons proceeded to repeat their performance of the first game of the series. They walloped the Bisons, 5 – 1 thus taking a nearly insurmountable lead in the seven game series. 8,202 gloomy fans filed out of the Aud. The final game was anti-climactic. The Bisons got wiped out, 6 – 1. Tony Wurzer concluded "it was a case of a team with not enough gunfire meeting a fully equipped battle cruiser."[61]

Despite the playoff debacle, the Bisons did have a satisfactory season. They did win the Eastern Division crown. The playoffs were another story. They would have to reload for the 1950-51 season. General Manager Art Chapman told whoever would listen that he was going to rebuild. Obviously many of the current team would not be back. Those who would return were the rookies that Chapman was pleased with. He wanted more of those speedy youngsters. He told people that he tried four this year and they worked out just fine. He was referring to Sid McNabny, Gordie Pennell, Paul Meger, and Hugh Currie. He figured that a few more like this quartet would give the Bisons enough scoring power. Also expected back were two veteran stars: Ab DeMarco and Knobby Warwick.

The Barons moved on to lose to the powerful Indianapolis Caps in the finals. The only thing left to do for the Bisons to wind up the 1949-50 hockey season was to hand out awards. The players could then scatter to the four winds to work seasonal jobs only to return in late summer to begin the cycle all over again. Paulie Meger accumulated

Paul Meger, Left Winger, joined the Bisons in 1949.
Photo: Tim Warchocki

the most accolades. Of the 10 coaches who voted, 8 named him as their choice as the American Hockey League Rookie of the year. For that he received a trophy and a $300 bonus. By today's standards that figure seemed miniscule; back then it was substantial. Meger scored the winning goal in seven games and was second in scoring for the Bisons with 66 points. The 21-year-old native of Barrie, Ontario, earned a place on the Montreal roster. In less than a year he had gone from Junior A to the Stanley Cup playoffs where he joined the Canadiens in their playoff series against the New York Rangers. Meger was the first rookie in the AHL to make the all star team. Bison teammates, Connie Dion and Ab DeMarco joined him. While Meger was busy picking up his awards and heading for Montreal, other Bisons had vacated their lockers and were on their way to other destinations. Coach Goldsworthy left for a scouting trip to Western Canada and then would be at the Jasper, Alberta Golf Lodge as the golf pro. Trainer Frank Christie headed to New York City where he operated a golf club concession. Wilf Field took up residence in Fort Erie where he would play golf and serve as the local pro. DeMarco left for North Bay, Ontario where he was engaged in three business ventures. Warwick would be playing semi pro baseball in Regina. Several stayed in the local area to follow various pursuits just as they had done in the past.[62]

Conditions began to change after 1950 for Buffalo Bison hockey as they did for hockey elsewhere and as they did for many sports in many areas of the country. In the 1950s, with the rapid spread of television, and with the almost equally rapid growth of suburbia, sport participation and sport spectatorship underwent significant and far reaching changes. There was also a proliferation of sports of all sorts in the 1950s.and beyond. These changes paralleled the tremendous growth of the Sunbelt and the decline of the Rustbelt. New cities and metropolitan areas throughout the South and Southwest replaced older Northeastern and Midwestern cities in the top 20 population lists. The various major leagues in all sports expanded significantly to accommodate the new urban areas.

At the dawn of the 1950s, the impact of the monumental changes that were beginning to occur was not clearly discernible to most observers. The 1950-51 Bison hockey season was somewhat similar to that of the previous season. The Bisons had a strong team; they held first place throughout the season. Then they ran into the Baron Buzzsaw in the playoffs and were obliterated, 4 - 1. But there were changes underway. A veritable "changing of the Guard" was occurring. The Bisons traded the legend, Murdo MacKay, at the beginning of the season. He would retire shortly thereafter. Ab DeMarco followed him a year later but was retained as a scout. DeMarco led the team in scoring in 1950-51 as he had in 1949-50, and would again for his third consecutive year, in 1951-52. In fact his 113 points in the '50-'51 season put him at the very top of the scoring list in the AHL. Connie Dion also recognized the writing on the wall and retired after the 1950-51 season.[63] During the '51-'52 season, Leroy Goldsworthy resigned. GM Art Chapman coached temporarily, then Murph Chamberlain was hired. He was a disaster and was quickly retired. Chapman again went behind the bench with the ever reliable, and ubiquitous, Freddie Hunt as his Assistant Coach. Chapman and Hunt finished the season. Edgar Danahy resigned the following year. Owner Lou Jacobs put William Joseph in charge. Chapman left the organization and Hunt was promoted to General Manager. Eddolls returned as player/coach. New faces abounded. Possibly reflecting the turmoil was the fact that the Bisons in 1952-53 were in last place. For most of the decade the Bisons were a fairly mediocre team. Whereas the Bisons often had sellouts in the

Ab DeMarco , leading scorer in 1949-50.
Photo: Tim Warchocki

late 1940s, in the following decade capacity crowds were infrequent. In the mid '50s, the Jacobs brothers sold the team to the Chicago Blackhawks. That proved unsatisfactory. The Jacobs wanted home ownership to assure that the team would be kept in Buffalo. They were fortunate that the Pastor Brothers, the owners of the local Pepsi franchise, stepped into the picture. Their ownership gave new life to the hockey club. The red Pepsi logo on the front of the game jerseys became a trademark.

Television had a disastrous effect on minor league hockey just as it had on baseball. The American Hockey League barely survived. In 1952 Tony Wurzer reported that plummeting attendance had the AHL skating on thin ice. There was talk of the league disbanding if attendance did not rise sharply. Many thought that that was a distinct possibility. Two owners of teams in the Pacific Coach League indicated that their league was near "rock" bottom. Wurzer reported that Buffalo and Cleveland, the two mainstays of the AHL, were both losing money and that attendance was half of what it was "in the halcyon years three seasons ago (1949)."[64] Buffalo used to average over 9,000; in the '50s the attendance average was near 4,500. The Bisons even experimented with playing Sunday afternoon games. That helped pick up attendance slightly and the matinee games were continued. The league itself had shrunk; for most of the decade there were only six teams in the AHL. Cleveland and Buffalo remained the stalwarts of the league, even Pittsburgh, almost a stalwart, dropped out of the AHL in the late '50s and did not return until the '60s. There was talk from time to time of Cleveland and Buffalo being invited to apply for membership in the NHL but that was wishful thinking. The Canadian powerhouses, Toronto and Montreal, were not about to allow any league expansion that did not include additional Canadian cities. None seemed ready at that time.

In the early 1960s, the on-ice fortunes of the Buffalo Bisons improved. In 1962-63 they captured their first Calder cup in 17 years. But just as quickly the bottom fell out again, and in the following season the Bisons ended up in last place. Problems with their parent team, the Chicago Blackhawks, hurt considerably. In the mid 1960s the Bisons were at the bottom of the AHL and attendance was only about 1700 per game. In fact the 1966-67 was called the low point in the Bisons' 34 year history.[65]

Things improved in 1967-68 with Fred Shero as Coach and Fred Hunt as General Manager. The Bisons made the playoffs. They did so again the following season. And then, in their very last year of existence, 1969-70, they hit the jackpot and won the Calder Cup. The Buffalo Bisons Hockey team went out of existence in a blaze of glory. In so doing it also helped set the stage for the Buffalo Sabres of the National Hockey League.

Once that happened, as every schoolboy knows, the glorious years of major league hockey were upon the city. A new era had begun, an era featuring the fabulous French connection of Gilbert Perreault, Rene Robert, and Rick Martin, steady sellouts of more than 16,000 in the newly refurbished Aud with its raised roof, topped off with a Stanley Cup finals appearance within 5 years in the league. Other heroes emerged to take their place in the Sabre sun: Jim Shoenfield, Danny Gare, Gerry Meehan, Pat LaFontaine and more. The cream of National Hockey League coaches were a part of the Sabres' history: Punch Imlach, Scotty Bowman, and Lindy Ruff. Stars abounded and many more achievements followed, including, near the end of the century, the construction of a state of the art facility that regularly held sellout crowds of more than 18,000 fans.

But it was back in those years immediately after World War II that the stage was set for the glorious Sabres years that would come later. In those postwar years the Buffalo Bisons established solid roots for the sport of hockey in Western New York. The Bisons were consistent winners, almost always a contender for the AHL championship. The fan support in Buffalo was excellent; the Bisons drew crowds that were second only to Cleveland in the American Hockey League. Moreover the crowds that those two AHL powers drew approximated crowds in the National Hockey League, and sometimes were actually larger. Buffalo was mentioned on more than one occasion as a possible new member of the NHL.

In the years that followed the post-1950 period, indeed throughout the last half of the 20th century, Buffalo hockey fans could harken back to the Golden Age of Buffalo Bison Hockey in the American Hockey League and thank the Lord for the solid underpinnings that were then created.

CHAPTER SEVEN

The Muscatos and Company

— Heirs to Jimmy Slattery —

Courier-Express

Buffalo, N.Y.

Record 13,178 Crowd Jams Aud To Witness Golden Glove Finals

Buffalo Courier Express - December 6, 1947

Phil Muscato (left) and Joe Maxim (right) fought three times in 1946 in the Aud. *Photo: D. Valenzuela, Buffalo News*

The ring sports, boxing and wrestling played a major role on the Buffalo sports scene in the years immediately following World War II. Both sports had been a vital part of Buffalo's sporting life for many decades prior to the war; each had received a boost with the construction of the Memorial Auditorium in 1940. Though World War II put some restraints on the development of those sports, as it did on all others, both boxing and wrestling were poised to enter a take off phase once the war ended. Both provided exciting entertainment for an ever growing number of fans in the late 1940s; in subsequent years things changed. Both sports were hurt by the widespread use of television at the national level. Boxing would have its ups and downs in the 1950s and the years that followed. Occasionally a large crowd would flock to Memorial Auditorium to see a marquee bout but not often. Wrestling continued to have a substantial following in Buffalo in subsequent decades even though the sport was viewed as somewhat less glamorous and perhaps a bit more artificial than it had been in the 1940s. But in the years immediately following the war, boxing and wrestling contests were well attended. Each sport had its cast of local favorites who were responsible in large measure for drawing large crowds to Memorial Auditorium and for enhancing Buffalo's place in the national sports spotlight in the immediate postwar era.

Buffalo had been the scene of boxing bouts dating almost as far back as the beginnings of the city itself in the early 1800s. Throughout the 19th century and into the early 20th century, prizefighting was affected by laws throughout the United States, especially by state legislation. Sometimes the sport of boxing was legal in New York State and sometimes it was not. When legal, boxing bouts were held in saloons or theaters, those being the venues of choice; when illegal, fights were staged in clearings in rural wooded areas or across the Niagara River in Ontario, Canada, often in a Fort Erie facility or in the Crystal Beach stadium. They might even be staged in remote, quaint places such as the Sugarloaf area of Port Colborne, 20 miles west of Buffalo on the Canadian shore. On occasion, fearless promoters, those willing to defy the law, would stage boxing bouts almost anywhere they could find room, though the backrooms of local saloons were favored.[1]

John L. Sullivan, the first truly national hero in any sport in the United States, appeared in Buffalo in the 1880s. The great John L. was famous for his traveling exhibitions that were undertaken in order to create more interest in prizefighting. Other boxers with broad appeal appeared in subsequent years. Actually it was the decade of the 1920s that gave Buffalo a national boxing reputation. The Roarin' 20s have often been referred to in American history as the decade that gave birth to the Golden Age of American Sports, or at least America's First Golden Age. It was a decade when spectators began to flock to mammoth arenas and stadiums in unprecedented numbers to watch and to worship heroes of mythic stature; it was the age of Babe Ruth, Bill Tilden, Jack Dempsey, Bobby Jones, and Red Grange. Boxing, with headliners such as Dempsey and Gene Tunney and promoters like Jack Kearns and Tex Rickard, was a major part of that sports era.

Buffalo participated in this rising sports culture; boxers in the fight game in Buffalo were an important part of the national fight scene. Jimmy Slattery was at the top of Buffalo sports. His name became a household word in Buffalo in the 1920s. He, arguably, became Buffalo's most famous fighter, Buffalo's first authentic athletic celebrity. The names of Jimmy Goodrich, Rocky Kansas, Tommy Paul, Benny Ross, Art Weigand, Frankie Schoell, and Lou Scozza were also well known. They were good fighters and they were very popular. Some were champions and wore championship belts at one time or another. Jimmy Goodrich won the lightweight championship in the mid 1920s. He earned that by knocking out a Chilean, Stanislaus Loayza. Goodrich wore the crown for only a half of a year then lost it to Rocky Kansas, before a huge crowd in Buffalo's Broadway Auditorium. Kansas, in turn held the title for not much longer than Goodrich, losing it a year later to Sammy Mandell in Chicago in July of 1926. Tommy Paul won a number of amateur championships, and in 1932 he won the World Featherweight title in Detroit. Jimmy Slattery's moment in the sun came in August of 1927 when he won a decision over Maxie Rosenbloom. This earned him the title of Light Heavyweight champion. But in December of 1927, Slattery lost his title to Tommy Loughran in Madison Square Garden. Three years later Slattery and Lou Scozza fought a memorable fight in the Broadway Auditorium before a full house. Slattery was in great shape at that time and he fought one of the best fights of his entire career. He hung on to win a split decision in the 15 rounder and thereby captured the vacant Light Heavyweight title.

Jimmy Slattery was one of the widely recognized heroes in Buffalo's early sport history; certainly a mythic figure of heroic proportions in Buffalo's famed Irish First Ward. Unfortunately he had some major troubles in later years. He contracted tuberculosis and moved to Arizona to try to recover. In 1946 a fundraiser featuring Baseball Manager Joe McCarthy and former heavyweight Jimmy Braddock, was held at the Hotel Lafayette. It raised more than $10,000 for the ailing Slattery. This helped him out financially but his personal and health problems continued to mount. He died in a $10 a week room in a decrepit Franklin Street hotel in downtown Buffalo in1960. Such was the fate of many other boxers too. Nevertheless Jimmy Sattery became and remained one of the legendary figures of Buffalo Sport History. Jim Braddock called Slattery "The greatest boxer in my time . . . I know from experience, I fought him."[2]

Professional boxing lost some glitter during the Great Depression of the 1930s. Later in the decade, when Joe Louis emerged as the Heavyweight Champion of the world, boxing appeared to be on the edge of one of its periodic revivals. That rebirth had to be postponed for several years because of the onset of World War II. Americans soon learned what was meant by the concept of "total war."America's professional athletes joined the military services in overwhelming numbers. For the next few years some of America's outstanding athletes were involved in the deadly game of military combat. Many others represented, not their city or college, but their regiment or division or fleet in sporting competition with other military units. The military life was particularly suited to staging boxing competitions. A winning stable of boxers was very important to the esprit d'corps of a division of soldiers. Joe Louis was simply the best known boxer to serve his country. Many young boxers from Buffalo also enlisted in the military service. A side effect, indeed a benefit of sorts, of military service was that many an aspiring pugilist was offered an opportunity to develop his skills as a representative of his military unit.

On the home front, boxing, like other sports, was put on the backburner for the duration of the global conflict, while more important goals were being pursued. But as the war against Germany and Japan entered its final phase, athletes and other sports figures began preparations for a return to peace time. In Buffalo and in the sport of boxing, this meant that Promoter Jack Singer was poised to act.

Jack Singer is now a legend; at the end of the war he was on his way to becoming one. He was born, Jack Zingerski, on Buffalo's famous East Side. He became Singer in 1923, when he changed his name legally because as a semi-pro ball player everyone called him Singer anyway. He had a lifelong love for the fight game. Back in the early days of the Great Depression he handled both Tommy Paul and George Nichols, two recognized champions. Despite the restraints of the Depression years and darkening clouds of the coming of World War II, Singer maintained his involvement in boxing. He opened Singer's Gym at 338 Washington Street in the early 1930s. It quickly became the local training ground for aspiring fighters and remained so for many years. Shortly after Memorial Auditorium opened, Singer decided to organize the Hudson Athletic Club. He did this in 1943 and the following year he began to offer fight cards. He started with a few bouts in the Eagles Auditorium and also at the old Vienna Auditorium on Pearl Street, but found that those facilities were too small. He then moved his boxing cards to Memorial Auditorium. *Buffalo Evening News* Sports Reporter Cy Kritzer recalled that Singer faced formidable odds in the early 1940s, not the least of which was a slim bankroll. Kritzer said that at the time that Singer received formal approval to operate the Hudson Athletic Club "boxing was a homeless waif…with about the same social standing in Buffalo as a lower Main Street derelict."[3]

Jack Singer had a profound knowledge of boxing, "a corner on brass faith in wartime sports, and the energy to do everything himself." Singer said he just wanted to break even, and that is about all he did in the war years. He did well enough, initially, with a program of six rounders. His efforts brought on healthy competition for the fight game. In 1943, The Fairview Athletic Club was formed. Dewey Michaels was the main promoter and Billie Mitchie the matchmaker. Dewey Michaels' place in Buffalo folklore is due to his operation of the Palace Burlesk Theater in the heart of downtown Buffalo. He was a recognized leader of the show business community. He was involved with a number of theaters in the city. He was "a Damon Runyon character complete with trademark hat and cigar and a penchant for being a pal to every personality and politico in Buffalo." His boxing promotion may have been secondary to the interests in the theater but after Jack Singer, Dewey Michaels was Buffalo's main boxing promoter.[4]

The boxing cards arranged by both the Hudson A.C. and the Fairview A.C. were naturally constricted during the Second World War. But when the war ended, things quickly changed. Germany surrendered in May of 1945. On August 6, the Atomic Bomb was dropped and Japan was now ready to come to terms. Just two days later, Charley Bailey, writing in the *Courier Express*, noted that both the Hudson Athletic Club and the Fairview Athletic Club were busy arranging an indoor boxing season. Both organizations lined up a number of newcomers of varying abilities, but it was Billy Mitchie of the Fairview Club who landed a marquee bout. He scheduled a September fight between Sugar Ray Robinson and Jimmy Mandell. At that time, Sugar Ray was recognized as the reigning, though uncrowned welterweight champion; he easily dispatched Mandell in a 5th round TKO. Only 4,500 fans attended in Memorial Auditorium, not many for a Sugar Ray bout, but then again he was just beginning his storied career. He had not yet been proclaimed as the world's greatest middleweight. Bailey colorfully described Sugar's style as "alternately a calm, keen-eyed sniper and a fiery swing-from-way-back gunner, scoring with an amazing number of punches." Mandrell, a Buffalonian of high hopes, did not submit meekly but he just didn't have it.[5]

Two and one half years later, March 16, 1948, Sugar Ray returned to Buffalo to fight Henry Brimm, Buffalo's top middleweight. A record throng of 11,904 was on hand in the

Aud. Robinson won, as expected, but just a year later, on February 15. 1949, the same two fighters fought again, before fewer than 7,000. Why this smallish crowd is impossible to figure out! Possibly it was because many fans had been led to believe that it would be a lopsided victory for Sugar Ray. If so they were in for a rude awakening. This time the "stylish" Brimm fought the great Sugar Ray to a draw. Joe Alli, of the *Courier Express*, who covered the sport of boxing for that newspaper during the '40s, called the slugfest "the most brilliant performance" of Brimm's career. This non-title contest really was a stunner; it was only the 3rd time in 94 fights that Robinson had not won. Alli's counterpart in the *Buffalo Evening News*, Frank Wakefield, piled on more superlatives, calling Brimm's achievement "miraculous," and said it somehow rated up there with Brimm's recovery from tuberculosis in Perrysburg, N.Y, and also his re-appearance after being reportedly killed in action on the beach of Normandy. This was sometimes called a third miracle. Henry Brimm was one of Buffalo's most outstanding middleweights of all time. He fought often and he always drew respectable crowds. He took on some of the best including, in the waning days of his career, middleweight champions Rocky Graziano and Bobo Olsen. He lost both those fights. But in his second to last fight, held in the spring of 1951, he staged a startling upset against Joey DeJohn. Brimm was a 3 – 1 underdog and yet out pointed his tough opponent.[6]

Another boxing legend of national stature who graced the ring in the Aud in the immediate postwar years was Willie Pep, the world's featherweight champ. Pep was the winner of 87 of his 88 professional fights. Pep had done double duty in WW II, being honorably discharged from both the Army and the Navy. Two months after V.J. Day, Pep met Mike Martyk. The latter, a St. Catharine's, Ontario lightweight, had won 11 straight, nine by knockouts. Some felt that Pep was ring-rusty from his long time in the service, and thus Martyk might have a chance. He did not. Charlie Bailey called Martyk courageous. More than 7,000 turned out to watch the "human buzz saw" from Hartford, Connecticut, knock out Martyk in the 5th round. Bailey, as colorful as ever, referred to Pep's punch as something that "combined the best features of a red hot poker and a stiletto." A few months later, Guillermo Papaleo, aka Willie Pep, met and decked Johnny Virgo in the 2nd round of their Hudson A.C. bout in the Aud.[7]

Sugar Ray Robinson – Middleweight Champion – fought Henry Brimm in the Aud. *Photo: Wikipedia*

Boxing's biggest celebrity in the 1940s and one of the greatest heavyweights of all time was Joe Louis. The Brown Bomber, as he was popularly known, did not actually fight in Buffalo in the post war era but he did visit the city often. He had close ties with a number of people in the area. Some of his managers were from Buffalo including his last one, Marshall Miles. Also Ann Montgomery, the owner of the "Little Harlem Hotel, was a good friend."

According to Jerry Collins, she lived near the Cloverbank Hotel on the Lake Shore Road in Hamburg where Joe Louis was a frequent guest.[8]

Sugar Ray Robinson and Willie Pep were the biggest celebrities to fight in the Aud in the 1940s. They had national stature. But there were several solid local fighters who became regulars in the downtown arena. A surprisingly large number of them achieved a high level of success and maintained it for at least a few years; while some only experienced it fleetingly. Welterweight Johnny Green, and Tommy Stenhouse a lightweight, had successful boxing careers. Green was a National Golden Gloves champion; then as a pro was rated among the top contenders in his division. Stenhouse began his boxing career at the Michigan Avenue YMCA in 1939. In World War II he was a member of the famous Tuskegee Airmen. That was the group of heroic Black men who enlisted in the military and served their country valiantly in Europe. Stenhouse's career as a lightweight contender began in 1946 and for two years he seemed virtually invincible. At one point he rode a streak of 14 consecutive victories. Henry Flakes, popularly known as Snow Flakes, a moniker he was not fond of, showed some promise as did Prentiss Hall, a highly regarded heavyweight. All these pugilists hailed from Buffalo. There were a number of other good boxers too, who fell geographically in the greater Buffalo orbit, and who fought often either under the auspices of Jack Singer's Hudson Athletic Club or Dewey Michael's Fairview Athletic Club. This group included Joe Matisi, the Binghamton Battler, the DeJohn brothers of Syracuse, and Lee Oma of Detroit. Many boxing enthusiasts actually considered Oma a virtual Buffalonian since he spent so much time in the Queen City. The same could be said for Matisi. He fought both Joe and Phil Muscato as well as Ezzard Charles; all in Buffalo. He actually fought only 28 times in his career, largely due to the fact that he lost five years while serving in the military in World War II.

Buffalo also had a fair share of quality amateurs during this era. When one thought of amateurs, one thought immediately of the Golden Gloves. The origins of the Golden Gloves tournaments date to the 1920s. Arch Ward of the *Chicago Tribune*, one of the era's great sports writers, came up with the idea of a youthful boxing tournament and served as its chief promoter.The Golden Gloves Tournament spread to most major cities throughout the country. In Buffalo and Western New York, the *Courier Express* became the sponsor for the annual extravaganza. Sports Editor Billy Kelly became the principal "on the scene" promoter and cheerleader. He spared few superlatives to boost the annual event. Kelly often referred to the Golden Gloves as the "Greatest Show of the Year." Other times it would be referred to as "The Greatest Array of Amateur Boxers ever in a Buffalo Ring." The *Courier*'s Good Fellows Club, a group of community minded sportsmen, carried the torch for the event.[9] The newspaper would begin publicizing the annual tournament in the waning days of summer. Applications would be printed and distributed throughout the counties of Western New York. Regular notices would appear in the newspaper once the fall school term had begun, urging the applicants to complete their forms before the deadline. Line ups were arranged, various preliminaries bouts would be staged under the guidance of groups such as the Amateur Athletic Union, the Butler Mitchell club with Sammy Sacco serving as director, and similar organizations. Various civic groups, mainly the American Legion posts, would pitch in to enlist as many participants as possible.

Preliminary fight cards were held in various gyms around Western New York. Once they were completed, there were two super nights of boxing staged in Memorial Auditorium. The semi-finals would be held near the Thanksgiving holiday, and then on either the first or second Monday in December, the finals for the 32 qualifiers, would be held. "Come as early as you like and stay as late as you like." That was the Chairman's urging. The fights would start at 6:00 pm and last sometimes, past midnight. Diehard fans, some accompanied by their children, would drag themselves out of the Aud in the wee hours of the morning. Bleary eyes caused by the late hour but even more so by the smoke-filled auditorium were commonplace. In those days, smoking was permitted and if you were one of those sitting in the cheap seats high up in the grey sections, you paid for your frugality by having to peer with watering eyes through the ascending layers of smoke in order to see the action in the ring some levels below.

Boxing promoters liked to emphasize the virile aspects of the sport. The sport was viewed as a great training ground for manhood. What better opportunity to serve this purpose than with the Golden Gloves tournament! The annual event was also viewed as a mighty instrument to be used in the fight against juvenile delinquency, which was a rising concern in many urban areas after the war. Juvenile delinquents were troublesome but the conventional wisdom was that those so-called delinquents were basically good boys. What they needed was more guidance; perhaps a closer relationship with their fathers. The Father-Son promotion for the Golden Gloves tournament was trumpeted far and wide; it was viewed as a major weapon in the war against J.D., Juvenile Delinquency.

Certainly the Golden Gloves program fit in nicely with the sport's beneficial role in lending an aura of respectability to certain ethnic groups. For years this had been, if not a stated objective, at least a result of the openness of the egalitarianism of the sport. Talented athletes could climb the ladder to success in America. Here was the land of opportunity where a youth, gifted with talented hands, could make it in the boxing ring. The English settlers became involved with boxing in colonial America. In the southern colonies, black slaves were occasionally rewarded with their freedom if they were victorious in the ring. In the mid 19th century, swarms of Irish immigrants arrived in the eastern cities of the United States. Many of the young men, a considerable number of whom were bachelors, gravitated to the sport. In the 20th century, many children of Jewish immigrants made a living with their fists. In the second quarter of the century, Italians were commonplace in the boxing arenas along with increasingly large numbers of Black Americans. Hispanics would become numerous in the ring as the 20th century drew to a close.

The Golden Glove tournaments in Buffalo reflected this ethnic diversity. Moreover the event was priced right so that the families and friends of the many boxers would have no trouble purchasing admission. No one could complain about the price of tickets; $1.50 for a reserved seat, $1.00 for the higher seats, sometimes considered in "nosebleed" territory. Tickets were sold at the *Courier Express* and also at Edwards Department Store, located at Pearl and Mohawk across from the Statler Hotel. Many of the church and community organizations had large numbers of tickets at their disposal. There were many freebies.

Thousands of tickets were sold annually; many of them, perhaps surprisingly, were actually used. The City of Buffalo benefited, so did all those promoters who were infused with the "feel good spirit" about this worthwhile effort. Financially a big percentage of the proceeds went, in this pre-politically correct era, to "The inmates of the orphan asylums." Today they would be referred to as "the underprivileged or the financially challenged." Obviously the participants too were beneficiaries. Invariably, in these post war years, the vast majority of the participants came from within the city itself. In the 1945 tournament, all the finalists were from the city except for a Niagara Falls AAU entry, and a Canisius College Chemistry major from North Collins. Participants came from all walks of life; they included steel workers, butchers and bakers, various white collar clerks and a Purple Heart veteran from the Battle of the Bulge. The tournament itself included 16 weight divisions involving novices and masters. Some of the fights were thrilling; others just plain boring. A budding pugilist might get in the ring and end up flaying away wildly with haymakers, another young lad might just stalk his opponent for three rounds. One of the most memorable bouts was the 1948 slugfest between Joey Giambra and Bobby Barnes, two crowd favorites. Giambra won.

The superlatives, the alliterations, the purple prose poured forth profusely from the typewriters of the local press. Fans were promised a "right merry evening of maul." They would watch "free swinging kids...scramble an opponents' features and send him into the Land of Nod." Some of the fighters would "bomb with brutality." The "brigand of belters" would entertain in a "festival of KO punching." The real fans were the "buck boys" those who purchased the $1.00 tickets and stayed through thick and thin. They were the backbone of the fight game.[10]

On Golden Gloves fight night, Lower Main Street from Shelton Square South was a sight to behold. On frosty, sometimes snowy, late autumn nights, hundreds, indeed thousands, of young boys accompanied by their fathers, along with groups of Boy Scouts, Altar Boys, and Boys Clubs, all properly chaperoned, trekked toward the Aud. They walked past the massive Ellicott Square Building, past the Hotel Worth, across the railroad tracks and the trolley tracks and into the arena. Often they would arrive just in time to escape the furious winds that blew off the western end of Lake Erie at that time of year.

In the 1940s there were at least 8,000, often more than 9,000 fans at the semifinals. The finals usually topped 10,000 and the all time record came on December 6, 1947 when 13,178 passed through the turnstiles, the largest ever for an Aud event to that time. Attendance for the finals continued in the five figure category into the 1950s but as that decade moved along the numbers began to decrease. The popularity of the tournament subsided and more young men began to participate in a variety of other athletic activities. Fight fans or former fight fans became more fickle. They became engrossed in an ever widening variety of sporting events.[11]

But in the 1940s, the Golden Gloves tournament was a big time event in Buffalo. In addition to the vastly popular Golden Gloves, and in addition to the occasional big name fight involving a Willie Pep or a Sugar Ray Robinson, and in addition to the bouts contested by a number of pretty good local boxers, in addition to all this magnificent array of boxing available for the fight fan in Buffalo, in addition to all those pugilists, there were the Muscato Brothers. When all is said and done, boxing in Buffalo in the half decade following WWII, was virtually synonymous with the name Muscato. Phil and Joe Muscato were born in Dunkirk, New York, on Lake Erie's shoreline approximately 45 miles south of Buffalo. But they were nurtured on Buffalo's vibrant West Side. By the 1940s, the heart of the Italian community had moved away from the vicinity of Swan Street and from the area behind City Hall near St. Anthony's Church. Now the landmark thoroughfares were Connecticut and Niagara Streets, and Porter Avenue, with Holy Cross and Holy Angels Churches serving as the main houses of worship. Joe or Phil would walk down bustling Connecticut Street while the admiring eyes of youngsters would be transfixed on their heroes. Occasionally the Muscato boys could be seen exercising or doing some informal sparing in the Holy Angels Elementary School playground on West Avenue. They would inevitably draw a crowd of worshipful fans. The Muscato Boys became, arguably, the best known pair of brothers in Buffalo Sports history. They dominated the boxing headlines in the late 1940s. One wag put it succinctly: "This was "Muscato country." Another observer who happened to be close to a Muscato victim, remarked, after Joe Muscato had won a close decision, that "The Muscatos get all the close votes in Buffalo." Regardless, the fact is that the Muscatos fought often and they fought well. They won often, especially in 1946 and 1947, and the local fans adored them.

The Muscato brothers in training on the shores of Lake Erie.
Photo: D. Valenzuela, Buffalo Evening News.

The Muscatos were not unlike thousands of other young men who took up the sport in the 19th or 20th century. Boxing would be their way up the economic ladder. As Dan Muscato, Joe's son remarked, the Muscato boys used their skills "to bring the family together and to put bread on the table." Joe Muscato was four years older than Phil. Both rose through the amateur ranks before World War II. Both were alumni of the Golden Gloves program. Phil continued to fight throughout most of the war years in Buffalo. Joe served in the Army from 1943 until the end of 1945. Toward the end of the conflict, Phil served in the Navy.[12]

With the return of peacetime, the brothers, Phil and Joe, would have their opportunity to pursue their goals before the hometown folks. In the waning months of 1945, as the country returned to normalcy, Phil Muscato beefed up his resume, by defeating opponents of varying skills. He beat a pretty good Prentiss Hall in September, KO'd Vince Pinipinella in October, and KO'd Johnny Denson, the "Indianapolis Irishman" in October in a bout that lasted 3 rounds. In November he defeated Willy Barrow in Cleveland, and on December 2 he stopped the "stocky Celt" Michael Hayes in the 4th round. By the end of the year, 1945, Phil was ranked #3 among the light heavyweight contenders, by the reputable *Ring Magazine*. This was the highest rating in a decade for a Buffalo pugilist. Phil was just behind Archie Moore, and the champ, Gus

Lesnevich. Boxing was definitely back as a vital part of the Buffalo sports scene.

1945 ended on a high note for professional boxing in Buffalo. Thirty-one cards in the Aud had drawn a total of 96,880 fans. The people of Buffalo seemed eager for boxing and the Hudson and Fairview Athletic Clubs were there to offer it. But they had to confront some issues. Both clubs complained about the high fees they had to pay for use of the Aud; especially vexing was the rental fee. Billie Mitchie actually withdrew from the Fairview A.C. citing the unreasonable rental fee that the Aud charged. Bob Stedler, Sports Editor of the *Buffalo Evening News*, pointed out that Buffalo's rental was the highest of any comparable city. Stedler discussed this issue with Jack Singer who agreed that it was tough going in Buffalo. Both clubs would continue in the boxing business but would continue to seek relief from the appropriate officials.[13]

On New Year' Day, 1946, Sergeant Joe Muscato was mustered out of the Army. Joe's boxing ability had been put to good use in the military. He had fought 45 bouts and had won the South Pacific Heavyweight crown. He had also helped supervise the army's athletic program in New Caledonia. In addition he saw some military action on Iwo Jima. He was wounded when fragments from Japanese bombs entered both his legs. According to his friend, sports reporter Frank Wakefield, Sergeant Joe, "as he lay in the dark tropical underbrush awaiting medics" figured that his fighting days both as a G.I. and as a boxer were over. But less than a year later, this recipient of the Purple Heart was back in Buffalo preparing to renew his career. His first post war bout in February 1946, precisely one year after the Battle of Iwo Jima, saw him KO Jimmy Crawford in the 3rd round.[14]

The New Year also rang in nicely for brother, Phil. He earned his 6th consecutive victory. This time the victim was Henry Cooper, Brooklyn Hebrew heavyweight;

Phil and Joe Muscato Returning from the War to the Ring. *Photo: D. Valenzuela, Buffalo Evening News*

the ethnicity of a boxer at that time was something often referenced. Then, Phil ran into a brick wall. Lee Oma ended Phil's win streak on January 28 in a ten round decision. Oma had been the favorite; his convincing victory proved no fluke. The bright side for the Buffalo fight scene was that this fight drew the largest crowd yet to witness fisticuffs in Memorial Auditorium. 11, 431 fans were in attendance, most of them there to cheer on Phil. Buffalo fight fans were not really disappointed. The consensus was that the native son did not lose any prestige in suffering the defeat.

Promoter Jack Singer was pleased with the way the fight scene was progressing in 1945-46. The $25,000 gate for the Muscato-Oma fight along with some other good money houses proved that Singer was succeeding. *News* reporter Frank Wakefield recognized that a big payday like the one that resulted from the Muscato-Oma bout was sufficient to convince promoters that Buffalo fans preferred the top weight class. The Muscato brothers were heavyweights, good heavyweights, and they were in demand. Jack Singer and Dewey Michaels knew on what side their bread was buttered.

The Muscatos continued to fight regularly, not just once or twice a year as has often been the case in recent decades but sometimes as often as twice a month. In the spring of 1946, Phil Muscato quickly got back on the winning track. On March 13, he was victorious over Gunnar Barland and a month later, he bested Joey Maxim, a rising star from Cleveland. More than 8,000 were treated to a "humdinger," and a "furious and sometimes spectacular fight." The *Courier Express* called this 10 round decision won by Phil, his "most important triumph."[15]

The next contest for Phil Muscato came on April 30, 1946. He knocked out Mikie O'Dowd in the first round. The ease with which he achieved that victory may have made Phil a bit cocky, because in a 12 round rematch with Maxim on May 14, Phil lost a split decision. Maxim was the latest find of Jack Kearns, former manager of legendary Jack Dempsey. One wonders if perhaps Jack Kearns may have been a factor in the outcome of the most recent Maxim-Muscato fight. Kearns was a New York City promoter who had considerable clout. He had helped to manage Jack Dempsey in the 1920s. Kearns complained to the New York State Athletic Commission about Buffalo boxing officials, asserting that they were doing a "home" job, and underscoring this by stating that "Buffalo is definitely a Muscato town." At this phase of his career, Phil appeared to be struggling; he was definitely in a down period. He lost to Tommy Gomez in June, and lost again to Maxim in August 2, 1946 in a bout held in Rochester.[16]

Meanwhile Brother Joe's star was in the ascendancy. Joe lost to Joe Matisi, the "Endicott Dynamiter," by a TKO. But Joe fought a tough aggressive battle. The nearly 9000 who witnessed this March 27 contest, agreed that it was a "most exciting bout." Joe's performance showed that he was back in top notch physical condition. He won his next four fights. Then, in November, his fortunes were reversed; he was stopped by Lee Oma. A month later, on December 10, he was KO'd by Melio Bettino.

`Generally, 1946 had been a pretty good year for boxing in Buffalo. Frank Wakefield in his year end summary for the *Buffalo Evening News* noted that the 39 ring shows arranged by the Hudson and the Fairview Athletic Clubs in the Aud emphatically lifted the Queen City "out of Boxing's Bush League."[17]

The next year, 1947, things started off well for Joe as well as for Phil. It proved to be the highpoint of the brothers' career. Joe did well in the early months but faltered later in the year, but Phil continued in top form through 1947 and into 1948.

The year opened with Phil avenging brother Joe's recent defeat at the hands of Lee Oma. Phil won a split decision over this tough battler from Detroit before nearly 10,000 on January 14, and this placed Phil back in the Top 10 list of heavies. Joe Alli of the *Courier* praised Phil for this crucial victory and called it one of his best. Phil then followed this with a quick KO of Bill Peterson, a former Indiana University football player. The "West Side Idol" won a close split decision over Lee Savold in March before nearly 9,000, actually 8,894, a fight in which he gave up 22 pounds. To prove that that victory was no fluke, he defeated Savold again the following month.[18]

Meanwhile Joe got back on the winning trail by defeating Johnny Shkor in February, then he KO'd Freddie Schott in March and KO'd Johnny Flynn in April. The Muscato boys were riding high in early 1947. Joe's swift knock out of Schott placed him among the top heavyweights, Joe was never "more impressive" especially with his power punches and solid left hooks. Schott had been

KO'D only once in more than 50 bouts.[19]

The superlatives were flowing freely. Phil's triumph over Savold in April before nearly 9,000 fans was a very popular victory and Wakefield said it established Phil as "Buffalo's foremost individual sports attraction." Savold, a 31 year old, Des Moines, Iowa, native had Phil on the ropes, knocked him rubber-legged and dropped him in the 2nd and again in the 3rd round. But Muscato showed why he was so popular, why he had become the "Queen City's top gate attraction." Phil roared back from almost certain defeat with a reckless audacity that kept Savold busy just protecting himself. Later in April, Phil lost to Walter Hafer but he quickly avenged that isolated defeat. Less than two months later he defeated Hafer. Then he went on a rampage, winning 12 out of his next 13 fights in a period covering the rest of 1947, all of 1948 and into January of 1949.[20]

Joe Muscato, the older of the brothers, had begun to show his age by the middle of 1947. In May Big Pat Comiskey of Paterson, New Jersey, with a 21-pound advantage, knocked him out in the second round, and a month later a 222 pound giant from Argentina, Abel Cestac, KO'D the 193 pound Muscato, again in round number two. These quick knockouts caused the New York State Athletic Commission to order Joe to rest for a while. He was put on the inactive list for three months.

Tommy Stenhouse , top Buffalo lightweight.

As Joe was winding down his boxing career, some other hometown boys made news. Henry Brimm, as already noted, hit the high point of his career early in 1949 in the draw he earned with Sugar Ray Robinson. Lightweight Tommy Stenhouse won often during these years; his best years were 1946 and 1947. Walter Kolby, welterweight, also had his best years in '46 and '47, then faded from the scene. Prentiss Hall, who had some good years from 1944 to 1946, was on the way out in 1947. Johnny Green, who was riding high in 1947, was shelved with an injury by the end of that year. Henry Flakes had begun to make a name for himself. Indeed twice in 1948 he defeated. Pat Comisky, considered by some to be a legitimate challenger for Joe Louis' title. Jack Singer liked him a lot and thought he should be rated near the top of the charts, but Flakes' good start came to a rather abrupt halt when he was suspended by the New York Athletic Commission because of an eye problem. Then trouble with the law brought a definite end to his career.[21]

The promotion of the fight game was also experiencing some changes. As Wakefield put it, the "promoters honeymoon is over, they were going to have to realize that the fans want fights deemed worthy of paying the price of admission." 1946 had been a record breaking year, and now, things were settling down; 1947 ended with both the Hudson A.C. and Fairview A.C. showing shrinking numbers in patronage. On the other hand each of the clubs had a couple of big paydays. The Hudson and the Fairview clubs had to adjust to promote fights that were fan-pleasers. They did so. The FAC's best effort came with the 9,400 fans who witnessed the Ezzard Charles – Joe Matisi fight. Charles had risen to the head of the heavyweight class. He defeated Joe Matisi. The Hudson's best turn out came with the Phil Muscato – Lee Savold fight. By this time Phil was easily recognized as the district's top fighter. Both clubs had come to see the wisdom of promoting fewer cards than previously.[22]

Cy Kritzer wrote a column commenting on the status of boxing in Buffalo. He noted that the boxing clubs usually found themselves in the red. Regardless, the fighters, the government, the fights fans and the city itself, all benefited. The Clubs deserved some help. Kritzer cautioned that the rental was too high and that the city should do a better job of accommodating the boxing clubs. The Auditorium Board of the City of Buffalo would have to do its share in assuring the success of boxing in Buffalo. Kritzer knew that the fight fans were shopping around. He recognized that they were big-name conscious. The promoters surely deserved some help to keep out of the red. Kritzer respected Singer's devotion to the fight game. He also knew that Singer was as much of a draw as the fighters he promoted. He was a real character somewhat amusingly admired for the way that he demolished the King's English. Jack Singer was well on his way to becoming a Buffalo legend. Kritzer called Singer's gym the best known training oasis in the cauliflower industry between New York and Chicago. On any given day, the *News* journalist noted, one could hike up some four flights at the 338 Washington Street site and find anywhere from 80 to 90 punchers busy at their craft.[23]

Dewey Michaels, Singer's counterpart at the Fairview Athletic Club himself was on his way to becoming a legendary figure in Buffalo. This was perhaps in part because of his fight promotion at the FAC but more probably because of his promotion of the famous or perhaps infamous, Palace Burlesk. The Palace, just a short distance from the boxing clubs, was noted not just for the appearances of Gypsie Rose Lee, Rose La Rose, and Blaze Starr, (no relation), but also because of the entire Burlesk show program; the colorful, sometimes corny slapstick comedians, and the aggressive sales barkers, who hawked their Eskimo Pies and their bags of popcorn, and especially their boxes of Cracker Jacks, each one guaranteed to have a valuable prize at the bottom of the box. There was a prize there but its value was questionable. Dewey's Burlesk House was universally recognized as one of the landmarks of Buffalo. If someone asked where he or she might find the Erie County Savings Bank, or Shelton Square, or Bonds Clothing Store for Men (buy a new suit and get two pair of trousers), the answer often would be: "right near the Palace Burlesk." Nine out of ten red blooded males, and a surprising number of females, would have no trouble locating the Palace.

Dewey Michaels' Fairview gym was also on Washington Street though further uptown, near Tupper Street. Frank Wakefield, Kritzer's colleague at the *News*, learned, that the Fairview gym was going to be dismantled; the site was rented to a printing shop. All the gym equipment there was to be sold. Fight fans were concerned. Michaels however emphasized that the Fairview A.C. was not going out of business. He would continue to promote fights, even without a gym. When needed, he would have access to other area gyms. One of the more popular was in the Butler Mitchell Boys' Club on Virginia Street.[24]

Singer and Michaels had done a splendid job in making Buffalo a big time boxing location. They continued to do so; they staged fewer bouts than they had in the two years immediately following the war, but they still were responsible for a number of headliners. 1948 opened with a bang. On January 20 Phil Muscato, won a unanimous 10 round decision; he upset Joe Matisi. The fight fans numbered 11,541, the largest professional crowd in WNY sports history in the Aud to that time. Phil fought a very smart fight. Stedler called it a "ripsnorting battle from the first bell" and asserted that Muscato offered a "remarkable demonstration of punching, stamina, and alertness." Not to be outdone, the *Courier* said that "Phil added another spectacular chapter to Buffalo's fistic history… in one of the greatest heavyweight battles ever staged in the Aud."[25]

Then Phil laid low for most of the remaining months in 1948. He did not fight again until October 19 when he beat Shamus O'Brien. In the meantime Phil got caught up in his business; too much so according to some observers. Phil had invested in a restaurant, named The Melody. It was actually a night club and popularly was simply known as "Muscato's." It was located on Main Street near Virginia. This business enterprise consumed a considerable amount of time and it was not a financial success.

Two major crowds highlighted the year, one at the Matisi-Muscato donnybrook, and the second at the Brimm - Sugar Ray bout. Both drew near capacity crowds to the lower Main Street arena. The year also witnessed the re-emergence of Joey DeJohn, native of Syracuse, but adopted Buffalonian and now referred to as the "Swan Street youth." In 1947 Joey DeJohn had had a 30 win streak ended by a tough pug-nosed Irishman, Peter Meade in the Aud. Meade was an experienced fighter; he had fought several fights in Madison Square Garden but he did not have an easy time with this young upstart. DeJohn had just turned 21 years old; he was fearless against this nationally known opponent. There was a terrific exchange of punches that kept the shouting fans on their feet. But the lack of experience and over-eagerness hurt DeJohn. He was going to have to learn how to pace himself and he did learn from this experience. 1948 was a good year for him. He set a new Aud record when he KO'd his middleweight foe, George "Sonny" Randle, just thirty-nine seconds into the first round. That was in November. A short time later, just a few days before the end of the year, DeJohn KO'd Ossi Harris. Joe Alli of the *Courier Express* called DeJohn the most promising middleweight title hope in a decade.[26]

Phil Muscato's return, late in 1948 after a long layoff through most of the year, saw him back on the winning side of the ledger. Four straight wins culminated with his toughest fight in a long time. This was a bout against Ted Lowery, in January of 1949. It was labeled "a brutal, free-swinging slugfest."Phil won it in a 10 round decision.

Joe Muscato, too, had some success on the comeback trail. Following a long layoff, Joe fought twice in early 1949, with wins over Willie Davis and Henry Jones, but Joe was running out of gas and he knew it. He took a few more months off, came back in September, lost again, then listened to his friends and decided it was time to retire. He decided to pursue other interests. According to fight historian, Jerry Collins, Joe wrestled professionally for a few years and then pursued an active and rewarding career helping in various athletic and recreational activities. This local hero was proudly giving back to his Western New York community.[27]

Unfortunately, Phil Muscato's retirement from the ring was more painful and more erratic. His first fight in 1949 was a victory over "Tiger" Ted Lowry. Two months later, Lee Oma gave Phil a boxing lesson before more than 11,000 fans in the Aud. In fact Oma was so elated with this victory that he indicated that he was ready for a big time bout against either Ezzard Charles or Jersey Joe Walcott. Phil obviously was not elated, but he did win a return bout over Ted Lowry just a month later. Unfortunately that proved to be just a slight bump up on the downward slope. Phil lost three more times in mid - 1949, then he indicated to Frank Wakefield that he would take only a couple more fights and call it quits. Wakefield thought that Phil seemed in fine physical shape but his mind was elsewhere, noting that Phil was harassed with numerous problems as proprietor of his new night club. So while his mind was on his shaky business ventures, Phil's boxing losses mounted.

In October he fought Archie Moore, a legitimate contender for the Joe Louis crown, in Toledo, Ohio. Muscato was knocked out in the 6th round. A little bit later, in fact a week before Christmas, he met Rocky Marciano "the sensational young New Englander" in Providence and was knocked down 4 times before the referee called it a TKO in the 5th round. Sadly he tried again, in May of 1950 and lost to Nick Barone by a knockout in the 4th. Only 3,201 diehards showed up at the Aud. Phil Muscato was done in New York State. The state athletic commission recommended Phil's license be cancelled and Phil's manager, Don Parisi, said he would not permit Phil to fight again. Stubborn to the end, Phil traveled to Seattle, 3,000 miles away, only to be knocked out in the first round by Henry Mathews. That spelled Finale.

The times, they were a 'changin.' The Muscato era was over. But it wasn't just the retirement of the Muscato brothers that spelled an end to an era. Fighters who had once looked to the Hudson A.C. or the Fairview A.C. for their chance to make a name for themselves now more and more looked to New York City. Joey DeJohn delivered a financial body blow to Jack Singer saying "My next fight! It's against Pete Mead in the Garden." Singer had hoped for a big payday in the Aud. But for those advancing or trying to advance toward a championship, Madison Square Garden in New York City was the answer. That was the media capital; that is where television was coming on strong. In late 1949 there were, already, boxing cards being televised from New York City on every night except Sunday. Fight fans in Buffalo sought out local saloons that "had the fight on TV." Buffalo boxing could no longer compete with "The Big Apple." Boxing from the Aud in downtown Buffalo could no longer compete with the televised bouts from Madison Square Garden.

Joey DeJohn, Syracuse Welter-weight, Regular in Buffalo .
Photo: Ring 44 program

Perhaps another sign of the times was that Joe Giambra who had made a big hit in 1948 in the Golden Gloves, was now going to ,make his professional debut, not in the Aud, but on the Frontier Boxing Club card at the Ft. Erie Arena. On a normal evening, about 1,500 fans would attend boxing in the newly renovated facility in Ft Erie. Jack Singer was still in charge, but having the fight in Fort Erie was an indication that the Aud was going to be used less often. Marquee bouts, when and if, they could be scheduled, would be held in Memorial Auditorium. Then, on November 5, 1949, Jack Singer died suddenly, felled by a massive heart attack. Singer's son, Jack Jr. would carry on. But the passing of the senior Singer seemed to mark the end of an era; it certainly could be regarded as another sign of the changing times.

In New York City itself, boxing was undergoing changes, and its promoters were being investigated. Boxing was being hurt by gambling charges. Joe Louis had retired then un-retired then retired again, so there was controversy as to how the next champion would be named.

This was a transition period. Big photogenic punchers were eagerly sought out. They were what the television moguls wanted and what the networks and arenas in New York City promised to deliver. Smaller cities would have to take the leftovers. Not as many young men were entering the field of boxing. Some of those who did were quickly dispatched into oblivion if they did not fit the television needs. Finesse in the sweet science, was not nearly as important as the ability to throw big wild haymakers. The odds were that one would land occasionally on some unknowing victim. That, presumably, would be sufficient to satisfy most of the new television viewers.

Buffalo's famous Aud would continue to hold fights in the future though not very often. Occasionally a genuine headliner would be held. In fact, late in 1950, a certified heavyweight championship fight was held in Buffalo, between Ezzard Charles and Fred Beshore. Only 6,298 attended; another sign of what was in store in the future. The Charles – Beshore fight drew the smallest title crowd in history. The Golden Gloves continued to be a significant local event at least for most of the 1950s. Gradually the tournament lost some of its appeal. The crowds were fair, not at all on a par with those in the years immediately following the Second World War. Some big local names would draw a sizeable following in Buffalo. Carmen Basilio was a great, middleweight champion in the 1950s. Popularly referred to as "the onion farmer from Canastota, New York," Basilio was a star attraction in Buffalo and throughout New York State. More than two decades later, Sugar Ray Leonard, the charismatic Welterweight Champion was set to defend his title against Roger Stafford in Buffalo in May of 1982. However an eye injury to Leonard led to the cancellation of the fight. Two years later, Livingston Bramble and "Boom Boom" Mancini met before a full house in Memorial Auditorium. Bramble wore the Lightweight crown after that bout. By the end of the century, Joe Mesi, "Baby Joe," had come on to the Buffalo fight scene as a young boxer of some promise. Things were different by then, even the Aud was closed.

The period immediately following World War II was a golden age for boxing in Buffalo. Fight fans were offered a wide spectrum of boxing fare ranging from thrilling amateur bouts to spectacular heavyweight contests. It was an era when more than 10,000 fervent fans packed Memorial Auditorium to watch Phil and Joe Muscato, and Henry Brimm and Sugar Ray Robinson as well as amateurs in the Golden Gloves tournaments. It was a golden age for Boxing in Buffalo. It was also a spectacular era for the sport of wrestling.

CHAPTER EIGHT

Two Georges

— Ed Don and Gorgeous and the Mat Men —

BUFFALO EVENING NEWS

Gorgeous G.s Act Still Gets Them - 11,160 Laugh, Boo as He Wins Again

Buffalo Evenng News - January 22, 1949

Gorgeous George grappling with the Angel. *Photo: D. Valenzuela, Buffalo News.*

As a spectator sport, wrestling's early history as well as its presence in Buffalo in the Golden Age of the 1940s was similar to boxing more than to any other sport. Wrestling grew in popularity after the Civil War. Wrestling matches were held at a variety of sites in Western New York in the 19th century. By the early years of the 20th century, wrestling came to be accepted as a legitimate sport. It became popular with area sports fans. In the 1920s and 30s, Buffalonians attended the contests in the Broadway Auditorium in sizeable numbers. Boxing and professional wrestling used that same venue and the sport attracted many of the same fans. By the 1940s professional wrestling had developed its showmanship aspect. Fans came for the show and the show was wrestling. It was professional wrestling, not to be confused with college wrestling. Professional wrestling was very different, very spectator oriented. For all of its showmanship and its zaniness and its gimmickry it was, certainly in the 1940s, still considered, at least, a quasi legitimate sport.

Two local authors have provided us with a good understanding of the meaning of professional wrestling in the middle decades of the 20th century. Dick Hirsch, a long time writer for the *Courier Express* often produced features in the Sunday Magazine section of that newspaper. On March 15, 1981, his article entitled: "Masters of the Mat," and subtitled: "Some Warm Memories of Buffalo's Meanest Wrestlers," appeared. He focused on the period from the Great Depression through the 1950s. That was the heyday of wrestling in downtown Buffalo. Hirsch put it this way: "They call it professional wrestling but it was much more than that. It was melodrama. It was strength. It was size. It was comedy. It was gymnastics. It was mayhem. It was showbiz. All of it for about a buck an' a half." Dan Murphy, a local devotee on wrestling, published a book in 2002 entitled: "Bodyslams in Buffalo." The book focuses on the period after the 1950s. Nevertheless much of what it says is appropriate for the earlier period. Murphy states: "pro wrestling is exactly the same as it always was. It's loud, it's uncouth, it's violent, it's funny, it's silly, and it's entertaining."[1]

In the period before the Second World War, the two most popular and influential people in wrestling in Buffalo were Monsignor Franklin Kelliher and Ed Don George.[2] Kelliher, a Catholic priest, was best known by his pseudonym, The Masked Marvel. The mask was his trademark, and fans never saw him without it when he wrestled in the years from 1928 to 1932. Then, when he finally lost a match, he was unmasked and that was the end of his professional wrestling career. The local bishop assisted in the unmasking and saw to it that his days as an active grappler were at an end. As a Catholic priest, Kelliher had other obligations. But he did continue to have a colorful and active career in sports. He was a local celebrity in Buffalo for many decades. For more than 30 years he served as the director of Boys' Town on Buffalo's West Side just a stone's throw from the Peace Bridge. That itself was significant since Kelliher had a close attachment to Canada and had often wrestled there. The Kelliher home served boys who were considered troublesome. Kelleher helped them become respectable; he helped them learn some skills. He took great pride in introducing them to the sports of wrestling and boxing. The Catholic clergyman was an important figure in the promotion of Golden Gloves boxing for many years. He retired to a comfortable ranch home on New Amsterdam Avenue in the upscale area of North Buffalo. There he had adequate space to showcase many of his trophies and memorabilia. He would continue to entertain guests, to reminisce, and to offer advice, well into the waning years of the 20th century.[3]

Ed Don George, began his professional wrestling career about the same time that

***Above:* Ed Don George, All Star college wrestler at Michigan and St. Bonaventure, was on the 1928 Olympic team. *Insert, right:* George , Navy Commander and promoter of the Aud wrestling program.**
Photos: D. Valenzuela, Buffalo News

Monsignor Kelliher did. George was a native of North Java, a tiny hamlet southeast of Buffalo. He graduated from Canisius High School in Buffalo and then had a colorful and varied collegiate career. He enrolled at St. Bonaventure University where he was a member of the football and wrestling teams. His final two years were spent at the University of Michigan; he was named Big Ten Champion wrestler. Later in life he was named to both the St. Bonaventure University and the University of Michigan Halls of Fame. He was a member of the 1928 Olympics team in Amsterdam and reached the finals. He then turned pro and was a wrestling title holder in the 1930s. His toughest match ever was against well known Strangler Lewis in 1930 in Wrigley Field, Los Angeles. He lost. Ed Don wrestled more than 100 bouts over the next dozen years. He joined the Navy in 1942. As a commander at a Naval Air Base in North Carolina he supervised a judo training program and he even managed to earn another degree at the University of North Carolina. Ed Don was released from the Navy in January 1946. He helped out Jack Herman, President of the Great Lakes Athletic Club with wrestling promotions. When matchmaker Jerry Monahan passed away in 1947, Ed Don assumed that position and continued serving as Buffalo's main wrestling impresario until the mid 1950s when he turned over those functions to Pedro Martinez.[4]

In the 1930s, life in America was dictated by the Great Depression. Wrestling was no exception. There was a sharp decline in attendance at wrestling matches. There were also some significant changes taking place in the sport. Lou Thesz, who later wrestled in Buffalo, was recognized as a champion. Scott Beekman, the latest authority on the sport called Thesz "a significant transitional figure in the history of professional wrestling." Beekman refers to the years from the 1930s to the 1950s as the era when wrestling moved from an emphasis on the skills of the sport to the age of television which emphasized showmanship. Thesz had genuine wrestling skills but also was very useful to promoters as a drawing attraction. He was sometimes referred to as the handsome young Hungarian from Missouri. Promoters began to have success drawing large crowds to the arenas by using gimmicks and calling attention to special physical features or behavioral characteristics of their subjects. Buffalo wrestling fans, promoters, and sportswriters did their best to make their own contributions to the gimmick business. Perhaps best remembered by fans would be the nicknames given to the wrestlers. The villains were the most memorable. Maurice "the French Angel" Tillet became the first to be a major draw. He was a big, bad, ugly guy, but he was the type that Buffalo fans eagerly paid to see because they loved to hate him.[5]

Toward the end of the 1930s, wrestling emerged from the Depression doldrums. The setting in Buffalo was ideal for the renewed interest in the sport. Buffalo was preparing itself for big crowds for other spectator sports too. Memorial Auditorium, the scene of Buffalo's glory days of professional wrestling, opened in 1940. The first sports attraction was held on October 18, 1940. It was a wrestling match. 6,267 fans turned out to watch the main event on the card that featured local hero Ed Don George against Jumpin' Joe Savoldi. Don George was described by the *Buffalo Evening News*, as the "The North Java Adonis;" he, being a native of that rural community in the southern tier. Savoldi was an ex-Notre Dame football player. Don George won; he pinned Savoldi in 26 minutes and 46 seconds.[6]

A year later the Japanese bombed Pearl Harbor. America was now in the global conflict, literally, "up to its neck." The promising beginning of a new era in sports ground to a halt with the coming of World War II. Many wrestlers either were drafted or enlisted. Wrestling did take place during the war, but it was low keyed. Sports venues scheduled abbreviated mat cards. The Great Lakes Athletic Club was primarily responsible for the wrestling cards held in the Aud in the 1940s. Jack Herman was president and Jerry Monahan was the matchmaker. The latter was in charge of promoting wrestling. He and Herman did a satisfactory job keeping wrestling afloat during wartime. A number of cards were held featuring Whipper Billy Watson and Frank Sexton, sometimes against each other, and other times against a villain such as Bob Wagner or John Katan. Those four were regulars and continued to be so after the war.

With the return of peacetime, wrestling was posed to embark on a new and wildly successful era. This was true for the national scene and it was true for Buffalo, now proudly boasting of its new, large downtown auditorium. The facility was considered one of the best in the country, perhaps second only to Madison Square Garden. Wrestling at that time was divided into various territories throughout the United States. Buffalo was the hub of its territory which covered most of upstate New York and extended west to Columbus, Ohio, south into Northern Pennsylvania, and north, over the border to Toronto, Canada. Wrestlers would perform throughout the circuit, perhaps one night on a card in Binghamton, then a few nights later the same wrestler would be pursuing his craft in Albany, and if a particular wrestler were good enough and had sufficient drawing power he would be on the card in Buffalo. The main attractions were held in Memorial Auditorium.

As the war neared its conclusion in 1945, the Great Lakes A.C. began work on the upcoming season. Just two days after V J Day, Jack Herman announced that a full card of events, 28 shows in all, had been scheduled to take place from mid September through April of 1946. A short time later, he indicated that 45,000 tickets, reserved seats, had already been sold. The GLAC was ready; so were the fans and the wrestlers and so were the sportswriters. The latter seemed to relish the opportunity to use their purple prose when assigned to wrestling events, employing more colorful adjectives and more alliterations than they could get away with when writing about any other sport.

The first big night of the new season was on October 20, 1945. 4,012 fans showed up, not a huge crowd, but those fans made a heck of racket and it seemed as though the Aud was near capacity. There were customarily five or six matches on the Friday night wrestling card usually topped by one headliner or feature. Sometimes, primarily so as not to offend the sensibilities of a prima donna, the promoter would line up a co-feature. This was the case on October 20: John Katan wrestled George Macricostos and Billy Watson was pitted against Walter Strols.

The climax in the first match came when Katan put a headlock on Macricostos and a chancery hold on the referee (in wrestling the officials were not immune from physical involvement) and bumped their heads together. Macricostos broke away, and after a series of maneuvers, the referee called the fall and awarded the victory to George "the Greek" Macricostos. Since this was a non-politically correct age, he was also called the Golden Greek. It was an age when references to ethnicity or race were commonplace; writers were not aware that they might offend someone with such references. Almost every match had a villain. This was Katan's role. Cy Kritzer of the *Buffalo Evening News* noted that Katan was the "villain who never steps out of character." Kritzer thought Katan deserved an Oscar for his antics and referred to Katan as "an expert on the anti-Emily Post rules of wrestling."[7] In the co-feature, Strols, a former Army Sergeant, could not match the speed of his opponent, who was universally known as Whipper Watson. The Whipper won in a one fall match that conveniently lasted just one hour. Watson was a local favorite and a regular participant for many years. He hailed from Toronto and had a very large following throughout the Niagara peninsula. The Whipper made some money from wrestling but he also made a good living from his interests in lumber, building, and soft drink companies. Two weeks later, on November 2, the top of the card featured two villains against each other which was somewhat unusual. John Katan and Bob Wagner were the grapplers. The *News* dubbed it the "Wrestling version of Murder Inc," and said it was for the "skullduggery championship." The two had met before. They were not friends. The press played up the nasty rivalry. Of course, that was normal practice and of course, each had a nickname. Katan was invariaibly referred to as Honest John Katan. Ray Ryan of the *Courier Express* said that the "Honest" essentially meant that he had never stolen the battleship, Missouri, or the equivalent thereof. The name "Bob Wagner" was invariably prefixed with "Strangler." In the Buffalo area, Strangler Bob Wagner had been recognized as the arch villain for the previous two years. It was said that the joust between these two villains, itself, would have "delighted the late lamented Marquis de Sade."[8] The announced crowd was 6,004. Many of those attended in the anticipation of seeing someone lose and not caring who it would be. It was a rough bout; at times both contestants were outside the ring, battling in the aisles. The finale came when Katan was knocked down under the ring and then was counted out. Wagner fled to the dressing room knowing that at least half the crowd would disagree with the outcome.

As wrestling got back into favor with local fans in the fall of 1945, Matchmaker Jerry Monahan made sure that Frank Sexton and Whipper Billy Watson would meet. They were without doubt the biggest attractions on the local wrestling scene. Both Sexton and Watson had been part of the regular Aud wrestling program for some time. They were arch-rivals. In one of their encounters, one that Sexton bitterly remembered, Sexton plunged through the ropes in the Aud and was counted out. They met again a short time later, and the contest ended in a draw. Monahan booked them for November 16, 1945. Sexton was looking forward to this tussle, the Whipper being the last man to defeat him, and Watson also was anxious for this rematch. The Canadian native had been tramping in the Canadian woods where he bagged some deer and was now hoping that this would be a sign of the luck he would need "to bag" his old rival.

Promoter Monahan felt that he could count on a big turnout. It was anticipated that large numbers of Watson's fellow citizens would come over the Peace Bridge from St. Catharines, and from Hamilton as well as from Toronto to cheer on their native son. Watson was also popular on the American side of the Niagara River. Handsome Frank Sexton, sometimes called "Black Thatched Frank" generated just as much excitement. He was actually from Columbus, Ohio and was sometimes referred to as "the Columbus Strongman." Since the capital of Ohio was in the Buffalo wrestling orbit, Sexton was considered a local favorite. The promoters created considerable interest in this wrestling card. An indication of this interest was seen when Glen Campbell, local Chevrolet executive, arranged for a delegation of 90 Chevy dealers and their employees to be his guests at the wrestling event. It is no wonder that the Great Lakes Athletic Club looked forward to November 16th as its big payday of the fall season.

Sexton and Watson put on a good bout. Each had some bright moments. The two popular grapplers did not disappoint the crowd of 6,721, largest so far of the young season. Watson held Sexton to a draw which was viewed as a genuine accomplishment since Sexton was recognized as the "the kingpin of the local wrestling ranks."[9]

The calendar year drew to a close with crowds averaging between 4,000 and 5,000 for the Friday night events. Those figures were not as disappointing as might appear to some observers. Half the Aud was usually filled and more importantly, the ground work was laid for larger crowds in the future. Indeed, in the closing years of the decade, the Aud would be the scene of a number of sellouts.

The first Friday in January again featured Billy Watson, this time against Jumpin' Joe Savoldi, the former football star. Naturally Savoldi's arsenal of wrestling tactics included tackles and dropkicks. 5,402 attended and watched Watson use his famous whip to slam his opponent to the canvas and achieve victory. Over the next several weeks, the Friday night cards featured a number of the regulars including Sexton, Watson and Wagner. Others, who would become familiar on the local scene in the months and years that followed, included Friedrich Von Schlacht, a 6'4" Teuton from Milwaukee, Chief Osley Bird Saunooke and Frank Taylor. Crowds continued to number about 6,000 and in one case, 7,000 turned out. All of these Friday night wrestling cards were viewed as preliminary to the highlight of the entire wrestling season, the annual night of the Parade of Champions. It was the pet production of America's oldest wrestling promoter, Jack Herman. It was first staged in 1939 and continued during and after the war. It was always a huge hit invariably drawing the largest throng of the wrestling season. This marquee event was scheduled for February 8, 1946. The annual date varied; it depended on when the matchmakers could arrange the most attractive matches.

Fans loved the annual extravaganza. They showed their appreciation by flocking to the event in unprecedented numbers. Wrestlers were eager to participate. In fact a week before the event, Whipper Watson threw down the gauntlet; He stated that he wanted to wrestle Frank Sexton or he would go on strike. Sexton was considered by many wrestling officials to be the reigning world champion or at least one of them and Watson wanted a crack at the title. Actually Watson held a title of his own, he was touted as the British Empire Champion. Sexton claimed to be the world title holder as a result of his defeat of Babe Sharkey in Baltimore earlier in the year. Watson appeared satisfied when he was offered some top flight opponents over the next several weeks and an eventual match against Sexton. The 1946 version of the Parade of Champions lived up to its reputation; the evening was a tremendous success. It attracted 10,317 fans. Cy Kritzer, referring to the number of matches on the card, called in a real six star hit. Frank Sexton and Chief Saunooke grappled in the feature event. Second billing went to Whipper Watson and Jim "the Goon" Henry, who claimed to be the Texas State champion. The star studded card also included Sandy O'Donnell, Honest John Katan, Sliding Billy Hansen and Friedrich von Schacht.[10]

In the feature, perennial favorite Frank Sexton had a majority of the fans on his side, including most of the females. They liked to call the handsome athlete, "The Columbus Cutie." But his fan club ended the evening a bit disappointed. Chief Osley Bird Saunooke, also known as the "Curvaceous Cherokee Indian" proved a tougher opponent than anticipated. In part this was because he had increased his weight in a fairly brief time period from 310 to 350 pounds. Sexton tried to whirl the Chief in a giant swing but failed. But Sexton caught a break when the Chief's knee popped out of joint, and the Chief was finished. In the companion event, Watson and Henry put on a 36 minute all star performance. It shattered all noise records and it wound up a draw.

Two weeks later Matchmaker Monahan had a very pleasant surprise. He rediscovered Henry DeGlane. Ed Don George had actually wrestled DeGlane back in the early 1930s. Henry made some money wrestling in America. The Frenchman was a holder of a world's heavyweight championship at one time. He returned to France and purchased a large farm. Then the DeGlane story turned mysterious. He ran afoul of the Nazi tyranny then sweeping the continent. His farm in Northern France was not far from the soon to be famous beaches of Normandy. There were rumors that he sold chickens to the Nazis and he was accused therefore of being a collaborationist with the enemy. That was disproved. Henri DeGlane was actually an underground leader for the French resistance movement. He did get privileges because he was a farmer, but he could use that to work against the Germans. He was allowed to ride his bicycle over the countryside. That enabled him to pick up valuable information such as where certain key bridges were mined. The *Buffalo Evening News* reported that on D Day DeGlane took his notes on German positions, jumped into his canoe, and paddled many miles to meet the Yanks coming into the beaches.

After the war, DeGlane returned to the United States. In Buffalo he was lined up to face Frank Taylor. The fans, 6,018 of them, read about DeGlane's life and concluded that he was an authentic hero. When he appeared in the Aud they lustily cheered on the 40-year-old veteran. DeGlane had no trouble pinning Taylor; in fact Charley Young remarked that he brought him "into camp with the ease of a champion." What caught Promoter Monahan's attention was the thunderous standing ovation that DeGlane received. Monahan lost no time in signing DeGlane for the main event for the following week, and then went to work to find a worthy opponent. He thought of Sexton or Watson. If he secured one of those, Monahan figured "we will have a match that will arouse nationwide interest." Sexton agreed to the match. In readying himself for the big event, DeGlane worked out in the Community Hall in Crystal Beach, Ontario, as wrestlers sometimes did. In fact he drew crowds of a few hundred spectators to the famous resort community. Some residents, no doubt tired of roller coaster and caterpillar rides, looked for some diversion. The match was held on the first day of March. The largest turnout of the season, 10,407, attended, even surpassing the Parade of Champions event. The enthusiastic crowd got its money's worth. The two Champions went back and forth to the delight of the crowd. Sexton concentrated on leglocks and toeholds which had DeGlane moaning. DeGlane had Sexton in trouble several times with a head scissors. DeGlane flipped Sexton across the ring and scored with a headlock." Sexton used a new hold, a combination of a back body drop with a headlock. He executed it expertly. Sexton caught DeGlane in midair and they went over backwards, with DeGlane's shoulders on the canvas. The sequence happened so quickly that before most knew what was happening, even DeGlane, Sexton had cleanly pinned him and won. The *News* called it a "wrestling classic."[11]

The crowd also was enthusiastic with the undercard. It featured Wladyslaw Talon, popularly known as "Iron Talun," against Ray "Sandy" O'Donnell. Both had drawing power, especially Talon. He had wrestled in Buffalo since the 1930s and invariably before the largest crowds of the season. Talon was a native of Poland; he spoke only Polish. He seemed made for Buffalo; he thrived in the Queen City with its huge Polish immigrant community. In no small way this was because of his close relationship with Teddy Thomas, one of the mainstay referees for wrestling. Thomas had been a wrestler himself; he also spoke Polish. The two became related, Talon married Thomas' sister. Talun was a giant of a man, 6' 8", mighty tall for those times; he weighed 320 pounds and was as strong as an ox. Indeed the nickname Iron came to him because it was believed that he could bend iron bars. Dick Hirsch noted that Talon was a natural for the blue collar town of Buffalo. He rode his bicycle on city streets to keep in shape; sometimes he would stop in a saloon on Buffalo's famous Polish East Side and order a kielbasa and a beer. The natives loved it. In 1951 he went to Hollywood to play the role of Goliath in the film David and Bathsheba. Talon's opponent, Sandy O'Donnell, sometimes referred to as "a hulk of Iowa wrestling machinery" had his own gimmick. He carried an extra $100 bill in his pocket to "shoot in the gym" against anyone who challenged his ability. He hoped that that would stir up the fans.[12]

Even before their meeting in Buffalo, there was bad blood between Talun and O'Donnell. They were supposed to have wrestled in Hamilton, Ontario earlier in the season but the bout was cancelled because of a weird sequence at the last minute. The combatants were taking instructions from the referee near the ring. Nearby was a swimming pool. Iron Talun decided to toss Sandy into the pool, bathrobe and all. Sandy, at best a poor swimmer, had to be rescued. The match never took place in Hamilton. However promoter Monahan, never one to miss a good opportunity, booked them for the Aud. The February meeting between Talon and O'Donnell was a thriller, a classic. The *Courier*'s Ray Ryan called it the best in years. It was marked by an epic brawl; part of the match was fought outside the ropes, some of it actually in press row. Sandy finally won.[13]

A week later, another quality match was staged. This one had a newcomer, Kaye Bell featured against Whipper Watson. The winner was promised a date with Sexton. Bell was an ex-football tackle from Washington State and had played with the Chicago Bears. He was considered a hero of the Bobby Soxers' set. Whipper had been putting on more beef. The more Watson wrestled the more weight he gained and he finally arrived at 235. He was recognized as a full fledged heavyweight. Now he and Bell were similar in build as well as in style and tactics. The match was a good one; the crowd of 6,732 loved it. Watson won. Many of the young women, the Bobby Soxers, were disappointed with the outcome. But their hero, Bell, tried to assuage them, saying that he had "No alibi, he just beat me." The customers got their money's worth because a very attractive undercard program had also been lined up. In the best of those companion contests, Jim "The Goon" Henry won by bashing Friedrich Von Schacht, the 6' 5" Teuton and landing him in the front row seats. He climbed back into the ring and Henry finished him with a body slam.[14]

The wrestling season continued through most of the spring but as the weather warmed up the crowds became a little slimmer. The Friday night cards still featured favorites such as Sexton and Watson, as well as Slidin' Billy Hansen and Chief Saunooke. Attendance was usually between 5,000 and 6,000.

In the first full season since the end of World War II, wrestling in Buffalo had returned big time. The locals loved it and Buffalo's reputation on the national wrestling scene grew. There were even better times ahead. Frank Sexton, the Aud's all star performer would be back along with many other regulars. The cast would include the villains, always fan favorites. There would also be plenty of "truer" wrestlers, sometimes referred to as the scientific wrestlers.

The mat opener for the 1946-47 season pitted Whipper Billy Watson, the pride of Toronto, against Ole Olson, the 6' 6" Swede. "Give Him the Whip" was the familiar cry as Watson's fans welcomed their hero. The Whip complied and emerged victorious before the 4,817 fans. A bigger crowd was anticipated by the promoters but probably should not have been, considering the busy fall sport calendar that was highlighted by the continuing successes of the Buffalo Bills football team. Several newcomers were on the undercard. Paul Boesch a much decorated war veteran, easily outlasted Jim Dolan of Kansas City. Kola Kwariani, a big Russian wore down Toronto's Pat Flanagan. Kola Kwariani, was a real character, one of those often found in the sport of wrestling. Temporarily, at least, this made him a marquee type wrestler. Kwariani claimed to wear the Russian wrestling crown. When he first appeared in Buffalo, he stopped in at the *Buffalo Evening News* offices and said that he was looking for a chess match but also he noted that he had a date to wrestle Frank Sexton. He fancied himself somewhat as a Cold War emissary. He dressed as a Cossack, with a sword dangling from his belt. He announced that there would be no war between Russia and the United States, though he probably had not discussed that with President Harry Truman nor with Premier Josef Stalin. He proceeded to discuss his lengthy wrestling background. He had been wrestling since the age of 12, most of it done in Russia. Now he was on tour.[15] Kwariani did get what he sought, a date with Frank Sexton in the Aud. It turned out as expected. Cy Kritzer, referring to Sexton, as wrestling's uncrowned champion, said that Sexton was able to "airplane-spin" the big Russian to defeat. The more than 6,000 spectators were satisfied. At least some of the onlookers regarded this as a victory for America in the Cold War.

Perhaps the real highlight of the fall wrestling season was the arrival in Buffalo of Primo Carnera. Affectionately called "Da Preem," Carnera had only recently proclaimed himself a professional wrestler. Earlier he had been a professional boxer. That earned him celebrity status. In 1933 he knocked out Jack Sharkey and became heavyweight champion of the world. The following year, he lost the crown to Max Baer. He then experienced a rather mediocre boxing career for a few years, returned to Italy and soon found himself a German prisoner of war. Once the war was over, he returned to the United States, a country he loved, and then turned to wrestling to make some money to send back to Italy so that he could bring his family to America. Americans loved him. The fact that he also donated money from his appearances to the Infantile Paralysis fund did not hurt his reputation. On December 6, 1946, Primo Carnera wrestled Iron Talun before the largest crowd of the season, a sellout of 12,014. He wasted no time in conquering Iron Talun. It only took him 6 minutes to demonstrate his skill at wrestling and he pleased the crowd. He said he found wrestling easier than boxing; wrestling was "not so hard as when Joe Louis hit me." It was Primo's 90th straight victory on this recent American tour.[16]

1947 started off with some of the old favorites still in good form. Frank Sexton beat Sandy O'Donnell, before more than 6,000, and Strangler Bob Wagner, now recognized as the chief villain on the local scene, was victorious over popular Vic Christy before nearly 7,000. Then a sad note hit the local wrestling scene. Jerry Monahan, the matchmaker for the Great Lakes Athletic Club for the previous two years, passed away at his home in Crystal Beach, Ontario. He had been suffering from an incurable ailment for nearly a year but had been able to remain active until very recently. Monahan was fondly remembered. Earlier he had had a respectable career as a wrestler in the western part of the United States, then he came to Buffalo to work with Jack Herman the President of the GLAC, in the promotion of wrestling. He was a significant figure in making the sport of wrestling a success in the Queen City.

Two weeks later, Jack Herman appointed Ed Don George, already one of the best known figures in local and national wrestling circles, to be his matchmaker, with the title of Vice President of the Athletic Club. Ed Don George did not miss a beat. Ed Don's first big challenge was the Parade of Champions, the annual extravaganza that had become the highlight of the wrestling season. It had become a classic, indeed a veritable wrestling institution. Even during the Second World War, the event drew more than 10,000 each year. In 1946, 10,317 had turned out to watch Frank Sexton defeat Chief Saunooke. Sexton again led the Parade of Champions program in 1947. This time, Sandy O'Donnell was selected as his opponent. 10,116 fans were thrilled by the "sheer artistry" displayed by Sexton. He invented two new holds which he worked successfully on O'Donnell. One was a full nelson manipulated with both feet, and the other was a pinwheel twist worked from a wristlock and a drop of the right leg. But Cy Kritzer concluded it was Sexton's sheer power and strength that finally subdued O'Donnell.[17]

For the spring of 1947, Ed Don George had one more card up his sleeve. He knew that Frank Sexton planned to leave on some sort of a world tour. But he thought that if he could schedule a match between Sexton and the Angel, Maurice Tillet, it would be a fantastic success. He was right. The event took place on May 2 and drew 11,763. Sexton beat the Angel. Most of the fans were pleased but many were in a dilemma because they also were fans of the Angel. Thousands swarmed around his dressing room before and after his battle with Sexton. The Angel might have been a gruesome looking figure but he was also likeable. When, for instance, during the clash, Sexton had to retire to his dressing room for a few minutes for some repairs, the Angel stayed in the ring and leaned over the ropes to shake hands with many of the assembled.

As it developed, Ed Don was able to stage a number of first rate wrestling cards in the closing months of the 1946-47 season. Bigger crowds than corresponding months in previous years turned out which was a testimony to Ed Don's expertise as a matchmaker. In one encounter Frank Sexton put the finishing touches on Bobby Bruns before 7,749 fans. Another Friday night saw Primo Carnera pin Wee Willie Davis before 9,411 fans. One event that did not turn out as well as expected featured Frank Sexton against Bronko Nagurski. There was a big build up promoting the match but fewer than 6000 fans showed up. Both contestants were well known, Sexton for his many wrestling accomplishments especially in the Buffalo area, and Nagurski for his gridiron feats that made him one of the most outstanding football players of the 20th century. Nagurski was an All American at the University of Minnesota. He played fullback on offense (one of the biggest backs of his era) and tackle on defense. In the 1930s he played professional football for the Chicago Bears. Following his retirement from football, he took up professional wrestling and was now making his Buffalo debut. Unfortunately Nagurski was recovering from an injury and was not in top shape. Sexton was able to pin the bulky football star. Both would return to grapple another day.

Meanwhile Ed Don George kept busy searching for new talent. When the new season, 1947- 48, rolled around, the match-maker had several newcomers ready to try out their talents before the Buffalo sports fans. Perhaps the most impressive of the new-comers was 6 foot 9 inch Texas "High" Lee. In his initial outing, he whipped his opponent, Tom Collins of Hamilton, Ontario with a bear hug in just over 7 minutes. A second new-comer, Angelo Cistodi, fresh from touring the lumber camps in the North Country won, with little trouble, over Buddy Curtis. Ed Don signed Lee and Cistodi for future engagements.

The first big card of the new season took place on October 3. It featured Friedrich Von Schacht against Frank Sexton. The latter, still the big local hero, found himself in more trouble than he had encountered in many of his recent bouts. At one point, handsome Frank was yanked out of the ring feet first and his body slammed on the terrazzo floor. But Sexton rebounded and proceeded to floor von Schacht where he was counted out by the referee while the 6,933 onlookers howled in delight. A month later, Sexton, again, beat von Schacht before almost 7,000.

While Ed Don George was sorting out wrestlers in the fall of 1947 to determine who would fit best into the spring schedule, he was also faced with the prospect of television playing a role in his future plans. Network television would make its formal debut in May of 1948 but for some months prior there were discussions taking place that focused on the role of the new medium and what impact it would have.

Experimental programming was going to take place, and wrestling was seen as one of the suitable events to be televised. Television would eventually, though not quite yet, take its place alongside newspapers and radio as a significant part of the sports scene in America. It would come to dominate virtually all sports. Most observers simply could not anticipate the revolutionary impact that television would have. Radio itself was a fairly recent development. Many sports figures had worried about radio's impact on attendance as recently as the 1930s. However by the mid 1940s radio was accepted and welcomed; rather than hurt attendance it was felt that it actually helped. Therefore many reasoned that television would have a similarly healthy impact on attendance. Ed Don George said he had seen television in Chicago and it had made new fans there and would do so in Buffalo. Boxing promoter Jack Singer indicated that he was very interested in having his boxing bouts on television. He felt that once fans had seen boxing on "TV," then they would want to attend in person. Baseball officials said essentially the same thing.[18]

On February 13, 1948, Buffalo's first television station, WBEN-TV, opened the new era in communications. 400 spectators were invited to the Hotel Lafayette that evening to watch the wrestling matches televised from Memorial Auditorium. The event was also billed as the first television program in the history of the city. Among those in attendance at this inaugural event, sponsored by RCA, were a number of radio dealers, and press and radio representatives. The wrestling contest pitted Friedrich Otto von Schacht against Lou Thesz. It was a good choice. Von Schacht was always entertaining; he was a true crowd pleaser. Lou Thesz, the old pro, had national stature. Thesz won, von Schacht verbally disputed the decision.The crowd itself was enthusiastic. Ed Kelly of the *Buffalo Evening News* described in detail how the filming and transmission took place. Cameras showed fans and celebrities as well as the action. Sports Editor Bob Stedler devoted his Saturday column to the historic event. He said that the reaction was generally good, as were the pictures and the coverage. The Lafayette Hotel observers liked what they saw, especially the close ups of the wrestlers. Stedler felt that new fans were made but he noted that the carnival spirit of a sports event was missing. The yelling and screaming were absent. In a separate news item, Ed Don George reiterated his conviction that the wrestling card on television made new fans.[19]

A week earlier the annual mid winter classic, the Parade of Champions had taken place. Ed Don anticipated the usual large turnout; Bob Stedler noted that the tradition of the classic would assure a huge crowd. Both were correct. In fact the Parade of Champions wrestling card produced the largest advance sale in history. Ed Don could have sold all the seats as reserved seats but wisely held back 3,000 for general admission. Those ticket buyers "are the backbone of any sports enterprise" the promoter affirmed. 12,365 fans passed through the turnstiles. It was a sell out, the largest wrestling crowd in Buffalo's history. More than 5,000 waited to get in but were disappointed. The main event on the star studded card was a crowd pleaser; it featured Frank Sexton against Strangler Bob Wagner, "The Portland Bulldog." Wagner had defeated every top wrestler of the past decade when each was at his best, except Sexton. The press played this up, emphasizing that Columbus Frank was the lone barrier to Wagner's perfect record. The big throng got its money's worth. "After 52 minutes of slams, tackles, gouging, elbow-smashing, blood, thunder, and crashing of bodies," Sexton received the decision of the judges. The crowd was ecstatic. For the 4th straight year, Sexton won the featured event in the Parade of Champions.[20] The overflow crowd also loved the undercard. Lou Thesz defeated George "KO" Koverly. Thesz won when he knocked Koverly over the ropes and KO hung outside with his feet entangled in the hemp. The referee counted him out while he was hanging upside down.

Following the successful Parade of Champions classic, the wrestling season seemed to meander along in the late winter and early spring until it reached a blazing climax at the very time that the coming of the age of television was a big news item. May 14, 1948 would witness the formal beginning of WBEN-TV. Whether television would attract new wrestling fans remained uncertain. But there was absolutely no doubt about another newcomer on the scene. Gorgeous George would draw thousands of fans and would do so over and over again.

Gorgeous George was an instant sensation in Buffalo. If one conducted a survey of old time Buffalonians today, there would seem to be little doubt that the one name in Buffalo sports history, from that time period, that many would recall above all others would be Gorgeous George.

He first set foot on Buffalo ground on May 11, 1948. He was scheduled for a match three days later. Gorgeous George was new to Buffalo, but he had been involved in the sport of wrestling for several years. His name

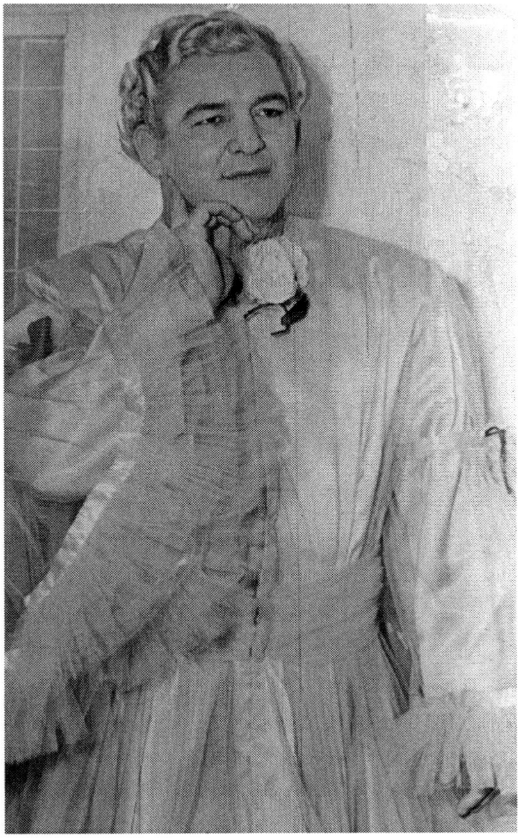

Gorgeous George, in one of his many satin robes.
Photo: D. Valenzuela, Buffalo News

originally was George Wagner. During the Depression years, he had wrestled on the West Coast where he established a name for himself as a good wrestler. He was not big. He stood 5' 9" and weighed 210, but he was solid muscle. He was tough, he knew many holds and. as he gained experience, wrestling experts came to regard him as one of the best in the business.

In 1943, George Wagner changed his name, legally, to Gorgeous George. He dyed his hair and donned exotic clothing. Overnight he became a dynamite gate attraction. He began to command a big sum of money for his appearances. At a time when the run of the mill wrestlers were making $8,000 to $10,000 a year, he was hauling in about $70,000 annually. He had three high-priced automobiles, a chauffeur and a valet. Gorgeous George owned 870 elaborate expensive robes, fashioned in all sorts of exotic colors. George was a precursor of some of today's overpaid sports celebrities who live a garish lifestyle.

Ed Don George attended the Rose bowl game in Pasadena on New Years Day, 1948 and while in Southern California he watched Gorgeous George perform. He was impressed. Knowing that Gorgeous was in demand in the cities of the Northeast, Ed Don George signed him for a May 14th date with Joe Page. Wrestling's latest sensation nationally, quickly became and would remain a dominant and compelling figure on the Buffalo wrestling scene for the next several years. Page was quickly forgotten.

As soon as he arrived in town, Gorgeous George left no doubt that he was an import straight out of Hollywood. He checked in at the Statler Hotel with his usual fanfare. As he approached his 16th floor suite he asked for James, his valet, to spray the doorway with disinfectant. Gorgeous George sniffed, nodded his approval, then he entered. Gorgeous George knew the promotion game. He knew what the fans wanted. He knew what it took to be a big time celebrity. As soon as he arrived, as was his custom, he headed to the beauty salon to have his signature hair style, his Lana Turner style blond curls, fixed properly.[21] On the night of his match in Memorial Auditorium, a tumultuous crowd turned out, Ray Ryan called it a turn away crowd of 11,845. His entrance on to the floor of the arena was a big part of his show. He wore one of the 80 silken robes that he had brought with him on his trip east. He hated germs with a passion. When he entered the ring, James, his valet, preceded him with his flit gun, spraying high and low, and all around. Ryan said that George was at this best before the bout. He posed for photographers, he sneered at some of the fans whom he asserted were beneath him, and when a spectator brushed against him he turned to his valet and said: "remind me to burn this suit tonight." Gorgeous George's entrance was stirring and exciting. Special music heralded his arrival. His valet disinfected the ring then parted the ropes for Gorgeous to enter. Quickly, the valet brushed a speck off his black velvet robe generously adorned with gold sequins. Once in the ring, his valet sprayed a perfumed disinfectant; George bore himself regally and sneered at the onlookers, the "peasants."[22] For many the bout itself was a bit anti-climatic. Gorgeous George showed not only showmanship but also acrobatic wrestling ability. He was no fluke as a wrestler. He proceeded to pin Joe Page. The crowd was actually somewhat disappointed. At the very least they had hoped to see Gorgeous George's hair pulled out.

The Buffalo public came to know Gorgeous George the celebrity more and more as time passed. On one occasion he slipped into one of his exotic robes, climbed into the back of a convertible, and was driven around busy Lafayette Square in the middle of downtown Buffalo. As crowds gathered, Gorgeous tossed out $1 and $10 bills to the onlookers. The highlight of the last part of the wrestling season was, once again, Gorgeous George. He was pitted against Strangler Bob Wagner. Another banner crowd of more than 10,000 turned out. The bout was quick but it was an absolute crowd pleaser. It was marked by plenty of action, some humor, and several colorful asides. Charley Young of the *News* said it best, "true, Gorgeous George lost a bloody, sensational battle to Wagner in only 7:25, but there was more action in those few minutes than in all the rest of the card combined." Ed Don George was so pleased that he was ready to sign up Gorgeous immediately and for a hefty figure for future features on his mat cards.[23]

In the summer of 1948 the Olympic games returned to the world of sports. The two previously scheduled Olympiads had been cancelled because of the Second World War. The first postwar games were held in London. Ed Don George, himself a former Olympian, spent time there and also traveled to Paris. Wrestling was undergoing a rebirth in Europe just as it was in the United States. Ed Don had traveled abroad to line up young wrestlers for future programs in Buffalo. He succeeded in doing that and newcomers began to appear on the Friday night mat cards in the 1948-49 wrestling season. But, as expected, Gorgeous George was again the top attraction. His appearance in the Aud on October 29 caused as much excitement as ever. He opponent was George Becker, another star imported from the west coast.

Before the bout began, the action was held up for more than 10 minutes in order to allow Gorgeous George's valet to spray the path into the arena presumably freeing the air of germs. Special rugs were laid down for the grand entrance. This worked up the fans. A new song entitled "Gorgeous George" blared over the microphones. Fortunately the song was quickly forgotten. Then Gorgeous George made his way toward the ring and the music changed to the strains of "Pomp and Circumstance." Everyone stood; no one wanted to miss any part of the show. George strutted like an Oriental potentate; he looked over his "subjects" contemptuously and in a low tone uttered "peasants be seated."

The bout did not last long. Referee Teddy Thomas called a quick fall at 18:16 in George's favor. Cy Kritzer claimed that the reason for the snappy decision was that the referee was not used to the germ killer mixed with perfume. It was called "intoxicating."[24] The crowd, detesting Gorgeous and all his antics, or at least pretending to, joined the defeated George Becker protesting the decision. Becker had tossed Gorgeous all over the place, but Gorgeous scored the only fall that counted and he pinned Becker. The

8,016 fans wanted George's scalp and Becker did everything but give it to them. Becker would have a chance for redemption against Gorgeous a few weeks later.

In the meantime, Frank Sexton proved that he still had drawing power. Ed Don had him take on Nanjo Singh, the "hustling Hindu." Singh offered 1,000 rupees to any opponent who could break his cobra hold, his signature weapon that he had presumably learned in the jungles of India. 8,457 showed up anxious to see if Sexton could do it. Singh's offer still stood since before he had a chance to finish Sexton off with it, Sexton rallied and pinned Singh. Sexton barely squeezed out a victory. Two weeks later Frank Sexton and Nanjo Singh met again. Singh, once again, could not get the cobra hold to work against Sexton. This time there was no doubt that Sexton was the winner. "Frank gave another inimitable lesson of strategy and holds."[25]

Meanwhile, the Gorgeous George – George Becker rematch took place. More than 9,000 were on hand. The result was similar to their previous outing. Becker dropped a hotly disputed fall to Gorgeous. It appeared to most fans that Gorgeous George had used the ropes illegally. The referee's decision provoked outrage. The crowd was up in arms. All sorts of things were thrown at Gorgeous. The ring was literally covered with liter. Becker and his brother, who was also his second, added their two cents. They attacked the winner, harassing him all the way to his dressing room, punching and berating him along the way.

Whether Gorgeous George appeared as the feature or whether a lesser known celebrity was the main attraction, large crowds continued. Buffalo was riding the crest of wrestling mania. The new calendar year, 1949, opened with Primo Carnera taking on High Lee. It was another very good drawing card.

A short time later, another perennial crowd pleaser, the French Angel, Maurice Tillet, appeared in Memorial Auditorium. Ed Don scheduled him to wrestle against Slidin' Billy Hansen. There were a number of "Angels" on the wrestling scene, from various parts of the wrestling universe. But the French one was the most famous and Buffalo was fortunate to have him appear on a regular basis. According to Ed Don, Tillet was the best draw over the years averaging 10,000 a performance. The Angel celebrated his 10th mat year, and 22nd appearance, in Buffalo by pinning Hansen. Tillet's manager shrewdly allowed the Angel to wrestle in any one city no more than three times per year. This made Tillet an even bigger attraction. This time 8,626 turned out in Buffalo's Aud. The Angel had just returned from drawing similar crowds in Rome, Lisbon, London, and Antwerp.

Meanwhile Gorgeous George had returned to Buffalo. He had been on the West Coast where he continued to be a sensation. In fact in 30 appearances in Los Angeles in recent years, he performed before a sold out arena 20 times. He continued to wrestle before capacity houses as he made his way east toward the mecca of indoor sports in America, Madison Square Garden. George's itinerary resembled that of a theatrical production headed for the Great White Way on Broadway. Buffalo and St. Louis had become known as two of the nation's best wrestling towns. Gorgeous George had "tried out" successfully in those two good sized cities, now he was ready for his debut in "The Big Apple." He was well groomed for his initial appearance in the Garden. He was a hit there; obviously it would not be his last trip to New York City.

Back in Buffalo, Ed Don George arranged for Ray Villmer, famous for his airplane spin, to be George's opponent. George was awarded a hotly contested fall over Villmer. As usual the fans were hissing and booing. The winner's striking turquoise robe with pink borders and long flowing sleeves just egged on the rowdy onlookers. A week later,

Gorgeous George wrestled again, and again he defeated Villmer. It was a throwback to their earlier battle. A month later, Gorgeous George and the Angel were on the same card, and they proved once again their drawing power when the largest crowd of the season, well over 11,000, turned out.

The Parade of Champions was held on April 8; as usual it was a box office success as 10,282 mat fans passed through the turnstiles. The appetite of every discerning fan was certain to be satisfied, such was the star studded mat card. Frank Sexton was featured in the feature. That had become a tradition. His opponent was "Tiny" Lee of Houston. Mike Kanaley of the *Courier Express* noted that Sexton used his specialty, the giant swing, as a softener, and then pinned his opponent with a reverse scissors. Ivan Rasputin, the bearded Russian, pinned Bobby Bruns, and Whipper Watson defeated Wee Willie Davis. Other matches on the Parade card included Sandy O'Donnell and Mike Sharpe. This "pair of mammoths" ended up in a draw, but their bout was filled with lots of action. It was a real crowd pleaser, as was the curtain raiser that "sent the card off to an arousing start" when Montreal's Larry Moquin blasted Mike Mihalakis into submission. Bob Stedler, sports editor of the *Buffalo Evening News* sang the praises of Ed Don George and the Parade of Champions. Stedler noted that the total attendance for the 11 years of the Parade's existence, including the 1949 figures, was 109,319. That was incredible. One of the main reasons for the success was the fact that Promoter Ed Don carefully filled the undercard with a cast of all star performers.[26]

In May the mat season drew to a close; it kind of whimpered away with only 3,339 paying customers passing through the turnstiles. It was almost summertime, and wrestling fans had plenty of other things to do in Buffalo during the warm months. Sexton closed out the season by pinning Ivan Rasputin in the featured finale. The low attendance figure was definitely not characteristic of a Sexton match.

Frank Sexton was undeniably the top wrestler in Buffalo during these immediate post-war years. He was an accomplished and skillful practitioner of the art of wrestling. He invariably drew large crowds; he was admired by the fans and the press. But the road to success had not always been smooth for Sexton. When he first started out on a career in wrestling back in 1938 he had "illusions of grandeur." He came to Buffalo from Columbus after a successful undergraduate career at The Ohio State University. He was a bit pushy; he more or less demanded some bookings. Jerry Monahan, who was then himself a wrestler, and had not yet become the matchmaker, advised Sexton to go out and learn how to wrestle. But Sexton would not listen. He signed for various local bouts. He would build up a lead and then, displaying his amateurishness, he proceeded to get fooled time and time again. He ended up losing 14 matches in a row. So he went to Monahan and asked for advice again. He was advised to take to the road. Sexton headed south and into the Midwest and then to Texas. He began to learn. Each time out he would work on some new holds.[27]

Frank Sexton served his apprenticeship. He lived out of a suitcase in dingy hotels, traveling thousands of miles on old buses and cinder sprayed railroads, performing in "tank" towns, before skimpy crowds, several nights a week. But he learned and he improved. He eventually made it to the top of the wrestling ladder in Buffalo. He became a perfectionist, a man of "10,000 holds" and a recognized champion. In the late 1940s, Frank Sexton was acknowledged as the king of wrestling in Buffalo.

In the summer of 1949 Ed Don George again went on a recruiting trip, this time logging more than 3,500 miles which in itself was somewhat of a feat in this early age of aviation. When he returned he announced that his travels convinced him that the wrestling revival was continuing and that television was giving it an assist. He also indicated that he would continue with the policy begun last season of televising the preliminaries for an hour each Friday night. He said that he was "keen to see the reaction of Buffalo fans to Seelie Samara, the 250 pound Negro, former British Empire champion." Promoters in Australia said Samara was the biggest drawing card there. Another prized prospect, who attracted Ed Don's attention, was Tarzan Kowalski, 22-year- old from Detroit. Both newcomers performed satisfactorily in preliminaries in the fall season.

The first major wrestling card in the fall of 1949 fell on November 11. It featured Gorgeous George against Mayes McLain. The semi final saw Angelo Cistoldi of Italy against Johnny Barend of Rochester. But the highlight of the evening proved to be the debut on the local scene of one of the great crowd pleasers of all time, Yukon Eric Holmback of Fairbanks, Alaska. In short order, he would come to rival even Gorgeous George, as a wrestling icon in the eyes of Western New York fans.

Yukon had arrived in Buffalo a few weeks earlier. He soon made his presence known. He stormed into Memorial Auditorium, marched right down to the ring and challenged any wrestler in the area. Twice he was tossed out of the Aud and his ticket money refunded. So Ed Don concluded that the only way to get Yukon "out of his hair" was to give him a spot on the November 11 card. He was scheduled to face Dan O'Connor, a pretty fair wrestler from Boston.[28]

7,535 fans were on hand for this Armistice Day wrestling show. It was the best turnout of the early season. Most paid their admission to watch the typical Gorgeous George extravaganza. His robe was pink satin trimmed with white lace on green insets. He had a jeweled golden clasp on his neck at a time when most fans did not even know what gold bling was. His entrance followed the usual pattern. His valet preceded him, carrying the silver tray bearing the silver atomizer; he sprayed everything in sight. Gorgeous followed with his haughty demeanor and gold locks and proceeded to toss gold Georgie pins to the fans. As for the match itself; it was not very exciting. George won, as expected. But the two other matches stole the show. Rochester Johnny Barend applied one of his flying head scissors holds that led to the downfall of Cistoldi. The crowd loved it but even more they loved Yukon Eric. O'Connor, punched, heaved and finally tackled Yukon but to no avail. Finally Yukon lifted O'Connor twice for a slam and a press and that was the match.

Ed Don was enormously impressed with Yukon. He took the time to furnish the press with information on his latest mat hero. Yukon Eric was born in Alaska; he worked there as a lumberjack and a dog team driver. Ed Don said he checked his own notebook and concluded that he had never seen a man like the enormous Yukon. He had the biggest chest on record, 67 ½ inches; he stood 6'2"and weighed 275 pounds. Ed Don received stacks of mail about Yukon, the fans loved him. He quickly signed him for a feature on November 18 against Angelo Cistoldi. Yukon took care of Cistoldi posthaste. It did not require much effort; the big Alaskan simply had too much power for his opponent. There were others on the Friday night card that made a big hit with the fans. These included Seelie Samara "the flashy Negro" and Tarzan Kowalski. Each of them won. Each hoped for a shot at Primo Carnera who was to headline the next wrestling card in the Queen City.

Yukon returned a few weeks later. On December 10 he faced Hi Lee. The crowds

Yukon Eric, Huge barrel-chested wrestler from the North.
Photo: D. Valenzuela, Buffalo Evening News

were getting better. Only 5,004 showed up for the Yukon-Cistold match, but almost 8,000 turned out for Yukon's tussle with Hi Lee. The crowd ogled and awed, and blinked their eyes in amazement at Yukon's 67 ½ inch chest as he took off his tundra type, checked woolen shirt, tightened the rope that held up his dungarees and went to work on his opponent. The Alaskan goldminer and woodsman turned professional wrestler, made short work of his opponent. He again demonstrated the same phenomenal power "that has made him the wonder of his fellow wrestlers, local gyms, and barbell salons."

Overnight, Yukon Eric had become a celebrity. His trademark outfit, huge dungarees, large enough to serve as a tent for 5 or 6 boy scouts, his plaid woolen shirt and lumberjack boots made him easily recognizable, which his size would have done anyway, as he made his way around Buffalo. He would stop at places such as the Alcobar Restaurant on Delaware Avenue in Kenmore where impressionable youngsters would stare in wonderment as this giant of a man literally lumbered out of his convertible.

In between the Yukon Eric appearances, Frank Sexton returned to the Buffalo scene. Sexton, it seems had to play second fiddle to both Gorgeous George and Yukon Eric, at least for a while. But the much admired Sexton was always welcomed by the Buffalo wrestling fans. Ed Don arranged for him to meet Seelie Samura, "the cool Negro matman," now also referred to as the "popular Negro grappler." Samura surprised the "sharps," as well as the 6,023 fans, by holding Sexton to a draw.

A week later, Yukon was again the feature, and this time it was his turn to take on Samura. 6817 of the regulars witnessed the two of them match each other for the first seven minutes. Then Yukon, the barrel chested tower of strength, turned ferocious and tossed Samura into a corner where he suffered a shoulder injury. This caused the referee to call the match for Yukon. On the night before New York's Eve, Yukon took on Ivan Rasputin. Promoters usually wrote off that particular night of the year, as a box office bust, but they were nicely surprised by the crowd of 9,484. It was the largest of the season to date. Yukon, with what was appropriately labeled his "Icicle hold," chilled Ivan. It was the Alaskan's 5th straight victory. Yukon also handily defeated Wee Willie Davis a week later for his 6th straight.

It appeared that everyone, or at least all major challengers, who wanted a shot at the huge lumberjack, would get the opportunity. Next for Yukon Eric was Nanjo "the Mad Hindu" Singh. The fight took place on January 20 before the second largest wrestling crowd of all time. Originally the turnstile figure was announced as 11,917. However a recount of ticket stubs and turnstile numbers was completed the day after the match and the new figure of 12,296 was disclosed. The *Buffalo Evening News* claimed that as many as 9,000 fans were turned away. The police estimated that when the 4,000 general admission tickets went on sale, there were more than 13,000 people trying to buy them. No standing room tickets were sold. The *News* also thought that television may have been partly responsible for the huge crowd. Many fans had seen Singh and his cobra hold on television previously and now wanted to see how Eric, their latest hero, would cope with his cobra wielding opponent.[29]

The majority of those in the arena that night were solidly behind Yukon Eric. He had won them over with his Paul Bunyon-like strength and his conventional or straight wrestling. But Singh was confident. In his two previous outings he had put his opponents out of commission with his famous cobra hold. Both victims were carried unconscious from the ring. Singh managed to get Yukon in his cobra hold but outside the ropes and when Singh was warned and would not get back, then Singh was counted out. Ed Don was happy because he believed the cobra hold was illegal and wanted the Alaskan to erase Singh from the local wrestling scene.[30]

Ed Don George lined up the two most successful grapplers he could find for the first Friday in March. That meant Yukon Eric of course, and Freddie Atkins, an Australian, who had recently held the British Empire crown. Atkins played the role of the villain, he punched, and kneed Yukon and ripped him with elbow smashes but the strength of Yukon prevailed once again. Referee Teddy Thomas, himself battered a bit by Atkins, awarded Yukon the victory. Yukon clearly showed that he was learning how to cope with villains. The crowd of slightly more than 5,000 was pleased.

Ed Don George then announced that he was leaving on a talent hunt to New York City as well as to the Midwest to line up the card for the annual Parade of Champions. The upstate A.C. sent an urgent cable to Frank Sexton who was in Europe, urging his return immediately so that he could take his usual spot on the Parade of Champions mat card.[31]

The annual Parade of Champions was held on March 31, 1950. Ed Don George had arranged an all star cast. His reward was an attendance that topped 11,000. The fans were not disappointed. Ed Don lined up Suni Warcloud, the Indian heavyweight wrestler. Warcloud was managed by Jim Thorpe, the greatest athlete of the first half of the 20th century. The giant Wee Willie Davis was Warcloud's opponent. Suni entered the ring wrapped in his Red Indian blanket and topped with an eagle feathered head dress. He then performed a little war dance. Thirteen minutes later he let out a big war hoop and produced a hold that he called an Indian death stretch. That hold tangled Davis' legs in something judo experts called a grape vine. Then Warcloud exerted pressure and Davis was forced to quit. War Cloud went into his victory dance and the Aud rocked with cheers.

There was much more to the evening's program. One might be tempted to compare it to a modern day all star rock concert. Kay "Samson" Bell was there in his shepherd's cloak and knee-high sheepskin sandals. He faced Maurice "the Angel" Tillet who needed no accoutrements, he had his easily recognizable face. The Angel had to withstand some rough tactics by Kay Samson Bell, before he finally clamped a bear hug on Bell and was awarded the victory.

There was Ali "Turk" Bey in his fez and carrying a prayer rug. He defeated Tiger Tasker in less than 13 minutes, when he grabbed Tiger around the middle and simply squeezed until he gave up. There was also Steve "Mr. America" Stanlee in his leopard skin. He took a terrific pounding from Dr. Len Hall, but recovered enough to earn a draw. There also was Laverne Baxter who used slashing backhand chops to soften up Ray

McClarity. In just over 12 minutes, McClarity caved in.

Without doubt it was the most action packed card of the season. The crowd was in a frenzy. They loved all the excitement, and the variety, the villains, the straight wrestlers, and the entire menagerie provided by Ed Don George and his company.

All of these bouts were worthy of the hearty applause given by the fans. Had the evening ended there, the fans would have left the Aud contented. But there was more. There was the Johnny Barend - Lord Blears contest, and that one stole the show. Lord Blears appeared in his homemade tunic and monocle. Johnny Barend was the guy without the "gimmick." What happened was this. Twenty minutes into the bout, Referee George Baltz said that Barend quit under the pressure of a leglock. Barend emphatically said he did not quit. He staged a sitdown in the middle of the ring. Many in the crowd wanted to see the bout continue. All sorts of things were tossed down on the ring. Chaos reigned. Special policemen, announcers, seconds, judges and miscellaneous staff tried and finally lured Johny Barend out of the ring. Barend left just in time for the next bout to begin, but not before a period of bedlam had taken place.[32]

Another successful Parade of Champions was now over. Once again it was another feather in Ed Don George's cap. But the season was far from over. Ed Don and company had embarked upon a marathon season; top flight wrestling cards would continue through the spring and well into the summer months. Ed Don was giving the public what they wanted and what they wanted was wrestling and lots of it complete with gimmicks, villains, newcomers, the whole works.

A week following the Parade, Suni Warcloud was again the feature. He was pitted against a relative newcomer, Laverne Baxter. It was a short but sweet match, the fans enjoyed it. Baxter instigated the fireworks. He promised that he "would scatter a few feathers around the ring" as he took on the celebrated Indian protege of Jim Thorpe, wearing his large fancy headdress. In the first few minutes the Aud crowd of 4,528 was howling as Baxter felled Warcloud with an elbow smash and pounded him with fists and knees with little regard for Referee Teddy Thomas' warnings. But Warcloud recovered, got the upper hand and let loose with his war whoop, went into his war dance and then applied a leg lock that finished off Baxter.

In mid-April, a Blears–Barend rematch took place. Again Blears won, again it was disputed. But the 8,386 customers got their money's worth, as they did with another of the undercard matches, that being the one between Laverne Baxter and Hi Lee. Many veteran mat customers were pleased with that outcome, glad to see Hi Lee lose. The fans felt that the main match featuring Suni Warcloud and Friedrick Otto von Schacht paled by comparison.

On the last Friday in April, Gorgeous George was featured against Lord Blears. The crowd of 9,032 got an eyeful. Gorgeous made his usual entrance. He wore a rose and pink chiffon creation, a pale orchid on the left shoulder, and a bouquet of roses "strategically placed so as to be crushed if Gorgeous sat down."[33] Jeffrey sprayed cologne, and Gorgeous paraded into the arena to the chords of Pomp and Circumstance. But Lord Jan Blears had his own routine. He tried to outdo Gorgeous, but did not quite succeed. He arrived in a royal purple robe. His valet, Captain Leslie Holmes assisted him in taking off his tunic and removing his monocle. Then the wrestling began and after trading holds and blows, George pinned Blears and was declared the winner. Blears protested. Captain Holmes reacted vigorously and he attempted to pin Jeffrey, his valet counterpart. In turn, Gorgeous pinned Captain Holmes and Lord Blears pinned Jeffrey. The crowd loved it; some of the fans thought that Barnum and Bailey's annual appearance in the Aud had arrived early this year.

Next one of the famous Duseks came to town. The brothers' Dusek, there were five of them, wrestled in various parts of the country, and were headliners if for no other reason then that there were five of them. Ernie Dusek was the toughest and fastest of the quintet. Ernie Dusek had had a good match in Omaha two weeks earlier. He was victorious over Primo Carnera. Ed Don George sought him out. However as Charley Young of the *Buffalo Evening News* noted, Dusek had Ed Don over a barrel. Dusek demanded that he wrestle Yukon Eric or he would move on to other pastures. Dusek got his wish. On May 12, before just 4,053 customers, Yukon finished off Dusek with little difficulty. Dusek tried all sorts of holds on Eric who proceeded to break all of them with the help of his massive chest. Then Dusek gave up. Such was the fleeting moment in the sun for one of the Duseks, the so-called famous Duseks, in the Memorial Auditorium wrestling program.[34]

The big names continued to appear in the Aud in the summer of 1950. The biggest night, August 4, featured two of the biggest celebrities, Gorgeous George against the Angel. This was Gorgeous George's 13th match in Buffalo. Though he claimed not to worry about the 13th he did go out of his way to wear the robe with orchid lining trimmed with rosettes, the same outfit that he had worn in his first Buffalo outing. In stark contrast the Angel appeared in his well worn robe and black tights. The two headliners tussled to the delight of the fans for a while. The end came when Gorgeous George launched a drop kick which struck the Angel in the back of the neck and flung him into the ropes. As the Angel rebounded George flung him on his back and Referee Teddy Thomas proceeded to beat the floor three times. The Angel disagreed. Most of the crowd of 10,935 was on the Angel's side, and they too voiced disagreement. The decision stuck. In the semi final, Suni War Cloud continued his winning ways with a triumph over Joe "Hammerlock" Montana. War Cloud was aroused by some of Montana's antics so he went into his war dance and ended up with an Indian death lock on Montana. By this time, War Cloud was recognized as one of the stars in the Upstate Athletic Club wrestling stable.[35]

The final mat program of the season took place on the last day of August. It featured two of the most recent stars in the Ed Don George's galaxy, Johnny Barend and Farmer Don Marlin. Both were experts in the use of their feet. Barend, the Rochester Flash, specialized in flying dropkicks, while Marlin, aka "Scaffler" relied on the mule kick. The new season was just three weeks away, and this meant that Barend and Marlin along with other local wrestlers were contending for Ed Don George's favor for future billing. Each hoped to land a feature spot on the upcoming fall program. Marlin the backwoods character clad in dungarees sometimes referred to as the Mule Kicker from Niles, Michigan, was the favorite. However Barend won, his drop kicks proved decisive. A surprisingly good Labor Day weekend turnout was thoroughly satisfied once again.

The crowd of 7,476 for the Barend-Marlin bout brought the total for the 1949-50 season to 265,396 fans. 42 shows had been held; the average crowd was more than 6,000 per evening. The total figure was nearly 100,000 more than the previous year. Wrestling topped all other sports in the Buffalo area in attendance for the 1949-50 season. The two local newspapers were in agreement; wrestling in Buffalo had hit its zenith. The *Courier* stated that the curtain was lowered "on the most successful season in Buffalo wrestling history." Cy Kritzer called it "a phenomenal wrestling season" and asserted that it "established Ed Don George as the East's top promoter." Ed Don George, himself, said he expected no problem filling his Friday night cards now that "Buffalo has been established as one of the three top wrestling centers of the country." Ed Don noted that "word of that 265,000 attendance we registered spread like fire throughout the wrestling firmament." He added "No more do I have to bid for the cream of the crop. Every top flight wrestler is making himself available for Buffalo shows."[36]

On the surface it appeared that the wrestling programs in Buffalo and elsewhere in the country would continue to be successful for the foreseeable future. But "Times were a-changing." Factors were at work that would erode the Buffalo sports scene as the decade wore on. Television sets began to be sold by the car load. Young families began to move to suburbia in increasing numbers. Moving vans loaded with all sorts of new appliances including Philco, Sylvania, and Dumont TV sets were part of the emigration. While the suburbs boomed in the 1950s, downtown Buffalo continued to be a vibrant scene of activity, though not quite as vibrant as in the 1940s.

As the new decade moved along, the old favorites of the mat continued to draw good crowds. Wrestling continued to be successful in Buffalo in the 1950s and into the 1960s. Ed Don George's Parade of Champions continued to be a blue ribbon event.

Ed Don George left the Buffalo scene in the mid 1950s. He turned over the district mat card to Pedro Martinez.[37] Pedro did well as a promoter. Many new faces appeared on the wrestling scene. Some cards drew sizeable crowds.

Among the new wrestlers, one, especially, stood out. That was Ilio DiPaolo. He had emigrated from Italy in 1951 and first wrestled in Buffalo in 1955. He met Pedro Martinez who became his father-in-law. Ilio became a regular star attraction on Pedro's Aud mat cards over the next decade. He wrestled his way into the hearts of Buffalo fans and remained there for years to come

Ilio DiPaolo - for many years, an Aud favorite.
Photo: Dennis DiPaolo.

DiPaolo was joined on the local scene by Dick Beyer. "The Destroyer," as Beyer was dubbed, was another big star of the era of the '50s and early '60s. In fact, he arrived on the scene already a celebrity. He had been an outstanding football player at Syracuse University. Along with the Gallagher brothers and DiPaolo, he was a mainstay of wrestling in Buffalo in that period. Tag wrestling became part of the Auditorium's wrestling cards. The well known Gallagher brothers, Mike and Doc, were regarded as a top flight tag team.

But the heyday of wrestling was coming to an end. The big crowds that one had come to expect regularly on Friday nights were diminishing. At the same time wrestling on the national scene was thriving. It was experiencing great success on television.

Under the tutelage of Vince McMahon, professional wrestling, with more gimmickry than ever, became a huge television success. McMahon earned a national reputation as wrestling's most successful promoter. Hulk Hogan became the national sensation of the mat game. In the last decade of the century, Buffalonians watched Hogan on cable television along with millions of other Americans. But no longer did thousands of fans travel to downtown Buffalo for the weekly wrestling cards. The evenings when hundreds of gentlemen dressed in coat and tie, and hundreds of ladies decked out in fine dresses worn under expensive furs filled the red seats in the Aud were past. So too were the nights when the blue and gray sections were filled with countless numbers of blue collar workers, the groups who would give the city one of its time-worn labels. Those nights too were history.

True, even in the latter decades of the 20th century, Buffalo, on occasion, proved to be a good place to stage wrestling matches. At least, on occasion, big name features might draw near capacity crowds. But there were also many evenings when only 3,000 or 4,000 fans would attend. That was the difference from the immediate postwar era. Even the blue collar label had become somewhat anachronistic.

Nevertheless, wrestling and its famous venue, the Aud, went out with a big bang. In June of 1996, a crowd "announced at 14,852, turned out for a program entitled "Wrestling Legends of the Aud." A large number of both wrestlers and boxers who had competed in the Aud at some point during the previous decades, was on hand. A short time later, the Aud would be closed permanently. It would give way to a new downtown arena, initially called the Crossroads Arena and eventually known as the HSBC Arena. The "Pretty Gray Lady of Lower Main Street," as Cy Kritzer had labeled it, had outlived its usefulness.

But the June finale in 1996 was much more than a tribute to the venerable old Aud. It was also a fitting "Tribute to Ilio DiPaolo" who had died as a result of an auto accident a year earlier.[38] DiPaolo had had a colorful and a championship career and had won his way into the hearts of Western New Yorkers. He was a restaurateur of renown, a great wrestler and an even greater human being. Ilio DiPaolo had become one of the most beloved and admired sports figures in the history of the city.

It was fitting that wrestling had opened the Aud and now it was closing the Aud. Professional wrestling had become an integral part of the Buffalo sports scene in the years immediately following World War II. Wrestling had been important before World War II and would continue to be so for a long time.

But it was in the years immediately following World War II that wrestling was a major player on the sports stage in Buffalo.Those were the years when Ed Don George manned the helm, and when Frank Sexton and Whipper Watson, along with Iron Talun and the Angel became increasingly popular. Crowds in excess of 10,000 were common. By decade's end they were joined by newcomers to the Buffalo wrestling scene, most famously Gorgeous George and Yukon Eric. They all played a role in making Buffalo a national hotspot for the sport of wrestling. They were main pillars of the golden age. Wrestlers with national reputations, as well as wrestlers known mainly to area fans, combined with the Buffalo fans themselves and the promotional work of matchmaker Ed Don George to give Buffalo a nation-wide reputation in the sport of wrestling, just as the city had earned in other spectator sports. No one who lived during those days would doubt that wrestling was an amazingly successful sport in Buffalo's Golden Age of Sports.

CHAPTER NINE

A Potpourri of Sports

— Something for every fan in the Queen City —

BUFFALO EVENING NEWS

Record 24,708 Crowd Sees Schindler Win 200-Lap Midget Race

Buffalo Evening News - September 2, 1948

Wild Bill Schindler in his famous "Offy" *Photo: Keith Herbst*

Football, Basketball, Baseball, Hockey, as well as Boxing and Wrestling were all principal components of Buffalo's Golden Age. Buffalo did very well with those major spectator sports in the 1940s. But the period also included several less well known or less celebrated sports. Some were team sports; others were individual sports. A few did not do very well; primarily they suffered from lack of interest. But others made their mark; in one way or another they contributed to the golden glow of Buffalo during the 1940s.

Doodlebugs in Civic Stadium

A colorful entry in the Buffalo sports world of the 1940s was Midget Auto Racing. The little racing machines, popularly known as Doddlebugs, seemed to be ideally suited to perform on the quarter mile track in Civic Stadium. The sport had a big though brief impact in Buffalo in the years immediately following the war. Crocky Wright in his "Midget Auto Racing History" stated that the midgets reached their all-time peak in popularity in the late 1940s and then slid to their lowest ebb, to near-oblivion."[1]

Actually the sport did have some limited success in the Buffalo area before World War II. But the war simply closed down the sport, for all practical purposes, "for the duration." Gasoline was needed for tanks, tires were needed for jeeps, and the race drivers were needed to serve in the armed forces to "to do their part." Which they did![2]

Just two weeks after the Japanese surrendered, the midget autos returned to Civic Stadium. On August 30, 1945, 18,002 fans filed into the Best Street facility. It was the largest crowd that had ever witnessed a midget auto race in Western New York. The local press was ecstatic. A week later, another impressive turnout, 20,000, showed up at Civic Stadium and the *Buffalo Evening News* bellowed: "Top Midget Drivers Sought after 38,000 Turnout Here." Top drivers from elsewhere in the East were needed in Buffalo. Fortunately, Ed Otto, a top Eastern operator, was hired and proved to be just what the doctor ordered. He was recognized for being upfront with the racers and giving them a fair share of the take. Otto brought in the best drivers from all over the country but especially from the Eastern Seaboard. He created more open competition and longer races were featured.[3]

In time Otto saw to it that the track was "gently banked" and that the surface was repaved. He added a guard rail to improve track safety. These were positive measures. Still injuries, indeed fatalities, continued to be a concern in the sport of midget auto racing. *Buffalo Evening News* beat reporter, Mike Calandra, zeroed in on the issue. He called the Civic Stadium track dangerous and said that "the first turn is fast becoming the most talked about curve in midget auto racing in the East." Three drivers met instant death there, the last in 1946, and more than 25 suffered serious injuries. On August 20, 1947 it almost happened again. That night three cars crashed, one literally jumping into the air and landing on one of the others. For a moment the spectators sat silent and horrified. Then the drivers scrambled out of their cars. Two of the drivers escaped without a scratch and the third suffered minor wounds. Fans breathed a sigh of relief. The fans in the stands were not exempt. On July 8, 1948 a spectator in Civic Stadium was hurt by a flying wheel; a driver lost a wheel on a turn, the wheel hit the guard rail and flew up and into the stands injuring the spectator.[4]

Overall the casualties did lessen and things did improve for midget auto racing. Indeed, under Ed Otto's guidance, midget auto racing came into its own in 1947 and then proceeded to enjoy a spectacular though short lived career. Ed Otto brought order to the midget program in Buffalo, but it remained for a one legged native of Long Island to bring creditability to the sport and to raise its popularity to new heights. That was Bill Schindler, popularly known as Bronco Bill. Bill Schindler was to midget auto racing in Buffalo, as Jim Kelly would be to the Football Bills, or Jimmy Slattery was to boxing. Each was regarded as virtually synonymous with his sport.[5]

Bill Schindler was no newcomer to auto racing. He was well known on the tracks along the Eastern Seaboard, especially those on Long Island and in New Jersey. In 1936, he suffered injuries in a big car race at the Mineola Fairgrounds on Long Island. Those injuries resulted in the amputation of his right leg just above the knee. The loss of the leg did not deter him in the least. If anything it made his accomplishments even more heroic and his will to win more steadfast. He continued to win on the track and came to be referred to, regularly in this pre-politically correct era, as the one legged wizard from Freeport, Long Island.

By the time that Bill Schindler came to Buffalo he was already an established star. He made his first appearance on June 11, 1947. It was a night for midget auto fans to remember. Bronco Bill stole the show. He piloted his Offenhauser to a triple victory before the 6,608 fans in what would be the first of many such victories. He soon established himself as the most dominant and successful driver in Buffalo history. Bill Schindler won "42 out of 46 races of all the races he entered during his three years appearing at the Stadium." He also won in other cities; he was victorious in "53 feature races back to back in 1947 and 1948." That was a record that would not be broken.[6]

There were other race car drivers in those years who also endeared themselves to the Buffalo fans. Some were from Western New York; Keith Herbst refers to these as the "Buffalo Gang" This group included Al Keller, Eddie Shaw, Speed McFee, PeeWee Southcott, and Eddie Lenz. Another favorite in 1947 was Al Bonnell the "Flying Dutchman" from Erie, Pa. He had been voted the most popular doddlebug in the country the previous year. Another was Ted Tappitt, a Long Island native and a hero of World War II. Tappitt won features throughout the East as well as in Buffalo during these golden years. There also was Eddie "The Fox" Shaw from Bellevue, New Jersey, aka the Bellevue Bullet, who thrilled 8,201 fans when he won the 25 lap special on June 24, 1947. He did so piloting his blue Ford and defeating Johnny Rice, who drove an Offenhauser. It was the first time that year that an "offy" was defeated in a feature. Another crowd pleaser was Duane Carter. Phil Ranallo, who covered auto racing regularly for the *Courier Express*, referred to Carter as "the accelerator happy offenhauser pilot" from Santa Monica, California. Only 5,209 fans showed up on a chilly July 23 but they watched the West Coast star emerge as a triple winner. One of his victories was the 25 lap feature. Rex Records from Stamford, Connecticut was also able to attract a host of vocal fans. Rex "reckless" Records, engaged Schindler in one of the most thrilling duels ever at Civic Stadium. Records roared off into the lead, but "Schindler's own reckless bids to take the lead on every curve brought the fans to their feet several times." Bronco Bill cut off Records on the sixth lap and stayed in front the rest of the way to win the 25 lap race. Schindler collected $375 for his triple win.[7]

The summer of 1947 was a splendid one for midget auto racing in Buffalo. The *Buffalo Evening News* was prompted to run a major story about the little cars. It began: "there's a screaming, screeching roaring infant in Buffalo's fast growing sport family – midget automobile racing." The *News* gave a brief historical overview noting that there had been some limited success before the war and immediately after the war, and then, focusing on the 1947 season, noted that "The speedy little doodlebugs became a permanent member of the family this season and local fans turned out 13,000 strong last Wednesday to make the 'adoption' official." Buffalo's fans and its midget autos were going full steam ahead, just like the rest of the nation. The most popular makes of the autos were the Ford V-8 60s and the Offenhausers. The latter, "the hottest little racer on wheels" captured the imagination of the racing fans. The "Offys" cost anywhere between $6000 and $13000. The drivers were earning more money than previously and the winners, racing several nights per week, could take home as much as $2000 per week. The doodlebugs were timed up to 125 miles per hour; they roared into turns at better than 40 mph, sometimes the wheels lifted off the ground. Waxing rhapsodic the *Buffalo Evening News* stated that they were "shining mechanical miracles of speed, paint and chromium, truly machines of color and beauty." Promoters attributed some of the success to the layout in Civic Stadium. It was a good place to watch a race. Moreover crackups were frequent; many fans enjoyed that.[8]

The highlight of the 1947 season was the Queen City Handicap held on September 10. 17,449 fans showed up; the largest crowd of the season. Schindler and Duane Carter were both entered in the 50 lap feature. The *Buffalo Evening News* called it: "The finest field of midget racing cars and drivers ever assembled in the East." It was a thriller. Schindler broke on top and led the whole way. Carter gave him a run for his money but in the 19th lap, he had car trouble and had to call it a night. Schindler proceeded to lap the field and won in the record breaking time of 14:11:17. No doubt he convinced the huge crowd that he was the nation's number one little car pilot.[9]

The final race of the glorious season of 1947 was held on October 1. Surprisingly Bronco Bill suffered two setbacks in races early in the evening. But he won the grand finale, the 100 lap feature, decisively. It was Schindler's 13th triumph in 15 whirls in 1947 around the local oval. All told in Buffalo and on other tracks, he now had established a world record of 50 feature wins in one season.

Schindler began the following year right where he had left off previously. On June 17, 1948 Bronco Bill had a triple victory and in his narrow victory in the 25 lap headliner he shattered his own track record. His new record time was 6:56:28. The straight-aways on the Civic Stadium track had been resurfaced to remove hazardous bumps. The track was "lightening fast."[10]

Schindler kept on winning, and kept on shattering records. Phil Ranallo's hyperbole caught the flavor of one of Schindler victories: "In the most thrilling race ever witnessed at Civic Stadium, Bill Schindler, the amazing amputee. . .the most talented chauffeur ever to grip the wheel of a midget auto" came from last place to win the 25 lap feature in a near-photo finish. Schindler had to start in last place, the 14th spot. Schindler worked his way up to the 3rd spot after eight laps but then had to bide his time as Eddie Lenz of nearby Colden, New York and Ted Tappitt set a blistering, blocking pace. On the very last lap, Schindler rocketed into the lead and stormed across the finish line, by just half a length to the delight of the standing, shouting 7,581 fans. Schindler remained unbeaten in a Buffalo headliner.[11]

Schindler's feat served as an appealing appetizer for the $7500 Eastern Open Midget Classic held on Labor Day weekend. Keith Herbst, referred to it as the 200 lap Indianapolis type classic. In the feature, the best from the west would be vying with the best of the east, along with some cornbelt favorites from the Midwest. Two of the greatest from the West, Duane Carter, the Santa Monica speedster, and Johnny Manta, the Los Angeles daredevil, were counted as very strong contenders as was Ted Tappett from Long Island. But the real favorite was the "one legged" champion from Freeport, Bill Schindler. It was tabbed the "greatest assemblage of drivers and cars ever." A record turnout, 24,708 fans showed up. Historian Herbst said "this was the all time highlight night at BCS; Huge crowd, huge field, huge purse." Eddie Otto deserved the credit for putting it all together.[12]

The race itself was a thriller. Schindler took the lead on the 16th lap but found a rookie from Connecticut, Buddy Chase, giving him a run for the money. Chase was in the runner up spot after the 50th lap; he then roared into the lead on the 102nd lap, and held the first spot until the 171st leap when he was forced to make a two minute pit stop. That lapse enabled Schindler to recapture the lead and Chase could not catch him.

It was a superb evening for midget auto racing in Buffalo. But an ominous sign also marked the evening. A stunt event involving two stock cars was part of the program. Joie Chitwoods' Daredevil racers cracked up two stock cars, putting on a show that pleased the spectators.

In the final race of the year, 7,851 racing fans saw the great Schindler finally defeated in a feature race, his first loss in a feature in two years. Al Bonnell, an excellent driver from Erie, Pennsylvania, ended Bronco Bill's reign. Bonnell was trailing, when Schindler was forced to make a pit stop. Bonnell then outmaneuvered Schindler to take the flag.

1949 was another good year for midget auto racing. Herbst labeled it "One last season in the sun." Actually, more sun would have helped the 1949 racing season. Poor weather reduced the number of programs. "King Doodlebug" as Schindler was dubbed by *Illustrated Speedway News* continued to win. He also suffered some defeats. July 13 was an especially big day for racing fans and for Bronco Bill. 14,654 turned out. In the 50 lap feature, Schindler again set a new track record. In so doing he defeated two of his top rivals, Duane Carter and Al Bonnell, who came in second, and third, respectably.[13]

A rather intriguing aspect of the July 13th program involved an unusual match up between a little car and a big car. Schindler challenged Bill Holland, the 1949 Indianapolis 500 winner. Holland, of course, won at Indy in his big car. The unprecedented match up in Buffalo called for two, five lap dashes. Schindler won them both. Phil Ranallo remarked that it was simply "a case of Schindler and his mighty midget, the black no.2 Caruso Offy, being too much for Holland in his $18,000 Offenhauser powered auto." Holland's car was just too big for the treacherous quarter mile asphalt track at Civic Stadium.[14]

The blockbuster race of the year was held on August 24. Ed Otto announced that that 50 lap race would be the official 1949 AAA national championship test. Drivers from all over the country indicated their intention to compete. Schindler, of course, would be there. But his reign as uncrowned king of midget auto racing was a little tarnished. He was no longer undefeated. He had come in second to Mike Nazaruk of East Meadow, Long Island in June and then in early August he was edged out of the winner's spot by Duane Carter. At the very end of the previous season he had lost to Al Bonnell. Still, as the *Courier Express* noted, he had amassed an amazing record over three years. In 31 features Bronco Bill was victorious 28 times. Nazaruk, Carter, and Bonnell, his three conquerors, would join Schindler in the August 24 extravaganza. The *Courier Express* called it "the most important auto race ever staged in Buffalo."[15]

The largest crowd of the year was in attendance. Nearly 20,000, actually 19,913 saw Henri Renard, heralded as "The Flying Dutchman from Long Island," capture the crown. Renard led for the entire 50 laps. He had won the coveted pole position. Schindler was right on his tail but was forced to slow momentarily when a car in front of him went out of control. Schindler ended up third. Renard pocketed $975 for winning the biggest race of the year.

Also on the program were stock car dashes. The stocks were a big hit; fans loved the smash ups and watching the cars being untangled. Ed Otto announced an all stock car racing card for the following Saturday. In fact the remainder of the 1949 schedule featured stock car races. 1949 was the last full season of regularly scheduled midget auto racing in Buffalo. "Almost overnight" the stock cars had become tremendously popular. A host of young men, some with the print barely dry on their driving licenses, could soup up an old jalopy and think seriously of entering it in a stock car race. Stock cars were cheaper and safer and to the delight of the fans they crashed often. No wonder the promoters welcomed them. Ed Otto turned to promoting them almost exclusively and when he left the scene to return to the east coast, Dewey Michaels took over the promotion of the stocks locally.[16]

By end of the 1949 season, Bob Cameron, the 21-year-old Kenmore native, and Bennett High School graduate, was already being hailed as the Bill Schindler of local stock car racing. Phil Ranallo in the *Courier Express* called him, "the Mighty Joe Young of local stock car racing." In September, 20,236 fans cheered Cameron as he flashed to victory in five races. Many other local boys became involved with the stocks. It was not only in Civic Stadium but at other sites, frequently county fairgrounds throughout Western New York, that the stocks were run. Often thousands attended. The future of auto racing was at hand.[17]

Midget auto racing had roared on to the Buffalo scene immediately at the end of World War II, sputtered for a while and then proceeded to take the area by storm. Then the midgets more or less sped into oblivion. For many years thereafter the midget auto saga of those post war years would be fondly remembered. Old timers especially recalled the slick little black offys, and the heroics of the one legged dynamo, Bronco Bill Schindler, who had captured the imagination of thousands during Buffalo's Golden Age of Sport.

Roller Derby

There was a basic similarity between Roller Derby and Midget Auto Racing. Each had a brief history before the war, managed a half hearted survival during the conflict then burst on the scene shortly after peace returned. Each made a big splash for a few years and then faded into oblivion by the end of the decade. Whereas midget auto racing was simply replaced by other forms of auto racing, roller derby reappeared under new guises in later years elsewhere in the country. Like the Cheshire cat, it had many lives.

Most Buffalonians recall the Roller Derby, but dimly, like a favorite old radio program such as the Lone Ranger or The Shadow. The last half of the '40s was "the golden age of the derby."[1] Some form of roller skating races date back at least to the 1920s in Chicago. In the 1930s in the midst of the Great Depression, Leo Seltzer began promoting dance marathons in the Windy city. Seltzer was looking for ways to utilize the coliseum in Chicago. The story goes that he used a kitchen table cloth to draw up his plans for the sport of roller derby. For the promotion of this new entertainment form he received an assist from his friend, Damon Runyon. He had the name trademarked and used it for a group of skaters who traveled to various Midwestern cities to compete.[2]

A roller derby game would involve two teams each with five players. One of the five was designated a jammer. The jammer was the scorer. The teams would start together in a pack. The jammers would be 20 feet behind the pack. The players skated in formation counterclockwise around an oval track. Points would be scored by the jammer when he passed the opposing pack. The rival team tried to block the jammer to impede his or her progress. The game was usually quite physical. Hair pulling and elbowing were quite common; players often ended up with bumps and bruises. They grew tired too since they were expected to skate an average of 50 miles per evening at up to 40 mph. The size of the oval track was about that of a college basketball court; it fit nicely in the center of Memorial Auditorium. The players wore football type helmets and used the blocking tactics of football, the lap stealing of the 6 day bike races, and the body contact of hockey.[3]

Seltzer had some trying moments with his invented sport. He barnstormed the country, setting up his $20,000 portable track wherever he could find permission to do so. Tickets were 10 cents; high-priced seats cost a quarter. He did not make a lot of money, perhaps a few hundred dollars for a fifteen game series. From the mid 1930s and into the war years, it was tough to sell.

The Roller Derby made its first appearance in Buffalo in the Broadway Auditorium in 1939. It received very little publicity. There were only a few games played annually for the next several years. But after the war the Derby picked up momentum reaching its height in Buffalo in the last years of the decade. The Buffalo team, known as the Buffalo Bisons, played a series of games, about 20 each year, sometimes in September, but usually in May. It was obviously a filler - type of sport, scheduled to fill the down time in Memorial Auditorium when the boxing and wrestling programs were winding down and basketball and hockey were not being played.

The Roller Derby resembled the Barnum and Bailey circus coming to town. The participants arrived in beat up Ford Pickups and old Chevy sedans. They headed for the laundry mat, did other chores, and smoked plenty of cigarettes. They brought the track with them from their previous engagement; they themselves proceeded to assemble it in the Aud.

Seltzer owned all the derby teams so he could change the rosters of each as he saw fit. Players played for different cities at different times of the year. But Seltzer made sure that certain players were identified with specific cities. Gerry Murray was Buffalo's ace, even though she was from Iowa. Year after year Murray was the captain of the Buffalo Bisons women's team. She was known as the pretty blue eyed Irish lass from Des Moines. She was a former vaudeville skater, played in a softball league in 1938 and then joined the Derby circuit.

Seltzer tried to have at least a few local girls on the team and he succeeded. It was a similar story with the men. Bill Bogash was the perennial captain as well as the big gun. Like Gerry Murray he was the one the fans identified with. The press, enamored with alliterations, referred to the Bison captain as Blastin' Bill Bogash.

The competitions in the Aud featured the Bisons against either Brooklyn or Chicago. Occasionally a team from Philadelphia would make an appearance. The crowds usually numbered between 3,000 and 4,000. Sometimes as many as 8,000 fans would show up. In one of the first post war contests in 1946, an excellent turnout of 7,005 fans witnessed a game that was as exciting as roller derby gets, Brooklyn nipped Buffalo, 17 - 16; Bill Bogash was the big gun for the Bisons with four points.

In May 1947 Buffalo began a 20-game series against Chicago in the Aud. Tryouts were held for local players and three Buffalo girls made the team. They were Ester Skorupa, who also used the name Bunny Shalley, and had attended East High School, Jena Porter an Oneida Mohawk Indian, and Julia Patrick, a graduate of South Park High School. Two local lads, Paul McGoldrick and Norm Fitzpatrick, made the men's team.

Nearly every night throughout the month of May Buffalo and Chicago clashed. Buffalo won more than Chicago accumulating a total of 245 points to the 238 for Chicago. The finale was held on May 31. Frank Wakefield who covered the derby for the *Buffalo Evening News* remarked that "Now that the madcap Roller Derbyists have finished their merry chase to nowhere," boxing and wrestling can return.[4]

Despite criticisms from sport "purists" the Derby continued to attract an enthusiastic following. It drew fans for a number of reasons. The women especially, attracted attention. Women athletes were somewhat of a novelty. The women's team received more publicity than the men did. On the one hand fans liked to see the women play a physical game, mixing it up with their opponents, pulling their hair, knocking them down, and dealing them body blows. On the other hand the press and the publicity people were careful to show that these women were not tomboy types; some were married and had children; they were family oriented. The photos in the newspapers that accompanied the game stories emphasized the women's femininity. The girls were attractive, often resembling the girl next door. Their uniforms were short enough so that their legs were featured. Since they wore white high top skates the picture gave the appearance that they were in high heels. The photos might be mistaken for mild cheesecake shots; perhaps imitative of Betty Grable's appealing photo of World War II fame.

Another important factor in the derby's popularity was the endless feuding that was carried on between Buffalo's Captain, Gerry Murray, and Chicago's Captain, Midge Brashun. Midge (from midget, she was only four feet eleven inches tall) was also known as "toughie." Murray and Midge glared at each other, they elbowed, they fought, they were penalized, they were thrown out of games, they were suspended, but they persisted in their feuds and the crowds loved it. One authority on the derby asserts that Midge's popularity derived from her role "as the anti hero, the woman the fans loved to hate." When the Roller Derby first appeared on television in New York City, even the sophisticated *New York Times* covered it and remarked that "women skaters captured the fancy of the crowd."[5]

Many of the fans were working class, blue collar types, and so were the skaters. The fans could relate to them. The players were bartenders, laborers, factory workers, housewives, and clerks. Moreover, roller skating was a popular pastime in Buffalo. There were several large indoor skating rinks in the city frequented by people of various

Above: Popular Roller Derby apponents Midge Brasuhn and Gerry Murray. *Photo: Game Program.*

ages. Adolescent young men, clumsy as they might be on skates, were willing to chance wearing them in pursuit of a voluptuous young female who they eyed gracefully gliding around the large oval rink. To abet the interest in skating, local amateurs were allowed to skate between periods when the Roller Derby teams were competing in the Aud. Also when in town the Roller Derby ran a midday school for Derby candidates. That certainly created additional fans. Finally for some fans, attending the Roller Derby was just something to do. The Derby filled a void in May and September, a time relatively quiet for other sports and other forms of entertainment.

Buffalo opened a 23 night stand in September 1948. Television had arrived in Buffalo a few months earlier, and the Roller Derby looked forward to having its games televised. Seltzer thought it would increase Derby attendance. It did, at least for a while. On September 26,824 fans were on hand; it was a record for opening night. Buffalo defeated Chicago 20 – 14. On the nights that followed, the teams alternated victories and defeats fairly regularly. Bogash and Murray were usually the stars for the home team, whereas Wild Bill Reynolds and Midge Brashun led the Chicago team. Attendance continued to be satisfactory. *Courier Express* Sports Editor Billy Kelly congratulated Charley Murray, the local derby promoter, for his role in the success of the Buffalo franchise.[6]

The Roller Derby returned to Buffalo in September of 1949. The Buffalo Bisons started a 16 day stand with Brooklyn. There were now four teams; they had hoped for six. There was a new wrinkle; the season would end with a world series of Roller Derby; the first ever such grand event. Things rolled along nicely for the Roller Derby in 1949. Seltzer was pleased with the televised Derby contests, first in Chicago then in Buffalo. Next he arranged for it in the Big Apple. Initially the Derby played in the armory in New York City but it quickly outgrew that venue and moved to Madison Square Garden. Seltzer thought he had died and gone to heaven.

The World Series featured the teams from Buffalo, Brooklyn, Chicago and Philadelphia. The series went back and forth between Memorial Auditorium and Madison Square Garden. Buffalo defeated all three opponents and won the World Series. There were no fireworks or parades to celebrate the feat. By that time the Roller Derby had run its course.

The Roller Derby and television seemed a natural fit in the late 1940s. By the early 1950s that natural fit was no longer natural. However, when television was in its infancy, it needed programming. It had time to fill and television executives were not sure how to fill it. The Roller Derby was available and seemed made to order for television. The game took place in a very limited space. The rules were simple. The action was fairly easy to follow. At the time television viewers had very limited fare. They could stare at the test pattern, which many people did, at least for a while. They could watch the trotting horses from Yonkers Raceway, and they could laugh at the Milton Berle show. There was very little else. But when programs became more available in the early fifties, then shows such as I Love Lucy starring Desi and Lucy easily replaced the Gerry and Toughie Roller Derby encounters. In 1951 the TV bubble for the roller derby burst; Roller Derby fell off prime time TV and that was its death knell. "Television exploited the derby and then discarded it, the first sport it wasted."[7]

Frank Deford, one of the county's most acclaimed sports writers, gave the Roller Derby some legitimacy when he wrote a book in 1971, entitled: *Five Strides on the Banked Track: the Life and times of the Roller Derby.* A 20th century fox film released in 1950 entitled

Fireball stirred a little interest in the sport. It starred Mickey Rooney as a tough jammer. The movie was not a big hit, but those who watched it found it enjoyable. Incidentally the film included Marilyn Monroe's first screen appearance, a small but sultry part.[8]

There always was a question as to whether Roller Derby was actually a sport. Many sports authorities would deny its legitimacy, claiming that it was just another form of entertainment; some would say it was equivalent to modern day professional wrestling. Of course, today, many would maintain that most professional sports are basically entertainment, at least to some degree.

Randy Roberts, a prominent sports historian, in "Winning is the Only Thing," his volume on the history of sports since World War II, asserts that critics who argue whether roller derby is a sport or not, miss the point. Television was in the entertainment business; it had time to fill. The Roller Derby served a purpose and it thrived on TV for a few years. Then the viewing public found other things to watch and so the Roller Derby, after 1951, returned to "its former obscurity."[9]

Still more sports events

There were a number of other sports that had a role to play in Buffalo's Golden Age. Unlike Midget Auto Racing and the Roller Derby, these sports had much earlier origins. Some date back to colonial times in America, others to the late 19th century. In one way or another, because of some specific event or some noteworthy development these merit consideration in this volume. Each had a role to play at some time in the postwar era, a role that was somehow special for the Golden Age. These included bowling, golf, high school football, horseracing and rowing.

Bowling

The American Bowling Congress held its annual tournament in Buffalo less than a year after the war ended; it was an overwhelming success. New money, thousands and thousands of dollars came gushing into the city. Merchants were happy. Every hotel room in downtown and near the downtown area was sold out. Wherever one looked, the sign: "No room in the Inn" was posted.

Bowling was very popular in Buffalo as it was in many cities of similar population size and similar ethnic composition. St. Louis, Milwaukee, Detroit, Cleveland, Cincinnati and Pittsburgh all shared Buffalo's fondness for the sport. It was popular where the German heritage was important and where beer flowed freely. The sport had been popular since the turn of the century. The first American Bowling Congress tournament was held in 1901. The following year, Buffalo served as host city for the second ABC tourney.

Bowling grew during the prohibition era of the 1920s and continued to attract participants through the Depression and World War II. Many industrial plants sponsored bowling leagues; in the Depression that was a way of boosting morale, and in the war years these extracurricular activities helped to relieve some of the tedium associated with the grueling work schedules of the war plants.

The ABC tournament had a voluntary three year blackout during the war. As soon as the war as over, Buffalo was asked to host the annual event. Billy Kelly, *Buffalo Courier Express* Sports Editor, noted that Buffalo was considered one of the top bowling cities in the nation; the city hosted 5 of the 42 championship tournaments, more than any other city.[1]

The tournament was planned for the spring of 1946. In August of 1945, just three days after the Japanese surrender, the Office of Defense Transportation lifted the restriction on travel to sports events. Plans proceeded swiftly and smoothly. It was announced that the bowling extravaganza would be held from March 14 through May 6 in the 74th Armory, sometimes referred to as the Connecticut Street Armory. The bowling officials and the entire Buffalo community were enthusiastic. George Obenauer, a local ABC officer, predicted that 30,000 out of town bowlers would converge on the city. Counting friends and families the number of visitors could reach 50,000. It was expected that more than $2 million would be spent by visitors. A community wide effort set up hundreds of booster clubs, from churches and industry and especially from service clubs such as Kiwanis, Lions, Rotary and the Knights of Columbus.[2]

Opening ceremonies in the 74th Armory were highlighted by welcoming speeches from United States Senator James Mead and Mayor Bernard Dowd. They spoke in front of a mammoth replica of the flag raising at Iwo Jima. The famous battle had taken place just one year earlier. An overflow crowd squeezed in for the opening ceremonies. It was announced at the outset that five records had already been established at the 43rd ABC tournament. There were 12,780 doubles teams, and more than 25,000 single entrants registered. Back in 1902 there had been just 300 registrants. $900,000 was received for entry fees. 42 teams from Canada registered as well as 195 teams from communities throughout New York State. All told there were almost 6000 teams and they came from 830 towns and cities from 35 states, and Hawaii and Canada. 62 days of bowling were scheduled on the 40 alleys.[3]

The top bowlers in the nation were headed to Buffalo. These included Andy Varipapa and Ned Day. Ranking right up there with them was Allie Brandt, the cream of the local crop. Allie Brandt arguably the most widely known and best bowler in Buffalo's history was a first team All American bowling team member. The Lockport native established a world record in 1939 when he rolled an 886 and won an ABC gold medal. Locally, he was a regular member of the Ideal Classic League.

An unforeseen development marred the early days of the tournament. Black bowlers were banned from participation. NAACP pickets protested the banning of a Negro team, as the term was then used; a team from the local Jesse Clipper Post of the American Legion. Representatives of the pickets were invited in to meet with ABC officials who pointed to their charter that said eligibility was limited to "white men" bowlers. The charter was written in 1895. Just one year later, in 1896, the Supreme Court, in the Plessy vs. Ferguson decision, legalized segregation in the United States. The pickets, Black and White, were peaceful; the NAACP said that its main objective was to obtain an interview. They got one, but not much else. No real progress was made.

Nevertheless, at least some Buffalonians were on record voicing their concern that the Black exclusion policy was wrong and should be changed. On April 7, Billy Kelly, the respected sports editor of the *Courier Express* in his widely read column noted that "It appears that the ABC will get away from Buffalo without doing anything at all about the 'male white' only clause." He added that no report had been made available and there is a "palpable disposition" to avoid the subject; he wryly concluded "Apparently the business sessions of the ABC are under perfect control." Mayor Dowd too voiced his concern. He requested that the ABC amend its rules.On the front page of the *Buffalo Evening News*, the Mayor said "on behalf of the people of Buffalo and officially as chief executive of your host city, I earnestly appeal to your organization to make such changes in your rules...to remove all possibility of discrimination...because of race, creed, or color." The ABC governing board took cover saying that it could amend but had to wait until local groups had the opportunity to consider the issue. Integration of the ABC would have to wait a little longer. Ironically at that very time, in May of 1946, Jackie Robinson, with the Montreal Royals of the Brooklyn Dodger baseball organization was being welcomed in his debut in Buffalo in Offermann Stadium just across town from the 74th armory.[4]

Meanwhile each day, the local newspapers published a listing of the scores of all the leading participants as well as a number of human interest stories on various participants. Crowds of 1,500 to 2,000 gathered each day to watch the bowlers roll away. But when Allie Brandt the home grown favorite bowled, the crowds were greater. Contributing to the success of the event was the Buffalo duet of John Gworek and Henry Kmidowski. They were typical hometown blue collar keglers. On March 10, Gworek left his shift early as foreman at General Mills to meet with Kmidowski, a former riveter at Bell Aircraft. They proceeded to set a tourney record of 544 for a doubles team. At the conclusion of the tournament in May it was announced that they had walked away with the doubles title for the entire tournament. All other championships went to "visiting firemen."[5] **Of great interest at the tournament was the unveiling of the revolutionary automatic pin setter machine.** It was developed by the American Machine and Foundry Corporation of Cheektowaga, the company that had taken over the Buffalo Arms plant of World War II fame. The machine was on exhibition and demonstrations were given. Eventually it would replace the pin boys, those youngsters who performed the dangerous and backbreaking physical labor of setting the pins and often had to dodge the 16 pound balls and the erratically flying bowling pins. They labored after school, evenings and on weekends for a paltry 5 to 10 cents a game; it was pin money.[6]

The 62 day ABC tournament came to a close on May 13. 23,954,100 pins had been knocked over and 155,688 admissions were sold. Bowlers and their fans purchased 15,000 cases of beer and 7,000 of soda pop, 50,000 cigars and 2,480 cartons of cigarettes. The tournament bowlers spent early 3 ½ million dollars in Buffalo. Included in that figure was what Gabby Hartnett paid for 20 alleys he had shipped back to his bowling establishment in the Windy City. Hartnett was the Buffalo Bison Baseball manager and was a former all star catcher for the Chicago Cubs.

ABC officials called the tournament "eminently successful." Buffalo would continue to be known as a good bowling town. Allie Brandt continued his success too; he was named to the 1946-7 all star team. 1947 was a great year for the 127 pound "mighty mite" from Lockport. In eight consecutive major events, he finished no lower that fourth and picked up a number of sizable checks. He won a classic in Detroit and another in New York City. He put on a stellar performance in the national match game championship in Chicago. He battled the great national champion Andy Varipapa right down to the wire; Varipapa needed a final strike in the last frame to win and he got it. In 1960 Allie Brandt was inducted into the ABC Hall of Fame. In 1991, one of first Buffalonians to be inducted into the newly established Western New York Sports Hall of Fame was Allie Brandt.

Meanwhile bowling's popularity had grown and spread in the Buffalo area. New stars emerged. These included Jim Schroeder and Jerry Back, and on the distaff side Phyliss Notaro, Cindy Coburn and her mother, Doris. Many new lanes were opened throughout Western New York. Bowling became a television hit. Bowling for Dollars, hosted by WBEN-TV's popular sportscaster Chuck Healy became a must watch program for bowling fans. Bowlers kept abreast of their sport by reading Joe Alli's regular column,

"Right Down Your Alley" in the sport pages of the *Courier Express* and its counterpart in the *Buffalo Evening News*, "Spares and Misses."

Golf

Golf, recognized as a sport in contemporary America, began to be played in the closing decades of the 19th century. Some activities, that resembled the game, were played much earlier, even in colonial days. The sport itself dates back to Scotland several centuries ago. In America in the 1890s wealthy businessmen and industrial magnates took up the sport, with the assistance of professional tutors from Scotland.

The turn of the century witnessed the beginnings of the country club movement in the United States and Buffalo shared in this. The Country Club of Buffalo, with little fanfare, hosted the United States Open in 1912. In 1926 the United States Open was again played in the Buffalo area, this time at the Park Country Club. In that decade golf's popularity spread throughout the country. Walter Hagen, as the first big time professional, did much to popularize the sport. Bobby Jones did so too. Jones became an authentic American hero after winning the Grand Slam, one of the truly great accomplishments in sports.

World War II saw limited golf played. Many tournaments were suspended for the duration of the conflict. Once the war was over, golf began to experience that same vigorous rebirth that characterized so many other sports. Buffalo shared in this rebirth. The city was given the opportunity to host the Western Open, at that time considered one of the major tournaments in golf. The Western Open had first been held in 1899 just a short time after the first U.S. Open. In Buffalo, after the Second World War, it was Albin Holder, the president of J. N. Adam's, one of Buffalo's largest department stores who sought out the Western Open. Holder was head of the sports foundation of J. N. Adam's; in that capacity he outbid 13 other cities for the right of Buffalo to host the 45th annual Western Open.[1]

Photo: Chip Clover

In fact not only was Holder personally responsible for securing the Western, but he oversaw the details for making the entire event a first class affair. Holder had experience with golf tournaments. He knew that the Western officials preferred a long course. Holder offered the Brookfield Country Club as the area course that would best fit that bill. Grantland Rice, the premier sportswriter of the era, complimented Holder and saluted Buffalo for holding the prestigious event. Rice maintained that it was 2nd only to the U.S. Open in prestige. A purse of $15,000, largest ever for the Western Open, was offered.[2]

The Western Open was held, July 29-August 1, 1948 at the Brookfield golf course.

It was located in Clarence, New York, about 20 miles east of Buffalo, in rolling farm country with acres of corn fields and herds of dairy cows for neighbors. Holder made sure the public had an excellent opportunity to witness the golf spectacle. The J.N. Adams department store did considerable advertising for the event. Busses ran regularly from the store in downtown Buffalo transporting fans directly to the entrance of the country club in Clarence. Tickets were priced at $1.60 daily and $3.60 for the weekend.[3]

Many of golf's luminaries were scheduled to participate including Lloyd Mangrum, Dr. Cary Middlecoff, and Masters Champion Jimmy Demaret. Frank Stranahan, the top amateur in the country also announced that he would be there. The number one golfer of the era also committed. That was Ben Hogan. His participation would assure that the golf tournament in Buffalo would make national and even international news. Bantam Ben was the man to beat. He had won the Reading Open a week earlier with a record 64. Hogan was the leading money winner of the year and was leading in Ryder Cup points.

For the two days prior to the opening, rabid fans had a chance to checkout their favorite pro while at practice. Thousands took advantage of the opportunity. Then, on opening day, 5000 followers of the links game invaded the course, a considerable number of them in the gallery following Ben Hogan.

Ben Hogan , Western Open Champion *Photo: Chip Clover*

On that first day, Clayt Haefner set a blistering pace with a 66. The following day, Haefner could not hold his lead; he shot a 77 and fell about twenty back in the pack. The real story of the second day of the tournament was "local boy makes good." The local golfer was Mike Parco. He made great copy for the sportswriters. He had turned pro back in 1937 but, subsequently, had not had many chances to participate in tournaments. During the war, he served in the Army Air Force, as a gunner, part of a B-17 crew that flew 24 combat missions over Germany. After the war, the Kenmore resident opened a driving range on Delaware Avenue in the Town of Tonawanda. In fact many of his neighbors found that his driving range was as popular for its charcoal broiled hot dogs as it was for its golfing opportunities. Mike Parco loved golf, played as much as he could, and jumped at the chance to play in the Brookfield Tournament.

Parco started off strong; he shot a 69 on the first day. Then he astonished many golf devotees with a 67 on the second day. His two day total of 136 was enough to make him the leader of the pack, one ahead of the indomitable Hogan. Parco's ace in the hole was that he knew how to play the winds at Brookfield. Some of the pros complained about the stiff breezes on the tournament's second day, but Parco was familiar with them. He played them perfectly, with low hook shots off the tee.

On the third day a crowd of 6400 turned out. Billy Kelly said it could have been larger but it was hard to find room to maneuver.

Kelly observed that the crowd was a cross section of Buffalo's diverse population. Many were there to cheer on home grown Mike Parco. Bob Stedler of the *News* added his two cents, asserting that "Buffalo is proving golf is a real spectator sport like baseball and football" The tournament also involved many local students, caddies and area club members who served as volunteers, helping out as marshals and in other capacities. Tom O'Connor, a Canisius High School student was typical. Later a Jesuit priest on the Canisius College faculty, and the college golf coach, O'Connor was a volunteer who shagged balls for the practicing pros. He also recalled vividly the excitement of watching Parco hit off the tees. On the third day Parco was teamed with Vic Ghezzi, 1941 PGA champion, and Ed "Porky" Oliver, a long driver from the State of Washington.[4]

Unfortunately Mike Parco did not do so well on Saturday. He posted a 75 and slid into third place. Porky Oliver moved into second place, and Hogan surged into the first position taking a three stroke lead. Hogan had a 70. Steve Doctor, of Audubon, was the closest Buffalonian behind Parco. After three days, Doctor had a total of 220. Parco had 211 and Hogan 207.

Sunday was Porky Oliver's moment in the sun. Oliver shot a 71 good enough to tie Hogan who came in with a 74. With Hogan and Oliver tied at 281 at the end of the regulation tournament, a Monday 18 hole playoff was necessary. Incidentally Parco had a 76 for a total of 287, good enough for eighth place.

On Monday, August 2, the playoff started a bit slowly for Hogan. The crowd was not overly warm toward Hogan. Bantam Ben was not known to be a very affable person. However when Hogan surged into the lead by the 6th hole the crowd changed. Fans sensed that they might see a bit of history in the making and they rallied behind Hogan. Sure enough Bantam Ben proceeded to shatter the course record of 66 with a 64 and he finished 9 strokes ahead of Oliver who took the clobbering good naturedly.

According to the *Buffalo Evening News*, Ben Hogan became the first player in golf history to win the big three in one year "the National Open, the National PGA and the Western Open." After the ceremonies, Hogan proved gracious and rode over to Mike Parco's driving range where, to the delight of a small gathering of surprised bystanders, he drove balls for about 20 minutes.

The *Courier Express* pronounced the tournament "a complete artistic success." Attendance figures hit 26,200 for the four day affair; if the two practice rounds on Tuesday and Wednesday were included it topped 30,000. The tournament was extremely well run. The press congratulated Albin Holder and J.N.Adams and all the Brookfield officials and club members for putting Buffalo "in the major golf spotlight nationally and internationally." The Western Open in 1948 had brought attention and fame to Buffalo.[5]

High School Football

If bowling hit the jackpot in one season, the spring of 1946, and golf did on one weekend in the summer of 1948, then high school football did it on one night in the autumn of 1948.

In the pre-war years, big headlines about high school football had come from the Midwest. In more recent decades they have come from the small towns in the large states of California, Texas and Florida; rarely from the Northeast. A major article in Sports Illustrated discussed the football crazed town of Odessa, Texas a few years ago. Friday Night Lights, a television program, commands a huge following attesting to high school football's elevated status in the Southwest. But long before Friday night lights there were Thursday night lights. Those were the lights that shown above the unbelievable 50,000 plus crowd that attended a high school football game in Civic Stadium in Buffalo on October 21, 1948.

High School football was big in the Buffalo city schools in the 1940s; it was really big. It was played before surprisingly large crowds. That was also true in the smaller cities and towns outside the city, those high schools in the municipalities that comprised the Niagara Frontier Football League. When those high schools met on the gridiron, it was not just parents and girlfriends who attended, but fans from the neighborhood and the community. Football games were big events. Often the attendance figures were impressive. But no crowd ever topped the mammoth turnout for the Kensington -Bennett game on October 21, 1948.

The turnstile count was 50,988. It was a verified count. It is still talked about to this day. Nothing like it had ever been seen in high school football and nothing ever would again. It was mind boggling.

As amazing and solitary as that figure was; there were other high school football contests in the 1940s that drew impressive numbers of fans.

The Buffalo high schools had competed for the Harvard Cup in football for several decades before 1948. In 1929 All High Stadium opened behind the recently built Bennett High School on Main Street, in what was then a newer section of the city. A record turnout of 19,704 attended the Harvard Cup championship game that year, a record not broken until 1948. The annual Harvard Cup game was played on Thanksgiving Day in All High; it always drew a sizeable crowd.

The outstanding high school football team during and at the end of World War II was from McKinley Vocational. Led by Chet Kwasek, Les Molnar and the MacKinnon brothers, the McKinley Macks captured the Harvard Cup for five consecutive years. Their supremacy culminated with the 1946 Turkey day championship win over Burgard Vocational, 7 -0, before 18,319 in All High Stadium.

The Niagara Frontier League rivaled the Buffalo's Harvard Cup League in terms of playing the highest caliber of high school football in Western New York. The NFL was not the typical suburban league that would become commonplace in the later decades of the 20th century. Rather the NFL was comprised of the teams from the high schools in the smaller municipalities scattered outside of the city of Buffalo. Included were North Tonawanda, Kenmore, Tonawanda, Lackawanna, Niagara Falls, LaSalle, Lockport, and Trott. The most dominant were the teams from North Tonawanda and Kenmore. They contested for the championship annually in the post war years.

In 1946, North Tonawanda and Kenmore were headed for a showdown. Both were undefeated and there was such widespread interest, that the school authorities moved the game from Kenmore Stadium to Civic Stadium. A then record attendance of 23,970 was on hand to watch Kenmore win, 13 – 7. A year later the same two schools clashed in the same place before 20,008; North Tonawanda won, 12 – 0.

Meanwhile Kensington had replaced McKinley as the dominant team in the city of Buffalo. In 1947, 14,353 watched Kensington defeat Lafayette 26- 0 in All High Stadium for the Harvard Cup. Bennett like Kensington had very good teams in several sports. In 1948 each football team got off to a flying start. As their annual date approached each was undefeated. The stage was set for a momentous High School football event.

The Principal of Kensington, Charles Monan, became the principal player in promoting the Ken-Bennett game as a major event in Civic Stadium. Monan had decided that his high school should become the juggernaut of high school athletics in the Buffalo system. He saw an opportunity to make a smash hit with the 1948 Kensington Bennett football game. He became chairman of a committee to make the arrangements for the game in Civic Stadium. The program supporting the game was named the Youth Participation Night. All the Buffalo high schools would participate and all would share in the proceeds to aid their own athletic programs. The game would be on television, it would be the first game under the lights, the first night game. It was expected that the game would break all previous attendance records, including the Kenmore - North Tonawanda game and even the Buffalo Bills - Cleveland Browns game of the previous year that had drawn 43,167.[1]

A community wide effort began in earnest and picked up considerable momentum. Neighborhood businesses were solicited for ticket purchases. It became a spirited community effort. All along Hertel Avenue the North Park Businessman's Association responded enthusiastically; so did the businesses on Parkside Avenue across from the Zoo. Cardina's general store, famous for serving unbelievable amounts of ice cream to area youth, was a center of activity for discussing the upcoming game. The merchants in the Kensington-Bailey area were just as involved if not more so. The coffee/ donut diners, the banks, the Mom and Pop grocery stores, the Red & White Superettes, and the big auto dealers on the Bailey Avenue auto showroom strip, all became part of the hoopla surrounding the Ken - Bennett night at Civic Stadium.[2]

Thursday night the stadium was a beehive of activity. Extra busses converged on Best and Jefferson carrying thousands of fans. The pre game activities witnessed hundreds of students participating. The action started when the two school bands gave the signal and the circus acts began. Student costumed performers leaped onto stages spaced at intervals around the stadium track. There were acrobats, tumblers, clowns, dancing Scottish lassies, cowboys on horseback, trick rope specialists, a German band and accordion players, and more. All 14 high schools were involved. One of the acts

Cardina's General Store, across Parkside from the Main Zoo entrance, was famous for its penny candy, Cherry Cokes, thick milkshakes and great comic books. *Photo: Joe Cardina*

featured a fully equipped girls' football squad from Hutch which ran through drills before the big game. Then the bands played again and the parade began. Drill teams performed and several floats crawled through the tunnel and on to the track. The noise from the crowd was deafening; louder than any late 20th century hard rock concert. The floats included a large stuffed tiger, a picturesque Rose Bowl replica, a Gay '90s shmoos, and from Burgard Vocational an atomic, hydromatic dynaflow training car.[3]

The bands and color guards massed at one end of the field, the two teams at the other end. The screaming got even louder as the individual players were introduced. Then all was quiet. All 50,988 spectators stood, bareheaded and at attention, for the singing of the National Anthem.

On the field at Civic Stadium a closely contested, hard fought struggle was anticipated. However Kensington dominated the game from the opening kickoff. The Knights surged ahead with three touchdowns in the first half. Following the third score, Harvey Yeates, Bennett's star fullback had a brief moment in the sun when he took the kickoff and galloped 79 yards for the lone Tiger touchdown. The final score was 26 - 8. The big guns for the Knights were quarterback Bobby Wilde and scatback Chris Frauenhofer,

The crowd was the story. 37,064 was the seating capacity in Civic Stadium. 50,988 attended. One student appropriately dubbed the event, "the elastic bowl." The all time stadium mark set the previous year for the Buffalo Bills–Cleveland Browns football game was easily surpassed. As expected the majority of spectators were students. But there were plenty of adults in attendance. 20,000 adult tickets had been sold in advance. The fans stood, sat, knelt, wherever they could find a few inches, in the aisles, on the track, in the end zone.[4]

Unfortunately there was a downside to the game, a critical injury to one of the Bennett players, Richard Dengler. He walked off the field in the third quarter on his own but his teammates told the coach that he did not look well. He was taken to the hospital; on the way there he lost consciousness. It was determined that he had a probable skull fracture. In the weeks that followed with countless prayers offered and best wishes extended and bedside vigils a daily occurrence, he showed some improvement. But unfortunately, he never fully recovered.

There were some other games played before very good crowds in that era. The following year, 1949, Kensington and Bennett again clashed in Civic Stadium. 13,251 fans turned out. That was about one quarter of the crowd of 1948, but nevertheless it was a very impressive crowd for high school football anywhere in those years. Kensington won again. Kenmore and North Tonawanda continued to be the strongest gridiron elevens beyond the city limits and continued to draw the biggest crowds. In 1949, more than 9,000 cramped into the North Tonawanda stadium and saw NT win again. In 1950, the game returned to Civic Stadium. More than 8,000 fans showed up to watch the Lumberjacks again defeat the Kenmore Blue Devils.

1948 was also the year that marked the renewal of the gridiron rivalry between Canisius High School and St Joe's Collegiate Institute after a 17th year hiatus. 10,559 turned out in Civic Stadium to witness a 14 – 9 Canisius victory. This, the most intense rivalry in Catholic High athletics, would continue to draw even larger crowds in the years that followed.

In the decades ahead, new rivalries in the growing suburbs would emerge. Games would be played before thousands of loyal fans. Arguments would continue as to which team was the best team ever. But no game would ever top the Kensington Bennett gridiron contest, the Ken-Ben game of 1948. In terms of community spirit, in terms of attendance it truly deserved to become a legend. The Ken Bennett game was a classic; it stands in a class by itself; it entered the history books as a one of a kind.

Horse Racing

Unlike Golf with its Western Open, and Bowling with the ABC tournament, and High School football with the legendary Ken Bennett game, horse racing in the 1940s had a different story to tell, as did the sport of crew. There was no particular marquee event, no blockbuster development that turned the entire eyes of the local sports minded community toward the horses or the rowers. It was simply a case of spectators and fans being drawn to various competitions in those sports, competitions that reflected well on the status of the city itself at that time in history.

Horseracing is recognized as the oldest organized sport in America. It dates back to pre-revolutionary days. Colonists by the mid 18th century acquired thoroughbred horses from England. Tracks were laid out, scheduled races were held, jockey clubs were formed and spectators were welcomed. Racing expanded in the 19th century. After the Civil War it became a big attraction in the New York City area. At the same time, famous race tracks such as Pimlico in Baltimore (1870) and Churchill Downs in Kentucky (1875) began operations.

Horseracing in the Western New York area, including nearby Canada, dates from that same era. The Grand Circuit of Trotters was organized in 1873; Buffalo was a charter member. The trotters and pacers, harness racing it was also called, raced at the Buffalo Raceway at the Erie County Fairgrounds in Hamburg, New York.[1] At the end of the century, in 1897, just across the international border of the Niagara River in Ontario, the Fort Erie race track opened. Buffalo fans now could watch the thoroughbreds. Usually there was just one meet at Fort Erie and that was in mid summer; the trotters sometimes raced in two meets each season. Both tracks were easily accessible. The Hamburg track was about ten miles south of the city of Buffalo; in the days after the Second World War it was probably a half hour drive to the pleasant little village of Hamburg. The Canadian track was even closer; it was accessible by car or bus by way of the Peace Bridge. A more colorful route, taken by many track regulars, was by ferry boat. A prospective bettor could board the ferry, appropriately at the foot of Ferry Street, and take the 10 minute boat ride across the swift flowing Niagara River to the Fort Erie dock. While on board the prospective wager could check out the racing form while listening to a banjo player, and take a side glance at a passing motorboat. Once embarked on the Canadian shore, if time allowed before he took the walk up the gently slopping road to the race track, he might stop at the Queens Hotel for a snack of cheddar cheese, Canadian bacon and a draft of O'Keefe's ale (Molsons and Labatts played second fiddle in those days). The hotels in Fort Erie, including the Anglo American, and the King Edward were actually legitimate hotels in the 1940s.

Both race tracks operated successfully in the first part of the 20th century. World War II put a damper on the races, but after the war the track business resumed. The crowds increased, in fact often attendance records were set, and the betting increased. Fort Erie had an unprecedented season in 1946, "the most gold lined in Ontario history." About 139,000 fans attended and they wagered more than $4,663,387.[2]

The crowds continued to be very good in the years that followed. More attendance records were set. 1947 was an even better year and 1948 was still better. Hamburg opened the 1948 harness racing season with the largest opening day throng in raceway history. 7500 were on hand on May 24, and they bet $104,841. It was a similar story when Fort Erie opened a month later.[3]

The headlines on the sport pages of the daily newspapers told the story best. "Record Racing season at Fort Erie," — "Betting at Fort Erie...1-day record set," —"2.726,610 wagered at Hamburg Track, new record is likely." — "11,000 Ft Erie Fans see Zapola capture Feature." — "12,000 see Valdina Herman take Statler at Fort Erie." — "turnstile and betting records both broke at Hamburg Racetrack."[4]

1949 was pretty much a duplicate of the 1948 season. Another opening night record crowd of 8,000 showed up at Hamburg. A record $137,867 was bet. A three horse photo finish in the very first race added to the excitement of the racing season. Across the river, Fort Erie also continued to set records. Tomos captured the Buffalo Purse in what was called a very good "off-day crowd." Less than a week later, 10,000, the largest crowd of the season, turned out to watch "His Jewel" win the Statler Cup. A week later, Gams took the Madigan purse before another 10,000 edging out His Jewel for the victory.[5]

The races at both Hamburg and Fort Erie were major attractions for Buffalonians in the post war years. Fans had the leisure time to attend the races; money appeared not to be a problem. For a few dollars, one could have a very pleasant afternoon at the track. But there were other factors accounting for the success of the two tracks.

The track proprietors themselves ran first class operations. They were not content to sit still and simply enjoy their current successes. Both tracks made major improvements. *Courier Express* sports editor, Billy Kelly himself a devoted racing fan, was effusive in his praise for everything that happened at Fort Erie. "To say the meeting (the 24 days of racing in 1947) was a financial and sporting success is an understatement." Kelly pointed to the crowds, the handle, and the condition of the track itself. He noted that the increased purses attracted better horses and the splendid work of the handicapper pleased the fans. The players received a better return than previously. Kelly complimented the management for taking care of the comfort of the public.[6]

A few weeks later, Kelly turned his attention to Buffalo Raceway. He praised that venue in much the same way as he did Fort Erie. A large advertisement in the *Courier* called attention to the fall meeting that would run from August 29 to November 8. The ad called the Hamburg track the "finest half-mile harness track in the United States." Kelly had ample praise for Jimmy Dunnigan, the president of Buffalo Raceway. Dunnigan presided over $100,000 worth of improvements on the track and in the grandstands. Kelly noted that two $10,000 purses offered for races midway through the 62-date harness meeting attracted some top notch trotters and pacers. In 1951, Dunnigan was recognized for his achievements when he was named Buffalo's Sportsman of the Year at the Buffalo Athletic Club's annual dinner.[7]

Support from Buffalo businesses and area service clubs gave a big boost to attendance. The Variety Club of Buffalo sponsored a day at the races at each of the tracks. Dewey Michaels, chief barker of the club, presented a trophy to the winning owner of the feature race. The Buffalo Club also sponsored a day at Fort Erie. Purses were offered by many of the downtown hotels, including the Statler, the Markeen and the Buffalo.

Fast tracks in excellent condition, comfortable settings, amenities and good wagering opportunities; these were important. Just as important was the abundance of good horses at both tracks. At the beginning of the meets there would be hundreds of splendid horses available. One who helped out in this respect was John

C. Montana, taxicab tycoon, and Buffalo sportsman. He made sure that some of his top notch horses were ready for Fort Erie, including those he had recently purchased in Lexington, Kentucky.[8]

Good press coverage especially in the morning *Courier*, was important for those planning a trip to the track. The daily selections were published, the handicapper had his say and Billy Kelly, the sports editor often furnished race information and anecdotal material in his column. Additional zest was added when the newspaper regularly published photos of dead heat finishes. In the days before television and instant replay, these gripping photographs did much to arouse interest in the viewers.

The drive out to the Hamburg Raceway or the trip across the border to Fort Erie was another of the many options open to Buffalonians in post war America. However should one not want to venture south to watch the trotters, nor bother with American and Canadian Customs, then a stop along the river to watch the oarsmen at the West Side Rowing Club was another option to consider.

The West Side Rowing Club

In the 1940s, The West Side Rowing Club, often referred to simply as the WSRC, was well on the way to becoming one of the most recognized and celebrated institutions in the entire city.

Rowing is one of the oldest sports in America. It traces its beginning to England where crews competed on the Thames River several hundred years ago. Cambridge and Oxford Universities were noted for their rowing rivalry. Yale and Harvard, imitating their English counterparts, engaged in the first American Intercollegiate Rowing competition in 1852. The sport grew in popularity, especially in colleges and communities in the New England and Middle Atlantic states. Urban locations that bordered bodies of water suitable for rowing became sites of the earliest clubhouses in the country.

Buffalo was one of those localities. The city owed its existence to water. It had a natural port; it dominated the eastern end of Lake Erie. The lake emptied into the Niagara River and that river took the water from the Great Lakes and swiftly moved it to and over the famous waterfalls that bore the river's name. The river served as the border between the United States and Canada. The swift currents in the river made rowing virtually impossible. However the Black Rock Channel, an extension of the Erie Canal, ran parallel to the river. It had been constructed to allow large commercial vessels to avoid navigating the river. The Channel served its commercial purposed extremely well; it aided considerably in the growth of the city of Buffalo. The sheltered channel also provided, as an afterthought, an ideal place for the sport of rowing. Boathouses of various types sprang up along the canal in the late 19th and in the early years of the 20th century. The one that gained permanency was named the West Side Rowing Club.

In the years before World War II, the dominant figures in the WSRC were Mike Broderick, Jim Griffin, and John Bennett. Broderick served as the president of the club from its infancy; he continued to serve in that capacity in the post war years. Griffin was the primary coach in the 1920s and 30s. Bennett, a Buffalo policeman, took over for Griffin and annually served as the unpaid coach of nearly 200 young oarsmen, or as the *Courier Express* sports writer Ray Ryan called them, "the sweep swingers." In the World War II period, Jim Hogan, an ex-football star at Canisius College, joined that illustrious trio.[1]

Appropriately, at the start of the first season following the conclusion of World War II, the West Side held ceremonies at its Bird Island club house honoring those who had served in the conflict. A monument was dedicated to the six club members who had fallen in combat. It was a solemn occasion that served to underscore the patriotism of the WSRC.

It did not take long following the end of the war for the West Side Club to make headlines on the water. In July of 1947, the "Bison" crew, as the *Buffalo Evening News* referred to the West Side oarsmen, took three trophies at the national races held in Detroit, including the coveted senior eight. John Bennett and Jim Hogan scored an easy victory for the pair-oared title, winning by four lengths. The senior four-oared crew with coxwain was victorious too.

A week later, the WSRC won the Royal Canadian Henley Regatta title at Port Dalhousie, (St. Catharine's) Ontario, edging out 16 of the "continent's outstanding rowing organizations." West Side officials began to talk seriously about sending crews to the 1948 Olympics to be held in London. First the West Side crews would have to earn the right to participate by winning in the trials at Princeton, New Jersey. Victory at Princeton became the focus of the rigorous training that the West Side oarsmen undertook in the first half of 1948.

To underscore the commitment, a new shell that would be used by the heavyweight crew at the Princeton tryouts was purchased for $1,500. It was named for Jim Griffin, the 90-year-old former coach, who returned to the Black Rock Channel for the dedication of the shell. In 1936 Griffin's four oared crew had earned distinction by winning the final Olympic tryouts in Philadelphia. That crew proceeded to finish fifth in the Berlin Olympics, which were the most recent ones, since the 1940 and 1944 games were cancelled due to World War II.[2]

West Side crews competed against the top crews in the United States in the tryouts in New Jersey. They performed heroically on Carnegie Lake at Princeton before losing the semi finals. The dream of earning a spot in the Olympics would have to be deferred for eight years. But those '48ers, prepared the path to future glory in Melbourne in 1956 when the crew of Jim McMullen, Doug Turner, Ron Cardwell, Jim Wynne and Coxie Eddie Masterson would carry the banner of the WSRC to the Olympics in that Australian city.

The West Side crews continued to do well at the Royal Canadian Henley in the late 1940s; in fact they dominated the Henley in those years. That dominance extended to the annual Labor Day races that the local club sponsored in the Black Rock Channel. The holiday weekend was a festive occasion for the Buffalo community. Bleachers were set up along the waterway affording excellent viewing. Many new fans were created.

Successes continued to come to the West Side rowers. The blockbuster event for the West Side Rowing Club in the Golden Age of Sports in Buffalo came in the last year of the decade. In January 1949 the announcement was made that the 75th annual Regatta of the National Association of Amateur Oarsmen would be held July 23-24 in the Black Rock Channel.

The city made preparations to roll out the red carpet and to make the event a memorable one for the entire city. Ed Atwill, a club stalwart, and Mike Broderick, perennial WSRC president and its guiding spirit, provided guidelines to a number of public spirited citizens at a luncheon at the Buffalo Club. Included were plans to surround the sporting spectacle with all sorts of water activities and exhibitions to entertain the public during the lengthy intervals between races. The oarsmen themselves had their eyes set on the coveted Julius Barnes Trophy, the team championship award. *Courier Express* Sportswriter Phil Ranallo asserted that the West Siders had good reason to feel confident; they had one of the strongest squads in the history of the club.[3]

As the date for the opening of the regatta approached, Buffalo became the rowing capital of the nation. Some 350 of the best oarsmen in the United States arrived in the city. The U.S. Naval Reserve Training Center provided cots, showers and other necessities for the visiting oarsmen. Big tents were erected on the Sea Scout Base for all the shells. A regular training table was set up at the Buffalo Yacht Club. Races would start at the Buffalo Yacht Club and finish at the West Side clubhouse. On the opening day, an estimated 10,000 fans were on hand to watch the WSRC take the lead by amassing 54 points. The senior four oared crew with coxswain won its race; the WSRC also had two seconds, a third and a fourth. Close behind was the renowned Vesper Club of Philadelphia, famous also for one of its members, Jack Kelly, known as the King of the Scullers. Vespers was in 2nd place with 46 points.

The local media did its part. Both the *Courier Express* and the *Buffalo Evening News* devoted ample space to the regatta. WBEN-TV, with Ralph Hubbell doing the commentary, announced that some of the events would be telecast. Local television was still in its infancy. Several local saloons had television sets sitting high above the back bar, so the devoted fans would not be denied the opportunity to witness the grand event.[4]

The second day was as exciting a day as one ever witnesses at a regatta. Billy Kelly, described it for the reading public: "The West Siders, trailing in the point standing with only three events to go, pulled the championship out of the fire in a manner which the throng of 15,000 will never forget. They took the 145 pound eight oared test, setting a national record to boot, then came back to rack up a sensational, hair line victory in the final race of the day, the senior heavyweight eight-oared grind." The two victories gave the WSRC a two day total of 114 points, a 23 point margin over the Vespers Club. The WSRC was awarded the Julius Barnes trophy, the coveted team award.[5]

A little over a week later, the West Side crews traveled across the international border on their way to participate in the Royal Canadian Henley in St. Catharines, Ontario. There, the senior eight streaked to a "smashing triumph." Overall the WSRC finished second to the host club. The West Siders had won the title the previous four years.[6]

A month later, at the 38th annual Labor Day Regatta the WSRC, once again paced by its senior heavyweight eight oared crew, "closed one of its most successful seasons in its long history," by sweeping to victory in five of eleven events. The star-studded seniors, already champions of North America by virtue of victories at both the United States National and the Royal Canadian Henley, proved to be an outstanding symbol of the Golden Age of Sports in Buffalo.[7]

The West Side Rowing Club would continue to be a vital part of the Buffalo sports scene in the decades that followed. In part that was due to veteran stalwarts such as Charley Fontana and Al Sauerwein and the coming on board at the end of the decade of novices including Doug Turner, Bob Uhl, and Bill Cotter. Under the tutelage of Cotter, the West Side facility and its athletes would earn ever greater accolades in future years. Cotter himself was acclaimed for undertaking the monumental task of rebuilding the clubhouse and boathouse and relocating it following the disastrous fire in the 1970s.

Bob Stedler, the respected Sports Editor of the *Buffalo Evening News*, found the secret of the success of the West Side Rowing Club in its unflagging spirit and its indomitable will and its refusal not to be sidetracked by adverse conditions. He singled out "the enthusiasm of the club's officials who devoted hours in their work with the oarsmen without any recompense except the satisfaction and thrill they get out of training winning crews... Buffalo is fortunate in having an organization of that kind."[8]

Other Sports

There were other things that happened in the wide world of sports, other sporting events, sports activities, and the individual achievements of outstanding athletes that brought attention and glory to Buffalo during its Golden Age. Then too there were other sports that just did not work out very well in Buffalo, or for that matter in any number of other cities.

6 day Bike Races

The 6 day bicycle races were very popular in the 1930s. The marathon races seemed to fit the mood of the Great Depression. Old timers from Buffalo when asked about sporting events they recalled from their youth would invariably bring up the 6 day bike races. The cyclists first came to Buffalo in 1934; the venue was the Broadway Auditorium, the predecessor of Memorial Auditorium. Several thousands fans, sometimes as many as 6,000 or 7,000, were present at the beginning of the race. After midnight, there might be as few as fifty lonesome souls left in the stands.

In March of 1946 Charley Murray, one of the area's premier promoters, met with officials of the National Cycling Association and mapped out plans for the postwar renewal of the races in the fall of 1946. They were also scheduled for Chicago and other Midwest cities.

They opened in Buffalo on October 4, 1946. 2,800 fans were on hand. Adults paid 50 cents, and children 10 cents. On subsequent days, about 2500 fans showed up daily. On the final day 3800 attended. The international team of Cesare Moretti of Italy and Rene Cyr of Montreal won the event by a single lap. The real loser was Cycling Enterprises, the sponsor. Not nearly enough fans attended; the promoters lost money. The moment in the sun for the 6 day races was the 1930s; it was over in the 1940s. The racers faded into nostalgia.[1]

Professional Basketball

Whereas the 6 day cycling sporting events could hark back to a somewhat successful past, professional basketball had a very checkered past; in the 1940s it was still attempting to establish its niche in the larger sporting world.

Professional basketball had been around since shortly after James Naismith invented the game. Unlike the college game, the professionals had a helter-skelter existence for many years. Robert Peterson, historian of the sport, notes that "for fifty years after its beginnings in the last years of the nineteenth century basketball (professional) was a stepchild on the national sport scene." The National Baske tball Association, the NBA, was not formed until 1949.[1]
`The professionals differed from the collegians in that they usually had full time jobs in the community where they played. What made them professional was that they would receive meal money and perhaps a few dollars for each game they played. The most successful team in the early years just happened to be the Buffalo Germans, a team organized at the Genesee Street YMCA near downtown Buffalo. The Buffalo Germans had an illustrious career; in 1904 they participated in a tournament held at the St. Louis World's fair in conjunction with the III Olympics. In effect basketball was a demonstration sport at the Olympics. The Buffalo Germans won the tournament and billed themselves as the world champions. A few years later the Germans went barnstorming. They won 111 consecutive games, a winning streak never challenged. Many years later that feat earned

them induction into the Basketball Hall of Fame in Springfield, Massachusetts, the first team to be so honored.

In the decades that followed other so called professional teams representing Buffalo would appear. Many other cities had similar experiences with professional basketball. Teams came and went and so did leagues. The most successful early teams were those that went barnstorming. The Original Celtics, the New York Rens, and the Harlem Globe Trotters were the most famous. By the mid 1930s a semblance of order had emerged in the broader professional ranks. Two groups achieved a measure of stability, the National Basketball League, and the Basketball Association of America. Nevertheless member teams continued to come and go. That continued to be the situation at the end of the Second World War.

Following the return to peace time conditions, Buffalo secured a franchise in the National Basketball League. Not surprisingly, the team's nickname was the Bisons. They joined the old baseball Bisons, the fairly new hockey Bisons, the brand new football Bisons (in 1947 to be renamed the Bills) and the Roller Derby Bisons. So why not five!

A group led by Leo Ferris and supported by the Erie County American Legion was granted the Buffalo franchise. A former Original Celtic star, Nat Hickey was named coach; he lined up a number of solid players. Mel Thurston, Lockport native and former Canisius star was first. Bob Gauchat, a practicing dentist and also a former Canisius star joined, as did Pop Gates. One of the first Black players in the league, Gates had several years of experience with other teams. Next Buffalo lined up a big man, in fact the biggest in the game at that time. Don Otten, former star at Bowling Green University, was just a shade shy of 7 feet tall. Billy Hassett, who had starred for Notre Dame and had played in the Aud against Canisius was also signed.

In October the team spent two weeks training in Elmira then returned to Buffalo for a gala welcome. A big parade that included numerous bands, drum corps and American Legion Units was staged. The team was also honored at a festive luncheon in the Hotel Statler. A week later the Buffalo Bisons, in their opening game, played the Syracuse Nationals and won, 50 - 39, before 4,182. Buffalo proceeded to win a few and lose a few in the weeks that followed, usually about 3,000 fans showed up. The outlook was dim.

The Bisons lost to the Fort Wayne Zollners, and then to the Oshkosh All Stars. They returned to the Aud to defeat the Anderson Indiana Packers, 52 – 50 in a thrilling overtime game marked by a big brawl. Unfortunately only 1,003 fans showed up. Financially the club was hurting; Leo Ferris was losing money. He tried to entice fans to buy stock, to give the fans a stake in the club, like the Green Bay Packers. He had no success.

A week later, on December 16, only 1,022 fans showed up for the loss to Sheboygan. That was the last straw. The decision was made to move the team to the Tri Cities (Moline and Rock Island, Illinois, and Davenport, Iowa.) by the end of the year. The Bisons then had a 5 – 8 record. General Manager Leo Ferris said that the club needed about 4,000 spectators a game to break even.

Meanwhile, just 70 miles to the east, in Rochester, pro basketball was doing quite well. College basketball was not a spectator attraction there whereas Buffalo had long been known as a place where college basketball thrived. Les Harrison, the owner of the Rochester Royals, was an old basketball hand. He had been involved with amateur and semipro teams since the 1920s. In the 1930s he took his earnings from his fruit and vegetable business and bought the Rochester Royals. He made them into a power in the National Basketball League and later in the National Basketball Association. Harrison knew the lay of the land; he knew that the colleges had Buffalo locked up. He saw Rochester as a middle sized city without colleges playing major basketball. It was an ideal setting for a new professional team to begin to have limited success.[2]

It was clear that professional basketball was not going to secure a foothold in Buffalo in the immediate postwar era. The pro game would make slow progress elsewhere. By the end of the decade the two leagues had solved some differences and formed the NBA, the National Basketball Association. Still, for some time to come, professional basketball was a very poor second cousin to major college basketball

Tennis

Professional tennis tried its hand at taking advantage of the upsurge in interest in sports following the Second World War. It ended up double faulting. In April 1946, the world professional tennis tour came to the Memorial Auditorium. Don Budge defeated Bobby Riggs before just 2,107 spectators. That was it for that season. Two years later, another attempt was made; this time 2,700 fans watched Jack Kramer defeat the irrepressible Riggs. *News* sportswriter Dick Johnston concluded that the "attendance just about proved that Buffalo is not a tennis town." Bobby Riggs decided to try his hand at promotion. In 1949, he staged a match between Kramer and Poncho Gonzales in the Aud before 2,600 paid admissions. Johnston was right; almost anyway. A short time later, a record crowd of 5,041 was on hand to watch Jack Kramer defeat Frank Sedgman. Regardless, tennis was not a successful spectator sport in Buffalo."[1]

Still More

Bike races, pro basketball and tennis were not golden in Buffalo in the 1940s. However there were still other events, simply by being hosted in Buffalo, that brought prestige to the City of Good Neighbors; that added to the golden glow.

In the first month of 1948, the Buffalo Tennis and Squash Club hosted the national professional squash racquets championship tournament. In March of the same year, the Buffalo Intercollegiate Hockey group hosted a four team college tournament in Memorial Auditorium. Dartmouth defeated Clarkson for the first place trophy. In September of 1948, the Buffalo Yacht club hosted the International Lightning Championships at the Canoe Club at Bay Beach on the Canadian shore.

Meanwhile Dr. Robert Westermeier was achieving national acclaim in shooting circles. Westermeier earned his stripes locally at the Buffalo Trap and Field Club. The high water mark of his career came in 1947 when he won the National Skeet Association in Syracuse by hitting 250 targets over a two day period. He did not miss a single one.[1]

In an era when women were not viewed as major players in the world of sport, two Buffalonians, Ethel Marshall and Bea Massman, were major exceptions. Both women worked at Bell Aircraft during the war, shades of Rosie the Riveter. Following the war they made headlines on the local sports pages. In 1947 Marshall won the U.S. National Badminton championship. She broke all records by winning it for seven consecutive years. Marshall amassed a total of 27 badminton crowns and Bea Massman won 14 U.S. titles. Both women also won several tennis championships. Marshall and Massman earned enshrinement in the U.S. Badminton Hall of Fame and both of these star athletes became charter members of the Greater Buffalo Sports Hall of Fame.[1]

Speedboats on the Niagara

Speed is often regarded as the key element in athletic success. At the close of the Golden Age of Buffalo sports, speed in the form of speedboat racing on the Niagara River commanded the attention of the public.

Speedboat races had been held on the Niagara River in the early years of the 20th century. In the 1920s, *Courier Express* Publisher Bill Connors, a widely known sports enthusiast, often took part in the races and often won. His presence greatly enhanced the sport. Then with the hard times of the Great Depression and the priorities of the Second World War, speedboat racing lapsed.[1]

In 1949 the races were revived with a vengeance. George Trimper, young Buffalo lawyer and speed boat aficionado along with Bob Schutt of the Buffalo Launch Club arranged for the International Speedboat and Powerboat Regatta to be held in Buffalo, on the Niagara River, on August 21-22, 1949.[2]

The regatta was a huge event. It attracted considerable attention not just in Western New York but wherever water sports were popular. Sportsmen of national reputation brought their boats to Buffalo. Big band leader Guy Lombardo, known for playing the sweetest music this side of heaven, brought his Tempo IV to compete in the unlimited hydroplane event. He would compete against Bill Cantrell, whose My Sweetie, was regarded as one of the fastest boats the world.

In the feature event of the regatta, Cantrell, aka the Kentucky Colonel, lived up to his top billing. He missed the record for a 15 mile race by a little over 1/10th of a second. His average speed was over 77 mph. He ended up a mile ahead of Guy Lombardo. George Trimper was the best known of the local speedboat contingent. Trimper seemed a natural. He lived in the Riverside section of the city, only a long stone's throw from the river. As a youth he was active in water sports and took an active interest in speedboat racing. Not surprisingly he served in the Navy in World War 11. Trimper became a recognized racing champion in the years after the war. In the 1949 regatta he piloted his boat, Wild Oats, to a second place finish in the Class D roundabout category.[3]

The area public warmly embraced the regatta. Dick Johnston, of the *Buffalo Evening News*, likened the Launch Club and adjoining area to a large county fairground. Picnickers seemed to be everywhere. Cars parked for miles along the River Road on Grand Island; yachts and crafts of all sizes were buoyed along the Buffalo side of the river. A public address system kept the fans informed. It boomed results up and down the banks of the river. It was heard by the patrons of the legendary Bedell House and Daverns Saloon as well as those youngsters who were diving recklessly off the pilings and the ferryboat into the river. The weekend regatta provided a festive occasion. All aspects of it were successful. Johnston said, "No accurate count could be made but estimates of the crowd ran from 50,000 to 100,000." Regardless of exact figures, the crowds were phenomenal. The success did not go unrewarded. The 1949 International Speedboat Regatta was judged to be the nation's best by the American Powerboat Association, the sport's governing body, as well as by the sport's two leading speedboat racing magazines.[4]

A few months later, Trimper was named Buffalo's Athlete of the Year. Cited as the holder of four world speedboat records two of them set in 1949, Trimper was honored as the athlete who contributed most to Buffalo athletics in 1949. Trimper's award came at the third annual March of Dimes dinner at the Hotel Statler. It was noted that he had "contributed greatly to regaining for speedboat racing a prominent position in the local sports picture."[5]

Buffalo hosted the regatta again in 1950 and with equally successful results, if not more so. There were many more entries than the previous year and probably more fans lining the course. It was hailed as the largest inboard meet in the United States. Throngs estimated at 50,000 or more were on hand each day; one estimate had the two day total at 200,000. This time George Trimper rose to the pinnacle. He piloted his Baby Loon to a "smashing victory" to open the 1950 regatta. Trimper raced in the Class E runabout category. That was the highlight of the first day. The second day belonged to Guy Lombardo. The well known band leader powered his Tempo IV to victory in the unlimited hydroplane event.[6]

Buffalo had made its mark in the sport of speedboat racing, just as it had in so many other sports. As the curtain came down on the Golden Age of Sports, perhaps it was fitting that water, that great resource for which the Niagara region was widely known, would be the scene for one of the last and one of the most successful sporting events of the era.

CHAPTER TEN

Conclusion

— Just How Golden Was the Golden Age —

The Golden Age of Buffalo Sports came to an end as the decade of the 1950s got underway. Most historical eras are not clearly defined with precise bookends marking either the beginning or the end. In the case of Buffalo's Golden Age the beginning was very precise. World War II ended in August of 1945. Peace returned, organized sports prepared to go full speed ahead. The Golden Age began. The end was less precise but the beginning of the 1950s is a convenient place to indicate that the era was passing. By then several sports had lost the Midas touch; some came to an abrupt end. Perhaps the Golden Age of Sports in Buffalo could be compared to the more familiar Golden Age of Radio in America. That Golden Age is generally acknowledged to be the 1930s but there were glimmers of it in the 1920s and surely aspects of it continued well into the decade of the 1940s.

Football was the first and biggest casualty. The Buffalo Bills and the Canisius College football teams no longer existed in 1950; Niagara's football team ended the following year, and St. Bona's, the year after that. The football program at the University of Buffalo lingered on for a few years before experiencing some changes for the better.

Big time boxing faded into oblivion in Buffalo, as it did in many comparable sized cities. There was just too much televising of the boxing matches from New York City. The era's most celebrated sports writer added his view complaining that there was "practically no heavyweight division left." Television demanded fighters, big, heavy punchers. Grantland Rice thought that too many heavyweights came up to the big time without having proper experience. The result was bad for boxing.[1]

Wrestling was hurt but not quite as much as boxing. The Aud still witnessed some large wrestling crowds, but they were infrequent and there were not nearly as many mat cards each season as there had been in the 1940s.

College basketball remained a very big attraction in Memorial Auditorium in the 1950s and 60s. The attendance remained especially strong for Little Three games. However the era that saw the dominance of the Garden and the Aud was over. Many of the big state institutions, especially in the West and the South, built large edifices on their own campuses. Often these arenas held more than 10,000 seats. Consequently the teams from those parts of the country no longer felt a need to be a regular part of the doubleheader programs in Buffalo.

Baseball and hockey had their ups and downs in the 1950s and 60s. In the 50s, television had an absolutely disastrous effect on minor league baseball. Attendance at minor league games was off 8 million fans in 1950 from its high in 1949. Buffalo was no exception. Even on July 4th weekends, the attendance would often be less than 2,000. In the mid 1950s there were frequently fewer than 1,000 fans in the seats of Offermann Stadium. The nail in the coffin came at the end of the decade when the venerable stadium was torn down, and a school was built, supposedly in the name of progress, on the site. The Bisons tried to succeed for a few years in War Memorial (formerly Civic) Stadium but couldn't do so. The Bison baseball team became extinct, at least temporarily.[2]

Hockey followed a somewhat similar route. The American Hockey League even contemplated disbanding in the mid-1950s. Occasionally a playoff contender would draw decent crowds in Buffalo. But the sport hit rock bottom by the end of the decade. It was much of the same in the 1960s before a championship team in 1969 gave way to the National Hockey League Sabres.

The Golden Age of Sports faded rather quickly. On the other hand, the city of Buffalo, generally, continued to do quite well in the decade of the 1950s. The Buffalo community continued along the road of economic prosperity and growth without major difficulties. At the beginning of the new decade, *Fortune* magazine, painted a rosy picture of the city. Buffalo ranked eleventh among the nation's cities in manufacturing. It was still the world's milling capital, and the inland port was bustling with activity. The magazine presented many examples of Buffalo's diverse industry, singling out Worthington Pump, Buffalo Forge, Wurlitzer, Wood and Brooks, Wickwire, American Brass, American Radiator, Fedders, the Chevrolet and Ford plants, Bell Aircraft and Twin Coach, Kittinger, Birge Wallpaper, Sylvania, Western Electric, Westinghouse, Durez Plastics and Hooker Chemical. It noted that the steel industry was booming. *Fortune* did point out that half of the large plants, those with 100 or more workers were absentee-owned but it did not regard that as a problem.[3]

Buffalo's auto plants set records in production in the 1950s. The *Courier Express* noted that "construction of the new Ford plant tied in with the Bethlehem steel program comprise the largest industrial expansion in the history of the Niagara Frontier."[4] Bethlehem was on track to employing 20,000 workers and the auto industry was not far behind, employing some 19,000 workers.

The city government functioned well at the dawn of the new decade. Politics were not as acrimonious as they would be later. In the early 1950s the two parties were nearly equal in terms of voter registration. Joseph Mruk was the Mayor; he was the first Polish American elected to that office; he was a Republican. *Fortune* magazine noted that Buffalo was one of the most highly organized, labor union cities, and yet often the workers voted Republican.

As the decade rolled along, the Chamber of Commerce fell into the habit of annually predicting continued prosperity, noting that each coming year would be better than the previous one. Employment reached record highs. Industrial production was unprecedented. The Korean War, 1950-53, proved to be a boon to industry. A headline in the *Buffalo Evening News* exclaimed: "military contracts of local plants at $100,000,000."[5]

Downtown Buffalo continued to be the hub of entertainment, business, and retail shopping. The city remained the center of cultural activities and sporting events. Nightclubs and music spots were thriving. The population of the city continued strong. The suburbs were beginning to grow but the city's population reached its highest point ever according to the census of 1950. The city population numbered 580,132. It had slipped merely from 14th position in 1940 to 15th a decade later.

Thus while significant changes were taking place in the sports scene in Buffalo, the city as a whole continued to be quite healthy. Buffalo manufacturing and industry, with steel, autos, and chemicals leading the way, continued to prosper.

However there were changes in the wind. At first there were the small ones, the kind that always seem to occur and pretty much are taken for granted. Some are simply cosmetic, the sort of changes that later become endeared to the nostalgic minded.

Buffalo's streetcars made their final run in July of 1950. Busses were the wave of the future. The trolleys made their final trips along the Hertel-Fillmore route and on Broadway and on Genesee Street. At the Broadway-Fillmore intersection, a celebration took place. As the *Courier* graphically described it: "The seven antiquated monsters shuffled warily out Broadway and though a jeering gauntlet of harassed citizens to an ignominious burial…the grim cortege …picking up rejoicing mourners anxious to get one last free dig into the vehicles' ancient hides before the end."[6] Ominously, perhaps, the triple AAA, the Automobile Association of America, celebrated its 50th anniversary at the same time.

The Niagara River Ferry Boat, navigating between Buffalo to Fort Erie for 75 years, made its final run in April of 1951. Increasing costs forced its exit. It would find a final resting place near the Bedell House on Grand Island. There, a generation of youngsters would be able to perfect their diving and swimming skills using the hulk as a base of operations.

Buffalo's largest maker of beer, the Lang Brewery, closed in 1950. The Larkin Building, designed by Frank Lloyd Wright, was slated for demolition that same year. The Lehigh Valley railroad announced it was ending its service. The sleek Black Diamond sped off into history. The imposing train station across the street from Memorial Auditorium would soon become a ghost palace.

The War Assets Administration announced that it was closing shop in 1950. It had successfully disposed of billions of dollars of government property since the end of World War II. Area youth could say goodbye to the army and navy surplus stores that had dotted Main Street, places where so many boy scouts and campers had purchased canteens, trenching tools and other treasures of military equipment.

Charlie Murray died in 1950. He was eulogized as one of Buffalo's premier athletic promoters. Jack Singer, the legendary boxing impresario, had predeceased him by a few months. Billy Kelly, longtime sports editor of the *Courier Express* retired. Doc Crowdle was getting ready to join Ned Irish in severing ties with the Memorial Auditorium doubleheader basketball program. The Jacobs family was also preparing to turn over the Bison hockey franchise as well as Offermann stadium to other interests. The Old Guard was passing from the scene.

Large scale, sweeping changes, with revolutionary impact, were just beginning to be recognized as the new decade dawned. The growth of suburbia, the rise of the Sunbelt, and the impact of television would change life fundamentally. The huge magnitude of the changes would become evident as the years rolled on; glimpses of them could be seen earlier.

Following the end of the war, returning veterans using Veteran Administration loans were able to secure affordable mortgages on "Levittown style" houses that were mass produced in the inner ring of suburbs. The towns of Tonawanda and Cheektowaga began to boom followed shortly by Amherst and West Seneca. Increasingly large number of automobiles was purchased; municipalities constructed bigger and better roads that allowed the new suburbanites to commute from home to work easier. The thruway was completed in 1954 and the spin-offs of it, the expressways around and into the city followed. These included the Main line, the Youngman and the Niagara sections of Interstate 90, and eventually the Kensington and Scajaquada. The latter two knifed through the heart of the city.

Retail shopping was an important part of the mushrooming suburbs. Shopping centers, plazas as they were called in Buffalo, made their appearance. The Sheridan Plaza and the University Plaza were the earliest. The gigantic Thruway plaza in Cheektowaga followed a short time later as did the Northtowns shopping center in Amherst as well as shopping centers in the Southtowns. Theaters, banks, and restaurants also became a part of the suburban scene.

The impact on downtown Buffalo began to be noticed. Department stores built branches in the new shopping centers. Retail business was drained off from downtown. Sometimes store closings resulted. Edwards department store was the first to go. By the end of the decade the J. N. Adams and Flint and Kent department stores followed the path to extinction. About the same time Buffalo area industry turned more and more to the suburbs for expansion and sometimes for relocation. Some entertainment venues, cultural activities and athletic events experienced losses in attendance. In the following decades downtown became a skeleton of the past.[7]

As the ring of towns around Buffalo grew, the city's population decreased. The population of the city of Buffalo fell from 580,132 in 1950 to 532,759, a decade later. What was true for Buffalo and its suburbs was true for the nation as a whole. Suburbs grew before and after the1950s, but it was during that decade that the most pronounced shift in population took place. "Suburbs during the 1950s grew...forty times as fast as the central cities."[8] However it was not just the suburbs that were siphoning off city population. The Sunbelt states and especially their cities attracted people from throughout the Northeast and the Midwest thereby helping to create the Rustbelt. Virtually overnight it seemed that some of those urban areas in the south and west became megalopolises. The warm weather, air conditioning, lower taxes, and other factors encouraged people and businesses to relocate to the Sunbelt. The impact on Buffalo began to be noticed in the 1950s; it would become an overwhelming force in the '60s and '70s. The Sunbelt cities of San Diego, San Antonia, Dallas and Houston all moved ahead of Buffalo. In 1960 Buffalo was ranked number 20; by the end of the century Buffalo had slid to number 50, just below Toledo.

The Buffalo metropolitan area (basically Erie and Niagara counties) had grown during the 1950s. But elsewhere, especially in the Sunbelt, the growth rate was much faster. By the end of the century the United States Census Bureau ranked the Buffalo SMSA (Standard Metropolitan Statistical Area) #43, with a total population of 1,170,111 one slot below Hartford, Connecticut.[9]

Sports, especially spectator sports, were affected by the suburban revolution and the rise of the Sunbelt. But nothing affected sports in Buffalo and in the United States more than television did. Television's impact on sports was decisive and far reaching; in fact it was revolutionary.

Demolition of Offermann Stadium, 1961. The Old Order Changeth. *Photo: Pat Farrell.*

Television was born prior to World War II. But the war gave it a still birth. Once peace returned, it was full speed ahead. New York City was naturally the nurturing place for television in the years immediately following the war. By the end of the decade, most major cities had at least one television station. WBEN began televising in Buffalo in mid 1948. Philco, Admiral or Dumont TV sets could be found in showroom windows and in saloons and other commercial establishments. Purchases for home use began in earnest in the 1950s and by the middle of the decade, three out of four families owned a set and were watching very limited programming, sometimes only a test pattern, as much as 35 hours a week.

Television's impact in the 1950s was especially hard on what sports historian Randy Roberts calls the arena sports, boxing, wrestling, and the roller derby. Throughout the country those sports suffered in terms of attendance. For example, in the late 1940s, 10,000 to 12,000 fans regularly watched the Friday night card at Madison Square Garden, a decade later "attendance had dropped to an average of a mere 1,200." Buffalo was not spared that fate in its arena sports. Benjamin Rader adds that "Attendance at major and minor league baseball as well as inner city high school sports dropped precipitously." When a lukewarm fan had the choice of attending a minor league game or watching Ted Williams or Mickey Mantle on television, the choice was most often the latter.[10]

Television, along with the rise of suburbia and to some extent the Sunbelt, had an influence on the fading of Buffalo's Golden Age of Sports. Each particular sport also had its own problems endemic to it that accounted for its status in the years ahead.

But hope springs eternal. Steve Weller, in 1959 a newly arrived sports columnist for the *Buffalo Evening News*, and one of the most talented sports writers ever to grace the local sports scene, had high hopes for a new golden era beginning in 1960. Ralph Wilson had just secured a franchise for the Buffalo team in the American Football League. Branch Rickey announced plans for a new baseball league, the Continental League, with Buffalo slated to be a charter member. Bison Hockey was on the verge of resurgence. Bison Baseball won the pennant in the International League and led that league in attendance with a record setting, 413,263.[11]

Alas that new golden era did not materialize. Every blue collar, red blooded Buffalo sports fan knows that there were definitely some years in the second half of the 20th century and in the early years of the 21st when a particular sport was golden. There were even times when two or three, concurrently, might be worthy of that label. But no one period of time or stretch of years, embracing a large number of major sports, was able to match the era immediately following the Second World War.

Just how Golden was the Golden Age of Sports in Buffalo???

Without a doubt, sports in Buffalo flourished in those years. Most of the time each of the teams was at least respectable on the field of play; often they were very, very good. Buffalonians were very generous in their backing of the athletes and the teams. Fans turned out in unprecedented numbers. The entire Buffalo community was overwhelmingly supportive.

Buffalo Bison baseball was a solid part of Buffalo's sports scene. Opening day crowds including a record breaking throng in1946, filled Offermann Stadium. As the decade drew to a close the Bisons brought home to the city the International Baseball League pennant. In September 1949, 40,000 fans welcomed the pennant winners at the mammoth New York Central Terminal. The baseball team's success was enhanced by the fact that the Triple AAA International League enjoyed an excellent reputation. The caliber of baseball played, at least at times, approximated that of the majors. At a time when the number of major league baseball teams was half what is was at the end of the century, the top teams in Triple AAA were quite special.

The Hockey Bisons fared similarly. They made the playoffs all but one year in the post war period. The Hockey team won the Calder Cup in 1946 and was the runner up to Cleveland in 1948. The Ice Bisons won the Eastern Division in 1950 and 1951 and again were the runner up to Cleveland in the race for the Calder cup in the latter year. Fans turned out in record numbers. Crowds often numbered more than 10,000 in the Aud. The crowds were second only to those in Cleveland. The top teams in the AHL were on the doorstep of the NHL, where only four American (and two Canadian) teams held sway.

College Football did well in Western New York. No one would argue that it was on a par or even near so, with Notre Dame, or Ohio State. But the teams representing Canisius, Niagara, St. Bonaventure, and the University of Buffalo performed admirably. They put fans in the stands and defeated some highly rated teams on the field of play. Winning seasons were commonplace. The victims of the Western New York teams included Louisville, Bowling Green, Bucknell, Marshall, Toledo, St. Louis, Fordham, San Francisco, and Boston University. Canisius and St. Bona even played in bowl games, both lost by just one point. Those same two elevens had battled in 1946 before 35,089 fans. That set the record for college football attendance in Western

New York. It remained in tact into the 21st century.

In the All American Football Conference, which proved to be a worthy and competitive rival of the National Football League, the Buffalo team did poorly in its first year. That changed and the Buffalo Bills from 1947 through 1949 made a name for themselves in professional football. The Bills drew very good crowds, better than those in many of the NFL cities. Buffalo made the playoffs in 1948, first defeating the Baltimore Colts then losing to the Cleveland Browns. Not many teams defeated the Browns in those years. The crowning achievements may have been in 1949 when the Bills twice tied the best team in all of professional football, and then went on to lose to those same Cleveland Browns by only 10 points in a post season contest. That came just a month before Buffalo was blindsided by the NFL.

There is little dispute that college basketball shone brightly in the post war years. On the five seasons from 1946-7 through 1950-51, a total of 20 seasons for the four western New York college teams, there were 17 winning seasons and only three losing ones. Niagara and St. Bona each earned a berth in the National Invitation Tournament. Canisius had done so in 1944. The NIT was then a more prestigious tournament than the NCAA. The four local quintets enjoyed victories against some of the top teams from throughout the entire United States. The Aud was the scene of numerous sell outs in those years. It could be readily understood why Buffalo's Memorial Auditorium was acknowledged to be the number two venue for college basketball in the United States, just a step behind Madison Square Garden.

When college basketball doubleheaders were not packing the fans into the downtown arena then boxing and wrestling were. Nationally ranked boxers, Willie Pep and Sugar Ray Robinson, fought there. Local heroes, Phil and Joe Muscato regularly drew more than 10,000 fans to their bouts. Yukon Eric and Gorgeous George did the same in wrestling, as did the Angel and Frank Sexton. Ed Don George's Parade of Champions annually drew a five figure crowd.

In Civic Stadium the Midget Auto Races drew eight to ten thousand spectators regularly and on special evenings that featured the likes of Wild Bill Schindler more than 20,000 would attend. In the limited time that the Roller Derby had center stage in the Aud, some 4,000 frantic followers of the game would attend and on occasion that figure would be doubled.

The Golden Age also included some special occasions, those one time sporting events that added additional glitter to the era. The American Bowling Congress' annual tournament in 1946 was held in Buffalo and it drew tens of thousands of participants and spectators who spent well over $2 million dollars in the Queen City. In golf, in 1948, the Western Open, then one of the premier golf tournaments, was held at the Brookfield Country Club. Over the four day period some 26,000 watched the great Ben Hogan on route to victory. The West Side Rowing Club annually drew throngs of onlookers who lined the banks of the Niagara River and the Black Rock Channel to watch the oarsmen in action. The horse races at Fort Erie and at the Buffalo Raceway drew steady crowds, well over 5,000 at each running, in those years.

Last but no means least, the crème de la crème of the post war period of Buffalo was a high school football game. The Kensington-Bennett game in 1948, attracted 50,988 spectators to Civic Stadium. That figure has never been matched; it has not even been approximated.

Those times really did glitter. The years

immediately following the Second World War were genuinely a Golden Age for Sports in Buffalo.

A half century later, when old timers reflected nostalgically on that period, there was no reason to exaggerate, no need for hyperbole. Thousands upon thousands of Buffalonians left the Queen City in the 1950s and '60s and even greater numbers exited in the decades that followed. They left the area, many against their wishes, for any number of reasons. Some moved to the big cities along the east coast, including Boston, New York City, Philadelphia, Baltimore and Washington. Others, many more in fact, moved to the cities and new urban areas throughout the South, Southwest, the Rocky Mountain area and the Far West. In their new environs, groups of ex-Buffalonians would gather periodically for mutual interests and to remember fondly the great city they had left behind.

The "exiles" would recall fondly stories from their youth, from high school and college years, those formative years that are so vivid in one's memories. They would gather at an annual Buffalo night or perhaps at a post Buffalo Bills game party, or a college reunion, or to watch the Sabres in the NHL playoffs. Perhaps it might be just a gathering of South Buffalonians held together by an allegiance to Cazenovia Park, or a group of former employees from Bell Aerospace. Sometimes it might just be several Buffalonians getting together for the sake of getting together.

On these occasions, conversations would inevitably turn to Roast Beef on Kummelweck, the Crystal Beach Boat, the Chez Ami, Sattlers, the Everglades on Hertel, Fish Fries and Ted's or Pat's Hot Dogs, Lerczaks, Sunset Bay and the Sherkston Quarry. Invariably sports would surface, and Golden Age memories would rise to the top: Offermann Stadium, George Ratterman, Ollie Carnegie (he did play a final year in the 1940s), Gorgeous George, Leroy Chollet and the Ken-Bennett game. Always the Ken-Bennett game! The *New York Times* once recalled that if all the people who claimed that they were at the New York Giants - Brooklyn Dodgers game in 1951 when Bobby Thompson hit the famous pennant winning home run were actually there, then the crowd must have numbered more than 800,000. The Ken Bennett game is like that. There must have been close to 2 million Buffalonians at Civic Stadium that warm October night in 1948. Well, so it seemed!

The immediate post war era, the late 1940s, was a unique one. It was a proud time for Buffalonians. It is an even prouder time for nostalgic, ex-Buffalonians to remember, to boast about, and even to tell tall tales about. Those really were the good old days; the golden age for sports-minded Buffalonians.

Demographic Data

Population tables constructed from US Bureau of the Census data illustrate population trends in the United States during the last century. Table I shows Buffalo as one of the top ten cities in the US in 1900.

Table I

Rank	Place 1	Population
1	New York city, NY	3,437,202
2	Chicago city, IL	1,698,575
3	Philadelphia city, PA	1,293,697
4	St. Louis city, MO	575,238
5	Boston city, MA	560,892
6	Baltimore city, MD	508,957
7	Cleveland city, OH	381,768
8	Buffalo city, NY	352,387
9	San Francisco city, CA	342,782
10	Cincinnati city, OH	325,902

In 1900 Buffalo was #8, ahead of Detroit, Washington, and Pittsburgh.

Buffalo gradually, but almost imperceptibly slid down the Census tables.
In 1950 Buffalo was still in top 15, but the sunbelt was beginning to move up.
Houston was in #14.

In 1960, at the end of the great boom of the suburbs and the sunbelt, the great Queen City of the Great Lakes found itself in #20 trailing not only Houston, but also San Diego, San Francisco, Seattle, San Antonio, New Orleans, and Dallas.

By the end of the century Buffalo found itself sandwiched between Toledo, and Wichita as the 50th largest city in the US.

Table II gives a detailed account of Buffalo's population.

Like most formerly industrial cities of the Great Lakes region—the so-called "rust belt"—Buffalo, has suffered through several decades of population decline brought about by the loss of its industrial base. The city's population peaked in 1950, when it was the 15th largest city in the United States. Its population has declined in every decade since, particularly during the two decades from 1960 to 1980, when the city lost nearly one-third of its population.

Table II

Historical Populations

Census	Pop.	% + / -
1830	8,688	-----
1840	18,213	110.1%
1850	42,261	132.0%
1860	81,129	92.0%
1870	117,714	45.1%
1880	155,134	31.8%
1890	255,664	64.8%
1900	352,387	37.8%
1910	423,715	20.2%
1920	506,775	19.6%
1930	573,076	13.1%
1940	575,901	0.5%
1950	580,132	0.7%
1960	532,759	-8.2%
1970	462,768	-13.1%
1980	357,870	-22.7%
1990	328,123	-8.3%
2000	292,648	-10.8%

FOOTNOTES

BEN = Buffalo Evening News
CE = Courier Express

Chapter 1

1. Mark Goldman, *High Hopes: The Rise and Decline of Buffalo, New York* (Albany: State University of New York Press, 1983), 61, 121, 128 ff.
2. Edward Dunn, *A History of Railroads in Western New York* (Buffalo: Canisius College Press, 2000), see especially Ch. 12.
3. Goldman, *City On The Edge* (Buffalo: Prometheus Books, 2007), 31.
4. Goldman, *Ibid.*, 17 ff.
5. Stephen Powell, *Rushing the Grolier – A History of Brewing in Buffalo* (Buffalo: Digital Print Services, 1996), 41 ff.
6. Sam B. Warner, *Streetcar Suburbs* (Cambridge: Harvard University Press, 1962). Provides details of suburban development in Boston. Similar development took place in Buffalo.
7. Joseph Bieron, *Postcard Views: A Walk Down Main Street Buffalo, New York, circa. 1910* (Buffalo: Buffalo Heritage Unlimited, 2007), esp. Chapters 3 – 7.
8. Goldman, *High Hopes*, 152 ff., 219 ff.
9. Goldman, *City on the Edge*, 133 ff. Allen C. Gadensky, *The Bison Shipyard Story* (Buffalo: Allen Gadensky, 2005). The Bison Shipbuilding Corporation was a wartime partnership of the Ernst Iron Works and the August Feine Company. Frank Eberl, interview by the author, Unistruct - Eberl Iron Works, May 20, 2008.
10. *BEN,* August 15, 1945.
11. *BEN*, September 2, 1945.
12. *BEN*, November 10, 1945.
13. *BEN*, December 29, 1945.
14. *BEN*, January 6, 1945, February 27, 1946. *CE*, January 1,1946.
15. *BEN*, *CE*, May 3, 1946. *CE*, June 6, 1947, October 10, 1946.
16. *CE*, January 20, 1946. *BEN*, November 22, July 18, 1947.
17. *CE*, June 24, 28, 1946. *BEN*, January 27, November 24, 1947. *CE*, August 5, 1947, February 25, 1947.
18. *BEN*, December 31, 1947. *CE,* August 15, 1948.
19. *CE,* July 6, 1949, February 11, February 1, 195

Chapter 2

1. Joseph Overfield, *The 100 Seasons of Buffalo Baseball (*Buffalo: Partners Press, 1985), 17-18. See also http://www.*NLBPA.com.*
2. Overfield, *Ibid.*, 160 ff.
3. Cy Kritzer, *BEN*, August 8, 15, 1945.
4. Kritzer*, BEN*, November 1-2, 1945.
5. *BEN*, March 9, 1946. Cy Kritzer, interview by the author, August 10, 1992. Kritzer, one of the most knowledgeable baseball men in the country, was a former president of the American Baseball Writers Group.
6. *BEN*, May 1, 1946. *CE*, May 1, 1946.
7. Robert Stedler, *BEN*, May 19, 1946. *Toronto Star*, April 1996.
8. Cy Williams, interview by the author, March 5, 2005. General Bass, interview by the author, May 4, 1998.
9. Overfield, *Ibid.*, 88.
10. Kritzer, *BEN*, November 1, December 4, 1946.
11. Stedler, *BEN,* December 4, Nov 1946, May 5, 1946. *CE*, December 3, 1946.
12. Kritzer*, BEN*, December 4, 10, 1946.
13. Earle Hannel, interview by the author, November 8, 2004.
14. Jerry Collins, interview by the author, November 15, 2004.
15. Williams, interview by the author, March 12, 2005.
16. Overfield, 89.
17. *CE*, July 9, 1948. Overfield, 89.
18. *BEN*, July 6, 1948.
19. Overfield, 93. James Burke, interview by the author, November 20, 2006.
20. Joe Alli, *CE,* May 4, 1949.
21. Billy Kelly, *CE*, June 17, 1949.
22. *BEN*, September 2, 6, 1949.
23. *BEN*, September 7, 1949. Overfield, 91.
24. *BEN*, September 7, 1949.
25. Overfield, 91.
26. Stedler, *BEN*, June 16, 1950.
27. Website: http://www.minorleaguebaseball.com,

28. David Greenman, interview by the author, May 20, 2008.

Chapter 3

1. Francis Dunn, Bus. Mgr of the Buffalo franchise, as noted in the *CE*, February 16, 1949.
2. Robert Peterson, *Pigskin: The Early Years of Pro Football* (New York: Oxford University Press, 1997), 66 ff.
3. Peterson, 69 ff.
4. Roy Sye, "Almost Champions," (*Coffin Corner*, Volume 25, 2003), provides basic information. See also Jeffrey Miller, *Buffalo's Forgotten Champions*, www.Xlibris.com: Xlibris Corporation 2007. Also J. Miller "The All American" Summer 2003, Volume 3 in Buffalo Bills Archive
5. Stan Grosshandler, *Professional Football Research Association*, http:www.footballre search.com.6. Grosshandler, PRRA.
7. *BEN*, August 3, 1945. *CE* February 28, 1946.
8. Kritzer, *BEN*, April 16, 1946.
9. *CE*, September 9, 1946. *BEN* September 9, 1946.
10. Stedler, *BEN*, June 11, 1947. Obituary in *Denver Post*, November 14, 2007.
11. *BEN*, June 6, 1947. George Ratterman, *Confessions of a Gypsy Quarterback* (New York: Coward-McCann, 1962), 27.
12. *BEN*, June 11, 1947.
13. Lawton Carver, International News, in *BEN*, August 26, 1947.
14. *CE*, August 23, 1947.
15. Kelly, *CE*, September 1, 1947. The Buckets Hirsch hit has been compared by many local wags with the Mike Stratton hit on Keith Lincoln, in the San Diego-Buffalo Bills championship game in 1964.
16. Wurzer, *BEN*, September 2, 1947.
17. Mike Kanaley, *CE*, October 5, 1947.
18. Kritzer, *BEN*, October 14, 1947. *CE*, October 14, 1947.
19. Kelly, *CE*, October 25, November 2, 1947.
20. Kanaley, *CE*, December 14, 1947. *BEN*, December 30, 1947.
21. Grantland Rice, *BEN*, December 30, 1947.
22. Kelly, *CE*, November 22, 1947. Stedler, *BEN*, November 23, 1947.
23. *Look Magazine* cited in *BEN*, October 12, 1948.
24. *BEN*, October 12, 1948. Collins, *The History of the Buffalo Bills and the All American Football Conference*, unpublished paper. Wells, "What If? The General; Manager if the Original Buffalo Bills Reminiscences," *Western New York Magazine*, Winter, 1999. Ratterman earned his degree from Notre Dame in 1949, later he earned a law degree from the Northern Kentucky Salmon P. Chase School of Law. He became a successful reform sheriff of Campbell County, Kentucky. He served as a pro football color commentator in the 1960s and also acted as General Counsel for the American League Players Association at the same time that Jack Kemp was the president of the union.
25. *CE*, August 29, 1949.
26. Connie McGillicuddy, unpublished paper in file of *Greater Buffalo Sports Hall of Fame Archives*, 2002.
27. *CE*, September 6, 1949. *BEN*, September 6, 1949. Ratterman, *Confessions of a Gypsy Quarterback*, 92. Richard Thompson, interview by the author, July 5, 2005. Many AAFC fans think that the Browns' undefeated 1948 season compares favorably with the more famous 1972 Miami Dolphins' season. *BEN*, September 5, 1949.
28. Kelly, *CE*, October 16, 1949. Kanaley, *CE*, October 10, 1949. Tarapacki, "The Rise and Fall of the Buffalo Bills," in *Buffalo Bills Archives* page 9, circa 2000.
29. *BEN*, October 16, 1949.
30. *CE*, September 9, 1948. Stedler, *BEN*, September 11, 1948. Rice in *BEN*, September 8, 1948.
31. Rice, *BEN*, September 17, 1948.
32. *CE*, October 26, 1948. *BEN*, October 27, 1948
33. Rice, *BEN*, December 10, 1948
34. *BEN*, December 22, 1948.
35. *CE*, April 25, 1949.
36. Stedler, *BEN*, May 14, June 3, 1949. Kelly, *CE*, June 3, 1949.
37. Stedler, *BEN*, May 14, 1949. Kelly, *CE*, May 15, 1949.

38. McGillicuddy, Greater Buffalo Sports Hall of Fame folder.
39. That bone, the "American" part, tossed to the old AAFC, lasted only a few weeks; the NAFL then became the NFL once again.
40. All quotes in December 1949 and January 1950 are taken from the *CE* and *BEN* unless otherwise indicated.
41. Thomas Tarapacki, in *Bills Archives.* Grosshandler in *Professional Football Research Association*, http://www.footballresearch.com. Peterson, *Pigskin*,165-66.
42. Kelly, *CE*, December 10, 13, 14, 18, 1949.
43. Wurzer, *BEN*, January 21, 1950. Ray Weil interview by the author, August 20, 2004.
44. Jack Ledden, *Cleveland Plain Dealer*, in *BEN*, December 12, 1950.
45. "PB: The Paul Brown Story," found in the Archives of *The Greater Buffalo Hall of Fame.*
46. Kritzer, "Bills – Not Far from Great," in *BEN*, September 22, 1963.
47. Collins, *The History of the Buffalo Bills*, *Ibid.*
48. Jim Wells, "What If," *Western New York Heritage*, Winter, 1999.

Chapter 4

1. The Ivy League was not actually organized as a formal conference until after WWII. It is officially known as the Ivy Group.
2. Kritzer, *BEN,* September 10, 1946. Kritzer reported that there were so many good veterans that some High School All Stars might not make the team.
3. Ray Jacobi, interview by the author, August 20, 2005.
4. Kritzer, *BEN*, September 10-13, 19, 1946.
5. *BEN,* September 12, 17, 1946. Ryan, *CE*, September 17, July 11, August 8, 1946.
6. *BEN*, September 21-22, 1946.
7. Ryan, *CE,* September 28, November 26, 1946.
8. Bona defeated Cornell, preseason. Cornell praised Bona's forward wall. *BEN,* October 31, 1949, *CE,* October 30, November 1, 1946.
9. Rick Azar, interview by the author, August 20, 2007.
10. Stedler, *BEN*, November 11, 1946. Game Balls were considered costly and scarce; they were not about to be given away freely.
11. E-mail from Phil Colella's daughter to author, August 10, 2006.
12. Kritzer, *BEN*, September 12, 1946. Bob Jerussi, future Canisius star, later played opposite Colella. In 1945 Jerussi, a High School student recalls watching the controversial play on Movietones Newsreel at the local theater in New York City. This might be considered the instant replay of the day. He was certain that Colella scored.
13. *BEN*, September 10, 1947.
14. *BEN*, September 20, 1947.
15. *Ibid.*
16. William Baird, a benefactor of U.B. did the same thing, i.e., taking the team to Point Abino, Ontario, before a big football game.
17. Ryan, *CE,* October 20, 1947.
18. Kritzer, *BEN*, October 22, 1947.
19. Ryan, *CE*, October 21, 1947.
20. Mike Quinlan, *Niagara Falls Gazette*, November 2, 1947.
21. Kritzer, *BEN*, November 24, 1947.
22. Stedler, *BEN*, November 17, December 10, 1947.
23. *Niagara Index*, December 1947.
24. Ryan, *CE,* January 21, 1948. Kritzer, *BEN*, January 20, 1948.
25. E-mail from Larry Felser to the author, July 10, 2006.
26. *Niagara Record*, Niagara University Archives, 1947.
27. Kritzer, *BEN,* September 9-12, 1948.
28. Jerussi, letter to author, August 20, 2006.
29. *Niagara Index*, September 24, 1948.
30. *U.B. Bee* in University of Buffalo Archives, Fall 1948. Stedler, *BEN*, October 23, 1948.
31. Ed Gicewicz, telephone conversation with author, August. 20, 2006.
32. *BEN*, October 24, 1948.
33. *BEN*, October 17, 1948. *CE*, October 17, 1948.

34. *The Griffin*, Canisius College student newspaper, Fall 1948. Jerussi, conversation with author, August, 20, 2006. Max McCarthy, Big Man on Campus, was the prime mover behind the chartering of the plane. Max became a successful U.S. Congressman from the Buffalo area.
35. Kritzer, *BEN*, November 3, 1948.
36. *BEN*, November 4, 1948.
37. *The Griffin,* Canisius College student newspaper, Fall 1948.
38. *BEN*, November 7, 1948.
39. *Ibid.*
40. Stedler, *BEN,* November 8, 1948.
41. Kelly, *CE*, November 13, 1948.
42. Gicewicz, conversation with the author, August.20, 2006.
43. Dick Stedler (brother of Bob of the *News), Union and Echo*, December 1948.
44. Kritzer, *BEN,* August 23, 30, 1949.
45. *BEN*, September 24, 1949.
46. Stedler, *BEN*, October 31, 1949.
47. Kritzer, *BEN*, October 31, November l, 1949.
48. *BEN*, November 7, 1949.
49. Kritzer, *BEN*, November 7, 1949.
50. *BEN*, November 14, 1949.
51. *BEN,* November 9, 1949.
52. *CE*, November 5-6, 1949; Gicewicz, conversations with by the author, August 20, September 20, 2006.
53. Kritzer, *BEN,* November 20, 1949.
54. Collins, "Buffalo's Triple Threat Backs." Unpublished article. Collins summarizes the accomplishments of the leading players and provides a plethora of statistics.
55. *BEN*, March 10, 1950. *The Griffin*, March 1950.
56. Stedler, *BEN,* February 8, March 15, 1950.
57. *Public Relations Scrapbook,* Canisius Archives, 1947-52.
58. Gicewicz, *Ibid.*
59. Wurzer, *BEN* August 24, 1950, reported by Jack Horrigan of UPI, *BEN*, March 15, 1952.
60. Kelly, *CE*, November 5, 1950.
61. Kritzer, *BEN*, December 30, 1950.
62. *CE,* February 8, 1952.
63. Don McLean, e-mail to the author, August 13, 2006. McLean was the voice of Bona sports over Olean Radio for many years. He recalls that in the victory over Louisville, (22-21) Johnny Unitas was the backup quarterback. When things were not going well, Unitas was put in the game. From that point on he was the starter. Thus the Bona game witnessed the "baptism" of one of the greatest quarterbacks in history.

Chapter 5

1. The Seelbach Trophy, established by Ned Irish in honor of Canisius Coach Allie Seelbach, who died prematurely of cancer, was awarded annually for upstate basketball supremacy in the 1940s and 1950s.
2. Ray Ryan, *CE*, November 13, 1945.
3. One of the most acclaimed World War II films, *Saving Private Ryan*, was based in part on Niland family members who served in the war.
4. *CE*, December 20, 1945; February.28 1946. One of Brown's teammates was Ray Meyer, the legendary coach of DePaul.
5. Enrollment statistics – thanks to Blair Foster, Registrar at Canisius College and Kathleen Delaney, archivist at Niagara University. *BEN*, November 19, 1946.
6. *Niagara Index,* Niagara Archives, 1946.
7. Ken Murray, conversation with the author, July 20, 2005.
8. *CE,* December 18, 20, 26, 1946.
9. The term "Negro" and words such as "slickest" were casually used in this pre-politically correct era. *CE*, December 27, 1946.
10. A third brother, Al, also matriculated at Canisius College in 1946. He reported for the team but left school shortly thereafter.
11. *CE*, January 26, 1947.
12. *BEN*, January 27, 1947.
13. Dan Parker, *The New York Mirror*, February 13, 15, 1947. Dick Young, *The New York Daily News*, February 15, 1947. *The Brooklyn Eagle*, February 14, 1947. *The New York Journal,* February14, 1947. *CE*, February 13-15, 1947. *BEN*, February 13,15, 1947.

14. *The Griffin,* February 21, 1947.
15. *BEN*, February 11, 15, 1947.
16. *CE*, February 14, 1947.
17. *New York World Telegram*, February 15, 1947, in *The Athletics Scrapbook* collection in Canisius College archives.
18. *BEN,* February.20, 1947.
19. L. Effrat, *The New York Times*, February 19, 1947.
20. Red Smith, *The New York Herald Tribune,* February 20, 1947.
21. Joe Niland, interview by the author, March 3, 2005.
22. *CE*, November 25-26, 1947. *BEN*, December 4, 1947.
23. Parker, *The New York Mirror,* November 13, 1947.
24. Dick Johnston, *BEN*, January 5, 1948.
25. *CE,* January 21, 1948.
26. Niland, interview by the author, December 10, 2005.
27. Correspondence with Don Harnett, correspondence with the author, February 10, 2005. There was a large round table at Bennie Powers' saloon. Jim Naples, Canisius Football star end, tended bar there. Later he secured the table for use in his upscale restaurant in downtown Buffalo, close to the Statler Hotel, aptly named "The Round Table."
28. *BEN*, October 7, November 23, 1948.
29. Figures for a sellout varied depending on the particular sport and also depending on Aud arrangements for a particular contest. College basketball would vary from 10,667 for every seat sold, to 12,000 if additional seats were set up on the Aud floor and also if standing room only tickets were sold.
30. Bob Stoetzel, interview and correspondence with the author, May 12, 2006. He noted that Coach Diddle had a colorful warm up drill. His players would dunk the ball (illegal during the game) with flaps on their warm up jackets flying all about. Some observers thought it was supposed to intimidate the opposition.
31. Don McMahon, interview by the author, August 29, 2006. McMahon notes that some students who could not get a 60-cent ticket would watch the game on TV at a lower Main St. bar and then at half time jump over the turnstile and watch the rest of the game inside the arena.
32. *CE*, January 22, 1949.
33. *CE*, February 3, 1949.
34. Everet Morris, *The New York Herald Tribune*, February 13, 1949.
35. *BEN*, March 14, 1949.
36. *Ibid.*
37. *The Sporting News,* February 20, 1949, cited in *BEN,* March 4, 1949.
38. *CE,* November 27, 1949.
39. *CE*, December 11, 1949.
40. *CE*, December 16, 1949. *BEN*, December 17, 1949.
41. *CE*, January 1, 1950.
42. *The New York Daily News*, February 10, 1950. *The Herald Tribune,* February 10, 1950.
43. *CE*, March 5, 1950.
44. Jack Laing, *CE*, March 9, 1950.
45. *CE*, December.8, 1950.
46. *BEN*, December 15, 1950.
47. *BEN*, December 27, 1950. *CE*, December 27, 1950.
48. *CE,* January 2, 1951.
49. Stedler, *BEN,* January 11, 1951.
50. McGillicuddy, interview by the author, July, 2005. Jim Burke, interview by the author, August 20, 2005. Don Hartnett, interview by the author, September 10, 2005.
51. *CE,* January 12, 1951. *BEN*, January 13, 1951.
52. *Ibid. CE*, January 23, 1951. *BEN*, January 23, 1951.
53. *Ibid.*
54. Kelly, *CE*, February 16, 1951.
55. *BEN*, February 16, 1951.
56. Kritzer, *BEN*, February 28, March 3, 1951.
57. Associated Press in *BEN*, March 10, 1951.

Chapter 6

1. Don Barnett, interview by the author, August 15, 2006.
2. Laing *CE*, September 15, 1945. Ralph Hubbell, C*ome Walk With Me,* (Englewood, N.J.: Prentice Hall, 1975), 31-2.

3. *BEN*, October 17, 1945.
4. Tim Warchocki, *Buffalo Bisons: Before the Blade*, (Carthage: Rama Publishing: 1999), 64 ff. Warchocki's book is a treasure of information for the entire history of the Bisons in the American Hockey League. Also Hall of Fame folders for the AHL in the National Hockey Hall of Fame in Toronto.
5. Wurzer, *BEN*, October 20. 1945, *CE*, October 28, 1945.
6. Laing, *CE*, November 4, 1945. Wurzer, *BEN*, November 1, 1945.
7. Laing, *CE*, November 4, 1945. Sellouts varied - See Chapter 5, footnote # 29.
8. Wurzer, *BEN*, November 14, 1945.
9. *Ibid.*, December.4, 1945.
10. Wurzer, *BEN*, November 20, 1945. Laing, *CE*, December 19, 1945.
11. Wurzer, *BEN*, January 24, 1946.
12. Wurzer, *BEN*, February 17, 19, 1946.
13. *BEN*, February 25, 27, 1946.
14. *CE*, February 25, 1946. Dan Amigone was host.
15. *CE*, March 1, 6, 1946.
16. Wurzer, *BEN*, March 21, 1946.
17. *Ibid.*
18. Wurzer, *BEN*, April 1, 1946. Wurzer referred to magazine salesman, which was a common side job in those days.
19. Stedler, *BEN*, April 12, 1946.
20. Kelly, *CE*, April 15, 1946.
21. Laing, *CE*, April 16, 1946. Wurzer and Stedler, *BEN*, April 16, 1946.
22. American Hockey League, *Red Book for Hockey*, 17, (Toronto: Hockey Hall of Fame, 1946). The capacities of all AHL arenas are listed.
23. Stedler, *BEN*, November 12 1946, February 16, 1947.
24. Kelly, *CE*, August 11, 1946.
25. *BEN*, August 12, 1946.
26. *BEN*, November 18, 27, 1946.
27. *BEN*, March 10, 1947.
28. *CE*, July 24, 1947.
29. *BEN*, September 25, October 7, 1947.
30. *CE*, October 4, 1947. *BEN*, October 14, 1947.
31. *BEN*, October 16-17, 1947.
32. *CE*, October 22, 1947.
33. Wurzer, *BEN*, October 20, 1947. Laing, *CE*, October 28, 1947.
34. Wurzer, *BEN*, October 17, 1947.
35. Laing, *CE*, October 22, 1947. Goalies did not wear masks in the 40s.
36. Laing, *CE*, October 29, 1947. Wurzer, *BEN*, October 29, 1947.
37. Wurzer, *BEN*, December 9, 1947.
38. Wurzer, *BEN*, December 11, 1947.
39. Kritzer, *BEN*, December 20, 1947. See also Michael McKinley, *Hockey: A People's History* (Toronto: McClelland and Stewart, 2006) and Brian McFarlane, *History of Hockey* (Toronto: Sagamore Publishing, 1997).
40. Laing, *CE*, December 27, 1947.
41. Wurzer, *BEN*, January 21, 22, 1948.
42. Interview with Hunt by Wurzer, *BEN*, November 27, 1948. Laing, *CE*, March 8, 1948.
43. Wurzer, *BEN*, April 9, 1948.
44. Laing, *CE*, April 12, 1948.
45. Laing, *CE*, September 9, 1948.
46. Wurzer, *BEN*, October 16, 1948.
47. Wurzer, *BEN*, October 18, 1948. Laing, *CE*, October 20-21, 1948.
48. Wurzer, *BEN*, November 12, 1948. Laing, *CE*, November 18, 1948. Sawchuk would go on to a storied career in the NHL.
49. Laing, *CE*, November 18, 22, 1948.
50. Wurzer, *BEN*, December 29, 1948, January 4, 1949.
51. Page one story in *CE*, January 18, 1949. *CE*, January 19, 1949. Young, *BEN*, January 19, 1949.
52. Stedler, *BEN*, January 19, 1949.
53. Tim Warchocki, *Before the Blade*, 91 FF. Laing, *CE*, February 10, 1949. Hubbell, *Ibid.* Barnett, interview by the author, July 10, 2006.
54. *BEN*, March 4, 1949. Laing, *CE*, March 21, 1949.
55. *Ibid. BEN*, May 15, 1949. Laing, *CE*, May 16, 1949.
56. *BEN*, September 5, 1949.
57. Laing, *CE*, November 29, 1949. Stedler, *BEN*, October 30, 1949.
58. Laing, *CE*, December 30, 1949.
59. Laing, *CE*, February 3, March 20, 1950.
60. Wurzer, *BEN*, April 3, 1950. Laing, *CE*,

April 3, 1950.

61. *BEN*, April 4, 1950. Laing, *CE*, April 3, 1950. Meger spent three years in the NHL. In early 1954 his skull was cut open; he spent a year in the hospital and then his career was finished.
62. Warchocki, 96 ff, notes that DeMarco in 1950-51 led in assists and scoring and was named MVP. He earned bonuses of $300 for being named to the AHL All Star team, $300 for leading the AHL in scoring, and $300 for MVP. He was a "rich" man.
63. *Ibid.*
64. Wurzer, *BEN*, January 5, 1952.
65. Warchocki, *Ibid.*, 90 ff.

Chapter 7

1. *BEN*, October 12, 1857. Lazurus vs. Harrigan, in sports card file in Library of the Buffalo and Erie County Historical Society (BME).
2. Collins, *When Boxing was Big in Buffalo, 1881-1951*, Unpublished manuscript. Tim Graham, *Boxing Illustrated, 1959* in *Buffalo News*, August 20, 2006.
3. Kritzer, *BEN,* February 25, 1946. Frank Wakefield, *BEN*, November 7, 1949. *Ring 44* Program, October 16, 1998.
4. Jim Bisco, *Western New York Heritage*, Spring 2006.
5. Charley Bailey, *CE,* August 8, September 17, 1945.
6. Alli, *CE,* January 5, 1946. Wakefield, *BEN,* February 19, 1946. Wakefield, a native of Massachusetts, came to work at the Buffalo Evening News as a young man. One of his first assignments was the famous Slattery-Suozo fight. Boxing became his specialty and he covered the sport for the next half century. Brimm, *Ring 44 Program,* October 16, 1998.
7. Bailey, *CE*, October 18, November 6, 1945. *BEN*, November 6, 1945, February 3, 1946.
8. Collins, *Ibid.*
9. Kelly, *CE*, November 30, 1945, *CE*, December 1, 2, 5, 13, 1945. *BEN*, December. 6, 1947.
10. *Ibid.*
11. Joe Cardina, interview by the author, August 12, 2007. Cardina handled promotions for the *Courier Express* in the late 1940s. *CE,* December 6, 11, 13, 1945, December 6, 1947.
12. Dan Muscato, quoted in *Buffalo News*, October 5, 2007.
13. Stedler, *BEN* December 5, 22, 1945. *CE*, January 6, 1946.
14. Wakefield, *BEN*, January 6, February 5, March 5, 1946.
15. *CE,* March 12, April 10, December 28, 1946.
16. *CE*, May 14, 1946. *BEN*, May 15, 1946.
17. *CE*, December 28, 1946. *BEN*, December 31, 1946.
18. *CE,* January 10, March 20, April 16,1946.
19. *CE,* March 20, April 16, 1947.
20. *BEN,* January 20, 21, 1948.
21. Collins, *Ibid., Ring 44 Program*, October 16, 1998. *BEN*, February 20-21, 1948. *CE*, February 18, 1948. *BEN,* July 3, 1948.
22. *BEN,* January 8, 1949.
23. *BEN*, November 6, 7, 1949.
24. Wakefield, *BEN*, November 20, 1949.
25. *BEN*, January 21, 1948. CE, January 21, 1948.
26. *CE,* January 20, 1949.
27. Collins, *Ibid.*

Chapter 8

1. Dick Hirsch, "Masters of the Mat" in *Sunday Magazine*, *Buffalo Courier Express,* March 15, 1981. Daniel Murphy, *Bodyslams in Buffalo* (Buffalo: Western New York Wares Inc., 2002).
2. Murphy, *Bodyslams,* 7 ff.
3. *Ibid.,* 13-14. Msgr. Franklin Kelleher, interview by the author, June 15, 1992.
4. *CE*, January 30, 1946. *BEN*, January 31, 1946, January 28, 1947. Collins, various unpublished works.
5. Scott Beekman, *Ringside: A History of Professional Wrestling in America.* (Westport, Conn.: Praeger Publishers, 2006), 64-86.
6. Bob Summers, "Memorial Auditorium Memories," in special supplement in *Buffalo News*, March 25, 1996, on the closing of Memorial Auditorium. Charley Young, in "100 Years of Sport," in special

supplement in *Buffalo Evening News*, helped make Buffalo a leading wrestling center in the 1940s.

38. Ed Don George worked in Cuba until Fidel Castro too over. Milt Northrup in Buffalo News, June 1996, wrote a splendid piece on Ilio Di Paolo. I had the pleasure of interviewing Ilio when we played golf in 1993.

Chapter 9

Midgets

1. Crocky Wright, *The Midgets Come East, Midget Auto Racing History: the Golden Era*, Volume 2 (Indianapolis: Crocky Wright Enterprises, 1979), 73.
2. Keith S. Herbst, *Daredevils of the Frontier* (Newburyport, Ma., Coastal 181 Publisher, 2006), various pages. Herbst's book has a superb collection of photographs of the midgets from the Depression to the waning days of the 1950s.
3. *BEN*, August 31, 1945, August 20, 1946. Herbst, *Ibid.* 19, 71. Also Herbst "A Distant Roar" *Western New York Heritage*, Summer 2007, 50. *BEN,* August 21, 1947. *CE*, July 8, 1949.
4. Phil Ranallo, *CE,* June 25, July 24, 1947. Mike Calandra, *BEN*, June 12, 1947.
5. Herbst, *Ibid.*
6. Ranallo, *CE*, June 11, 1947. *BEN*, September 2, 1947
7. Herbst, *Ibid.,* 50 ff. Ranallo, *CE*, *Ibid.*
8. *BEN*, September 11, 1947. Crowds numbered usually between 6,000 and 7,000 but more than 10,000 turned out for the bigger races.
9. *BEN*, September 2, 11, 1947.
10. *CE,* June 17, 1948.
11. *CE*, August 25, 1948.
12. Herbst, *Ibid.*, 82-87.
13. Herbst, *Ibid.*, 89. *BEN,* September 16, 1948. Nat Kleinfeld, *The Bill Schindler Story* (New York: Witness Productions, 2002), 75.
14. *CE*, July 14, 1949.
15. *BEN*, August 19, 1949. *CE*, August 20, 1949.
16. Herbst, *Ibid.*, 93.
17. *CE*, September 10, 1949.

Roller Derby

1. Frank Deford, *Five Strides on the Banked Track: The Life and Times of the Roller Derby* (New York: Little, Brown, 1971), 16.
2. Wikipedia (Internet), *Roller Derby. BEN,* August 27, 1949.
3. Wikipedia, *Ibid. BEN*, September 8, 1949.
4. *BEN,* June 2, 1947.
5. Keith Coppage, *Roller Derby to Roller Jam* (New York: Squarebooks, 1999).
6. *CE*, September 17, 1948.
7. Deford, *Ibid.*, 17, 97, 104.
8. Coppage, *Ibid.*, 25.
9. Randy Roberts, *Winning is the Only Thing* (Baltimore: The Johns Hopkins University Press, 1989), 102.

Still More Sports Events

Bowling

1. *CE*, September 3, 1945.
2. *CE*, August 18, 1945.
3. *BEN*, October 19, 1945. *CE*, February 23, 1946.
4. *BEN*, March 13, 1946. *CE* March 7, 17, 1946. (Japanese, Chinese, and Hawaiians were also excluded).
5. *CE*, April 7, 1946. *BEN,* March 19, 1946. *CE*, March 11, May 14, 1946.
6. *CE*, February 4 1946. *BEN,* May 14, 1946. *CE*, May 14, 1946.

Golf

1. *BEN,* January 12, 1948.
2. *BEN*, July 24, 1948. *CE*, July 18, 1948.
3. *BEN,* July 16, 1948.
4. *BEN*, July 31, 1948. *CE,* July 31 1948. Interview with T. O'Connor by the author, July 2005. O'Connor was Golf Coach at Canisius College in the 1980s.
5. *BEN*, August 3, 1948. *CE*, August 2-3, 1948.

High School football

1. J. Sullivan, *Buffalo News*, September 21, 1999.
2. Joe Cardina and Wayne and Helen Reilly,

interview by the author, April 29, 2007.

3. Bob Feeney, *BEN,* October 21, 1945.
4. *BEN*, October 22, 1945. *CE,* October 22, 1945.

Horseracing

1. *CE*, August 29, 1947.
2. *BEN*, August 2, 1946.
3. *CE,* May 24, 1948.
4. *BEN*, June 28, July 1, 28, 1948. *CE*, July 5, 10, 29. 1948.
5. *CE*, August 3, 1948. *BEN*, July 29, 1948. *CE,* May 24, July 10, 1949.
6. *CE,* August 1, 1947.
7. *CE,* August 25, 28, 1947.
8. *CE,* January 14, 1948.

Rowing

1. *CE,* April 19, 1952. E-mail from Bill Cotter to the author, March 6, 2006.
2. *BEN,* June 24, 1948.
3. Ranallo, *CE,* July 21, 1948.
4. Johnston, *BEN*, July 21, 1949. Stedler, *BEN*, July 22, 1949.
5. Kelly, *CE*, July 26, 1949.
6. *CE*, July 30, 1949.
7. Ranallo, *CE,* September 5, 1949.
8. *BEN*, July 28, November 12, 1947.

Other Sports

Six Day Bike Races

1. *CE,* March 31, June 18, September 9, October 3-11, 1946. *BEN*, October 6-11, 1946.

Pro Basketball

1. Peterson, *Cages to Jumpshots* (New York: Oxford University Press, 1990), 3.
2. *CE*, December 30, 1945. Peterson, *Ibid.*, 137. Les Harrison, interview by the author, August 10, 1995.

Tennis

1. *BEN*, January 6, 1948.

Still More

1. *CE*, August 10, 1947. *BEN.* August 11, 1947. *CE*, September 11, 1948. Richard Westermeier Jr., interview by the author, July 9, 2008.
2. Website: http:www.buffalosportshalloffame.com, 1991. *CE,* April 8, 1947. *BEN*, March 21, 1947. *CE,* March 29, 1948. *BEN*, April 18, 1947.

Speedboat

1. *CE,* August 23, 1949.
2. *CE*, August 20, 1949.
3. *CE*, August 21, 1949.
4. *BEN*, August 20, 22, 23, 1949. *CE*, January 17, 1950.
5. *CE,* January 11, 1950.
6. *BEN,* August 18-19, 1950. *CE*, August 18, 1950.

Chapter 10

1. Rice, *BEN*, April 6, 1950.
2. *CE,* October 22, 1950. *BEN*, November 16, 1949. On June 2, 1954 only 573 fans attended. *CE*, June 2, 1954.
3. "Made in Buffalo," *Fortune Magazine*, Vol. 44, July 1950.
4. *CE*, February 11, 1950.
5. *BEN*, December 30, 1950.
6. *CE*, July 8, 1950.
7. *BEN,* November.12, 1952. December 30, 1953.
8. Richard Polenberg, One Nation Divisible (New York: Penguin Books, 1980), 127-9.
9. *United States Bureau of Census*, Internet Release Data, June 15, 1998.
10. Randy Roberts, *Winning Is The Only Thing* (Baltimore: The Johns Hopkins University Press, 1989), 97-108. Benjamin Rader, *American Sports* (Upper Saddle River, N.J.: Prentice Hall, 2004), 242-256.
11. Steve Weller, *BEN*, December 26, 1959.

Bibliography

In the acknowledgment section of the introduction I have mentioned other sources that include: Interviews, archival material, and newspapers.

Interviews: listed in Introduction.

Archival material: Including game programs, press guides and year books for football and basketball in the archives of: Canisius College, Niagara University, St. Bonaventure University, and the University of Buffalo. I also used the Buffalo Bills Archives, the Archives of the Professional Hockey Hall of Fame, and the Archives of the Professional Football Hall of Fame.

Newspapers: All copies of the Buffalo Evening News and the Buffalo Courier Express for 1945-1951, and selected issues for other years. Also use has been made of the Cleveland Plain Dealer and the Niagara Falls Gazette as well as several other newspapers as they appeared in various scrapbooks.

Books:

Angelo, Mark, OFM. *The History of St. Bonaventure University*. St. Bonaventure University Archives: The Franciscan Institute, 1961.

Axthelm, Peter. *The City Game*. Lincoln: University of Nebraska Press, 1999.

Beekman, Scott. *Ringside: A History of Professional Wrestling in America.* Westport, Conn.: Praeger Books, 2006.

Baseball Encyclopedia. *The Complete and Definitive Record of Major League Baseball.* New York: MacMillan, 1996.

Bieron, Joseph. *Postcard Views: A Walk Down Main Street Buffalo, New York, circa 1910.* Buffalo: Buffalo Heritage Unlimited, 2007.

Boddy, William. *Fifties Television*. Urbana: University of Illinois Press, 1990.

Boyd, Herb. *Pound for Pound.* New York: Harper Collins, 2005.

Brady, Charles. *Canisius College: The First 100 Years*. Buffalo: Holling Press, 1970.

Brown, Paul, with Jack Clary. *PB: The Paul Brown Story*. New York: Atheneum, 1980.

Brown, Richard, and Bob Watson. *Buffalo: Lake City in Niagara Land*. Buffalo: Windsor Publications, 1981.

Buffalo Veterans Boxers Association, Ring 44. *Annual Hall of Fame Dinner Banquet Program*, 2006-2008.

Cappetta, Gary. *Bodyslams, Memoirs of a Wrestling Pitchman.* Jackson: Little, Brown, 2000.

Chapman, Mike. *Encyclopedia of American Wrestling*. Champaign: Leisure Press, 1990.

Coenen, Craig. *From Sandlots to the Super Bowl: The National Football League: 1920 to 1966.* Knoxville: U of Tennessee Press, 2005.

Cohen, Stanley. *The Game They Played.* Telander, 1977.

Collins, Jerry. *On the Sidelines, 100 years of the Best in Local Sports Reporting*. Buffalo: Bates Jackson, 2006.

- - -. *The Bond of the Ring*. Buffalo: North Delaware Printing, 2008.

Conley, Joseph. *The Story of the Little Three: 1904 – 1975.* Self-published.

Coppage, Keith. *Roller Derby to Roller Jam.* New York: Squarebooks, 1999.

Daley, Dan, and Bob O'Donnell. *The Pro Football Chronicles.* MacMillan, 1990.

Davies, Richard. *America's Obsession: Sports and Society Since 1945*. Belmont.: Wadsworth, 1994.

Dillaway, Diana. *Power Failure*. Amherst: Prometheus Books, 2005.

Dunn, Edward. *A History of Railroads in Western New York*. Buffalo: Canisius College Press, 2000.

Eberle, Scott, and Joseph Grande. *Second Looks: A Pictorial History of Buffalo and Erie County*. Norfolk: The Donning Company, 1987.

Eklund, Clarence. *Forty Years of Wrestling*. Buffalo: Univ. of Wyoming Press, 1947.

Gadensky, Allen C. *The Bison Shipyard Story*. Buffalo: Allen C. Gadensky, 2005.

Goldman, Mark. *City on the Edge*. Buffalo: Prometheus, Books, 2007.

- - -. *City on the Lake*. Buffalo: Prometheus Books, 1990.

- - -. *High Hopes: The Rise and Decline of Buffalo, New York*. Albany: State University of New York Press, 1983.

Halberstam, David. *Summer of '49*. New York: Avon Books, 1989.

Herbst, Keith. *Daredevils of the Frontier*. Newburyport, Ma.: Coastal 181, 2006.

The Hockey News. *Century of Hockey*. Toronto: McClelland and Stewart, 2000.

Hubbell, Ralph. *A Man Remembers*. Buffalo: Niagara Frontier Services, 1972.

- - -. *Come Walk with Me*. Englewood: Prentice Hall, 1975.

- - -. *Across a Crowded Room*. Buffalo: Partners Press, 1983.

- - -. *They Still Can Smell the Roses*. Buffalo: Partners Press, 1991.

Isaacs, Neil. *All the Moves: A History of College Basketball*. Philadelphia: Lippincott Co., 1975.

Jares, Joe. *Whatever Happened to Gorgeous George?* Englewood Cliffs: Prentice Hall, 1978.

Kleinfield, Nat. *The Bill Schindler Story*. Witness Production, 2002.

Klinkenborg, Verlyn. *The Last Fine Time*. New York: Alfred Knopf, 1991.

Kunz, George. *Buffalo Memories*. Buffalo: Canisius College Press, 2002.

LeBow, G. *The Wrestling Scene*. New York: Homecrafts Division, 1950.

Leibling, A.J. *The Most of A.J. Leibling*. New York: Simon & Schuster, 1954.

- - -. *The Sweet Science*. New York: The Viking Press, 1956.

Leveratte, Marc. *Professional Wrestling, The Myth, The Mat, and American Popular Culture*. Lewistown: Edwin Mellen Press, 2003.

Levy, Alan. *Joe McCarthy*. Jefferson: McFarland and Company, 2003.

MacCambridge, Michael. *America's Game*. New York: Random House, 2004.

Maiorana, Sal. *Relentless: The Hard Hitting History of Buffalo Bills Football*. Buffalo: Western New York Wares, Inc., 2003.

McFarlane, Brian. *History of Hockey*. Toronto: Sagamore Publishing, 1997.

McKinley, Michael. *Hockey: A People's History*. Toronto: McClelland and Stewart, 2006.

Mead, Chris. *Champion Joe Louis.* New York: Scribner, 1985.

Miller, Jeffrey. Buffalo's Forgotten Champions. www.Xlibris.com: Xlibris Corporation, 2007.

Murphy, Dan. *Bodyslams in Buffalo*. Buffalo: Western New York Wares, Inc., 2002.

Naylor, Barney. *James Norris and the Decline of Boxing*. Indianapolis: Bobbs-Merrill Co., 1964.

Oriard, Michael. *King Football.* Chapel Hill: Univ of North Carolina Press, 2001.

Overfield, Joseph. *The 100 Seasons of Buffalo Baseball*. Buffalo: Partners Press, 1985.

- - -. *Buffalo Bison Sketch Book,* 1953.

Percy, John. *Buffalo-Niagara Connections.* Buffalo: Western New York Heritage Press, 2007.

Powell, Steven. *Rushing the Growler: A History of Brewing in Buffalo.* Buffalo: Digital Print Services, 1996.

Pope, Kristian, and Ray Whebbe, Jr. *The Encyclopedia of Professional Wrestling*. Iola: Kraus Publications, 2001.

Peterson, Robert. *Pigskin: The Early Years of Pro Football.* New York: Oxford University Press, 1997.

- - -. *Cages to Jumpshots: Pro Basketball's Early Years.* New York: Oxford University Press, 1990.

Polenberg, Richard. *One Nation Divisible*. New York: Penguin Books, 1980.

Rader, Benjamin. *In its Own Image: How TV has Transformed Sports.* Englewood Cliffs: Prentice Hall, 2004.

- - -. *American Sports*. Upper Saddle River: Prentice Hall, 2004.

Ratterman, George. *Confessions of a Gypsy Quarterback.* New York: Coward-McCann, 1962.

Roberts, Randy. *Winning is the Only Thing: Sports in America since 1945.* Baltimore: Johns Hopkins University Press, 1989.

Rosen, Charles. *Scandals of '51*. New York: Holt, Rinehart, 1978.

Ross, Charles. *Outside the Lines*. New York: New York University Press, 1999.

Schnabal, James. *U.S. Army in the Korean War.* Washington, D.C.: Office of Military History, 1972.

Stedler, Dick. *Stedler's Sports Stories*. Buffalo: Faith Publications, 1954.

Sullivan, Neil. *The Minors: 1876 to the Present.* New York: St. Martin's Press, 1990.

Swados, Robert. *Counsel In the Crease.* Amherst: Prometheus Books, 2006.

Testa, Judith. *Sal Maglie*. DeKalb: Northern Illinois University Press, 2007.

Tygiel, Jules. *Baseball's Great Experiment: Jackie Robinson and His Legacy*. New York: Oxford University Press, 1983.

Vogel. Michael, Ed Patton and Paul Redding. *America's Crossroads*. Buffalo: The Heritage Press, 1993.

Wallace, Malcolm. *And They Were Giants: The St. Bonaventure Football Book.* St. Bonaventure: The Franciscan Institute, 1989.

Warchocki, Tim. *Before the Blade.* Carthage: Rama Publishing, 1999.

Warner, Sam Bass. *Streetcar Suburbs*. Cambridge: Harvard University Press, 1983.

Watterson, John. *College Football.* Baltimore: Johns Hopkins University Press, 2001.

White, G. Edw. *Creating the National Pastime; Baseball Transforms Itself, 1903 – 1953.* Princeton: Princeton University Press, 1996.

Williams, Joe. *TV Boxing Book.* New York: Van Nostrand, 1954.

Wright, Crocky. *The Midgets Come East*, 1980. *Eastern Midget Racing 1945-1951,* Vol. 2. Indianapolis: Crocky Wright Enterprises, 1980.

Articles:

Adelman, Melvin. "Making Money…The Case for the 1946 Cleveland Browns," *Proceedings of the North American Society for Sports History*, 2004.

Beaudet, Paul. "The Growth of Buffalo's Suburban Zone," *Niagara Frontier,* Autumn 1971. Publication of Buffalo and Erie County Historical Society.
Collins, Jerry. "The History of the Buffalo Bills and the All American Football Conference," Unpublished article.

- - -. "Buffalo's Triple Threat Backs," Unpublished article.

- - -. "Made in Buffalo," *Fortune Magazine,* Fortune Magazine Pub. Co., Vol. 44, July 1951.

Hirsch, Dick. "Masters of the Mat," *Sunday Magazine, CE*, March 15, 1981.

Kritzer, Cy. "The Bills: Not Far From Great," *BEN*, September 22, 1963.

Lomax, Michael. "Detrimental to the League: Gambling and the Governance of Professional Football, 1946-1963," *Journal of Sport History,* Summer 2002

Summers, Robert. "Memorial Auditorium Memories," Buffalo News, March 25, 1996.

Sye, Roy. "Almost Champions," *Coffin Corner*, Vol. 25.

Tarapacki, Thomas. *The Rise and Fall of the Buffalo Bills*. In Buffalo Bills Archives.

Young, Charlie. "100 Years of Sports, *BEN*, September 14, 1980.

Western New York Heritage Magazine:

Bisco, Jim. "Burlesque in Buffalo," Spring 2006.

- - -. "Big Time at Little Harlem," Winter, 2006

Keenan, Peter. "A Salesman's Walk Downtown," Summer 2006.

Picard, Clarence. "Hockey Before Helmets: The Bisons and Championship Hockey in Buffalo," Winter 2008.

Wells, Jim. "What If? The General Manager of the Original Buffalo Bills Reminiscences," Winter, 1999.

Herbst, Keith. "A Distant Roar," Summer, 2007.